Lecture Notes in Computer Science   1482

Edited by G. Goos, J. Hartmanis and J. van Leeuwen

Springer

Berlin
Heidelberg
New York
Barcelona
Budapest
Hong Kong
London
Milan
Paris
Singapore
Tokyo

Reiner W. Hartenstein Andres Keevallik (Eds.)

Field-Programmable Logic and Applications

From FPGAs to Computing Paradigm

8th International Workshop, FPL '98
Tallinn, Estonia, August 31 – September 3, 1998
Proceedings

Springer

Series Editors

Gerhard Goos, Karlsruhe University, Germany
Juris Hartmanis, Cornell University, NY, USA
Jan van Leeuwen, Utrecht University, The Netherlands

Volume Editors

Reiner W. Hartenstein
University of Kaiserslautern, Computer Science Department
PO Box 3049, D-67653 Kaiserslautern, Germany
E-mail: hartenst@rhrk.uni-kl.de

Andres Keevallik
Tallinn Technical University
Raja 15, Tallinn EE-0026, Estonia
E-mail: akeev@cc.ttu.ee

Cataloging-in-Publication data applied for

Die Deutsche Bibliothek - CIP-Einheitsaufnahme

Field programmable logic and applications : from FPGAs to computing paradigm ;
8th international workshop ; proceedings / FPL '98, Tallinn, Estonia, August
31 - September 3, 1998. Reiner W. Hartenstein ; Andres Keevallik (ed.). -
Berlin ; Heidelberg ; New York ; Barcelona ; Budapest ; Hong Kong ; London ;
Milan ; Paris ; Singapore ; Tokyo : Springer, 1998
  (Lecture notes in computer science ; Vol. 1482)
  ISBN 3-540-64948-4

CR Subject Classification (1991): B.6-7, J.6

ISSN 0302-9743
ISBN 3-540-64948-4 Springer-Verlag Berlin Heidelberg New York

Typesetting: Camera-ready by author
SPIN 10638774   06/3142 – 5 4 3 2 1 0   Printed on acid-free paper

Preface

This book features papers first presented at the 8th International Workshop on Field-Programmable Logic and Applications (FPL'98), held in Tallinn, Estonia, August 31 to September 3, 1998.

The FPL'98 workshop was organized by the Tallinn Technical University and the University of Kaiserslautern, in co-operation with the University of Oxford, as a continuation of seven already held workshops in Oxford (1991, 1993, and 1995), in Vienna, Austria (1992), in Prague, Czech Republic (1994), in Darmstadt, Germany (1996), and in London, UK (1997).

Field-programmable logic is no longer merely a niche technology being limited to logic synthesis mainly. An increasing number of papers go toward coarse grain field-programmable platforms. More and more authors view this area as an emerging new computing paradigm. In the future the universities should teach both, procedural programming and structural programming (programming in space vs. programming in time).

The growing importance of field-programmable devices is demonstrated by the wide variety of applications described in the submitted papers for FPL'98. This time, we had 86 submissions, the second largest number in the history of FPL workshops (also see http://xputers.informatik.uni-kl.de/FPL/index_fpl.html). The highest number of submissions was received for FPL'94 in Prague, Czech Republic: 116 submissions (Springer LNCS Vol. 849, also see http://link.springer.de/series/lncs/).

The list below shows the distribution of origins of the papers submitted to FPL'98 (some papers were written by an international team):

Australia	2	Latvia	1
Belarus	1	Philippines	1
Belgium	1	Portugal	1
CzechRepublik	1	Russia	1
Estonia	1	Slovenia	1
Finland	2	Spain	4
France	4	Switzerland	1
Germany	20	Tunisie	1
HongKong	2	USA	14
Hungary	3	United Kingdom	17
Israel	1	Yugoslavia	1
Japan	5		

The FPL'98 Technical Program offers an exciting collection of regular presentations and posters covering a wide range of topics. From the 86 submitted papers the very best 39 regular papers and 30 high quality posters were selected. All selected papers are included in this book.

We would like to thank the reviewers and the members of the Technical Program Committee for reviewing the papers submitted to the workshop. Our thanks go also to the keynote speaker and to the authors who wrote the final papers for this issue.

We also gratefully acknowledge all the work done at Springer-Verlag in publishing this book.

June 1998

Reiner W. Hartenstein, Program Chair
Andres Keevallik, General Chair

Program Committee

Organizing Committee

Table of Contents

Accelerators

System Architectures

Applications (1)

Hardware/Software Codesign

System Development

Algorithms on FPGAs

Applications (2)

Tutorial

Miscellaneous

New CAD Framework Extends Simulation of Dynamically Reconfigurable Logic

David Robinson, Gordon McGregor and Patrick Lysaght

Dept. Electronic and Electrical Engineering,
University of Strathclyde,
204 George Street,
Glasgow, G1 1XW
United Kingdom

Fax: +44 (0) 141 552 4968
e-mail: d.robinson@eee.strath.ac.uk

Abstract. New design methods and tools are needed to improve the process of designing dynamically reconfigurable logic. This paper reports on the revision and extension of Dynamic Circuit Switching (DCS), a CAD tool for specifying and simulating dynamically reconfigurable systems. The work introduces a new design framework, which exploits existing design practices where feasible, and proposes a new design flow for reconfigurable logic.

1. Introduction

One approach to the problems posed by the design of dynamically reconfigurable systems is to accept the limitations of current simulation technology and seek to solve the problem without attempting to simulate dynamic circuit behaviour. Designs are configured onto FPGAs and debugged by interactively monitoring their execution on the target architectures. This technique is in common use and is valid for small and prototype designs. There are many fundamental problems with this *ad hoc* approach to the design of dynamically reconfigurable systems. Two of the most critical are that it assumes that configuration bitstreams are available for the design in the target FPGA and that a verified reconfiguration controller is also available. To get to this stage in a design requires a great deal of effort and yet one is still only evaluating design options; the design may fail for any number of reasons at this late stage. Furthermore, design iteration is very complex and is not guaranteed to yield an acceptable solution. In an era of ever reducing time-to-market and increasing design complexities, this empirical approach is untenable.

The focus of the work reported here is to identify a structured design flow for dynamically reconfigurable logic and to extend current CAD tools to create a framework that supports the new design methods. The key to this approach is to identify opportunities to improve the performance evaluation of designs as early as possible in the design cycle. Relatively crude estimates of parameters such as circuit area and reconfiguration time may be sufficient to eliminate candidate designs and hence reduce the design space. The goal is to identify how and where this type of information can be extracted in the design flow and how best it may be incorporated into the design methods and tools. By iterating in the design cycle as early as possible, and using best estimates of parameters that cannot be precisely quantified until later design stages are complete, the overall number of design iterations can be reduced.

This paper is organised into five further sections. Section two reviews Dynamic Circuit Switching and describes a number of improvements that have been made to it. Section three presents a new CAD framework and introduces two new CAD tools and shows how they integrate with DCS into the overall design flow. In section four, the challenges of back annotating dynamically reconfigurable tasks are described. Section five addresses the issues of back annotation of reconfiguration delays. Conclusions and future work are presented in the last section.

2. Extending Dynamic Circuit Switching

Dynamic Circuit Switching was the first reported tool to allow the simulation of dynamically reconfigurable systems [1]. This software allows the designer to model system behaviour during reconfiguration intervals. The dynamically reconfigurable design is modelled by inserting virtual switching components and control modules to model dynamic reconfiguration. The simulation can be performed before the time consuming technology mapping phase, an advantage still held over subsequently reported methods [2, 3]. Simulating the system at a high level of design abstraction allows the designer to explore the design space more effectively. DCS was recently revised and re-written to target designs that are specified exclusively in VHDL. The following new features have been introduced:
- Separate reconfiguration file
- Support for multiple levels of design hierarchy
- Resource contention management
  - Task grouping
  - Reconfiguration port

The original version of DCS used a distributed scheme for specifying reconfiguration information. Individual tasks were annotated with attributes that specified their reconfiguration details. In the current version of DCS, the reconfiguration information is integrated into a single reconfiguration file. This re-organisation was motivated by practical experience and the more general change from schematic methods of design entry to textual circuit specification.

The move to VHDL highlighted the need to extend DCS to support hierarchical design descriptions, which in turn, further reinforced the importance of moving to a single reconfiguration file.

Task grouping is a new technique that has been introduced to simplify the management of dynamic circuits. It is applied to groups of tasks that have the potential to conflict with one another because their floorplans overlap. Because these task groups are not mutually exclusive in space, they must be mutually exclusive with respect to each other in time, or resource contention will result. Task grouping introduces the concept of a mutually exclusive group, called a mutex group, to collect those tasks whose physical locations overlap on an array. The mutex group is used as a simulation artefact to perform a pseudo design rule check that highlights potential contention for array resources.

Access to the reconfiguration port during simulation is now controlled by a revised arbitration scheme which models the fact that access to the physical port is limited. DCS assumes that there is only one configuration port, in line with current FPGA technology, but this can be changed by the user to model multiple FPGA systems, or a hypothetical FPGA with multiple configuration ports. Port access becomes an issue when the activation and deactivation of multiple tasks occur simultaneously. As only a limited subset of these tasks can be processed, some method of arbitration must be implemented. The arbitration scheme is responsible for the sequencing of reconfiguration events in an orderly manner.

In addition to the extensions to DCS, two new modules have been added and an overall CAD framework has been defined. In the light of these changes, the revised simulation component of DCS has been re-named as DCSim. The two new modules are called DCSTech and DCSEst and are introduced along with the new CAD framework in the next section.

3. CAD Framework

The CAD framework, shown in Fig. 1 presents a new environment for designing reconfigurable systems that co-exists with current design tools and practices. This framework allows the specification and simulation of dynamically reconfigurable designs and addresses many of the challenges inherent in the production of working hardware.

The new software tools, DCSim, DCSTech and DCSEst, are shown shaded in the diagram. DCSTech and DCSEst appear in a number of places because they are accessed at different stages in the design flow and perform different functions. Timing information is currently transferred between the design tools using SDF (Standard Delay Format).

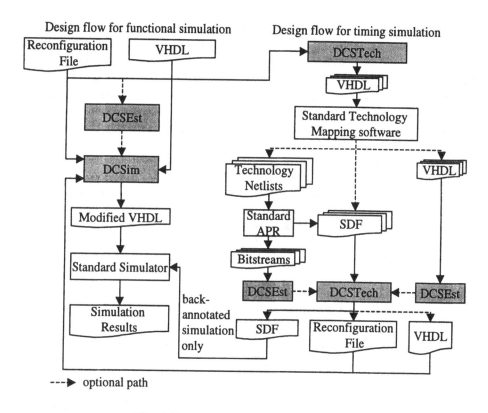

Fig. 1: Proposed DCS CAD framework

The design flow begins at the top-left of the diagram with a set of VHDL design files and a reconfiguration file. The latter specifies the reconfigurable aspects of the design. DCSim combines the two sets of files to produce a modified VHDL design that is used to provide functional simulation.

Two further simulation options exist within the framework. Both of these provide timing simulations, with increasing degrees of accuracy. The first uses timing estimates produced by technology mapping software, such as synthesis tools. The second option makes use of back-annotated timing information, created by APR tools, to provide a more accurate simulation. Both of these simulation flows are shown on the right of the diagram.

The VHDL design files are modified by DCSTech to allow processing by the technology-dependent mapping tools. After the design has passed through the technology mapping software, the designer can choose to use the timing estimates produced by the technology mapper or proceed to the APR stage. Both paths create multiple SDF files which are re-combined and modified by DCSTech to correspond the structure of the initial design. The functional simulation flow is repeated but this time the SDF file is passed to the simulator to provide a timing simulation.

The three simulation paths each require estimates of the time taken to reconfigure individual tasks. These can be supplied by the designer, based on previous experience, or are estimated by DCSEst. DCSEst can be invoked at most stages of the design flow. Initial values can be obtained from the high level VHDL design descriptions. Later in the design cycle, the device-specific VHDL design or the actual bitstreams are used to provide better estimates. DCSTech is responsible for integrating the new estimates into the reconfiguration file prior to each simulation.

Once the back-annotation stage is complete, the design cycle can move into the implementation phase. The bitstreams that have been generated to gain back-annotated timing information are in fact the configurations that are required in the final application. Unlike a conventional "static" FPGA design, this does not represent the end of the design cycle. Further design elements need to be considered such as the reconfiguration controller and overall system design. This design flow is an area ongoing research [4].

4. Back-Annotated Timing

Timing information can only be obtained after a design has been processed by device specific tools. Initially, DCSTech is responsible for decomposing the complete dynamically reconfigurable design into a set of component designs that are each, in themselves, static. These designs can be processed by current tools whereas the composite dynamic design cannot. DCSTech splits the design files based on the reconfiguration specifications contained in the reconfiguration file.

If the design contains n dynamic tasks, then $n+1$ separate designs must be created; one for each task and one more that contains only the static elements of the design (the static design). In the static design, all dynamic tasks are replaced with "reserved" components. These components reserve an area on the array to prevent the placement of circuitry in areas where the dynamic tasks will eventually reside. All tasks that are linked by a mutex group are replaced by a single reserved component that encompass all the tasks elements in the group. Signals that connect to a task must be locked into position in both the static design and the task design. This ensures that the routing is continuous in the dynamic design. Constraints such as task placement and area requirements (in the form of rectangular bounding boxes) may be specified for each task, Fig. 2. Each of the $n+1$ designs are processed by synthesis and APR tools.

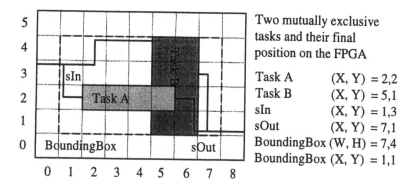

Two mutually exclusive tasks and their final position on the FPGA

Task A	(X, Y) = 2,2
Task B	(X, Y) = 5,1
sIn	(X, Y) = 1,3
sOut	(X, Y) = 7,1
BoundingBox (W, H) = 7,4
BoundingBox (X, Y) = 1,1

Fig. 2: Co-ordinates required by DCSTech

Once the designs have been processed, the timing results obtained can be recombined to create an SDF timing file for the dynamically reconfigurable design. The $n+1$ SDF files produced by the technology specific tools are modified to match the original hierarchy of the dynamically reconfigurable design and then combined into one file.

The DCSTech tool is used to encapsulate all interactions with technology dependent tools. The tool dependent aspects of DCSTech have deliberately been isolated from the core software. This has the advantage of allowing new devices to be targeted by creating a new function library to interface with the device design software.

5. Estimation of Reconfiguration Latency

The reconfiguration latency for a task can be broken down into five constituent latencies, Fig. 3. These latencies are determined by both system (t_{ACK}, $t_{CONTROL}$ and t_{INIT}) and circuit parameters (t_{REMOVE} and t_{LOAD}).

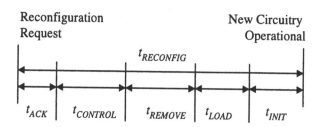

Fig. 3: Reconfiguration latency (reproduced from [5])

The expert system proposed by Lysaght [5] would generate estimates for t_{ACK}, $t_{CONTROL}$ and t_{INIT}. The remaining latencies, t_{REMOVE} and t_{LOAD} are initially estimated by the designer based on previous experience.

t_{REMOVE} and t_{LOAD} are related to the size of the bitstream for the task, which in turn is dependent on the task area. The calculation of area estimates is common in high level synthesis [6, 7] and low power design [8]. Estimation from the behavioural level gives the earliest indication of circuit area. Performing a simple scheduling and binding on the circuit yields estimates that include the area contribution from registers, steering logic and controllers [9]. Area estimation from structural VHDL is obtained by summing the size of every component in the design. Accurate component sizes may be obtained from vendor-supplied libraries. A placement and global routing step can be used to determine the area contributions from wiring and wasted space. Once the circuit area is known, the size of the bitstream can be predicted.

Calculating the t_{REMOVE} and t_{LOAD} latencies from the circuit area is an area of active research. The configuration time for a task differs depending on its position and orientation on the array. Configuration acceleration mechanisms, such as wildcarding, or advanced techniques, such as only configuring the changes between tasks [10], may be used to reduce the configuration time.

6. Conclusions and Future Work

The CAD framework marks an advance in the design and development of reconfigurable systems. An integrated environment of tools and methodologies has been developed that co-exists with existing CAD design flows. The evolution of the original DCS principles, from a simulation tool to a more complete framework for the implementation of dynamic designs, is accelerating as new components are completed. The extraction and APR of dynamic tasks represents a significant step towards implementing the final reconfigurable design.

Many areas of the framework require further research, such as reconfiguration latency estimation, specification of dynamic systems, high level synthesis for minimum configuration time and configuration controller synthesis. The framework provides an essential platform for this research.

7. References

[1] Lysaght, P., Stockwood, J.: A Simulation Tool for Dynamically Reconfigurable Field Programmable Gate Arrays. In: IEEE Transactions on VLSI Systems, Sept 1996
[2] McGregor, G., Lysaght, P.: Extending Dynamic Circuit Switching to Meet the Challenges of New FPGA Architectures. In: Field Programmable Logic and Applications, pp 31-40, Luk, W., Cheung, P., & Glesner, M. (Eds) 1997

[3] Kwiat, K., Debany, W.: Reconfigurable Logic Modelling. Integrated System Design, December 1996 (www.isdmag.com)

[4] McGregor, G., Robinson, D., Lysaght, P.: Hardware/Software Co-design Environment for Reconfigurable Logic Systems. ibid

[5] Lysaght, P.: Towards an Expert System for a priori Estimation of Reconfiguration Latency in Dynamically Reconfigurable Logic. In: Field Programmable Logic and Applications, pp 183-192, Luk, W., Cheung, P., & Glesner, M. (Eds) 1997

[6] Ohm, S. Y., Kurdahi, F. J., Dutt, N., Xu, M.: A Comprehensive Estimation Technique for High-Level Synthesis. In: Proceeding of 8th International Symposium on System Synthesis, 1995.

[7] Xu, M., Kurdahi, F.: ChipEst-FPGA: A Tool for Chip Level Area and Timing Estimation of Lookup Table Based FPGAs for High Level Applications. In: Proceeding of Asia and South Pacific Design Automation Conference, 1997.

[8] Nemani, M., Najm, F.: High-Level Area Prediction for Power Estimation. Custom Integrated Circuits Conference, 1997

[9] De Micheli, G.: Synthesis and Optimization of Digital Circuits, pp155-158, McGraw Hill, 1994

[10] Hadley, J. D., Hutchings, B. L.: Design Methodologies for Partially Reconfigured Systems. In: Peter Athanas and Kenneth L. Pocek, editors. Proceedings of the IEEE Workshop on FPGAs for Custom Computing Machines, pages 78-84, Los Alamitos, California, April 1995. IEEE Computer Society, IEEE Computer Society Press.

Pebble: A Language for Parametrised and Reconfigurable Hardware Design

Wayne Luk and Steve McKeever

Department of Computing, Imperial College, 180 Queen's Gate,
London SW7 2BZ, UK

Abstract. Pebble is a simple language designed to improve the productivity and effectiveness of hardware design. It improves productivity by adopting reusable word-level and bit-level descriptions which can be customised by different parameter values, such as design size and the number of pipeline stages. Such descriptions can be compiled without flattening into various VHDL dialects. Pebble improves design effectiveness by supporting optional constraint descriptions, such as placement attributes, at various levels of abstraction; it also supports run-time reconfigurable design. We introduce Pebble and the associated tools, and illustrate their application to VHDL library development and reconfigurable designs for Field Programmable Gate Arrays (FPGAs).

1 Introduction

Many hardware designers recognise that their productivity can be enhanced by reusable designs in the form of library elements, macros, modules or intellectual property cores. These components are developed carefully to ensure that they are efficient, validated and easy to use. Several development systems based on Java [1], Lola [2], C [3], ML [5], VHDL and Ruby [7] have been proposed. While the languages in these systems have their own goals and merits, none seems to meet all our requirements of:

1. having a simple syntax and semantics;
2. allowing a wide range of parameters in design descriptions;
3. providing support for both word-level design and bit-level design;
4. supporting optional constraint descriptions, such as placement attributes, at various levels of abstraction;
5. including facilities for developing designs reconfigurable at run time.

From our previous work [7] and others, it is also important for design tools to:

6. produce reusable hardware libraries in industrial-standard languages;
7. facilitate multiple means of validation, from formal verification to executing on a hardware platform;
8. enable automatic generation of documentations.

The purpose of this paper is to introduce a language, called Pebble, which is designed to meet the above requirements. Section 2 provides an overview of Pebble, showing how it meets requirements 1–3. Section 3 outlines the development tools for Pebble on which the design flow is based, showing how requirements 6–8 can be satisfied. Section 4 deals with requirement 4: it describes how placement constraints can be captured and how descriptions such as ABOVE and BESIDE provide a useful abstraction. Section 5 presents an approach for developing reconfigurable designs in Pebble, covering requirement 5. User experience with Pebble is reported in Section 6, while concluding remarks are given in Section 7.

2 Language Overview

Pebble is an alias for *Parametrised Block Language*. The two primary objectives for Pebble are to facilitate the development of efficient and reusable designs, and to support the development of designs involving run-time reconfiguration. Much of our previous work is based on VHDL, which has been used for both library development [7] and simulation of reconfigurable components [11].

The complexity of VHDL and the associated tools, however, has led us to believe that a simpler approach will provide a better foundation on which to build abstractions and tools. A simple language would be both easy to learn and to use. More importantly, it would form a core language satisfying our immediate requirements while amenable to extensions. Moreover, since most VHDL vendors have their own dialect of VHDL, it would be easier to generate vendor-specific VHDL from a single standard library database than to maintain different library databases, one for each VHDL dialect. In any case, the complexity of existing industrial languages such as Verilog or VHDL makes them difficult to include experimental features, such as language support for run-time reconfiguration.

Pebble can be regarded as a much simplified variant of structural VHDL. It provides a means of representing block diagrams hierarchically and parametrically. The basic features of Pebble are outlined below [10].

- A Pebble program is a block, defined by its name, parameters, interfaces, local definitions, and its body.
- The block interfaces are given by two lists, usually interpreted as the inputs and outputs. An input or an output can be of type WIRE, or it can be a multi-dimensional vector of wires. A wire can carry integer or boolean values.
- A primitive block has an empty body; a composite block has a body containing the instantiation of composite or primitive blocks in any order. Blocks connected to each other share the same wire in the interface instantiation.
- For hardware designs, the primitive blocks can be bit-level logic gates and registers, or they can, like an adder, process word-level data such as integers or fixed-point numbers; the primitives depend on the availability of corresponding components in the domain targeted by the Pebble compiler.
- The GENERATE-IF statement enables conditional compilation, while the GENERATE-FOR statement allows the concise description of regular circuits.

Pebble has a simple, block-structured syntax. As examples, Fig. 1 contains a Pebble description of a multiplexor which is a primitive component for Xilinx

```
BLOCK mux [c,x,y:WIRE] [z:WIRE]
BEGIN
END;
```

Fig. 1. A multiplexor description in Pebble, with control input c, data inputs x and y and output z. The empty body indicates that it is a primitive block.

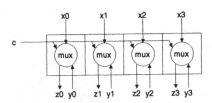

Fig. 2. An array of multiplexors described by the Pebble program in Fig. 3.

6200 FPGAs, while Fig. 3 describes the multiplexor array in Fig. 2, provided that the size parameter n is 4.

In more complex descriptions, the parameters in a Pebble program can include the number of pipeline stages or the pitch between neighbouring interface connections [7]. Different network structures, such as tree- or butterfly-shaped circuits, can be described parametrically by indexing the components and wires.

Pebble supports the use of annotations and constraint descriptions. Annotations contain optional information that does not affect the functional behaviour of Pebble programs. The use of annotations for guiding the Pebble compiler and for automatic documentation generation will be described in Section 3. The use of constraint descriptions to provide, for instance, abstract and concrete placement information will be presented in Section 4.

The semantics of Pebble depends on the behaviour of the primitive blocks and their composition in the target technology. Currently a synchronous circuit

```
BLOCK muxarray (n:GENERIC) [c:WIRE, x,y:VECTOR (n-1..0) OF WIRE]
                           [z:VECTOR (n-1..0) OF WIRE]
        VAR   i
BEGIN
  GENERATE FOR i = 0..(n-1) DO
    mux [c,x(i),y(i)] [z(i)]
END;
```

Fig. 3. A description of an array of multiplexors (Fig. 2) in Pebble. The external input c is used to provide a common control input for each mutiplexor.

model is used in our tools (Section 3), and special control components for modelling run-time reconfiguration are also supported (Section 5). However, other models can be used if desired. Indeed Pebble can be used in modelling any block-structured systems, not just electronic circuits.

Advanced features of Pebble include support for modules which improves reusability and facilitates interface to components in other languages, including behavioural descriptions. Discussions about these features are beyond the scope of this paper.

3 Development Tools and Design Flow

We have developed a compiler for Pebble which can produce either a flattened netlist for simulation, or a parametrised description in structural VHDL. Pebble programs can be compiled into the netlist format for the Rebecca simulator, which can be used for cycle-accurate numerical or symbolic simulation at word-level, bit-level, or a mixture [7]. Automatic mapping between word-level and bit-level blocks is under development. Pebble descriptions can also be translated into formats suitable for verification systems such as HOL [4].

Pebble programs can be compiled into parametrised VHDL while preserving their hierarchy and parametrisation. The resulting VHDL code may contain compiler-generated names, but they can be replaced by user-specified names annotated in the Pebble source code. Section 6 includes more details about the parametrised VHDL libraries generated from Pebble; users of these VHDL libraries do not need to know Pebble.

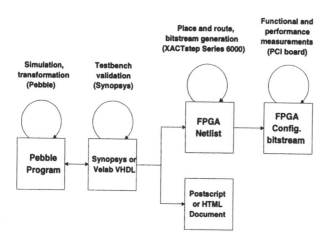

Fig. 4. Design flow for our Pebble-based system. Synopsys and Velab are VHDL tools, and XACTstep Series 6000 is the implementation tool for Xilinx 6200 FPGAs.

Fig. 4 shows the major elements in our design flow. Synopsys is a well-known industrial system which deals with VHDL synthesis; Velab and XACTstep Series

13

6000 are implementation tools for Xilinx 6200 FPGAs; and a PCI-based platform [9] for evaluating designs. We have also developed a Library Documentation Tool (LDT), which automatically produces library documentation in various formats such as Postscript and HTML [7]. The documentation is generated from information annotated in a specific format in the Pebble source; this method reduces the number of files to be maintained.

4 Constraint Description and Abstraction

It is often useful to have the ability to include information about layout or timing in a hardware description. Such information provides a means of guiding design tools to produce an optimised design, or to generate improved estimates of design properties such as critical path delay or reconfiguration time.

Placement information is particularly important for FPGAs for two reasons. First, optimal resource usage is often necessary in FPGA design, since the density and speed of FPGAs are much less than those of custom integrated circuits in similar technologies. Second, precise control over the placement of components is required to minimise reconfiguration time, since components at identical locations common to two successive configurations do not need to be reconfigured.

A number of design languages, such as Lola [2], VHDL [7] and Lava [12], include mechanisms for specifying placement information. Pebble provides a facility similar to these languages. For example, a halfadder containing an **xor2** gate beside an **and2** gate can be described by the Pebble program in Fig. 5.

```
BLOCK hadd (x,y:GENERIC) [a,b:WIRE] [cout,sum:WIRE]
BEGIN
   xor2 [a,b] [sum ] MAP rloc IS "X,x,Y,y,";
   and2 [a,b] [cout] MAP rloc IS "X,(x+1),Y,y,"
END;
```

Fig. 5. A Pebble program describing a halfadder with an **xor** gate on the left of an **and** gate. The values x and y denote the (x,y) co-ordinates of a block; for instance if x=8 and y=3, then the **xor** gate will be placed at (8,3) and the **and** gate at (9,3).

While placement information helps to optimise the layout, it is usually tedious and error-prone to specify. Pebble provides high-level descriptions for placement constraints, abstracting away the low-level details. These descriptions are compile-time directives for the Pebble compiler to project co-ordinates onto designs, generating a tree representing placement possibilities. The two main descriptions are BESIDE, which places two or more blocks beside each other, and ABOVE, which places blocks vertically. These descriptions allow blocks to be placed relatively to each other, without the user providing the coordinates of

14

their locations. Using them, the halfadder example in Fig. 5 becomes the one in Fig. 6(a), while the multiplexor array in Fig. 3 becomes the program in Fig. 6(b).

```
(a) BLOCK hadd [a,b:WIRE] [cout,sum:WIRE]
    BEGIN
       BESIDE (xor2 [a,b] [sum ],
               and2 [a,b] [cout])
    END;

(b) BLOCK muxarray (n:GENERIC) [c:WIRE, x,y:VECTOR (n-1..0) OF WIRE]
                               [z:VECTOR (n-1..0) OF WIRE]
          VAR   i
    BEGIN
       BESIDE FOR i = 0..(n-1) DO
           mux [c,x(i),y(i)] [z(i)]
    END;
```

Fig. 6. (a) A Pebble program using BESIDE to describe the halfadder shown in Fig. 5. (b) A Pebble program describing an array of multiplexors placed beside one another, as shown in Fig. 2. The only alteration to the Pebble description in Fig. 3 is to replace the reserved word GENERATE by BESIDE.

To illustrate further how ABOVE and BESIDE abstract from placement details, consider the description in Fig. 7(a) which specifies that blockC will be placed above blockA and blockB. Without using ABOVE and BESIDE, to place blockC one needs to calculate the width of blockA and the larger of the height of blockA and blockB as in Fig. 7(b). The calculations may involve the generic parameters to these blocks, hence Fig. 7(a) provides a significant simplification.

```
(a)    ABOVE ( blockC [cin] [cout],
             BESIDE ( blockA [ain] [aout],
                     blockB (n) [bin] [bout] ) );

(b)    blockA      [ain] [aout] MAP rloc IS "X,x,Y,y,";
       blockB (n) [bin] [bout] MAP rloc IS "X,(x+widthA),Y,y";
       GENERATE
         IF heightA >= heightB THEN
           blockC [cin] [cout]  MAP rloc IS "X,x,Y,(y+heightA)" END
         IF heightA <  heightB THEN
           blockC [cin] [cout]  MAP rloc IS "X,x,Y,(y+heightB)" END;
```

Fig. 7. (a) A description with nested ABOVE and BESIDE. (b) An alternative with explicit co-ordinates. heightA and widthA denote the height and width of blockA.

A more complex example is a pipelined incrementer [7]. A fully-pipelined incrementer, with a rectangular layout suitable for Xilinx 6200 FPGAs, is shown in Fig. 8. In this design, the core array of halfadders are placed along the diagonal of the block, with triangular-shaped arrays of registers for signal re-alignment placed above and below the halfadder cells.

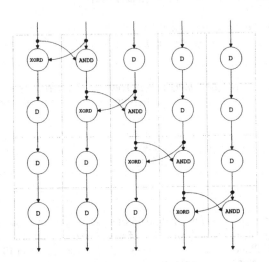

Fig. 8. A fully-pipelined 4-bit incrementer. The components XORD and ANDD correspond to xor and and gates with a latched output.

```
ABOVE FOR i = 0..(n-1) DO
  BESIDE (
    BESIDE FOR j = 0..(i-1) DO
    D [w(i,j)] [w(i+1,j)],
    XORD [w(i,i),w(i,i+1)] [w(i+1,i)],
    ANDD [w(i,i),w(i,i+1)] [w(i+1,i+1)],
    BESIDE FOR j = (i+2)..n DO
    D [w(i,j)] [w(i+1,j)] ) ;
```

Fig. 9. Pebble description of the pipelined incrementer in Fig. 8, where n is 4. w(0,0)..w(0,n) are the input wires for the top row of halfadders, and w(0,0) is the carry-in. w(n,0)..w(n,n) are the outputs at the bottom, and w(n,n) is the carry-out.

The corresponding Pebble code (Fig. 9) contains an ABOVE loop, the body of which contains a BESIDE of the four components found on each row of the array of cells. The first component is itself a BESIDE loop of registers D, whose size increases from zero for the top row of cells to n-1 for the bottom row. On the right of this BESIDE loop, there are the xor and and gates with a register at each of their outputs, which correspond to XORD and ANDD in Fig. 8. The fourth component in a row of cells is another BESIDE loop of registers, whose size decreases from n-1 for the top row of cells to zero for the bottom row. For clarity, the clock and clear signals for registers are not shown. The corresponding code with explicit co-ordinates is too large to be included here.

It is possible to extend this design so that the number of pipeline stages can be controlled by a parameter [7]. The resulting description can be used to produce implementations with different trade-offs in resource usage and performance.

5 Support for Reconfiguration

Pebble supports the development of run-time reconfigurable circuits based on the model for reconfigurable designs in [8]. In this model, a component that can be configured to behave either as A or as B is described by a network with A and B connected between two control blocks. The control blocks, RC_DMux and RC_Mux, route the data and results from the external ports x and y to A or B depending on the value of *cond* (Fig. 10). Each control block will be mapped either into a real multiplexor or a demultiplexor to produce a single-cycle reconfigurable design, or into virtual ones which model the control mechanisms for replacing one configuration by another. If the reconfiguration sequence is known at compile time, then control blocks which model the run-time selection of components in a particular sequence can be used [6]. At present Pebble descriptions are translated into the EDIF format, for which a set of tools has been developed to produce reconfigurable designs [8]. We are exploring language support for reconfiguration by having, for instance, a RECONFIGURE-IF statement (Fig. 11).

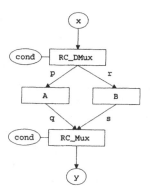

Fig. 10. A design that can behave either as A or as B, depending on the value of the input wire *cond* connected to the control blocks RC_DMux and RC_Mux.

6 Experience

Pebble has been in development since early 1997. In the following we report our experience with Pebble in three applications: hardware library development,

```
(a)    BLOCK AB [x,cond:WIRE] [y:WIRE]
       BEGIN
          RECONFIGURE IF cond THEN
             A [x] [y]   END
          ELSE
             B [x] [y]   END
       END;

(b)    BLOCK AB [x,cond:WIRE] [y:WIRE]
       VAR p, q, r, s: WIRE
       BEGIN
          RC_DMux [cond,x] [p,r];
          A [p] [q];
          B [r] [s];
          RC_Mux [cond,q,s] [y]
       END;
```

Fig. 11. (a) A Pebble block showing how the RECONFIGURE IF statement captures the circuit in Fig. 10. (b) An alternative Pebble block describing the same design, with variables p, q, r and s representing the internal wires.

implementation of video-processing hardware, and student design projects.

Our previous work on parametrised hardware libraries involved VHDL87 from Synopsys [7]. Since then Xilinx introduced Velab, a fast VHDL93 elaborator which is issued free of charge. Because of the differences in the two VHDL dialects, many of our libraries have to be rewritten. Following the design flow in Fig. 4, over 30 libraries have now been recast in Pebble and most can target both Synopsys and Velab.

Pebble libraries have been used in various applications, particularly for video processing. To enable video experiments, a real-time video interface has been built for a PCI-based board with a Xilinx 6200 FPGA and two megabytes of memory [9]. Case studies include linear and non-linear filtering, edge detection, image rotation, colour identification and motion detection.

Pebble has also been used in many student projects. Because of the simplicity of the language and the tools, students usually master the basic techniques rapidly and complete complex designs much faster than using VHDL. As an example in a group project for first-year undergraduates, a convolver which took more than four weeks to design in VHDL was finished in Pebble within the first week of the project.

7 Concluding Remarks

Pebble has served as a focus for our research on languages and tools for developing hardware in general and reconfigurable circuits in particular. Its simplicity facilitates design construction, parametrisation and validation. It supports circuit descriptions at various levels of abstraction, allowing designers to selectively control a design step such as placement when desired. Designs can be captured and analysed at different levels of detail, since they can be expressed using non-implementable components such as RC_Mux (Section 5) and converters between word-level and bit-level data. Current and future work includes support for passing blocks as parameters and for polynomial constraints, optimisations such as retiming and partial evaluation, interface to high-level tools and run-time environments, and backends for various FPGAs and custom VLSI implementations.

Acknowledgements

Our thanks to the many Pebble developers, users and advisors, particularly Florent Dupont-De-Dinechin, Douglas Grant, Patrick Mackinlay, Richard Sandiford, Seng Shay Ping, Nabeel Shirazi, Dimitris Siganos, David Stacey and Markus Weinhardt, for their help and suggestions. The support of Xilinx, Interval Research, Hewlett Packard Laboratories Bristol and the UK Engineering and Physical Sciences Research Council (Grant Number GR/L24366, GR/L54356 and GR/L59658) is gratefully acknowledged.

References

1. P. Bellows and B. Hutchings, "JHDL – an HDL for reconfigurable systems", in *Proc. FCCM98*, IEEE Computer Society Press, 1998.
2. S. Gehring and S. Ludwig, "The Trianus system and its application to custom computing", in *Field-Programmable Logic, Smart Applications, New Paradigms and Compilers*, LNCS 1142, Springer, 1996.
3. M. Gokhale and E. Gomersall, "High-Level compilation for fine-grained FPGAs", in *Proc. FCCM97*, IEEE Computer Society Press, 1997.
4. M.J.C. Gordon, "Why Higher-Order Logic is a good formalism for specifying and verifying hardware", in *Formal Aspects of VLSI Design*, G. Milne and P.A. Subrahmanyam (eds.), North Holland, 1986.
5. Y. Li and M. Leeser, "HML: an innovative hardware description language and its translation to VHDL", in *Proc. CHDL'95*, 1995.
6. W. Luk, "Systematic serialization of array-based architectures", *Integration, the VLSI Journal*, 14(3), February 1993.
7. W. Luk, S. Guo, N. Shirazi and N. Zhuang, "A framework for developing parametrised FPGA libraries", in *Field-Programmable Logic, Smart Applications, New Paradigms and Compilers*, LNCS 1142, Springer, 1996.
8. W. Luk, N. Shirazi and P.Y.K. Cheung, "Compilation tools for run-time reconfigurable designs", in *Proc. FCCM97*, IEEE Computer Society Press, 1997.
9. W. Luk, N. Shirazi, S. Guo and P.Y.K. Cheung, "Pipeline morphing and virtual pipelines", in *Field Programmable Logic and Applications*, LNCS 1304, Springer, 1997.
10. W. Luk, S. McKeever and M. Weinhardt, *A Tutorial Introduction to Pebble*, Technical Report, Imperial College, 1998.
11. P. Lysaght and J. Stockwood, "A simulation tool for dynamically reconfigurable field programmable gate arrays", *IEEE Trans. VLSI*, 4(3), September 1996.
12. S. Singh, *Lava*, http://www.dcs.gla.ac.uk/~satnam/lava/main.html.

Integrated Development Environment for Logic Synthesis Based on Dynamically Reconfigurable FPGAs

Valery Sklyarov, Ricardo Sal Monteiro, Nuno Lau, Andreia Melo,
Arnaldo Oliveira, Konstantin Kondratjuk

Department of Electronics and Telecommunications, Aveiro University,
Campo Universitário, 3810 Aveiro, Portugal
skl@inesca.pt; {ricardo, lau, andreia, arnaldo}@ua.pt; k.kondr@usa.net

Abstract. The paper discusses the models, methods and software tools included in an Integrated Design Environment for Logic Synthesis (IDELS) that has been developed in Visual C++ and can be used for PC computers running under Windows 95/98. It is able to solve a range of problems related to the design of digital systems and their components based on dynamically reconfigurable FPGAs of the XC6200 family. The paper focuses primarily on the integrated features, the basic capabilities and the main packages of the environment itself, rather than the details of how it was implemented. However, the basic ideas behind the methods used, and some of the approaches to implementing the environment are considered, together with some of the problems that we had to address.

1. Introduction

Models of digital circuits can be visualized at different levels of abstraction [1], each of which shows specific features of interest with their associated details. We will consider here two main abstractions, the architectural level and the logic level. The architectural level of abstraction is characterized by a set of operations. In the logic level of abstraction, a circuit evaluates and calculates a set of logic functions. In general, when we are using FPGAs we have to combine architectural, logic, and topological levels. Indeed, if we do not pay particular attention to the last level, in many cases we will be prevented from completing our design because of routing problems since it is very common that some connections cannot be routed. In practice, the problem can be solved by applying some constraints that will be taken into account by the software, such as XACT6000 [2,3].

For many practical applications (embedded applications in particular [4]), digital systems are heterogeneous and their specification may change continuously. In this case we need to provide them with the flexibility and extensibility necessary to accommodate this. In some instances this can be achieved by exploiting field programmable technology, but for the general case this is not sufficient because the particular methods of the design must be adapted to this technology. Since the behavior of digital systems and their components is determined by control circuits, to provide the system with the properties of flexibility and extensibility, we have to be able to modify the control algorithms after the scheme for the control circuits has been implemented in hardware. For some applications it is also desirable to be able to modify their functionality during run-time. An attractive technique that might be used for such purposes, is based on partial dynamic reconfiguration. Unfortunately, the established approaches to architectural, logic, and topological synthesis cannot be applied directly, so we need to develop new models, methods, and software tools that provide:

- design of virtual control circuits, i.e. circuits that implement dynamically modifiable control algorithms;
- design of virtual digital controllers based on virtual control circuits surrounded with supplementary logic, which simplifies vector-based operations [5];
- design of reconfigurable datapath components;
- a working design environment for dynamically reconfigurable FPGAs.

This paper is organized in seven sections. Section 1 is this introduction. Section 2 clarifies the problem considered in the paper and specifies the target requirements. Sections 3, 4 and 5 present the basic techniques developed for virtual control circuits, virtual controllers and the datapath. Section 6 contains a description of the Integrated Design Environment for Logic Synthesis (IDELS), which is considered as working tools for dynamically reconfigurable FPGAs. The conclusion is in section 7.

2. Problem Definition

We have already mentioned that traditionally digital systems and their components can be modeled as a composition of a datapath and a control circuit. The latter is responsible for pure control such that inputs and outputs are considered as individual one-bit signals represented by boolean variables, for example $x_1,...,x_L$ for inputs $1,...,L$, and $y_1,...,y_N$ for outputs $1,...,N$. This kind of device may be used not only as a component of more complicated digital system, but also autonomously for embedded applications in such a way that the device is considered as an embedded controller. For many practical cases the capabilities of pure control are limited for embedded systems and we have to extend them in order to handle both individual binary signals and multi-bit vector signals [5]. In principle such an extension might be visualized as a primitive datapath. However, for many practical applications, the treatment of multi-bit signals can be modeled by some well-known operations applied to the relevant boolean vectors in such a way that we are dealing with boolean functions and boolean equations. This possibility allows us to introduce and to consider models and methods oriented towards embedded controllers. That is why we have specified three different areas for our research, pure control circuits, digital systems decomposed into a datapath and control units, and digital controllers to be visualized as a pure control circuit surrounded by extra logic for handling boolean vectors. Note that the last case has been considered in detail in [5].

There are many different methods and tools that can be applied to describe the behavior of pure control units [1,6,7, etc.]. We are using graph-schemes (GS) [6] for such purposes, as well as their varieties, such as extended GS [5], hierarchical GS (HGS) [8] and parallel HGS [9]. The proposed synthesis technique (see section 3 below) enables us to provide a formal conversion of a given GS (HGS) to the corresponding virtual control circuit physically implemented within a dynamically reconfigurable FPGA, such as XC6200 family. The virtual property of a circuit makes it possible to have just a part of the entire circuit implemented in hardware at any given time. When another part, not currently implemented in the FPGA, is needed, it will be loaded in place of some part that is currently not required. This process is hidden and automatic.

We have already mentioned above that a digital controller can be visualized as a composition of a pure control unit plus extra logic that is used to handle boolean vectors. The behavior of the pure control unit can be described with the aid of GS (HGS) and the corresponding synthesis approach can be used. The extra logic is responsible for processing boolean vectors and it is linked with the associated pure control unit to help the unit carry out the following kinds of operations:

- calculating the value(s) of boolean function(s). For instance, we might want to calculate the value of the function $X = A.B + C.D$, where A, B, C and D are n-bit operands, and X is an n-bit result that we want to obtain. The same target can be specified for a system of boolean functions;
- testing the values of boolean functions. Suppose, for example, we have to examine the results of the expression $A.B + C.D < 1010$, where A, B, C and D are 4-bit boolean vectors and the result is one-bit value;
- providing support for switch-case statements in such a way that the result of a calculation is an n-bit value $x_1,...,x_k$ that might be interpreted in different ways;
- providing various loops similar to "for" and "while" loops in C/C++ languages.

This list could be extended with many other application-dependent operations that generally correspond with constructions common to general purpose programming languages, such as C and C++. All these operations can be implemented in circuits formally synthesized with the aid of sequential and combinatorial optimization however, for many practical cases, this leads us to design irregular circuits that in general are not compliant with our requirements such as modifiability and extensibility. We have proposed another technique that can be characterized as stack-oriented calculations using reverse Polish notation (see section 4 below).

The design technique for a datapath is mainly based on traditional methodology [1]. The only new facilities that have been provided are related to dynamic reconfiguration (see section 5 below).

3. Control Circuits Design

The proposed technique provides the formal conversion of a given behavioral specification (that is a set of GSs or their varieties) to a hardware implementation (which is a configured FPGA of the XC6200 family). This technique is founded on the following general sequence of steps:

1. Behavioral specification of the control algorithm by GSs (HGSs).
2. Applying optimization technique to the GSs (HGSs), based on the methods described in [6]. The primary purpose is to minimize the numbers of rhomboidal and rectangular nodes of the GSs.
3. Synthesis of structural VHDL code with minimal components taken from the Xilinx PRIMS library for FPGAs of the XC6200 family from the behavioral description [5].
4. Translation of the code from the previous item into an EDIF file with the aid of the VELAB elaborator [10].
5. Processing of the EDIF file using XACT6000 [3] to carry out mapping, placement and routing of the control circuit for a particular type of FPGA, such as XC6216, obtaining the FPGA configuration information.
6. Loading configuration information (described by CAL and SYM files) into FPGA RAM. In the case of the FireFly™ PC board Annapolis, the procedure is based on commercially available libraries, such as RALLib [3] and Annapolis [11], and original software developed by the authors of this paper.

The contribution of the authors is mainly covered by point 3 and partially by points 1 and 6 above. Let us consider them in more detail.

Control algorithms (see point 1) are described using a comprehensive graphical editor that incorporates user-friendly interface supporting run-time debugging facilities (see point 6). In summary it allows:

- the rapid and effective description and editing of both GSs and HGSs;
- emulation of control sequences generated by the control algorithm, i.e. specification of input variables and monitoring of desired output signals;
- run-time debugging facilities that make it possible to observe in parallel input/output sequences from real hardware and from software emulation. The user may specify break points at FSM states and control the number of clock pulses that drive the control circuit at each step.

The synthesis tools (see point 3) use two methods of FSM synthesis. The first method enables us to construct a FSM on the basis of one-hot encoding technique [5,12]. In the second method [5,7] the output register of the FSM is simultaneously used as the state register. This method allows explicit states to be avoided. We can visualize such output vectors as implicit states.

We assume that virtual control circuits have been specified by a set of HGSs. Any individual HGS in the given set is considered to be a relatively autonomous component, which in particular cases might be reused in future products. The proposed technique provides for automatic swapping of the HGSs available in the FPGA and stored in external RAM. Each HGS that is loaded into the FPGA is associated with some window in the configuration RAM. When necessary, a new HGS can be loaded into this window during run-time. The proposed swapping mechanism is fully automatic and completely hidden from the end user. We have proposed to build the control algorithm in such a way that it is ordered hierarchically and all its components are HGSs with a limited number of nodes. In fact this is not a difficult constraint. If necessary, any complex HGS can be decomposed into simpler HGSs that satisfy our requirements. For the current implementation, we assume that a maximum of four HGSs can be loaded into an FPGA simultaneously. However the overall complexity of a control algorithm is practically unlimited. The limitation on the size of an HGS is necessary for it to fit in one of the predefined windows in configuration RAM. All four windows are identical and have a predefined numbers of inputs and outputs. During the swapping process, all links with the corresponding window will be temporary suspended. This is permitted for FPGAs of the XC6200 family, which allow partial dynamic reconfiguration [2].

4. Design of Digital Controllers

The main ideas of the proposed approach were considered in [5]. They are based on the use of a pure control unit (see previous section) surrounded with supplementary logic that provides helper functions (see section 2). Since we have already considered all the steps for synthesis of a pure control circuit, we will concentrate here on the structural organization of helper logic that is dealing with boolean vectors and extending the facilities of the original behavioral specification. The supplementary logic also allows us to specify GSs (HGSs) that can contain (see also section 2):

- rhomboidal nodes with boolean functions, i.e. expressions with boolean vectors, that have to be calculated;
- conditional branches or switch-case statements;
- loops with preconditions (such as the "for" loop in C) and post conditions (such as the "do-while" loop in C);
- operational nodes allowing boolean function(s) and boolean equation(s) to be dealt with;
- operational node of HGSs that can invoke virtual macrooperations [13], i.e. other HGSs that might be identified only during run-time;
- operational nodes for which we can specify the duration of clock pulses (we call such GSs extended GSs). The corresponding control circuit is modeled by a FSM with a run-time alterable clock.

The distinctive feature of all these extensions is the necessity to deal with boolean vectors, i.e. we would want to provide the desired processing of individual binary signals together with the treatment of multi-bit variables. The resources available within FPGAs of the XC6200 family allow them to be structured in such a way that they will directly implement any operation with boolean vectors of a reasonable length. Note that any cell of an FPGA can be reconfigured to implement any boolean function of two variables with very high speed (300 ns for a clock frequency of 66 MHz [14]). A composition of n cells allows any given function to be applied to boolean vectors of size n, and allows a reconfigurable unit (that is the kernel of a logic processor) for handling boolean vectors to be constructed. The idea here is to convert boolean function(s) to reverse Polish form, then to store all the required operations in stack memory, and finally to sequentially extract these operations from the stack and execute them on a single reconfigurable logic processor based on modifiable FPGA cells. This technique has at least two advantages. Firstly it only requires cells to be reconfigured. Since we do not need to alter routing resources, this is easier and faster. Secondly the implementation is very well suited to possible future modifications and extensions.

5. Datapath Design

It has been already mentioned that the basic contribution of the authors in this area is aimed at exploitation of methods and tools for partial dynamic reconfiguration. The problem of a reconfigurable datapath design has been divided into two, the design of the core of the datapath that carries out arithmetic and logic computations, and the design of the structural components of the datapath, such as widely used blocks whose functionality can be altered slightly (counters, shift registers, multiplexers, decoders, etc.). We have assumed that the design of the core can be based on the approach considered above (see section 4). The structural components can be viewed as standard elements belonging to some predefined library such as MACROS available with VELAB [10].

The design of the core of the datapath is based on reverse Polish notation and mainly follows the ideas that we discussed earlier. Depending on the target, this technique can be applied to either logic or arithmetic computations. In fact we are dealing with universal computational units that can be implemented using dynamically reconfigurable cells without any specific restrictions on the required functions, be they arithmetic, logic, algebraic or others.

Another technique is the design of predefined frames (templates), which contain reprogrammable (reconfigurable) elements with modifiable functions from a predefined set. For example, each FPGA cell can be characterized by a set of feasible functions that might be realized by configuring built in RAM. Any composition of cells can be seen as a reconfigurable unit with a predefined set of possible configurations provided by its reconfigurable cells and its modifiable routing resources. We assume that most of the connections between elements within a particular frame are fixed and cannot be changed. This requirement has to be taken into account for various hierarchical levels above the cell level. The objective is to make the scheme more structural in order to achieve the minimum possible number of changes to implement any required modifications or extensions. Generally speaking, each frame is considered to be a template for a finite number of related applications. The customizing of the base frame (implementing, for instance, a set of desired arithmetic operations) is carried out by configuring (reconfiguring) FPGA cells with the minimum possible number of modifications to routing resources. For many practical cases (see, for example, section 4) we are able to avoid re-routing altogether.

In order to construct standard parameterizable blocks with predefined functionality the following work has been done:

1. We have created a library of components that are similar to the macros considered in [10] and in XC6200 of Xilinx. It includes circuits for different synchronization modes, various kinds of stacks, circuits supporting dynamic swapping of FPGA areas, and so on.
2. We are planning to use well-known combinatorial methods for the synthesis of combinational schemes [15] with some predefined constraints [3,14]. The topological constraints specify some recommendations to relevant software such as XACT6000 [2]. The constraints are not mandatory, but we generally predict good results if they are taken into account. Performing logic synthesis accordingly to the approach mentioned above provides a bridge between logic and topological steps and it allows many problems to be avoided.
3. We are developing a package of IDELS, which will be used for the synthesis of reusable functional blocks. It is based on predefined VHDL self-constructed frames that can be slightly extended in order to be completed and implemented in hardware.

6. Integrated Design Environment for Logic Synthesis

Integrated Design Environment for Logic Synthesis (IDELS) has been developed at the Electronics and Telecommunications Department of Aveiro University. It enables us to solve a variety of design problems for dynamically reconfigurable FPGAs of the XC6200 family and in general it has the following primary components:

1. Integrated development subsystem for pure control circuits design. This is based on commercially available software, plus software tools developed by the authors that combined allow the design steps considered in section 3 to be carried out.
2. Integrated debugger with modifiable debugging resources such as externally accessible components of arbitrary circuits implemented within an FPGA with support for dynamic reconfiguration.
3. Library which is composed of graphical images and structural VHDL codes. At any step, any component of the design can be included into the library for future use. In addition, we can use any existing VHDL code based on components of the library for XC6200 FPGAs, such as macros available with VELAB elaborator [10].
4. We are currently working on the subsystem of IDELS that provides the design of datapath and digital controllers based on the techniques discussed in sections 4 and 5.

All the software has been developed in Visual C++ (currently version 5.0) under Windows 95/98 environment. Since the first subsystem (see point 1 above) has been described in detail in section 3, we will skip it here and concentrate on the components 2 and 3.

The debugger has a comprehensive user-friendly interface, and it provides for loading the design and working with the FPGA implementing the design. It is primarily based on software developed by the authors. If it is used in conjunction with a PC board, such as FireFly™ of Annapolis, the low-level access to the board has been organized via the RALLib library [3] and the Annapolis C++ classes [11]. Inputs of the debugger can be:

- SYM file, which is produced by XACT6000 and defines placements of circuit components within the FPGA;
- optional RAL file, which is also produced by XACT6000 [3] and defines data for the dynamic reconfiguration of individual FPGA cells;
- optional structural VHDL code for the circuit based on components of the PRIMS library for FPGAs of the XC6200 family.

The first file gives information about readable and writable components of the debugged circuit. Data from any readable component of FPGA can be displayed during run-time. Any writable component of the FPGA can be changed during run-time from the debugger resources. Tracing facilities have also been provided so we can observe historical values for all readable components represented as waveforms.

RAL file is used when dynamic reconfiguration is required. Currently the debugger supports two different ways of making run-time modifications. The first allows the functionality of any modifiable cell to be changed, i.e. any cell that can be identified and recognized by data from the RAL file. The second way of making modifications allows templates (groups of cells) to be constructed. For example, we can create a template for any primary component of an arithmetic and logic unit. This template will specify all possible configurations that we intend to implement in future. Information about these configurations will be kept in internal structures of IDELS (and ultimately in relevant files). Later this information will be used to reconfigure both the individual components and any number of grouped components with the repeated template. In other words any predefined configuration can be automatically replicated.

Structural VHDL code is read by IDELS and converted to a visually represented structural scheme. The scheme is composed of all structural components that were present in VHDL code. If you click any component you can see all its connections with the other components. You can also observe input and output run-time values while debugging. For convenience, facilities for dragging components of the structural scheme have been implemented.

The debugger provides comprehensive run-time support for modularity and hierarchy. Modularity makes it possible to observe/modify values of a tangible entity, which is a component at a given level within the design hierarchy. Since each level reflects a user-dependent abstraction, it can be rearranged during run-time if necessary. This allows the abstraction that will be most appropriate to each debugging task to be created. Let say we want to examine a set $Rh_1,...,Rh_K$ of K registers, and each register Rh_k has the size G. For one debugging task, we would want to consider such entities (modules) as $Rh_1,...,Rh_K$, which implies a horizontal level of abstraction composed of some rows $1,...,k,...,K$. On the other hand we might want to examine a vertical level of abstraction composed of some columns $1,...,g,...,G$, i.e. entities $Rv_1,...,Rv_G$ where each entity Rv_g is visualized as a column g (bit g) within the given set of registers. The debugger permits the given hierarchical tree of the circuit to be rearranged in any reasonable way specified by the designer. We have already mentioned the differences between the topological hierarchy and the logic (architectural) hierarchy, so the capability of IDELS to build precisely the hierarchy that we want gives significant benefits.

The debugger provides powerful synchronization facilities, such as:

- step by step synchronization with the aid of clocks forced by the designer. Each clock pulse is generated when you press a particular key on the keyboard;
- generation of a local clock sequence with any frequency that can contain any desired number of clock pulses;
- free-running local clocks;
- global clocks with any frequency permitted by the FireFly™ board;
- local and global reset facilities.

The debugger provides support for a large number of mechanisms that are common to general purpose software, such as:

- specifying the required observable (readable and writable) components;
- setting break points;
- generating any desired (arbitrarily distributed in time) sequence of input (intermediate) vectors preliminary stored in the respective files;
- storing all intermediate debugging information in a file within a predefined period of time.

7. Conclusion

In the previous discussion, we have described the primary components of the Integrated Design Environment for Logic Synthesis (IDELS). IDELS is being developed as a standard Windows application. All the components have been designed in the Visual C++ environment (version 5.0). The first version of IDELS has been preliminarily tested for different design tasks. All experiments have been performed with the Annapolis FireFly™ PC board based on the XC6216 FPGA. We have performed synthesis, implementation in FPGA, debugging and testing of a variety of digital devices, such as pure control circuits described by graph-schemes, virtual control circuits described by hierarchical graph-schemes, and autonomous digital components of datapath and embedded controllers. The correctness of the functionality was checked using external and internal tools. In the first case a multi-channel logic analyzer (Hewlett Packard 1650A) externally connected to FPGA pins via the PC board mezzanine connectors was used. Thus all required waveforms were evaluated and examined in real time. In the second case we have used the debugger facilities of IDELS. The capability for dynamic reconfiguration has been tested with the aid of designed modifiable computational units. The preliminary results have shown that the majority of target requirements have been satisfied. We are going to continue working in the directions described in this paper. The most immediate task is to complete the IDELS subsystem that will provide formal synthesis of reconfigurable computational units and control circuits described by parallel hierarchical graph-schemes. The other problem we are addressing is the design of digital systems as a composition of so-called hardware objects [7] for which we would want to combine the methods of digital synthesis with the technique of object-oriented analysis and design.

References

1. Giovanni De Micheli: Synthesis and Optimization of Digital Circuits. McGraw-Hill, Inc., (1994)
2. Xilinx: XC6200 Field Programmable Gate Arrays, Xilinx Product Description (Version 1.10). April 24 (1997)
3. Xilinx: XACTstep Series 6000 User Guide. (1997)
4. Stepen Edwards, Luciano Lavagno, Edward A.Lee, Alberto Sangiovanny-Vincentelli: Design of Embedded Systems: Formal Models, Validation, and Synthesis. Proceeding of the IEEE, vol. 85, no. 3, March (1997) 366-390
5. Valery Sklyarov, Nuno Lau, Ricardo Sal Monteiro, Andreia Melo, Arnaldo Oliveira, Konstantin Kondratjuk: Design of Virtual Digital Controllers Based on Dynamically Reconfigurable FPGAs. Proc. of Workshop on Digital System Design: Architectures. Methods and Tools, Vasteras, Sweden (1998)
6. S.Baranov: Logic Synthesis for Control Automata. Kluwer Academic Publishers (1994)
7. Valery Sklyarov, Antonio Adrego da Rocha, Antonio de Brito Ferrari: Synthesis of Reconfigurable Control Devices Based on Object-Oriented Specifications. In :Advanced Techniques for Embedded Systems Design and Test. Kluwer Academic Publishers (1998) 151-177
8. Valery Sklyarov, Antonio de Brito Ferrari: Synthesis of Control Devices Described by Hierarchical Graph-Schemes. Springer-Verlag (1998) 181-191
9. Antonio Adrego da Rocha, Valery Sklyarov, Antonio de Brito Ferrari: Hierarchical Description and Design of Control Circuits Based on Reconfigurable and Reprogrammable Elements. Proc. of the International Workshop on Logic and Architectural Synthesis - IWLAS'97, Grenoble, December (1997) 73-82
10. Xilinx: Velab, VHDL Elaborator for XC6200 (v0.52). Internet at URL http://www.xilinx.com/apps/velabrel.htm (1998)
11. Annapolis Micro Systems, Inc.: XC6200 PCI Board C++ Interface. Included in FireFly™ Board Documentation.
12. Valery Sklyarov, Antonio de Brito Ferrari: Design and Implementation of Control Circuits Based on Dynamically Reconfigurable FPGA. Proc. of IEEE International Conference on Electronics, Circuits and Systems, Lisbon (1998)
13. Valery Sklyarov, Antonio Adrego da Rocha, Antonio de Brito Ferrari: Applying Procedural and Object-Oriented Decomposition to the Logical Synthesis of Digital Devices. Proc. of the Second International Conference on Computer-Aided Design of Discrete Devices CADDD'97, Minsk (1997) 15-20.
14. Annapolis Micro Systems, Inc.: FIREFLY™ Tutorials. Included in FireFly™ Board Documentation. November (1997)
15. A.Zakrevskij: Combinatorial Problems over Logical Matrices in Logic Design and Artificial Intelligence. Electrónica e Telecomunicações, vol. 2, No 2 (1998) 261-268.

Designing for Xilinx XC6200 FPGAs

Reiner W. Hartenstein, Michael Herz, Frank Gilbert

University of Kaiserslautern
Erwin-Schrödinger-Straße, D-67663 Kaiserslautern, Germany
Fax: ++49 631 205 2640, email: abakus@informatik.uni-kl.de
www: http://xputers.informatik.uni-kl.de

Abstract. With the XC6200 FPGA Xilinx introduced the first commercially available FPGA designed for reconfigurable computing. It has a completely new internal architecture, so new design algorithms and software is needed. Due to the fact that most applications are in the research area, the number of sold units seems to be small. Because of this progress of design tools for this architecture is rather low. This paper discusses the problems, which appear during designing for the XC6200 FPGAs. A dedicated design flow is presented and demonstrated on an example application.

1 Introduction

The XC6200 is an FPGA that has been designed to be used in two broad classes of applications. The first class is the conventional role of a general-purpose ASIC device for logic integration. The other role is that of an intelligent peripheral that can operate as a memory-mapped coprocessor in microprocessor systems. This is largely due to the advanced FPGA to CPU interface. The design philosophy appears to have been driven by the desire to produce a FPGA optimized for reconfigurable computing.

Designing for the XC6200 is similar to other FPGA families, but some limitations apply. The design software is still in a beta state and progress is slow, as the commercial use is low. Not all features are implemented yet and some are still buggy. Further routing of irregular structures is very difficult because of few routing resources of the target architecture. A lot of problems during application implementation have to be solved manually. Therefore most design flows directly start at gate level where directly the logic blocks of the FPGA are programmed (e.g. Lola [Lo98]). This is like a step back into the stone age of hardware design. To alleviate this drawback in this paper a dedicated design flow for the XC6200 FPGA family is proposed. A few steps appear similar to other FPGA technologies. But due to XC6200 specific problems each single step shows differences to other technologies. Designing consists of five steps: Design Creation, Logic Synthesis, Netlist Generation, Place and Route and Simulate Design with Timing Information. As stated before this looks familiar, although Netlist Generation is mostly a part of the Logic Synthesis step.

The paper is structured as follows. First in the next section the structure of the hardware is briefly introduced. After sketching the limitations of available design software the dedicated design flow is presented, which is mainly based on predefined macro cells. Its benefits are demonstrated with an generic 3x3 linear filter with configurable weights for image processing. This application benefits from the processor interface, which allows to change filter coefficients without reconfiguration of the complete device. To simplify the design process the control part of the design is synthesized. Performance results will justify the introduced method.

2 Overview on the Xilinx XC6k and the VCC HOT Works Board

Architectural Overview on the XC6200 Series [GL97]

The XC6200 is based on a fine-grained, sea-of-gates architecture. The XC6216 consists of an array of 64 x 64 core cells surrounded by 256 input-output ports. Every logic cell can implement any combinatorial logic function of two inputs. Each cell can also implement a D-type flip-flop which can be used to register the cell's combinatorial function. Cells have nearest neighbor connections to their North, South, East and West neighbors. The device has a hierarchical busing scheme. Cells are organized into blocks of 4 x 4, 16 x 16, and so on, increasing by a factor of four each time. A set of fast buses is associated with each size of block. Access to these fast buses is via routing switches that are adjacent to the cells on periphery of the respective blocks.

The processor interface is a 32-bit wide data bus that may also be configured for 16 or 8 bit operation. The XC6200 has been designed to appear in system as random access memory. All data registers on the array are accessible, making it possible to interface with user logic via the processor interface alone. Registers are addressed in columns via a map register. Up to 32 of the 64 registers in column may be read from or written to by nominating their appropriate row position in the map register. This can be extended so that all of the 64 registers in a column may be written by a single 8-bit operation. This is particularly useful in reconfigurable computing applications.

For further information, please refer to the Xilinx XC6200 datasheet at [Xi98a] and some application notes at [Xi98b].

The HOT Works PCI-XC6200 Development System

The proposed design-flow and the implemented examples are tested on the HOT Works PCI Board by Virtual Computer Corporation [Vc98]. The board architecture allows the XC6200 to be accessed by a host CPU via the PCI-bus. The board consists of:

- a XC6216 for the user-designs
- a XC4013 implementing the PCI bus interface
- up to 2 MBytes of fast SRAM for user-data
- a programmable clock-generator.

The XC6216, the SRAM and a set of configuration registers are mapped to the memory space of the host CPU. This allows the host CPU to read or write the SRAM memory of the board and configure or read or write the user FPGA and the user design. For an introduction to the XC6200 Development System refer to [NG97], further information can be found at [Xi97a].

3 Design-Flow for the Xilinx XC6200

This chapter will describe a VHDL-based design flow for the XC6200. First, all parts of the development process (design libraries and software) are described. Then the general design flow, the use of the software, problems and limitations concerning the single design steps are discussed.

The design environment consists of five parts (figure 1). First, a VHDL-simulator is needed to validate the VHDL design description. Then behavioral VHDL must be synthesized in primitive gates of the target technology, therefore a synthesis tool with a corresponding technology library is required. The output format of the synthesis tool will be VHDL. To transform the VHDL netlist in the EDIF-input-format of the place-and-route tool a small program will be used. The place-and-route software is the last tool to mention in the design environment.

Technology Library

Basic part of the development process is a technology library. The primitives of this library are any two-input gate functions, any 2:1 multiplexer, constant 0 or 1, buffer, inverter and D-type register. Technology libraries for the XC6200 family exist for the Viewlogic schematic entry tool and the Synopsys Design Compiler. In our design environment Synopsys is utilized.

Using a textural description of the target technology, the Synopsys Library Compiler generates, in addition to a primitive library for the Synopsys Design Compiler, also a VITAL [Vi95] compliant technology library for VHDL-simulation and back-annotation. The VITAL library provides behavioral models of all primitive gates with default timing. The default timing can be overridden by exact timing values calculated by the Place-and-Route-software using SDF data (Standard Delay Format). The Synopsys library is included in the SunOS version of XACT Step 6000 only.

Simulating the design

As the synthesis primitive library can be used only with the Synopsys Design Compiler, the VITAL library is vendor independent. The VITAL library can be simulated with any VHDL simulator such as Synopsys' VSS, Model Technology's V-System or Mentor Graphics' QuickHDL. V-System and QuickHDL have two advantages compared to VSS. First both provide a VHDL foreign language interface to their simulators. This feature can be used for co-simulation of hardware and software [Xi97a]. Then, both support VHDL'93 standard, which is necessary for the coding technique shown in the following. Because of this QuickHDL it is chosen for simulation. Setting up the VITAL library for QuickHDL simulation is similar to VSS, described at [Xi97a]. For information about Quick-HDL design libraries refer to [Me97].

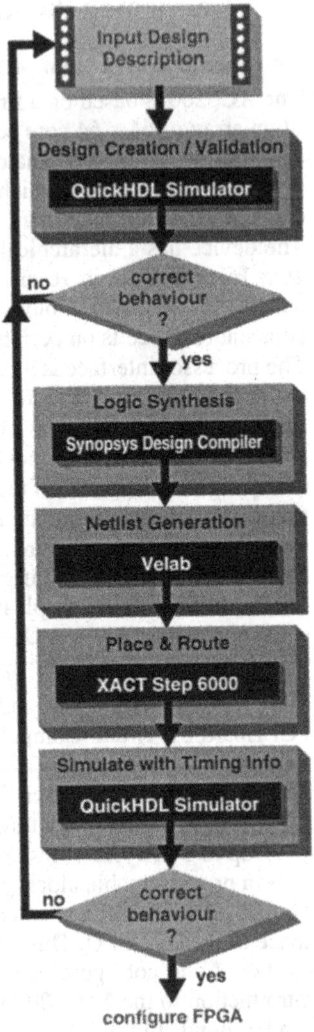

Logic Synthesis

Fig. 1. XC6200 Design Flow

As a technology library of the XC6200 family is provided for Synopsys Design Compiler, logic synthesis of behavioral VHDL can be done with some limitations. First the Synopsys Design Compiler can not synthesize pad-cells, which are needed for user IOBs (Synopsys creates only input/output-buffers). Therefore a top-level structural description of the I/Os has to be provided manually by the designer. Second, some design information such as the pinout or placement can only be attached by user defined attributes, which are not supported by Synopsys Design Compiler.

Another big disadvantage of logic synthesis is a problem of the Xilinx Place-and-Route software XACT Step 6000. Placement and routing of larger non-hierarchical designs without placement information results in bad designs. Hierarchical designs with pre-placed macro-cells for adders, subtractors and other regular structures are necessary to allow manual floorplanning. As a consequence, only pure state-machines without datapath (<100 primitive gates) should be synthesized with Synopsys. Synthesis of RTL-VHDL of larger designs (>1000 primitive gates) as for other FPGA technologies is not practicable at the moment.

Netlist Generation

For the datapath a well structured hierarchical design is necessary. Cells of regular structure, such as adders and multipliers, should be preplaced using user-defined attributes and instantiated in larger cells such as pipelines. The result of this design style is hierarchical VHDL-netlist of instantiated components and technology primitives. The input netlist format of XACTStep 6000 is EDIF. To transform VHDL-netlists to EDIF a small tool called VELAB is used [Xi97b]. VELAB is a free VHDL analyser and EDIF netlist generator for the XC6200 family provided by Xilinx. One of its major features is the ability to generate parametrized attributes.

Placement and Routing

XACTStep Series 6000 [Xi96] is a graphical tool for XC6200 family designs. This system is a back-end tool with EDIF as its primary input. The XACTStep Series 6000 editor preserves the hierarchy of the input design. This hierarchy information is used to support both top down design through floorplanning and bottom up design through either manual or automatic techniques. In addition, fully automatic place-and-route is supported. The graphical editor gives full access to all resources of the XC6200 family architecture [NG97].

In practice, the automatic techniques need a lot of manual assistance. Even when using preplaced structures floorplanning and manual placement is unavoidable. The automatic router often fails in routing the top-level design. Therefore placement and routing is not an automated design step as for most commercial FPGA technologies. A lot of manual work and design experience is essential for acceptable results. Timing constraints can not be set, timing analysis of the post-layouted design has to be done interactively by choosing source and destination cells in the graphical editor.

Design Step	Design Tool	Version
Design Validation (1), Simulation (5)	Mentor Graphics QuickHDL	v8.5_4.6c
Logic Synthesis (2)	Synopsys Design Compiler	1997.08
Netlist Generation (3)	Xilinx Velab (freeware [Xi97b])	0.52
Place & Route (4)	Xilinx XACT Step 6000	1.1 beta build 4

Table 1.   Summary of the used design software

3.1   The XC6200 Specific Design Flow

As mentioned in the introduction the design flow for the XC6200 family consists of five steps (figure 1): Design Creation, Logic Synthesis, Netlist Generation, Place and Route and Simulate Design with Timing Information. In the following the architecture specific characteristics of this design flow will be explained by treating each design step in detail.

Design Creation / Validation

First, the design is described and a testbench is written in VHDL. Then the design is simulated and its specification is validated until the behavior of the design is satisfactory. The design has to be specified in a synthesizable subset of VHDL (RTL). The testbench may also include VHDL-statements which are not synthesizable.

Unfortunately the Xilinx place and route software XACT Step 6000 is unable to place and route designs of logic-cell usage larger than 15% to 25%. To handle larger designs, floorplanning and manual placement must be done. To support floorplanning regularity and hierarchical information is necessary. In addition, very regular substructures such as adders, multipliers and other operators should be preplaced. In the applied design methodology for the XC6200 family, a design is partitioned in three entities: a top-level entity, a control unit (finite state machine) and a datapath unit. The datapath is restricted to primitive gates and macro-cells of primitive gates. The macro-cells [XC98] used in the datapath unit are included in a predefined design library. This library may be extended by the designer if a specific macro is not available.

Figure 2 illustrates this design step. Design Creation is an iterative process of writing/modifying VHDL code and simulation. All parts of the design apart from the technology library may be edited. Even the macro-library may be extended, if new regular substructures are needed. Writing a testbench forcing all input ports and verifying automatically the results simplifies this iterative process. Validating the design needs no interaction if no errors occur. Unfortunately two versions of the top-level description are necessary. The reason is that it is not possible to simulate the behavior of a special type of register (RPFDs) and there is no functional equivalent for pad-cells. RPFDs (Register Protected D type Flip-Flop) can only change value by reconfiguration. To simulate the behaviour of a RPFD it must be replaced by a UP_RPFD, which is a RPFD with a simplified processor interface. In future releases of XACT Step 6000 the mapping software will automatically replace a UP_RPFD by an ordinary RPFD. All these cells are included in the VITAL simulation library delivered with the Xilinx software.

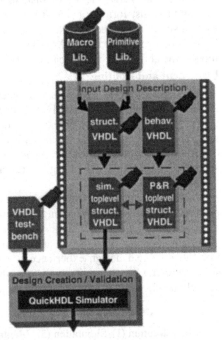

Fig. 2. Step1, Design Creation / Validation

If simulation results meet the design requirements, this step is finished. Further iterations may be necessary if the following design steps demand a redesign, e.g. timing requirements are not met or placement information has to be added for future enhancements.

Logic Synthesis of behavioral VHDL

This design step transforms the part of the design given in behavioral VHDL (e.g. finite state machines) into a structural description of technology gates. Using the Synopsys Design Compiler for the synthesis of XC6200 family technology gates is described in [Xi97c]. There a detailed introduction in setting up the Synopsys environment and a step by step explanation of the synthesis is given. However minor differences appear to our design flow:

1. First, no pad cells are needed, as they are instantiated in the top-level description.
2. The output format should be VHDL as the complete EDIF-netlist will be generated in the next design step with VELAB.

As indicated in figure 3 some modifications must be done. The netlist generated by the Synopsys Design Compiler will report errors when processed directly by VELAB. Synopsys writes a package declaration in the beginning of the netlist, which is not necessary and must be deleted, because it is not allowed in VELAB. Further, if ports of type std_logic_vector are used, Synopsys writes signal-assignments to a vector, which are also not accepted by VELAB. They need to be converted into bitwise assignments. To automate this modifications an awk-script [XC98] has been written. After this design step all design information consists only of structural VHDL description files.

Netlist Generation with VELAB

VELAB is a free VHDL analyser and EDIF netlist generator for the XC6200 family. It can be downloaded from the Xilinx homepage at [Xi97b]. In this design flow, VELAB is used to generate a EDIF netlist for placement and routing and a second VHDL netlist for simulation (see figure 4).

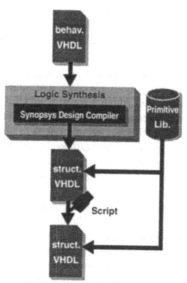

Fig. 3. Step 2, Logic Synthesis of behavioral VHDL

The reason not to use Synopsys Design Compiler for netlist generation is, that it ignores all user defined attributes. But this is the only way to add placement information to the design. Macro library elements (e.g. adders, multipliers) need to be preplaced, because of the bad placement and routing results of the Xilinx XACT Step 6000. Preplacing is further useful if datapath registers have to be accessed via the processor interface. Adding placement information to user attributes is only supported by VELAB. VELAB accepts only a subset of VHDL, especially all structural parts. For a detailed description refer to [Xi97b]. One of the most useful features for preplacement of regular devices is its ability to handle parametrized attributes. This feature allows preplacement of devices with generic parameters such as size or layout. The macro-library used in the proposed design flow is based on this feature.

As illustrated in figure 4 VELAB is used to generate two separate files. Therefore the top-level structural description for place-and-route (and of course all other design-files) are fed into VELAB to generate the EDIF netlist as an input to XACT-Step 6000. The top-level description for simulation is processed to a VHDL-netlist. This netlist is used for simulation of the placed and routed

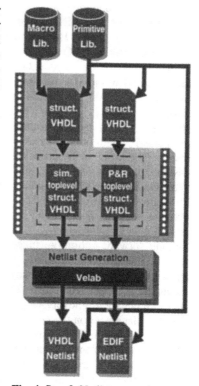

Fig. 4. Step 3, Netlist generation

design with the exact timing parameters calculated by XACT Step 6000.

Place-and-Route

Placement and routing is an important step in the design flow. In contrast to other FGPA-technologies where floorplanning is optional, it is an essential part for most designs. XACT Step 6000 is a graphical tool allowing both manual floorplanning and automatic place and route. Unfortunately fully automatic place and route mostly fails or leads to bad results.

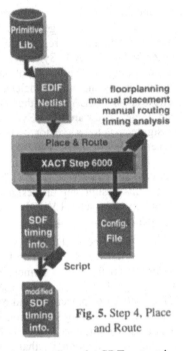

Figure 5 gives an overview to the place and route design step. The EDIF-netlist generated by VELAB is placed on the FPGA and all nets are routed. The configuration information of the FPGA is written to a CAL-file. A complete list of all nets and their corresponding delays are calculated for timing analysis. Setting up timing constraints for placement and routing and an automatic timing report is not supported. For a detailed analysis of critical paths source and destination nets are chosen from a list of all nets. The analysis information may be exported to a text file or used as an input to a standard spreadsheet. For timing simulation of the layouted design two other forms of timing extraction are supported, a delay table for the View-logic Simulator, and SDF (Standard Delay Format),

Fig. 5. Step 4, Place and Route

which is used in most VHDL simulators. In the proposed design flow the SDF output is used as an input to the QuickHDL simulator. For the reason of bugs in both the VITAL technology library of the XC6200 family and the SDF-writer of XACT Step 6000 some modifications of the SDF-file are necessary. These bugs may be fixed in a future release of XACT Step 6000, meanwhile an awk-script [XC98] does the modifications.

XACT Step 6000 is based on a bottom-up strategy. That means that one level of hierarchy is first placed and then routed, when all units of the lower design level are already placed and routed. In most cases manual floorplanning is necessary to achieve adequate results. The basis of the proposed method is the library of preplaced macro-cells for design units of high regularity such as adders or multipliers. Using this library elements avoids to floorplan at gate level. Because unstructured elements such as the synthesized FSM are more difficult to place, it is recommended to simplify the control logic as much as possible. Straight and short connections between the design units is the major goal of manual floorplanning.

Straight forward bottom-up placement is not recommended because of a placement must be found which simplifies not only the connections of the actual design level but also of the higher design hierarchy levels. That may be one of the major problems of a automatic place-and-route procedure. If the nearest-neighbor connection is not sufficient, higher routing levels such as length-4 or length-16 must be used restricting the possible placement on the next design hierarchy level. Therefore it is recommended to route the design on the top hierarchy level (except for the preplaced macro-cells).

Manual routing of the design is not well supported by Xilinx software. To completely route a design the sequence of the routed nets is an important issue. The order chosen by the software often leads to bad results. A good order would be to start with the obvious connections such as the neighbor-connections. Next, all critical nets should be routed. Critical nets include the timing-critical nets and the nets which are difficult to route or even failed during automatic routing. Then all nets connecting I/O-cells should be routed. Last, all other nets are routed.

Note that the placement & routing guidelines reflect our experience with XACT Step 6000. They may not be best for all designs. As a consequence of using the above method only a limited design utilization can be achieved because the elements of the implemented macro-library are optimized for timing rather than high device utilization.

Simulating Design with Timing Information

After placement and routing of a design the exact timing-parameters are known. The VHDL-netlist generated by VELAB and the SDF-timing-information calculated by XACT Step 6000 can be simulated again using the QuickHDL-simulator (see figure 6). If a testbench has been created in step 1 it may be used here again simplifying this design step. If the testbench validates all design results and the simulator does not report any timing conflicts the design is correct under the tested conditions and the FPGA may be configured. Timing violations may be corrected by a different placement and routing leading back to step 4, but if the design does not show the correct behavior the whole design process starting with step 1 must be iterated.

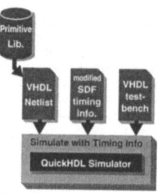

Fig. 6. Step 5, Simulate Design with Timing Information

4   Generic 3x3 Linear Filter for Image-Processing Example

The generic 3x3 linear filter processes an image by moving a 3x3 window over it (figure 7) and applying the following formula:

$$p_0^{new} = \frac{1}{j} \cdot \sum_{i=0}^{8} p_i \cdot k_i$$

Fig. 7. Operation of a 3x3 Image-Transformation

This operation on an m*n-pixel image results in an image of size (m-2)*(n-2). All pixel-values are assumed to be an 8-bit grayscale value (0 to 255). Fig. 8 shows some filter coefficient examples.

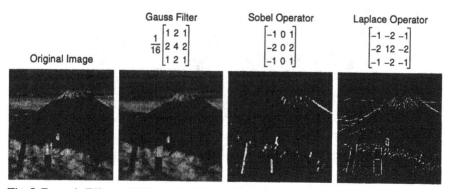

Gauss Filter
$$\frac{1}{16}\begin{bmatrix} 1 & 2 & 1 \\ 2 & 4 & 2 \\ 1 & 2 & 1 \end{bmatrix}$$

Sobel Operator
$$\begin{bmatrix} -1 & 0 & 1 \\ -2 & 0 & 2 \\ -1 & 0 & 1 \end{bmatrix}$$

Laplace Operator
$$\begin{bmatrix} -1 & -2 & -1 \\ -2 & 12 & -2 \\ -1 & -2 & -1 \end{bmatrix}$$

Original Image

Fig. 8. Example Effects of Different 3x3 Linear Filter Operators

In this implementation of the filter, the coefficients k_i are signed integer numbers in the range from -16 to 15 (5 bit) and $j=2^n$ with n element of [0:8].

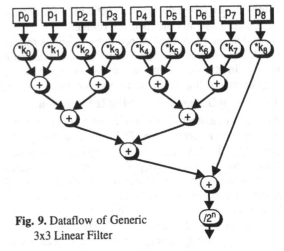

This leads to the dataflow-graph shown in figure 9. For multiplication of the coefficients k_i constant coefficient multipliers are used, which are included into the macro library. For macro implementation the description in [Xi97d] is modified for negative constants and higher device-utilization.

Fig. 9. Dataflow of Generic 3x3 Linear Filter

Fig. 10 shows the layout of the placed and routed generic 3x3 linear filter design. Because of the used preplaced macro cell elements, the constant-multipliers are always placed at the same location. Therefore the weights can be exchanged by only reconfiguring the related cells.

The design is working at a clock frequency of 25 MHz, where the computational pipeline is processing one pixel in two clock cycles. The design utilizes 2373 logic cells of the XC6216 (58%). Implementation details and more application examples can be found in [Gi98].

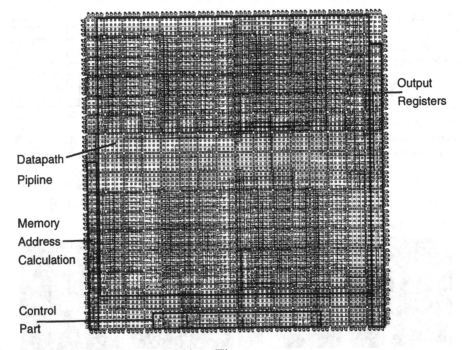

Output Registers

Datapath Pipline

Memory Address Calculation

Control Part

Fig. 10. Layout of the Generic 3x3 Linear Filter

5 Conclusions

A dedicated design flow for the Xilinx XC6200 FPGA series has been introduced to overcome problems of the available design software. The proposed method recommends partitioning of designs in a control part and a datapath. All regular structures of the datapath should be implemented with a macro library. This library has been implemented and is extendable for future designs. Its use has been proven on several examples [XC98], whereas an image processing example was presented.

Future work will be software support for dynamic reconfiguration and data access via the fast map interface.

6 References

[Gi98]   Frank Gilbert: Development of a Design Flow and Implementation of Example Designs for the Xilinx XC6200 FPGA Series; Diploma Thesis, University of Kaiserslautern, Kaiserslautern, May 29, 1998. Download from [XC98].

[GL97]   Gordon McGregor, Patrick Lysat: Extending Dynamic Circuit Switching to Meet the Challenges of New FPGA Architectures; Proceedings of 7th International Workshop, FPL'97 London, UK, Sept. 1997. LNCS 1304. Springer 1997

[Lo98]   http://www.lola.ethz.ch/lola/

[Me97]   Mentor Graphics Inc., QuickHDL User and Reference Manual, 1997

[NG97]   Stuart Nisbet; Steven A. Guccione: The XC6200DS Development System; Proceedings of 7th International Workshop, FPL'97 London, UK, Sep. 1997. Lecture Notes in Computer Science 1304. Springer 1997

[Vc98]   http://www.vcc.com

[Vi95]   VITAL ASIC Modelling Specification; Draft IEEE 1076.4; New York October 1995; http://www.vhdl.org/vital

[Xi98a] http://www.xilinx.com/partinfo/6200.pdf

[Xi98b] http://www.xilinx.com/apps/6200.htm

[Xi97a] Xilinx Inc., Application Note XAPP 087: Co-Simulation of Hardware and Software, http://www.xilinx.com/xapp/xapp087.pdf, San Jose, CA, USA, 1997

[Xi97b] Xilinx Inc., Velab: VHDL Elaborator for XC6200, http://www.xilinx.com/apps/velabrel.htm, San Jose, CA, USA, 1997

[Xi97c] Xilinx Inc., Synthesis and simulation of a circuit in VHDL, using the Synopsys toolset, Synopsys_flow.pdf, XACT 6000 Synopsys Interface Documentation

[Xi97d] Xilinx Inc., Application Note XAPP 082: A Fast Constant Coefficient Multiplier for the XC6200, http://www.xilinx.com/xapp/xapp082.pdf, San Jose, CA, USA, 1997

[Xi96]   Xilinx Inc., XACT Step Series 6000 User Guide, Scotland, UK 1996

[XC98]   Xputer Lab's XC6k Pages: http://xputers.informatik.uni-kl.de/ reconfigurable_computing/XC6k/index_xc6k.html

Perspectives of Reconfigurable Computing in Research, Industry and Education

Jürgen Becker, Andreas Kirschbaum, Frank-Michael Renner, Manfred Glesner

Darmstadt University of Technology
Institute of Microelectronic Systems
Karlstr. 15, D-64283 Darmstadt, Germany
Fax: ++49 6151 16 4936
e-mail: {becker, andreask, renner, glesner}@mes.tu-darmstadt.de

Abstract. The paper presents an overview on perspectives of reconfigurable computing in research, industry and education, whereas some past, present and future developments as well as trends are sketched from the authors point of view. It is tried to stress the perspectives of such promising, flexible and cheap computing systems within these three communities, but also to identify present disadvantages in order to accelerate future developments, and to force more interrelations between industry and academic fields.

1. Introduction

Configurable Computing demonstrates currently its potential of achieving high performance improvements for a wide range of applications like image processing [1], [2], [3] and compression [4], morphology [5], feature extraction [6], computational chemistry [7], object tracking [8], fuzzy controlers [9] among many others. The obtained performance results deliver an order of magnitude improvement over general purpose microprocessors. Due to this real speed-up potential a lot of researchers have built corresponding (re)configurable prototype systems for a large number of applications.

In general, computer system designers have always to find the right balance between speed and generality in evaluating corresponding trade-offs in performance and cost. Two main options exist for implementing the required functionalities:

- general-purpose microprocessors or microcontrollers that perform many different functions relatively slowly, or in contrast
- custom hardware circuits, known as application-specific integrated circuits (ASICs), providing precisely functionalities needed for specific tasks.

Now another option is offered by the new developments in integrated circuits during the last years: large, fast, field-programmable gate arrays (FPGAs), highly tuned hardware circuits that can be modified at almost any point during use. The area is very promising and receives now more and more popularity, proved also by the first published article on this subject from the main stream periodical "Scientific American" [10]. FPGAs consist of arrays of configurable logic blocks (CLBs) that implement the logical functions of gates. Both the logical functions as well as the interconnections between the corresponding blocks can be altered by sending signals to the chip. Thus, in FPGAs the CLBs can be rewired and reprogrammed repeatedly, long time after fabrication. Although Gerald Estrin of the University of California at Los Angeles proposed configurable computing in the early 1960s [11], this subject is still a young field with its first demonstrations a few years ago. Current FPGAs with up to 100.000 gates are still unable to exploit the full potential of this fundamentally new technique.

The final performance achieved by an application implemented on a reconfigurable platform depends not only on the underlying hardware itself, but also strongly on the characteristics (e.g.

amount of available parallelism) of the application, as well as on the application development environments (CAD tools, compiler etc.). Therefore, these two additional main aspects have to be considered when customized reconfigurable computing systems are built:

- the data dependency and control structures of potential applications have to be reviewed in order to identify simultanously occuring operations for outperforming a microprocessor [12]. Application samples with references to the papers can be found in [13], and an overview on possible speed-ups within this area is given in [14], and
- the availability and possibility of suitable programming environments for such "structurally programmable" platforms is essential. Obviously, it exists a "software gap" between software compilers and compilers for custom computing machines [15]. Most environments resemble the synthesis of ASICs and require techniques of the hardware/software co-design area. Thus, due to the complexity of the design space a hardware expert is needed in most of the cases for programming such platforms.

First, the paper outlines selected research in reconfigurable computing, focusing on hardware architectures, and development environments. In chapter 3, current industry aspects of reconfigurable systems are viewed, showing their potential in performance, as well as in prototyping and realizing core-based designs. Finally, the perspectives of such platforms are discussed for internet-based education by giving a course proposal.

2. Selected Research in Reconfigurable Computing

Since the performance of applications implemented on a customized reconfigurable computing system depends strongly on the application structure itself, the underlying hardware architecture, and its corresponding development environment, this chapter outlines some selected recent research work within its two main aspects:

- hardware architecture,
- development environments.

2.1 Hardware Architectures

Many different reconfigurable hardware architectures have been developed and built, which provide flexibility to tune the hardware structures to the applications to be implemented. Dependent on required performance/cost trade-offs, the architectures of such FPGA-based Custom Computing Machines (F-CCMs) range from universal emulation systems to more specialized custom computers. Emulation systems are developed as general as possible, not considering the different characteristics of potential applications to be implemented. In contrast, custom computer architectures are tuned to the characteristics of application classes, e.g. with similar data manipulation or communication structures. In [16] the pros and cons of emulation systems and custom computers are explained on the system level. Therefore, this subsection discusses the architecture structures of the reconfigurable devices used in such F-CCMs, because of their relevance to the performance of implemented applications. The device architecture structures can be divided into:

- fine-grained FPGAs (bit-level),
- coarse-grained arrays (word-level), and
- hybrid solutions (mixtures of fine- and coarse grained).

2.1.1 Fine-Grained Hardware Architectures

Fine-grained sea-of-gates device architectures consist of arrays of so-called configurable logic blocks (CLBs), surrounded by reconfigurable routing channels of different length and flexibility. Such bit level architectures are well-suited for logic controller applications and intelligent periph-

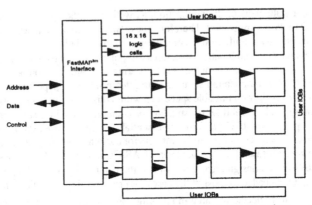

Figure 1. XC6200 Block Diagram with FastMAP^{tm} Interface

eral implementations. A recently available dynamically reconfigurable device is the XC6216 from Xilinx, consisting of 64x64 CLBs surrounded by 256 I/O ports (see figure 1). The XC6216 has a hierarchical routing structure, whereas fast routing channels are associated with the different sizes of blocks consisting of several CLBs (4x4, 16x16). An important feature of this device is its dynamic reconfiguration capability, realized by accessing the address location of each CLB by simply writing to the corresponding configuration memory space, e.g. the reconfiguration signals have been made accessible for user logic parts on the device. For further details see the data sheet of this device in [17].

2.1.2   Coarse-Grained Hardware Architectures

Coarse-grained device architectures consist of arrays of processing elements (PEs) with a wider datapath, e.g. 32 bit, in order to implement more complex applications efficiently [18], [19], e.g. computation-intensive arithmetic operations [20], [21]. In the following, two examples of such architectures will be explained briefly.

A dynamically reconfigurable device is the KressArray [21], being less overhead-prone and more area-efficient than fine-grained FPGAs. Figure 2 illustrates a 4 by 8 rALU device example. The KressArray is a generalization of the systolic array — an area-efficient and throughput-efficient datapath design style known, using wiring by abutment of optimized full-custom cells. Each PE can perform all C-like relational and logical operations, as well as integer-based arithmetic operations like additions, subtractions, multiplications and divisions. Moreover, PEs can be used as routing elements, in order to avoid global array communication. A mapper called

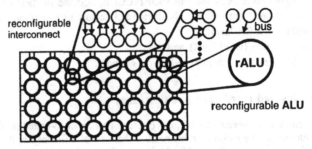

Figure 2.   Example of a KressArray (buses not shown).

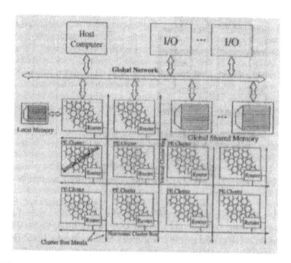

Figure 3.   Hierarchical Hardware Architecture of the Prototyping System PEDAM

DPSS (data path synthesis system) is used as synthesis tool for mapping operations optimized onto this device, e.g. in using only local interconnects between neighbouring PEs [21].

In [22] a hierarchical coarse-grained architecture consisting of several PE-clusters has been developed, incl. its prototyping environment PEDAM (see also section 2.2). The PEs communicate via a local static network of point-to-point channels synchronized by data-transfers. The ability to dynamically control the datapath with a processing element allows a flexible mapping of irregular algorithms onto this prototyping system, e.g. computation-intensive dataflow-oriented applications. The overall system architecture of the prototyping system is shown in figure 3. According to the hexagonal topology of the system each PE has six static interconnection links to its six direct neighbors. The prototyping system is data-driven and consists of multiple processor arrays, called "clusters", which comprise an arbitrary number of PEs. The amount of PEs per cluster depends on the complexity of the subgraph, which is mapped onto that cluster and can be controlled by inserting different types of integrated processor-chips. Each processing element can be configured in respect to the bitwidth of the datapath. Typical operations of the datapath are logical-, arithmetic- and comparison-functions. More complex operations like multiplication and division are not directly supported in order to minimize the area of a PE but can be emulated by a sequential program. A PE is microprogrammed and includes a local instruction memory. Six on-chip peripheral dataregisters are used for interprocessor communication. Point-to-point communication between two arbitrary PEs inside a cluster is established via a fast global communication bus. This intracluster-bus is controlled with a optimized message-based communication protocol. Buses of different clusters are independent of each other, so that intramodule communication can be parallelized. Message exchange between two clusters is realized with a matrixbus network consisting of row- and column-buses. A separate router for each cluster controls data sending/receiving and routes data packages either to appropriate rows resp. columns.

2.1.3   Hybrid Hardware Architectures

Hybrid device architecures are mixtures between fine- and coarse-grain structures, e.g. several reconfigurable fine-garined CLBs are clustered to one coarse-grained PE for implementing more complex operations. Here, one application-driven example, tuned to the telecommunication area, will be outlined.

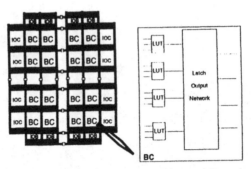

Figure 4.   *PROTEUS-Lite* Architecture Overview

In [23] a hybrid telecommunication-based architecture *PROTEUS-Lite* has been introduced. *PROTEUS-Lite* is a look-up table (LUT)-based device comprising of regularly placed *Basic Cells* (BCs), *I/O blocks* (IOBs) and routing resources (see figure 4). Each BC has four 3-input/1-output LUTs and one 5-input AND-gate. Additionally, an output network of latches is provided. Such a BC structure makes it easy to implement basic functions for telecommunication circuits, e.g. pattern matching. The routing resources consist of a hierarchy of local (neighbouring LUTs), middle and long lines. For details about this device and its dedicated CAD system see [23].

2.2   Development Environments

Since the user acceptance of reconfigurable hardware platforms strongly depends on the quality of their programming environments, this aspect will also be discussed here. Most environments resemble the synthesis of ASICs and require hardware design knowledge and techniques of the HW/SW codesign area. The following historically evolved steps can be distinguished: first, hardware experts used low level schematic entry tools including module generators. Second, text-based entry tools for hardware description languages (HDLs) were used for generating automatically larger designs. Third, applications were described in subsets of standard programming languages, not requiring necessarily hardware experts. Due to the lack of space, please see [14] for an overview and corresponding references on such programming environments for configurable computing systems. The final step for a high user acceptance is to use for both, the software (host) as well as the reconfigurable hardware accelerator, a common programming language. An example for such a partitioning compiler is provided in [31]. The co-compilation environment CoDe-X (Co-Design for Xputers) generates both automatically: sequential microprocessor code, and configuration code for dynamically reconfigurable Xputer-based accelerators, including "vertical" parallelizing code optimizations and transparent communication/synchronization handling. CoDe-X represents one step in the direction of closing the still existing "software gap" for reconfigurable platforms. For further details please see [31].

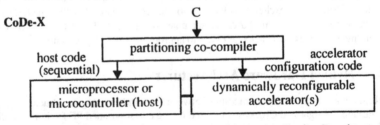

Figure 5.   Co-Compiler CoDe-X for Host/Accelerator Application Development.

The PEDAM-environment [22] for the hierarchical coarse-grained hardware architecture introduced in section 2.1.2 targets the design of mechatronic, application-specific algorithms, which have to be evaluated in a hardware-in-the-loop-simulation together with the mechanical system environment. Starting with a Hardware-C-like specification a control-dataflow-graph of the algorithm is constructed and finally mapped to a planar, regular field of homogeneous and programmable PEs.

3. Industry Aspects

The flexibility of this novel promising technology and its reported impressive performance results in the research area forced companies to build commercial CCMs. Moreover, several CCM-building companies have been founded, resulting in the availability of professional reconfigurable machines. Some examples of such CCMs are:

- ACE-12 Reconfigurable Compute Engine by Methalithic Systems Inc. (MSI) [24],
- WILDFIRE from Annapolis Micro Systems Inc. (AMS) [25], based on the Splash-2 CCM [6],
- EVC1, the DVC1 Transformable Computer, and the H.O.T. Works Board incl. development system from Virtual Computer Inc. (VCC) [26],
- Spectrum CCMs from Giga Operations Corp. [27],
- PCI Pamette V1 from Digital [28],
- the ProTest board from Biel School of Engineering [30], among others.

For a complete list of available commercial and non-commercial CCMs see [29].

3.1 FPGA to ASIC Migration

Modern integrated circuit design often relies on reconfigurable components for its product life-cycle management. As shown in figure 6 reconfigurable components (e.g. FPGAs) are used in product phases where low numbers of devices are needed, i.e. in production ramps as well as final phases of product life-cycles. Here reconfigurable components reduce system and device development time, assure fast time to market and provide flexibility at the expense of higher device costs. Even unplanned production peaks can be controlled with additional FPGA devices.

Nevertheless, the mainstream of the product is still covered by ASICs which are less expensive but have to be ordered in higher production numbers. Additionally, ASICs require higher Non Recovering Engineering (NRE) costs and introduce a long turn-around time. Therefore, efficient migration paths enable the usage of both reconfigurable and hardwired solutions in different phases of the product-life cycle. During migration the designers usually have to retarget the design to a different architecture, which results in a completely different timing behavior, mainly due to changed interconnection wire lengths and capacitances. Therefore, industry developed several smooth migration paths. Actel offers a mask-programmable Sea-of-Gates-Array (MPGA) as replacement for their Antifuse-FPGAs, which is derived automatically out of the

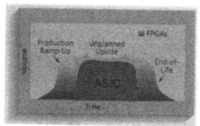

Figure 6.   Typical Product Life-Cycle (Xilinx)

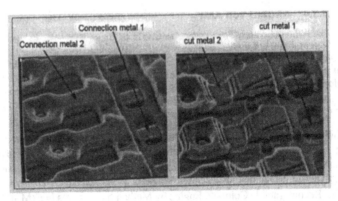

Figure 7.   LPGA Process

original FPGA netlist. Xilinx also uses a mask programmable version of their SRAM-based FPGAs as hardwired replacement for mass production. These devices are not only functional- but also architectural- and pin-compatible to the original FPGA. Only the reconfigurable elements including the configuration circuitry has been replaced by maskprogrammable interconnections. Therefore, the area and consequently the price of the device is significantly higher than that of a pure Gate Array solution. Laser-programmable Gate Arrays (LPGA) are another interesting replacement strategy offered by ChipExpress for designs originally targeted to Actel, Altera, Lucent, QuickLogic or Xilinx FPGAs. On prefabricated wafers all possible connections are realized via two metal layers. When personalizing the chip unnecessary connections are destroyed by a laser micro-machining system. Using special cutting windows connections on both metal layers can be eliminated (figure 7). A 200K design will take about two hours of laser processing.

3.2   IP-based Design

Currently new strategies for realizing complex systems in reduced design times are under development, using already available modules, called core cells. Major challenges in such IP-based design methods are the integration and coordination of test, diagnosis and debugging capabilities into the overall design flow. The FPGA vendors Xilinx and Altera have also developed core generators for generating and delivering parameterizable cores optimized for the corresponding FPGA-architectures. An overview on the Xilinx Core generator concept is shown in figure 8. Especially interface analysis and verification of the IP-based components is a key issue. During interface analysis the operation of one or more IP-components has to be checked with respect to its surrounding environment. Traditional simulation approaches can be used to carry out component as well as first rudimentary system tests. Unfortunately, they soon run out of

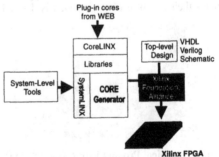

Figure 8.   Overview on Xilinx Core Concept

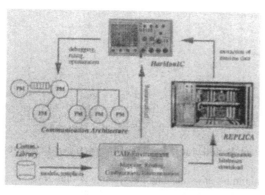

Figure 9.   Prototyping with REPLICA

steam when system complexity increases or simulation models for some subcomponents or the system environment are not available. Rapid system prototyping will help to speed up the verification process and enable the designer to include existing (hardware) IP-components into the prototype which is physically connected to its environment. REPLICA [32] is a rapid prototyping system focusing on the emulation of realistic intermodul communication. The system is integrated in a design environment for embedded mixed hardware/software systems (DICE [33]). REPLICA facilitates design space exploration of embedded IP-based systems as well as the validation and the test of IP interfaces. The reconfigurable system architecture allows prototyping of different communication topologies types and IP-protocols and is supported by a powerful toolkit for automatic system configuration (figure 9). A reconfigurable hardware monitor HarMonIC [34] is integrated into the prototyping platform and physically connects to user-defined points within the communication architecture of the prototype. Main task of the non-intrusive monitoring are the observation, extraction and visualization of real-time data about IP-interface activities.

REPLICA is based on a scalable and reconfigurable system architecture. Up to six *Processing Modules* such as processors, ASIPs, IP-components etc. can be plugged into the prototype. Connectivity is established by SRAM-based bit-oriented FPID (Field Programmable Interconnect Devices) switches, which are used to route one or more signals via a non-blocking switch matrix. Some communication links may require additional hardware resources such as memory, glue logic, synchronization circuits etc. These resources will be allocated on the *Interface Modules* which comprise FPGAs, FPIDs and Dual-Port Memories.

4.   Perspectives in Education

The flexibility, increasing performance, and good performance/cost trade-offs of reconfigurable devices, boards, and computing engines promise tremendous perspectives for industrial users, especially small and medium enterprises (SMEs). Therefore, a large demand on corresponding know-how can be expected among these companies in the near future. The universities are potential candidates for satisfying these teaching requirements. Current computer science curricula do not create awareness, that hardware has become soft, nor, that hardware, structural and sequential software are alternatives. Principles and applications of dynamically reconfigurable devices as basis of new computing based on *structural programming* should be included in academic and industrial main courses to increase the potential of this emerging technology.

Here, the structure and contents of a FPGA-course system on different severity levels is briefly outlined, which increases the understanding of reconfigurable circuit architectures and

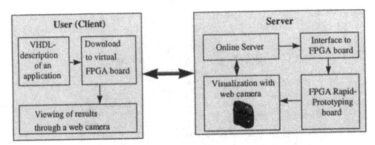

Figure 10.   System Architecture Concept of Internet-based Structural Programming

their structural programming environments for systematic high-level design. This includes an introduction into the area and its applications, cost/performance trade-offs (e.g. for SMEs), fine-/coarse-grained and hybrid device architecures, overview on vendors and corresponding design tools, and the structural programming process including examples from different areas. The focus of this course proposal is the concept how to implement realistically practical application examples over the internet in programming online a reconfigurable PCI-bus based extension board (H.O.T. Works [26], PCI Pamette V1 [28], or ProTest [30]). An overview on the system architecture suggestion of internet-based structural programming and success control is given in figure 10. The inclusion of such a concept into a course system would provide access to structural programming of real hardware through the internet for a broad variety of participants, e.g. students, industry participants etc.. For details about this course proposal and its content see [35].

5.   Conclusions

An overview on perspectives of reconfigurable computing in research, industry and education has been tried to present, which cannot be complete due to the large number of activities in this field. Due to the increasing throughput requirements of general-purpose microprocessor-based systems, today's workstations need more and more add-on accelerators for graphic, multimedia etc. applications. But there are also next-generation microprocessors under development whose hardware supports limited amounts of FPGA-like reconfiguration. Thus, future computing machines might download new hardware configurations for such reconfigurable add-on hardware as they are needed. This would be much more flexible and cheaper than hardwired ASIC solutions, e.g. for frequently altered telecommunication protocol applications. Moreover, the flexibility and cheapness of such devices can be very attractive for embedded system solutions and low volume products, especially for SMEs. Since the authors believe that future computing machines and digital systems 10 years from now will include a strong mix of sequential programmable hardware and structural programmable reconfigurable devices, the interrelations in research, industry and education communities have to become closer in order to accelerate a wider acceptance of this promising technology, e.g. to improve the performance of reconfigurable hardware devices and architectures, and to close the still exisiting software gap for a better user acceptance.

6.   Literature

[1] P. Athanas, A. Abbot: Real-Time Image Processing on a Custom Computing Platform, IEEE Computer, vol. 28, no. 2, pp. 16-24, Feb. 1995.
[2] R. W. Hartenstein, J. Becker et al.: A Novel Machine Paradigm to Accelerate Scientific Computing; Special issue on Scientific Computing of Computer Science and Informatics Journal, Computer Soc. of India, 1996.
[3] D. Ross, O. Vellacott, M Turner: An FPGA-based Hardware Accelerator for Image Processing; Proc. of Int'l. Workshop on Field-Programmable Logic and Applications, 3rd Int'l. Workshop On Field Programmable Logic And Applications, Oxford, September 7-10, 1993.

[4] R. W. Hartenstein, J. Becker et al.: A Reconfigurable Machine for Applications in Image and Video Compression; Europ. Symp. on Advanced Networks and Services, Conf. on Compression Technologies & Standards for Image & Video Compression, Amsterdam, The Netherlands, March 20-24, 1995.

[5] T. H. Drayer, W. E. King, J. G. Tront, R. W. Conners: A MOdular Reprogrammable Real-Time Processing Hardware, MORPH; FCCM'95, IEEE Computer Society Press, Napa, CA, April 1995.

[6] A. L. Abbott, P. M. Athanas, L. Chen, R. L. Elliott: Finding Lines and Building Pyramids with Splash 2; IEEE Workshop on FPGAs f. Custom Computing Machines, FCCM'94, IEEE Computer Soc. Press, Napa, CA, pp. 155-161, April 1994.

[7] J. Becker, R. W. Hartenstein et al.: High-Performance Computing Using a Reconfigurable Accelerator; Proc. of Workshop on High Performance Computing, Montreal, Canada, July 1995.

[8] M. Shand: Flexible Image Acquisition Using Reconfigurable Hardware; FCCM'95, IEEE Computer Society Press, Napa, CA, April 1995.

[9] T. Hollstein, A. Kirschbaum. M. Glesner: A Prototyping Environment for Fuzzy Controllers; 7th Int'l. Workshop On Field Programmable Logic And Applications, FPL'97, London, UK, Sept.1-3, 1997, Lecture Notes in Computer Science 1304, Springer Press, 1997.

[10] J. Villasenor, W. H. Mangione-Smith: Configurable Computing; Scientific American, June 1997.

[11] G. Estrin: Organization of Computer Systems: The Fixed-plus Variable Structure Computer; Proc. of the Western Joint Computer Conference, pp. 33-40, 1960.

[12] R. J. Peterson, B. L. Hutchings: An Assessment of the suitability of FPGA-Based Systems for Use in Digital Signal Processing; 5th Int'l. Workshop On Field Programmable Logic And Applications, FPL'95, Oxford, UK, Sept. 1997, Springer Press, 1997.

[13] A. DeHon: DPGA-Coupled Microprocessors: Commodity ICs for the Early 21st Century; IEEE Workshop on FPGAs f. Custom Computing Machines, FCCM'94, IEEE Computer Soc. Press, Napa, CA, April 1994.

[14] R. W. Hartenstein: An Overview on Custom Computing Machines; Workshop on Design Methodologies for Microelectronics, Invited Paper, Smolenice Castle, Slovakia, Sept. 1995.

[15] R. Kress: Configurable Computing - The Software Gap; Proc. of Reconfigurable Architectures Workshop RAW'97, held in coonjunction with IPPS'97, Geneva, April 1-5, 1997.

[16] W. H. Mangione-Smith, B. L. Hutchings: Configurable Computing: The Road Ahead; Proc. of Reconfigurable Architectures Workshop RAW'97, in coonjunction with IPPS'97, Geneva, April 1-5, 1997.

[17] Xilinx, Inc.: The Programmable Logic Data Book, 1996

[18] B. Mangione-Smith (Coord.): Task Force on Configurable Computing Systems; in Proc. of 30th Annual Hawaii Int'l. Conf. on System Science (HICSS-30), January 7-10, Wailea, Maui, Hawaii, USA, 1997.

[19] A. DeHon: Reconfigurable Architectures for General-Purpose Computing; Ph.D. thesis (Technical Report 1586), MIT Artificial Intelligence Laboratory, September, 1996.

[20] C. Ebling, D. C. Cronquist, P. Franklin: 6th Int'l. Workshop On Field Programmable Logic And Applications, FPL'96, Darmstadt, Germany, Sept. 23-25, 1996, Lecture Notes in Computer Science 1142, Springer Press, 1996.

[21] R. Kress: A Fast Reconfigurable ALU for Xputers; Ph.D. Thesis, University of Kaiserslautern, 1996.

[22] M.-D. Doan: Eine Hardware/Software-Entwurfsumgebung für das Rapid-Prototyping von rechenintensiven anwendungsspezifischen Algorithmen in der Mechatronik. D17 Darmstädter Dissertationen, TU Darmstadt, 1997.

[23] T. Miyazaki, A. Takahara, M. Katayama, T. Murooka, T. Ichimori, K. Fukami, A. Tsutsui, K. Hayashi: CAD-oriented FPGA and Dedicated CAD System for Telecommunications; 7th Int'l. Workshop On Field Programmable Logic And Applications, FPL'97, London, UK, Sept.1-3, 1997, Lecture Notes in Computer Science 1304, Springer Press, 1997.

[24] N. N.: Special Report: FPGAs as Reconfigurable Processing Elements; B. Fawcett (ed.) XCELL, Xilinx, San Jose, CA, Issue 16, First Quarter 1995 FPGAs.

[25] N.N.: WILDFIRE Custom Configurable Computer WAC4010/16; Document #11502-0000, Rev. C, Annapolis Micro Systems Inc., April 1995.

[26] Virtual Computer Corporation: http://www.vcc.com

[27] N. N.: Giga Ops: G-800 Dynamically Reconfigurable Accelerator Mother Board; Preliminary Documentation, Rev. 0.5, Giga Operations Corporation, Berkeley, 1993.

[28] Digital Equipment Corporation: http://www.research.digital.com/SRC/pamette

[29] S. A. Guccione: List of FPGA-based Computing Machines; http://www.io.com/~guccione/HW_list.html, last updated February 10, 1998

[30] ProTest, Biel School of Engineering, http://www.isbiel.ch/I3S/e.html

[31] J. Becker: A Partitioning Compiler for Computers with Xputer-based Accelerators; Ph.D. dissertation, University of Kaiserslautern, Germany, 1997.

[32] A. Kirschbaum, M. Glesner: Rapid Prototyping of Communication Architectures.In IEEE Workshop on Rapid System Prototyping. p. 136-141, Chapel Hill, USA,June 1997.

[33] M. Gasteier et al.: An Interactive Approach to Hardware/Software Co-Design.In Int. Workshop on Logic and Architecture Synthesis, p. 211-218, Grenoble,France, Dec. 1996.

[34] A. Kirschbaum, J. Becker, M. Glesner: Run-Time Monitoring of Communication Activities in a Rapid-Prototyping Environment. In IEEE Workshop on Rapid System Prototyping, Leuven, Belgium, June 1998.

[35] J. Becker, F.-M. Renner, M. Glesner: Perspectives of Reconfigurable Computing in Education; Proc. of 2nd European Workshop on Microelectronics Education, The Netherlands, May 14-15, 1998.

Field-Programmable Logic: Catalyst for New Computing Paradigms

Gordon Brebner

Department of Computer Science
University of Edinburgh
Mayfield Road
Edinburgh EH9 3JZ
Scotland

Abstract. This paper discusses the changes in computational viewpoint that have been, or are being, facilitated by the advent of Field-Programmable Logic. To quote the FPL'98 workshop aim, the paper is concerned with exploring the evolution 'from tinkertoy to parallel computing paradigm'. The central point is to discourage thinking in terms of just 'hardware' and 'software', with FPL being considered within the former category. This may have been appropriate for initial FPL applications, but is inappropriate when seeking to exploit its full potential. A summary of the revised viewpoint is that both control flow and data flow methods should be equally accessible to the algorithm designer, and also that flexibility in architectures should be made available as an aid to designing algorithms.

1 Introduction

The main catalytic effect of Field-Programmable Logic (FPL) is indicated in its very name: logic circuitry can be programmed, that is, it can be regarded as 'soft'. This fact is one driving force for a review of the traditional roles of things like hardware and software, and circuits and programs. There are other, related, driving forces, including the emergent fields of:

- hardware/software co-design;
- custom computing machines; and
- algorithms for configurable parallel computers.

So far, research into hardware/software co-design *per se* has mainly been a separate area from research into field-programmable logic, although many papers on the use of FPL include hardware-software partitioning as a feature of system design. In contrast, custom computing machines have been at the heart of FPL research activity, evidenced in particular by the highly-successful series of IEEE Symposia on FPGAs for Custom Computing Machines. Hartenstein *et al* present a very good discussion of the relationship between the fields of hardware/software co-design and custom computing machines in [7]. In tandem with these two very practically oriented areas, there has been much interest in configurable computers within the parallel algorithms community, in particular through the reconfigurable mesh model [1]. It is natural to ask what links there are between this area and the more practical areas, given that all are concerned with reconfigurability.

This paper presents a rather more general discussion of the new digital computing paradigms[1] that lie ahead as a result of these driving forces. Thus, the concern is with how computing systems implement required functions, rather than the equally-important question of how a user specifies functional requirements in the first place. However, consideration of the concerns addressed here is essential to thoughful consideration of the latter question.

The new paradigms offer an exciting vision to those who currently only see FPL as a mechanism for easy prototyping and cheap glue logic, or for enabling occasional field upgrades of computer system 'hardware'. The author believes that the key to this vision is to stop regarding FPL as being merely a functionally-equivalent alternative to ASICs (one helpful step in this direction is to stop using the suggestive terms 'hardware' and 'software').

The central discussion points of the paper follow in the next five sections. Section 2 discusses a fundamental paradigm change in system design: from a world where there is:

- higher-level algorithm/program/software design on one side; and
- lower-level architecture/circuit/hardware design on the other side

to a new world with:

- programs/circuits;
- algorithms/architectures; and
- softness/hardness

as three distinct design trade-offs. Section 3 examines this new world more closely, identifying that these three trade-offs can recur at different levels of abstraction within designs.

After the review of the new world, Section 4 focuses on programmability itself, examining how it can manifest itself within system components. In Section 5, there is a discussion of the different characteristics of computational circuits and interconnected processing elements — although both have a basic graph-style abstract structure, they have differing computation properties, and so it seems reasonable to distinguish between them. After this, Section 6 briefly examines the role of memories in the new computational world. Finally, Section 7 draws some conclusions, and points to the major research problems that lie ahead.

---

[1] There is no attempt here to address analogue computing paradigms, although most of the ideas related to digital circuitry will carry over to analogue circuitry.

2   The fundamental paradigm change

Control flow v. data flow

A central feature of the traditional engineering of computer systems is that, at some point, there is a stage of partitioning of the system into hardware components and software components; even in the enlightened world of hardware/software co-design, there is, by definition, the notion of separate hardware and software components.

The fundamental paradigm shift suggested by field-programmable logic, and related developments in reconfigurable systems, is that there is a more natural basic choice, which is between:

− control flow approaches; and
− data flow approaches.

To date, consideration of these two approaches, and their relative merits and demerits, has largely been the domain of computer architecture and programming language specialists. However, now seems the time to place them in front of a larger audience. Here, control flow is typically exemplified by sequential program execution, where instructions cause data manipulation. At a low-level, this includes microprocessor and DSP instruction sequences, and at higher levels, programs in imperative and functional languages. Data flow is exemplified by interconnected processing elements with data moving between elements, not under some central programmed control. At a low level, this includes logic circuitry, and at higher levels, interconnected ALUs or even interconnected processors. Another interpretation of these approaches is control flow as 'computing in time' and data flow as 'computing in space'.

To a very large extent in the past, control flow approaches have been associated with the software designer, and data flow approaches with the hardware designer. This has been forced by the underpinning technology respectively available to these classes of designer. A main impact of FPL should be that a data flow approach can be made available to the software designer, as an alternative form of programming. One noteworthy existing example is the field of systolic arrays, which uses a data flow approach with constrained interconnection and timing constraints. Control flow approaches are already made available to hardware designers in many cases, principally through the use of state machines.

This general world of control flow v. data flow matches a world that is well-familiar to those specialising in complexity theory and the analysis of algorithms. There, there are control flow-style models, such as the Turing Machine and the Random Access Machine, and data flow-style models, such as boolean circuits and algebraic circuits. In this more abstract world, algorithm designers are often comfortable with working in terms of circuits, rather than programs, not feeling encumbered by extra baggage associated with the circuits having a hardware nature.

One further development of the control flow and data flow theme is to envisage algorithms that make use of both approaches in combination. This might be termed 'control flow/data flow co-design'. It is an effect already achieved at a high system level when hardware/software co-design is employed. Here, however, there is no general presumption about what is hard and what is soft.

Algorithms v. architectures

As a consequence of focusing on the choice between control flow and data flow styles, a new interpretation can be placed on the traditional notions of 'algorithm' and 'architecture'. Currently, the prevalent situation is that algorithms are seen as a software (and control flow) matter and architectures are seen as a hardware (and data flow) matter, and so it is necessary to fit algorithms to fixed architectures.

In the new view of computing paradigms, a better interpretation of these notions is that an algorithm specifies a special-purpose computation, described in terms of an architecture which supplies a more general-purpose computational mechanism. This is a particular instance of a layered implementation, considered in more general in the next section. A key point however, is that the architecture need not be considered as a fixed and given entity. That is, an implementor can use algorithm/architecture co-design to develop an algorithm supported by an apt architecture. The architecture may supply a control flow model, a data flow model, or a combination of both if this is convenient for algorithms to use. FPL is a technology that, together with conventional processors, enables such co-design, in its most general form, to be used as a routine implementation method.

Hardness v. softness

Given the above paradigm shift, the hardware/software issue now occupies a separate dimension to the control flow/data flow issue, and also a separate dimension to the algorithm/architecture issue. This dimension is concerned with the benefits of hardness:

- first, at some point, use of hardware is necessary to give a physical basis for computation;
- second, hardware may give better brute-force performance than software.

That is, the business of hardness v. softness is decoupled from the nature of the computational model being implemented. A processor core is an example of a control flow model implemented in hardware; an FPL device is an example of a data flow model implemented in hardware — in both cases, the hardware provides a physical basis that can run an effectively-infinite range of different algorithms. Processors are sufficiently mature and well-understood artifacts that it is possible to have instruction set architectures that are relatively stable over time. This is not the case for FPL devices at the moment, but the author is confident that more stable 'instruction set architectures' will emerge over time. Some initial thoughts on what a less device-dependent ISA might be like are contained in [4].

3 Layered implementation

The key feature of selecting between control flow and data flow approaches to computation is that choice need not occur at only one level of a system design. That is, a conventional approach of partitioning a system at the topmost level only is just one special case of a more general model. At any level of abstraction of the detail of a system, a specification of required system or sub-system behaviour might be implemented using either model or, indeed, a co-design using both.

This general idea offers a possible reconcilation for the theological debates in the configurable community that concern the best granularity for interconnected processing elements. At one level, a data flow model with chunky processing elements may be apt; however, either in implementing these elements or for other computation at the same level, simpler processing elements may be used. This flexibility essentially arises from convincing the designer that there is not an unbreakable commitment to hardware at any particular stage.

In order to implement a model at a higher level of abstraction in terms of a lower level, the notions of simulation and emulation are relevant. These two terms are used with different meanings by different people. To paraphrase the Oxford English Dictionary, simulation is the use of a computer model to imitate that conditions of a process; and, to quote the OED, emulation is 'the technique by which a computer or software system is enabled to execute programs written for a different type of computer, by means of special hardware or software'.

In the conventional FPL world, the most usual case of simulation is that a software program is being used to imitate the behaviour of a hardware circuit. Simulation methods also occur in the complexity theory and analysis of algorithms community — for example, results on how Turing Machines can simulate boolean circuits, and *vice versa*, are well-known and well-understood.

In this new setting, concerned with layered implementation, the notion of emulation is the more relevant. A control flow model might emulate a data flow model, and a data flow model might emulate a control flow model. For example, the first direction might be when a program for a processor is used as a simulator of programmed logic circuitry, and the second direction might be when programmed logic circuitry is used to implement a simple processor core (e.g., [5]).

Thus, the mapping between a higher-level model and a lower-level model may be orchestrated from either the higher level or the lower level. The first case corresponds to traditional compilation, and the second case corresponds to emulation. From the higher level, a control flow or data flow description of a component is converted into a form executable by a programmable lower-level implementation (for example, program compilation, automatic place and route for FPL). From the lower level, a programmable implementation is programmed so that it can perform emulation by interpreting a description of a higher-level component. The key point in both cases is that the mapping may involve crossovers between control flow and data flow in either direction. Further, in both cases, the higher level component might be considered as being the 'algorithm', and the lower level component the 'architecture'. However, note that the algorithm might, in turn, be implementing an architecture for a higher level.

4 Three-level programmability

Notice that the discussion in the previous section leant heavily on the notion of programmability of a lower-level component. Considering an overall system, then it is perfectly natural for its behaviour to be programmable, either directly by a human user or more subtly as an adaptive system reacting to its environment. It is only at the lowest level of committing to hardware (for example, for a block on a chip) that there is no underlying programmable component. With current developments, such as the Virtual Socket Interface (VSI) [8] for system-on-chip design, one might even argue that there is an element of programmability at the chip level.

In trying to understand the novelty that arises from the programmability of FPL, it is useful to identify three different levels of programmability that apply to control flow models (i.e., to programming). In order of increasing frequency over time, these are:

- different programs can be executed;
- executing programs can be modified;
- dynamic behaviour through choice in control flows.

Of these, the first and third are perfectly normal, but the second is generally viewed as very bad practice nowadays — mostly because understandability (and hence more obvious correctness) is deemed more important than any possible performance gains.

For data flow models (i.e., circuits), a similar three-level classification of programmability can be derived, and this reflects types of FPL research carried out and also continuing. In the same order as above, these are:

- different circuits can be executed;
- executing circuits can be modified;
- dynamic behaviour through choice in data flows.

Many examples of FPL applications use only the first level: a device can be used to execute different circuits, in sequence over (perhaps lengthy) time. Indeed, if this level of programability is not used, then it is questionable why FPL is being used in the first place.

It appears that there is a much stronger case for indulging in the second level of programmability in data flow models than there is in control flow models. This is due to the weaker nature of the third level compared to that in the control flow model, where there is considerable run-time flexibility in the order that data items are processed and the operations that are performed on them. Incorporating equivalent flexibility directly into a particular circuit will result in an extremely large circuit, with many components redundant at any particular instant in time. Dynamic modification of circuitry is an attractive alternative that allows efficiency in circuit size. The extreme end of the scale is when different circuits time share an execution medium, that is, there is dynamic replacement of circuitry, rather than mere modification.

Note that there is an alternative approach when dealing with circuits that may have an excessive size, but include temporal redundancy. This is to employ virtual circuitry (a.k.a. virtual hardware), where circuits may have large sizes, and an operating system is used to manage the problems transparently (e.g., [2,3]). However, such methods of disguising circuit modification during execution do not preclude other, finer-grain, applications. As an example, parameter passing is one way of incorporating dynamic behaviour into control flow programs. Modification of executing circuits can be used to achieve a similar effect in a data flow model, by 'folding' parameter values into the functionality of the circuitry. It is also possible to modify data flows by changing interconnections between components.

What is currently lacking is any systematic way for controlling the extent of in-execution circuit modification — one practical reason for this has been the fact that partially-reconfigurable FPL technologies have only recently emerged to motivate consideration of these problems in detail.

5   Distinguishing circuits and networks

The preceding discussion does not deal with the class of regular parallel architectures very well. At first sight, a parallel architecture with interconnected processing elements might seem a natural candidate that fits the data flow model. This is acceptable for something like a systolic array; however, it is not entirely apt for less-constrained cases where the processing elements are conducting more random-style programmed communication. This can be expressed loosely as a distinction between MIMD and SIMD styles, to use the archaic terminology of Flynn [6], but the author prefers to avoid this famous taxonomy, since it rather constrains thinking to the models that seemed feasible many years ago.

To deal with this tension, it seems tempting at first to try to abstract away any differences, either using the fact that both are essentially graph-based, or using a more abstract model of communicating processes. However, the author believes that it is worth making a distinction, when discussing architectures at least. The following are criteria for differentiating circuits and networks of interconnected elements:

- tighter coupling v. looser coupling;
- communication each time step v. more asynchronous communication;
- randomish (by design) topology v. more structured topology.

In time, a more thorough definition will be necessary. For now, note that the first points in each item capture the essence of data flow, whereas the second points in each item capture the essence of interconnected control flow elements. In terms of using these different classes, the first involves continous attention to communication, wheras the second involves communication as a backdrop to computation.

This distinction points to interconnection as an important third technique, in addition to the control flow and data flow techniques (not forgetting the interconnection also occurs implicitly within the data flow model). In regular parallel architectures, the interconnection is between control flow entities. More interestingly, interconnection is important in order to co-design systems from control flow and data flow components. For example, at a low level of abstraction, the interconnection of a processor core with an FPL array is a very important issue.

Like the other two components, interconnection can often be programmable itself, either by programming of the interconnection fabric or by packet routing switches. This makes additional fluidity available to the algorithm/architecture designer. One further extension, that fits within the overall general model, is the use of active interconnections, where data flow, or perhaps control flow, function is inserted within the interconnection.

6 The role of memory

As a final piece in the overall picture of the new paradigm for computing, the role of memory must be considered. This is a significant adjunct to control flow, data flow and interconnection.

First, memory is necessary as the means of recording state information in both the control flow and data flow models, a fact which is very familiar. In the control flow model, memory is used for things like processor registers, cache memory and main memory, which are essential as repositories for the data being manipulated during the control flow. In the data flow model, memory is used for things like input and output registers and, in sequential circuitry, for internal latches, flip-flops and registers. Pipeline registers and buffers may be used to affect the timing characteristics of synchronous data flow models.

Second, memory is necessary as the means of recording the programmed features in both control flow and data flow models. In principle, this use is a special-case of the first use, in that the memory contains data for a lower-level implementation of the programmable model. This is fairly self-evident for conventional stored-program computers, where the same memory is used to hold both programs and data. Paradoxically, however, the contents of the memory are being used at two different levels of implementation. The observation is less evident in most present-day FPL technologies, since these incorporate special-case configuration memory distributed across the FPL array, which is disjoint from memory used to store data processed by the array. Furthermore, the interfacing of these two types of memory is often significantly different. However, this does stress that two implementation levels are involved.

Third, memory may act as a subsititute for direct interconnection, effectively simulating an all-to-all, but sequential rather than parallel, interconnect. In the context of parallel computation, the relative merits of shared memory versus explicit inter-processor communication are much debated. Rather than rehearse

these arguments here, there is one observation worth making. The use of memory
for interconnection might be seen as offering a further reference point using the
criteria for differentiating interconnected processing elements and the data flow
model. Its properties are:

- loose coupling;
- very asynchronous communication;
- random topology

In other words, it is a variant on physical interconnection that enables random
interconnections, with arbitrarily-large latencies, between processing elements.

Finally, memory may be a substitute for use of a control flow or data flow
component, by facilitating computation through lookup tables if an algorithm
designer deems this efficient. For a limited number of inputs, with limited ranges
of values, this can be considered as the ultimate in programmed components.
This use establishes memory as not only a necessary adjunct to the control flow
and data flow models, and interconnection, but also as a first-order component
in its own right.

7 Conclusions and major problems

This paper has introduced a revised view of the system design process, to reflect
an age of configurability and programmability in components once regarded
as fixed. The author firmly believes that such a global view is needed before
tackling the huge problems associated with the practicalities of designing in
such a framework.

These problems include the notations used for describing designs, the tools for
processing these notations and the compilation/emulation used for implementing
higher-level views in terms of lower-level views. The hope is that there can be
a softening of barriers between the tool sets used for hardware design and for
software design. Ultimately, the problems also include the design of future novel
hardware, to act as the physical basis for the revised design process.

It is also the hope that algorithm designers might have a higher profile in the
world of configurable computing, with the incentive of being able to contemplate
both control flow/data flow co-design, and algorithm/architecture co-design to
obtain solutions that have very good performance, but perhaps without having
to delve into the mysteries of real hardware to achieve these benefits.

Acknowledgement

The author thanks the participants in the February 1998 Dagstuhl-Seminar on
Dynamically Reconfigurable Architectures, for the wide-ranging technical discussion that helped him to form a more general view of the subject.

References

1. Ben-Asher, Peleg, Ramaswami and Schuster, "The Power of Reconfiguration", Journal of Parallel and Distributed Computing, **13**, 1991, pp.139–153.
2. Brebner, "The Swappable Logic Unit: a Paradigm for Virtual Hardware", Proc. 5th Annual IEEE Symposium on Custom Computing Machines, IEEE Computer Society Press 1997, pp.77–86.
3. Brebner, "Automatic Identification of Swappable Logic Units in XC6200 Circuitry", Proc. 7th International Workshop on Field-Programmable Logic and Applications, Springer LNCS 1304, 1997, pp.173–182.
4. Brebner, "Circlets: Circuits as Applets", Proc. 6th Annual IEEE Symposium on Custom Computing Machines, IEEE Computer Society Press, 1998.
5. Donlin, "Self Modifying Circuitry — A Platform for Tractible Virtual Circuitry", Proc. 8th International Workshop on Field-Programmable Logic and Applications, Springer LNCS, 1998.
6. Flynn, Some Computer Organisations and their Effectiveness", IEEE Trans. on Computers, **21**, 1972, pp.948–960.
7. Hartenstein, Becker and Kress, "Custom Computing Machines vs. Hardware/Software Co-Design: From a Globalized Point of View", Proc. 6th International Workshop on Field-Programmable Logic and Applications, Springer LNCS 1142, pp.65–76.
8. VSI Alliance Architecture Document, VSI Alliance, 1998.

Run-Time Management of Dynamically Reconfigurable Designs

N. Shirazi, W. Luk and P.Y.K. Cheung

Department of Computing, Imperial College, 180 Queen's Gate,
London SW7 2BZ, UK

Abstract. A method for managing reconfigurable designs, which supports run-time configuration transformation, is proposed. This method involves structuring the reconfiguration manager into three components: a monitor, a loader, and a configuration store. Various trade-offs can be achieved in reconfiguration time, the optimality of the reconfigured circuits, and the complexity of the reconfiguration manager. We consider methods of reconfiguration and ways of exploiting run-time information available at compile time, and study their impact on design trade-offs. The proposed techniques, implementable in hardware or software, are supported by our tools and can be applied to both partially and non-partially reconfigurable devices. We describe the combined and the partitioned reconfiguration methods, and use them to illustrate the techniques and the associated trade-offs.

1 Introduction

Exploiting the run-time configurability of FPGAs has been regarded by many as the key to overcoming their reduced capacity and speed compared with custom integrated circuit implementations. The approach will, however, only be valid if the time for reconfiguring the FPGAs does not outweigh its benefits of increasing capacity. Techniques are required to manage reconfigurable resources efficiently at run time; such techniques may also provide abstractions which hide low level details from users when appropriate.

This paper presents a method for efficient run-time management of reconfigurable designs, which involves structuring the reconfiguration manager into three components: a monitor, a loader, and a configuration store. The method can be implemented in hardware, software, or a combination of both. It can be applied to dynamically reconfigurable systems containing one or more FPGAs, which may or may not support partial reconfiguration. Techniques such as run-time transformation and partitioning the reconfiguration manager can be used to optimise configuration store usage or to reduce reconfiguration time.

Our work complements related research on tool development and run-time support for reconfigurable systems [1], [2], [3], [4], [8], [10]. The important aspects of our work include: (a) exploitation of compile-time information for optimising run-time performance, (b) flexibility of implementing the reconfiguration manager in hardware or software, (c) support for both partially reconfigurable and non-partially reconfigurable FPGAs.

2 Framework Overview

This section provides an overview of our framework for reconfiguration management. Details of the components in this framework will be presented later. While the discussion below centres on one dynamically reconfigurable FPGA, the framework can be extended to deal with multiple devices.

In this framework, the reconfiguration manager contains three components: a monitor, a loader, and a configuration store (Figure 1). The monitor maintains information about the configuration state, which may include the type and location of the circuits currently operating in the FPGA. When the conditions for advancing to the next configuration state – such as receiving a request from the application or from the FPGA – are met, the monitor notifies the loader to install the new circuit at particular locations on the FPGA. In situations such as image processing, as long as the image size is fixed, the number of cycles for many operations are data independent and can be determined at compile time. The monitor can then be simplified to contain a few counters.

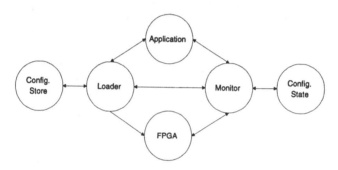

Fig. 1. Framework for reconfiguration manager.

The loader, on receiving a request from the monitor, configures the FPGA using data from a configuration store. When finished, it signals the monitor for completion, and normal operation can resume.

The configuration store contains a directory for the circuit configurations. The configurations are usually stored in the form of address-data pairs, where the data specify the configuration for an FPGA cell while the address indicates its location in the FPGA. A transformation agent can be used to transform or compose circuit configurations at run time; such details will be discussed later.

Our framework can be used to construct generic or customised reconfiguration managers. A generic reconfiguration manager can deal with a variety of applications, and is therefore likely to be more complex and less efficient. A customised reconfiguration manager is developed for one or a few applications, and can be optimised at compile time based on knowledge about run-time conditions. It is often more efficient, compact and simpler than a generic reconfiguration manager, but is not as flexible.

3 Design Flow

The proposed run-time management techniques are supported by a model [6] and the associated development procedure [7] for reconfigurable designs. There are six steps in this procedure: decomposition, sequencing, partial evaluation, incremental configuration calculation, simultaneous configuration generation, and validation. Reusable libraries [5], prototype tools [7], [9] and FPGA-based evaluation platforms [6] supporting these steps have been reported.

For this paper, we shall focus on the sequencing step. In this step, the design is captured as a network with control blocks connecting together the possible configurations for each reconfigurable component, together with the sequence of conditions for activating a particular configuration for each control block. In the next section, we shall describe how compile-time information captured in the activation sequence can be used to optimise the reconfiguration manager.

The above procedure can be explained using our model [6] for reconfigurable designs. In this model, a component that can be configured to behave either as A or as B is described by a network with A and B connected between two control blocks. The control blocks, RC_DMux and RC_Mux, route the data and results from the external ports x and y to either A or B at the desired instant, depending on the value c on their select lines (Figure 2). Each control block will be mapped either into a real multiplexer or demultiplexer to form a single-cycle reconfigurable design, or into virtual ones which model the control mechanisms for replacing one configuration by another [6]. We shall see how this model can be used in developing and optimising the reconfiguration manager in later sections.

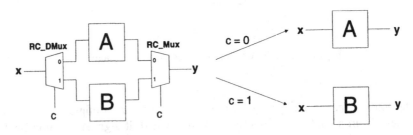

Fig. 2. A static network modelling a design that can behave either as A or as B, depending on the select value c for the control blocks RC_DMux and RC_Mux.

4 Monitor

The purpose of the monitor is to keep track of the configurations in the FPGA. The monitor also contains information about possible transitions to the next state from a particular state.

Since run-time conditions usually require rapid capture and may involve a large amount of data, part of the monitor often resides on the dynamically reconfigurable FPGA, and is mainly used for data-driven reconfiguration. The monitor checks for the user condition that activates reconfiguration. If the user condition for the next configuration is met and the desired configuration is not in a usable form on the FPGA, the monitor notifies the loader to introduce the configuration. When finished, the monitor may signal the completion of the configuration process if required.

The monitor includes one or more reconfiguration state machines. These state machines can be produced from our tools automatically and are based on the activation sequence from the user specifying the reconfiguration conditions (Section 3). A reconfiguration state machine indicates which configuration to load from the configuration store.

There are three possibilities for the monitor operation depending on the information in the reconfiguration sequence available at compile time.

(a) The duration for which the current configuration remains valid is known at compile time, and the next configuration is also known.

(b) The duration for which the current configuration remains valid is not known, although the next configuration is known.

(c) Both the duration for which the current configuration remains valid, and the next configuration, is not known.

Case (a) is the simplest: a timing mechanism such as a counter could be included in the monitor to indicate when the next configuration will be loaded. This happens, for instance, in video processing when the hardware reconfigures to a known next state after a fixed number of frames whose size is also known. Recall that RC_Mux/RC_DMux pairs are used to indicate the reconfigurable regions, and that changing the value on their select lines corresponds to reconfiguring between components delimited by the RC_Mux/RC_DMux pair (Figure 2). For case (a), these select lines will be connected to the timing mechanism.

For FPGAs supporting partial reconfiguration such as Xilinx 6200 devices, this means that partial reconfiguration will be performed after a fixed duration; for non-partially reconfigurable FPGAs such as Xilinx 4000 devices, entire chip configurations will be swapped. Provided that there is enough FPGA resources, one can implement the RC_Mux/RC_DMux pairs and the associated configurations as physical components on the FPGA to produce a single-cycle reconfigurable design [6], [9].

Case (b) requires inputs from run-time conditions, from the FPGA or from application software, to decide when the next configuration is required. In this case, the select lines of the RC_Mux/RC_DMux pairs are connected to the source that triggers reconfiguration. The same is true for case (c); however, since the choice of the next configuration is determined at run time, all possible next configurations will have to be produced at compile time or at run time.

Our scheme allows an abstraction layer above the RC_Mux/RC_DMux level. A mapping function can be defined that relates a value from the user design to the corresponding RC_Mux/RC_DMux pairs. In the constant adder example provided in Section 8, a user only needs to supply an integer constant which is then mapped to selecting the corresponding RC_Mux/RC_DMux pairs that indicate the reconfiguration to be performed.

Sometimes the designer can determine whether reducing the reconfiguration time, or optimising the size or speed of the new circuit, should take priority. For instance, one configuration may contain circuit elements usable by its successor, but in an suboptimal way. One can then decide whether to reduce the reconfiguration time and tolerate a suboptimal circuit, or to have a longer reconfiguration time in return for a better circuit. Alternatively, circuit elements from the next configuration can be included in the current configuration, such that circuit behaviour is preserved while reducing reconfiguration time. Facilities for estimating reconfiguration time will be useful [8].

5 Loader

The purpose of the loader is to carry out the reconfiguration of the FPGA, as specified by the select value for the RC_Mux/RC_DMux components. On receiving a request from the monitor, the loader obtains the location of the requested configuration from the configuration directory, extracts the configuration from the configuration store and then initiates the configuration process. On completion, the loader may, when appropriate, set a new clock speed for the new circuit. It then signals the monitor for completion, and normal operation can resume.

The software version of the loader runs on the host processor. API functions are provided to facilitate design development by hiding the mechanisms used for performing run-time reconfiguration. We follow an object-oriented approach, treating an RC_Mux/RC_DMux pair as objects which load a new configuration when the value on their select lines changes. When an object is created, the configuration data associated with the RC_Mux/RC_DMux pair are loaded into the host's main memory to ensure fast configuration of the FPGA. The resulting facilities are similar to those supported by JERC [4].

To improve reconfiguration speed, we have developed a scheme to implement the loader in hardware. This enables dynamic reconfiguration to be performed at the maximum speed that the FPGA can handle. This is difficult to achieve by loading configurations from a loosely-coupled processor, for example an FPGA co-processor board that resides on a PCI bus.

A handshaking scheme is used to synchronise the user design with the reconfiguration manager, since the reconfiguration manager can be clocked faster than the user design. This allows multiple configuration cycles to occur in a single compute cycle, thus reducing reconfiguration overhead.

6 Configuration Store and Run-Time Transformations

The configuration store contains three components: a configuration directory, a repository for configuration data, and a transformation agent (Figure 3). The configuration directory and the configuration data can be arranged as shown in Figure 4. If required, the transformation agent transforms a configuration before loading it into the FPGA; this can be used in minimising configuration store usage, as discussed below. For performance critical applications, the transformation agent can itself be implemented in hardware. If the next configuration can be predicted at compile time or at run time before it is required, there may be sufficient time for a software transformation agent to perform its tasks.

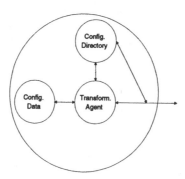

Fig. 3. Configuration store architecture. The configuration store is connected to the loader as shown in Figure 1.

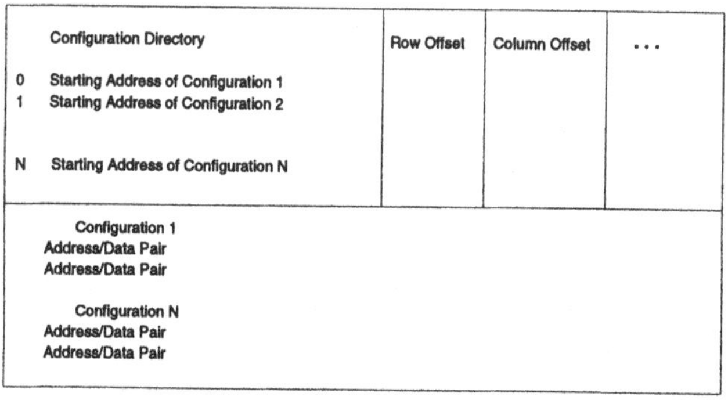

Configuration Directory	Row Offset	Column Offset	. . .
0 Starting Address of Configuration 1			
1 Starting Address of Configuration 2			
N Starting Address of Configuration N			

Configuration 1
Address/Data Pair
Address/Data Pair

Configuration N
Address/Data Pair
Address/Data Pair

Fig. 4. Possible data arrangement in the configuration store, showing the configuration directory (top left), transformation parameters (top right) and configuration data (bottom). Row Offset and Column Offset are examples of transformation parameters for the configuration data which can be produced at compile time or at run time.

Fast storage is often scarce. To minimise configuration storage, three transformation methods are explored. The first method covers regular circuits: if the same configuration information is used in two or more locations of the FPGA, an offset (Figure 4) can be added repeatedly to the address of the base configuration to produce the required configurations. Our tools automatically calculate these offsets and the number of replications, and place them as transformation parameters in the configuration store. The replication of configuration data at the row and column offsets are generated by the transformation agent during reconfiguration of the FPGA.

The second method is to maximise sharing of lower-level components in the design hierarchy: for instance the same adder configuration can be used in producing different kinds of multipliers. This method is an extension of the first method to support hierarchical representations of configuration data.

The third method adopts a small number of configuration templates, which can be transformed by operations such as stretching or partial evaluation, for building the actual configuration bitstreams at run time. This method is particularly useful in, for example, producing constant-coefficient adders or multipliers. Further parameters can be included to support specific transformations.

All three transformation methods assume that the configurations are relocatable [10], and work best when there are minimum constraints on the placement of the circuits. These methods can be implemented in hardware to reduce their run-time overhead. While other configuration store architectures may result in greater utilisation, they may do so at the expense of increasing reconfiguration time or complicating the transformation agent.

7   Reconfiguration Methods

This section presents two reconfiguration methods, and assesses their impact on our framework. An example will be considered in Section 8; further case studies, such as arithmetic and video processing designs, are under development.

Combined reconfiguration method. For a design with n configurations, there are $n(n-1)$ possibilities of changing from one configuration to another. If the reconfiguration sequence is known at compile time, then we can generate incremental configurations instead of full configurations [7]. At run time, the transformation agent produces the required configuration from incremental configurations, including the computation of offsets (Section 6). For devices supporting partial reconfiguration or simultaneous reconfiguration, there will be an improvement in reconfiguration time since only the parts that change need to be reconfigured.

However, if the reconfiguration sequence is only available at run time, then up to $n(n-1)$ configurations will need to be generated at compile time. Alternatively the configurations will have to be produced on demand at run time.

Partitioned reconfiguration method. An alternative method is based on the principle that more efficient implementations can often be obtained by moving the RC_Muxes and RC_DMuxes to a lower level of description [6]. For the above example, this method is applicable if the n configurations can each be decomposed into m components, so that each component is controlled by its group of RC_Mux/RC_DMux pairs. m reconfiguration state machines are generated, one for each group of RC_Mux/RC_DMux pairs, so that the design can be configured to be one of the n possible configurations.

At run time, the required configuration is produced by the transformation agent from data for each of the m components. The reconfiguration state machine in the monitor for each component determines if the conditions for transition have been reached; if so, it signals the loader to load the appropriate partial configuration.

In this example, the partitioned reconfiguration method reduces the number of partial reconfigurations from $n(n-1)$ to an application-specific value depending on m. However, the reconfiguration manager is more complex than that for the combined reconfiguration method, since there are now m reconfiguration state machines instead of one. This method may not be able to take advantage of simultaneous reconfiguration techniques, unless the relevant control information (such as wildcard data for the Xilinx 6200 FPGA) can be computed rapidly [7]. Finally, a mapping function may be required to produce the appropriate control information for the m state machines; this will be illustrated in the next section.

8 Constant Adder

In this example, a bitslice of a variable adder is partially evaluated, resulting in the two circuits shown in Figure 5(a) which correspond to a constant zero adder and a constant one adder. Our tools [9] automatically find the reconfigurable regions in these two designs and insert RC_Muxes and RC_DMuxes to delimit the reconfigurable regions, resulting in the bitslice in Figure 5(b). This bitslice can then be replicated to give a constant adder of a particular size. For a Xilinx 6200 FPGA, the use of a constant adder in place of a variable adder reduces the size by 50%, and increases the speed by 33%.

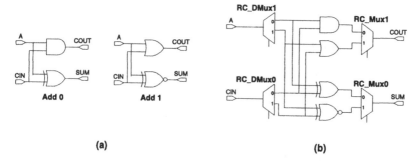

(a)   (b)

Fig. 5.   (a) Two circuit bitslices for adding a constant zero or a constant one. (b) A circuit that can be reconfigured to implement either of the circuits in (a), by a value at the select lines of the control components RC_Mux and RC_DMux. The same value is used for all four control components.

Combined reconfiguration method. In this method, the user specifies the constants in the command file along with the duration between reconfigurations if available. The configuration state diagram in Figure 6(a) is produced by our tools. If the duration between reconfiguration is known at compile time, then a timing mechanism will be included in the monitor to trigger the reconfiguration automatically. If the duration is not known, then the monitor keeps track of the configuration state so that, when the conditions for reconfiguration occur, it requests the loader to initiate the reconfiguration.

For this method, the ease of reconfiguration comes at the expense of increasing the amount of configuration data. For each bit that differs between two successive constants, two configurations cycles are needed in the Xilinx 6200: one for reconfiguring the XNOR gate to the XOR gate, and the other for reconfiguring the OR gate to the AND gate. Our tools can take advantage of device-specific optimisation such as wildcarding in the Xilinx 6200, thus reducing the amount of reconfiguration cycles between the constant "1111" and "0000" [7]. There are a total of 20 configuration words for the reconfiguration sequence in Figure 6(a). In general, if the design needs to reconfigure between all 2^n different constants, up to $2^n(2^n - 1)$ configurations may have to be generated and stored.

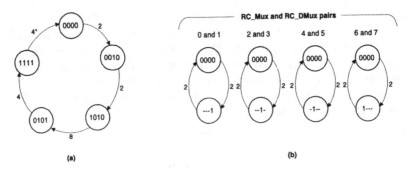

(a)   (b)

Fig. 6. (a) State diagram for incremental configuration of a 4-bit constant adder using the combined reconfiguration method. The number of configuration words involved in a transition is shown next to the corresponding edge. The asterisk indicates that the number of configuration words has been reduced by wildcarding. (b) State diagram for configuring each bitslice individually. RC_Mux/RC_DMux pairs correspond to the ones in Figure 5(b). A dash indicates a don't care condition for a particular bit.

Partitioned reconfiguration method. An alternative is to partition the adder into bitslices, and calculate the configuration needed for each bitslice to add a 0 or 1. To change a constant, a mapping function is defined that selects the appropriate RC_Muxes/RC_DMuxes for each bitslice shown in Figure 5(b). The monitor has access to a reconfiguration state machine for each bitslice, which determines if its bit of the constant has changed; if so, it signals the loader to load the appropriate partial configuration. The configuration for each bitslice is stitched together by the transformation agent to form the required configuration.

This method significantly reduces the amount of configuration data for an n-bit constant adder. Four configuration words are needed for each bitslice. Apart from the component at the least significant bit position due to the external carry input, the configuration bits for the bitslices are the same, except for an address offset. Hence we only need to store the configuration bits for the component at the least significant bit position and the repeating bitslice. During reconfiguration, the transformation agent in the configuration store adds the corresponding offsets to reconfigure the bitslice. There are only 8 configuration words needed to be stored using this method.

9 Summary

This paper presents a framework for efficient run-time management of reconfigurable designs, which exploits compile-time information for optimising run-time performance. The reconfiguration manager can be implemented in hardware or software, and supports both partially and non-partially reconfigurable FPGAs. Current and future research includes refining and extending our framework and tools, exploring their use in multi-tasking systems, and applying them to realistic applications.

Acknowledgements

The support of Xilinx, Interval Research, Hewlett Packard Laboratories Bristol and the UK Engineering and Physical Sciences Research Council (Grant Number GR/L24366, GR/L54356 and GR/L59658) is gratefully acknowledged.

References

1. G. Brebner, "A virtual hardware operating system for the Xilinx 6200", in *Field-Programmable Logic, Smart Applications, New Paradigms and Compilers*, LNCS 1142, Springer, 1996.
2. J. Burns et. al., "A dynamic reconfiguration run-time system", in *Proc. FCCM97*, IEEE Computer Society Press, 1997.
3. S. Cadambi et. al., "Managing pipeline-reconfigurable FPGAs", in *Proc. FPGA98*, ACM Press, 1998.
4. E. Lechner and S.A. Guccione, "The Java environment for reconfigurable computing", in *Field Programmable Logic and Applications*, LNCS 1304, Springer, 1997.
5. W. Luk, S. Guo, N. Shirazi and N. Zhuang, "A framework for developing parametrised FPGA libraries", in *Field-Programmable Logic, Smart Applications, New Paradigms and Compilers*, LNCS 1142, Springer, 1996.
6. W. Luk, N. Shirazi and P.Y.K. Cheung, "Modelling and optimising run-time reconfigurable systems", in *Proc. FCCM96*, IEEE Computer Society Press, 1996.
7. W. Luk, N. Shirazi and P.Y.K. Cheung, "Compilation tools for run-time reconfigurable designs", in *Proc. FCCM97*, IEEE Computer Society Press, 1997.
8. P. Lysaght, "Towards an expert system for a priori estimation of reconfiguration latency in dynamically reconfigurable logic", in *Field Programmable Logic and Applications*, LNCS 1304, Springer, 1997.
9. N. Shirazi, W. Luk and P.Y.K. Cheung, "Automating production of run-time reconfigurable designs", in *Proc. FCCM98*, IEEE Computer Society Press, 1998.
10. M.J. Wirthlin and B.L. Hutchings, "A dynamic instruction set computer", in *Proc. FCCM95*, IEEE Computer Society Press, 1995.

Acceleration of Satisfiability Algorithms by Reconfigurable Hardware

Marco Platzner and Giovanni De Micheli

Computer Systems Laboratory, Stanford University
Stanford, CA 94305, U.S.A.
marco.platzner@computer.org

Abstract. We present different architectures to solve Boolean satisfiability problems in instance-specific hardware. A simulation of these architectures shows that for examples from the DIMACS benchmark suite, high raw speed-ups over software can be achieved. We present a design tool flow and prototype implementation of an instance-specific satisfiability solver and discuss experimental results. We measure the overall speed-up of the instance-specific architecture that takes the hardware compilation time into account. The results prove that many of the DIMACS examples can be accelerated with current FPGA technology.

1   Introduction

The *Boolean satisfiability problem* (SAT) is a fundamental problem in mathematical logic and computing theory with many practical applications in areas such as computer-aided design of digital systems, automated reasoning, and machine vision. In computer-aided design, tools for synthesis, optimization, verification, timing analysis, and test pattern generation use variants of SAT solvers as core algorithms. The SAT problem is commonly defined as follows [1]: Given

- a set of n Boolean variables $x_1, x_2, \ldots, x_n$,
- a set of literals, where a literal is a variable x_i or the complement of a variable $\bar{x}_i$, and
- a set of m distinctive clauses $C_1, C_2, \ldots, C_m$, where each clause consists of literals combined by the logical *or* connective $\vee$,

determine, whether there exists an assignment of truth values to the variables that makes the Conjunctive Normal Form (CNF)

$$C_1 \wedge C_2 \wedge \ldots \wedge C_m \tag{1}$$

true, where $\wedge$ denotes the logical *and* connective.

Since the general SAT problem is NP-complete, exact methods to solve SAT problems show an exponential worst-case runtime complexity. This limits the applicability of exact SAT solvers in many areas. Heuristics can be used to find solutions faster, but they may fail to prove satisfiability.

The SAT problem is a *discrete, constrained decision problem* [1]. A straightforward but inefficient procedure to solve it exactly is to enumerate all possible truth value assignments and check if one satisfies the CNF. Many of the improved techniques that have been proposed to solve SAT problems eliminate one variable from the CNF at a time. There are two basic methods: *splitting* and *resolution*. Resolution was implemented in the original Davis-Putnam (DP) algorithm [2]. Splitting was used first in Loveland's modification to DP, the DPL algorithm [3]. In splitting, a variable is selected from the CNF and two sub-CNFs are generated by setting the variable to 0 and 1, respectively. The iterative application of splitting generates a *search tree*; a leaf of the tree denotes a full assignment of values to variables. Most practical SAT solvers use the splitting technique and combine it with *backtracking*. Backtracking searches the search tree in a depth-first order and thus avoids excessive memory requirements.

A general template for backtracking SAT solvers is described in [4] and includes 3 steps: decision, deduction, and diagnosis. In the decision step, a variable is selected for the next assignment. In the deduction step, information is inferred from the current partial assignment. This information is then used to guide the search process, e.g., to prune the search tree. If the current partial assignment leads to a contradiction, a diagnosis step can be used to analyze this situation and to avoid running into the same contradiction in future.

Existing software SAT solvers use a wide variety of backtracking methods and strategies for decision, deduction, and diagnosis. GRASP [4] is a sophisticated SAT solver that implements all steps of the described template. We use GRASP as software reference system in our work. The powerful strategies that are implemented by sophisticated SAT solvers reduce the number of variable assignments required to find a solution or to prove that there is no solution. However, these strategies can be computationally very expensive.

The goal of our work is to speed up exact SAT solvers by exploiting the fine-grain parallelism in the SAT problem instances. For each new problem instance (CNF), a new hardware is generated that reflects the particular structure of the CNF. This class of hardware architectures is called *instance-specific* and relys on fine-grained reconfigurable computing structures, e.g., FPGAs. Instance-specific SAT solvers use less powerful strategies than software solvers for decision and deduction; diagnosis methods in hardware have not been reported at all. The advantage of SAT in hardware is that the deduction step can be implemented very fast. This is because many deduction strategies operate on values in 2-, 3-, or 4-valued logic and show large amounts of fine-grained parallelism. This makes fine-grained parallel computing structures, such as FPGAs, an optimal target.

2   Related Work

In this section, we mention related projects that apply reconfigurable hardware to solve the SAT problem. Zhong et al. [5] [6] described an instance-specific architecture to solve SAT problems that uses Boolean constraint propagation as deduction strategy and models the variables in 4-valued logic. They simulated their architecture and reported speed-ups in the order of several magnitudes for the DIMACS benchmarks [7]. Their prototype translates a SAT problem into a logic description in VHDL. This description is partitioned and mapped onto an array of Xilinx XC4K FPGAs by an IKOS logic emulation system. Suyama et al. [8] proposed an architecture for SAT that combines a forward checking technique with non-chronological backtracking. They model the variables in 2-valued logic. Their tool flow also targets the Xilinx XC4K line.

In [9], an instance-specific architecture for SAT problems in arbitrary Boolean expressions was presented. This architecture uses a strategy similar to the PO-DEM algorithm for automatic test pattern generation. The same architecture is used in [10], with an emphasis on a fast hardware compilation. To address this issue, the use of Xilinx XC62xx FPGAs is proposed which allows to develop SAT-specific tools for synthesis, partition, placement, and routing.

3 Hardware Architectures

The basic architecture for backtracking search is shown in Figure 1 and consists of three blocks: i) an array of finite state machines (FSMs), ii) a datapath, and iii) a global controller. Each variable of the CNF corresponds to one FSM. The FSMs are connected in a one-dimensional array; each FSM can activate its two neighboring FSMs at the top and at the bottom. The datapath is a combinational circuit that takes the variables as input and computes outputs that are fed back to the FSMs. The global controller starts the computation and handles I/O communication. All the architectures presented in this section consist of these three blocks. However, they differ in the modeling of the variables and the used deduction strategy, which is reflected in the actual implementation of the datapath and the FSM.

3.1 Architecture CE

CE (CNF evaluation) models the variables in 3-valued logic. A variable can take on the values $\{0, 1, X\}$, where X denotes an unassigned variable. The datapath computes the 3-valued result of the CNF expression. Initially, all variables are unassigned which also leads to CNF value X, and the global controller activates the top-most FSM. The state diagram for an FSM is shown in Figure 2. An activated FSM assigns 0 to its variable and checks the resulting CNF value. If the CNF value is 1, the partial assignment already satisfied the CNF and the computation stops. If the CNF value is 0, the partial assignment made the CNF unsatisfiable. In this case, the FSM assigns the complementary value to its variable. If the CNF value is X, the partial assignment did neither satisfy the CNF nor did it make the CNF unsatisfiable. In this case, the FSM activates the next FSM at the bottom. If both value assignments have been tried, the FSM relaxes its variable by assigning X to it, and activates the previous FSM at the top. When the first FSM relaxes its variable and activates the global controller, the SAT problem is proven to be unsatisfiable. By this procedure, the array of interconnected FSMs implements chronological backtracking.

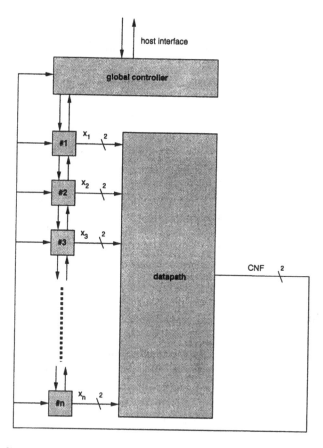

Fig. 1. Block diagram for the basic architecture (CE), consisting of an array of FSMs (#1 ... #n), a datapath, and a global controller. The variables x_i and the CNF are modeled in 3-valued logic.

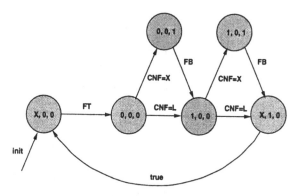

Fig. 2. State diagram for an FSM of the architecture CE. The inputs are FT (from top) and FB (from bottom) that activate the FSM, and the 3-valued CNF. The output signals displayed inside the states are the variable value, and the signals TT (to top) and TB (to bottom) that activate the previous and next FSM.

3.2 Architecture CEDC

CEDC (CE + don't cares) extends CE by introducing don't care variables. Don't care variables are unassigned variables that appear only in clauses that are already satisfied. For example, the assignment $(x_1 \leftarrow 1)$ for the CNF

$$(\bar{x}_1 \vee x_2) \wedge (x_1 \vee \bar{x}_3 \vee x_4) \wedge (x_2 \vee \bar{x}_4) \tag{2}$$

makes x_3 a don't care variable. Don't care variables cannot change the CNF value and should not be selected for assignment. This strategy is similar to *clause-order backtracking* in software.

The don't care condition for a variable is a Boolean function of $x_1, \ldots, x_n$ and can be easily derived from the CNF. In the above example, the don't care condition for variable x_3 is $(x_1 \vee x_4)$. In the architecture CEDC, the datapath computes the CNF value and the don't care conditions for all variables in parallel. The FSM accepts an additional input, the don't care condition for its variable. If the FSM is activated while this condition is set, it passes control directly to the next or previous FSM.

3.3 Architecture IM

IM (propagation of implications) exploits logical implications that are caused by value assignments. For example, the assignment $(x_1 \leftarrow 1)$ for the CNF in Formula 2 implies the variable x_2, i.e., x_2 must be assigned 1 to satisfy the first clause. An implied variable can in turn imply other variables. An implication condition can be derived from the CNF for every literal. In the above example, the implication condition for x_2 is $(x_1 \vee x_4)$. If both literals of a variable are implied, a contradiction has occurred. To model the variables, IM uses 4-valued logic with the values $\{0, 1, X, C\}$, where C denotes the contradiction.

An FSM in this architecture sets its variable according to value assignments or value implications. If a contradiction occurs, the FSM sets a local contradiction flag. The datapath takes as input the variables as well as the local contradiction flags and generates as output the implications for all literals of the CNF and a global contradiction flag in parallel.

Resolving logical implications in CNFs is known as the *unit-clause rule* and is the basic mechanism in the DP algorithm. The iterative application of the unit-clause rule is called *Boolean constraint propagation*. Using this method in instance-specific hardware was first proposed by [5]; a detailed description of the datapath and the FSM can be found in [6].

3.4 IMCE, IMDC

IMCE and IMDC are combinations of the previous architectures. IMCE combines propagation of implications with the evaluation of the CNF expression. This can be helpful in cases, where a partial assignment already satisfies the CNF, but the IM strategy continues to assign values to unassigned variables. IMDC combines propagation of implications with don't cares, and has potentially the most deductive power.

4 Simulation

In order to compare the different architectures we have implemented a program in C, that solves SAT problems by simulating the different hardware architectures. The simulator estimates performance and hardware cost. The performance is measured in number of visited levels in the search tree, number of value assignments, and number of clock cycles. The hardware cost is estimated in number of gates (NOT and 2-input AND/OR) and flip-flops (FFs).

In this paper, we report on simulation results for three benchmark classes from the DIMACS satisfiability benchmarks suite [7]: class *par* (instances from learning the parity function), class *jnh* (randomly generated instances), and class *hole* (instantiations of the pigeon hole problem). These classes are well-suited for evaluation, as they include examples with long software runtimes.

Table 4 presents the simulation results for the architecture IM. The speed-up S_{raw} is defined as t_{sw}/t_{hw}, the ratio of software and hardware execution times and does not include the hardware compilation time. The speed-ups in Table 4 are remarkably high and motivate solving SAT in instance-specific hardware. Similar speed-up numbers have also been reported in [5]. Excellent candidates for instance-specific hardware are SAT problems, where high raw speed-ups are combined with long software runtimes. The estimation further shows that for the targeted FPGA line (Xilinx XC4K), the combinational logic dominates the hardware cost. Although the estimation of hardware cost is not very accurate, most of the examples in Table 4 should fit into one FPGA.

The comparison of the different hardware architectures relative to each other revealed the following facts:

- The architectures can be divided into two groups, {CE, CEDC} and {IM, IMCE, IMDC}. Inside each group, the performance differences are below 1%.
- For classes *par* and *jnh*, IM performs at least 100 x better than CE; for class *hole*, IM performs about 10 x better than CE.
- The estimated hardware cost for IM is at most twice the cost for CE.

Hardware is used more efficiently be IM, as this architecture achieves with at most twice the hardware cost a performance at least 10 times better than CE. However, CE may be an option when the hardware resources are limited. Further, the performance measure counts clock cycles. Architectures that have more complex hardware designs will also have lower clock frequencies. CE is less complex than IM and will very likely lead to faster FPGA designs.

The results presented in this section depend strongly on the benchmark class. The exact trade-offs between the architectures in terms of performance and hardware cost must be evaluated for each new benchmark class.

5 Prototype Implementation

The design tool flow of our prototype implementation is shown in Figure 3 and consists of three parts: the front-end, the generator, and the back-end. The front-

benchmark	variables	clauses	t_{sw} [s]	simulated number of cycles	S_{raw} at 10 MHz	hardware cost (Kgates)
par16-1-c	317	1264	203.03	63171	32140	30 K
par16-1	1015	3310	321.25	158934	20212	87 K
par16-2-c	349	1392	3111.20	225408	138025	32 K
par16-2	1015	3334	1009.00	422295	23893	88 K
jnh16	100	850	2.11	20052	1052	26 K
jnh19	100	850	0.11	6432	171	26 K
hole7	56	204	4.56	351042	129	4.7 K
hole8	72	297	54.98	4342574	126	6.1 K
hole9	90	415	627.52	60162652	104	7.3 K
hole10	110	562	7616.40	922461250	83	9.7 K

Table 1. Simulation results for examples from the DIMACS benchmark suite. The table shows the problem size in number of variables and clauses, the runtime of the software SAT solver GRASP, the simulated number of cycles for the IM architecture, the raw speed-up at an assumed clock frequency of 10 MHz, and the estimated hardware cost. GRASP was executed with parameters +bD +dDLIS on a Pentium-II/300MHz/128MB RAM PC platform running Linux.

end reads a SAT problem and checks for special cases, such as clauses that are always satisfied, reorders the variables and computes the assignment order. The generator compiles this modified SAT problem into a configuration bitstream for a Xilinx XC4K device. The back-end loads the bitstream onto the FPGA and waits for the end of the computation. If there is a solution, the back-end reads the FPGA register configuration, and extracts the variable values. The generator consists again of two blocks. The first block is the generation of the FPGA netlist, the second block invokes the Xilinx M1 design implementation tools for mapping, placement, and routing.

The architectures presented in Section 3 consist of the three blocks array of FSMs, datapath, and global controller. The global controller and the single FSM depend only on the chosen architecture, they do not change with the problem-instance. Therefore, these components are pre-designed, i.e., they are specified in Verilog HDL, synthesized and optimized by Synopsys FPGA Express II, and stored in a library as FPGA netlists. At hardware generation time, the required number of FSMs is instantiated and placed. Placement is done for two reasons: First, placing the FSMs allows the back-end to extract the result of the computation by the read-back facility of the FPGAs. Second, placement of the FSMs results in faster designs. The datapath depends totally on the problem-instance and is generated directly as FPGA netlist.

Our prototype is implemented on a PC platform running Windows NT4.0. As reconfigurable resource we use a Digital PCI Pamette board, which is equipped with 4 FPGAs of the type Xilinx XC4020. In our current experiments, we use only one of these FPGAs for implementing the SAT architecture.

The overall runtime for computing a SAT problem in hardware consists of the hardware compilation time, t_{comp}, the time for configuring the FPGA, t_{config},

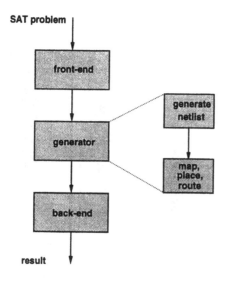

Fig. 3. Prototype design tool flow.

the actual hardware execution time, t_{hw}, and the time for reading back and extracting the result, t_{read}.

$$t_{overall} = t_{comp} + t_{config} + t_{hw} + t_{read} \qquad (3)$$

The overall speed-up $S_{overall}$ is then given by $t_{sw}/t_{overall}$. With our design tool flow, the times for FPGA configuration and read-back can be neglected compared to the hardware compilation time, which itself is strongly dominated by the Xilinx design implementation tools. At the time of this writing, we have successfully compiled and run CE architectures for the *hole* benchmark class. The examples *hole7* to *hole9* can be mapped onto one Xilinx XC4020, for *hole10* an FPGA of type XC4025/XC4028 is required. All the FPGA designs run at 20 MHz. Table 5 and Figure 4 present the experimental results

benchmark	t_{sw} [s]	t_{comp} [s]	t_{hw} [s]	S_{raw}	$S_{overall}$
hole7	4.56	134	0.181	25.14	0.03
hole8	54.98	249	2.398	22.93	0.22
hole9	627.52	439	35.229	17.81	1.32
hole10	7616.40	597	567.255	13.43	6.54

Table 2. Experimental results for the CE architecture and the *hole* benchmark class. The table shows the GRASP runtime, the hardware compilation time, the hardware execution time, and the resulting speed-ups.

The results show that we could generate faster designs as assumed in Section 4. The execution times of hardware and software SAT solvers increase with the

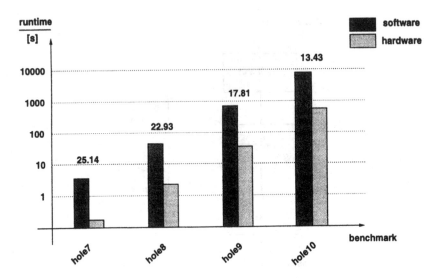

Fig. 4. Software runtime t_{sw}, hardware runtime t_{hw}, and the resulting raw speed-up S_{raw} for the CE architecture and the *hole* benchmark class.

problem size more rapidly than the hardware compilation time. This leads to a *cross-over* point in the overall speed-up around *hole9*, i.e., here the SAT solver in reconfigurable hardware is for the first time faster than the software SAT solver. For *hole10* we achieve a speed-up of 6.54, which reduces the runtime from more than 2 hours in software to about 20 minutes in hardware.

For the *hole* benchmarks, the architecture IM requires about 10 times less clock cycles than CE. This would lead to an overall speed-up of 8.77 for *hole10*, assuming the same hardware compilation time than for CE. However, IM for *hole10* will not fit onto one FPGA XC4025.

6 Conclusion, Further Work

We have presented different architectures for solving SAT problems in instance-specific hardware. These architectures offer trade-offs between performance and hardware cost, depending on the benchmark class. Simulations revealed that for larger problems from the DIMACS benchmark suite, instance-specific SAT solvers can achieve significant raw speed-ups over software SAT solvers. We have implemented a prototypical design tool flow and discussed first experimental results. The results show that architectures with less deductive power can be competitive when the hardware compilation time is not neglectable compared to the hardware execution time. This is the case for all currently implemented benchmarks.

As the density of FPGAs increases, many interesting SAT problems can be accelerated by instance-specific hardware. Although FPGA-based computing machines still require relatively long compilation times, instance-specific architectures are promising for hard SAT problems, where software algorithms show a long runtime.

Further work includes:

- Implementation of instance-specific architectures for minimum-cost problems. A SAT problem with unit cost or integer cost values assigned to the variables forms a minimization problem. Finding minimum-cost solutions to SAT problems is a frequent task in CAD algorithms.
- Application of the instance-specific SAT solver to CAD tools. CAD applications have to be found, that generate SAT problems that are hard to solve in software, i.e., problems that have a relatively small number of variables but show long software runtimes.

Acknowledgment

This work was partially supported by the Austrian National Science Foundation *FWF* under grant number J01412-MAT. We would also like to thank Alessandro Bogliolo and Luca Benini for their contributions and discussions in the early phases of this work.

References

1. Jun Gu, Paul W. Purdom, John Franco, and Benjamin W. Wah. Algorithms for the Satisfiability (SAT) Problem: A Survey. *DIMACS Series in Discrete Mathematics and Theoretical Computer Science*, 35:19–151, 1997.
2. M. Davis and H. Putnam. A computing procedure for quantification theory. *Journal of the ACM*, (7):201–215, 1960.
3. M. Davis, G. Logemann, and D. Loveland. A machine program for theorem proving. *Communications of the ACM*, (5):394–397, 1962.
4. J. Silva and K. Sakallah. GRASP – A New Search Algorithm for Satisfiability. In *IEEE ACM International Conference on CAD '96*, pages 220–227, November 1996.
5. Peixin Zhong, Margaret Martonosi, Sharad Malik, and Pranav Ashar. Implementing Boolean Satisfiability in Configurable Hardware. In *Logic Synthesis Workshop*, May 1997.
6. Peixin Zhong, Margaret Martonosi, Pranav Ashar, and Sharad Malik. Accelerating Boolean Satisfiability with Configurable Hardware. In *IEEE Symposium on FPGAs for Custom Computing Machines*, April 1998.
7. DIMACS satsifiability benchmark suite, available at *ftp://dimacs.rutgers.edu/pub/challenge/sat/benchmarks/cnf/*.
8. Takayuki Suyama, Makoto Yokoo, and Hiroshi Sawada. Solving Satisfiability Problems on FPGAs. In *International Workshop on Field-Programmable Logic and Applications (FPL)*, pages 136–145, 1996.
9. Miron Abramovici and Daniel Saab. Satisfiablity on Reconfigurable Hardware. In *International Workshop on Field-Programmable Logic and Applications (FPL)*, pages 448–456, 1997.
10. Azra Rashid, Jason Leonard, and William H. Mangione-Smith. Dynamic Circuit Generation for Solving Specific Problem Instances of Boolean Satisfiablity. In *IEEE Symposium on FPGAs for Custom Computing Machines*, April 1998.

An Optimized Design Flow
for Fast FPGA-Based Rapid Prototyping

Jörn Stohmann, Klaus Harbich, Markus Olbrich, Erich Barke

Institute of Microelectronic Systems, University of Hanover,
Callinstr. 34, D-30167 Hanover, Germany
{stohmann, harbich, olbrich, barke}@ims.uni-hannover.de

Abstract. In this paper, we present an optimized design flow to map Register-Transfer-Level (RTL) netlists onto multiple-FPGA architectures. Our FPGA-dedicated method fully exploits design structure by letting the basic design steps technology mapping, hierarchical partitioning, floorplanning and signal flow driven placement, interact. This efficiently reduces runtime and yields design implementations of higher performance and better resource utilization than published before.

1 Introduction

Since a couple of years, FPGA-based rapid prototyping systems [1, 2] have become very popular in digital design verification. In such systems, a digital circuit is mapped onto programmable devices implementing a hardware prototype, which can be connected to an existing hardware environment for in-circuit functional verification. Traditional design flows to map a design to the FPGA target are derived from ASIC flows. They neither do consider specific demands of FPGA designs nor do they take advantage of high-performance FPGA properties like fast-carry chain logic. Today, the implementation of designs into emulation systems is performed in a straightforward step-by-step design flow, as illustrated in Figure 1. It includes synthesis, partitioning, mapping, placement and routing. As stated by [3], synthesis algorithms mainly address glue logic optimization and do not consider regular structures, like adders or multipliers. Partitioning algorithms yield good solutions for small designs, however, they often can not satisfy the demands of today's complex designs. The same is true for traditional mapping algorithms which are based on gate-level netlists [4, 5, 6, 7]. Since structural information is lost during synthesis, each design step has to be accomplished at high-volume gate-level netlists. This yields very long runtimes, low FPGA utilization and low clock rates.

In this paper, we present a new approach to map Register-Transfer-Level netlists directly onto the programmable FPGA devices. The proposed implementation system includes automatic partitioning, mapping, floorplanning and placement. In contrast to traditional design flows, these steps are realized as interacting processes.

All structural information is kept and taken into account during implementation. Our FPGA-dedicated design flow yields high FPGA utilization and high design clock rates, while runtimes of the algorithms are very short.

The paper is organized as follows. Section 2 gives an overview of the complete system and describes the interactions of the implementation processes in detail. Since our approaches to module generation and high-level partitioning have been recently published in [8, 9], only the modifications are shortly described and we will focus on the new floorplanning method, which is necessary to complete the optimized design flow, in Section 3. In Section 4, we present some experimental results. Finally, Section 5 provides concluding remarks.

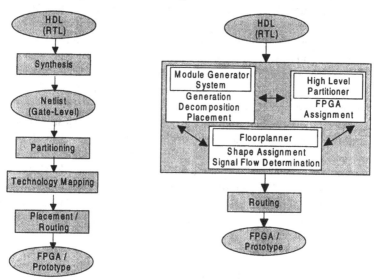

Fig. 1. Traditional design flow

Fig. 2. New RT-Level Rapid Prototyping design flow

2 System Overview

Our proposed Rapid-Prototyping design flow is illustrated in Figure 2. Partitioning, mapping and floorplanning are combined within one main process with data exchange between the interacting subprocesses.

First, an RTL netlist is translated into a hierarchical design database, preserving the original circuit hierarchy, the circuit modules and their interconnections. Then, each RTL module is directly mapped to the FPGA logic blocks by a module generator system in order to satisfy designer's demand on minimum CLB consumption or on maximum design clock rate. Additionally, components exceeding FPGA's pin or CLB capacity are automatically decomposed. The computation time to map the entire design depends only linearly on the number of RTL components. Thus, even very large designs can be handled since runtimes of the module generators are very short. After mapping, each RTL component is described by a CLB netlist. In case that components have been decomposed, for each part a separate CLB netlist is generated. All information about mapping and decomposition, like CLB count and cut lines, is added to the database and used by the partitioning program.

Partitioning is performed at RT-Level, where each element - even adders and multipliers - is represented by one node or in case of decomposed components by several nodes. This yields very short runtimes, even if traditional partitioning algorithms are used, since netlist complexity is very low. Another advantage is, that area consumption can unambiguously be measured in terms of "CLBs" and not in terms of "Equivalent Gates", since all components are already mapped.

Thus, the exact measurement allows very high CLB utilizations of the FPGAs. However, high utilization enlarges the placement and routability problem. We overcome this difficulty by integrating an FPGA-specific floorplanner into the optimized design flow, which directly interacts with the partitioner and the module generators. When the partitioner has distributed the modules to the multiple-FPGA architecture, the floorplanner determines optimum shapes for each component and arranges the blocks with respect to the design signal flow. This guarantees short interconnections between the components and simplifies routing. Based on these floorplans the module generators perform a structure driven placement considering their inherent knowledge about individual module properties, component's shape and internal signal flow. This combination of floorplanning and generator based placement leads to high-density and regular CLB distributions which tremendously speed up the final routing step accomplished by FPGA vendor's tools as explained in Section 3.3.

3 RTL Design Implementation

3.1 Module Generator System

Synthesis of datapath components often results in poor implementations in terms of logic resource usage and performance [3]. Furthermore, it suffers from very long computation times. Several module generator approaches to overcome these problems were published which can be divided into two classes, softmacro and hardmacro generators. Hardmacros [16] are tailored to a specific FPGA architecture. They fully exploit the specific FPGA features, like fast-carry logic. However, they are bound to one specific architecture, fixed in shape and their complexity is limited by the FPGA's capacity. Softmacros [10, 11] are more flexible because they are described in terms of generic cells or boolean equations. If they exceed FPGA's capacity, they have to be decomposed by traditional partitioning programs. Another major drawback is that mapping and placement of the macros have to be done by time consuming algorithms since structural knowledge will be lost during synthesis.

Our generators combine the benefits of both, flexibility of softmacros and FPGA-specific implementation of hardmacros. They perform mapping as well as structural decomposition and placement. A generic FPGA model, introduced in [12], ensures

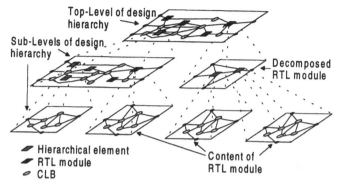

Fig. 3. Hierarchical graph representation

full exploitation of FPGA features during each design step and permits the application to a widespread range of commercial FPGAs. Module specific knowledge is implemented within the generators allowing an easy determination of optimum cut lines for decomposition and a signal flow driven placement. This yields CLB distributions which can easily be routed by the FPGA vendor's tools.

We have implemented a library of module generators based on the definitions of the Library of Parameterized Modules [13]. Up to now, our library includes multipliers, adders, comparators, registers and finite state machines. A detailed description of the module generation approach can be found in [8, 12]. To cope with either minimum delay or minimum area implementations, we provide two different generators for each LPM element. For example, multipliers are implemented using either the Modified-Booth (high speed) or the Pezaris structure (small area). Control path elements and glue logic are synthesized to gate level, clustered and then mapped by a modified version of the well known TOS program [7].

3.2 High-Level Partitioning

The main problem in partitioning is complexity. A lot of heuristics have been published [14, 27] in this area. New approaches considering high level design information [15] or design hierarchy [9] show good results even with todays design complexity. The main disadvantage of these approaches is, that they are still based on gate-level netlists, thus requiring time consuming synthesis, which also implies a tremendous increase in complexities.

In our new approach, we drastically reduce the complexity by keeping the structural information (e.g. design hierarchy) and considering it during partitioning. The recursive High-Level-Partitioner (HLP) is based on [9], but modified to interact with the module generator system. Thus, no FPGA utilization estimation steps are required, since all design elements are exactly measured in terms of CLBs.

The algorithm is based on a hierarchical graph representation, shown in Figure 3, which is directly derived from design hierarchy and modified regarding RTL modules. The hierarchy levels of RTL modules are created by the generators instead of the graph construction algorithm. The optimum module decomposition performed by the generators is directly embed into the hierarchical graph. Starting at the top level, the recursive HLP procedure is performed at each hierarchy level H_i. All levels, which meet FPGA's pin and CLB constraints are stored as a block in a temporary partition. Then, at each level H_{actual} different merging strategies, based on connectivity matrix and vector binpacking, can be used for optimization. Although most of RTL designs can be partitioned very fast at high level, designs containing huge amounts of glue logic have to be partitioned with traditional k-way algorithms, but again with lower complexity due to CLB level representation.

3.3 Floorplanning and Placement

In contrast to traditional rapid prototyping flows, which often yield unefficient FPGA utilizations of about 20-30%, the combined module generation and partitioning processes generate solutions with low FPGA count and very high utilization. However, if FPGA utilization increases, the runtimes for placement and routing will drastically rise, too. Thus, the runtime gain of mapping and partitioning would be lost during placement and routing. In Table 1, the drastical increase of the runtime is shown in case of different multiplier designs using Xilinx' ppr tool.

To bridge the gap between high resource utilization and short placement and routing runtimes, we integrate an FPGA-dedicated floorplanner and a generator based structural placement step into the optimized design flow. In contrast to the common ASIC floorplanning problem [17], the task of placing module components on FPGAs has different objectives. Area bounds are given by FPGA size, therefore, the problem is not to minimize area, but to fit the module components in the FPGA's array. In addition to mirroring or rotating the component shapes, the floorplanner has also to specify the height to width ratio and to determine a module distribution with short interconnections. Up to now, only a few automatic FPGA floorplanners have been published [18, 19]. In our approach, all components are treated as rectangular subareas on the FPGA's CLB array. By assigning a signal flow direction to each component, the floorplanner can control the CLB placement inside the component's shape. Based on the module structure, optimum connection positions at the edges of the component's shapes are determined and grouped to busses.

Table 1. Runtimes to place and route different multipliers onto an XC4013-5. PPR: Placement and routing performed by Xilinx' ppr tool; ODF/PPR: Placement done by module generators, routing done by Xilinx' ppr. Results are given in [min:sec] (Sparc10).

Multiplier Width	4	6	8	10	12	14	16	18	20
FPGA utilization	3%	6%	11%	17%	25%	34%	44%	56%	69%
PPR (flat netlist)	00:25	01:06	02:48	05:14	08:45	15:19	19:46	28:53	44:37
ODF/PPR	00:33	00:44	00:53	01:04	01:20	02:09	03:05	03:37	04:35

The floorplanner uses slicing trees, to represent the topological placement of the components [20]. Although this leads to a restriction in possible arrangements, it is of less importance than the possibility to change component shapes.

To determine optimum floorplans, we consider three objectives: bus length between components, proper shape of components and routing area between components, noted as F_B, F_S and F_A, respectively. The total cost F is given by

$$F = F_B + f_S \cdot F_S + f_A \cdot F_A \text{ , with weights } f_S \text{ and } f_A.$$

Bus lengths are estimated using the following calculation. Considering a net with k ports at positions $\vec{V}_i$ with $i = 1, ..., k$, the center of gravity $\vec{S}$ is calculated first. Then, the Manhattan distances between all ports and the center are accumulated:

$$L = \sum_{i=1}^{k} \left\| \vec{V}_i - \vec{S} \right\| \text{ , with } \vec{S} = \frac{1}{k} \sum_{i=1}^{k} \vec{V}_i$$

This estimation of net length L is easy to perform and takes the routing tool's ability of making spider connections into account. A bus length L_{bus} is estimated by the weighted arithmetical mean of the MSB and LSB net length. The weight N corresponds to the number of bus nets. In order to weight long busses, bus lengths are squared to compute F_B.

$$L_{bus} = N \cdot \frac{L_{msb} + L_{lsb}}{2} \quad \text{and} \quad F_B = \frac{1}{n} \sum_{i=1}^{n} L_{bus_i}^2$$

The floorplanner uses information about module's structure to determine an optimum shape ($W_{i_{opt}}, H_{i_{opt}}$) for each component i. Additionally, special capabilities of the target FPGAs can be considered. For example, in case of the Xilinx XC4000 a high height to width ratio is required to take full advantage of the fast-carry logic. The deviation of a component shape from the optimum one, is estimated by

$$F_S = \frac{1}{m} \sum_{i=1}^{m} \left(\left| W_i - W_{i_{opt}} \right| + \left| H_i - H_{i_{opt}} \right| \right)^2$$

for each of the m components within an FPGA.

Finally, the routing area F_A is estimated to ensure that there are enough routing channels to make connections between the module components.

F is computed hierarchically on the slicing tree. Even incomplete trees can be evaluated. Partial results are stored in the slicing tree nodes. Thus, a recalculation of an altered tree demands only few actions when most subtrees were not touched.

As mentioned, the floorplanner takes into account module structure and FPGA capabilities. This information is given by a simple expert system, called "WiseMan", which includes methods for determining optimum shapes and assigning busses to shape edges.

Our method consists of two steps: A floorplan is built-up by a constructive algorithm and then optimized by a genetic approach. The constructive floorplanning algorithm starts with an initial forest consisting of simple one-node trees for each component. Here, a component represents either a netlist element or a part of a decomposed element. Then, two trees of the forest are considered at a time and all

```
ConstructiveFloorplanner (C):

Create initial forest
```
$$T = \left\{ t \mid t_i = node(c_i) \right\}$$

while Number of trees > 1 {

   find t_i, t_j, that maximizes

$$\frac{\sum_{busses(t_i,t_j)} buswidth}{N_{leaf}(t_i) + N_{leaf}(t_j)} ;$$

   find combination for t_i and t_j

   that minimizes cost $F(t(t_i,t_j));$

   replace t_i and t_j by new $t(t_i,t_j);$ }

shrink outer shape to FPGA size

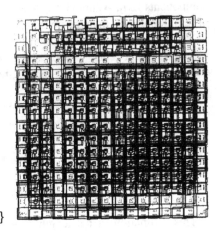

Fig. 4. Pseudo code of the constructive algorithm

Fig. 5. Placement of two adders feeding a multiplier onto a Xilinx XC4005 device

combinations of cut type (vertical or horizontal) and order are evaluated to construct a new tree with minimum cost, which replaces the original one. This step is repeated until all trees of the initial forest are combined within one slicing tree. If one of the considered trees is a leaf representing a component, several suggestions for optimum shapes and signal flows are taken from the "WiseMan". A pseudo code description to determine a cut tree for a given component set $C = \{c_1, \ldots, c_n\}$ is given in Fig. 4.

Since the given floorplanning problem has many degrees of freedom like position, shape and signal flow direction, an iterative genetic optimization algorithm was chosen to improve the constructive algorithm's solution. Because genetic algorithms have been proved to succeed in floorplanning [21], only special features of our approach are described here.

The presented algorithm performes genetic operations directly on slicing trees instead of using gen-strings [22]. Thus, time consuming translations of the gen-string solutions to slicing trees are avoided. Compared to other genetic algorithms this approach is very fast. Since good start solutions are provided by the constructive algorithm, floorplans are achieved in a few seconds.

Finally, all information about shapes and signal flow directions is passed to the module generators to accomplish the placement. Taking these assignments and the inherent structural knowledge into account, we yield very regular CLB distributions. The module generator based placement has linear time complexity. Furthermore, the routing is done within a few seconds up to a few minutes even if FPGA vendor's routing tools are involved. As demonstrated in Table 1 for ODF/PPR, runtimes are up to ten times lower, particulary for large components, while the routing quality is identical to the results achieved by PPR. In every case, the runtimes for floorplanning and placement are less than one minute on a Spac10.

As an example, Figure 5 shows a routed FPGA that contains two 10-bit adders, one at the left and one on top, providing input to a 10-by-10 bit Pezaris multiplier.

4 Experimental Results

We have implemented our approaches to RTL mapping, high-level partitioning and floorplanning in C++ running on SUN workstations (Sparc10). For data storage and data exchange an object-oriented database [23] is used.

To demonstrate the benefits of our approach, we have applied the FPGA-dedicated design flow to several circuits. The first design is a 32-by-32 array multiplier, the second one is an ALU, both taken from [24]. The other benchmarks are industrial designs: The third is a twelve-bit echo generator, the fourth is an echo compensator and the fifth is a 32 bit datapath of a video application circuit. The characteristics of the examples and the FPGA devices are listed in Table 2.

For benchmarks I and II the results for number of FPGAs, number of CLBs, average IO utilization, and average CLB utilization achieved by our approach are compared to a recently proposed functional partitioning approach [14], marked as FP in Table 3. In case of the multiplier (I), the number of XC3090 FPGAs could be reduced by a factor of two. For the XC4005, we yield the same results. For the second benchmark we yield as well compact design implementations reducing the number of CLBs and number of FPGAs by a factor of two. In all cases, our approach yields partitions with higher CLB utilization and, with the exception of XC4005, lower IO utilization than published before.

Table 3. Comparison of traditional design flows (MARS/Quest) and a recently published method (FP) [24] to our optimized design flow (ODF)

Table 2. Characteristics of the benchmark circuits and FPGA devices

Circuit	#IOs	#Eq.Gates
I	128	11810
II	47	5325
III	294	35000
IV	146	18654
V	60	5880

FPGA	#IOs	#CLBs
XC3090	144	320
XC4005	112	196
XC4010	160	400
XC4013	182	576

Circuit	Method	#FPGA	#CLBs	ØCLB	ØIO	T [min]
I	FP	7	1910	.85	.58	--
XC3090	ODF	4	1008	.92	.44	--
I	MARS	17	1606	.48	.80	126
XC4005	FP	6	1022	.86	.77	--
	ODF	6	1007	.97	.87	16
II	FP	2	694	.87	.58	--
XC4010	ODF	1	342	.82	.29	--
III	Quest	13	3085	.41	.75	235
XC4013	ODF	10	2247	.39	.71	160
IV	MARS	14	1332	.54	.66	224
XC4005	ODF	6	739	.62	.70	58
V	MARS	5	744	.65	.66	95
XC4005	ODF	3	456	.78	.57	38

Further, we compared our optimized FPGA-dedicated design flow (ODF) with two traditional Rapid-Prototyping flows MARS [24] and Quest [25]. The HDL synthesis to yield a netlist, that can be passed to the emulation software, was accomplished by Synopsys Design Analyzer using DesignWare Components [10]. Benchmarks I, IV and V were targeted to XC4005 and benchmark III to XC4013. For the examples, the number of FPGAs is reduced by 59% (I), 32% (III), 58% (IV) and 40% (V) due to the lower CLB count of the generator-based mapping approach. The total implementation time is drastically reduced by 87% (I), 22% (III), 74% (IV) and 60% (V). Especially in case of the array multiplier this tremendous savings are accomplished by the module generator which performs both, design mapping and partitioning. In case of benchmark V the HLP algorithm shortens partitioning runtime from 50 minutes to 38 seconds and yields a very compact implementation with an average CLB utilization of 78%. Note, that for benchmark III the runtime of the synthesis step is not considered, since the design description was already targeted to an industrial library. Thus, the speedup of using module generators instead of synthesis could not be taken into account.

The example given in Figure 5, was placed by the generators and routed by Xilinx's ppr-tool. Floorplanning and placement were performed in less than 30 seconds and for routing only 4 minutes were required by ppr. Most of the internal routing is done within the given shapes leaving the outer resources untouched. This ensures routability even for high CLB utilization rates. Since the CLBs are placed signal flow driven, the routing structure is very regular yielding a high performance emulation frequency of about 10 Mhz.

5 Conclusion

In this paper, we have presented an FPGA-dedicated design flow that includes RTL module mapping as well as high-level partitioning and floorplanning-based placement. In contrast to traditional approaches, these steps are performed by interacting subprocesses. Since RTL modules are directly mapped to FPGA logic blocks, no logic-level synthesis is required and structural information is kept as well as used during each design step. Additionally, partitioning complexity is drastically reduced. We have demonstrated, that module decomposition and high-level partitioning can overcome the known IO bottleneck and yield very good results regarding number of FPGAs and CLB utilization while runtimes of the implementation algorithms are very short. Further, we have introduced a floorplanning approach to determine module shapes and signal flow directions with respect to module properties and FPGA features. Although we do not address the routing problem, we have shown that signal flow driven placement strongly supports the routing step leading to a regular routing structure and a good usage of FPGA resources.

References

[1] M. Butts, J. Batcheller, J. Varghese; "An Efficient Logic Emulation System", ICCD,1992, pp.138-14

[2] D. M. Lewis, D. R. Galloway, Marcus van Ierssel, J. Rose, P. Chow; "The Transmogrifier-2: A 1 Million Gate Rapid Prototyping System", FPGA, 1997, pp. 53-61

[3] P. K. Jha, N. D. Dutt; "High-Level Library Mapping for Arithmetic Components", Trans. on Very Large Scale Integration (VLSI) Systems, Vol. 4, No. 2, 6/1996, pp. 157-169

[4] R. Murgai, N. Shenoy, R. K. Brayton, A. Sangiovanni-Vicentelli; "Improved Logic Synthesis Algorithms for Table Look Up Architectures", ICCAD, 1991, pp. 564-567

[5] R.J. Francis, J. Rose, Z. Vranesic; "Chortle-crf: Fast Technology Mapping for Lookup Table-Based FPGAs", DAC, 1991, pp.227-233

[6] J. Cong, Y. Ding; "FlowMap: An Optimal Technology Mapping Algorithm for Delay Optimization in Look-up Table Based FPGA Design", IEEE Transactions on Computer-Aided Design of Integrated Circuits and Systems, vol. 13, Jan. 1994, pp.1-11

[7] C. Legl, B. Wurth, K. Eckl; "A Boolean Approach to Performance-Directed Technology Mapping for LUT-Based FPGA Designs",DAC,1996,pp.730-733

[8] J. Stohmann, E. Barke: "A Universial Pezaris Array Multiplier Generator for SRAM-Based FPGAs", ICCD, 1997, pp. 489-495

[9] D. Behrens, K. Harbich, E. Barke; "Hierarchical Partitioning", ICCAD, 1996, pp.470-477

[10] Synopsys - DesignWare Components Databook, Version 3.4a, 1994

[11] Quickturn - HDL-ICE - Reference Manual, 1996

[12] J. Stohmann, E. Barke: "An Universial CLA Adder Generator for SRAM-Based FPGAs", FPL, 1996, pp. 44-54

[13] Library of Parameterized Modules, Proposed Standard 2.0, 1992

[14] J. Cong, M. Smith; "A Parallel Bottom-Up Clustering Algorithm with Applications to Circuit Partitioning in VLSI Design",DAC,1993, pp. 755-760

[15] D. Behrens, K. Harbich, E. Barke: "Circuit Partitioning Using High Level Design Information", IDPT, 1996, pp.259-266

[16] Xilinx - X-BLOX - User Guide, 1994

[17] P. Pan, C. L. Liu; "Area Minimization for Floorplans", IEEE Trans. on Computer-Aided Design, vol. 14, no. 1, pp. 123-132, 1995.

[18] H. Krupnova, C. Rabedaoro, G. Saucier; "Synthesis and Floorplanning For Large Hierarchical FPGAs", FPGA, 1997, pp. 105-111

[19] J. Shi, D. Bhatia; "Performance Driven Floor-planning for FPGA Based Designs", FPGA, 1997, pp. 112-118

[20] T. R. Mueller, D. F. Wong, C.L. Liu; "An Enhanced Bottom-Up Algorithm For Floorplan Design", ICCAD, 1987, pp. 524-527

[21] J. P. Cohoon et. al.; "Distributed Genetic Algorithms for the Floorplan Design Problem", Trans. on Computer-Aided Design, vol. 10, no. 4, pp. 483-491, 1991

[22] M. Rebaudengo, M. S. Reorda; "GALLO: A Genetic Algorithm for Floorplan Area Optimization", Trans. on Computer-Aided Design, vol. 15, no. 8, pp. 943-951, 1996.

[23] Objectivity - Objectivity/DB 3.5 - Guide, 1995

[24] W.-J. Fang, A. C.-H. Wu: "A Hierarchical Functional Structuring and Partitioning Approach for Multiple-FPGA Implementations", ICCAD, 1996, pp. 638-643

[25] PiE Design Systems - MARS III Emulation System Tool, 1993

[26] Quickturn Design Systems - Quest 4.2.3, 1994

[27] L. A. Sanchis; "Multiple-way network partition-ing", IEEE Transactions on Computer, vol. 38, no. 1, pp. 62-81, 1989

A Knowledge-Based System for Prototyping on FPGAs

Helena Krupnova, Vu DucAnh Dinh, and Gabriele Saucier

Institut National Polytechnique de Grenoble/CSI,
46, Avenue Felix Viallet, 38031 Grenoble cedex, France
{bogushev,dinhduc,saucier}@imag.fr

Abstract. This paper presents a knowledge-based system for ASIC prototyping on FPGAs. ASIC prototyping is known to be a difficult task. The rapid increase of densities and speeds of FPGAs, as well as sophisticated architectural features require changes in prototyping methodologies. FPGA prototypes should often work at real speeds. Obtaining efficient implementations demands reach design experience and perfect knowledge of the FPGA technology. The interest is in accumulating knowledges and reusing parts of previous designs. The idea was to facilitate prototyping by creating the knowledge-based system which stores the designer skills in form of technology-dependent design rules and reuse blocks.

1 Introduction

Prototyping is the translation of IC design from an ASIC technology rich in features to the less sophisticated FPGA technology. Prototyping an ASIC with FPGAs is a difficult task because of two reasons: (1) a lot of submicron ASIC features cannot be implemented directly on FPGAs; (2) FPGA prototype should work at real speeds. When prototyping on FPGAs, it is important to have fast and efficient software flows and obtain a high-quality FPGA implementations.

FPGAs rapidly evolve towards higher densities and speeds and are based on advanced architectural features. The recent FPGAs exceed 100K gates capacities and 100 MHz speeds. The latest architectures incorporate embedded memories, enhancements of logic blocks, sophisticated interconnect topologies and hierarchical structuring.

Due to the fast FPGA evolution, the challenge is to cope with increasing chip densities and follow the new architectural FPGA features such as embedded memories, dedicated arithmetical resources, rapid interconnections, etc. to reach high-quality prototyping on FPGAs. Obtaining efficient implementations requires high design experience and perfect knowledge of the target FPGA technology. That is why, a big interest is in (1) accumulating knowledges and skills and (2) reusing parts of previous designs.

This paper presents a knowledge-based system for ASIC prototyping on FPGAs, which consists of (1) rule-based system aimed at overcoming the difficult technology transformation stages in prototyping; (2) Web-based reuse block catalog for gathering the reuse block information. To achieve efficient prototyping, the knowledge-based system detects in the HDL description or netlist, specific blocks (RAM, ROM, ALB, DSP, etc.) for which there exist dedicated mapping strategies or FPGA cores. The search for FPGA cores is performed using the reuse block catalog. These specific blocks are handled as black boxes in migration or synthesis from ASIC to FPGA. Subsequently, in the target FPGA technology, these black boxes are replaced by IP cores. The remaining blocks of the design are treated as glue and migrated in a conventional way.

In this paper we describe both the prototyping environment and applications on industrial examples. The paper is organized as follows. The next section outlines the general prototyping flow. Section 3 presents the knowledge-based system. Section 4 describes the reuse block catalog invoked by the knowledge-based system. Section 5 explains the block wrapping strategy for instantiation of the reuse blocks during the prototyping. Finally, section 6 gives two examples of knowledge-based system operation on industrial circuits. In the first example the RAM, ALU and shifter blocks and in the second example, FIFO buffers are processed by the knowledge-based system.

2 The Prototyping Flow

The general prototyping flow is depicted in Fig. 1. The prototyping starts from HDL description. Firstly, the design analysis is performed and critical blocks are extracted. They are processed by the knowledge-based system, the task of which is to assist in the prototyping of specific circuit entities. The knowledge-based system may invoke the search in the reuse block catalog. If the corresponding block is found, it will be instantiated in the design. The reuse blocks already mapped on the target FPGA technology are ignored during the synthesis and replaced by "black boxes". The rest of the design is synthesized in a traditional way by one of the available synthesis tools. The synthesized design is partitioned using the hierarchy-driven partitioning method ([1]). Partitioned design is passed to the FPGA vendor's place and route tool which generates the bitstream files for FPGA programming. The bitstream files are downloaded in the FPGAs plugged in the prototyping board.

3 The Knowledge-Based System

As the FPGA technologies evolve, it becomes more and more difficult for the prototyping engineers to be permanently updated on all the architectural features of different FPGA devices and dedicated properties for implementing different blocks.

The task of the knowledge based system is to assist in the prototyping of specific circuit entities. The focus is on entities that require more efficiency than an automatic re-mapping or migration process which is valid for glue logic. Basic critical blocks are ROM, RAM, latches, clock trees, buses, tri-state buffers, etc.

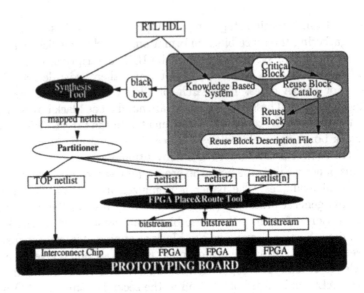

Fig. 1. General prototyping flow

This list of critical blocks is expandable and is related both to the source ASIC technology and the FPGA target technology.

The general objective is to store the knowledges such as (1) designer skills, (2) technology features and (3) previous experience in form of reuse blocks. Once the new design is considered, composing blocks are processed one by one and all accumulated skills related to these blocks are retrieved in the data base. The unique features of the design are processed manually, and accumulated knowledges, related to these new features are add to the knowledge base. As said above, these knowledges have to be updated on a regular basis due to technology evolution.

The knowledge based system has a modular structure with following main parts:

(I) the FPGA technology information including an FPGA device data base. It includes the information concerning FPGA architectural features and critical FPGA resources represented as a resource vectors;

(II) a rule based system consisting of "mapping strategies" for critical blocks. This part is itself modular and organized in pairs defined as *[critical design item, FPGA destination technology]*.

The knowledge-based system gives an implementation rules and solutions on the target devices. It interacts with the reuse blocks catalog and may invoke the search in the reuse block database for the corresponding block. If such a block is found, then it will be instantiated in the design.

To illustrate this process, let us consider a very common block such as an embedded RAM and a target technology for prototyping of Altera FLEX10K. The characteristics of the ASIC RAM are extracted from the VHDL description,

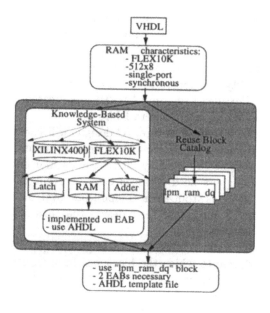

Fig. 2. RAM block treatment with KBS

as shown in Fig. 2, and passed to the knowledge-based system in form of request. The request includes the information on block type, target technology and block-specific parameters. For RAM example the parameters include the RAM word length which is equal 8 and RAM depth (number of words) which is equal to 512, single port/dual port, synchronous/asynchronous. The request is transferred to the knowledge-based system and to the reuse block catalog. The knowledge-based system outputs the implementation rules for the given block, if exists. The reuse block catalog outputs the list of blocks which correspond to the given block. For the RAM example the knowledge-based system produces at its output (as shown in Fig. 2):

- the number of Embedded Array Blocks (EAB) which should be used ([2]) - 2 EABs are necessary for implementing 512x8 RAM;
- the name of the parameterized block corresponding the closest to the required block - "lpm_ram_dq";
- the AHDL (Altera Hardware Description Language) template containing the parameterized block call and having the interface which corresponds to the VHDL block interface.

4 Reuse Blocks Catalog

The reuse was a common design practice for many years ([3],[4],[5],[6]). The FPGA vendors make oncoming effort to speed up FPGA design through block reuse. The first attempts were done through offers of LPM (Library of Parameterized Modules) and macro block libraries which evolved into reuse partnership programs. The new design methodologies use the pre-built megafunctions. The successful development of megafunctions requires close cooperation between intellectual property developers and PLD vendors. As an example, the Altera Megafunction Partners Program (AMPP) was created to bring the advantages of megafunctions to users of Altera PLDs ([8]).

According to [5], in the future, IC designs will contain several reused functional blocks from several internal and external sources, mixed with some functional blocks designed specifically for that particular design. The authors of [7] suggest that designers need to focus on 25 percent of the design that differentiates their systems from their competitors' systems. They should not have to recreate the 75 percent of their design that has already been designed by countless of engineers.

The reuse blocks are classified in three groups ([9]) according to their "hardness", or the degree to which the block has been targeted toward a particular fabrication process (*soft,firm,hard* blocks). The described above knowledge-based system interacts with created reuse blocks catalog containing the information on the FPGA reuse blocks which may be used for prototyping on FPGAs. A reuse block *taxonomy* was introduced to classify blocks into families and subfamilies with respect to their functionality. It is represented as a tree with nodes being the keywords characterizing block families and leafs being the reuse blocks.

5 Block Wrapping

The most often encountered problem when reusing blocks is that the parameters of the reused block do not correspond exactly to those of the HDL block. Even if the rule-based system estimates that the reuse block generally correspond to the specified block, some signals may be missing in the reuse block or be interpreted differently. Two cases are possible.

In the first case, a reuse block covers all the features of the design block, and possibly has additional functionalities. In this case, the design needs only a subset of the reuse block modes of operation and (or) pins. The unused modes should be disabled, and unused pins should be set to constant values, or should be combined with used pins.

In the second case, the reuse block does not cover all the features of the design block. The reuse blocks often implement only the core features, whereas the ASIC block may need some supplementary requirements. In this case, an additional logic should be used to complete the missing signals and functionalities.

In both cases, the reuse block should be *wrapped up* to establish an interface between the ASIC and the reuse block pins and functionalities. The wrapping is performed by creation of an envelope around the reuse block with IO pins corresponding to the ASIC block pins. In the case of soft blocks, this correspondence is performed in HDL description. In the case of firm and hard blocks wrapping is performed at the netlist level and possibly by using the specific

FPGA vendor language (for example, AHDL for Altera). The envelope template is automatically created by the knowledge-based system. But in particular cases the template should be completed manually by the user. The envelope may require additional logic to realise the missing ASIC features. The knowledge-based system also contains the knowledges about the completing of some missing functionalities. It may output the rules for implementing of a set of known features.

As an example of block wrapping, let's take the implementation of two different single-port RAM blocks in Altera FLEX 10K technology. As was shown in Fig. 2, the knowledge-based system outputs the AHDL template containing the call of the "lpm_ram_dq" blocks proposed by the reuse block catalog for the described RAM. The proposed block has address and data buses, write enable, and input and output clock signals. The first ASIC RAM example which we consider requires in addition an output enable signal, which is not available in the LPM RAM. The designer should manually add a buffer on the output bus in the AHDL template. Block wrapping is shown in Fig. 3a.

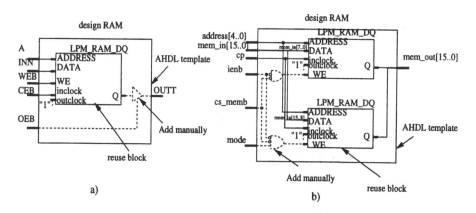

Fig. 3. RAM wrapping: a) ASIC RAM requiring output enable; b) ASIC RAM working in 8/16 bit mode

The second example is more complicated. The ASIC RAM works in 8/16 bit mode and requires in addition a chip select signal. The knowledge-based system contains the corresponding rule for implementing the bit-slice blocks. According to this rule two 8-bit LPM RAM blocks are instantiated. When the circuits works in 8-bit mode, only the lower-bit RAM is activated. In a 16-bit mode both RAM blocks are activated. The implementation is shown in Fig. 3b. The additional logic should be added manually in the AHDL description to implement the chip select, mode signal and input enable signal. The manually add logic is shown by dotted lines in Fig. 3.

6 Prototyping of Industrial Examples

6.1 Microprocessor Example

The case study example is a 16-bit microprocessor which will be prototyped in the Altera FLEX 10K technology. To allow all interfaces to targeted applications work in real time, it is required that the microprocessor prototype work at 10MHz frequency, i.e. a system cycle time is limited to 100 ns.

The microprocessor contains an instruction latch and decoder, state machine, status register, 32-word by 16-bit RAM, barrel shifter, ALU and accumulator (see Fig. 4). The ALU contains a 16-bit adder. The microprocessor may execute byte and word instructions. All instructions, except immediate instructions are executed in a single clock cycle.

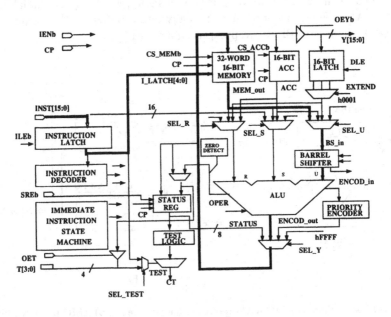

Fig. 4. Microprocessor structure

The most critical path of the microprocessor (drawn in bold in Fig. 4) is activated when executing an instruction which uses RAM block as data source and destination and requires an operation of the barrel shifter and the ALU adder. The critical path traverses the instruction latch, activating the asynchronous memory read, then goes through the barrel shifter and ALU and writes the operation result into the memory. The critical blocks are the memory, barrel shifter, ALU and instruction latch.

The automatic blind "glue" mapping of all the design blocks on the Altera FLEX 10K produces an implementation working at only 5.5 MHz. In this implementation, all blocks are mapped as glue logic, without processing by the knowledge-based system. The Altera FLEX 10K devices contain an embedded array for implementing memories and dedicated carry chains for implementing arithmetical functions ([2]). For more efficient implementation, the critical blocks of the microprocessor were processed one by one by the knowledge-based system, as described in the following subsections, and replaced by the corresponding Altera parameterized blocks found in the reuse block catalog applying the described wrapping strategy. The Altera MAX+Plus II place and route tool has the dedicated implementation strategies for these blocks, which allows the use of FPGA chip embedded memories and arithmetic features.

In this section, we will consider the case when the Hamiltonian $H(x)$ is autonomous. For the sake of simplicity, we shall also assume that it is C^1.

32-word by 16-bit RAM The 32-word by 16-bit RAM is a single-port RAM with a 16-bit latch at its output. For byte instructions, only the lower eight bits are written into. For word instructions, all 16-bits are written into. When implemented on FLEX 10K device as "glue", the propagation delay of this RAM is 50.2ns.

The Altera FLEX 10K devices are the first FPGAs to contain embedded array blocks (EAB) ([2]) which can be used to efficiently implement memory and logic functions. The implementation of RAM on EABs is carried out by call of the Altera dedicated macro blocks, as shown in the previous section. Being implemented like in Fig. 3b, RAM has a propagation delay of 24.6ns, which is twice faster than the "glue" implementation (see Table 1).

Table 1. LPM implementation versus "glue" implementation

	"Glue" implementation	LPM implementation
RAM	50.2ns	24.6 ns
ALU	100.3ns	39.9 ns
Barrel Shifter	40.53ns	41.8ns

ALU The microprocessor contains a 16-bit ALU with adder to perform arithmetical operations. The ALU is capable of operating on either one, two or three operands, depending upon the instruction being executed. Mapped directly on FLEX 10K, it has a delay of 100.3 ns.

To increase the ALU performance, there exists the possibility to replace the adder by an Altera macro block *lpm_add_sub* found in the reuse block catalog. To implement 8 and 16-bit modes, two 8-bit LPM blocks should be instantiated, in the same way as it was done for RAM (Fig. 3b). Being implemented as a macro block, the adder uses the dedicated carry chains which significantly accelerates speed ([2]), as shown in Table 1.

Barrel Shifter The 16-bit barrel shifter is used as one of the ALU inputs and permits data rotating from either the RAM, the accumulator or the data latch. Data bits shifted out at one end of a barrel shifter re-appear at the other end. Barrel shifters are known to be time-critical applications because shifted data traverses multiple layers of multiplexers. But in this case, no block with speed-optimized architecture was found in the reuse block catalog. The propagation time of the area-optimized macro block *lpm_clshift* found in the reuse block catalog is more than one produced by the "glue" mapping, as shown in Table 1. The glue implementation is maintained in the final version. Propagation delay values given in Table 1 are obtained when placing blocks separately on FLEX 10K chip. These values include also the delay due to the I/O element, which is about 9-10ns. So, when evaluating delays of blocks inside the whole placed design, the propagation delay values will be smaller that values presented in Table 1.

6.2 Image Processing Circuit Example

The industrial example considered here is an image processing circuit containing a two-dimensional convolver which uses FIFO buffers. The FIFO buffers store input pixel matrices until they are ready for processing. Each FIFO buffer is implemented as an interleaved memory buffer which contains two RAM blocks for storing consecutive odd and even data words. The design requires three different types of FIFO blocks: 16 instances of 1024x8 FIFO blocks, 1 instance of 1024x10 FIFO block and 1 instance of 1024x1 FIFO block. The total number of memory bits required is about 150,000.

In the first step, FIFO blocks are extracted during VHDL synthesis and processed by the knowledge-based system which gives the strategy for their implementation in FLEX 10K devices. The reuse blocks catalog does not contain any block corresponding to the interleaved memory FIFO in FLEX 10K ([10]). The proposed strategy is to descend till RAM blocks and perform RAM processing with the knowledge-based system. RAM blocks of each FIFO buffer will be implemented in the Embedded Array Blocks (EABs), and the surrounding control logic in the Logic Array Blocks (LABs). The FLEX10K EABs provide 2,048 bits of memory which may be configured as 256x8, 512x4, 1,024x2 or 2,048x1. The design requires three different types of RAM blocks: 512x8, 512x10 and 64x8. They will be implemented by combining EABs ([11]).

Performing the EAB combining, the knowledge-based system estimates the number of EABs needed for each type of RAM. The total number of EABs needed for the design is equal to 72. The chosen FLEX EPF10K70RGFP240 device has 9 EABs. The FIFO blocks are finally assigned by partitioner to 9 devices as shown in Fig. 5.

7 Conclusion

This paper presents the knowledge-based system for ASIC prototyping on FP-GAs. As the prototyping is generally a complicated process, the interest is in

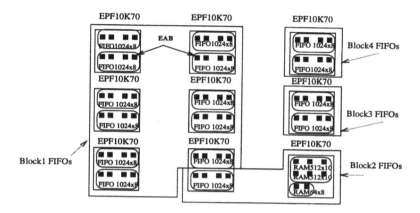

Fig. 5. Assigning FIFO buffers to FPGAs

accumulating knowledges and making them available to the large number of designers. The proposed knowledge-based system solves this problem by storing (1) the knowledges about the specific features of the target FPGA technology; (2) the previous design experience in form of reuse blocks. This makes it possible to automatize prototyping and to obtain the efficient design solutions on FPGAs.

References

1. Krupnova, H., Abbara, A., Saucier, G.: A Hierarchy-Driven FPGA Partitioning Method. Proc. 34-th ACM/IEEE Design Automation Conference (1997) 522–525
2. Altera Data Book: FLEX 10K Embedded Programmable Logic Family Data Sheet (1996)
3. Lehmann, G., Wunder, B. Muller Glaser K. D.: A VHDL Reuse Workbench. Proc. EURO-DAC (1996) 412–417
4. Jha, P. K., Dutt, N. D.: Design Reuse through High-Level Library Mapping. Proc. of the European Design and Test Conference (1995) 345–350
5. Girczyc, E., Carlson, S.: Increasing Design Quality and Engineering Productivity through Design Reuse. Proc. 30th ACM/IEEE Design Automation Conference (1993) 48-53
6. Mariatos, V., Senouci, S-A., Bertrand, M. C., Saucier, G., Kikides, J.: A Library of Reuse Blocks for FPGAs. Proc. European Design&Test Conference, User Forum volume (1997) 609–633
7. Lytle, C., Beachler, R.K.: Using Intellectual Property in Programmable Logic. Proc. European Design&Test Conference, User Forum volume (1997): 125-129
8. Altera AMPP Catalog (1997)
9. VSI Alliance: Architecture Document. http://www.vsi.org/library.html (1997)
10. Altera Application Note 66: Implementing FIFO Buffers in FLEX 10K Devices (1996)
11. Altera Application Note 52: Implementing RAM Functions in FLEX 10K Devices (1995)

JVX - A Rapid Prototyping System Based on Java and FPGAs

Robert Macketanz, Wolfgang Karl*

Lehr- und Forschungseinheit Informatik X
Rechnertechnik und Rechnerorganisation (LRR-TUM)
Institut für Informatik der Technischen Universität München
Arcisstr. 21, D-80290 München, Germany
{macketan, karlw}@in.tum.de

Abstract. The paper describes the JVX[1] system which combines hardware/software codesign aspects with rapid prototyping techniques. Applications for embedded systems written in Java are translated into a VHDL description. The hardware platform of the JVX system consists of FPGAs facilitating the execution of the synthesized VHDL code, and the communication with the interpreted Java byte code via a PCI interface. The JVX system enables the generated hardware parts and corresponding Java byte code of an application to be mutually exchanged allowing the developer to find a good tradeoff between the hardware costs and performance requirements.

1 Introduction

The development of complex embedded systems requires sophisticated tool support in order to be able to complete a correct design in time. The main problem is to find a good tradeoff between hardware costs and performance constraints.

The hardware/software codesign approach allows to achive the best design results while meeting the requirements mentioned above. In the growing market for embedded systems, development has to be economically balanced. Therefore, the main goal is a fast design approach with tools supporting the development and test phases in order to minimize the time spent. Rapid prototyping employs techniques based on a prototype for test and evaluation phases which allows problems and pitfalls to be avoided later during mass production.

The paper describes the JVX system which combines hardware/software codesign aspects with rapid prototyping techniques. Applications for embedded systems written in Java are translated into a VHDL description. The hardware platform of the JVX system consists of FPGAs facilitating the execution of

---

* We would like to thank Prof. Dr. Klaus Buchenrieder, Christian Veith, Andreas Pyttel, Dr. Rainer Kress, and Viktor Preis from Siemens AG ME ZT 5 for their support, and their helpful comments.
[1] JVX stands for the combination of Java, VHDL, and FPGAs from Xilinx within one system.

the synthesized VHDL code and the communication with the interpreted Java byte code via a PCI interface. With the JVX system, a developer can find a good tradeoff between the hardware costs and performance requirements since it allows the application's Java byte code to be mutually exchanged with the synthesized hardware parts.

Other rapid prototyping development tools like the COSYMA system [4, 11, 13], use specification languages that are in some way derived from well-known programming languages like C in order to take the step from software to hardware. COSYMA uses an extended C dialect called C^x for system specification. Other approaches use hardware descriptions like plain VHDL and extract some parts in software. The POLIS system [16], based on the ptolemy simulation system [6, 12, 5] uses CFSMs[2], and offers a wide variety of description kinds like Esterel[3], StateCarts [7], formal data flow diagrams [9], or a subset of VHDL [2]. Other approaches do not require a special description language or methodolgy, but offer an intermediate format and an encapsualtion for the different parts of an application, that are submitted in a heterogeneous way. The CoWare system [18] offers this. The VULCAN system [10] takes another way, it extracts software parts from a specification in hardware-C.

Common to all these approaches is, that they extend or cut down the description languages to fit both sides – hardware and software – in the best way. The JVX system neither uses extension nor restriction of the description language. The developer is in no way confined to a subset of Java. If the compiler is unable to translate some part of the application into VHDL, this part will be left as software. So, the limitations of the compiler do not force the developer to use only a subset of Java.

2 Description of the JVX System

The JVX system consists of three main parts, a compiler to generate VHDL from a Java input (the 'J' and the 'V'), an interpreter, which executes Java byte code and also triggers the hardware, hardware, a FPGA board (with FPGAs from Xlinix Inc., the 'X'), which is connected through a PCI interface to the machine running the interpreter.

The JVX system takes an already debugged and tested Java application as input, which will be translated either into bytecode and VHDL equivalent. The VHDL parts are then synthesized and mapped on the FPGAs with external tools like the SYNOPSYS design compiler. During this step the generated VHDL is fitted into a 'frame', which provides glue logic to transfer parameters to the VHDL code, to trigger execution and to return any computed value. At this point, the developer decides, which parts of the application to execute on hardware, and which not. After instrumenting the interpreter, one is able to measure execution time for the parts of the application, that are interpreted in software, and the others, executed on hardware. Based on the simulation times and required chip

---

[2] Codesign Finite State Machines, a description based on finite state machines with certain extensions.

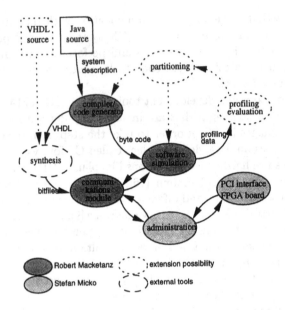

Fig. 1. The JVX system

area , the development is used to optimize the application while figuring out the optimal balance between hard- and software parts.

In the simulation, communication between the Java interpreter and the synthesized hardware is done via a PCI bus interface card [15].

The parts drawn dotted in Fig. 1 mark possible extensions and are projected for future development.

The platform hosting the PCI interface card for the FPGA board, compiler, and interpreter is an ordinary personal computer running under Linux as operating system. All other software was planned and written portably and tested under both Linux and Solaris (on a Sparc).

In the following sections, the three main parts will be described in detail.

2.1 The Java to VHDL Compiler

The Java to VHDL compiler is based on a free Java to bytecode compiler called guavac [8] which has been extended to generate a VHDL representation from Java methods as well as the ordinary bytecode.

The compiler's way to generate VHDL from a Java program is to look at a single method, not at basic blocks, statements of other low-level parts. Accordingly, the object oriented aspects in Java were left out. This sight looks clearer and easier than a concentration on smaller parts of a program, and also implies less overhead. Also, there is no need to transfer any context information to and from the generated hardware part other than parameters and results.

The compilation comprises three phases, parsing the input, matching the Java grammar and traversing the resulting expression tree in order to generate byte code and VHDL.

A method in Java is translated into a state machine in VHDL, with the same semantics as the method. The generation of a VHDL representation of a method breaks complex expressions within that method into atomic ones up to a single statement.

The Fig. 2 shows the way the compiler breaks up the expression "$a = b+c-d$" into atomic parts (in this case an addition, a subtraction and an assignment). The compiler automatically obeys the precedence rules for Java expressions via the scanner and parser grammatics.

Fig. 2. Expression breaking

The compiler translates every atomic statement (generated by the step described above) into a state. It connects these states with transitions it computes from the context of the atomic expressions. Fig. 3 shows the generated (simple) state machine from the example above. Note, that the transitions in this case do nothing, they just ensure the order for the execution of single statments. Any of

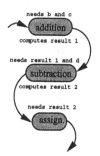

Fig. 3. Generated states

the statments together with their transitions to the next state now are inspected to detect dependencies. As one can see from the Fig.3, the addition needs the values of b and c, and produces a result called '1'. The subtraction needs this result and d and produces an result called '2'. Finally, the assignment to a needs this result.

The compiler generates for every of these intermediate results a signal in VHDL, which is used to transport and buffer the intermediates. As a side effect, the synthesizer software can use these intermediate signals to generate a pipelined hardware, with the intermediates as register stages. These result in faster execution.

Not every statment has a result which is needed by other statments; for example, in the fragment "a=b+c; d=c+b;", there is no dependency between the two expressions, although they both require the same input variables.

The dependencies and resulting transitions in the state machine are 'static', in terms that there are no decisions taken at runtime, the states are just connected one after another. A typical program consists however not only from such simple expressions. The Java to VHDL compiler translates control structures like if, or loops expressed with for or while as follows.

The conditional expression is translated like any other expression, giving a Boolean result stored in an intermediate register. This Boolean is evaluated *at runtime*, and depending on its value, the next state in the state machine is computed.

Similarily, the loops are translated: in this case, the compiler has to remember the entry state for the loop body, and to fill in the jump to the state *after* the loop body after translating it.

Not every possible construction in Java can be translated into a proper VHDL equivalent. These constructions are forced by either memory allocations and memory access or simply by bloating the needed FPGA area. Memory references have not been implemented to simplify the VHDL 'frame' around the methods mentioned above, and to simplify communication between the interpreter and the FPGA board. Size limits force to leave out the support for wide numerical types like floating point, which use most of the FPGA routing capacities.

Some of the function and data element modifiers public, private, static and synchronized are treated especially while generating VHDL: The key words public, private are evaluated at compile-time, not at runtime; any method referencing class member variables cannot be translated due to memory accesses, therefore any function with the modifier static can be translated. Each method which is executed in hardware only exists in *one* instance, as if it was declared with the synchronized key word. The VHDL generation does not take care of synchronized blocks within a method, as the whole method is executed synchronized in hardware On violations of these rules, the compiler stops to generate VHDL for the current translated function, emits an error message and continues to translate the other methods. This behaviour makes the system easy to use, as one can start the compiler to work on arbitrary any project written in Java; each synthesizable method then is automatically generated as VHDL, where the ones which violate the above restrictions are left for the software part.

2.2 The Interpreter and Support Programs

The JVM interpreter included in the JVX-System is based on the free JVM kaffe [20]. It was extended with an interface to the hardware of the JVX system. This interface in conjunction with a database (for translated methods) and the PCI drive is used to execution the application. The database is used to present the developer a friendly interface where one can tell the system, which methods should be executed in software (supporting the JIT technique on certain machines), and which in hardware. The interpreter can be used like any standalone JVM, in case the JVX hardware is not available.

Internally, The JVM interpreter used for the JVX system marks the methods (after loading them from a .class file) different according to their attributes like static or synchronized. This mechanism was used to mark methods, which are to be executed in hardware also as synchronized. The current implementation does not support more than one simultaneous accesses to the hardware. Thus, any call to execute a method in hardware goes through one 'call gate' that is marked as synchronized internally in the JVM.

The interpreter itself was also extended with a communication facility, in order to be able to talk to the hardware. This communication library was designed to establish a connection between interpreter and hardware interface; it supports either the interpreter running and hardware installed on one machine or on different ones, connected via ethernet. In the case both the interpreter and the hardware are installed and running on the same machine, it uses shared memory to establish a fast communications channel, otherwise, a simple BSD socket connection is used.

Measuring of the executed time is done within the interpreter which uses several ways for that. The user can tell the JVM, whether it should measure standard time (via the gettimeofday system call) or system or user time (computed via getrusage). The developer can tell the interpreter, which measuring method to use.

2.3 The Hardware

The hardware part of the JVX project consists of two major components, as there are the interface to the JVM (database, kernel driver, and PCI hardware) and the FPGA board including the VHDL 'frame' for the generated Java methods. The type of FPGA used was a Xilinx XC4025/4028 [21].

It has the ability to talk to the PCI kernel driver and serves on the other side as communication partner to the JVM interpreter. Queries are sent from the interpreter to that database at the beginning of each simulation to request the methods which should run as hardware. While running, the interpreter sends execution request to the database for every method call it has registrered to simulate as hardware. Such requests cause the database to look up, whether the current method already is loaded on a FPGA.Otherwise, a 'free' FPGA will be located (or will be 'freed' after a LRU rule) and loaded with de design file for the method.

The driver on the Linux machine directly talks to an PCI interface card, to transfer parameters to the synthesized method, to trigger the execution and to and to get the result back.

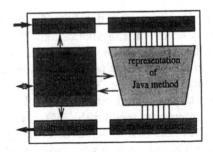

Fig. 4. Frame for Java method

Chosen as PCI interface card was a deveopment kit from AMCC Inc., the AMCC-S5933 [1], which provides serial (FIFO) and parallel data transfer paths. It is connected to the FPGA board via a bidirectional driver board for amplification and 'cleaning' of the signals

The FPGAs are placed on a custom board from the TU Braunschweig called "Weaver board" which has sockets for four Xilinx XC4025/4028. Any of these FPGAs can be loaded with one method representation, so that calls to up to four different methods do not cause reloading of the FGPAs contents.

A VHDL representation of a Java method is fit into the frame (4 by a shell script and then synthesized as one block. This frame is used to transfer the parameters to the method, start the execution and so on.

The 'frame' contains logic to transfer the input parameters from and to the PCI bus with serial conversion in between.

The method accesses the input parameters in the upper transfer register and the result in the lower transfer register fully parallel. The block marked as 'control' serves as trigger for loading the input and output registers, it also sends a signal back to the PCI board, when the method signals the finishing of its computation.

3 Preliminary Results

The JVX system was designed to check the possibilities and limitations, that a translation from a software description to hardware can show. Due to the limited time available for planning, implementing and testing of the system, not all aims that were discussed have been reached. Below, the actual results and future work and planning are discussed.

3.1 Current State

In the current state of development, the system is able to translate simple methods into VHDL, to automate the synthesis of hardware, and to run a sample program with some methods simulated in hardware and some executed in software. As a simple demonstration, the following program was used:

```
class demonstration {
  public static void main (String[] args) {
      int a = 17,  b = 4;
      System.out.println("mutliply "+a+" and "+b);
      int itres = badmult(a,b);
      int normres = normmult(a,b);
      System.out.println("Results "+itres+" and "+normres);
  }
  public static int badmult(int a, int b) {
      int c=0, d=0;
      for(;c<a;c++)
        d+=b;
      return d;
  }
  public static int normmult(inta, int b) {return a*b;}
}
```

The method badmult was then translated into VHDL, synthesized and run on the FPGAs. As expected, such implementation of an multiplication could not be faster than the simple one modeled in Java. Other tests, where the method normmult was executed in hardware, the communication overhead from the interpreter to the hardware and back via database and PCI driver, was much greater than the execution time.

The FPGA type that was used for these experiments (a XC4025) showed a utilization as in the table 1 ('FG' and 'H' are function generator blocks on the FPGA which can be used to model high level functions easily):

	I/O Pins	FG	H	flip-flops	busses
avail.	256	2048	1024	2048	128
badmult	34	420	43	330	8
control.	139	454	156	363	72
total	173	874	199	693	80
%	54%	42%	19%	31%	62%

Table 1. Example measurements

The 'avail' row determines the possible FPGA usage, the 'badmult' row that used only for the method equivalent, and the 'control.' the space used for the frame around the method. The last two rows determine the total usage and the percentage. The FPGA is rather unused with such a little method, the synthesizer software recommends a 4008 FPGA type for that design.

After developing the JVX system to this point, there showed up some interesting research topics: It is possible to generate parallel processes in VHDL for every independent subexpression. Similariliy, a technique like 'inlining' methods into each other can be used after detecting closed call chains (method calls which take place only in one module or class).The compiler also can be extended to produce high level VHDL (a behavioural description) rather than the expression-for-expression and step-by-step way. Most of the work to produce 'good' (in terms of speed and little area covering on the FPGA) then is left to the VHDL synthesizer.

As the hardware has been extended with partial reconfigurable FPGAs, the restriction of only *one* method in hardware at one time is falling. The number of parallel methods in hardware should only be limited by the FPGA's resources.

These extensions and research topics are currently under development, although most work has to be done in partitioning, when the resultig designs do not fit anymore on one single FPGA.

4 Conclusion

Currently, work is in progress to port the JVX system to a different hardware base. After reworking the kernel driver and some of the VHDL frame parts, a working solution based on an integrated board from VCC [19] has been finished. This board contains an integrated PCI chip (actually a XC4013 with Xilinx' PCI core), 2 MB of local SRAM memory and a XC6216 chip, which is partially reconfigurable. The faster interface can be used for a semi-parallel parameter transfer to the method (the number of available I/O pins is still not much), eg. transferring the parameters via the processor bus into the right registers on the FPGA. This is called semi-parallel, because the transfer of all parameters cannot be done in *one* bus cycle, but instead it can be done in a burst manner in far less cycles than serialized.

The JVX system supports this hardware too, avoiding the slow download of FPGA configurations via the serial line and the parallel-serial-parallel transformations of parameters and results which were necessary on the Weaver board design. Currently, the local SRAM on the FPGA board is not used, but some thoughts have been made to use this facility like a local, fast, reconfigurable, and inexpensive co-processor.

References

1. AMCC. *PCI Matchmaker Developer's Kit Technical Reference Manual.* Applied Micro Circuits Corporation, 1996.
2. W. Baker. Application of the synchronous/reactive model to the vhdl language. Technical report, U. C. Berkeley, 1993.
3. Berry, G.; Corunné, P.; Gonthier, G. The synchronous approach to reactive and real-time systems. 79. IEEE Proceedings, September 1991.
4. Brenner, Th.; Ernst, R.; Könenkamp, I.; Schüler, P.; Schaub, H.-C. A prototyping system for verification and evaluation in hardware-software cosynthesis. Internet - WWW http://sueton.ida-ing.tu-bs.de/cosyma/cosyma/cosyma.html, Institut für Datenverarbeitungsanlagen, Technische Universität Braunschweig, 1996.
5. J.T. Buck. *Scheduling Dynamic Dataflow Graphs with Bounded Memory Using the Token Flow Model.* PhD thesis, U.C. Berkeley, 1993.

6. Buck, J.T.; Ha, S.; Lee, E.A.; Messerschmitt, D.G. Ptolemy: a framework for simulating and prototyping heterogeneous systems. *International Journal of Computer Simulation*, special issue on Simulation Software development, Januar 1990.

7. Druzinski, D.; Harel, D. Using statecharts for hardware description and synthesis. *IEEE Transactions on Computer-Aided Design*, Juli 1989. 8(7).

8. David Engberg. Guavac home page. Internet - http://HTTP.CS.Berkeley.-EDU/~engberg/guavac/, 1997.

9. Fuggetta, A., Ghezzi, C. et. al. Formal data flow diagrams. *IEEE Transaction of Software Engineering*, 1986.

10. Gupta, Rajesh K.; De Micheli, Giovanni. Hardware-software cosynthesis for digital systems. *IEEE Design & Test of Computers*, 10(3):29–41, September 1993.

11. Henkel, Jörg; Ernst, Rolf; Ye, Wei; Trawny, Michael; Brenner, Thomas. Cosyma: ein system zur hardware/software co-synthese. Internet - WWW http://sueton.ida--ing.tu-bs.de/cosyma/cosyma/cosyma.html, Institut für Datenverarbeitungsanlagen, Technische Universität Braunschweig, 1997.

12. Kalavade, A.; Lee, E.A. A hardware-software codesign methodology for dsp applications. *IEEE Design and Test of Computers*, 10(3):16–28, September 1993.

13. Lagnese, E. Dirkes; Thomas, D.E. Architectural partitioning for system level design. In *ACM/IEEE DAC*, 26th, pages 62–67, 1989.

14. Robert Macketanz. Hard- und Softwarebasiertes Simulationssystem für Applikationen in hochsprachlicher Beschreibung. Master's thesis, Technische Universität München, Lehrstuhl für Rechnertechnik und Rechnerorganisation/Parallelrechner, 1997.

15. Stefan Micko. Entwicklung einer Plattform zur Co-Emulation von Hardware/Software-Systemen. Master's thesis, Technische Universität München, Lehrstuhl für Rechnergestütztes Entwerfen, 1997.

16. POLIS. POLIS Files. *Internet - WWW http://www-cad.eecs.berkeley.edu/Respep/Research/hsc/polis_files.html*, 1995-1997.

17. T. Lindholm, F. Yellin. *The Java Virtual Machine Specification*. The Java Series. Addison-Wesley Longman, Inc, first edition, 1997.

18. Van Rompaey, Karl; Verkest, Dirk; Bolsens, Ivo; De man, Hugo. Coware - a design environment for heterogeneous hardware/software systems. Number 0-89791-848 in 7/96. EURO-DAC '96 with EURO-VHDL '96, 1997.

19. VCC. Virtual computer company homepage. Internet - http://www.vcc.com/, 1997.

20. Tim J. Wilkinson. Kaffe, a jit and interpreting virtual machine to run java(tm)* code. Internet - http://www.kaffe.org/, 1997.

21. Xilinx. *The Programmable Logic Data Book*. Xilinx Inc., San Jose, California, 1994.

Prototyping New ILP Architectures Using FPGAs

by Joy Shetler, Brian Hemme, Chia Yang, and Christopher Hinsz

Abstract. We are developing a set of custom computer applications coupled with FPGAs and other physical hardware that can be used to emulate an entire processor with monitor functions. This environment provides a working processor research platform complete with operational software that will allow productive computer architecture research to be conducted at both the upper division undergraduate level and at the graduate theses level. The focus of the research component is to devise and test Instruction Level Parallelism (ILP) techniques and mechanisms. The rapid-prototyping platform developed for this effort can be used for several upper division computer architecture and microprocessor courses. The ideas we develop are to be incorporated into the microprocessor and computer architecture curriculum. To implement this system, we have developed a set of VHDL modules to allow for control and monitoring of the processor, a basic operating system with a set of test applications, and a reconfigurable assembler as well as utility and interface applications.

1 Introduction

Increased parallelism within computer systems, both hardware and software, has been the hallmark of the recent generation of computers. New ILP (Instruction Level Parallelism) computer architectures are being pursued aggressively in the academic arena. Increases in speed for a single threaded, pipelined processor have been achieved by superpipelining, superscalar or VLIW (Very Long Instruction Word) architectures. Rather than implementing each candidate solution, researchers typically rely on simulation techniques to discover the most advantageous combination of mechanisms and resources. Simulating and implementing new designs can require special hardware platforms and extensive software resources. Currently, over 80 billion instructions are used to simulate new microprocessor designs. Software simulations require high speed, costly workstations with large disk space requirements. To overcome these problems, many researchers have used abstract simulation techniques. These simulations fail to take into account the physical constraints and problems associated with these designs including the logic implementation, circuit loading effects, and pinout.

Recent advances in FPGAs and reconfigurable hardware have made emulation attractive for candidate designs and opened up new techniques for implementing many components. Emulation techniques involve using hardware configured to perform as the target computer. Using a hardware rapid-prototyping environment to develop and test new processors has several advantages over software simulations. A rapid-prototyping system requires less computation time, provides more accurate models of the hardware and requires less memory capacity. This makes a rapid-prototyping system attractive for use in a university setting.

2 Design Goals

The project was inspired by our desire to create and test new computer architectures. Many schools across the world are conducting computer research using FPGAs. Schools such as Brigham Young University [4] and UC Berkeley [2] are performing research on reconfigurable computing. Others, such as the SPACE design done at University of Strathclyde in Glasgow Scotland [8], are performing studies on basic computer research and design. At Cal Poly [6][12], we wished to conduct research on multithreaded processors, VLIW (Very Long Instruction Word) computing and reconfigurable CPUs, yet there was no hardware or software available to support these projects or to incorporate these ideas into our undergraduate courses. A development environment needed to be constructed before considering any advanced work.

2.1 Support for Multithreaded Architectures

Traditional single-issue processors have many drawbacks. Problems such as data, structural, and control dependencies minimize the throughput of a processor [11]. The basic approaches to reducing the penalties concentrate either on using software or hardware to enhance the performance of a single instruction stream or thread.

In the VLIW approach [5], a compiler breaks an application program into many small units called basic blocks. This process requires rearranging the order of execution (which can be done by a compiler or within the hardware). A set of instructions are combined within a basic block into a very long instruction buffer. There are some drawbacks with the VLIW model. First, the performance is heavily dependent upon the compiler technology. The second drawback is increased complexity in hardware support. Since the VLIW is a multiple-issue processor, it requires more hardware (such as functional units, memory bandwidth, and register file bandwidth). Third, out-of-order execution makes it harder to implement a precise interrupt. Some techniques such as history buffer or reorder buffer can ensure in-order completion; however, this increases the hardware complexity.

Multiple-issue pipelined or superscalar architectures improve performance by increasing the instruction bandwidth and providing multiple functional units. However, since a superscalar implementation issues multiple instructions during each clock cycle, it may suffer the same drawbacks as the VLIW architectures.

Alternatively, multithreaded architectures [9][12] have emerged as a better solution. Multithreaded architectures are more efficient than the traditional pipelined architectures because control and data dependencies are reduced or minimized. There are two basic models, fine-grained and coarse-grained. For the fine-grained model instructions are fetched from a set of ready threads and then interleaved among those from other threads during each clock cycle. The coarse-grained model allows a thread to execute until it is stalled (for example on a cache miss). Then the processor switches to another ready thread. Normally, this type of architecture provides a mechanism for a fast context switch to minimize the context switch cost. This model minimizes memory latency to improve performance. Memory latency can be hidden by switching from one thread to another available thread. The performance of a multithreaded architecture is limited by problems such as network latency and thread synchronization. Dependencies on compilers and concurrency of an application program also restrict processor utilization.

The complexities of both the software and hardware based solutions may not be determined without many attempts [7]. The "final" solution may not be optimal for many applications. To prove our ideas we needed to provide a development platform that could provide better results than traditional simulation methods. While some real world problems might be difficult to model, a design implemented using FPGAs would provide more accurate results, allow greater flexibility as well as coordinate with our educational goals.

2.2 Educational Goals

Our educational goals [4][10] were to: teach basic architectures using FPGA modeling and emulation; teach advanced architectural concepts in the upper division curriculum; allow experimentation; interface to the Windows NT environment as the host system; and provide a platform that students in the lower division, upper division and graduate levels could share. All of these goals can be easily justified. New technology and concepts should be rapidly incorporated into the curriculum at a level easily accepted by the students. There is a critical industrial need for graduates trained in the advanced computer architecture concepts and techniques. Emulation has become the most practical method of testing new ideas in computer engineering. Students would learn basic concepts using the platform in lower division classes and then reuse the platform later on in the curriculum to learn advanced material. Introducing students to state of the art design and debugging techniques to acquire the skills necessary for entry level positions in industry. In summary, we had resources and ideas and needed to implement the software and hardware that could support these efforts.

2.3 Hardware Development Issues

To adequately devise such a system, we needed some rather large FPGAs as well as some custom support software beyond that supplied by the typical FPGA vendor. The physical hardware consists of two main components: an Altera Flex 10k70 University Program board and a custom memory board [1]. An Altera BitBlaster is required to program the FPGA. A serial line connected to an RS232 to TTL level converter circuit is used to connect the workstation to the Flex device. The Altera University Program board is a demo board from Altera that contains a Flex 10k70 device and a MAX 7128. The board supplies power to both devices as well as a set of headers, switches, buttons and LEDs to interface to the devices.

The memory consists of four 1Mx4 SRAM chips, for an addressable memory space of 1M by 16 bits (1 word). Each of the chips is a Motorola MCM6249WJ35 with a 35 ns memory access time. With the current memory interface this would limit the maximum processor clock frequency to 14MHz (1/35 ns x ½) since the memory interface must be clocked at twice the rate of the processing unit. The memory is mounted on a custom circuit board laid out using Orcad and manufactured in the Cal Poly Industrial and Manufacturing Engineering laboratory. Serial line conversion is handled with a TC232CPE IC which comes in a standard 14 pin DIP package. The RS232 level signals are connected to a connector that plugs directly into a workstation com port. Two external clocks are needed, one for the serial subsystem and one for the processor and monitor systems. For this project, both clocks were connected to a single oscillator running at 4.9152MHz. This frequency can be divided down to produce a 9600 baud rate clock.

3 Initial CPU Design

Our initial goal [6] was to create a CPU that was powerful enough to run a basic operating system but simple enough to leave plenty of room for expansion. A load-store RISC type processor was chosen for its simpler structure over a CISC type machine. To make the design practical and current, the processor was pipelined and supports register forwarding. The basic processor lacks external interrupts. The only supported interrupt is the TRAP instruction (software interrupt).

A simple processor replacement model (pseudo processor) was created to test the monitor module. The pseudo processor outputs counts or constant values on its port and the monitor logs these values as if they represented the state of a working CPU. The CPU and pseudo CPU share the same port map, therefore, to switch to the actual processor only required a library change and a single name change in the port map.

Due mainly to the limitations in the number of available I/O pins the CPU was limited to 16 bits. This only allows for an addressable memory space of 64k. While rather small, 64k should be enough to load a small operating system and a few test programs and should be sufficient for research purposes. To double the memory space, the CPU addresses words, not bytes. The processor can then address twice the physical memory as a normal byte addressable 16 bit processor.

The CPU is composed of four stages. The instruction fetch resolves the address based on the contents of the PC (program counter), BP(Base Pointer) and mode bit. This effective address is sent to memory and the data returned from the fetch is latched to the second stage. The second stage is the decode and register fetch. The instruction is decoded and the fields are placed on the correct buses and all jump instructions are resolved. The execution stage, stage three, contains two functional units, an ALU (Arithmetic and Logic Unit) and a shifter. The ALU can perform addition, subtraction, and the bitwise operations NOT, AND, XOR, OR and CMP (compare). All data is assumed to be integer; floating point math is not supported. This stage does not contain a pipeline register. Data to the following stage is latched into the register file immediately at the beginning of the cycle if the instruction was complete and a write back was requested. If an instruction requires that a result be placed into a register the fourth stage will send the control bits and data to the register file thus initiating a save operation. Since the register file performs the same function, an additional pipeline register is not needed.

A very limited instruction set was selected based on the review of several processors including the MIPS R3000 and the Motorola 68000. The instruction set was augmented to provide instructions to support a fully functioning operating system. This evaluation used a basic software simulator and assembler [12]. These tools allowed for the concurrent development of the operating system and processor. The processor currently supports 24 instructions. The opcodes use 6 bits (allowing up to 64 instructions) for the instruction with the following 10 for the arguments. The instructions are divided up into four types: register to register, immediate, jump and shift type instructions.

4 Software Requirements

Software packages were needed to handle serial communication with the processor system and to parse the data returned from the CPU into a readable format. Specific pieces of software were also needed to support different test circuits such as the memory test. The software developed includes: an assembler, a serial communication interface, a simple serial communication program for testing, two programs to support the memory test circuit, a program to convert the binary dump of CPU memory into a readable hex file and a program to parse the hex file into fields. The lasercrt.exe program allows the user to capture and print the display of an HP logic analyzer. All the programs except the assembler were written as 32-bit Windows programs and will run under NT or 95. The assembler was written as a console application that can execute under DOS or any version of Windows. All the code was written in C++ with Borland compilers, the Windows programming was done using Borland's C++ Builder Professional.

The main design philosophy of the assembler was to allow instructions to be added without rewriting the assembler code. The current assembler uses an initiation file (oasm.ini) to load in the supported instructions, their format and opcodes. New instructions that comply with the existing formats can be easily added to the instruction set. The user can also add or change the pneumonic for the existing instructions.

4.1 VHDL Models

To ease testing and reuse, every main block of the VHDL code was implemented as a library. These modules can be incorporated into another design by simply including the correct library and providing a port map. This makes reuse a simple act and aids reliability by providing a clear separation between components. The possibility of accidentally modifying working code while working on a different module has been eliminated. The project is composed of the following VHDL blocks: an RS232 interface, a memory interface, a monitor circuit, a 16-bit CPU, a 16-bit pseudo CPU (to test the monitor), a simple echo circuit (to test the serial connections and the RS232 interface), an echo program (to test the memory interface as well as the physical serial setup and VHDL interface), and a memory test module (to verify that all 1M addresses of memory function properly). An overview and functional description of each follows.

The RS232 package interfaces any VHDL program to an RS232 serial line. The package will convert incoming serial data into a bit vector to be read by the controlling program. The package converts bit vectors from the controlling program into serial format for transmission. The RS232 package supplies RDRF (Receive Data Register Full) and TDRE (Transmit Data Register Empty) bits to report status to the controlling module. Data reads and writes to the RS232 package are handled with two separate read and write strobe lines.

To test the serial interface, a simple module was designed that performed a hardware echo of data sent over the serial line. This test module is used to test future additions or changes that are made to the serial interface and to verify that the serial port is operational. A VHDL module similar to the serial tester was developed. This module would take data over the serial line and save it to memory. The address is then incremented and the data found in memory is sent over the serial line. The data read out of memory can be used to verify that the values returned are not due to line capacitance. This test module uses the same interface software as the serial port test circuit.

After the memory and serial interface are functional, the memory must be tested to verify that the addressing is working properly and each memory location is functional. This test uses a VHDL module that will write the lower 16 bits of the address to every location in memory. Once the data is written, every location will be read and then output over the serial line. The data can be examined to determine if there are any errors and for which bits and/or address the errors occur. This test module requires a vastly different interface to the workstation then the previous tests. This module has no need for a serial input line but places a very large amount of data out the serial port.

4.2 Windows Interface Programs

The serial test program (STEST.EXE) is a quick way to send data over a selected serial port at different settings. Shell.exe is a robust serial interface program that allows for data to be transmitted to the processor either as a file, ASCII string or a hexadecimal value. This program is used to send data to the hardware, to visually examine the hardware's response, and input data as an ASCII string by pushing a button.

MTEST (MTEST .EXE) is simply a program that will allow a quick connection to a serial port and be able to either visually view received data or save the data to a file. The program will only allow for the data to be viewed on screen or saved to a file, not both because Windows NT can not perform both functions without missing some serial data. For large serial dumps, the user can save the data to a file to be viewed later.

The Memory Data Evaluator (EVAL.EXE) program is run on a file created with the MTEST program described previously. MTEST should have been run while the hardware was loaded with the memory test module. If the hardware is working correctly, the data file should contain an increasing 16-bit count from zero up to 65535. This count should be repeated sixteen times because the address is 20 bits and the data is just the lower 16 bits of the address. EVAL will examine the file and determine if any of the data is incorrect. The program will return the total count of bytes evaluated and the total number of bytes with errors. EVAL will also sum up the number of times a bit error occurred for each bit. EVAL will display the first ten errors encountered.

The user shell (SHELL.EXE) is the main program used to interface the CPU. The program is written with threads, the transmit and receive portions are written as independent threads. Shell.exe also allows hex program files to be sent in a format that the monitor can easily load into memory. The serial interface will concurrently take data received on the serial port and display it in the window and/or save it to a file. The received data can be converted to hexadecimal before being displayed, if desired. Windows NT has difficulty handling a large number of interrupts while updating a window at the same rate.

The Binary to Hex Converter (HEX.EXE) program is used to convert a binary file to a file containing the data in readable hex format. The data is saved eight hexadecimal words to a line with the optional addition of line numbers followed by colons. An ASCII representation of the hexadecimal data is appended to the end of every line. Characters that are not displayable in ASCII will be represented as a period. The ability to remove an "echoed code dump" is also available. The monitor echoes all the data from the download mode.

The Data Parser (PARSE.EXE) organizes the data returned from a CPU run. The data must first be run through the HEX program to convert to hex and add line numbers. PARSE will locate line number 10000 in the file (which should be the head of monitor memory space) and then dumps the data to the window.

4.3 Monitor System

The monitor is a rather large and complex block of VHDL that supplies the CPU with a clock, a reset, memory, and a memory mapped serial interface. The monitor watches the CPU every cycle and saves the current state of the machine to upper memory (memory beyond the 64k available to a 16-bit CPU). The monitor provides the following services: the ability to load a bootstrap file into memory over the serial line, a means to reset the CPU (to run the bootstrap), a method of dumping the contents of memory over the serial line (for inspection), a simple memory interface to the CPU, and a memory mapped serial port for the CPU.

The monitor code is designed to facilitate data logging of every cycle of the CPU. The test procedures for the CPU can be easily customized. The only current limitation is that there are only 14 points in every CPU cycle for writing data to memory. The CPU's clock cycle relative to the monitor would have to be halved to allow another sixteen pieces of data to be saved to memory every CPU cycle. Alternatively, the clock speed of the CPU could be increased with a reduction in the amount of data that is logged.

4.4 Scheduler

The main purpose of the scheduler is to fetch an instruction among a set of active processes. For a multithreaded architecture, there will be more than one process running at the same time. A mechanism is required to maintain a given number of available processes. Conceptually, an instruction queue links a process to an input stream, where the processor fetches instructions from one of those input streams. There will be a set of registers associated with each instruction queue, and the linking information is maintained in the status register. When the number of processes exceeds the number of instruction queues, all unscheduled processes are kept in the waiting queue. A modified version of a round-robin scheme is used to fetch an instruction from the instruction queue.

During each clock cycle, the scheduler searches through the instruction queues; if the queue is valid and the process state is "running", then the instruction in the queue is fetched into the register renaming module. Otherwise the scheduler moves to the next queue. Instruction input is dynamically altered based on the availability of processes. Better performance is obtained over the traditional round-robin scheme. The base register allows the operating system to set up the context of a user program. The base register is only used in user mode to allow programs to execute at different memory locations, and to protect the operating system which is in the lower mode. The LBP (Load Base Pointer) instruction is a privileged instruction, and only can be executed in the supervisor mode.

4.5 Operating System

The Operating system maintains a set of processes and manages all global resources associated with the environment. There are two versions of the operating system, a single-task single-user operating system for the base model and a multi-task single-user system for the multithreaded model. The organization of the operating system can be divided into three major components, memory management, process management, and service request. In both models, there is a set of data structures (a process table, memory table, event table, and various queue structures) that are maintained by the operating system. These data structures are protected by supervisor mode. By default, all other programs are running in user mode and have restricted access to these structures.

The base architecture is a word addressable machine with a 64k word addressable space. This space is divided into 32 2k word pages with the first two pages reserved for the operating system. A central manager maintains the bitmap to ensure race conditions never occur, and the serialization of requesting a free page is done via a message queue mechanism. The system memory consists of three parts: operating system code space, global data space, and a vector table. The system code space begins at the physical memory location 0x1000, and is extended to cover a 4k address space. During initialization, the operating system rearranges the system memory space to the final operation state.

The global data space contains structures such as the process table. For the base model, the operating system structures are simple. A process table has a fixed number of entries to keep track of the status of the processes. Each entry is reserved according to the process ID number. In the multithreaded model, additional fields are needed to support multitasking. The page and base addresses indicate the contents of the base register associated with that process, and the user stack contains the logical address of a process. During the creation of a process, the operating system assigns a process ID number based on the availability of the process table. Once an entry is allocated, the process ID is then placed at the end of the ready queue waiting to be scheduled.

For the base model, a service request is performed by switching to the operating system mode. The service code and the return PC address are fetched from the user stack, and the service routine corresponding to the service code is called. The modified model has a more complex design. Since more than one process may make a request at the same time, there might be more than one copy of the operating system running. To resolve this problem, one of four instruction queues is designated for the operating system. Hence, there is always a thread running at all times.

In terms of implementation, the operating system can be divided into the following blocks: initialization, main loop, and service controller. During the initialization phase, all data structures are initialized within the operating system address space. The vector table is set up, and all service routines are attached to their corresponding entry. Once this is completed, the OS is in an endless loop with three primary functions: schedule the next ready process to run, parse and execute user commands, and service any service requests.

5 Future Work

The complexity of the design that can be tested is limited by the size of FPGAs currently available. The Altera Flex 10K30 has 30,000 gates on a single chip, which is barely large enough for the base model. For the multithreaded model, a 10K70 (70,000 gates) is required. Once larger FPGA devices become available, additional enhancements could be implemented to improve overall performance.

There are some limitations to the existing base architecture. First, the size of address and data buses should be extended to 32 bits wide. Currently, the number of general purpose registers are limited by the instruction size. Limitations on the address and data lengths also limit the number of registers and total memory capacity. Second, implementations of hardware interrupt support should be included. The only means of switching from user to system mode is via software trap. For the base mode this problem might not affect overall performance. A multitasking operating system is desired for more complex systems since multitasking is more efficient. By implementing hardware interrupts, not only can multiple programs be executed at the same time on the base model but the addition of interrupts also allows external IO devices to be added. Thirdly, there is only a small number of test programs available, more complex and diverse programs are required.

Acknowledgements

This material is based upon work supported by the National Science Foundation under Grant No. MIP-9624967. We would also like to thank Matt Brown, Thompson Lewis and Prof. James Harris for their contributions to the success of our projects.

References

1. Altera, 1996 Data Book. San Jose, Altera, 1996
2. Berkeley Reconfigurable Architecture, Systems and Software Group. http://HTTP.CS.Berkeley.EDU/Research/Projects/brass/
3. Don Bouldin, et.al. "Report of the 1993 Workshop on Rapid Prototyping of Microelectronic Systems for Universities", Computer Architecture News, June 1994, pp. 19-26
4. BYU Electrical Engineering's Configurable Computing Laboratory. http://splish.ee.byu.edu/
5. Christian Iseli and Eduardo Sanchez, "Spyder: A Reconfigurable VLIW Processor using FPGAs", Proceedings IEEE Workshop on FPGAs for Custom Computing Machines, April 1993, pp. 17-24
6. Hemme, Brian. "An Expandable Computer Architecture Research Platform" Thesis California Polytechnic State University, San Luis Obispo, CA 1998.
7. J. L. Hennessy and D. A. Patterson, "Computer Architecture - A quantitative Approach." 2nd Edition, Morgan Kaufmann Publishers, Inc., 1995.
8. Reconfigurable Architecture Group at Glasgow Scotland. http://www.dcs.gla.ac.uk/research/fpga/
9. J. Shetler and S. Butner, "Multiple Stream Execution on the DART Processor", 1991 Int.Conf. on Parallel Processing, August 1991, pp. I92-I96
10. Joy Shetler, "Mentoring Graduate and Undergraduate Students in Microelectronic Systems Architecture Education and Research", 1997 ASEE/IEEE Frontiers in Engineering Conference Proceedings, Session F2B.4, CD-ROM
11. D. Wall, "Limits of Instruction-Level Parallelism", Proc. of the 4th Int. Conf. on Architectural Support for Programming Languages and Operating Systems, April 1991, pp. 176-188
12. Yang, Chia. "A Multi Context Uniprocessor: Another Multithreaded Architecture." Thesis California Polytechnic State University, San Luis Obispo, CA 1997.

CAD System for ASM and FSM Synthesis

Samary Baranov

Computer System Department, Center for technological Education Holon , 52 Golomb St,
P.O. Box 305, Holon 58102, Israel
baranov@barley.cteh. ac.il

Abstract. For hardware realization of computer programs (for the realization of software as hardware) it is very important to represent, to transform and to synthesize very complex Finite State Machines (FSM). This work contains the first report about CAD system Synthesis1 for design of FSMs with hardly any constraints on their size, that is, the number of inputs, outputs and states. Synthesis1 implements automatically various transformations of an Algorithmic State Machine (minimization, composition, decomposition etc.) and synthesis of FSM's logic circuit as (a) multilevel circuit with gates from a predefined library; (b) with standard LSI and VLSI circuits without memory, such as PLA(s,t,q) – programmable logic arrays with s inputs, t outputs and q horizontals; (c) with standard LSI and VLSI circuits with memory, such as PLAM(s,t,q,r) – programmable logic arrays with s inputs, t outputs, q horizontals and r memory elements; (d) matrices circuits on the chip with a minimization of the chip area; (e) with LUTs (Look-Up-Tables) for FPGA technology.

1. Introduction

Why is it so important to synthesize Finite State Machines? There are at least two serious reasons:

1. FSM, or a control unit, is unique in each project. To design a data path you can use very large library units from the previous projects. It is not possible for FSM since you cannot use former projects for new FSM design.

2. In the latest few years, the share of FSMs in each project was considerably increased. There are also some reasons for this tendency:

(a) realization of software as hardware;
(b) complex specialized processors with very complex embedded functions;
(c) parallel processors with complex control.

However, with Synthesis1 you need not even construct FSM. You can design your control unit without any knowledge about FSM - about states, transitions, inputs and outputs. The only thing you should do is to represent the behavior of the designed digital system as an Algorithmic State Machine (flowchart). Moreover, you should not think about minimization of your Algorithmic State Machine (ASM) - Synthesis1 will minimize it.

You should only concentrate on the correctness of the behavior presented as ASM. And if it is difficult for you to describe the whole behavior as one ASM, you can present separate subbehaviors by several ASMs and Synthesis1 will combine them into one minimized ASM.

2. The Structure of Synthesis1

CAD System Synthesis1 contains three subsystems.

2.1 Algorithmic State Machine Transformer

Algorithmic state machine (ASM) is a directed connected graph, containing one initial and one final vertex and a finite set of operator and conditional vertices, connected in such a way that: (i) every output is connected with only one input; (ii) every input is connected with at least one output; (iii) every vertex is located at least in one of the paths leading from an initial vertex to a final one.

One of the logical conditions from the set $X = \{x_1, ..., x_L\}$ is written in each conditional vertex. It is possible to write the same logical conditions in different conditional vertices. The operator Y_t which is the subset of the set of microoperations $Y = \{y_1, .., y_N\}$ is written in each operator vertex. It is possible to write the same operator in different operator vertices. The example of ASM G_1 is shown in Fig. 1. The operators are written near the operator vertices in this ASM.

ASM in Synthesis1 is presented in VHDL or as a two-connected list (a text file also). The following procedures are implemented in ASM Transformer:

Show ASM. This procedure displays a picture of ASM on the screen.

Print ASM. This procedure prints a picture of ASM into a post-script file.

Check ASM. This procedure verifies the correctness of ASM.

ASM minimization. This procedure minimizes the number of vertices in ASM. For example, ASM G_1 in Fig. 1 containing 17 vertices was obtained with Synthesis1 as a result of minimization of ASM G_2 in Fig. 2, containing 25 vertices. One of the results of ASM minimization is the minimization of FSM, constructed for this ASM, and of the logic circuit for this FSM. Thus, in our example, FSM S_2 implementing ASM G_2 contains 7 states and 27 rows in its transition table. The logic circuit of FSM S_2 contains 39 gates, the total number of inputs into these gates is equal to 89 and the gate equivalent for this circuit with the use of the library Class for CAD system Synopsys is equal to 71. The FSM S_1, constructed for ASM G_1, contains 6 states and 21 rows. There are only 28 gates with 61 inputs in its logic circuit. The gate equivalent for this circuit is equal to 53.

ASMs combining. This procedure combines separate ASMs into one ASM and minimizes the number of vertices in this ASM [1]. Note, that ASM in Fig. 2 was constructed by combining four ASMs with the total number of vertices equal to 38.

ASM decomposition. This procedure decomposes a given ASM into a set of component ASMs with given constraints on the number of logical conditions (input variables), microoperations (output variables) and vertices.

ASM extraction. This procedure extracts private ASMs from combined ASM.

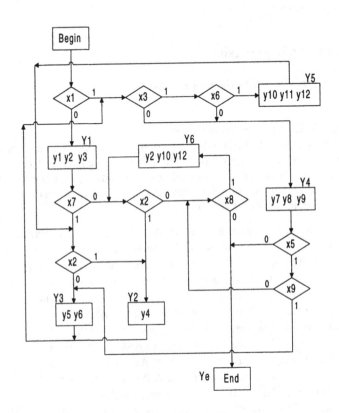

Fig. 1. ASM G_1

2.2 Finite State Machine Synthesizer

The following procedures are implemented in FSM Synthesizer:

Constructing of FSM transition table. An ASM description in VHDL or ASM as a two connected list are the inputs to this procedure which constructs 24 various types of FSMs tables for Mealy, Moore and their combined model. The output of this procedure is FSM in VHDL, BLIF or a text file with an FSM table. In Synthesis1, there exist procedures for transformation of FSM into special FSM representation in CAD systems Synopsys and Compass. FSM Mealy S_1 implementing ASM G_1 is shown in Fig. 3.

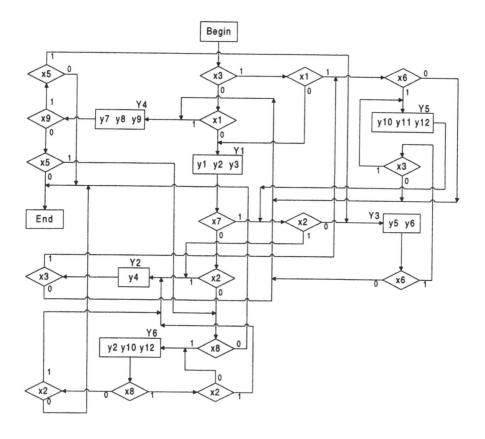

Fig. 2. ASM G_2

State assignment. FSM in VHDL or a text file with an FSM table are the inputs to this procedure. A text file with FSM table, containing states, codes and input memory functions, is the output of this procedure. A designer can also enter his/her own state assignment from the keyboard. FSM Synthesizer implements *log* or one-hot state assignments.

FSM decomposition. This procedure decomposes a given FSM into a set of connected component FSMs with given constraints on the complexity of component FSMs (a number of inputs, outputs, states and rows in their transition tables) [2, 3].

2.3 Logic Circuit Synthesizer

Logic circuit synthesis with gates. FSM in VHDL or a text file with an FSM table are the inputs into this subsystem of Logic Circuit Synthesizer, multilevel logic circuit in VHDL or a netlist as a text file are its output. A designer can enter constraints on

a1	a5	x1*x3*x6	y10y11y12	1
a1	a6	x1*x3*~x6	y7y8y9	2
a1	a6	x1*~x3	y7y8y9	3
a1	a2	~x1	y1y2y3	4
a2	a3	x7*x2	y4	5
a2	a3	x7*~x2	y5y6	6
a2	a3	~x7*x2	y4	7
a2	a4	~x7*~x2*x8	y2y10y12	8
a2	a1	~x7*~x2*~x8	--	9
a3	a5	x3*x6	y10y11y12	10
a3	a6	x3*~x6	y7y8y9	11
a3	a6	~x3	y7y8y9	12
a4	a3	x2	y4	13
a4	a4	~x2*x8	y2y10y12	14
a4	a1	~x2*~x8	--	15
a5	a3	x2	y4	16
a5	a3	~x2	y5y6	17
a6	a3	x5*x9	y5y6	18
a6	a4	x5*~x9*x8	y2y10y12	19
a6	a1	x5*~x9*~x8	--	20
a6	a1	~x5	--	21

Fig. 3. FSM S_1 implementing ASM G_1

the number of inputs in gates and/or to the number of levels (the length of a maximum path) in the logic circuit. A special procedure finds the level of the circuit (if the circuit was constructed without constraints on the number of levels) and the distances of each gate from the input and to the output. Another procedure checks that the logic circuit really implements FSM and, if this procedure finds a lack of correspondence, it localizes the incompatibility. The designer can define his/her library, containing gates AND, OR, INV, NAND, NOR, etc. and two-level library elements with one output only. A netlist constructed for FSM S_1 (Fig. 3) is shown in Fig. 4. In this netlist, the number of the gate is written in the first column, type of the gate – in the second, inputs of the gate – in the third (t_i is the output of the i th flip-flops, x_j is the input of FSM, e_p is the output of the p th gate). In the fourth column, the outputs of the logic circuit are written (y_n is the n th output of FSM and d_r is the input of the r th flip-flop). It is not a mistake that work time is equal to zero, it is really less than the minimal time quantum for IBM PC with 200Mhz.

Synthesis of logic circuits with Look-Up-Tables (LUTs) for FPGA technology. The design problem for an FSM logic circuit with LUT(k) is formulated as follows: it is necessary to decompose a logic circuit into such subcircuits (cells, or LUTs) that each cell implements one function with not more than k inputs or two functions with not more than $k-1$ inputs, but in the latter case, the common number of inputs into a cell

1	AND	~t1 ~t2	15	AND	~t3 ~x1 e1	y3 y1
2	AND	~t1 t2	16	OR	e10 e6	
3	AND	~t2 t1	17	AND	x2 e16	y4
4	AND	x7 e3	18	AND	~x2 e6	
5	OR	e2 e4	19	AND	x9 e11	
6	AND	t3 e5	20	OR	e18 e19	y6 y5
7	OR	t3 x1	21	AND	x8 e14	
8	AND	e1 e7	22	AND	x3 x6 e8	y11
9	OR	~t3 ~x7	23	OR	~x3 ~x6	
10	AND	e3 e9	24	AND	e8 e23	y9 y8 y7
11	AND	~t3 x5 e2	25	OR	e21 e22	y10 y12
12	AND	~x9 e11	26	OR	e15 e21	y2 d1
13	AND	~x2 e10	27	OR	e24 e22	d2
14	OR	e12 e13	28	OR	e17 e15 e20 e22	d3

```
*** Report ***

Start time: 03:06:98  09:17:34.290
Stop time:  03:06:98  09:17:34.290
Work time:            00:00:00.000
Number of input variables: 11
Number of output signals: 15
        10 OR gates with 2 inputs
        14 AND gates with 2 inputs
        3 AND gates with 3 inputs
        1 OR gates with 4 inputs
Total number of gates: 28
Total number of inputs: 61
  The number of inputs in one gate is equal to 2.1786
Gate EqUvalent for the circuit: 53.000000
```

Fig. 4. Netlist constructed by Synthesis1 for FSM S_1

should also not exceed k inputs. FSM in VHDL or a text file with an FSM table are the inputs to this subsystem, its output is a text file with a netlist containing LUTs. Synthesis1 allows to construct circuits with $k=4-8$. As in the synthesis of logic circuits with gates, a special procedure checks that the logic circuit really implements FSM and, if this procedure finds a lack of correspondence, it localizes the incompatibility.

Synthesis of logic circuits with Programmable Logic Array (PLA). FSM in VHDL or a text file with an FSM table are also the inputs into this subsystem of Logic Circuit Synthesizer. The designer should also enter the maximal numbers of inputs (s), outputs (t) and rows (q) in the PLA used. The output is the text file with programming tables for PLAs.

Matrix realization of FSM. FSM in VHDL or a text file with an FSM table are the inputs into this subsystem, its output contains programming tables for each matrix in the multimatrix logic circuit. The techniques used here minimize the chip area. They are based on the circuit presentation as a composition of matrices, input variables replacement and special methods for state assignment and microinstructions coding. At the same time, this subsystem constructs a classical two-matrix logic circuit. Our experiments showed that a multimatrix realization reduces the chip area by 30-40%.

3. Experiments with Synopsys, Xilinx, Altera, Leonardo and Synplify

The results of comparative experiments with VLSI CAD Systems Synthesis1 and Synopsys, Xilinx, Altera, Leonardo, Synplify are generalized in Tables 1-7. Table 1 contains the results of experiments with Synopsys and Synthesis1 for 52 FSMs. The experiments are arranged into four groups. 12 examples with gate equivalents from Synopsys does not exceeding 300, are placed in the first row. The total gate equivalent for these 12 examples is equal to 2713 for Synopsys and only 1757 for Synthesis1 (64.8%). 12 examples with gate equivalent from 300 to 600 are placed in the second row, 14 examples (from 600 to 900) – in the third etc. As seen from this table, Synthesis1 reduces the logic circuits by halves and minimization is increased for more complicated circuits. Tables 2–7 contain the results of experiments with FPGA cells XC-3000 and FLEX8000. The reduction of the chip area (number of LUTs) for circuits constructed by Synthesis1 is equal to 70.3% for Altera (FLEX8000), 62.4% for Synopsys (FLEX8000), 61.3% for Leonardo (XC-3000), 54.3% for XILINX (XC-3000), 50.4% for Synplify (FLEX8000) and 42.3% for Leonardo (FLEX8000). Each experiment with Altera or Xilinx went on from 10 min to 3.5 hours on Pentium-200, while it took not more than 3 sec with Synthesis1. Parameters of FSMs in these experiments are presented in Table 8.

Table 1. The experiments with Synopsys (Library CLASS) and Synthesis1

Gate Equivalent	# Examples	Synopsys	Synthesis1	%
< 300	12	2713	1757	64.8
300 – 600	12	5503	3308	60.1
600 – 900	14	10273	5414	52.7
> 900	16	18601	7966	42.8
Total	52	37082	18445	49.7

Table 2. The experiments with Xilinx (FPGA XC3000) and Synthesis1

Number of LUTs	# Examples	Xilinx	Synthesis1	%
< 60	12	544	298	54.8
61 – 120	9	821	430	52.4
121 – 200	15	2402	1126	46.9
201 – 350	15	3737	1573	42.1
Total	51	7504	3427	45.7

Table 3. The experiments with Altera (FLEX8000) and Synthesis1

Number of LUTs	# Examples	Altera	Synthesis1	%
< 150	15	1556	786	50.5
151 – 400	11	3210	1165	36.1
401 – 600	13	6471	1779	27.5
> 600	9	7483	1827	24.4
Total	48	18720	5557	29.7

Table 4. The experiments with Synopsys (FLEX8000) and Synthesis1

Number of LUTs	# Examples	Synopsys	Synthesis1	%
< 150	14	1425	692	48.6
151 – 300	11	2458	1130	46.0
301 – 450	12	4512	1721	38.1
> 450	12	6848	2186	31.9
Total	49	15243	5729	37.6

Table 5. The experiments with Leonardo (FPGA XC3000) and Synthesis1

Number of LUTs	# Examples	Leonardo	Synthesis1	%
< 60	13	587	493	84.0
61 – 140	11	1050	552	52.6
141 – 200	16	2656	1248	47.0
> 201	11	4553	1134	24.9
Total	51	8846	3427	38.7

Table 6. The experiments with Leonardo (FLEX8000) and Synthesis1

Number of LUTs	# Examples	Leonardo	Synthesis1	%
< 100	16	1046	842	80.5
101 – 190	12	1856	1373	74.0
191 – 260	11	2428	1608	66.2
> 261	10	4602	1906	41.4
Total	49	9932	5729	57.7

Table 7. The experiments with Synplify (FLEX8000) and Synthesis1

Number of LUTs	# Examples	Synplify	Synthesis1	%
< 100	16	1046	842	80.5
101 – 190	12	1856	1373	74.0
191 – 260	11	2428	1608	66.2
> 261	10	4602	1906	41.4
Total	49	9932	5729	57.7

Table 8. The parmeters of several FSMs in experiments

Examples	State	Input	Output	Rows
acdl	22	16	27	215
amtz	85	23	52	261
bull	24	44	13	281
cow	24	49	24	261
gol	58	18	64	228
kobz	29	19	53	231
md	59	22	53	388
ort	56	61	48	214
oshr	55	19	72	213
rafi	52	18	70	248
ratm	73	19	57	234
roiz	35	17	53	251
v1_10	18	15	18	264
v11_20	18	14	29	367

4. Conclusions

Synthesis1 is a comprehensive and effective system for synthesis and optimization of very complex FSM. It is easily interfaced with other CAD systems using VHDL or their special formats supported by Synthesis 1. Owing to very high operating speed, Synthesis1 allows to make experiments inaccessible for most of other CAD systems. Thus an hour it is possible to execute tens or even hundreds of experiments with very complex FSMs by changing the number of inputs in elements, rank of logic circuit, number of inputs into LUTs, number of inputs, outputs and rows in PLA etc. Such experiments allow to find a better version for a logic circuit among many possible ones and to optimize parameters of library cells, LUTs, PLAs etc. Formal transformations of ASMs (minimization, composition and decomposition) with an automatic synthesis of FSMs, implementing these ASMs, also allow a part of high-level synthesis for digital systems to be automated.

References

1. Baranov, S.: Logic Synthesis for Control Automata. Kluwer Academic Publishers, Boston - London - Dordrecht, (1994)

2. Jozwiak, L., Kolsteren, J.: An efficient method for the decomposition of sequential machines. Microprocessing and Microprogramming. 32, (1991) 657-664

3. Baranov, S., Bregman, L.: Synthesis of automata from elements with given constraints on their complexity. Journal of Microcomputer Applications. 17, (1994) 227-237

Fast Floorplanning for FPGAs*

John M Emmert, Akash Randhar and *Dinesh Bhatia*

Design Automation Laboratory,
ECECS Department
University of Cincinnati,
Cincinnati, OII 45221–0030

Abstract

Floorplanning is a crucial step in the physical design flow for FPGAs. In this paper, we use min-cut based successive bipartitioning to floorplan circuits for application to FPGAs. The primary motivation of this work is reduction of execution time required to accomplish the floorplanning step of device mapping. Our method includes clustering to enhance circuit performance and terminal propagation to reduce total wire length and enhance circuit routability. The floorplanner is intended to take predefined macro based designs as input. Using the Xilinx xc4000 series of FPGAs as the target architecture, we have demonstrated effective and fast floorplanning on a collection of designs.

1 Introduction

Field Programmable Gate Arrays (FPGAs) have become very prevalent in every possible design scenario. Since their introduction in the mid 1980s, FPGA device architectures have undergone significant changes. Devices with an ability to map 100,000 gate equivalent designs have become common and new research and commercial development has shown the promise of one million gate equivalent devices in the near future[12]. While technological innovations are easily facilitating higher density devices, not much progress has been made towards CAD tools facilitating the implementation of large designs. Once the device density reaches one million gates and beyond, the design complexity will fall close to what we currently have for custom ASICs. These new high density FPGAs will require new and innovative methods for rapidly mapping circuits to device architectures.

In this paper, we present a min-cut successive bipartitioning based floorplanner for mapping macro based designs to high density FPGAs. Our approach makes use of precharacterized macros [2] that are used during the application design process as well as during the physical mapping process. Figure 1 illustrates the design flow. The subsequent netlist defining the interconnection of macros is used to floorplan the design for an FPGA device.

Breuer [2] suggested a min-cut based floorplanning approach for general VLSI circuits. We adapt this approach and make use of combinational *force directed clustering* along with *Fiduccia Mattheyses* [1] successive bipartitioning to relatively place macros within

---

* This research is partially supported by contract number F33615-96-C1912 from Wright Laboratory of the US Air Force and a grant from Lucent Technologies

[2] Components in the library include macros like adders, multipliers, shifters, decoders, and more. These macros have fixed size, expressed in terms of number of logic blocks. In addition, each block also has a shape with logic blocks optimally preassigned within the predefined shape. Such a preplacement of logic blocks within a shape boundary helps in precharacterizing the performance of the macro. Also, after floorplanning, macros can be forced to retain their shape thus avoiding the need of reassigning logic blocks within macros after floorplan completion.

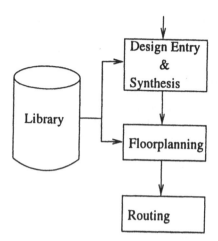

Fig. 1. *The floorplanning based design flow.*

partitions. This is followed by *legal placement* within each partition. During legal placement, flexible macros are reshaped and all macros are assigned a physical location. For flexible macros, any intra macro placement is accomplished using simulated annealing. Finally, compaction is performed on the floorplanned design to minimize the overall area.

The floorplanning problem has been studied extensively in VLSI CAD, but relatively little work has been done in the area of FPGA floorplanning for macro based designs. Shi has proposed a force directed method for macro based FPGA floorplanning [5, 6]. Mathur proposed a combination of net based and path based approaches for timing driven floorplanning [7]. Simulated annealing based approaches have been suggested [9], but they are not efficient in terms of execution time. Various other techniques suggested for general VLSI floorplanning have been adopted for FPGAs [11][2]. In this paper section 2 defines the floorplanning problem and illustrates each step in our floorplanning approach. Section 3 presents benchmarks circuits, test results, and test analysis.

2 Floorplanning

Macros are a collection of relatively placed configurable logic blocks (CLBs). They can be *hard* (of fixed area and shape) or *soft* (of fixed area but flexible shape). The goal of floorplanning is to determine a valid physical location for each macro and the dimensions and internal placement for each flexible macro. More formally stated:

Given : A set of macro blocks $M = \{m_1, m_2, ..., m_n\}$, with area $a_1, a_2, ..., a_n$ respectively.
Objective : Assign a width w_i and height h_i to each flexible block $m_i \in M$ and assign a physical location to each macro $m_i \in M$ such that the following constraints are satisfied:

1. the area of the mapped circuit is $\leq$ the area of the target FPGA,
2. the circuit delay is minimized, and
3. the circuit is 100 % routable.

2.1 Definitions

Partition Segment: A set of modules generated by bipartitioning is called a partition segment. Bipartitioning of a set generates two partition segments.

Segment Number: A unique number assigned to each *partition segment*.

Parent Partition Segment: A partition segment is *parent* to all modules it contains.

Cardinality of Partition Segment: The number of modules in the segment.

Area Slice: An area slice is a block of area on the FPGA generated by *cutlines*. Each *partition segment* is mapped to one and only one area slice, and each area slice has one and only one partition segment mapped to it.

Pseudo Module: A pseudo module is a module of size zero, introduced by the process of *terminal propagation*. A pseudo module is always contained in a *partition segment*.

Coordinates of Partition Segment: The coordinates of a *partition segment* are the coordinates of the area slice, to which it is mapped. They are represented by top left and bottom right coordinates of the area slice.

2.2 Successive Bipartitioning

Successive bipartitioning is the process of dividing the design into multiple segments, such that the cardinality of each segment is less than or equal to a constant, K. We start with the input design as the initial partition segment and assign it to the whole FPGA area. We continue to bipartition the segments, until the terminating condition (cardinality of each partition segment $\leq K$) is satisfied. With every bipartitioning of a segment, the area allocated to that segment is also divided into two area slices. Then, we allocate each new partition segment to an area slice.

Following describes the process of successive bipartitioning. A queue is maintained to keep track of partition segments which are candidates for further bipartitioning. A partition segment is a candidate for further bipartitioning if and only if the cardinality of the segment is $> K$. The queue is initially loaded with the original design. In one pass of successive bipartitioning, the head of the queue is bipartitioned. At the same time, the area of the target FPGA is sliced into two parts by a *vertical cut*, and each area slice is allocated to a segment obtained as a result of the bipartitioning. Out of these two partition segments, eligible candidates for further bipartitioning are loaded into the queue. The process stops when the queue is empty. It should be noted that vertical cuts of the target FPGA are followed by horizontal cuts and horizontal cuts are followed by vertical cuts in an alternating pattern. This process of iterative bipartitioning effectively forms a *partition tree* whose nodes are H or V indicating horizontal or vertical cuts respectively, and leaf cells of the tree are the partition segments with $\leq K$ modules. Each of these leaf cells has an area slice assigned to it on the FPGA. A possible order of cuts is shown in Figure 2 (A), and the corresponding partition tree is shown in Figure 2 (B). A two dimensional integer array keeps track of which segment numbers are mapped to which FPGA CLBs. Integer values at the (x, y) indices of this array, correspond to the segment numbers occupying the CLB slots on the FPGA. Since all leaf nodes of the partition tree are mapped to the array, the physical area of the FPGA is allocated by the tree nodes. Each of these nodes contains $\leq K$ macros. Hence, effectively mapping the groups of macros to localities on the FPGA.

We perform connectivity based clustering to form the initial partition for input to the FM bipartitioning algorithm. We extract two clusters out of the initial macro set, M. Each contains macros which are densely connected. Since initial clusters are further operated on by the partitioner to refine the cutset, execution speed takes precedence over quality during clustering. Therefore, a simple greedy method is used to obtain the clusters.

The FM partitioning algorithm, being iterative in nature, is highly dependent on the quality of the initial cut. Hence a good initial cut produced by clustering, remarkably improves the performance of the FM bipartitioner. Table 1 demonstrates cutset improvement for clustered input relative to random input for the FM bipartitioner.

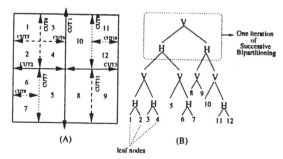

Fig. 2. *(A)-A possible order of cuts. (B)-Corresponding partition tree.*

	Cutset by FM Partitioner	
Design	Random	Clustered
CKT1	62	40
Mult16	79	45
MultRace	57	50
CLA	148	82
CPU	58	73

Table 1. *Cutset after first cut on input netlist.*

Terminal Propagation: The purpose of terminal propagation is to provide knowledge of inter-partition connections to modules in each partition [3]. This aids in reducing total interconnection length of the placed design. We begin with preprocessing of existing pseudo terminals. The pseudo terminals, which were unlocked during *clustering*, belong to one of the sub partitions generated by the *FM partitioner*. They are initially unlocked. During preprocessing, we first lock such pseudo modules. If a pseudo module belongs to a partition segment $p_i \in P$ and its previous lock position was (x, y), then given a horizontal cutline its new lock position is $(x, \frac{BRY(p_i)+TLY(p_i)}{2})$. ($BRY(p_i)$ and $TLY(p_i)$ return the bottom-right and top-left coordinates of the partition segment $p_i \in P$ respectively.) Similarly, given a vertical cutline its new lock position is $(\frac{BRX(p_i)+TLX(p_i)}{2}, y)$. After allocating the new lock positions to all unlocked pseudo modules, we lock the corresponding pseudo modules in every module *pair*, such that the relative lock position of the *pair* of modules is maintained.

After this preprocessing, we introduce a new pseudo module for each cut-net in both of the subpartitions. These new pseudo modules are located on the center of the cut-line. Hence, a new pair of pseudo modules belonging to two different partitions but locked to adjacent positions are introduced. Hereafter, when any pseudo module of this pair is moved to another location, the other pseudo module is also moved to maintain the same relative position. In this manner the pseudo modules form an intermediate connection that draws modules connected to these pseudo modules closer together (see figure 3).

In figure 3, the modules m_i and $m_j \in M$ are cut by the first vertical cut V_1. At this point, two pseudo modules (shown as circles) are introduced and locked to the the center of the cutline V_1. After the horizontal cut H_1, the module m_i is placed in the top partition. Because of this movement, the pseudo module in the partition of m_i moves to the center position on the previous vertical cut-line in the new partition of m_i. This causes the corresponding pseudo module (m_j) of the pair to be attracted to the top partition during partition H_2. In the absence of any bias from the pseudo module, the module m_j could go in the top or bottom partition made by horizontal cut H_2 But as a result of the pseudo modules, m_j has a bias to go to the top partition. This will reduce the cutset by one and m_j will remain close to m_i. For the same reason, the two modules will tend to remain in nearby partitions during subsequent cuts.

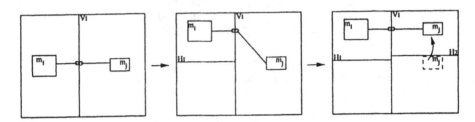

Fig. 3. *Terminal propagation : pseudo modules.*

2.3 Legal Placement

At the end of successive bipartitioning, each leaf node of the partitioning tree contains a maximum of K macros. Also, each leaf node is mapped on the target FPGA. In effect, it gives a locality on the FPGA chip corresponding to a leaf node, within which, macros contained in the leaf node should be placed. Legal placement is performed individually on each leaf node to decide the exact location and shape of macros contained in them. First, we decide relative placement of macros inside each partition. Then, we place hard macros. Finally, we process soft macros and place them. Processing of soft macros includes reshaping and deciding CLB placement inside the reshaped macro. Legal placement is also largely responsible for highly compact floorplans. This is achieved during reshaping and placement of soft macros. We place the macros maintaining actual rectilinear boundaries of the modules under consideration, figure 4.

Relative placement of Macro Blocks: To obtain relative placement of macros inside a partition, we perform an exhaustive search for the best relative placement (least total wire length). Since there are a maximum of K modules in each partition, there are $K!$ combinations to be explored in this search. Experimentally we found $K = 3$ to be a manageable value. K values beyond 3 require other methods for placement [4].

During macro block placement pseudo modules, introduced during *terminal propagation*, are still present at the boundaries of the partition. These give the direction from which each net enters or exits the partition. While deciding the relative placement of modules inside a partition, we account for wire length for connections among various macros as well as the pseudo modules in the partition. This takes care of both inter-partition and intra-partition connections. Hence an attempt to limit global minimum wire length is made.

To identify the best arrangement out of all possible permutations of macros inside a partition, we first compute the number of connections between macros within the boundary of the partition. Next, we calculate the number of connections between each module in the partition and the left boundary of the partition. Then the right boundary. Finally we exhaustively place the modules in a horizontal direction based on the number of connections.

Hard Macros: We performed *successive bipartitioning* and *relative placement* while considering module size only. No attention was paid to module dimensions. This may result in partitions that despite having enough area, are not wide enough or tall enough to accommodate a fixed $m_i \in M$. In case of such a discrepancy, we place the macro in free space of adequate dimensions nearest to the location allocated to it. Suppose the decided module location is (x, y). If this location can not accommodate the hard macro $m_i \in M$, then m_i is placed at a location $(x + \delta x, y + \delta y)$, where $|\delta x|$ and $|\delta y|$ are minimum, and location $(x + \delta x, y + \delta y)$ can accommodate the hard macro.

Soft Macros: We reshape soft macros to fit in the dimensions of the space allocated to their *leaf cell* in the partition tree. This is done by sequentially allocating available CLB slots on the FPGA to macros in the partition segment. This allocation is done in a snake like fashion (even columns start from the top row, odd from the bottom). The method of CLB assignment is such that we first fill the column of available space beginning from the first row of the column. After a column is filled the next successive column is filled starting from the last row up to the first row. The remaining CLBs of the macro start occupying the available CLB slots in the next column. This process is continued until all CLBs inside the macro are placed. If a high degree of compactness is desired, the next soft macro starts where the previous one ends. Hence the shape of the soft macros can be nonrectangular, which helps in placing the macros in the minimum possible space (figure 4). But if less compactness is desired, the next macro starts from the top row of the next column. In this case the shape of macros is always rectangular.

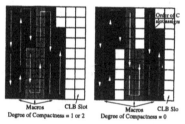

Fig. 4. *Legal Placement: Example nonrectangular shaped of macros.*

Simulated Annealing for Intra Macro Placement: CLBs inside each soft macro are placed using simulated annealing [10]. The constraints for placement are minimum total wire length and minimum longest wire. In this step both intra module connections and inter module connections are considered. Hence a global picture is in view while attempting wire length minimization.

2.4 Compaction

After legal placement, we have a valid floorplan. This floorplan has tightly placed modules inside each leaf cell of the partition tree, but the floorplan may have some unused CLBs surrounding the placed area inside leaf cells. This is illustrated in figure 5(A). During compaction, we work on the floorplan generated by the legal placement step and strive to eliminate such unused space from within the bounding box of the floorplanned layout. We are constrained by the fact that we cannot disturb the relative placement of the macros. We perform compaction by eliminating unutilized rows and columns of CLBs from the floorplan if any exist inside the boundary of the placed design. Partially empty rows and/or columns are left as they are. This ensures that relative placement obtained so far is respected. This step is carried out only if a high degree of compactness is desired. Figure 5 illustrates an example floorplan before and after compaction. After any compaction, we have our final floorplan.

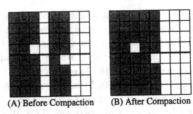

(A) Before Compaction   (B) After Compaction

Fig. 5. *Compaction example for high degree of compactness.*

3   Results and Analysis

All results reported here were obtained on a SUN-ULTRA 2300, running solaris 2.5 (with
the exception of the force directed floorplan of the CLA design, which was obtained on a
SUN-SPARC 5). Table 2 describes various benchmark circuits used to test the floorplanner
[8]. In this table, column 1 defines the benchmark circuit names. Columns 2 and 3 (labeled
#CLB and #Macro) define the number of CLBs and number of macro blocks used for each
of the bench mark circuits. Columns 4 and 5 (labeled Part and #CLB) define the target
FPGA part and the total number of CLBs available on the target FPGA part. Column 6
gives the percentage of CLB utilization by the benchmark circuit on the target FPGA part
$\left(\frac{column2}{column5}\right)$.

Design	#CLB	#Macro	Part	#CLB	%Util
Ckt1	180	9	4005	196	91.8%
Ckt2	200	10	4006	256	78.1%
Mult16	576	16	4020	784	73.46%
Mult16	576	16	4025	1024	56.25%
MultRacc	618	23	4020	784	78.82%
MultRacc	618	23	4025	1024	60.35%
CLA	607	128	4020	784	77.42%
CLA	607	128	4025	1024	59.27%
CPU	674	168	4020	784	85.87%
CPU	674	168	4025	1024	65.82%

Table 2. *Benchmarks circuits used for testing.*

Table 3 gives the CPU execution time required by our floorplanner [8], the Xilinx XACT
PPR floorplanner, and the force directed floorplanner [5] to floorplan the various benchmark
circuits. In this table columns 3 and 4 (labeled Macro) give the execution times for the Xilinx
PPR tool using macro based input circuits. In this table and subsequent tables, column 3
provides data for the default placement effort (=2) and column 4 provides data for the
maximum placement effort (=5). Columns 5 and 6 (labeled Flat) give the CPU time for
executing the Xilinx PPR tool on the flattened input circuits (circuits are flattened and
macro hierarchy is removed). In this table and subsequent tables, column 5 provides data
for the lower, default placement effort and column 6 provides data for the highest placement
effort. Column 7 (labeled FD) gives the execution time for the force directed floorplanner
[5], and Column 8 (labeled This Work) gives the execution time for our floorplanner.
   The data in table 3 indicates our floorplanner exhibits a fast execution time relative
to the other methods tested. This fast execution time by our floorplanner is possible be-

cause of the linear nature of the FM bipartitioning algorithm. It was shown that the FM bipartitioner can bipartition a hypergraph with n terminals in $O(n)$ time [1]. This will enable our floorplanner to handle very large circuits in an extremely short amount of time. Table 3 shows the time required by Xilinx increases monotonically as the size of the input design increases. On the other hand, our floorplanner is substantially faster when number of macros is larger. Hence when the average size of the macros is small compared to the design size our floorplanner is substantially faster. But when the design has fewer macros our floorplanner does not greatly outperform Xilinx PPR The force directed floorplanner takes the longest time to floorplan the larger designs. The most time consuming process in the force directed floorplanner is reshaping of the macro blocks. For circuits where the percentage of utilization of the target FPGA is low (reshaping is not performed) the force directed floorplanner is extremely fast. Our floorplanner is faster for circuits with a higher percentage utilization of the target FPGA.

Design	Part	CPU Time (sec)				FD	This Work
		XACT					
		Macro		Flat			
CKT1	4005	NA	NA	42	153	NA	8
CKT2	4006	17	27	45	217	11	12
Mult16	4020	123	174	195	1408	14	81
Mult16	4025	127	175	197	1483	14	81
MultRacc	4020	NA	NA	308	1428	NA	90
MultRacc	4025	143	170	302	1460	NA	90
CLA	4020	172	294	297	1458	NA	32
CLA	4025	158	273	291	1400	5hr	32
CPU	4020	247	563	412	2937	NA	36
CPU	4025	210	385	418	3035	NA	36

Table 3. *Execution times for various algorithms.*

Table 4 describes performance characteristics of the mapped circuits. It gives the maximum operating frequency for each of the benchmark circuits floorplanned by the various tools [8]. Maximum frequency (F) was calculated from the worst case delay (D) reported by the Xdelay tool from the Xilinx tool set $(F = \frac{1}{D})$. After importation into the Xilinx tool, the floorplanned designs were routed using the Xilinx PPR tool, and the routed designs were analyzed using the Xdelay timing analysis tool.

Columns 3 and 4 give the maximum operating frequency for the macro based benchmark circuits floorplanned by the Xilinx PPR tools. Columns 5 and 6 give the maximum operating frequency for the flattened benchmark circuits mapped by the Xilinx PPR tools. Column 7 gives the operating frequency for the benchmark circuits floorplanned by the force directed tool. Column 8 (labeled H) gives the operating frequency for the benchmark circuits floorplanned by our floorplanner with a high degree of compactness, and column 9 (labeled L) gives the operating frequency for the benchmark circuits floorplanned by our floorplanner with a low degree of compactness.

Performance is a critical metric for floorplanned circuits. A fast floorplanner that results in circuit maps with very low maximum operating frequency is not acceptable. Table 4 shows the operating frequency of our floorplanned designs have performance characteristics similar to those of the commercial tools (except mult16 on xc4025). The table also shows performance characteristics for our floorplanned designs are at least as good of those that were successfully floorplanned by the force directed floorplanner.

Design	Part	Frequency (MHz)					
		XACT			FD	This Work	
		Macro		Flat		H	L
CKT1	4005	NA	NA	5.8	6.0	NA	5.7	NA
CKT2	4006	4.5	4.7	5.1	5.7	4.8	4.9	4.7
M16	4020	13.5	13.7	13.7	13.7	13.6	13.8	13.4
M16	4025	13.6	13.8	13.4	12.9	13.2	13.4	13.3
MultR	4020	NA	NA	10.6	10.0	NA	10.7	10.3
MultR	4025	9.6	9.9	9.8	9.7	NA	10.1	9.5
CLA	4020	8.5	8.8	8.4	8.6	NA	8.54	8.4
CLA	4025	7.5	7.5	8.1	8.9	6.7	8.1	7.9
CPU	4020	6.6	6.7	7.8	7.8	NA	7.1	6.9
CPU	4025	5.5	6.9	7.1	7.9	NA	6.9	6.9

Table 4. *Maximum operating frequency for floorplanned benchmark circuits.*

Table 5 shows the bounding box of the placed designs for various runs of the benchmark circuits [8]. In this case the bounding box is described by the number of CLBs required to accommodate the floorplanned circuit. Obviously the flat designs require the fewest total CLBS since they are the most compact. Since inevitably macro based floorplans of circuits with fixed shaped macros cannot be 100% area efficient, the macro based floorplans require more CLB area and hence a larger bounding box area than flat designs. This is part of the cost of using a fast executing, macro based floorplanner. When high area utilization of the FPGA is required this becomes a factor and a tradeoff between execution time and area utilization may be required. Our floorplanner addresses this issue by reshaping the soft macros to reduce the overall area required by the mapped circuit. The effective reshaping and packing of macros by our floorplanner allowed it achieved feasible placement for all of the test runs.

Design	Part	Bounding Box					
		XACT			FD	This Work	
		Macro		Flat		H	L
CKT1	4005	NA	NA	182	182	NA	196	NA
CKT2	4006	240	240	200	200	240	210	240
M16	4020	675	675	506	506	576	625	672
M16	4025	702	702	506	506	576	625	672
MultR	4020	NA	NA	644	644	NA	729	784
MultR	4025	992	992	1024	1024	NA	729	864
CLA	4020	628	628	584	584	NA	625	784
CLA	4025	650	650	676	676	780	625	1024
CPU	4020	756	756	616	616	NA	702	784
CPU	4025	736	736	640	640	NA	702	870

Table 5. *Smallest bounding box area for floorplanned benchmark circuits.*

4 Conclusions

In this paper we have described the implementation of a large scale macro based floorplanner that exhibits fast execution when compared to industry standard Xilinx tools. Due to predesigned macros, the floorplanner need not address the problem of CLB level placement for all of the macros. Only soft macros, whose shapes are changed during the floorplanning process must be placed. In the majority of cases, the overall approach resulted in mapped circuits whose performance was similar to that of the circuits produced by the Xilinx tools.

The successive bipartitioning method is ideal for initial floorplanning of very large circuits. It quickly divides the circuit into sections that can be assigned to various areas on the FPGA. With the addition of clustering to improve the initial cutsets and terminal propagation to limit the total wire length the quality of the floorplan is greatly improved. In the future we expect that library based design approaches will become fairly common right from synthesis to physical mapping. Thus, floorplanning will play a significant role in both area estimation during synthesis and final mapping during late stages of the design. In our future work, we will integrate this floorplanning methodology with performance driven algorithms to enhance the performance of mapped designs [4]. We will use the successive bipartitioning method with clustering and terminal propagation in the early stages of floorplanning for very large designs. In the latter stages we incorporate performance enhancing methods to aid in the final assignment and placement of the macro blocks.

References

1. C. Fiduccia and R. Mattheyses, "A Linear time Heuristic for Improving Network Partitions", Proc. of DAC, pp.175-181, June 1982.
2. M. Breuer, "A class of min-cut placement algorithms", Proc. of DAC, pp. 284-290, 1980.
3. A. E. Dunlop and B. W. Kernighan, "A Procedure for Placement of Standard-Cell VLSI Circuits", IEEE Transactions on Computer-Aided Design, pp. 92-98, January 1985.
4. J. M. Emmert and D. K. Bhatia, "Fast Placement Using TABU Search for Total Wire Length Minimization", University of Cincinnati, ECECS Technical Report, 1998.
5. Jianzhong Shi, Akash Randhar and Dinesh Bhatia "Macro block based FPGA Floorplanning" Proc. of Intl. Conf. on VLSI Design, January 1997.
6. J. Shi and D. Bhatia, "Performance Driven Floorplanning for FPGA Based Designs" Proc. of ACM Symposium on Field Programmable Gate Arrays, February 1997.
7. A. Mathur and C.L. Liu, "Compression-Relaxation:A New Approach to Timing Driven Placement for Regular Architectures" IEEE Transactions on CAD of Integrated Circuits and Systems, pp. 597-608, June 1997.
8. A. Randhar, "Macro Based Floorplanning for FPGAs" Thesis: University of Cincinnati, December 1997.
9. C. Sechen "Chip Planning, Placement, and Global Routing of Macro/Custom Cell integrated Circuits Using Simulated Annealing" in Proc. of DAC, pp. 73-80, June 1988.
10. A. Subramaniam and D. Bhatia "Timing Driven Placement for Logic Cell Arrays" University of Cincinnati, ECECS Technical Report, 1994.
11. D.F. Wong and C.L. Liu "A new method for floorplan design" Proc. of DAC, pp. 101-107, 1986.
12. www.xilinx.com.

SRAM-Based FPGAs : A Fault Model for the Configurable Logic Modules

M.Renovell[1], J.M.Portal[1], J.Figueras[2], Y.Zorian[3]

[1]LIRMM-UM2 161 rue Ada
34392 Montpellier Cedex France
renovell@lirmm.fr
[2]UPC Diagonal, 647
Barcelona Spain
figueras@eel.upc.es
[3]Logic Vision Inc. 101 Meta Drive
San Jose CA 951 10 USA
zorian@lvision.com

Abstract. The configurable logic cells of the SRAM-based FPGA are mainly described as an interconnection of functional logic module. In this paper, we state that the stuck-at fault model can be used on such a description when multiplexer-based module are under consideration. To validate this assumption, the following step are realized. A test sequence is generated for the functional description assuming a stuck-at fault model of the input/output. The test sequence is applied, on a logic gate implementation assuming a stuck-at fault model of the gates nodes and then, on a transmission gate implementation assuming a short fault model. In the both case the fault coverage is 100%.

1. Introduction

Field Programmable Gate Arrays (FPGAs) are digital devices that can implement logic circuits by programming the required function [1,2]. One important class of FPGA is the SRAM-based FPGAs which can be easily reprogrammed any number of times. Testing of these SRAM-based FPGA chips has only recently been addressed [3-12]. In the recently published works, different FPGA test aspects are considered. As an example, Inoue and al. address the problem of testing look-up table in [5], Huang and al. focus address the problem of testing the configurable logic in [6], Stroud and al. focus on BIST for FPGA in [7] and Lombardi and al. focus on diagnosis in [8]. Following this approach, the authors have proposed a test procedure targeting the interconnect structure of SRAM-based FPGAs in [3], then another test procedure targeting the configurable logic cells in [12]. The work presented in this paper concerns the test of the configurable logic modules of SRAM-based FPGAs. The fundamental discussion of this paper concerns the definition of an adequate fault model for the multiplexer-based logic modules.

The paper is organized as follows. Section 2 presents and discusses the usual logic cell representations of commercially available SRAM-based FPGAs. It is pointed out that (i) usual representations mainly include multiplexer-based modules such as FPGA-mux and Look-Up-Table (LUT) and (ii) the detailed implementation of these modules is not given. It is consequently proposed to use the classical stuck-at fault model on the multiplexer inputs and output. In section 3, following the recommendation of section 2, a test sequence is generated using the stuck-at fault model on the inputs and output of FPGA-mux and mux-based LUT. In section 4, different logic gate implementations of the multiplexer are considered. For each possible logic gate implementation, the proposed test sequence is validated since the coverage for the stuck-at fault model on the logic gate implementation is 100%. In section 5, a transmission gate implementation of the multiplexer is considered. The proposed test sequence is again validated using SPICE since the coverage for an exhaustive list of shorts is 100%. Finally section 6 gives some concluding remarks.

2. The fault model

A typical SRAM-based architecture consist of an m*m array of cells with interconnect elements. Each logic cell is made of an interconnection of configurable logic modules. For example the Xilinx XC4000 family configurable logic cell [14] presents 12 multiplexers, 3 look up table and 2 flip-flops and can be connected to the interconnect elements through 12 operative inputs, a clock input, 4 outputs. The configuration inputs of a configurable logic cell are not usually represented, but they can be of around 60 for this Xilinx cell. That means that the total of operative inputs plus configuration inputs is around 70, making impossible an exhaustive test of the cell.

A classical deterministic test approach is consequently applied to the cell implying first the choice of adequate fault models and then the computation of deterministic test vectors targeting these fault models. The logic modules are represented at the functionnal level and appear as black boxes without any information on the actual logic or electrical implementation. To our knowledge, most of the commercially available FPGAs use this type of representation making difficult the choice of an adequate fault model.

In this section, we propose to use the classical stuck-at-0 and stuck-at-1 fault model on the functional representation called here the "FPGA representation". As a matter of fact, we consider stuck-at-0 and stuck-at-1 on all inputs and output of the functional modules. Obviously, the use of this fault model on such a representation must be validated. The principle of the validation includes 3 steps:
1. A sequence is generated for a given module using the stuck at fault model on the inputs and the outputs.

2. Different implementations of the given module with logic gates are considered. The above generated test sequence is applied to each implementation using the stuck-at fault model on the logic gates. A classical fault coverage is derived and discussed for each version of the module.
3. Another implementation of the given module with transmission gate is considered. The above generated test sequence is applied to this transistor level implementation using the short fault model on the transistors. A short fault coverage is derived with SPICE and discussed.

3. The test sequence

Most of the modules in a SRAM-based FPGA logic cell are built with classical multiplexers. As illustrated in figure 1, a LUT can be also built with a classical multiplexer with SRAM cells connected to the data inputs. That means that considering the FPGA-mux and the multiplexer-based LUTs, all the modules in the Xilinx XC4000, except the 2 flip-flops, are built with classical multiplexers. For this reason, we focus in this paper on a test sequence for a classical multiplexer using the stuck-at fault model on the multiplexer inputs and output.

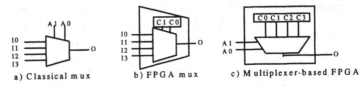

Fig. 1. Multiplexer-based modules

Test vectors						Detected faults	
I0	I1	I2	I3	A1	A0		
0	1	1	X	0	0	I0 stuck-1, A1 stuck-1, A0 stuck-1	Vector 1
0	X	1	0	1	0	I2 stuck-0, A1 stuck-0, A0 stuck-1	Vector 2
1	0	X	1	0	1	I1 stuck-1, A1 stuck-1, A0 stuck-0	Vector 3
X	0	0	1	1	1	I3 stuck-0, A1 stuck-0, A0 stuck-0	Vector 4
1	X	0	1	1	0	I2 stuck-1, A1 stuck-0, A0 stuck-1	Vector 5
1	0	0	X	0	0	I0 stuck-0, A1 stuck-1, A0 stuck-1	Vector 6
X	1	1	0	1	1	I3 stuck-1, A1 stuck-0, A0 stuck-0	Vector 7
0	1	X	0	0	1	I1 stuck-0, A1 stuck-1, A0 stuck-0	Vector 8

Table 1. Test sequence for the classical Multiplexer

Table 1 gives the test sequence generated by a commercial ATPG tool for the stuck-at-0/1 of the inputs and the output of the classical multiplexer of figure1.a. In the 8 vectors generated test sequence, we can note that each multiplexer address is activated twice allowing to test the stuck-at-0 and the stuck-at-1 of each data input. When the stuck-at of a data input is tested it is possible to test the stuck-at of the address bit by setting the adjacent data inputs to the opposite value. For the module representation, the fault coverage is noted:

$$FC_{module/IO\text{-}stuck\text{-}at}(\text{Classical-Multiplexer}) = 100\%$$

Note that the test sequence has been generated for a classical multiplexer and must be now adapted to a FPGA-mux and to a multiplexer-based LUT. Indeed, the sequence of table 1 includes some don't care values that are chosen in order to minimize the number of test configurations. The reconfiguration process of a FPGA is an extremely time consuming process and so the number of test configurations must absolutely be minimized.

Figure 2 illustrates how this sequence is applied to a multiplexer-based LUT. In fact, the completely specified sequence is split into two parts: the bits corresponding to the data inputs and the bits corresponding to the address inputs. The data inputs of a classical multiplexer correspond to the configuration bits of a multiplexer-based LUT. It appears that the don't care values of the configurations (data) bits can be adequately used in order to have only 2 test configurations. The first configuration (0110) corresponds to the XOR function and the second configuration (1001) corresponds to the XNOR function. For each test configuration, an exhaustive sequence (00, 01, 10, 11) must be applied on the operative (address) inputs.

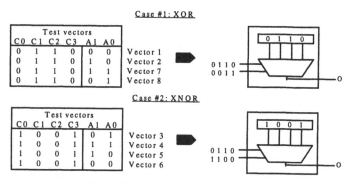

.**Fig. 2.** Test of the multiplexer based-LUT

For a FPGA-mux, the same approach can be used as illustrated in figure 3. In case of a FPGA-mux, we obtain 4 test configuration (00, 01, 10, 11).

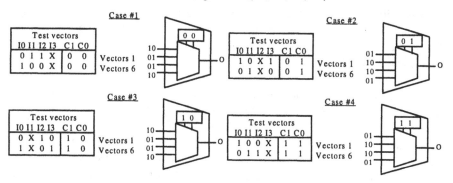

Fig. 3. Test of the FPGA-mux

For each test configuration, two vectors must be applied on the operative inputs. Here again, the don't care values can be chosen in order to obtain the XOR and XNOR vectors.

Note that the resulting completely specified test sequence is the same after adaptation to the FPGA-mux and to the multiplexer-based LUT. This sequence is given in table 2. It is absolutely obvious that the adaptation of the sequence by choosing the don't care values does not change the original fault coverage. Consequently, the corresponding fault coverage for the FPGA-mux and for the multiplexer-based LUT with regard to the stuck-at-0/1 of the module inputs and output is:

$$FC_{module/IO\text{-}stuck\text{-}at}(FPGA\text{-}mux) = FC_{module/IO\text{-}stuck\text{-}at}(multiplexer\text{-}based\ LUT) =$$
$$FC_{module/IO\text{-}stuck\text{-}at}(Classical\text{-}Multiplexer) = 100\%$$

| \multicolumn{6}{c}{Test vectors} |
I0	I1	I2	I3	A1	A0
0	1	1	0	0	0
0	1	1	0	1	0
1	0	0	1	0	1
1	0	0	1	1	1
1	0	0	1	1	0
1	0	0	1	0	0
0	1	1	0	1	1
0	1	1	0	0	1

Table 2. completely specified test sequence

4. Validation with logic gate implementation

The completely specified test sequence guarantees the detection of the module inputs and output stuck-at faults but no guaranty is given concerning the fault inside the module. For large modules, the ratio of internal to external nodes can be important, making the faults on internal nodes hard to detect by a sequence generated only for the external faults. In this section, the completely specified test sequence is validated with faults on internal nodes considering a large variety of logic implementation for the classical multiplexer. Basically, two types of logic implementation can be considered: the first one is called the '2 layers' implementation and the second one is called the 'tree' implementation.

For the 2 layers implementation, any path between a data input and the output includes 2 logic gates. Many implementation of this type can be found, but the most classical are the AND-OR, the OR-AND, the NAND-NAND and the NOR-NOR implementations. Here also two types of logic 2 layers implementations can be considered the first one without decoder and the second one with decoder. In the first case, the first layer gate have n+1 inputs for a n address bits multiplexer, and in the second case, the first layer gates have only 2 inputs whatever the number of address bits.

On the basis of the 2 layers implementation, the classical stuck-at-0/1 fault model can be used in relation with the logic gates and nodes. A fault simulation using a commercial fault simulator has consequently been performed to validate the efficiency of the completely specified test sequence. Table 3 shows that a 100% fault coverage is obtained whatever the implementation: AND-OR, OR-AND, NOR-NOR, NAND-NAND, with or without decoder. Whatever the 2 layer implementation, the properties of the multiplexer are such that we can write:

$$FC_{Logic-2layers/Istuck-at}(Classical-Multiplexer)=100\%$$

Multiplexer	AND-OR	OR-AND	NOR-NOR	NAND-NAND
With decoder	100 %	100 %	100 %	100 %
Without decoder	100 %	100 %	100 %	100 %

Table 3. Fault coverage for different '2 layers' implementations

Considering now another logic gate implementation called the tree implementation, a path between a data input and the output includes a number of gates proportional to the size (n address) of the module. In fact, in the tree implementation a multiplexer with n bits address input is build as a 'binary' tree of 2^n-1 multiplexers called elementary multiplexers with 1 bit address. Figure 6 illustrates the tree implementation of a 2 bit address multiplexer made of $2^3-1=7$ elementary multiplexers. In order to validate the efficiency of the completely specified test sequence on the tree implementation, we first analyze some properties of the sequence with regard to this particular structure.

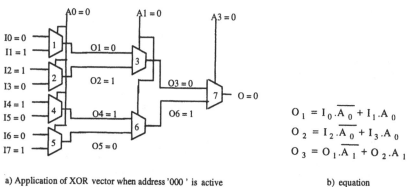

a) Application of XOR vector when address '000 ' is active

b) equation

$$O_1 = I_0.\overline{A_0} + I_1.A_0$$
$$O_2 = I_2.\overline{A_0} + I_3.A_0$$
$$O_3 = O_1.\overline{A_1} + O_2.A_1$$

Fig. 4. 'Tree' implementation

For a classical multiplexer with n address bits, the completely specified test sequence includes 2.2^n vectors. As an example in table 2, for a n=2 address bit multiplexer, we obtain $2.2^2=8$ test vectors. As another example for the 3 address bit multiplexer of figure 4, the test sequence activates address '000' and applies the XOR and XNOR vectors, then activates '001' and applies the XOR and XNOR vectors and so on until address '111'. Figure 4 illustrates the activation of address '000' and application of the XOR vectors. Due to a specific property of the multiplexer, we can observe that application of a XOR (01101001) and XNOR (10010110) vectors on the primary inputs implies that each elementary multiplexer receives the XOR (01) and XNOR (10) vectors. In a general manner, the XOR and XNOR function can be defined as an exclusive function Xf, composed with the same symetric properties then the XOR and XNOR ones, like illustrated below for an 8 bits function:

$$Xf\ (b,notb,notb,b,notb,b,b,notb)$$

For the elementary multiplexers of the first layer, this property can be easily demonstrated due to the multiple symmetries of the XOR and XNOR vectors. It is clear that each elementary module receive the (b, not b) vectors. It is also possible to demonstrate this property for the elementary multiplexers of layers 2 and 3 because of the intrinsic function of the multiplexer. According to the Xf function properties, we can substitute I0 for b, I1 for not-b, I2 for b, I3 for not-b into equation of figure 4 and we obtain:

$$\left.\begin{array}{l} O_1 = I_0.\overline{A_0} + I_1.A_0 \\ O_2 = I_2.\overline{A_0} + I_3.A_0 \\ O_3 = O_1.\overline{A_1} + O_2.A_1 \end{array}\right\} \implies \left.\begin{array}{l} O_1 = b.\overline{A_0} + \overline{b}.A_0 \\ O_2 = \overline{b}.\overline{A_0} + b.A_0 \end{array}\right\} \implies \begin{array}{l} O_1 = O_1 \\ O_2 = \overline{O_1} \\ O_3 = O_1.\overline{A_1} + \overline{O_1}.A_1 \end{array}$$

The previous equations demonstrate that the elementary multiplexers of the second layer also receives the XOR and the XNOR vectors. Of course, we can repeat this demonstration for any layer in the multiplexer and for any active address. Finally, when a completely specified test sequence of size n (2.2^n vectors) is applied to a classical multiplexer with n address bit, each elementary multiplexer receives a completely specified test sequence of size 1 (2.2^1 vectors). This important property has 2 consequences:

- Inter module consequence:
  Each elementary multiplexer receives the completely specified test sequence and consequently all the elementary multiplexer input and output stuck-at fault are detected. In other words, all the inter-elementary multiplexers stuck-at fault are detected:

$$FC_{Module/IO\text{-}stuck\text{-}at}(\text{Elementary-Multiplexer})=100\%$$

- Intra module consequence:
  Each elementary multiplexer receives the same specified test sequence and consequently the fault coverage of the intra-elementary multiplexers faults is the same for all the modules. That means that the coverage of the intra-elementary multiplexers fault for a n bit address multiplexer is equal to the intra-elementary multiplexers fault coverage of a single elementary multiplexer:

$$FC_{tree/Intra\text{-}fault}(\text{Classical-Multiplexer})= FC_{xxx/Intra\text{-}fault}(\text{Elementary-Multiplexer})$$

We assume now that the elementary multiplexers are implemented with 2 layers of logic gates. According to the intra-module property, the stuck-at fault coverage for a complete n address bit multiplexer is equal to the stuck-at fault coverage of an elementary multiplexer. The beginning of this section demonstrates that the stuck-at fault coverage for an elementary multiplexer implemented with 2 layers of logic gates is $FC_{Logic\text{-}2layers/stuck\text{-}at}(\text{Elementary-Multiplexer})=100\%$. Consequently, we can say that:

$$FC_{tree/stuck\text{-}at}(\text{Classical-Multiplexer})=FC_{Logic\text{-}2layers/stuck\text{-}at}(\text{Elementary-Multiplexer})=100\%$$

Finally, both the 2 layers and the tree implementations using logic gates exhibit a stuck-at fault coverage of 100%. This coverage is obtained with a sequence generated for inputs and output stuck-at fault. Obviously, this property is specific to the multiplexer module.

5. Validation with transmission gate implementation

The previous section validates the completely specified test sequence on classical multiplexers implemented with logic gates. However, the multiplexer are often implemented with transmission gate instead of logic gates. Taking into account that the implementation with transmission gates is in fact a tree implementation, we can use the intra-module property demonstrated in the previous section. In this case the fault coverage for a complete n address bit multiplexer is equal to the fault coverage of an elementary multiplexer implemented with transmission gates:

$$FC_{tree/Intra-fault}(\text{Classical-Multiplexer}) = FC_{trans-gate/Intra-fault}(\text{Elementary-Multiplexer})$$

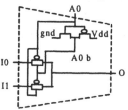

Fig. 5. Transmission gate based Mux 2-to-1

The test of transmission gate implementation must be performed with fault model related to transistors. We use here the short fault model. In the elementary multiplexer of figure 5, we consider the exhaustive list of shorts between electrical nodes. Of course, the completely specified test sequence is validated here by performing SPICE simulation on the transmission gate of figure 5. In order to have realistic electrical results, the SPICE simulations are performed with inverters that control the elementary multiplexer inputs or load the output.

Nodes	A0	A0 b	I0	I1	O	Vdd	gnd
A0	xx	3.82V/0V	0.10V/5V	3.48V/0V	1.02V/5V	5.00V/0V	0.00V/5V
A0 b	xx	xx	3.50V/0V	2.00V/5V	3.65V/0V	5.00V/0V	0.00V/5V
I0	xx	xx	xx	3.20V/0V	1.41V/5V	5.00V/0V	0.00V/5V
I1	xx	xx	xx	xx	1.41V/5V	5.00V/0V	0.00V/5V
O	xx	xx	xx	xx	xx	5.00V/0V	0.00V/5V
Vdd	xx	xx	xx	xx	xx	xx	xx
gnd	xx	xx	xx	xx	xx	xx	xx

Table 4. SPICE simulation results of the transmission gate shorts (*faulty / fault free voltage*)

Each inverters is designed in a very classical way trying to equilibrate the p- and n-channel transistors. This last point is very important because it determines the 'strength' of transistors fighting through a short.

Table 4 gives the result of the SPICE simulation for the exhaustive list of short in the elementary multiplexer of figure 5. The first value corresponds to the faulty circuit and the second one to the fault free one. As it could be expected, the shorts with the power supply VDD or the ground GND result in a non ambiguous faulty value 5.00V/0V or 0.00V/5V. On the other hand, shorts involving nodes different from VDD or GND result in ambiguous intermediate voltage such as 3.82V/0V, 0.10V/5V... In order to propose a realistic interpretation of the results, we consider that the logic threshold of the gates driven by the elementary multiplexer can vary from 2.00V to 3.00V. It must absolutely be noted that all the intermediate voltages are out of the uncertainty zone of 1V for the logic thresholds. This allows to declare the short detected in any case without any ambiguity.

Finally, we can say that the completely specified test sequence allow to detect 100% of the elementary multiplexer short faults. And using the intra-module property we can also say that the fault coverage for a classical n address bit multiplexer is:

$$FC_{tree/Intra-fault}(\text{Classical-Multiplexer}) = FC_{trans-gate/Short}(\text{Elementary-Multiplexer})$$

6. Discussion and conclusion

For commercially available SRAM-based FPGAs, the configurable logic cells are usually described as an interconnection of functional modules such as LUT or FPGA-multiplexers. The use of the stuck-at fault model an such a description could be quite controversial. In this paper we state that the stuck-at fault model can be used on such a description when multiplexer-based modules are under consideration.

In order to demonstrate the validity of using this stuck-at fault model in such a conditions, the following experiment is reported:
1. A test sequence is generated for a classical multiplexer using the stuck-at fault model on the inputs and output.
2. The don't care values of the sequence are specified taking into account the minimization specificity of SRAM-based FPGAs.
3. The completely specified test sequence is applied to the classical multiplexer, for different implementations with 2 layers of logic gates. In any case, the stuck-at fault coverage for internal nodes is 100% validating the proposed squence.
4. The completely specified test sequence is then applied to the classical multiplexer for an implementation with a binary tree of logic gates. In this case, the stuck-at fault coverage for internal nodes is shown to be 100% validating again the proposed sequence.
5. The completely specified test sequence is finally applied to the classical multiplexer for an implementation with transmission gates. The short fault

coverage for internal nodes is shown to be 100% validating once again the proposed sequence.

This experiment covers a large set of possible implementations of the classical multiplexer proving that the generated sequence is efficient in detecting internal fault whatever the actual implementation. The stuck-at fault model can consequently be efficiently used on the inputs and outputs of multiplexer-based FPGA modules such as FPGA-multiplexers or multiplexer-based LUT. Note that FPGA-multiplexers or multiplexer-based LUT represent the majority of the modules in the logic cells of SRAM-based FPGAs. Consequently, classical fault simulators or test pattern generators can be run efficiently on the usual description of FPGA logic cells with the stuck-at fault model.

7. Reference

[1] S.D.Brown, R.J.Francis, J.Rose, S.G.Vranesic: Field Programmable Gate Arrays, Kluwer Academic Publishers, 1992.

[2] S.M.Trimberger (ed): Field Programmable Gate Array Technology, Kluwer Academic Publishers, 1994.

[3] M. Renovell, J.M.Portal, J. Figueras and Y. Zorian: Testing the Interconnect of RAM-Based FPGAs, IEEE Design & Test of Computer, Vol.15, n°1, Jan-March 1998, pp. 45-50.

[4] C. Jordan and W.P. Marnane: Incoming Inspection of FPGAs, Proc. of IEEE European Test Conference, pp. 371-377, 1993.

[5] T. Inoue, H. Fujiwara, H. Michinishi, T. Yokohira and T. Okamoto: Universal Test Complexity of Field-Programmable Gate Arrays, 4th Asian Test Symposium, pp. 259-265, Bangalora, November 1995, India.

[6] W.K. Huang and F. Lombardi: An Approach for Testing Programmable/Configurable Field Programmable Gate Arrays, 14th IEEE VLSI Test Symposium, pp. 450-455, Princeton, NJ, USA, May 1996.

[7] C. Stroud, P. Chen, S. Konala, M. Abramovici: Evaluation of FPGA Ressources for Built-In Self Test of Programmable Logic Blocks, Proc. of 4th ACM/SIGDA Int. Symposium on FPGAs, pp. 107-113, 1996.

[8] F. Lombardi, D. Ashen, X.T. Chen, W.K. Huang: Diagnosing Programmable Interconnect Systems for FPGAs, FPGA'96, pp. 100-106, Monterey CA, USA, 1996.

[9] W.K. Huang, F.J. Meyer, N. Park and F. Lombardi: Testing Memory Modules in SRAM-based Configurable FPGAs, IEEE International Workshop on Memory Technology, Design and Test, August, 1997.

[10] R.O. Durate and M. Nicolaidis: A test methodology applied to cellular logic programmable gate arrays, in R.W. Hartenstein and M.Z. Servit (eds), Lecture Notes in Computer Science, Field Programmable Logic, Springer-Verlag, pp. 11-22, 1994.

[11] T. Liu, W.K. Huang, F. Lombardi: Testing of Uncustomized Segmented Channel FPGAs, Proc. of ACM Int. Symp. on FPGAs, pp. 125-131, 1995.

[12] .M. Renovell, J.M. Portal, J. Figueras and Y. Zorian: Testing the Configurable Logic of RAM-based FPGA, IEEE Int. Conf. on Design, Automation and Test in Europe, pp.82-88, Paris, France, Feb 1998.

[13] Xilinx: The Programmable Logic Data Book , San Jose, USA, 1994.

Reconfigurable Hardware as Shared Resource in Multipurpose Computers*

Gunter Haug and Wolfgang Rosenstiel

Universität Tübingen
Sand 13
Tübingen/Germany

Abstract One of the intended applications of the Xilinx XC6000 family is to be used as reconfigurable coprocessor to accelerate software. This approach has failed so far because of the lack of software support. First, there was no programming method similar to conventional coding. Second, there was no run time environment integrated in the operating system. Both will be presented in this paper.

1   Introduction

Approaches to use FPGAs as reconfigurable coprocessors so far always suffered from two problems. First, the hardware required for communication with the host processor occupied an unacceptable large part of the resources available on the FPGA and second, this communication was so slow that the gained acceleration came to naught. The new Xilinx XC6200 family [1] aims to solve both of these problems.

The chips are accessed via an SRAM interface, i. e. the host sees them as part of its memory. Besides the configuration bits, which determine logical behaviour and routing, all internal flip-flops of the XC6200 are accessible for reading as well as for writing. This ensures a high performance, since a 32 bit input or output value can be exchanged between the host and the coprocessor by a single load or store operation. Furthermore, the host can switch the coprocessor's clock on and off without glitches by an internal coprocessor register.

In order to make use of the hardware features of the new Xilinx chip series in workstations and PCs easily, a system is presented which synthesizes hardware out of threads coded in C. The threads are part of the C-program running on the host processor. In this paper this system will be referred as the *Hardware Thread System* (HTS). The run time environment required will be called the *Universal Coprocessor System* (UCS).

Hardware software partitioning is accomplished by the user; he has to mark threads he wants to have synthesized (hts_fork ...). This method has two advantages: The algorithm can be tested fully as software in advance before

* This work was supported in part with funds of the Deutsche Forschungsgemeinschaft under reference number 322 1040 within the priority program "Design and design methodology of embedded systems"

being synthesized. Moreover the programmer always knows which parts of his program he wants to go into hardware. Therefore, he can code these parts in a "synthesis fiendly" manner. Figure 1 shows a diagram of the design flow.

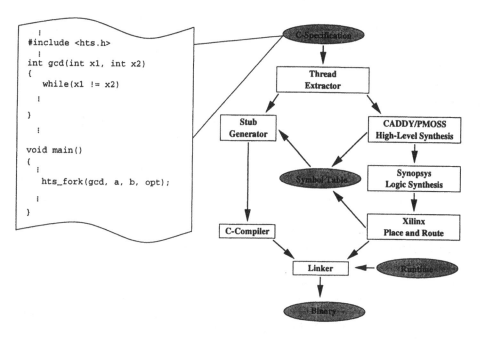

Figure 1. Design Flow

Like all other resources of a computer system, the reconfigurable coprocessor is controlled by the kernel. Simply speaking, when a program is started from disk, the kernel takes the configuration data out of the binary file and configures the coprocessor. When the scheduler of the kernel decides to take a process using the coprocessor off the main processor, a calculation which may be running on the coprocessor can continue as long as no other process wants to make use of this resource. If another process wants to engage the coprocessor, its clock is switched off by the kernel and the state of all its flip-flops is stored in the buffer RAM. Then the state which was saved with the last context switch, as well as the required configuration information, is transferred from the buffer RAM to the coprocessor. Finally, the clock is switched on again.

The remainder of this paper will first describe the hardware as well as the compile time and run time software. Then, a small example followed by a conclusion is given.

2 Hardware

For the hardware platform, a specially designed PCI card is used. Besides the reconfigurable coprocessor XC6216 (XC6264 as soon as available), it consists of the controller (XC4013e) and buffer/data RAM. The block diagram of the card is shown in figure 2. The RAM of the card can be mapped into the memory address space of the host; nontheless the controller can transfer data between reconfigurable coprocessor and buffer RAM without disturbing the host.

Besides the coupling to PCI bus, the controller also handles the design and state data. The PCI part and the coprocessor part of the controller are decoupled by a FIFO; they run at different clocks (see below).

In order to undertake a context switch, the controller first stores the state of all flip-flops of the interrupted process in the buffer RAM. Then the con-

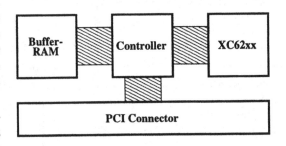

Figure 2. Hardware

figuration and state data of the process to be set on again are transferred from the RAM into the coprocessor. This procedure is only triggered by the kernel; no further software support is required. If a program is started which wants to make use of the coprocessor, the kernel has to write the program's configuration data into the buffer RAM. Meanwhile a possibly on-going computation on the coprocessor can continue. After the data has been transferred, the running process can be superseded by the new one.

The buffered configuration data is of variable length and is stored in the RAM of the card. To trigger a replacement procedure, the software on the host (kernel) only has to write the source and destination addresses of the two datasets in the appropriate registers of the controller. The length of the configuration data is also stored in the RAM. The length of state data is fixed. The number of configurations that can be buffered in the RAM of the card, i. e. the number of processes which can share the coprocessor, depends on the designs; even with fully used XC6216, more then ten configurations fit into the buffer RAM. The time the controller needs for a context switch also depends on the length of the configuration data. It is in the range of a few ten micro seconds.

Finally, the controller assumes the task of a programmable clock generator, which delivers two clock signals to the coprocessor. The first one, clk_i, is the PCI clock divided by 1, 2, 3 or 4. The second one, clk_p, is adjustable between 200 kHz and 50 MHz in 256 steps. clk_i and clk_p are controller internal signals. Either of them can be connected to the GClk pin of the coprocessor via a multiplexer. The other one (i. e. the one not connected to GClk) is connected to G1 pin of the coprocessor. The coprocessor part of the controller is always clocked by the signal connected to the GClk pin.

3 Software

The software is devided into two parts: Tools which generate the binary out of the source files at compile time (see Figure 1), and the run time environment which allows the execution of the binaries. Both parts will be described in the following sections.

3.1 Run Time Software (UCS)

The run time software is a slightly extended Linux system. Linux was chosen for many reasons. The most important are: It is free and the sources are well documented. It is ported to many platforms (although currently UCS only runs on Intel systems). Last but not least, it is UNIX-like.

The extensions include: four new system calls to add, remove and manage configurations; a modified scheduler to handle the coprocessor; and a new device to map the coprocessor's flip-flops into a Linux process's address space. The process list data structure has been extended by one field in order to determine whether a process uses the coprocessor, and if it does, where to find the configuration. Finally, a new structure, the configuration list, has been added.

The new system call `ucp_add_config` loads a configuration into the buffer RAM. Therefore, a pointer to a data structure in the main memory of the host that contains the length of the configuration data, a pointer to the configuration data itself, clock generator settings and coprocessor internal register settings are required as arguments. The return value of the call is an identification tag (*config-ID*). The added system calls `ucp_rm_config` and `ucp_run_config` both need a config-ID as an argument. `ucp_rm_config` deletes a configuration from the buffer RAM while `ucp_run_config` executes a configuration already present in the buffer RAM on the coprocessor. The last system call added is `ucp_clk`. It is used to switch the clock of the coprocessor on and off.

The scheduler has been extended to keep track of each process's use of the coprocessor. By looking into a process's process list entry the scheduler knows whether a process uses the coprocessor, and if so, which configuration the process wants to run. If the scheduler decides to run a process using the coprocessor, it stops the coprocessor by switching off the clocks. Then the state of the configuration running so far is written to the buffer RAM. The new configuration data, as well as the fomerly saved state are transferred to the coprocessor[1]. Finally, the clock generator and internal coprocessor data is written and the clocks are switched on again — the context switch is, as far as the coprocessor is concerned, complete.

---

[1] The reload procedure for the state data is slightly more complicated than described since the clock may not be turned off while writing a flip-flop. Therefore, the coprocessor's flip-flops are first configuered with the protect bit set. The clock is turned on and the state data is written. Although the circuit is running, nothing changes, because all flip-flops are protected. Then the clock is switched off again and the coprocessor is reconfigured with the protect bits reset.

Furthermore, a new device has been added: /dev/ucp. It is a memory device similar to /dev/mem (or /dev/fb under Solaris), wherein the state bits and internal registers of the coprocessor can be found. Via the system call mmap, a process is able to map this memory into its address space. A process is only allowed to open this device if it has registered itself as a coprocessor user by calling ucp_add_config and ucp_run_config before.

Programs not using the coprocessor, i. e. normal Linux programs run on the modified system without changes. The extension of the Linux operating system is not bound to the Hardware Thread System described in the next section. It is possible, for instance, to code the hardware functions in high level VHDL. A specification on RT-level can also be considered to achieve high performance and a good gain of the hardware resources. In this case, the data transfer and synchronisation between host and coprocessor has to be implemented by the user. Another possibility is to replace HTS by a system where the complete specification is written in Java. Besides the increasing popularity of Java, the advantage is that threads are a integral part of the Java language definition.

3.2 Code Generating Tools (HTS)

Existing tools were used as much as possible. First, this could be done in the case of the C compiler, where GNU-gcc is used. Second, the whole synthesis is accomplished by readily available, partially commercial tools. The design flow is described in detail in the following; it is also shown in Figure 1.

The Thread Extractor finds functions, which are arguments of hts_fork calls, in order to feed them to synthesis. The hts_fork and hts_join calls are replaced by handles which are further processed by the Stub Generator. As far as it is statically possible, the Thread Extractor recognizes functions which are called within hardware functions. Cases where this is not decidable during compile time are rejected. Function hierarchies are supported by the high level synthesis tool used. If more than one instance of a function is forked concurrently, it is also noticed by the Thread Extractor. Each instance is synthesized with a uniquified name. This means, many threads of one function actually run in parallel on the coprocessor. The handles for the Stub Generator, of course, have to be set according to the unique names. Actually, the Thread Extractor is a C parser. Here, it was possible to resort to existing software of the DTS (*Distributed Thread System*, [8], [9]).

The extracted functions are fed to the high level synthesis system PMOSS [4], [5] or CADDY [10]. An RT level VHDL description is the result of the high level synthesis. In excess of the variables specified in the source text (including parameters), two registers are inserted: a result register for the return value and a ready bit. The ready bit is also the reset for the controller of the hardware function. Out of this RT level VHDL description, the Synopsys Design Compiler synthesizes an EDIF netlist which is passed to the XACT6000, the Xilinx place and route tool. Besides the configuration data, which is fed to the linker as ELF object file, XACT6000 produces a symbol table file where the addresses of the registers of the design within the coprocessor's address space can be found.

Out of the source text with the handles, the Stub Generator produces a program that can be compiled. Therefore, the handles are replaced with calls to small generated functions, the *stubs*. A stub, which is called instead of a hts_fork, sets the ready bit to reset the controller of the hardware function, writes the arguments passed to the registers of the coprocessor, and finally resets the ready bit to release the controller; the calculation starts. The addresses of the registers are known out of the symbol table produced by the place and route tool. The stub called instead of hts_join is a function that waits actively until the ready bit of the synthesized circuit is set. Then it reads out the result register of the circuit and returns that value.

The source program with the stubs inserted is compiled and linked together with the configuration data for the coprocessor and the startup code to an ELF binary.

When a program is run, the startup code loads the configuration data into the buffer RAM by calling ucp_add_config, and than calls ucp_run_config to bring this configuration into the coprocessor. After that, the device /dev/ucp is opened and mapped into the address space of the process. Now main can be called as usual. Before the process is teminated, the configuration is removed from the buffer RAM by calling ucp_rm_config.

4   Related Work

The idea to use FPGAs as coprocessor is almost as old as FPGAs, many publications on that issue can be found. In the following the difference between the approach presented in this paper and some of the others is described.

The PRISM-II system [6] to some extent is similar to the system presented here. The major differences are the hardware used and the run time software. The PRISM-II hardware platform is not an extended multipurpose computer (PC or workstation) as in our system but a board with processor and FPGAs. Therefore no operating system is required whereas the integration of the coprocessor into the operating system (UCS) is one of the main features of the system presented in this paper.

The PRISM-II system [6] and many other approaches [3] use the Xilinx XC4000 family FPGAs. Systems based on this chips always suffer from two disadvantages: reconfiguration is slow and data transfer has to be done via I/O pins of the FPGA. With the XC6200 FPGAs used in the system presented here reconfiguration is very fast and all registers on the chip can be accessed directly via the SRAM-like interface of the XC6200.

SPACE 2 [2] is a system based on the Xilinx XC6200 family. In contrast to the system presented in this paper, SPACE 2 is large and expensive. It is not integrated in the scheduler of the operating system running on the host machine, so no task switching is supported. Finally the code genaration is completely different. While in case of the HTS presented here, the ease of use for the programmer is the major goal, performance is it in case of the SPACE 2 system. Therefore instead of a high level language structural VHDL, Lola [7] or even schematic entry is used.

5 Results

The presented system suffers from the early development state of the Xilinx place and route software. To make routing possible, many placement modifications by hand are required. Even after such modifications, the routing results of the tool are not sufficient. Considering the improvements industry made with place and route tools for other chips (e. g. the Xilinx XC4000), it can be expected that XACT6000 will reach an acceptable state reasonably soon.

The problems of the place and route software so far restrict HTS/UCS to smaller examples. But even with a small algorithm the possible accelaration can be demonstrated. As example, the calculation of the greatest common divisor (GCD) utilizing the Euklidian Algorithm is taken.

The C specification of the algorithm shown in Figure 3 has been fed to gcc (with -O2 on Linux), as well as to CADDY. The assembler code which is the result of gcc is shown in Figure 4, while the circuit generated by CADDY is shown in Figure 5.

```
int gcd(int x1, int x2)
{
  while(x1 != x2)
    if(x1 > x2)
      x1 -= x2;
    else
      x2 -= x1;
  return (x1);
}
```

Figure 3. gcd.c

The assembly listing only shows the loop. Building of the stack frame, transfer of arguments to registers, and so on are not shown. It is easy to see that x1 and x2 are stored in eax and edx. The comments have been added by hand. A loop consists of five instructions. Such a small loop will fit entirely into cache. Considering the percentage of branch instructions, an average execution time of 1.5 clock cycles per instruction

```
.L1:
cmpl %edx,%eax   ; compare operands
je .L3           ; equal: that's it
jle .L2          ; less: else branch
subl %edx,%eax   ; then branch
jmp .L1          ; once again
.L2:
subl %eax,%edx   ; else branch
jmp .L1          ; once again
.L3:
```

Figure 4. gcd.s

can be assumed on a Intel Pentium CPU. Therefore the execution time for the whole loop on a 200 MHz engine will be approximately 40 ns. The number of loops required for a whole calculation is, of course, data dependant. To make comparison with the coprocessor version possible, it is assumed to be 10000 (the GCD of 10000 and 1 was calculated in the experiments). Neglecting the overhead for function calls, this results in 2500 calculations per second on a Pentium-200 platform.

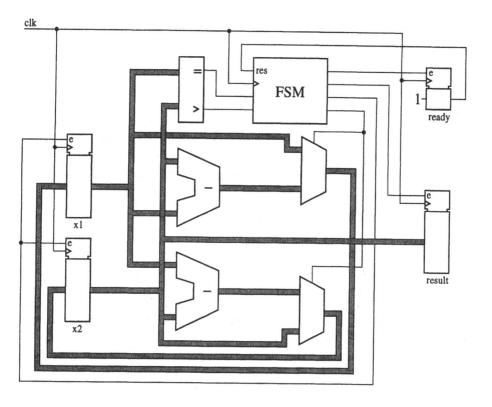

Figure 5. Cicuit synthesized by CADDY

Figure 5 shows the circuit synthesized by CADDY as a block diagram. Besides the functionality of the GCD, the figure demonstrates the working method of the HTS.

The circuit has no ports but the clock. All registers are read and written via the XC6200 processor interface. The stub called instead of the hts_fork writes its arguments to the registers x1 and x2. Then the ready bit is set to zero, releasing the controller (FSM) from the reset state. The controller sets the ready bit to one when the calculation is finished. By doing so, the controller puts itself into the reset state; none of the registers will change anymore. The stub inserted for the hts_join waits until the ready bit changes to one, reads the register labeled "result" and returns this value to its caller. The controller is blocked until the next calculation is started.

CADDY is adjustable to synthesize either for better performance or for smaller area. With priority to speed rather than to area, CADDY synthesizes a GCD circuit that has a controller with only one state for each loop iteration. The execution time for the loop is the clock cycle time. This is achieved by concurrently calculating both differences while doing the comparison of the operands in parallel (see Figure 5).

To determine the area the circuit requires on the coprocessor a look on the components has to be taken. The host can only access the registers of a circuit as one word in its memory if they are arranged as "tall towers", e. g. the logic blocks representing the bits are situated one above the other. For this, it is also useful to give functional units and multiplexers the shape of upright rectangles. The height (in logic blocks) of the rectangles is the word length. The width of the circuit (in logic blocks) is constant. In case of the GCD it is 18 logic blocks including the controller, which is quite small. Another possibility is to leave gaps between the cells of the registers. This makes routing easier. Using this technique, the functional units can be placed closer together. For the GCD a width of ten logic blocks including the controller for one instance is achieved. The XC6216 has an array that is 64 logic blocks high and 64 logic blocks wide. With a word length of 32 bit, six instances of the GCD can be placed in the coprocessor; with 16 bit, twelve instances fit into the chip. This does not depend on whether gaps ar left or not.

The possible clock frequency also depends on the word length. With 16 bit the circuit runs at 33 MHz, with 32 bit, only at 16 MHz. Under the same assumptions as above and with a fully loaded coprocessor, 9600 32 bit calculations per second are achieved. With 16 bit word length, even 38400 calculations per second are reached.

These theoretical results have been compared to measured execution times. In reality the software version was slightly faster than expected; the hardware vesion met the predictions almost exactly. The results demonstrate that the system can gain very high acceleration for applications which are easy to parallelize (factor 4 to 16 in the example). Many of these applications, such as image processing, only require word lengths of 16 or 8 bit improving the accelaration that can be expected even more.

6   Conclusion

In this paper, a complete system accelerating software with reconfigurable logic has been presented. A look has been taken at the hardware, at the extensions of a Linux system to administrate the hardware, and at the front end for programming. With a small example, it has been demonstrated that for certain applications, a great accelaration can be achieved.

At this point, HTS/UCS is in an experimental state. It is necessary to enlarge the class of applications that are accelerated. Therefore, two extensions of HTS have to be implemented.

First, it should be possible to reconfigure the coprocessor dynamically during process execution. Currently all synthesized functions are loaded into the coprocessor by the startup code. In a later version, functions which are called in parallel are grouped together. These groups are synthesized; the resulting configuration data sets are only loaded to the buffer RAM by the startup code. The stub belonging to a function tests whether the coprocessor is already configured appropriately. If not, the right data is brought to the coprocessor by a ucp_run_config call.

Second, global variables should be supported. That means that the main processor as well as the coprocesser must be able to access these variables. This can be done by placing these shared variables in the RAM of the coprocessor card. The controller of the card functions as an arbiter. Appropriate hardware has to be synthesized for the coprocessor. Applications like image processing will benefit from this extension: The image can be written into a global array by the main processor. While it is being processed by the coprocessor, the main processor can accomplish other jobs.

The presented system supports debugging in a very easy way: As the synthesis is done out of a C specification, the code can be verified completely in software before it is synthesized. It would also be possible to use a HW/SW codebugging approach as described in [11].

References

1. Xilinx Inc.: XC6200 Field Programmable Gate Arrays Datasheet, San Jose CA, USA Oktober 1996
2. B. Gunther: Space 2 as a Reconfigurable Stream Processor. 4th Ann. Australian Conf. on Parallel an Real-Time Systems 1997
3. D. Galloway: Transmogrifier C Hardware Description Language and Compiler for FPGAs. Proceedings of 3nd FCCM, Napa, April 1995
4. J. Gerlach, H.-J. Eikerling, W. Hardt, W. Rosenstiel: Von C nach Hardware: ein integratives Entwurfskonzept. 1. GI/ITG/GMM Workshop Allgemeine Methodik von Entwurfsprozessen, Paderborn, März, 1996
5. J. Gerlach, W. Rosenstiel: PMOSS: Eine integrative Umgebung zum HW/SW-Entwurf. GI/ITG/GMM Fachgruppentreffen 3.5.7/5.2.2/5.7, Paderborn, Juni, 1996
6. M. Wazlowski, P. Athanas, H. Silverman et al: PRISM-II Compiler and Architecture. Proceedings of 2nd FCCM, Napa, April 1994
7. N. Wirth: Lola System Notes. Technical Report No. 236, Institute for Comuter Systems, ETH Zürich, June 1995
8. T. Bubeck: Eine Systemumgebung zum verteilten funktionalen Rechnen. Interner Bericht WSI 93-8, Wilhelm-Schickard-Institut der Universität Tübingen, 1993
9. T. Bubeck, W. Rosenstiel: Verteiltes Rechnen mit DTS (Distributed Thread System). In Marc Aguilar, Editor, Proceedings of the '94 SIGPAR-Workshop on Parallel and Distributed Computing, p. 65-68, Fribourg, Switzerland, 1994
10. P. Gutberlet, W. Rosenstiel: Interface Specification and Synthesis for VHDL Processes. Proceedings of the 2nd EURODAC, 1993
11. G. Koch, U. Kebschull, W. Rosenstiel: Co-Emulation and Debugging of HW/SW-Systems. ISSS '97, Belgium-Antwerp, September 97

Reconfigurable Computer Array: The Bridge between High Speed Sensors and Low Speed Computing

Scott H. Robinson[1], Michael P. Caffrey[2], and Mark E. Dunham[1]

[1]Los Alamos National Laboratory, Space Engineering, NIS-4 MS-D448,
Los Alamos, New Mexico USA 87545
{shr, mdunham}@lanl.gov
[2]Los Alamos National Laboratory, Space Data Systems, NIS-3 MS-D440,
Los Alamos, New Mexico USA 87545
mpc@lanl.gov

Abstract. A universal limitation of RF and imaging front-end sensors is that they easily produce data at a higher rate than any general-purpose computer can continuously handle. Therefore, Los Alamos National Laboratory has developed a custom Reconfigurable Computing Array board to support a large variety of processing applications including wideband RF signals, LIDAR and multi-dimensional imaging. The boards design exploits three key features to achieve its performance. First, there are large banks of fast memory dedicated to each reconfigurable processor and also shared between pairs of processors. Second, there are dedicated data paths between processors, and from a processor to flexible I/O interfaces. Third, the design provides the ability to link multiple boards into a serial and/or parallel structure.

1   Computational Challenges

In modern digital remote sensing applications the need to continuously process enormous amounts of data is always present. Front-end sensors can easily generate a 100 megabytes per second or more of raw data. The ultimate goal is to reduce massive amounts of raw data down to answers that are useful and can be reasonably understood, stored or transmitted. Our challenge is to develop systems that continuously process data efficiently, are flexible to changing requirements and do it all at a reasonable system cost.

Los Alamos National Laboratory[1] (LANL) has a number of these types of computational challenges. As part of the Laboratory's research into lightning, RF propagation and astrophysics, there is a strong requirement for processing wideband RF data. Analog-to-digital converters running at rates of 100M samples per second and more support this work. Currently, snapshots of RF data are recorded, relayed back to the

---

[1] The University of California operates Los Alamos National Laboratory for the United States Department of Energy under contract W-7405-ENG-36. Publication LA-UR-98-2510.

laboratory and analyzed. Before system performance can improve significantly, the analysis of this data must move closer to the sensor and occur continuously.

Another effort with a great need for real-time signal processing at the Laboratory is a large and ongoing LIght Detection And Ranging (LIDAR) research program. The needs include: determining the range to a target when using a laser and detector operating from a moving platform; data filtering and signal averaging to increase the signal-to-noise ratio; return pulse integration and pattern recognition. Current upgrades will increase the laser-firing rate, add multiple laser frequencies, incorporate pointing information and expand the catalog of recognized return signals. In order for this work to continue, LANL must improve the signal processing hardware of the system beyond what is currently available from general purpose computers and DSP's.

Multi-dimensional imaging is another area of intense research at the Laboratory and has its own computational challenges. Multi-dimensional image data are traditionally collected in the form of datacubes with spatial, spectral and/or time information on each axis. Analysis of these datacubes requires the application of complex image processing algorithms. Again, generally available hardware is incapable of providing the data throughput required by these systems.

All of these efforts put severe demands on the signal processing hardware and data throughput requirements. For proper system operation it is critical that signal processing takes place continuously at the full rate of the incoming data. However, these problems share common characteristics that can be mutually addressed. A key to processing is the fact that the data has dependencies that are block oriented. Although these blocks can be large, they are relatively independent of each other. This allows pipelined operations to be performed on blocks of data either in serial or parallel pipe configurations. Related to this is the system characteristic that data latency is not critical. Therefore, additional pipeline stages can be added to allow throughput to increase or to provide other system functionality without affecting overall computational performance.

2   LANL Developed RCA Board

To meet the signal processing challenge of the systems described, the Space Engineering group and several Space Science groups at the Laboratory have joined together to develop a Reconfigurable Computer Array (RCA) board. The RCA-2 board bridges the gap between high speed front-end ASIC's and low speed back-end general purpose computers. The board was specifically designed to process large amounts of data with block oriented dependencies at high throughput rates. Additionally, the RCA-2 board can be reconfigured to meet the needs of individual systems and can deliver the required computational horsepower at a reasonable cost.

The goals of the project were to design a board that: 1) could support continuous data throughput of at least 100 Mbytes per second; 2) could provide the ability to link multiple boards together into a serial and/or parallel processing structure; and 3) could be configured to a wide range of signal and image processing requirements.

These goals translated into three key design features. First, around each reconfigurable processor the design provides a large amount of fast memory to support block oriented processing without resource contentions. Second, the design provides dedicated data paths between processors, and from a processor to a flexible I/O interface. These wide data communication channels keep blocks of data moving continuously through the board. Finally, the design provides three flexible, high speed input/output ports to allow data to move between boards as required by the processing algorithms. These I/O ports are accessible at the front panel. The RCA-2 board uses small daughter cards to adapt to different input or output data formats. With three front panel ports, two separate input data streams can be processed together to produce one output data stream. Alternatively, one stream of input data can be processed to create two streams of output data.

3 Function Description

Figure #1 shows the RCA-2 board and labels the major components. The design is implemented on a 'C' size VXI card that measures 233mm in width by 340mm in length. Attached to the board in daughter card location #1 is an input card. An output card is attached at daughter card location #3. Daughter cards measure 78mm in width by 142mm in length.

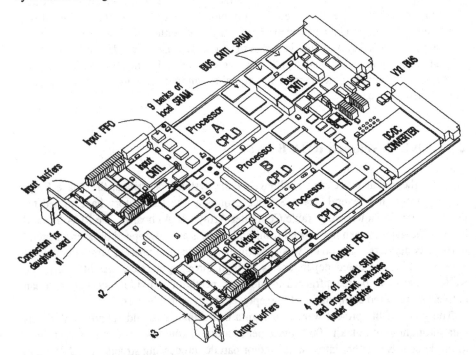

Fig. 1. Drawing of the RCA-2 board with an input and an output daughter card attached.

Figure #2 shows the functional blocks of the RCA-2 board and the data paths between them. Each functional block is described in more detail below.

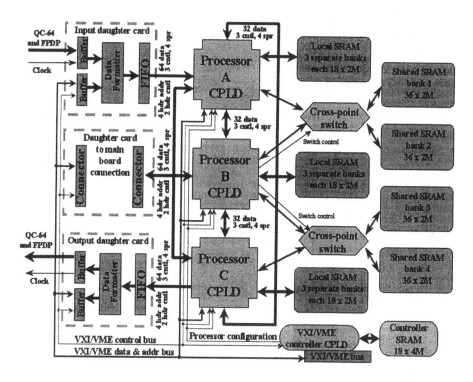

Fig. 2. Functional block diagram of the RCA-2 board and the input and output daughter cards.

3.1 Core Processing CPLD

The processing core of the board is created with three Altera[2] 10K130V SRAM based Complex Programmable Logic Devices (CPLD's). The 10K130V implement Altera's architecture for the FLEX 10K series of parts (see the Altera data book for a full description of the architecture). The 10K130V have 6,656 logic elements each with a 4-input look-up table, a flip-flop and interconnects. Eight logic elements are grouped into logic array blocks for a total of 832. In addition to logic array blocks there are 16 embedded array blocks that provide 32Kbits of memory. Signals passing on and off the chip go through one of 464 user I/O cells. Signals between logic array blocks, embedded array blocks and I/O cells are routed with global interconnects that run the full length and width of the device.

The RCA-2 design team selected the Altera FLEX 10K series as the system processor for several reasons. First, to accomplish complex algorithms, the large amount

---

[2] Altera Corporation, 101 Innovation Drive, San Jose, California USA 95134.
http://www.altera.com.

of logic available in the 10K130V is required. Second, to accommodate the desired memory and data path connections, a large number of I/O pins are needed, which the Altera part supplied. Finally, with complex logic and lots of I/O connections, a large supply of long-line routing resources is needed to support designs. The global interconnects provided by Altera will be relied on to meet these routing requirements.

Power to the CPLD is provided by two separate sets of pins. One set of power pins, VCC_INT, supplies power to the internal core logic and requires 3.3 volts. (The 3.3 volt supply is created by an onboard DC/DC converter from the 24 volt supply available on the VXI backplane.) The second set of power pins, VCC_IO, supplies power to the I/O cells and can be driven by either 5 or 3.3 volts. Even when driven by 3.3 volts, the I/O cells are tolerant of 5 volt inputs. The RCA-2 board uses 3.3 volts for the I/O cells.

The RCA-2 board uses the 10K130V in the 599-pin Pin-Grid-Array (PGA) package. Altera will also be producing the 10K250A in a pin compatible package. The 10K250A nearly doubles the number of logic array blocks available and increases the number of embedded array blocks to 20. Altera has announced that the new 10K250E will be available in the same package. The FLEX 10KE series uses an advanced 0.25-micron, five-layer-metal CMOS SRAM process technology. This results in a smaller die, faster chip speeds and lower power consumption. However, the FLEX 10KE requires 2.5 volts for the internal core logic.

To accommodate both the 10K and 10KE series of parts, the RCA-2 board uses a separate power plane to supply VCC_INT. The VCC_INT plane supplies all the internal core logic power pins for all three CPLD processors and the system controller CPLD (discussed later). When using the current FLEX 10K series, the VCC_INT plane would be strapped to the 3.3 volt supply. When the new 10KE series parts are used the VCC_INT plane would need to be powered by a separate, 2.5 volt external supply. The separate VCC_INT plane will allow the performance of the board to be extended as the newer parts become available.

3.2 Local Processor Memory

Connected to each processor CPLD are three independent banks of synchronous static RAM. The RCA-2 board uses Zero Bus Turnaround (ZBT) SRAM from Micron[3] that can support either a read or a write operation on each clock cycle. Micron currently produces SRAM parts that have 18 bits of data and are 128K deep. They have announced plans to produce parts as large as 1M deep. Each bank of local memory has two chips for a maximum size of 18 bits by 2M. These parts can support clock rates of greater than 100 MHz.

Since each bank is independent, the processor can perform read or write operations on each bank simultaneously without bus contention. Additionally, because of its synchronous operation, the memory fits cleanly with algorithm implementations inside the CPLD processor. This provides maximum flexibility to provide storage for

---

[3] Micron Technology, Incorporated, 8000 S. Federal Way, Boise, Idaho USA 83707-0006. http://www.micron.com/mit.

intermediate results, for coefficients and can provide large circular buffers for delaying data.

3.3 Shared Memory

To provide a large data block transfer capability between pairs of processors, two banks of shared memory were created. These banks of shared memory are between processors A and B, and between processors B and C. All data, address and control signals between the processors and the shared memory go through a large cross-point switch. The cross-point switch was built using bus exchange switches from IDT[4]. This allows each processor to have complete control of the bank of shared memory that it is connected to without contention. Once one processor has written a complete data block, the two banks of memory are exchanged, making the data immediately available to the second processor. Then, while the second processor works on the new block of data, the first processor can start creating the next block of data.

Each bank of shared memory is created with 4 chips of ZBT SRAM for a maximum size of 36 bits by 2M. Exchanging the banks of memory is controlled by a signal from processor B. One entire bank of memory can be exchanged with the other bank in one clock period. The shared memory fully supports the pipeline processing of block oriented data by allowing one processor to exchange a complete data block with its neighboring processor.

3.4 Dedicated Data Paths

Processors A and C each have a dedicated connection to I/O daughter card location 1 and 3 respectively. These connections are 77-bits wide. The daughter card design and the configuration of the Altera processor determine how these bits are used. LANL has developed input and output cards (discussed later) that determine the functions of these buses.

Processor B also has a 77-bit connection to daughter card location 2, but it is not a dedicated connection. Instead, this bus is also connected to processors A and C. This shared bus has several uses. Of course it can provide a data path between the daughter card and processor B. However, the main use is to allow two input streams of data to be brought together in one processor. Or, alternatively, to allow two output streams of data to be produced by one processor. Since this bus is fully shared by processors A, B and C, the design provides the flexibility to steer the data where it needs to go. An additional use of this shared bus is for inter-processor communications if daughter card location 2 is not used for I/O.

Normal inter-processor communication takes place between processors over a 39-bit bus. The three processors are connected in a ring; A to B, B to C and C to A. As with the other data paths, the functions of these bits are determined by the configura-

---

[4] Integrated Device Technology Inc., 2975 Stender Way, Santa Clara, California USA 95054. http://www.idt.com.

tion of the processors. LANL has adopted the initial convention that these buses would contain 32 bits of data, three control signals and four spare signals.

3.5 I/O Daughter Cards

Each of the three daughter card locations on the RCA-2 board provides two, 100-pin connectors. One connector is the data path connection from the daughter card to the Altera CPLD's plus ground connections. The second connector provides VXI bus access directly to the daughter card. Also included on the second connector are ground connections and various voltages from the backplane to power the daughter card. There is room at the edge of the daughter card for an 80-pin front panel data connector.

Although intended to provide a flexible front panel interface, daughter cards can fulfill other functions based on their design. One such function would be a high speed data path between a CPLD processor and the VXI bus. Another daughter card design might not implement any I/O functions at all but provide expanded memory resources instead. The design of a daughter card can be tailored to the requirements of the system and the algorithms being implemented.

For initial RCA-2 operations, LANL has developed an input daughter card and an output daughter card for high speed I/O. These daughter cards can implement both the Front Panel Data Port (FPDP) interface standard sanctioned by VITA[5] and the open QuickComm-64 (QC-64) standard from Catalina Research[6]. The cards provide First-In-First-Out (FIFO) memory for 64-bits of data going to or coming from the CPLD processor on the RCA-2 board. These FIFO's provide elastic buffers between cards, eliminating the requirement that all boards in the system must be synchronized and operate in lock step. LANL sees this as critically important for implementing block-oriented pipeline processing in a system containing multiple boards.

The QC-64 interface standard allows data to be transferred either as a continuous stream or as a packet. With packets of data, QC-64 allows header and trailer information to be appended to the data. All data transfers are synchronous with the front panel clock signal and are coordinated by three control signals. When transferring packets of data, two additional control signals are used to indicate when valid data begins and when it ends. These same signals control the transfer of header and trailer information. Header and trailer data is inserted in the place of normal sensor data and is further qualified by a 4-bit address indicating the function of the information. All data, header address and header control signals pass through the FIFO's.

Based on the QC-64 interface standard, LANL has initially assigned functions to the 77-bit bus from the daughter card to the CPLD processors. These functions are: 64 bits of data, 3 data control signals, 4 bits of header address, 2 header control signals and 4 spare signals.

---

[5] VMEbus International Trade Association, 7825 East Gelding Drive, Suite 104, Scottsdale, Arizona USA 85260. http://www.vita.com.
[6] Catalina Research Incorporated, 1321 Aeroplaza Drive, Colorado Springs, Colorado USA 80916. http://www.cri-dsp.com.

The function of the header and trailer information has not been fully defined. Since this information can travel with the data as it flows through the board, it will provide unique capabilities when implementing block-oriented pipeline processing. Information that might be included in the header could be gain, offset, start time and other sensor scaling information. For example, the current setting of an automatic gain control circuit could effect how a CPLD processor handles the data. Time stamps are especially valuable so that a processor can match together two blocks of data coming from separate sources. Trailer information might include an exponent value when implementing block floating-point representation.

3.6 VXI Interface

The RCA-2 board provides VXI bus access to each CPLD processor and to each daughter card. To each processor there are 8 bits of address and 18 bits of data from the backplane. The 18 bits for the data bus corresponds to the size of the local memory data bus. The VXI connection to the daughter cards includes 8 bits of address and a full 32 bits of data. The system controller CPLD supplies decoded VXI bus control signals and takes care of interrupts.

Through this VXI bus interface, data can be written to or read directly from any of the processors or daughter cards at standard VME bus rates. The main use of the VXI bus interface is for configuration, control and reporting functions. Examples of these functions include loading configuration files for the processors, loading coefficient values and monitoring the board's performance. These operations are expected to occur infrequently.

3.7 System Controller CPLD

The RCA-2 board uses an Altera 10K50V CPLD in a 356-pin Ball Grid Array (BGA) package to provide the VXI bus interface and to load configuration data into the processors. Altera has announced that a 10K100E will also be available in this package.

The system controller CPLD is automatically configured when power is turned on from onboard EPROM. Attached to the system controller is a local bank of ZBT SRAM. This bank has four chips for a maximum size of 18 bits by 4M. The controller also has a full VXI interface with 32 bits of data, 31 bits of address in addition to all data, address and interrupt control signals. These control signals are decoded and provided to the rest of the board. Depending on the configuration of the controller CPLD, the board can be either a memory mapped VME device or a VXI dynamically configured board.

The controller has separate passive serial configuration links with each of the board's CPLD processors. To load a processor, a configuration file is first written across the backplane and stored in the controller's bank of SRAM. Then, when commanded, the controller reads the file and writes it out the requested configuration link. If the maximum amount of controller SRAM is installed, there is enough memory to store more than 32 different configuration files for the 10K130. This allows the files to be pre-loaded on the board so reconfiguration of a processor can be done as quickly as possible.

4 Theory of Operation

The RCA-2 board is primarily designed to support pipeline operations on blocks of data. In its most basic operation, the data streams onto the board from the front panel directly to a CPLD processor. This processor then operates on the data, using local memory as needed. After its last operation on the data, the processor then writes it to a bank of shared memory. When the entire block of data has been written, the banks of shared memory are exchanged and processing begins on the next block of data. Blocks of data move from processor to processor as required by the algorithm. After the third processor has finished, the data is written directly to the front panel.

Obviously there is tremendous flexibility to how data is handled and how algorithms are mapped to the RCA-2 board. For particular applications, passing data directly between processors may perform better than exchanging shared memory banks. Still other applications may alternate blocks of data between two processors and use the third processor to accumulate the results. These application related questions can only be answered by first understanding the requirements and the algorithms of a specific system.

A fundamental principle of the RCA-2 board design was to keep application data off the backplane bus or any other bus having more than one data transmitter. This principle led to the board's heavy use of dedicated data paths between processors and between the front panel data ports and processors. The board does have one data path with more than two components, that is the connection between daughter card #2 and all three CPLD processors. However, this data path allows two data streams to be joined or created by one processor as discussed above. For any given application, this shared data path should still comply with the 'only one data transmitter' rule.

By relying on dedicated data paths for moving data, the data throughput rate of a system is not dependent on the performance of the backplane bus. Therefore, additional RCA-2 boards can be added to a system without affecting data throughput. This would not be true if all the boards in a system relied strictly on the backplane to move data.

5 Processor Logic Development

Before the RCA-2 board can perform useful work, the CPLD processors must be properly configured. This requires a designer to translate signal processing algorithms into logic implemented in the Altera 10K130V devices. These algorithms may be initially presented to the designer as a series of mathematical formulas or as Matlab, DSP or 'C' code. It is then the designer's responsibility to translate the algorithms into schematics or to VHDL, Verilog or some other RTL-level code. In addition to the algorithm, the designer must also incorporate data flow, memory interfaces, process coordination, system control, error handling and the other functions required to keep a system running correctly. All of this must then be partitioned across several CPLD processors and possibly across multiple boards. Finally, the logic must be placed and routed inside the CPLD's. In today's design environment, this is *not* a trivial effort.

To support logic development for the CPLD processors, LANL is developing a VHDL representation of the RCA-2 board, the two daughter cards and the VXI backplane. This representation will include behavior models for the ZBT memories, the FIFO memories, the cross-point switches and the VXI bus master CPU. To this testbench the designer would add the logic design of the three CPLD processors for simulation. This VHDL testbench will allow the designer to concentrate on developing his specific application code and to functionally test it at an early stage. A testbench of a complete system might include several RCA-2 boards, daughter cards and models of system specific boards all plugged into a backplane with front panel ports linked together.

LANL is also developing standard VHDL code at the RTL level that provides a basic VXI bus interface, a memory interface, daughter card interfaces, and allows configuration files to be loaded into the CPLD processors. Additionally, there is a package of code being developed that allows extensive testing of a board for diagnostic purposes. As application code is developed for the board, LANL intends to create a library of other useful routines.

6 RCA-2 Performance

At the time this paper is being written, no testing of the RCA-2 board has yet taken place since the board is currently being assembled. As test results become available, they will be posted to the project's web page at http://www.lanl.gov/rcc.

7 Conclusions

Los Alamos National Laboratory has specifically designed a reconfigurable computer board to support high speed processing of large blocks of data. Programmable logic is the key link between high speed, application specific, front-end sensors and slower speed general purpose computers. It is understood that the architecture of one reconfigurable processor, combined with its local memory, will not provide ideal implementation of all algorithms. However, by linking multiple processors and multiple boards together with high speed data paths, many algorithms can be implemented allowing an enormous increase in computing power and data throughput. Los Alamos National Laboratory believes that reconfigurable computing technology is a critical component of modern digital remote sensing systems.

A Reconfigurable Engine for Real-Time Video Processing

W. Luk, P. Andreou, A. Derbyshire, F. Dupont-De-Dinechin, J. Rice,
N. Shirazi and D. Siganos

Department of Computing, Imperial College, 180 Queen's Gate,
London SW7 2BZ, UK

Abstract. We describe the hardware and software extensions that transform a PC-based low-cost FPGA system into a reconfigurable engine for real-time video processing. The hardware extensions include a daughter board for the FPGA system which handles analog and digital colour video conversion. The software extensions include reusable libraries, development tools and a run-time environment. Applications include linear and non-linear filtering, edge detection, image rotation, histogram equalisation, colour identification, motion tracking, and creation of video effects. Our system has been used for research involving video processing, run-time reconfigurable circuits, and hardware/software co-design.

1 Introduction

Real-time video is becoming increasingly popular with the proliferation of low-cost video cameras, camcorders and other facilities. Real-time video processing, however, is among the most demanding computation tasks [1]. Application-specific integrated circuits can deliver implementations optimal in speed and size, but they are often inflexible, expensive and time-consuming to develop. Digital signal processing chips and general-purpose microprocessors often include hardware support for processing video or multimedia data, but there may be drawbacks. First, such hardware support may not cover a particular user-specific task; second, the system architecture and low-level software, such as interrupt control, can cause significant delay if not carefully optimised.

This paper describes the hardware and software extensions which transform an FPGA-based board into a reconfigurable engine for real-time video processing. The board we use has a user-reconfigurable Xilinx 6200 FPGA and two megabytes of static memory, and is available from multiple vendors for around 1000 US dollars. The key aspects of our work include: (a) the development of hardware and software components for a flexible, powerful and low-cost video processing engine, and (b) the use of techniques such as run-time reconfiguration and hardware/software codesign for optimising high-performance designs. A variety of application examples will be used to illustrate our approach.

Our work is inspired particularly by the VTSplash project [1] at Virginia Tech, which enhanced a multi-FPGA system hosted in a SPARC-workstation with monochrome video facility. Other FPGA-based video processing environments are based on the VME system [3], the transputer framework [11], or

FPGAs without partial reconfigurability [4]. Our system is PC-based, supports partial FPGA reconfiguration at run time, and can deal with colour video.

2 Framework

All of our designs for the video engine fit into the framework shown in Figure 1, which serves as a guide for structuring systems dealing with high-speed data streams. There are hardware elements PRE and POST for pre-processing and post-processing such streams. In the context of this paper, the PRE element accepts a video stream as input, performs the required processing such as subsampling or feature extraction, and passes the result to POST. The POST element performs further processing, such as labelling the features identified by PRE, before producing the output video stream. The mapping of hardware components into PRE and POST may not be unique, and they are often arranged in the form of a pipeline [1].

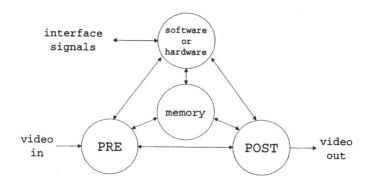

Fig. 1. A framework for structuring video designs, where PRE and POST are hardware elements for pre-processing and post-processing data. The hardware and the software components can be situated on the same or different boards.

Both PRE and POST may communicate with the memory or other hardware or software components. Reusable interface libraries have been developed to facilitate implementations involving the interactions between these components. A common situation is for PRE to extract features in the incoming video which can be described efficiently, since the feature descriptions can then be passed to a software procedure for further analysis using a low bandwidth link. Control information, such as configuration data, may also be sent from the software component to the hardware elements.

Run-time reconfiguration can be applied to this framework in several ways. First, the PRE and POST elements may be connected to video interface chips, and we will explain in Section 4 how reconfiguration techniques can be used to move seamlessly between changing the settings of these chips and processing the video data. Second, run-time reconfiguration can be used for optimising design size and speed by supplying a customised implementation at the appropriate time. In particular, there are techniques for effective reconfiguration of pipeline structures [9].

The scheme in Figure 1 has been shown to be useful not only for experiments involving video processing and run-time FPGA reconfiguration, but also for research in hardware/software partitioning and co-design. Software components are often better suited for some forms of processing than hardware components, for instance when irregular, data-dependent or floating-point computations are involved. The key to effective co-processing is to identify techniques and applications such that: (a) the hardware and software components perform tasks which match their capabilities, and (b) the communications between them do not overload the hardware/software interface.

As an example, we have developed a motion tracker which has a hardware component extracting motion information from an image and sending it to a software tracking procedure. The hardware component performs mainly regular and parallel computations at high speed, while the software component performs mainly irregular, sequential and floating-point operations less suitable for hardware implementation. Since for each video frame only a small amount of data are passed between the hardware and the software, the bus connecting them does not become a bottleneck. Further details of this application, and several others, will be discussed in Section 5.

3 Hardware

Our aim is to minimise efforts on system development, while the result should be flexible, low-cost and sufficiently powerful for real-time video operations. Flexibility and cost considerations motivate the use of a cheap but expandable FPGA-based board, preferably one capable of run-time reconfiguration. Performance consideration motivates specialised hardware support for video data transfer and for common operations such as hue, saturation and brightness control.

The approach that we adopt involves a low-cost development system based on the Xilinx 6200 FPGA, and a daughter board that we designed for interfacing the FPGA to real-time video sources and sinks (Figure 2). The hardware for the development system is a board which can contain either a Xilinx 6216 or a Xilinx 6264 device, on which the PRE and POST elements in Figure 1 can be implemented. The board has four 8-bit wide memories organised into two banks, and each bank can be accessed from either of the two address busses [10].

The FPGA board is interfaced to the PC through the PCI bus, but the PCI bus has often been found to be the bottleneck for real-time transfer of large image data [12]. To overcome this problem, we built a daughter board for converting between analog composite video and its digital version. The digitised video is sent to the FPGA board through a mezzanine connector. After processing, the result can be passed back to the daughter board for conversion into composite

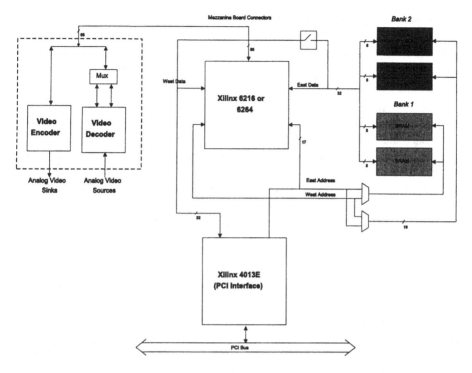

Fig. 2. Xilinx 6200 PCI system. The multiplexor Mux selects either the control ports or the data ports to connect to the mezzanine connector.

video for display. The display speed is only limited by processing delay, since we avoid using the PCI bus for transfer of uncompressed video. In essence, this method achieves high performance by eliminating system bus saturation and by shortcutting operating system delays.

The daughter board contains a video decoder and a video encoder, both from Brooktree Corporation. The decoder converts analog video, such as PAL or NTSC signals, to various digital formats, such as 24-bit or 16-bit RGB or YCrCb; the encoder performs digital to analog conversion. These chips also support other functions, including brightness and colour control. Since the number of lines on the mezzanine connector is limited, a scheme has been devised to share the control and data signals to the video decoder using a multiplexor (Figure 2). This method supports 24-bit colour input and output at the expense of losing video data whenever the settings of the decoder are adjusted.

4 Software

The software that has been developed for our reconfigurable engine include: (a) support for controlling the video interface chips, (b) memory interfaces,

(c) arithmetic and other building blocks in the form of parametrised libraries, (d) interface to software components, and (e) infrastructure for developing user applications involving real-time video. There are also compilation tools supporting run-time reconfigurable designs, and visualisation tools for debugging implementations.

The video interface chips described in the preceding section are powerful but require low-level programming. The programming involves specific data transfer protocols (such as I^2C and MPU) with complex timing constraints, which should be hidden from the designer of a video processing application. We adopt an approach which splits a video operation into two distinct phases. The initialisation phase involves setting up the FPGA to program the video interface chips through FPGA registers, with the multiplexor in Figure 2 selecting the control ports of the video decoder. A software library has been developed which transparently loads in an FPGA programming file defining all the required registers and their wiring to the relevant FPGA pins. There are high-level functions facilitating the configuration of the video interface chips to select the picture format, the colour depth and image intensity.

In the video processing phase, the registers linked to the programming of the video interface chips are frozen. The user design can access the video stream through standard interface components in various hardware description languages. The transition between the initialisation phase and the video processing phase is achieved by partially reconfiguring the Xilinx 6200 FPGA; this improves speed and minimises effects of transients on the video interface chips. The partial reconfiguration step is part of our framework for developing run-time reconfigurable systems, and is supported by various tools such as ConfigDiff [8].

Other components dedicated to the video daughter board include a memory interface capable of performing a read and a write cycle to the memory in each pixel clock cycle, and an address generator which produces the coordinates of the current pixel on the screen based on various clock and sync signals. Facilities are also available to enable the memory to be used as a double buffer, by using video synchronisation signals and a state machine generating the address and read/write signals. In the case of a line buffer, the current pixels are written to one memory bank while the pixels on the previous line are read from the other. This is reversed after each line, so a read and a write can be performed simultaneously. This method is less demanding on timing than attempting to read and write to the same SRAM bank in one cycle. The memory interface components have been demonstrated on various applications to be described in the next section.

Tools for application development consist of a compile-time environment and a run-time environment. The compile-time environment consists mainly of the development tools [8] and reusable libraries [5] for FPGA design. Hardware descriptions can either be expressed in VHDL or in the Pebble language [6], which can be regarded as a simple variant of VHDL used particularly by those without much background in electronics. Over 30 parametrised libraries have been developed in Pebble and VHDL, including various kinds of adders, multipliers and memory access circuits with different tradeoffs in processing speed and size. These libraries are also compatible with our tools for automating the production of run-time reconfigurable designs.

The run-time environment includes software libraries for monitoring and controlling the FPGA and the daughter board from the PC host. A graphical user interface has also been developed for design visualisation, debugging and demonstration. In all, the software extensions provide an infrastructure for rapid design implementation and for design reuse.

5 Applications

A variety of applications have been developed using this reconfigurable engine, including various forms of linear and non-linear filtering, edge detection, image transformation, histogram equalisation, colour identification, motion tracking and creation of video effects, all of which run at real-time rates.

One-dimensional operations. A variety of one-dimensional operators have been developed for our video processing system. These operators include binomial and median filters, and Sobel edge detectors. Often software is used in changing various settings by writing to registers on the FPGA, or in controlling run-time reconfiguration where customised circuits are downloaded onto the FPGA at the appropriate instants [7]. Memory can be used in transposing a video frame so that a two-dimensional operation can be obtained from composing two one-dimensional operations [2].

Colour detection. This application is used to detect a user-specified colour in the incoming video. The implementation filters out the other colours of the spectrum and only allows the detected colour to pass through. The processing is performed at a resolution of 640 by 480 pixels using 24-bit RGB colour.

Two different approaches were attempted. The first approach specifies the target colour by a range of values for each colour component. The detection is performed using six 8-bit comparators computing the maximum and minimum values for each colour component. Their outputs are combined to produce a signal representing the presence of the target colour. This design is sensitive to lighting conditions, since the criteria for colour identification are absolute.

The second approach identifies the target colour by the differences between the three colour components. For each pair of colours, the difference is calculated and then a comparator checks whether the difference is greater or smaller than a specified colour threshold. This method allows for more tolerance in brightness fluctuation, although further improvements can be achieved using another colour system such as HSV. The designs are reconfigurable at run time to enable the detection of a new target colour.

Image rotation. This application takes a video image and rotates it by an angle θ. This is accomplished by multiplying the co-ordinates of the incoming image by the formulae $x' = a \times x + b \times y$ and $y' = c \times x + d \times y$, where the coefficients $a = d = cos\,\theta$ and $b = -c = sin\,\theta$. Other transformations can be obtained by different coefficient formulae. Our design, which can complete four multiplications in two cycles, consists of two multipliers (Figure 3). The value of y is constant for the duration of each line; hence the products $y \times sin\,\theta$ and $y \times cos\,\theta$ can be performed at the blanking interval between lines, and in the remaining time the multipliers calculate the products involving x. The processing is performed on a 24-bit colour image at a resolution of 320 by 480 pixels; full resolution can be achieved by pipelining the multipliers. The encoder and decoder circuits convert coordinates to memory addresses and vice versa.

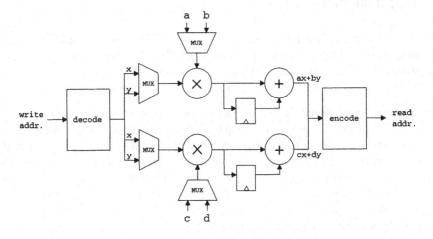

Fig. 3. Matrix multplier for image rotation design.

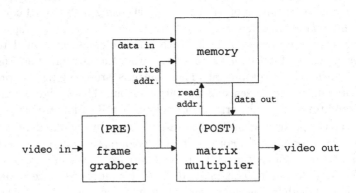

Fig. 4. System organisation for image rotation design.

The overall organisation is shown in Figure 4. The pre-processing step consists of optionally subsampling the image using a frame grabber and storing the result to memory. The matrix multiplier described above transforms the write address signals to read address signals, which can be used to extract a rotated image from memory and send it to the video output.

Histogram equalisation. Histogram equalisation has the effect of improving image contrast. Our design for histogram equalisation is similar to that for image rotation (Figure 4). The alterations include: (a) in addition to the frame grabber, the pre-processing step also involves generating a lookup table in memory which corresponds to a transformation function derived from the intensity histogram of the grabbed image; (b) the post-processing step consists of using the lookup table to transform the incoming video stream. Some calculations in the pre-processing step can be performed in software. This method can also be used to implement other computations involving lookup tables.

Edge detection. The edge detector described here is an example of a two-dimensional operator capable of processing full-rate, greyscale video derived from averaging the colour components. The gradient components of an image are computed by difference operators in the x and y direction. The difference operators are word-pipelined at every stage to keep the combinational delay within the pixel clock period. An edge is marked if the x or y gradient is above a given threshold; the thresholds are held in programmable registers and can be altered by software.

Video effects. Several examples involving video effects have been developed. We describe here an application to detect, in the video stream covering a sports event, a sign indicating an advertisement which will be replaced by another advertisement more appropriate for the local viewers. The task is complicated by the motion and zooming of the camera, and also by objects, such as the sportsmen, partly obscuring the sign.

The general solution to this problem requires processing power which is out of reach of the hardware described in this paper. However, if we assume that the camera rotates but does not translate, the position and size of the sign in the picture can be deduced from the angles and zoom values of the camera. From this information the software computes, for each video frame, the region holding the sign and writes this information to the FPGA for post-processing.

The POST component compares, for each pixel of the region containing the advertisement sign, its colour and the colour of the corresponding pixel in the initial advertisement scaled appropriately. The two pixels will be the same if nothing is obstructing the advertisement sign, in which case the pixel of the first advertisement is replaced by the corresponding pixel in the second. Otherwise there are objects in front of the sign which must be preserved in the image, so the incoming pixel will be transferred to the output.

Other applications have shown that appropriate scaling and restriction of the search space of the advertisement sign is straightforward. The main challenge is to decide whether two pixels have the same colour. We found that simple checks, such as comparing each colour in a pixel to within a certain range of the same colour in the corresponding pixel, are often too sensitive to lighting conditions.

We are currently exploring various colour representations and local algorithms, which may be able to produce a better result.

Motion tracking. Our motion tracker contains a hardware part and a software part. The PRE component of the hardware part consists of a differencer and a counter array; the POST component labels the detected moving objects in the output video stream. The software part contains a Kalman filter to minimise the effect of noise on the tracker performance (Figure 5).

A simple way of identifying motion is to compute the difference of the corresponding pixels in two consecutive video frames. The result is then thresholded to give a binary value for each pixel. The differenced frame is divided into blocks corresponding to different regions of the image. The amount of motion in each block can then be recorded by a counter; for instance an array of 64 counters will be required for a design with 8 by 8 blocks. A counter selector keeps a record of the current position of the incoming pixels on the screen, and enables the appropriate counter to increment accordingly.

Several FPGA-based implementations of motion trackers have been reported ([3],[11]). The advantages of our counter-based design include simplicity, flexibility and scalability. For instance, this method enables each pixel to be processed independently of the others within one cycle, so no inter-frame processing is necessary. Our method is also scalable: the availability of more hardware allows a larger counter array, and will usually lead to better performance.

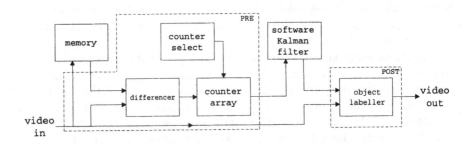

Fig. 5. A design for motion tracking.

The main function of the PC is to calculate the statistically 'best' estimate of the position and size of the object. Kalman filtering provides a method for making this estimate. It considers the statistical models of signal and noise to give optimum response to the actual motion, while giving minimum response to the noise present in its detection. Our Kalman filter involves mainly floating-point operations, and is best implemented in software. The post-processing on the FPGA consists of hardware for labelling the detected objects in the video stream, the locations of which are supplied by the PC.

6 Conclusion

Despite its simplicity and low cost, our reconfigurable engine has proved to be an effective vehicle for experimenting with run-time reconfiguration and hardware/software codesign techniques for video applications. We have shown that the PC can be used as the host to the video engine, and as a co-processor for executing complex, data-dependent and floating-point operations. Current and future work includes exploring further multimedia and other applications using our system, refining our framework and tools, and retargeting them to cater for other FPGA-based platforms.

Acknowledgements

Thanks to Stuart Nisbet for help in developing the video interface board. The support of Xilinx, Interval Research, Hewlett Packard Laboratories Bristol, INRIA, and the UK Engineering and Physical Sciences Research Council (Grant Number GR/L24366, GR/L54356 and GR/L59658) is gratefully acknowledged.

References

1. P.M. Athanas and A.L. Abbott, "Real-time image processing on a custom computing platform", *IEEE Computer*, February 1995.
2. M. Aubury and W. Luk, "Binomial filters", *Journal of VLSI Signal Processing*, vol. 12, 1996.
3. P. Dunn, "A configurable logic processor for machine vision", in *Field Programmable Logic and Applications*, W. Moore and W. Luk (editors), LNCS 975, Springer, 1995.
4. F. Lisa, F. Cuadrado, D. Rexachs and J. Carrabina, "A reconfigurable coprocessor for a PCI-based real-time computer vision system", in *Field-Programmable Logic, Smart Applications, New Paradigms and Compilers*, LNCS 1142, Springer, 1996.
5. W. Luk, S. Guo, N. Shirazi and N. Zhuang, "A framework for developing parametrised FPGA libraries", in *Field-Programmable Logic, Smart Applications, New Paradigms and Compilers*, LNCS 1142, Springer, 1996.
6. W. Luk and S. McKeever, "Pebble: a language for parametrised and reconfigurable hardware design", this volume.
7. W. Luk, N. Shirazi and P.Y.K. Cheung, "Modelling and optimising run-time reconfigurable systems", in *Proc. FCCM96*, IEEE Computer Society Press, 1996.
8. W. Luk, N. Shirazi and P.Y.K. Cheung, "Compilation tools for run-time reconfigurable designs", in *Proc. FCCM97*, IEEE Computer Society Press, 1997.
9. W. Luk, N. Shirazi, S. Guo and P.Y.K. Cheung, "Pipeline morphing and virtual pipelines", in *Field Programmable Logic and Applications*, LNCS 1304, Springer, 1997.
10. S. Nisbet and S.A. Guccione, "The XC6200DS development system", in *Field Programmable Logic and Applications*, LNCS 1304, Springer, 1997.
11. I. Page, "Constructing hardware-software systems from a single description", *Journal of VLSI Signal Processing*, Vol. 12, 1996.
12. S. Singh and R. Slous, "Accelerating Adobe Photoshop with reconfigurable logic", in *Proc. FCCM98*, IEEE Computer Society Press, 1998.

An FPGA Implementation of a Magnetic Bearing Controller for Mechatronic Applications

Frank-Michael Renner, Jürgen Becker and Manfred Glesner

Darmstadt University of Technology,
Institute of Microelectronic Systems,
Karlstr. 15, D-64283 Darmstadt, Germany,
Tel: (+49) 6151 164937 – Fax: (+49) 6151 164936
{renner|becker|glesner}@mes.tu-darmstadt.de

Abstract. In this paper we describe the implementation of an integrated magnetic bearing controller for mechatronic applications[1]. First, a brief overview of the mechatronic application is given. The design process for an FPGA implementation is described and details of the individual modules within the design process are given. The magnetic bearing controller is implemented using a graphical high-level approach. From this implementation a VHDL description is automatically generated, partitioned onto several FPGAs and transferred to a printed circuit board located at the test rig.

1 Introduction

The essential requirements of a marketable magnetic bearing system, like high availability, reliability, simple handling and efficiency, can be fulfilled by integrating separate tasks, for example

- sensorless position detection of rotors (self-sensing magnetic bearing),
- consideration of non-linear properties of the components of the closed-loop,
- on-line determination of optimal control parameters (adaption)

into an integrated magnetic bearing system. Today the majority of magnetic bearing systems in operation are classically arranged mechanic-electronic systems of which the components (controller, power amplifier, electro magnets, sensors, signal conditioning) are assembled additively. In order to reduce the disadvantages of this conglomerate, like expensive production, high support expenditure and small capacity, magnetic bearing systems must be developed with the aim of both functional and structural integration.

Integrated mechanic-electronic systems allow improved and completely new functions that were not realizable before. For example, the dynamical stiffness and damping of the magnetic bearing can be adapted to the momentary optimal operating point of the rotor and unbalance forces can be compensated on-line. For this purpose non measurable quantities are determined from non measurable

---

[1] This project is funded within the special research program 241 (IMES) by the German Research Foundation (DFG)

ones via analytical relations and also influenced specifically. As a consequence, tasks of process management (coordination, optimization, adaption) and monitoring with fault diagnosis are possible. Thus the integrated mechatronic bearing develops to an 'intelligent' actuator.

The realization of the integration, both functional and structural, is done using digital signal processors (DSPs) as software prototypes, field programmable devices (FPGAs) as hardware prototypes and application-specific integrated circuits (ASICs) as the final realization on which the problem's solutions are implemented as real-time algorithms. They must be adapted to the properties of the mechanical process by exhaustion of all capabilities of the programming language. This leads to process-coupled information processing with intelligent characteristics and to the functional integration of all components.

This paper is organized as follows. In the following section we describe the magnetic bearing system as the starting point for the controller implementation. In section 3 we describe the high-level specification for application specific integrated components for mechatronic systems. Section 4 covers the Rapid-System-Specification designflow while Section 5 describes the hardware prototype using field programmable logic. Our conclusions appear in Section 6, which also gives an outlook to the final magnetic bearing system realization.

2 The Integrated Magnetic Bearing System

Today, performance requirements of rotating machinery parts are highly increasing with respect to speed of rotation, low level of vibration, power to weight ratio, working-precision, life expectancy and cost. To meet these demands the mechan-

Fig. 1. The magnetic bearing system

ical system is normally designed using passive techniques. However, the needed performance is often not achievable using these passive techniques and therefore active systems are designed to meet these demands. These active systems are capable of monitoring the rotor position permanently and reacting intelligently with an appropriate information processing unit. With the actuators the rotor position can be influenced in real time.

The realization of an active system, we refer to it as an integrated mechatronic system, requires a combination of the fields of electrical and electronic engineering, information sciences and mechanical engineering.

The aim is to develop a self-contained actuator device suitable for engineering applications (see Fig. 1) which is externally controllable, operating as a "black box". This will be achieved by including the following properties:

- nonlinear modeling of the magnetic bearing system,
- sensorless determination of the rotor position without the use of additional displacement sensors,
- design of control strategies which consider the behavior of the rotor, electromagnets and power amplifier and
- conception and production of an ASIC.

Areas where these magnetically suspended rotors can be used include vacuum pumps and centrifuges in high purity manufacturing, high speed rotating machines where high precision and low levels of vibration is needed and gyroscopes in navigation instruments.

3   High Level System Specification

The information processing part of an integrated magnetic bearing consists of different representations. On one side there is control algorithm part, which is a dataflow oriented representation of the control algorithm, on the other side there is a controlflow oriented part, realizing for example the communication with the outside world and the configuration of the system after reset.

Fig. 2 shows the general designflow considered in our work. Starting from system requirements and information processing algorithms, dataflow graphs for the information processing part and finite state machine models for the control part are captured in high-level visual environments. Starting from the high-level specification of the algorithms for information processing, our goal is to turn around such designs for mechatronic systems in a few weeks, focusing on common-off-the-shelf (COTS) components, [GL+97].

The wide range of different algorithms to be considered for magnetic bearings make it impossible for the designer to know in advance the detailed characteristics of the system to be developed. However, for these information processing algorithms, synchronous dataflow has been proved to be a natural representation, [CKL96], [Pt96]. One of its strengths is the exposing of parallelism by expressing only the actual data dependencies existing in the algorithm. Dataflow is a well-known programming model in which a program is represented as a directed graph, where the vertices represent computation and edges represent FIFO (first-in-first-out) queues that direct data values from the output of one computation

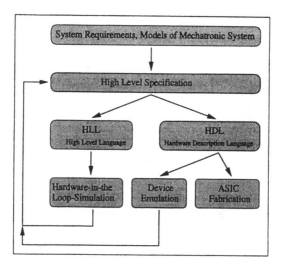

Fig. 2. Designflow for mechatronic systems

to the input of the following computation. Data precedence between computations are thus represented by edges. Actors consume data (or tokens) from their inputs, perform computation on them and produce certain number of tokens on their outputs, [Sr95]. The dataflow models implemented within the magnetic bearing application is the SDF - Synchronous Data Flow - model proposed by Lee and Messerschmidt, [LM87]. The SDF model poses restrictions on the firing of actors: the number of tokens produced (consumed) by an actor on each output (input) edge is fixed and known at compile time. The advantage of dataflow graphs is its formalism for block-diagram based visual programming, which is an intuitive specification mechanism for digital signal processing. The functional building block executes a specific algorithm but the eventual implementation depends upon the particular design steps the designer wishes to follow.

For the modeling of the behavior of the controlflow oriented part of the magnetic bearing controller an extended finite-state-machine (FSM) description was created based on Statecharts, [DH89]. The language was primarily for specifying reactive systems, which are essentially event-driven and control-dominated, for example controllers in communication networks. Statecharts are an extension of the traditional FSM description including three additional features: hierarchy, concurrency and communication, [i-L94].

A Statechart comprises different states and transitions, which are activated depending on a combination of conditions and events. The strategy of design decomposition with hierarchy significantly reduces the exponential increase in states and transitions. This design method was used before to model a CAN-Bus Controller, [KR+96], [Etsch94].

Using this level of abstraction lets designers (computer engineers, electrical engineers as well as mechanic engineers) complete the tasks at a very early design stage as efficiently as possible.

4   Rapid System Specification Designflow

Our approach (see Fig. 3) is based on the commercial tools Signal Processing Worksystem (SPW) from the Alta Group of Cadence Design Systems and ExpressV-HDL or Statemate from i-Logix. Starting from system requirements

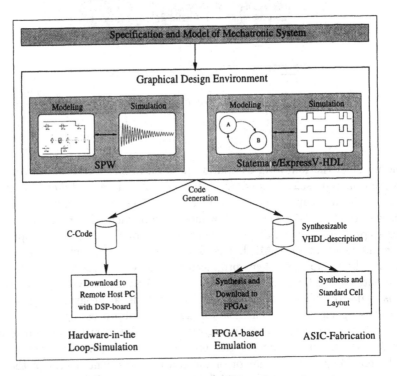

Fig. 3. Our detailed designflow for mechatronic systems

and information processing algorithms, dataflow and controlflow graphs are captured in a high-level block-diagram based visual environment. After verifying the algorithm the designer has the choice

1. to rapid-prototype the system as a software prototype using COTS components, like DSP microprocessors, AD/DA converters, or
2. to emulate the system as a hardware prototype based on FPGA components or
3. to develop an Application Specific Integrated Circuit (ASIC).

One of the key aspects in our approach is that designers are able to start step 2 and 3 from the same representation of the graphs instead of having to re-specify and reevaluate the system specification into a lower level hardware description language like VHDL.

The dataflow of the algorithm is captured in a graphical editor using functional blocks provided by SPW as well as custom coded blocks. The functionality of the algorithm can be evaluated by simulating the system within SPW. After successful simulation, a C description of the whole design can be automatically generated from SPW targeting a DSP processor. The C Code can be transferred to a remote PC located at the test rig. After successful compilation the machine code is downloaded to the prototyping board and can be used within the mechanical system for a hardware-in-the-loop simulation. Thus, different algorithms for magnetic bearings can be evaluated in a short turn-around time without having to consider the resulting hardware. This part of the rapid-prototyping approach has been described earlier, [LRG97].

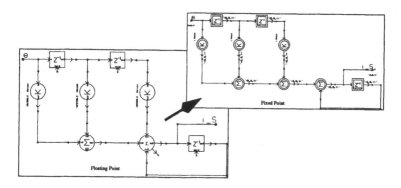

Fig. 4. Dataflow graph of the control algorithm (from floating to fixed point)

With successful validation of the rapid software prototype, the next step is to generate automatically a hardware prototype. First, the floating point to fixed point conversion has to be performed. This can be either done manually by replacing all floating point cells with fixed point cells or automatically with the built-in conversion tool (see Fig. 4). After simulation of the fixed point system the VHDL code of the dataflow part can be generated automatically. However to be able to put this system onto an FPGA a supervising controller has to be implemented as well. This represents the work to be done to move from a software prototype to a hardware prototype.

The controlflow oriented part is modeled with ExpressV-HDL from i-Logix as a hierarchical finite state machine (FSM) using the key advantages of ExpressV-HDL: hierarchy and concurrency. The controller has to initialize registers upon reset, sets default parameters for the dataflow oriented algorithm and monitors the interface to an external PC if a change of parameters occurs. The functionality of the controller can be graphically simulated within this tool in order to verify it's correct behavior. After successful simulation the VHDL Code of the controlflow oriented part can be automatically generated as well.

In this way the complete information processing part for the magnetic bearing system can be implemented using high-level graphical environments which can be used by electrical and computer engineers as well as mechanic engineers without having to consider the actual hardware structure of the final system at this early design stage.

5 Hardware Prototyping

After generation of the VHDL code for the controlflow and dataflow oriented parts of the system the functionality is synthesized onto Field Programmable Devices, like FPGAs in order to evaluate the functionality of the information processing part within the dedicated hardware environment. According to Fig. 5

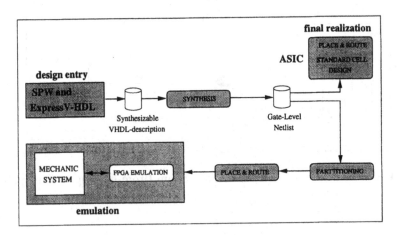

Fig. 5. Hardware Prototyping Designflow

the hardware prototype of the information processing part for integrated magnetic bearings is generated as follows: The controller is completely specified using the graphical design environments SPW and ExpressV-HDL (see Section 4). The generated VHDL Code is fully synthesizable. A standard synthesis tool (Synopsys Design Compiler) is used to get the gate-level netlist of the design in the target technology (standard cells or FPGAs for prototyping). After a manual partitioning of the design to multiple FPGAs (see Fig. 6) and placement and routing of each FPGA, the generated bitstream can be downloaded immediately to the FPGA based printed circuit board (PCB) which is currently developed for this purpose. After a few hours (varying with the chosen generic parameters of the design) the prototype of the information processing part will be ready for testing in its real process environment.

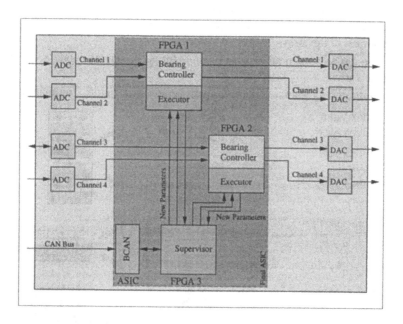

Fig. 6. Layout of the FPGA-based printed circuit board

Because of the unknown complexity of the various control algorithms to follow only 2 channels are controlled by one FPGA, containing the dataflow oriented bearing controller itself, and an additional controlflow oriented finite state machine called "Executor" receiving new parameters by the master controller, called "Supervisor". After reset, the "Supervisor" initializes the parameters of the bearing controllers and the registers of the BCAN-ASIC, an CAN-Bus (Controller-Area-Network) Controller, developed previously with ExpressV-HDL as a hierarchical finite state machine and currently in production. The BCAN-ASIC realizes the connection of the magnetic bearing system to an external PC which monitors its operation, allowing a changing of parameters and sensing the state of the bearing system. In an initial design the control algorithm implements a fully parallel PID controller. FPGA 1 and FPGA 2 (see Fig. 6) are both programmed with the same design consisting of the bearing control algorithm and the "Executor". The generated code for FPGAs 1 and 2 consists of 640 lines VHDL code and 612 lines for FPGA 3 (the "Supervisor"). Mapping these designs onto Xilinx 4013 FPGAs we get the following results:

FPGA 1 & 2: Bearing Controller and "Executor"

	No. used	Max. Available	% used
Occupied CLBs	413	576	71%
Packed CLBs	237	576	41%
Bounded I/O Pins:	50	192	26%
F and G Function Generators:	474	1152	41%
H Function Generators:	57	576	9%
CLB Flip Flops:	58	1152	5%

FPGA 3: "Supervisor"

	No. used	Max. Available	% used
Occupied CLBs	182	576	31%
Packed CLBs	87	576	15%
Bounded I/O Pins:	67	192	34%
F and G Function Generators:	174	1152	15%
H Function Generators:	30	576	5%
CLB Flip Flops:	100	1152	8%

This prototyping environment will be used in the next months to determine the optimal control algorithm for the magnetic bearing system. After evaluation of different algorithms within the real process environment the final step will be the production of an ASIC containing

- all 4 sensing channels,
- the "Executor", which will be adapted to 4 instead of 2 channels by just changing one parameter,
- the "Supervisor" for initialization of the components and
- the BCAN controller for the communication with the outside world.

6 Conclusions

In this paper we have presented an approach for designing mechatronic magnetic bearings by capturing the specification with an high-level graphical environment, automatically generating VHDL code of both the dataflow oriented part as well as the controlflow oriented part of the magnetic bearing controller. To rapid-prototype the system within its real process environment the functionality of the control system is mapped onto several FPGAs on a printed circuit board which will be located at the test rig. This system will be used to evaluate different control algorithms for the magnetic bearing with respect to the quality of the controller, throughput of the information processing part, time delay needed for the analog/digital and digital/analog converters and area needed for silicon production. The final realization of the information processing part will be an ASIC

containing the different blocks described in this paper. The last step includes the verification of the magnetic bearing system consisting only of the magnetic bearing itself and the power amplifier including the ASIC controller.

References

[LRG97] Le, T. and Renner, F.-M. and Glesner, M.: Hardware-in-the-loop Simulation – A Rapid Prototyping Approach for Designing Mechatronics Systems. IEEE Int. Workshop on Rapid System Prototyping, Chapel Hill, USA (1997)

[GL+97] Glesner, M. and Le, T. and Doan, M.-D. and Kirschbaum, A. and Renner, F.-M.: On the Methodology and Design of Application Specific Processors for Mechatronic Systems. Proc. of the 4th Int. Workshop on Mixed Design of Integrated Circuits and Systems, Poznan, Poland (1997)

[L+93] Lipsett, R. et al.: VHDL: Hardware Description and Design. Kluwer Academic Publishers, Boston (1993)

[CKL96] Chang, W.-T. and Kalavade, A. and Lee, E. A.: Effective Heterogeneous Design and Cosimulation. NATO ASI Series, Vol. 310, chapter in Hardware/Software Co-design, Kluwer Academic Publishers (1996)

[Pt96] Ptolemy's Group: The Almagest, Ptolemy 0.6. User's manual, volume 1, University of California at Berkeley, USA (1996)

[Sr95] Sriram, S.: Minimizing Communication and Synchronization Overhead in Multiprocessors for Digital Signal Processing. PhD thesis, Dept. of EECS, University of California at Berkeley, USA (1995)

[LM87] Lee, E. A. and Messerschmidt, D. G.: Synchronous Data Flow. Proc. of the IEEE (1987)

[DH89] Drusinsky, D. and Harel, D.: Using Statecharts for Hardware Description and Synthesis. IEEE Transactions on Computer-Aided Design (1989)

[KR+96] Kirschbaum, A. and Renner, F.-M. and Wilmes, A. and Glesner, M.: Rapid-Prototyping of a CAN-Bus Controller: A Case Study. Proc. of the 7th IEEE Int. Workshop on Rapid System Prototyping (RSP), Thessaloniki, Greece (1996)

[i-L94] i-Logix, Inc, Andover: ExpressV-HDL User Reference Manual V3.1, 1994

[Etsch94] Etschberger, K.: CAN Controller Area Network, Grundlagen, Protokolle, Bausteine, Anwendungen. Carl Hanser Verlag München, Wien(1994)

Exploiting Contemporary Memory Techniques in Reconfigurable Accelerators

R.W. Hartenstein, M. Herz, T. Hoffmann, U. Nageldinger

University of Kaiserslautern
Erwin-Schrödinger-Straße, D-67663 Kaiserslautern, Germany
Fax: ++49 631 205 2640, email: abakus@informatik.uni-kl.de
www: http://xputers.informatik.uni-kl.de

Abstract. This paper discusses the memory interface of custom computing machines. We present a high speed parallel memory for the MoM-PDA machine, which is based on the Xputer paradigm. The memory employs DRAMs instead of the more expensive SRAMs. To enhance the memory bandwidth, we use a threefold approach: modern memory devices featuring burst mode, an efficient memory architecture with multiple parallel modules, and memory access optimization for single applications. To exploit the features of the memory architecture, we introduce a strategy to determine optimized storage schemes for a class of applications.

1 Introduction

Custom computing machines [1][2] have been a promising research area for the recent years. These systems have shown the potential to achieve high performance for a variety of applications. Combining conventional microprocessors with accelerators featuring field programmable logic, custom computing machines make use of both traditional sequential code for the processor and structural code for the reconfigurable accelerator.

Naturally, the research on reconfigurable computing has focused mainly on the accelerator architectures themselves. However, experiences from traditional computers have shown, that the overall system performance depends also strongly on the peripheral parts. Especially the memory interface has shown to be a potential or existing bottleneck, which can extremely reduce the performance of the system.

The custom computing scene has avoided this problem by building the memory with fast SRAMs. However, SRAMs are still bigger and more expensive than DRAMs. Thus, it is worth thinking about using widespread DRAMs for large memories to be used for reconfigurable computing. As DRAMs are much slower than SRAMs, additional concepts have to be developed to speed the memory up.

For processors based on the so-called von Neumann paradigm, different methods have been developed to increase the memory bandwidth. The approaches can be distinguished into the following groups:

- Memory devices
- Memory architecture
- Compiler techniques

The most direct way to enhance memory access is the development of faster memory devices. This approach aims to reduce the physical data access time. In this field, a large variety of devices, especially in the DRAM sector, have been developed. Often, those devices also offer enhanced data access for consecutive data words (burst mode), with fixed or variable length.

Apart from the development of fast memory devices, special memory architectures have evolved to increase the memory bandwidth. The best known examples are caches [3] and interleaved memories with skewing schemes [4]. Caching relies on the locality

principle, which is basically an observation of normal program behavior. Though caches have shown to provide a remarkable speedup to memory accesses, the real efficiency of a cache depends on the application and can hardly be predicted. For interleaved memories, the classic examination by Budnik and Kuck [4] showed, that this architecture provides speedup only for certain access sequences. This is still true, although there has been remarkable research to increase the number of access sequences which take advantage of the interleaved memories, e.g. [5][6].

The third approach for faster memory access uses compiling techniques to adapt applications for utilizing memory architectures. Such techniques have been published for multiprocessors with shared address space [8], where the performance of a shared cache is enhanced by reducing disadvantageous cache-line replacements. Also, loop transformations can be used to increase the data locality in caches [7].

In this paper, we present an approach to improve the memory access for a reconfigurable architecture. Our target hardware is the MoM-PDA (Map-oriented Machine with Parallel Data Access) [9], which is based on the Xputer machine paradigm [10]. In our approach, we combine the three basic techniques mentioned above: We use a special memory architecture with parallel banks, which provides global speedup by supporting the execution model of the architecture. The memory is built of modern Multibank DRAM (MDRAM) devices [11], which feature support for interleaving by their internal structure as well as a fast burst mode for access of consecutive data words. Furthermore, we introduce strategies to utilize the memory architecture by examination of the data access sequences of applications and rearrangement of the application data.

The paper is structured as follows: In the next section, the target hardware MoM-PDA and the basic concepts of Xputers are introduced. Then, the compilation framework for the architecture is sketched briefly. In Section 4, a memory architecture for the MoM-PDA is described. After this, a data rearrangement strategy for this architecture is proposed. In the next section, performance results are given, and finally, the paper is concluded.

2 Target Architecture MoM-PDA

The MoM-PDA is an architecture based on the Xputer machine paradigm [10]. This non von Neumann paradigm provides high computation power for a large variety of computations. Especially for algorithms, where the same operation is performed on a big amount of data, Xputer-based accelerators achieve high speedup factors [12]. Such algorithms are found in many applications from multimedia, image and digital signal processing. The basic components of an Xputer-based machine and their interconnect are shown in Fig. 1.

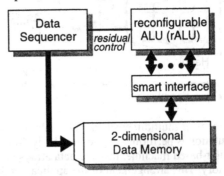

Fig. 1. Basic structure of the MoM-PDA architecture

The main difference between the Xputer and the so-called von Neumann paradigm

is, that an Xputer is controlled by a data stream rather than by an instruction stream. Thus, an Xputer features a data sequencer instead of an instruction sequencer. At run time, the data sequencer generates an address stream for the memory according to the data access sequence of the application. The resulting data stream is then fed into a reconfigurable ALU (rALU), which performs the required computation onto the data. The rALU is coupled to the memory by a smart memory interface, which contains a register file to store intermediate results and data, which is needed several times. This way, memory cycles are saved.

To execute an application, both the data sequencer and the reconfigurable ALU need to be configured before the computation. Once this is done, the machine can process a large amount of data without a change in this configuration. Thus, no instructions need to be fetched from memory during execution. The memory is used only for data. To make the mapping of multidimensional data arrays easier, the data memory is organized two-dimensionally. In contrast to traditional processors, which have an instruction set depending on the capabilities of the ALU, the data sequencer of the Xputer is only very loosely coupled to the reconfigurable ALU. So, the rALU and the data sequencer can be exchanged easily.

For the current prototype MoM-PDA, a novel sequencer hardware [9] and a novel memory architecture have been developed. The sequencer can implement a large number of generic address sequences. For the description of one sequence, only a few parameters are necessary. Multiple sequences can be concatenated or nested. The data memory comprises several (two in the prototype) parallel memory modules, which allow parallel access to data words. Each module is connected to the rALU via an own data bus and to the data sequencer via an own address bus. The data sequencer is capable of generating two independent address streams for each module.

The reconfigurable ALU of the MoM-PDA is implemented using the coarse-grained KressArray [13]. The KressArray resembles a mesh-connected array of configurable processing elements. In contrast to FPGAs, which offer only a one bit wide datapath, the processing elements can implement all operators of the language C for 32 bit words. Thus, the KressArray can easily implement a datapath for an application specified in a high level language.

The general execution model of an Xputer, which applies also to the MoM-PDA, is illustrated in Fig. 2. In many applications, the application data is typically arranged in

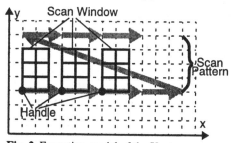

Fig. 2. Execution model of the Xputer

arrays, which may be one- or multidimensional. The data is traversed in nested loops, where a certain computation is performed in the loop body. In order to execute such an application on an Xputer-based machine, first the data arrays are mapped onto the two dimensional data memory. This arrangement of the application data is called data map. The data words, which are consumed or created by one execution of the datapath in the rALU are contained in a rectangular subarea of the data map, which is called scan win-

dow. The location of the scan window inside the data memory is determined by a reference position, the so-called handle (see Fig. 2). The traversal of the application data, which is normally done by loops, is performed by moving the scan window over the data map and performing the computation configured in the rALU in each step. The resulting movement pattern of the scan window is called scan pattern.

According to the execution model described above, a data map, a scan pattern and a rALU configuration have to be supplied in order to process an application on an Xputer. A compilation environment for this purpose is sketched in the next section.

3 Compilation Framework for the MoM-PDA

For the mapping of applications onto the MoM-PDA and other Xputer-based accelerators, the compilation environment CoDe-X [14] has been developed. CoDe-X is capable to compile applications specified in a high level language onto a system comprising a host and an Xputer-based accelerator.

CoDe-X accepts a description in a superset of the C language. The input program is in the first step partitioned in a set of tasks for the host and a set of tasks for the accelerator. This partitioning is driven by a performance analysis, which minimizes the overall execution time. Also, the first level partitioner performs loop transformations on the code to improve the performance.

The accelerator tasks are then processed by the X-C [15] compiler, which accepts a

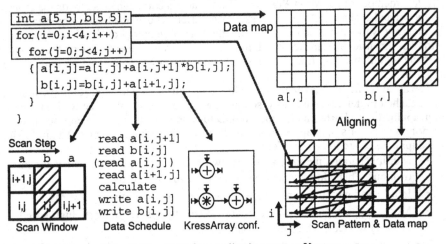

Fig. 3. Mapping of an application onto an Xputer

subset of X-C as input language. A course sketch of this second compilation step is illustrated by an example in Fig. 3. The X-C compiler performs a second level of partitioning by dividing the input up into code for the data sequencer and code for the rALU comprising the KressArray. First, the data arrays of the application are mapped onto the data memory. Basically, each array becomes a two-dimensional area and needs a scan pattern to access the data. If the loop structure allows it, several arrays can be aligned [15] to form one data area, so only one scan pattern is needed for multiple arrays (see Fig. 3). The scan pattern is generated from the loop structure. In the example, there are two nested loops whereof a so-called video scan is derived.

The loop body holds the information for the calculation to be performed onto the data. The variable references in the loop body combined with the scan pattern determine the scan window for the application. In the example in Fig. 3, there is only one

scan window due to the alignment of the two data arrays. The functions in the body itself are then transformed into a KressArray configuration by the Datapath Synthesis System (DPSS) [16]. For the topic of this paper, the configuration and the computational structure is of less importance. However, according to this structure and the ordering of the operators, the DPSS also determines an optimal data schedule. This schedule describes the sequence for reading and writing the data words inside the scan window. In the example in Fig. 3, the value of a[i,j] is the same as a[i,j+1] from the previous iteration. This can be seen by the overlap of two consecutive scan windows by one column. The DPSS recognizes this overlap and generates three schedules for the start of a new scan line, the positions in-between, and the last position of a line. The value a[i,j] has to be read from memory only at the beginning of each scan line. For all other positions, the according value from the last step is taken, which has been stored in the smart memory interface. In Fig. 3, this situation is illustrated by the parentheses around the read operation for a[i,j] in the data schedule.

It can be seen from the description above, that the smart memory interface performs a similar task as a cache in a conventional computer. The difference is, that this caching is not indeterministic. Instead, the reusable data is identified by the DPSS and only this data is stored. Thus, the smart memory interface needs much less capacity than a normal cache.

4 Memory Architecture

The data memory of the MoM-PDA uses a novel architecture, which supports the execution model and enables high-speed access. As described above, the logical organization of the memory is two-dimensional. This suits the execution model of the Xputer paradigm with two-dimensional scan patterns. It has shown, that this concept supports the mapping of many algorithms, e.g. from image processing, which are performed on multidimensional arrays.

The architecture of the data memory should provide a global means of improvement, like a cache or interleaved memory, so that one can expect a higher bandwidth for common applications. Furthermore, the architecture should support the enhancement of memory access for single applications by data rearrangement strategies. The following speedup features are to be considered:

- Multiple parallel memory modules (two in the prototype) with each using its own bus. This allows concurrent access to two data words.
- Interleaved memory banks, supporting access to sequential data words.
- More support for sequential data words by using modern high-speed memory devices, which offer a burst mode.

For the implementation of the memory architecture, we selected MDRAMs [11] from Siemens. An MDRAM features internally up to 36 independent banks. For our architecture, we have chosen devices with 32 banks. Reading and writing to and from a bank is done in bursts with variable length. An access to a bank requires an activation command, followed by the desired operation (read or write) and concluded by a precharge. The 32 banks can be activated independently from each other.

The resulting memory architecture using two parallel modules consisting of MDRAMs with 32 banks is shown in Fig. 4. The rows of the two-dimensional memory are alternately mapped onto the two memory modules, allowing parallel data access for two adjacent rows. Rows, which are in the same module are assigned to different banks of the MDRAM, allowing interleaved memory access within a module. Within a row, which resembles an MDRAM bank, the burst mode can be used. Thus, the memory architecture offers different speedup features in both dimensions. To address the memory modules, the two parrallel address streams from the data sequencer pass a burst control unit, which

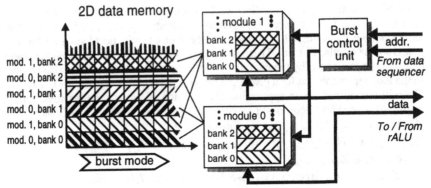

Fig. 4. Two-dimensional memory architecture

handles memory refresh and bursts. As the burst length is limited to 32 words, the burst control unit has to split bursts, if they reach over two horizontally neighbored banks.

5 Data Rearrangement Strategy

The memory architecture described above provides a basic means of enhancing the memory access. However, the memory bandwidth depends on the arrangement of the data according to the corresponding scan pattern. For many applications, this arrangement can be changed in a way to exploit the memory architecture, resulting in a higher bandwidth.

In this section, we will show for a specific application class, how the memory bandwidth can be enhanced. For simplicity, the algorithm is shown for max. two-dimensional data arrays, but the methods can be adapted to higher dimensions. We will utilize the compiler environment, which provides the data arrays and the according access sequences of an application in explicit form (see Fig. 3). Hereby, we assume, that the data arrays are not yet aligned.

Before the optimization strategies are discussed, we will introduce some naming conventions. Although all the information for the algorithm are provided as scan pattern parameters, we will mainly use terminology from the original loop structure to improve understandability. A two-dimensional loop nest L with index variables $i_1,...,i_n$, i_1 being the index of the innermost loop, can be rewritten so that each loop starts at 0 and ends at its limit N_l-1, $l=1,...,n$ (we use C notation). The loop body contains variables $v_1,...,v_m$, which are generated or consumed, depending if they appear on the left or right side of an assignment. The set of v_k in L, which are generated is called $GV(L)$, the set of consumed v_k is called $CV(L)$. Each v_k is addressed by an index function $f_k(i_1,...,i_n)$: $Z^n \rightarrow Z^2$ with $f_k(i_1,...,i_n) \rightarrow (x,y)$. An example loop nest is shown in Fig. 5a), with one variable v_1. The index function for v_1 is $f_1(i_1,i_2) = (3-i_2,i_1)$.

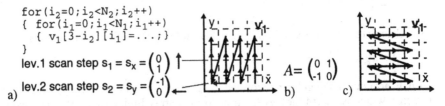

Fig. 5. Example application and scan pattern (a), transformation matrix (b), opimized scan pattern (c)

The index function $f_k(i_1,...,i_n)$ defines vectors determining the step direction of the scan pattern for v_k. There is one vector for each index variable i_j, $j=1,...,n$. The vector for the innermost loop is called level 1 scan step or s_1, the vector for the next loop level 2 scan step or s_2 and so on (see also Fig. 5a). These vectors can directly been derived from the scan pattern description generated by the compiler environment. The vectors could also be derived from the loop representation for a given f_k: $s_j = f_k(i_1,...,i_j+1,...,i_n) - f_k(i_1,...,i_j+1,...,i_n)$.

We will now introduce an application class, which allows a quite intuitive optimization strategy. Consider a loop nest L, which satisfies the following conditions:

1. $\forall\, v_k, v_l \in CV(L) \cup GV(L)$: $v_k = v_l \rightarrow f_k = f_l$;

2. $\forall\, v_k \in CV(L)$: $f_k(i_1,...,i_n) = (c_0+c_1i_1+...+c_ni_n, d_0+d_1i_1+...+d_ni_n)$;
   $c_0,...,c_n \in Z$; $d_0,...,d_n \in Z$;

3. $\forall\, v_k \in GV(L)$: $f_k(i_1,...,i_n) = (c_0+c_1i_1+...+c_ni_n, d_0+d_1i_1+...+d_ni_n)$;
   $c_0,...,c_n \in \{-1, 0, 1\}$; $d_0,...,d_n \in \{-1, 0, 1\}$;

4. $\forall\, v_k \in CV(L) \cap GV(L)$: $f_k(i_1,...,i_n) = (c_0+c_1i_1+...+c_ni_n, d_0+d_1i_1+...+d_ni_n)$;
   $c_0,c_2,...,c_n \in \{-1, 0, 1\}$; $d_0,d_2,...,d_n \in \{-1, 0, 1\}$; $c_1 = 0$; $d_1 = 0$;

The first condition demands, that there is only one access pattern for each variable. The next two conditions are due to the capabilities of the current compilation environment, which can handle only linear combinations of index variables for index functions. The third condition additionally requires from variables to be written, that the step width of their access sequence is at most one. The last condition means, that variables, which are written are not addressed using the innermost scan step s_1. Such variables can be buffered in the smart memory interface. This situation appears often in applications with multiply-accumulate operations.

For applications satisfying the above conditions, the access sequence of the data words is directly given by the scan pattern (i.e. the scan window has the size 1 by 1). The strategy to enhance the memory performance for such applications tries to exploit the burst mode of the memory for the innermost, time critical loop. This is done by rearranging the data map and the scan pattern in using a transformation matrix, so that the most relevant scan step points into the burst direction. After the rearrangement, the data is distributed onto parallel modules.

The transformation matrix is derived from the both most relevant scan steps. A scan step is considered not relevant, if it is the null vector or if it has the same direction as a scan step of a lower level. The algorithm for calculation of the transformation matrix A works as follows:

- Determine the most relevant scan step s_x:
  $s_x = s_j$, $j = \min(1,...,n)$ and $s_j \neq 0$
- Determine the second most relevant scan step s_y:
  $s_y = s_k$, $k = \min(j+1,...,n)$ and $s_k \neq 0$ and $\neg \exists\, l \in Z$: $(ls_k = s_x \vee ls_k = \binom{1}{0})$
  If there is no such s_k, then set:
  $$s_y = \binom{0}{1}$$
- Calculate the transformation matrix A by solving the following equations:
  $$A \times s_x = \binom{1}{0} \qquad A \times s_y = s_y$$

A data array v_k can then be transformed to v_k' using $v_k(x,y)' = A \times v_k(x,y)$, plus an offset vector, which is determined by the transformed array limits. Like the data, also the scan pattern is rearranged by calculating new scan steps $s_k' = A \times s_k$.

For the example in Fig. 5a, the transformation matrix and the result of the transformation are shown in Fig. 5b and Fig. 5c respectively. It can be seen, that A performs a clockwise turn by 90 degrees.

After the rearrangement of the arrays and the scan patterns, the parallel modules of the memory architecture are exploited. This is done by trying to align multiple arrays (see also Fig. 3). The alignment algorithm runs as follows:

- If $CV(L) = \emptyset$ or $GV(L) = \emptyset$ then distribute the arrays alternately onto adjacent rows of the memory.
- If there are arrays in both $CV(L)$ and $GV(L)$ then assign the variables in $CV(L)$ to one module and the variables in $GV(L)$ to the other one.
- In case there are more than one variable in one module, use vertical alignment of the arrays.
- Create a scan pattern and a scan window for each memory module and the aligned arrays.

To illustrate the algorithm, some examples are given in Fig. 6. The matrix-matrix

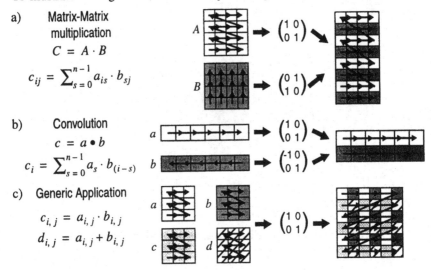

a) Matrix-Matrix multiplication
$$C = A \cdot B$$
$$c_{ij} = \sum_{s=0}^{n-1} a_{is} \cdot b_{sj}$$

b) Convolution
$$c = a \bullet b$$
$$c_i = \sum_{s=0}^{n-1} a_s \cdot b_{(i-s)}$$

c) Generic Application
$$c_{i,j} = a_{i,j} \cdot b_{i,j}$$
$$d_{i,j} = a_{i,j} + b_{i,j}$$

Fig. 6. Examples illustrating the transformation (a),(b) and aligning (c) of data

multiplication and the convolution (Fig. 6a,b) can be optimized, because the write operation to the current data word c_i or c_{ij} respectively does not take place in the innermost loop. Thus, the current value of c_i or c_{ij} can be stored in the smart memory interface, without needing any memory access. The example in Fig. 6c illustrates the aligning of more than two arrays.

Under certain conditions, both the rearrangement and the aligning may result in a higher usage of memory. E.g. If s_1 is not parallel to either the x or the y coordinate, the transformation will shear the data array, resulting in a bigger area. In order to make the class of transformable applications as big as possible, we did not forbid such situations by adding more conditions. The trade-off between the memory usage and the speed has to be considered by a post processor, which is not covered in this paper.

Furthermore, we did not consider any time for the actual computation to be performed on the data. Considering the generic example in Fig. 6c, it is obvious, that the results would have to be written in the same speed, as the input is read. In reality, this can hardly be reached. For the example, both read and write burst would probably have to be interrupted to allow the computation to take place. Also, one would expect a delay

between the start of the read burst and the writing back of the results. However, both a delay and an interrupt do not influence the usability of the resulting storage scheme.

6 Memory Performance

Some estimated access times for our approach are given in Table 1. The times are given in microseconds, assuming a cycle time of 15 ns, and calculated for two of the sample applications in Fig. 6 with different problem sizes. The applications are the matrix-matrix mul-

Table 1. Performance of the presented memory architecture

Appli-cation	Size of one array	Single word access			Without transformation			With transformation		
		FPM	BEDO	MDR	FPM	BEDO	MDR	FPM	BEDO	MDR
MAT	4 x 4	10.8	10.8	12.72	5.28	4.56	5.16	4.56	3.12	3.36
	40 x 40	9720	9720	11640	3984	3480	3600	3048	2040	1320
CON	20 x 1	18	18	19.8	7.05	9.75	11.4	7.05	5.31	4.65
	200 x 1	1530	1530	1833	475.5	772.5	924	475.5	322.5	197.7

tiplication (MAT, Fig. 6a) and the convolution (CON, Fig. 6b). The problem size is specified by the dimensions of one input array, i.e. not the resulting aligned array. We consider three different types of devices: Fast Page Mode DRAM (FPM), Burst Enhanced Data Out DRAM (BEDO) [17], and MDRAM (MDR) [11]. The first situation in the left major column represents the worst case where all data words are accessed without exploiting any burst or fast page modes and without parallel access. The other two columns assume the proposed parallel memory architecture, built from the different device types. The right column contains access times with the rearrangement strategy applied. The middle column contains theoretical values, assuming that the existing data ordering is exploited for burst mode and access to parallel banks is possible. These figures are only for examining the efficiency of the algorithm in optimizing the burst mode, as in reality, parallel access would not be possible without a proper data arrangement.

For the calculation, we assume, that the FPM DRAMs can read or write data with 5 cycles for the first word and 3 cycles for any other word in the same page. Words in the same row of the two dimensional data memory are supposed to be also on the same page. For the BEDO DRAMs, we assume, that they work exclusively in burst mode with a maximum burst length of 4. The first word is accessed in 5 cycles, the next three in 1 cycle each, for reading and writing. The MDRAMs also use burst mode exclusively. The maximum burst length is 32 words, a read burst needs $5+n$ cycles, a write burst $4+n$ cycles, where n is the burst length.

Though the figures in Table 1 describe the theoretical peak performance, they show the efficiency of the proposed architecture and the transformation strategy. Comparing different devices, the MDRAMs have a poor performance for single word access, as MDRAMs use exclusively bursts, which involves a rather long initialization time for read accesses. This disadvantage can also reduce the performance for small data sizes, as the application MAT with 4 x 4 arrays shows. Looking at the second column, it can be seen, that BEDO devices with shorter bursts are superior, if the data is not properly arranged. However, the combination with the proposed algorithm provides dramatic speedups for large array sizes, which justifies the use of MDRAMs.

7 Conclusions and Future Work

We have shown a memory architecture for the MoM-PDA, which uses high-speed DRAMs. The memory supports the two-dimensional memory model of the machine paradigm and offers high bandwidth due to the use of two parallel modules. We have presented a strategy to exploit the burst mode of the memory and the parallel modules for a class of applications. The algorithm makes use of the compilation framework for the MoM-PDA, which provides the explicit data access sequence. The next aim is to extend the group of optimizable algorithms. A promising approach tries to rearrange the data words inside the scan window. This kind of optimization is quite complex, as there are many constraints. With a combination of several techniques we are confident, that a high memory bandwidth can be achieved for many applications.

References

1. R.W. Hartenstein, J. Becker, R. Kress: Custom Computing Machines vs. Hardware/Software Co-Design: From a Globalized point of view; Proc. of the 6th Intl. Workshop of Field Programmable Logic and Applications FPL'96, pp. 65 - 76, Springer LNCS, 1996.
2. W.H. Mangione-Smith, et. al.: Seeking Solutions in Configurable Computing; IEEE Computer, Dec. 1997.
3. D.A. Patterson, J.L. Hennessy: Computer Architecture, A Quantitative Approach; Morgan Kaufmann Publishers, 1990.
4. P. Budnik, D.J. Kuck: The Organization and Use of parallel Memories; IEEE Transactions on Computers, Dec. 1971.
5. K. Kim, V.K. Prasanna: Perfect Latin Squares and Parallel Array Access; Proc. Int. Symposium on Computer Architecture, ACM Press, 1989.
6. A. Deb: Multiskewing - A Novel Technique for Optimal Parallel Memory Access; IEEE Transactions on Parallel and Distributed Systems; Vol. 7, No. 6, June 1996.
7. M.E. Wolf, M.S. Lam: A Data Locality Optimizing Algorithm; Proc. of the SIGPLAN'91 Conf. on Programming Language Design and Implementation, pp. 30 - 44, Toronto, Canada, June 1991.
8. J. M. Anderson, S. P. Amarasinghe and M. S. Lam: Data and computation transformations for multiprocessors; Proceedings of the Fifth ACM SIGPLAN Symp. on Principles and Practice of Parallel Processing, July 1995.
9. R.W. Hartenstein, J. Becker, M. Herz, U. Nageldinger: A Novel Universal Sequencer Hardware; Proceedings of Fachtagung Architekturen von Rechensystemen ARCS'97, Rostock, Germany, September 8-11, 1997.
10. R.W. Hartenstein, A. Hirschbiel, K. Schmidt, M. Weber: A Novel Paradigm of Parallel Computation and its Use to Implement Simple High-Performance-HW; Future Generation Computer Systems 7 91/92, p. 181-198, North Holland.
11. N.N.: Siemens Multibank DRAM; Ultra-high performance for graphic applications; Siemens Semiconductor Group, Oct. 1996.
12. R.W. Hartenstein, J. Becker, R. Kress, H. Reinig: High-Performance Computing Using a Reconfigurable Accelerator; CPE Journal, Special Issue of Concurrency: Practice and Experience, John Wiley & Sons Ltd., 1996.
13. R. Kress: A Fast Reconfigurable ALU for Xputers; Ph.D. dissertation, University of Kaiserslautern, 1996.
14. J. Becker: A Partitioning Compiler for Computers with Xputer-based Accelerators; Ph.D. dissertation, University of Kaiserslautern, 1997.
15. K. Schmidt: A Program Partitioning, Restructuring, and Mapping Method for Xputers; Ph.D. dissertation, University of Kaiserslautern, 1994.
16. R. W. Hartenstein, R. Kress: A Datapath Synthesis System for the Reconfigurable Datapath Architecture; Asia and South Pacific Design Automation Conference, ASP-DAC'95, Nippon Convention Center, Makuhari, Chiba, Japan, Aug. 29 - Sept. 1, 1995.
17. N.N: The Burst EDO DRAM Advantage, Technical Note TN-04-41, Micron Technology Inc., 1995

Self Modifying Circuitry -
A Platform for Tractable Virtual Circuitry

Adam Donlin

Department of Computer Science, University of Edinburgh,
Mayfield Road, Edinburgh EH9 3JZ, Scotland.

Abstract. The performance advantages, gained in early virtual circuitry systems, are being recouped through advances in general purpose processor architectures and have resulted in a questioning of the tractability of applying virtual circuitry in a general software environment. Two primary limitations of existing virtual circuitry systems are highlighted and the Flexible URISC is introduced as an array resident minimal processor architecture. Performance results of a prototype implementation of the Flexible URISC architecture demonstrate how peripheral bus bandwidth limitations are overcome by the increased bandwidth available to an array resident configuration, communication and computation agent. A discussion of the programming environment of the Flexible URISC is given, and provides the medium for identifying how the Flexible URISC's single instruction – *move* – effectively minimises the hardware/software divide.

1 Introduction

Increased FPGA density and flexibility has done much to improve the tractability of virtual circuitry[1], yet exploitation of custom hardware co-processing has remained the elusive attribute of a restricted set of application classes. General purpose processor systems, as has been revealed by case study[7], have also been successful in recouping a significant amount of the readily available performance advantages gained by early virtual circuitry systems. Key issues in sustaining this elusiveness stem from bandwidth constraints imposed by the environment in which virtual circuitry is typically deployed, and the complexities of negotiating the hardware/software divide. An a-typical setting for a virtual circuitry system is one where an FPGA is coupled to a host processor system via the host peripheral bus. The FPGA works exclusively as a slave co-processor, under the management of software component executing on the host processor. Virtual circuitry systems have been classified into various forms[1] yet all are typically applied in this common setting and, hence, are constrained by its common trappings.

---

[1] For reasons discussed in [2], the term virtual circuitry is used in preference to virtual hardware

The primary aim of this paper is to present an alternative environment for the deployment of virtual circuitry, in which the limitations of the traditional virtual circuitry environment have been addressed. The following section provides a brief introduction to the Ultimate RISC architecture. Section 3, presents a discussion of a *Flexible* Ultimate RISC (Flexible URISC) whilst section 4 explores technical requirements and implementation issues. The prospect of self modifying circuitry is introduced in section 5 and it's exploitation to support tractable virtual circuitry is discussed in section 6. Section 7 discusses a programming environment for the Flexible URISC and characterises both runtime and compile-time versions of the system.

2   The Ultimate RISC

The Ultimate RISC(URISC)[6] is a minimal processor architecture with only one instruction: *move memory to memory*. Computation is achieved by migrating devices onto the system bus, then mapping those devices into the memory space of the URISC processor core. For example, the core of the URISC machine possesses no ALU; instead, an ALU component resides on the system bus and its registers are mapped into the memory space of the URISC core. By moving operands to and from the memory addresses corresponding to the registers of ALU components, arithmetic computations may be performed.

The datapath of the URISC core, the Instruction Execution Unit(IEU), is particularly lean, consisting of only four registers, an incrementor, a simple decoder, and some basic multiplexors. The primary responsibility of the core is to implement the move instruction and, since move is the only instruction, no operand decoding is necessary. Unconditional jumps are possible by moving the target address into the memory mapped Program Counter(PC). Conditional jumps are made by adding the contents of a memory mapped ALU condition code register to an branch address that is then written back to the PC. This allows the destination of the jump to be offset by the truth or false value contained in the condition code register.

The lean resource requirements of the URISC control and data paths increase the feasibility of a configurable logic implementation, yet the static nature of the standard URISC machine excludes any benefits of dynamic reconfiguration. The remainder of this paper, therefore, focuses on the Flexible URISC machine.

3   The Flexible URISC

Figure 1 shows the abstract and physical implementations of a Flexible URISC system on an FPGA. Here, dynamic reconfiguration is used to vary the devices which are currently resident on the system bus. Specifically, the Flexible URISC core resides on the FPGA, alongside a set of Swappable Logic Units(SLUs)[1]. There is a direct correspondence between the set of SLUs resident on the configurable array and the devices currently resident on the Flexible URISC system bus. Indeed, the input and output registers of each SLU are mapped into the

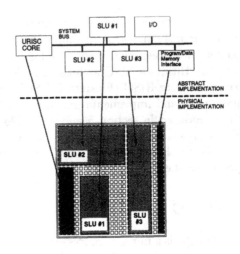

Figure 1. The Flexible URISC Architecture

memory space of the Flexible URISC allowing each SLU device to be accessed in the same manner as a piece of static hardware. Using dynamic reconfiguration, SLUs are dynamically placed and replaced, allowing the set of available devices on the URISC system bus to dynamically expand and contract.

The Flexible URISC exploits a memory-style co-processor interface, such as the FastMap^{tm} processor interface[3] of the Xilinx XC6200 series FPGA[8]. Notedly, there is no explicit implementation of a system bus utilising the configurable routing resources of the FPGA. The Flexible URISC can, instead, exploit the random access nature of the co-processor interface to move instruction operands to and from the input and output registers of the SLUs resident on the array. This limits the amount of interfacing logic required by SLUs to standard input/output registers and allows flexible SLU placement and relocation on virtually any unoccupied array area of appropriate dimensions. Provided additional compiler complexity can be justified, SLU geometry may also be irregular and chosen for the efficient implementation of the functionality being modelled. In this case, the Flexible URISC is acting primarily as a communication agent, transferring operands between SLUs and memory. A more detailed discussion of the use of the Flexible URISC in this rôle has already been undertaken in earlier work[2].

Given that the Flexible URISC has a minimal instruction set interface, the fact that the interface comprises of a move instruction is more significant than the fact that only a single instruction is employed. As discussed in section 7, the single Flexible URISC move instruction has inherent benefits in negotiating the hardware/software boundary. The main focus of this paper, and the following sections is to consider the further benefits gained from exploiting the co-processor interface to provide the Flexible URISC a rôle of being a combined communication, computation and configuration agent.

4 Technical Implementation and Requirements

A prototype of the Flexible URISC core has been implemented using Xilinx XC6200 series Reconfigurable Processing Units (RPUs) and a Xilinx XC6200DS compliant prototyping board. A primary novel contribution of the Flexible UR-ISC system is the presence of an *array resident* configuration agent. By this, it is meant that the Flexible URISC core is capable of dynamically reconfiguring the FPGA device upon which it is currently residing. At an abstract level, this is simply a matter of mapping the configuration memory of the FPGA into the memory map of the Flexible URISC core.

Some key technological advances in the XC6200 RPUs have made the implementation of an array resident configuration agent possible. The ability for user array logic to access the internal control logic of the RPU, such as the configuration address and data busses, is fundamental. The "Open Architecture" of the XC6200 series is an important non-technical feature, allowing essential access to detailed information regarding the low level programming interface and bit-stream formats. Since the Flexible URISC machine must interface directly with the configuration interface of the RPU, specific details regarding this interface must be available.

Additionally, since the FastMap^{tm} interface presents a memory style interface, only a narrow semantic gap need be bridged in mapping the FastMap^{tm} into the Flexible URISC's address space. The amount of interfacing logic required to map the configuration memory into the overall memory map of the URISC core, therefore, is minimised. In total, three conceptually distinct memory interfaces must be mapped into the memory map of the Flexible URISC core. System RAM for holding program and data segments is a basic requirement, derived from a standard URISC machine. In addition to configuration memory, it is also necessary to map the state memory of the user logic resident on the array into the URISC memory space. Mapping of user logic state facilitates the use of the Flexible URISC core as an inter-SLU communications agent.

User state memory is also accessed via the FastMap^{tm} interface and the act of mapping configuration memory also maps state memory into the address space. Extra measures are necessary, however, as state memory cannot be accessed directly, in the same manner as configuration memory. State memory is, instead, addressed by horizontal column and a series of masking registers are used to select the desired bitfields. Managing masking registers could be implemented within the processor core but, instead, is implemented as a system level software task to uphold the simplicity and purity of the Flexible URISC implementation.

5 Self Modifying Circuitry

By mapping the host FPGA's configuration memory into it's own memory space, the Flexible URISC gains the interesting attribute of self-reference. Circuitry exploiting this self-referentiality to drive the internal FastMap^{tm} control, address and data busses, can be considered "self-modifying".

5.1 The Self Modification Taboo

Traditional software which has access to its program text and data segments has the potential for self reference, and hence, self modification. In modern software engineering practices, however, the exploitation of such properties is rare and taboo. For large software systems, this is a justified notion as the unruly application of self modification makes systems particularly difficult to debug.

Efficiency, however, is a primary reason for exploiting self modification. Limited memory, storage, and processing time in early computer systems justified the use of self modification to gain increased code flexibility whilst limiting resource utilisation. Contemporary virtual circuitry systems find themselves in an analogous situation to early software systems. FPGA device densities, although improving, are still considered limited and configuration penalties remain high. Performance advantages are therefore to be gained from exploiting self modification as the technique for altering the configuration of a resident circuit. The main benefit for self modifying circuitry is the reduced time spent on configuration. The availability of partial reconfigurability is key in allowing the self modifying circuit to remain active whilst part of the datapath is modified.

6 Practicable Virtual Circuitry

Increased device level performance in FPGAs has resulted from advances in fabrication technologies, combined with partially reconfigurable architectures. Bottlenecks on the host peripheral bus have become a primary limitation restricting the deployment of virtual circuitry within general software systems. Most FPGA development cards interface an FPGA with a main processor system via the host's PCI bus. Interactions between the FPGA and host must be mediated against other devices resident on the PCI bus.

The self contained nature of the Flexible URISC allows peripheral bus bandwidth limitations to be avoided. As a self-modifying system, the Flexible URISC has direct, unmediated access to the host FPGA's FastMap^{tm} programming interface. Program and circuitry data, stored in on-board SRAM, is directly accessible to the Flexible URISC via a dedicated, on board memory bus. The combination of both these properties within the Flexible URISC core allows for the high bandwidth transfer of program and circuitry across the dedicated memory bus and the fast direct reconfiguration of the host FPGA by self-modification.

System Level Integration(SLI) is a promising approach in combating bandwidth limitation directly through deep sub-micron fabrication and Intellectual Property(IP) cores. Although the widespread fabrication and availability of such "System on Chip" devices is unlikely within the near future, it should be noted that the Flexible URISC is an equitable present day prototype of such single die solutions. Rather than physically integrating processor and cell array IP cores on a single die, the Flexible URISC core is tightly integrated with the configurable array by residing on it. Directly interfacing with the host array's configuration interface serves to further tighten the integration. Experiences and performance results gained from the Flexible URISC system should therefore parallel those to be gained in the SLI environment.

The choice of processor core to be integrated on the same die as an FPGA highlights another attribute of the Flexible URISC system. Integrating a complex processor core on the same die as an FPGA results in a system which has a traditional separation between hardware and software. To exploit the custom computing facilities of the integrated FPGA, it remains necessary to traverse between the notion of software, defined by the instruction set of the integrated processor core, to the notion of hardware, defined the custom circuitry implemented on the FPGA. In this situation, a significant hardware/software divide remains between the integrated processor and configurable array.

6.1 Prototype Performance

Since program data and circuitry reside within on-board SRAM, the bandwidth available over the dedicated SRAM interface sets an upper bounds on the rate of self modification and overall performance. The simple task of filling a buffer with a known constant was used to determine the number of instructions being executed within a given time period. The approximate memory bandwidth could be derived given that filling a single buffer cell requires a single move instruction, each move instruction costs 16 clock cycles and uses 4 memory cycles. Bandwidth grows linearly and at a modest clock speed of 8MHz, the observed bandwidth of 8Mb/s is particularly promising, especially considering the maximum reported bandwidth of 7Mb/s for first generation XC6200DS systems. Simple application of pipelining will increase the performance of the prototype further.

7 The Flexible URISC Programming Environment

7.1 System Context

The Flexible URISC's self-contained and self modifying nature makes it an autonomous processing system. The programming environment should, however, take into account the relationship between the Flexible URISC and any host processing system. To clarify; the primary system context, an autonomous Flexible URISC, comprises of a central RPU combined with RAM and NVRAM devices. RAM is primarily used to store program code, data, and SLU bitstreams. NVRAM provides an appropriately flexible storage medium for the Flexible URISC boot configuration. To facilitate a stand alone system, the Flexible URISC is capable of processing immediately at the end of the configuration cycle.

In the traditional approach to virtual circuitry, a software component executing on the host processor provides runtime virtual circuitry management. Integrating the Flexible URISC and a general purpose processor system effectively results in the creation of a closely coupled multiprocessor system. The metaphor is furthered by exploiting a shared memory interface to facilitate communication between processors. Notably, the Flexible URISC retains entire responsibility for management and implementation of the virtual circuitry model.

7.2   The Flexible URISC Model of Virtual Circuitry

Two primary models of virtual circuitry, the Sea of Accelerators and the Parallel Harness, have been defined in [1]. Both of these systems can be implemented on the Flexible URISC. Indeed, the definition of Sea of Accelerators gives some consideration to the use of a PC-host software agent to transfer data between SLUs, although traditional bandwidth limitations suggest the intractability of this technique.

Rather than simply implementing one of these models, however, the Flexible URISC provides enough facilities to consider a third model of virtual circuitry – the *Sequential Algorithmic* Model. Contextually, this model is a midpoint between the Sea of Accelerators, which exploits no routing, and the Parallel Harness model of explicit hard routing. The Sequential Algorithmic model implements efficient *software* routing and utilises the communications agent abilities of the Flexible URISC to effect processing. The model is sequential as a result of the serialising effect of processing move instructions within the Flexible URISC core. A Flexible URISC program defines, via a series of move instructions, the order of transfer of operands between system bus SLUs. The precise order of system bus transfers can be explicitly described in a lengthy series of moves. More attractive, however, is the potential to exploit the computational SLUs on the system bus to allow an *algorithmic* definition of complex communication patterns.

7.3   Programming Model

Programming the Flexible URISC in its native instruction set is undesirable. Hand construction of large programs solely with move instructions and absolute addressing as the only addressing mode would be cumbersome and error prone. Given this, a suitable formalism for the expression of a Flexible URISC program must be selected. Some initial consideration is given, however, to the overall development and execution model of a Flexible URISC program.

The Flexible URISC exploits a series of pre-defined SLUs as elements of execution, avoiding the costly run-time derivation of in-line hardware modules, as suggested for the self-configuring processor[5]. The Flexible URISC departs from the traditional virtual circuitry execution model in which processing involves combining periods of traditional software execution interspersed by periods of hardware custom co-processing. In contrast, the Flexible URISC insists *all* computation is performed in custom hardware modules. Whilst this model was not particularly tractable in previous systems, the technical features of the Flexible URISC used to support the Sequential Algorithmic virtual circuitry model increase the feasibility of hardware execution.

Since the Flexible URISC is essentially a dataflow machine, the programming formalism should adequately capture dataflow information. C, despite its ubiquity, requires additional compiler complexity to derive a suitable dataflow between instruction SLUs and has no intrinsic ability to represent dynamic reconfiguration. Functional languages, alternatively, capture dataflow information in a more readily accessible manner and higher order functions have some ability to represent dynamic reconfiguration.

7.4 Narrowing the Hardware Software Divide

Whilst the single move instruction effects computation by moving operands between system bus SLUs, the same instruction also effects reconfiguration when transporting configuration data between system memory and the host FPGA's configuration memory. The point to be noted is that the same instruction is used to both configure and compute and the transition between effecting computation and configuration is highly transparent – effectively being an attribute only of the source or destination address of the move instruction. Given a series of Flexible URISC move instructions, instructions for computation and instructions for configuration are not immediately discernible.

As well as bridging the gap between computation and configuration, the move instruction narrows the boundary between hardware and software. Considering the software tier of a Flexible URISC program to be the microcode style program defining the movement of operands and the hardware tier to be the processing of operands by system bus SLUs. No processing of any interest may occur independently, on any single tier. Realistic processing, instead, involves a move to transfer operands between tiers. *i.e.*, transferring operands from system RAM to and from state memory of the host FPGA. The Flexible URISC provides a single instruction which transparently negotiates the hardware/software and computation/configuration boundaries. Effectively, the move instruction is a single interface to hardware, software, and dynamic configuration.

7.5 Static and Dynamic Environments

Two styles of Flexible URISC environment are envisioned. A compile time system providing a highly efficient implementation of a pre-defined configuration schedule and a dynamic system implementing a primitive operating-system style demand configuration system.

The static environment is a compile time system which trades performance against flexibility. At the cost of system flexibility, the burden of runtime decision making is avoided by extracting a static reconfiguration schedule. The dynamic approach, which supports increased flexibility, is more applicable in a general software environment where no static reconfiguration schedule is available.

Loss of flexibility in the static environment is offset by increased opportunities to apply a number of performance enhancing techniques. A novel approach to reconfiguration, for example, is applicable. Traditional virtual circuitry systems employ distinct phases of computation and configuration. Configuration phases are immediately followed by computation phases intended to take maximum advantage of the newly configured circuitry, recouping any reconfiguration penalty. Notedly, processing must halt for a significant period whilst configuration is underway. Utilising the information contained in the static reconfiguration schedule, however, allows the advance determination of configuration deadlines.

This, combined with the Flexible URISC's ability to transparently mix configuration and computation instructions at a very fine grain, allows the compiler to begin configuration *in advance* of the execution of dependant computation instructions. Fine grain intermixing of configuration instructions allows a minimum impact on the level of computation instructions being processed. The lack of a static reconfiguration schedule in the dynamic environment restricts the application of such interleaved configuration and computation. Any application of the technique would be analogous to probabilistic page pre-fetching in virtual memory systems.

Further, technology specific techniques, may be exploited in the compile-time environment. As discussed in [2], careful alignment of system bus SLU interfaces and choice of map register values allows, multiple independent moves to be made in a single instruction. Wildcarding may also be exploited to implement multicasting.

The dynamic environment, in the model of a primitive operating system, implements two levels of programming. A privileged "system program" is charged with the responsibility of implementing demand dynamic reconfiguration of the host FPGA. Dynamic environment programs express computation dataflow and contain definitions of the appropriate system bus SLUs to effect the defined computational dataflow. In contrast to static environment programs, which contain integrated configuration, computation and circuitry definitions, no configuration dataflow is defined in user programs. The system program, instead, defines a general configuration dataflow for all user programs.

A dynamic environment compiler supports the use of a "procedural" interface to access the facilities of the system program. Upholding the operating system metaphor, user programs make Flexible URISC "system calls" to request, for example, the placement of a particular system bus SLU. Signalling a return to the traditional model of configuration followed by computation, system calls in the dynamic environment block the caller. Following a model of co-operative multitasking, blocking system calls allow the system program to resume executing, begin the demand paging process or possibly context switch to an alternative user program. A pre-emptive multitasking system is conceivable, but requires increased complexity in the Flexible URISC core, to introduce timing interrupts.

8   Conclusions and Future Work

Literature has shown that traditional performance gains in virtual circuitry systems are waning in the light of significant increases in the raw processing power of general purpose processors. It is the belief of the author, however, that virtual circuitry still has a significant contribution to make to the general field of computing. The advent of "Systems on Silicon" is perceived as a particularly promising new environment allowing virtual circuitry to be successfully integrated with a general software system, avoiding technical bandwidth limitations that have choked existing systems.

The Flexible URISC has been introduced as a combined computation, communication and configuration agent. By exploiting its ability for self-reference and self-modification, the Flexible URISC represents a practical midpoint between existing virtual circuitry systems and future SLI systems. A basic analysis of the prototype implementation has shown the Flexible URISC has the potential to combat the technical limitations of the existing virtual circuitry environment. This result provides some initial evidence of advantages to be gained by systems exploiting SLI.

Future plans for the Flexible URISC involve the development of its programming environment. This facilitates the use of the Flexible URISC as a vehicle for exploring the application hardware/software co-design when the boundaries between hardware/software are minimised. A planned application area for the Flexible URISC is Dynamic Protocol Construction, within the field of active networking[4]. This research is supported by UK EPSRC Grant 96307386.

References

1. G. Brebner. A Virtual Hardware Operating System for the Xilinx XC6200. In R. W. Hartenstein and Manfred Glesner, editors, *Proc. 6th International Workshop on Field-Programmable Logic and Applications, FPL'96*, pages 327–336, Darmstadt, Germany, September 1996. Springer-Verlag.
2. G. Brebner and A. Donlin. Runtime Reconfigurable Routing. In José Rolim, editor, *Parallel and Distributed Processing*, volume 1388 of *LNCS*, pages 25–30. Springer-Verlag, 1998.
3. S. Churcher, T. Kean, and B. Wilkie. The XC6200 FastMap^{TM} processor interface. In W. Moore and W. Luk, editors, *Field-Programmable Logic and Applications : 5th international workshop*, volume 975 of *LNCS*, pages 36–43, Oxford, United Kingdom, August/September 1995. Springer-Verlag.
4. A. Donlin. A Dynamically Self-Modifying Processor Architecture and its Application to Active Networking. Working Paper, University of Edinburgh, September 1997.
5. P. C. French and R. W. Taylor. A self-reconfiguring processor. In D. A. Buell and K. L. Pocek, editors, *Proceedings of IEEE Workshop on FPGAs for Custom Computing Machines*, pages 50–59, Napa, CA, April 1993.
6. D. W. Jones. The Ultimate RISC. *Computer Architecture News*, 16(3):48–55, June 1988.
7. M. Shand. A Case Study of Algorithm Implementation in Reconfigurable Hardware and Software. In *Proc. 7th International Workshop on Field Programmable Logic and Applications*, volume 1304 of *LNCS*, pages 333–343. Springer, 1997.
8. Xilinx. *The Programmable Logic Data Book*. Xilinx Inc, San Jose CA, 1996.

REACT: Reactive Environment for Runtime Reconfiguration*

Dinesh Bhatia, Parivallal Kannan, Kuldeep S.Simha,
Karthikeya M. GajjalaPurna

Design Automation Laboratory,
ECECS Department
University of Cincinnati,
Cincinnati, OH 45221-0030

Abstract

Field programmable gate array based computing machines have successfully demonstrated the performance advantages for a large class of compute intense problems. However, in most of the applications executing on FPGA based reconfigurable hardwares, the burden of careful design and mapping rests on the end user. Motivated with the task of making reconfigurable and adaptive computing more comprehensible to a software programmer, we have defined the REACT architecture. REACT consists of a dynamically and partially reconfigurable hardware platform supported by a collection of advanced analysis, compilation, and scheduling tools to allow maximum reconfigurability exploitation. The tools supporting REACT computing environment are portable to support other forms of reconfigurable processing hardware units. In other words, the tools completely hide the implementation details of a particular function in the hardware.

1 Introduction

In recent years we have witnessed the evolution of high speed general purpose microprocessors. Many of the commercial microprocessors implement a mix of RISC and CISC concepts [16]. A CISC machine can deliver high performance, if the available complex instruction set is effectively utilized by the compiler. However, in the absence of intelligent compilers, and also the complexity involved in finding a match for complex instructions from the user specifications, CISC machines could deliver equal or little higher performance than their RISC counterparts. Even in the presence of complex instruction set a still higher complex operation will have to be represented in terms of smaller complex instructions. This does not guarantee optimum performance. With an ability to customize the instruction set, it is easy to obtain a very high performance. The static nature of the general purpose microprocessors hinders such attempts. A viable alternative medium to implement the customization could be found in programmable logic, mostly implemented using Field Programmable Gate Arrays(FPGAs).

FPGA based computing machines allow application specific custom computing. They provide a rapid prototyping environment for custom hardware with higher flexibility compared to ASICs and higher performance compared to general purpose computers. A variety of custom computing machines [3] have been designed, and demonstrated to outperform supercomputers in solving problems such as text searching, DNA

---

* This research is partially supported by contract number DABT63-97-C-0029 from Defense Advanced Research Projects Agency (DARPA) and contract number F33615-96-C1912 from Wright Laboratory of the United States Air Force.

Comparison, and image processing algorithms. A common feature of all these machines is that they are highly static in nature and include a lot of overhead in designing the application for hardware and synthesizing to an array of FPGAs. In other words the user needs to understand the underlying hardware architecture and should also be proficient in hardware design techniques. Several research attempts [2] are being made to generate hardware mappings from a high level language.

The recent evolution of dynamically reconfigurable FPGAs, provides a processor friendly and efficient medium for high performance computing. The existing custom computing board architectures [3] incur a high overhead when communicating between the host CPU and the programmable logic [12]. Such overhead limits the applicability of this approach to a class of algorithms that have a combination of high computational complexity and low communication overhead. The ability of dynamically reconfigurable FPGAs to partially reconfigure in very short reconfiguration times provides a very convenient medium for the compilers, to synthesize a custom hardware implementation of complex instructions, from a high level language specification. The instructions synthesized by the compiler are dynamic in nature. This customization provides a very high performance implementation.

2 Related Work

The architectures using the Xilinx fine grained XC6200 family of FPGAs range from single chip systems like Hades [9], and 6200DS [10] to multi-chip systems like ACE [17]. These hardware architectures are supported by software tools for programming. Typically these environments consist of a schematic capture or HDL design specification tools that translate designs to the target chip configuration. They are also supported by runtime libraries for memory access and partial reconfiguration at runtime. However, it demands a profound hardware knowledge from the users.

Hybrid architectures combining conventional processors with configurable logic resources are beginning to evolve like GARP [2], NAPA [13], and RAW [19]. These architectures are supported by high level compilers. The RAW [1] compiler aims at exploiting the instruction level parallelism, while the NAPA C compiler [7] aims at the co-synthesis of the pragma-annotated program to an executable combined with hardware configuration.

Our goal is to develop a compiler framework that analyzes and identifies the tasks in the program for the potential candidates for hardware execution. The analysis takes into account the practical overheads involved in the target hardware architecture and annotate the code with directives. One such potential area is loops in the programs. The annotated code is further optimized to minimize the overheads. Finally the code generator produces the software executable, the hardware configurations and the necessary synchronization. The compiler framework is supported with a rich set of physical design tools that perform fast and efficient mapping of the tasks on the hardware. Such an environment provides a transparent abstraction to an end user while providing massive performance gains.

3 REACT : Overall Environment

The REACT environment consists of a custom high performance adaptive computing environment, capable of fine, medium and coarse grain reconfiguration. Although

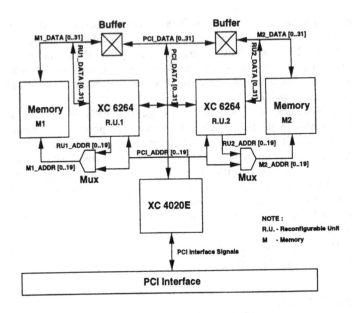

Fig. 1. *REACT : Hardware Architecture*

FPGAs evolved as devices for logic prototyping, their ability to effectively implement application specific execution has made them ideal for high performance computing. The static reconfiguration overheads become a considerable bottleneck in the performance [15]. Also, to extend the range of applications that can exploit the high performance of adaptive computing systems, it is highly essential that adaptive systems are partially reconfigurable. Partial reconfigurability keeps the reconfiguration overheads to a minimum. In order to be able to co-execute alongside a general purpose microprocessor, a very convenient interface to the microprocessor should be readily available. The REACT environment provides an effective medium for exploiting partial reconfigurability. In order to allow easy mapping of applications, a compilation environment facilitates the analysis, optimization, and mapping of applications on reconfigurable core. Detailed description of the REACT hardware environment is provided in Section 3.1.

A good Adaptive Computing System should also have a transparent user environment, that enables users with little or no hardware experience to conveniently reap the benefits of a high performance computation. Our earlier efforts [14] to develop a statically Reconfigurable Adaptive Computing Environment(RACE) highlighted the necessity to integrate a compiler support [8] that provides a higher level of abstraction to end users. The REACT architecture incorporates a library based approach for the hardware designers and a compiler directed software support for the software programmers. Detailed description of the REACT software environment is provided in Section 3.2.

3.1 REACT : Hardware Architecture

Time consuming and compute intensive applications can take an inordinate amount of time to execute on fixed CPU architecture based platforms. The ideal solution for such applications would be to implement them on custom hardware. However the flexibility of general purpose computing is lost and hence such solutions prove to be very costly solutions. A compromise is to have both flexibility and high performance using reconfigurable hardware. The reconfigurable unit could act as a co-processor and could thus speed up the execution of any application. Execution of an application on the hardware is in most cases orders of magnitude faster than the software execution. However, Reconfigurable computing includes the overhead of reconfiguring the hardware and the data transfers to and from the main memory into the reconfigurable platform from the fixed CPU architecture platform.

The main concern in reconfigurable computing is

- Reducing the reconfigurable overhead
- Reducing the data transfer time

An architecture of a co-processor board, taking these into consideration has been visualized and has been christened NEBULA.

NEBULA Architecture The environment for reconfigurable computing in this project consists of a host machine (Intel Pentium II @ 300MHz) connected to the NEBULA co-processor board through the PCI bus.

The NEBULA architecture is depicted in Figure1. It comprises of two reconfigurable units with local memory directly accessible by the host CPU through the PCI interface. The configuration data for the reconfigurable units and the data for the applications are transferred from the host memory using the PCI interface. The features of NEBULA are as follows :

- **Local Bus Standard - PCI:** The data transfer overhead could be reduced by transferring the data at a very high rate. Also if the size of data that is transferred in one data transfer cycle is increased, the data transfer time would significantly reduce. The PCI interface provides a 32-bit data interface which can operate at 33MHz. This would reduce the data transfer overhead significantly compared to other existing bus standards.
- **Memory organization:** One of the main issues in the design of the reconfigurable architecture is the provision of a local memory or a global memory. The provision of global memory would involve implementing a large memory which can be accessed by all the reconfigurable units and the system CPU. With the implementation of global memory comes the problem of addressing memory management and preventing memory access conflicts. Provision of local memory for the RUs on the other hand makes them independent units which can perform parallel computations without conflicting access of memory. NEBULA provides a large local memory of 1Mbytes for each RU. Thus highly data intensive applications can be implemented on this architecture.
- **Reconfigurable Units & Logic Capacity:** NEBULA provides two XC6264 reconfigurable units giving a total logic equivalent of 128000 to 200000 gate capacity. A 70 bit wide bus connects the two units. Very large applications could be partitioned and mapped onto the RUs. The XC6200 family of FPGAs from Xilinx provide very fast reconfiguration capability. Moreover, partial reconfiguration is supported. This would also reduce the reconfiguration overhead since the hardware need not be completely reconfigured for minor changes in the design. The swapping of computational units within the RUs is very feasible since they provide partial reconfigurability.

- **Clocking:** The PCI interface supports a 33Mhz clock. The data transfers to and from the on-board memory would take place at 33MHz. The data transfer size being 32bits, a high data transfer rate of 132 MByte/sec is achievable. The RUs have a choice of using the PCI 33Mhz clock or an onboard programmable clock which is anywhere between 2MHz-100MHz.
- **Provision of Interrupt** A single interrupt line is provided from NEBULA to the host processor. The cause for an interrupt could be any of the following.
  - Interrupt from any of the RUs
  - Parity errors on the address and data buses
  - A clock interrupt to emulate a design in the RUs

Design implementation options A design could be implemented on the NEBULA board in three different ways.

- The reconfigurable units could have separate designs loaded onto them and execute two different applications in parallel.
- A large design could be partitioned and mapped into the reconfigurable units so as to execute a single application.
- A large design could be partitioned in time (temporally partitioned) [6] and executed by mapping the temporally partitioned design onto the board.

3.2 REACT : Software Architecture

The software architecture for the REACT environment consists of a compiler directed approach and a Library based approach. The compiler directed approach provides means for directly mapping applications on a co-executing hardware. The analysis phase of the compiler extracts components of an application that will gain the most by reconfiguration. In other words the analysis partitions the application into what might look like hardware software co-design. In the library based approach the reconfigurable core acts more like a co-processor. A library of hardware functions is created using synthesis tools and is called from within the user application. Thus, procedures and functions that take excessive time to execute on general purpose machines can be synthesized as hardware functions and then directed for execution on reconfigurable core.

Compiler Driven Software Environment A compiler for an adaptive computing system should address many issues such as providing language extensions for reconfigurable computing, analyzing the parts of an algorithm, which when executed in the hardware results in maximum performance of the entire system. Other issues include program transformation for performance enhancement, code generation and runtime code optimization. The compiler should also be independent of the target adaptive computing architecture.

Efforts [4] have been made for code generation for variable instruction set reconfigurable architectures, using the concept of templates and sub-templates supported by an assembler framework. The framework generates bitstreams for reconfiguration, from annotated C program written using hardware libraries. Such an approach demands a highly skilled programmer fully familiar with the underlying hardware. The REACT compiler analyzes the program for potential for reconfiguration, determines performance gain and selects program points where reconfiguration should take place

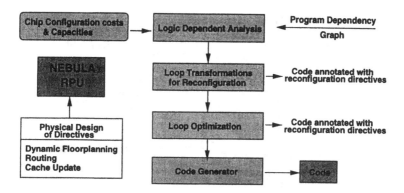

Fig. 2. *REACT Software: Compiler directed flow supporting adaptive computing.*

and then provides a mechanism for its implementation through code generation [11]. Figure 2 illustrates the issues involved in providing a compiler support for Adaptive Computing.

- **Logic dependent analysis:** It deals with program analysis, space-time cost analysis of operators and their hardware implementations, reconfiguration cost analysis and produces an annotated code with reconfiguration directives. Given a Program Dependency Graph [11], and chip configuration costs and capacities, Logic dependent analysis phase tries to exploit the hardware functionalities to implement conjunctive operators(combination of various arithmetic operators), concurrent operators, variable operand widths, strength reduction of an operator into separate operators.
- **Loop transformations:** Loops offer a lot of potential for parallel execution. Loop optimizations such as loop splitting, statement reordering within the loops and unrolling of loops are performed to exploit the parallel hardware execution capabilities of the hardware. It is then supplemented by a run time model analysis to analyze the overheads and gains.
- **Architecture dependent Analysis:** The final cost of execution is estimated by incorporating architecture dependent parameters into the compilation model. A separate architecture dependent analysis phase enables the compiler to be retargeted towards different adaptive computing architectures. The architecture dependent parameters include, the available data memory and the configuration transfer times, etc., that help to come up with an estimate of the cost of the implementation in a particular hardware architecture.

  After the loop transformation and loop optimization, the code gets annotated with reconfiguration directives. In other words those localities of code that will gain most speed up due to hardware implementation are identified. These localities are then synthesized, and mapped on the NEBULA architecture. The execution flow as directed by the program dependency graph is retained and the complete execution takes place as a single threaded operation. The execution is controlled by a scheduler [5].
- **Code Generation:** The code generation phase translates the potentially reconfigurable parts of the Program Dependency Graph, to the hardware configurations and the remaining parts to the software execution on the host processor. The code generation phase uses the hardware control functions from the Library that

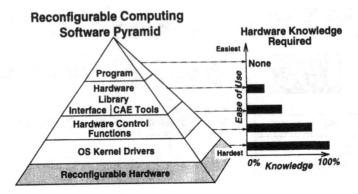

Fig. 3. *REACT Software: Library based facilitating the implementation of large functions as hardware objects.*

provide an abstract interface to the underlying hardware in terms of configuring the board, accessing the data memory. The code generation phase also provides the communication interface and synchronization between the hardware and the software executions through data transfer in terms of inputs and outputs. With a convenient FASTMAP interface available for the XC6200 [20], the entire configuration memory and its registers can be accessed as a memory access.

Library Based Software Environment The software environment built around the REACT architecture can be represented as a pyramid as shown in Figure 3. The pyramid is a representation of various levels of abstraction of the underlying adaptive computing environment. The higher the level in the pyramid, lesser is the knowledge required by the user about the adaptive hardware. The compiler driven environment occupies the peak of the pyramid. The library based approach can be visualized as a library of functions or objects provided in a high level language with various levels of abstraction for the user. The user can use the objects provided at the higher levels of abstraction or can start building new objects from the lower levels of abstraction according to his requirements. Our approach is to provide a complete prototyping environment to the user wherein he can customize things to his requirements, rather than imposing him with a fixed set of utilities.

- **Abstraction Levels:** At the bottom of the pyramid lies the reconfigurable hardware. The next level of abstraction is the operating system's kernel device drivers and functions, which allows a user to pass data and necessary signals to REACT without having to know all of the handshaking signals and protocols required to perform the operations. Nevertheless, few programmers care to deal with kernel function calls, which can be rather esoteric and hard to use. Consequently, easy to use functions have been created to make programming REACT and reading back data values much simpler. Using these *hardware control functions*, a programmer does not have to know how to configure the REACT controller for data transfers, nor the intricacies of how to program the FPGAs. A similar work has been done with the RACE environment [14].
   For a person who is strictly a programmer with little or no hardware experience, having a library of hardware control functions would be very difficult to use since

he would not have any hardware applications designed to work with the control functions. The hardware library includes custom mapped functions and applications designed by a hardware engineer to work on the Adaptive Computing System. The library functions utilize the hardware control functions to program the system and return the data from the hardware to the calling program. With the hardware library in-hand, the end-user of the hardware system can be someone who has no idea of what is happening in the hardware or any knowledge of the hardware system. The programmer simply knows that calling a function from the hardware library will result in the function being implemented on the Adaptive Computing Platform. Such a system now becomes attractive because anyone can use it without any detailed knowledge and benefit from the speedup by implementing in hardware.

Software : The Complete Picture A Software support is very essential for an Adaptive Computing Environment to exploit its power. Two different environments are available to the user to harness the higher performance of the Adaptive Computing Environment. Both the approaches differ in their levels of abstraction and the Compiler driven approach takes the support of the library based approach, when it comes closer to the hardware. Such a robust prototyping environment can accommodate users with various levels of exposure to the hardware, to fulfill their needs with the Adaptive Computing environments.

4   Applications

To demonstrate the gains and overheads with the Adaptive Computing Environment, the REACT environment applies the adaptive computing methodologies to solve Numerical Algorithms widely used in areas such as Analog and Mixed signal simulation. The Analog simulation methods requires solving large, sparse sets of first order non-linear differential algebraic equations. The set includes a static core set of equations and dynamic auxiliary equations. The dynamically reconfigurable Adaptive Computing Environment is well suited to exploit the parallelism and also the dynamic nature inherent in the applications. Efforts are being made to implement compute intensive Numerical Analysis Kernels on the Adaptive Computing Environment. Other such problems in the areas of Signal and Image processing are also under study. In addition several applications have been implemented on the REACT prototype architecture that is built around HotWorks card from Virtual Computer Corporation [18]. These include parallel adder multiplier, parallel array multiplier, Image scaling.

References

1. Anant Agarwal, Saman Amarasinghe, Rajeev Barua, Matthew Frank, Walter Lee, Vivek Sarkar, Devabhaktuni Srikrishna, and Michael Taylor, The Raw Compiler Project, Proceedings of the Second SUIF Compiler Workshop, Stanford, CA, August 21-23, 1997.
2. BRASS : Berkeley Reconfigurable Architectures Systems and Software, www.cs.berkeley.edu/projects/brass.
3. Duncan A. Buell, Jeffrey M.Arnold, Walter J.Kleinfelder, Splash2 FPGAs in Custom Computing Machine, IEEE Computer Society Press, 1996.

4. David A. Clark and Hutchins B.L., Supporting FPGA Microprocessors through Retargetable Software Tools, Proceedings of the IEEE Workshop on FPGAs for Custom Computing Machines, April 1996.

5. Karthikeya M. Gajjala Purna and Dinesh Bhatia, Temporal Partitioning and Scheduling for Reconfigurable Computing, Proceedings of IEEE Workshop onF-PGAs for Custom Computing Machines, April 1998 (Extended Abstract).

6. Karthikeya M. Gajjala Purna and Dinesh Bhatia, Emulating Large Designs on Small Reconfigurable Hardware, Proceedings of IEEE International Workshop on Rapid System Prototyping, June 1998.

7. M.B. Gokhale and J.M. Stone, NAPA C: Compiling for a Hybrid RISC/FPGA Architecture, Proceedings of the IEEE Workshop on FPGAs for Custom Computing Machines, April 1998.

8. Arun B.Hegde, C to Synthesizable VHDL, Master's thesis, Department of ECECS, University of Cincinnati, Jan 1998.

9. Stefan H.-M. Ludwig, The Design of a Coprocessor Board Using Xilinx's XC6200 FPGA - An Experience Report, 6th International Workshop on Field-Programmable Logic and Applications, FPL96, Darmstadt, Germany, Sept. 23-25 1996.

10. Staurt Nisbet, and Steven A. Guccione, The XC6200DS Development System, 7th International Workshop on Field-Programmable Logic and Applications, FPL97, London, England, Sept. 1997.

11. Santosh Pande, Ram Subramanian and Lakshmi Narasimhan, Analysis and Transformations for Compiling for Reconfigurable Architectures, Department of ECECS, Technical Report TR /98/ECECS, University of Cincinnati, 1998.

12. Rahul Razdan, PRISC : Programmable Reduced Instruction Set Computers, Center for Research in Computing Technology, Division of Applied Sciences, Harvard University, Technical report TR-14-94.

13. C. Rupp, M. Landguth, T. Garverick, E. Gomersall, H. Holt, J. Arnold and M. Gokhale, The NAPA Adaptive Processing Architecture, Proceedings of the IEEE Workshop on FPGAs for Custom Computing Machines, April 1998.

14. Doug Smith, Dinesh Bhatia, RACE: Reconfigurable and Adaptive Computing Environment, Field Programmable Logic: Smart Applications, New Paradigms and Compilers, Proceedings of 6th Int. Workshop on Field Programmable Logic and Applications,FPL 96, Darmstadt, Germany, Sept. 23-25 1996. See http://www.ececs.uc.edu/dal.

15. J.Douglas Smith, RACE : A Reconfigurable and Adaptive Computing Environment, Master's thesis, Department of ECECS, University of Cincinnati, June 1997.

16. William Stallings, Computer Organization and Architecture : Designing for Performance, Fourth Edition, Prentice Hall, 1996.

17. TSI-Telsys Inc. ACE Card, User's Manual, version 1.0,

18. Virtual Computer Corporation, http://www.vcc.com/products/pci6200.html

19. Elliot Waingold, Michael Taylor, Devabhaktuni Srikrishna, Vivek Sarkar, Walter Lee, Victor Lee, Jang Kim, Matthew Frank, Peter Finch, Rajeev Barua, Jonathan Babb, Saman Amarasinghe, and Anant Agarwal, Baring it all to Software: Raw Machines, IEEE Computer, September 1997, pp. 86-93.

20. Xilinx Corporation, XC6200 Field Programmable Gate Arrays, April 1997.

Evaluation of the XC6200-Series Architecture for Cryptographic Applications

Stephen Charlwood, Philip James-Roxby

Digital Systems and Vision Processing Group
School of Electronic and Electrical Engineering
The University of Birmingham
Birmingham B15 2TT, United Kingdom
S.M.Charlwood@bham.ac.uk, P.B.James-Roxby@bham.ac.uk

Field-programmable gate arrays have been established as a suitable platform for implementing cryptographic algorithms since they provide much of the performance gains achievable through the use of custom hardware, whilst retaining the reconfigurability and ease of development benefits commonly associated with software. However, the efficiency with which a cryptographic algorithm can be implemented on a programmable device is dependent on the architecture of the device itself. Through a discussion of common cryptographic operations, and the implementation and testing of two algorithms, A5 and a reduced block-size variant of Blowfish, the suitability of the XC6200-series architecture for cryptographic applications is evaluated.

1 Introduction

The ultimate success of electronic commerce depends upon public confidence in the security and confidentiality of the transactions involved. Cryptographic algorithms play an essential role in achieving both these aims. Modern cryptography employs a combination of symmetric or *secret key* algorithms for encrypting data and asymmetric or *public key* algorithms for managing keys [1]. Existing public-key algorithms such as RSA are too slow to support bulk data encryption and are therefore used to encrypt the keys used by the symmetric algorithms [2]. The overall performance of systems using this approach is therefore critically dependent on the performance of the symmetric algorithm used.

The software implementations of symmetric algorithms are often computationally expensive and therefore the use of field-programmable gate array technology is considered as an efficient alternative. Gains may be made through the use of reconfigurable logic in the area of implementation inefficiency and through the exploitation of parallelism. Where operations are not well suited to today's 32-bit general-purpose microprocessors, configurable logic can be programmed with an optimised solution and therefore overcome many of the architectural constraints that general-purpose processors are subject to.

The XC6200 series is a family of fine-grain, sea-of-gates, SRAM-based FPGAs developed by Xilinx, Inc. (a full treatment of these devices may be found in [3]). The architecture of the XC6200 series is based on a dense array of simple, configurable logic blocks known as *cells*, surrounded by user-configurable input/output blocks (IOBs). Each cell includes a 2:1 multiplexor-based function unit for implementing the logic function(s) intended by the user and a routing area for inter-cell communication. It is possible to directly read or write to any register in the device or any area of configuration memory via a 32-bit wide processor interface. Sections of the device can be reconfigured without disturbing circuits running in other areas of the device. These features combine to make the XC6200-series devices, referred to by Xilinx as *reconfigurable processing units*, particularly suited to coprocessor applications.

This paper presents an evaluation of XC6200-series devices for cryptographic applications. The primitive operations of important block ciphers are identified, and an evaluation of their implementation on XC6200-series FPGAs is given. Stream ciphers are treated similarly, and two case studies are presented; a reduced block-size variant of Blowfish and A5, the encryption algorithm used in GSM, the European standard for digital cellular telephones.

2   Block Ciphers

Table 1 presents common block cipher operations, and was compiled from a survey of important cryptographic algorithms [2, 4-15]. Block ciphers frequently have two phases of operation: *key setup* and *data encryption*. For algorithms where these phases are distinct, only operations that form part of the data encryption phase have been included, since this phase has the greater effect on overall performance.

Modular addition or subtraction	Blowfish, CAST, FEAL, GOST, IDEA, LOKI97, RC5, RC6, SAFER K-64, TEA, Twofish
Bitwise XOR	Blowfish, CAST, DEAL, DES, FEAL, GOST, IDEA, LOKI91, LOKI97, Madryga, MISTY, MMB, RC5, RC6, SAFER K-64, Serpent, TEA, Twofish
Bitwise AND/OR	MISTY
Variable-length rotations	CAST, Madryga, RC5, RC6
Fixed-length rotations	DEAL, DES, CAST, FEAL, GOST, Serpent, RC6, Twofish
Non-circular shifts	Serpent, TEA
Modular multiplication	CAST, IDEA, RC6, MMB (constant multiplier)
Substitution	Blowfish, DEAL, DES, LOKI91, LOKI97, Twofish
Permutation	DEAL, DES, ICE, LOKI91, LOKI97

Table 1. Common cryptographic operations in symmetric block ciphers.

The bitwise logic operations are clearly candidates for hardware implementation, especially where the word-lengths used do not match those of existing general-purpose microprocessors. Fixed length rotations, non-circular shifts and simple permutations also map well onto hardware but can consume significant routing resources, depending on the routing architecture of the FPGA. The ease with which these operations can be implemented on XC6200-series devices varies with circuit placement since not all cells have access to the fast bypass routing that is available. Variable-length rotations cannot efficiently be implemented in hardware or software. The remaining operations, modular arithmetic and substitution, along with the implementation of the Feistel structure in hardware are treated in more detail below.

2.1 Modular Arithmetic

As can be seen from Table 1, modular arithmetic (also known as finite-field arithmetic) is commonly used in block ciphers, with modular addition or subtraction being the most popular operation. This type of arithmetic is well-suited to implementation on microprocessors, which operate on fixed word lengths, since the range of all intermediate values, and also the result of any computation is limited. Although multiplication is a very effective diffusion primitive [12] and many modern microprocessors have dedicated hardware multipliers, multiplications are still intrinsically expensive instructions and a recent analysis recommended against their use in the design of new block ciphers [16]. To implement multipliers on FPGAs, it is usually necessary to use techniques such as distributed arithmetic rather than a direct implementation of a standard multiplier [17].

Modular addition and subtraction operations are used in a large number of significant algorithms, including at least four of the algorithms submitted recently as candidates to replace the current U.S. standard, DES. The implementation of circuits on the XC6200 for binary addition and subtraction modulo 2^n was investigated. A variety of different adder types exist, which basically differ in the way that carry signals are propagated: for a full treatment see [18]. The fine-grain architecture of the XC6200 cell results in long propagation delays for adder circuits containing gates requiring high fan-in or fan-out (such as carry-completion, carry-lookahead and carry-skip adders). These circuits also consume significantly more logic resources than the more basic carry-ripple type. On an XC6200, carry-select adders proved to be faster than both carry-ripple and carry-lookahead adders; a more thorough investigation into the implementation and performance of adders on the XC6200 series devices is currently underway. An n-bit, modulo 2^n 2-stage carry-select adder requires $5n-5$ cells compared to $3n-2$ for a carry-ripple adder.

2.2 Look-Up Tables

The term look-up table (LUT) is used to refer to any method of storing information, either in hardware or software, from which individual elements can be randomly selected. Substitution operations in cryptographic algorithms are often described in the form of *substitution boxes* or *S-boxes*, which may be implemented using LUTs. The information contained in these S-boxes may be random (e.g. GOST), chosen (e.g.

DES), key-dependent (e.g. Blowfish) or the result of a complex expression (e.g. SAFER K-64). If S-box data represents the result of a complex expression then by storing pre-computed data in a look-up table, the amount of time taken in evaluating the expression becomes dependent on the method by which information is retrieved from the LUT, rather than the calculation itself. This improves performance where the expression to be evaluated is computationally expensive.

XC6200-series devices have a multiplexor-based cell architecture. Look-up tables can be implemented using 2:1 multiplexors by means of a multiplexor tree, using registers to store LUT entries. The use of registers allows the contents of such a look-up table to be modified extremely quickly via the microprocessor interface. If the LUT entries are not required to change rapidly, then there are two methods of reducing the area requirements of a given LUT. The first method is to connect the inputs of the multiplexors to the output of a cell providing a constant-0 or constant-1, and using each cell providing a constant output to drive multiple multiplexor inputs. The amount of circuit area saved using this method increases with the size of the LUT. Another method, illustrated in [17], uses the SRAM configuration memory rather than registers or hard-wired inputs to store the LUT entries and replaces the first two levels of multiplexors in the multiplexor tree with a single level of 2-input gates. This results in the greatest saving in terms of area. Both methods require reconfiguration of the device at run-time in order to change the contents of the S-boxes. This is possible since the XC6200-series devices support partial reconfiguration and the bitstream format is open, but requires additional processing and therefore introduces delay. Depending on the nature of the application, this delay may not be significant compared to the total processing delay and therefore should not be considered a drawback.

As the number of input bits (or index width) increases, the number of 2:1 multiplexors required to implement a single bit of LUT storage increases significantly. The speed at which data can be retrieved is dependent on the number of levels in such a multiplexor tree. For a multiplexor tree with between 2^{k-1} and 2^k entries that uses registers to store data, k levels of multiplexors are required (i.e. one level for each bit of index width). Using configuration memory to store LUT entries reduces the number of levels of cells required by one. Although look-up tables become extremely inefficient with regards to the area required to implement them as the index width increases, they are an extremely useful method of accelerating complex functions, and broad LUTs with small indexes can be implemented easily on XC6216 devices due to the fine-grain architecture and availability of registers.

2.3 Feistel Networks

Feistel networks are a general class of *iterated block ciphers*, which are block ciphers whose cryptographic strength is based on the use of simple functions, iterated many times. Before processing by a Feistel network, data blocks are split into two sub-blocks, L_i and R_i (the left and right halves of the data block), and then these sub-blocks undergo a number of rounds of processing. A single round of processing is defined by the expressions given below. One complete pass through the network is concluded by swapping the left and right halves of the data block.

$$L_i = R_{i-1}$$
$$R_i = L_{i-1} \oplus f(R_{i-1}, K_i)$$

This structure is used by DES and also by many others, including Blowfish, CAST, FEAL, LOKI97, GOST and DEAL. The structure will continue to be popular since it has been extensively analysed over the past 20 years and its suitability as a basis for cryptographic algorithms is well understood. The key feature of each processing step is the function, f, which serves to combine data with some key-dependent information, K_i. Through the use of the bitwise exclusive-OR (XOR) operation, the effect of the function f can be guaranteed to be reversible. This function, known as the *round function* can be made arbitrarily complex provided that the inputs to the function can be reconstructed at each stage. This allows the same algorithm to be used for both encryption and decryption.

As can be seen from Table 1, bitwise XOR operations are used by all the block ciphers investigated, including those not based on Feistel networks. XC6200 cells can be configured to provide any Boolean function of two inputs with the option of the output being registered. Due to the fine-grain architecture of the XC6200, a large number of cells are available and therefore, in terms of device area, pipelining such operations is inexpensive. However, while the round function is being calculated, neither the left- or right-half data values are modified. This means that additional registers are required to delay these values until they are needed. Although the round function can be made arbitrarily complex, if fewer the clock cycles required then less area is wasted in delay lines. This may mean opting for a less complicated round function, or a function which can be accelerated through the use of parallelism.

The swap operations at the end of each round are easily implemented in hardware providing that routing resources are sufficient: direct connections can be made between one set of registers and the inputs to the next operation. The routing architecture of the XC6200 is hierarchical and effectively four types of cells exist, each varying in their degree of access to fast bypass routing. This often results in additional placement constraints in order to achieve consistent levels of performance, and will affect the ease with which core libraries can be developed for the series.

2.4   Case Study: Blowfish-16

Blowfish is a variable-length key, 64-bit iterated block cipher based on a Feistel network and developed as a drop-in replacement for the ageing DES algorithm [5]. It was designed to be suitable for implementation using both general-purpose processors and specialised hardware, and therefore avoids operations that are known to be inefficient in software such as variable-length shifts and bitwise permutations. The development and optimisation of a variant of this algorithm, using a 16-bit block size, is illustrated here. The test platform used was a Xilinx XC6200 development system PCI plug-in board with a single XC6216 reconfigurable coprocessor.

The encryption of a block of data, x, using the Blowfish algorithm can be described by the following pseudocode:

```
divide x into two halves, xL and xR
for i = 1 to 16
         xL = xL XOR Pi
         xR = xR XOR F(xL)
         swap xL and xR
swap xL and xR (undo the 16th swap)
xR = xR XOR P17
xL = xL XOR P18
recombine xL and xR
```

P_i are key-dependent values that effectively permute the data. The 18 values of P_i constitute the *permutation array* or *P-array* and are each half the block size in width. The round function F(xL) is based on both input and key data, and for the 16-bit variant of Blowfish is calculated using the following expression:

$$F(xL) = ((S_{1,a} + S_{2,b} \bmod 2^8) \text{ XOR } S_{3,c}) + S_{4,d} \bmod 2^8$$

$S_{n,m}$ refers to the mth entry in the nth S-box. The size of the S-boxes and the P-array are dependent on which variant of the algorithm is being used.

The Blowfish algorithm requires random access to information within its S-boxes. The options available to the designer are the use of random access memory (fast local memory is available on the XC6200 development system board), or the use of look-up tables. Blowfish-16 requires S-boxes with a 2-bit index. If registers are used to store the S-box entries (avoiding the need to reconfigure the device at run-time), then 224 cells are required. If partial reconfiguration is supported then area requirements can be reduced to as few as 32 cells.

An implementation of Blowfish-16 has been developed that does not require the use of partial reconfiguration. Versions with both a single, and all sixteen rounds of processing were investigated. In the single-round version, since the values in the P-array do not need to be accessed randomly, an 8-bit wide barrel shifter was used to store the values and the output from the barrel shifter was updated once per round. After each round, the swap operation was performed, and mirror registers were used to reduce the overhead to a single cycle. During development, support for global clock control was not available and therefore an alternate clocking scheme was used. This prevented cells being configured to contain both a gate and a register, since one of the cell inputs was used for the clock. This increased the area occupied by the circuit. In trying to minimise the circuit area, pipelining was avoided and this allowed the contents of registers to be temporally sensitive (the clocking scheme used provided clock signals only to those elements of the circuit that required them). The total number of cells required for this implementation was 603, and 19 API calls were required to process a single 16-bit block. Using configuration memory to store S-box entries reduced cell requirements to 411 but did not affect throughput.

Each round required 7 cycles at the global clock speed for completion, which meant that the entire algorithm required a total of 113 cycles (16 rounds at 7 cycles per round plus one for the final permutations using P_{17} and P_{18} in parallel). The circuit was clocked at 20MHz and achieved a throughput of 119KB/s which was comparable to the performance of an optimised software implementation running on a 90MHz Pentium. The same software implementation running on a 300MHz Pentium II achieved 1,744 KB/s, almost a factor of 15 faster. By implementing only a single round of the algorithm, the circuit developed was effectively performing the same operations as a general-purpose microprocessor, but was being clocked 15 times more slowly. The pipelining of a single-round implementation of the algorithm would improve performance, as would the use of carry-select adders (the greatest propagation delays between registers were found to be due to the adders in the round function), but not significantly. Order-of-magnitude performance improvements were determined to be realisable only with a fully-pipelined implementation.

In pipelining the design, the area requirements of the circuit increased significantly since each round requires its own S-boxes. However, since the value of the P-array used in any one round is static, there is no need for P-array values to be stored in registers (any value XOR a constant value can be implemented at no cost in an XC6216, since all cell inputs and outputs can be inverted). Pipelining also allows use of the global clock since the registers are not temporally sensitive. When using global clock, cells can be configured to provide both a 2-input gate and a register, which reduces the amount of space required by the adders. The fully-pipelined version requires 252 cells per round, plus 32 cells for I/O registers and would be capable of processing one block per cycle. The fastest data can be written to the XC6200 is two cycles of the global clock [3], thus 5 cycles per block would be required: 4 for data I/O and one to advance the pipeline. The throughput at 20MHz would be 8MB/s. Fast 8-bit carry-select adders have been developed that can be clocked at over 40MHz. Assuming that the addition operation would represent the worst-case propagation delay in the circuit, then throughputs of 16MB/s could be achieved. The penalty for this is that the number of cells required increases by 416.

3 Stream Ciphers

Most stream cipher designs are secret [2]. Table 4 presents common stream cipher operations, and was compiled from a survey of published algorithms [2, 19-20].

Modular addition or subtraction	RC4, SEAL, TWOPRIME, WAKE
Bitwise XOR	A5, Nanotcq, RC4, SEAL, TWOPRIME, WAKE
Non-circular shifts	WAKE
Substitution	RC4, TWOPRIME, WAKE

Table 2. Common cryptographic operations for symmetric stream ciphers.

Despite the fact that the majority of military encryption systems are based on *linear feedback shift registers* (LFSRs) [2], of the algorithms shown in Table 3, only A5 and

Nanoteq are LFSR-based. RC4, SEAL and WAKE use operations commonly used in block ciphers and TWOPRIME is based on cyclic counters. The implementation of LFSR-based stream ciphers is discussed here using A5 as an example.

3.1 Linear Feedback Shift Registers

Two common types of linear feedback shift registers (LFSRs), Fibonacci and Galois configurations (described in [2]), have been implemented on the XC6200. These types differ only in the way they feed back information. The complexity of implementing Fibonacci LFSRs, which are used in A5, depends upon the number of bits affecting the feedback function. As the number of taps increases, so does the fan-in (and therefore propagation delay) of the XOR operation required in the feedback function. Galois LFSRs are much faster, since all the XOR operations can be done in parallel and the most significant remaining delay is that associated with the distribution of the output bit to the feedback XOR gates.

Due to the nature of LFSR-based stream ciphers, arithmetic or bit-level parallelism cannot be exploited. However since XC6200-series cells each provide a single register and the density of cells is high, extremely compact implementations may be developed allowing parallelism at the algorithm level to be exploited. By replicating the circuit within the available device area, the device I/O requirements increase linearly with the number of instances of the circuit used. While this may not be a concern when XC6200-series devices are not used in a coprocessor role, when all communication with the device is via the 32-bit processor interface then performance becomes limited by the communication bandwidth of the processor interface.

3.2 Case Study: A5

A5 is the encryption algorithm used in GSM, the European standard for digital cellular telephones. The algorithm itself has not been officially disclosed, but the major features are known and an estimated implementation was released in a post to the sci.crypt newsgroup [19]. The algorithm uses the outputs from three Fibonacci LFSRs to generate a pseudo-random bitstream (the *keystream*). The algorithm is well suited to implementation in hardware due to the simplicity of the LFSRs [21].

A5 is a relatively low complexity algorithm, designed to be area-efficient when implemented in hardware. It is recognised as inefficient in software, due to the bit-level operations on variable-length operands [2]. Although in its application to mobile telephony, the algorithm would only be required to achieve a throughput of 64Kbit/s (the bandwidth of a standard digital voice channel), A5 is treated here as a general-purpose encryption algorithm which could be applied to channels with much larger bandwidth requirements.

Since A5 is a bitstream cipher, in order to maximise the efficient use of the processor interface, 32 bits of keystream were generated and encryption performed on 32-bit blocks. Three calls to the API were required to encrypt 32 bits of data: one to write the original data, one to initiate the clocking mechanism and one to read the encrypted data back. This may be reduced still further since circuits on an XC6200 can detect that a register write has occurred and act immediately [3]. A throughput of 1,022KB/s was achieved using an XC6216 clocked at 22MHz. An optimised software version running on a 300MHz Pentium II achieved a throughput of only 499KB/s. This corresponds to 23 cycles/byte for A5 implemented in hardware and 588 cycles/byte for A5 implemented in software. The performance of A5 in hardware was limited by the rate at which data could transferred over the PCI bus interface (the performance of the PCI interface on the development platform used is far lower than the theoretical peak transfer rates given in the definition of the PCI standard).

The limiting factors in the clock speed of A5 were its unusual clocking scheme (which the global clock lines cannot distribute) and the feedback functions of the three LFSRs used. The implementation of A5 in hardware required 215 cells, although the keystream generator which is the basis of A5 requires only 84 cells.

4   Conclusions

The development work performed has shown that XC6200-series architecture is suitable for implementing highly-pipelined cryptographic algorithms based on Feistel networks using the most popular cryptographic primitives. However, the block size of an algorithm affects efficiency and as block and key lengths increase (the latest block ciphers are 128-bit and a minimum of 90-bit keys has been recommended for security by a panel of experts [1]), the constraints associated with a 32-bit wide host processor interface will become increasingly significant. To avoid this problem, closer coupling of the reconfigurable coprocessor and the host is necessary.

Most new algorithm designs cite efficiency in software as a design objective, and by tailoring these designs to particular processor architectures, it becomes increasingly difficult for FPGAs to achieve performance improvements in the area of implementation inefficiency. Since FPGA clock speeds are currently well below those of general-purpose microprocessors, to achieve the order-of-magnitude performance improvements necessary to justify the use of hardware, sufficient logic resources to support fully-pipelined designs need to be available. However, as network communication bandwidths increase, hardware-oriented algorithms will be developed and the use of hardware-based encryption will become unavoidable in order to meet the high performance requirements.

The XC6200-series architecture is not suitable for implementing gates with high fan-in or fan-out due to the linear increase in propagation delays with the number of inputs or outputs respectively. Also, the availability of routing to cells in different locations relative to cell block boundaries varies, which affects the performance of translated instances of a given implementation. In order to achieve maximum performance, designs that make use of architecture-specific features are required, which means that circuit implementations are not portable between technologies.

References

[1]M. Blaze, W. Diffie, R. Rivest, B. Schneier, T. Shimomura, E. Thompson, M. Wiener, "Minimal Key Lengths for Symmetric Ciphers to Provide Adequate Commercial Security", available on the Internet from http://www.counterpane.com/

[2]B. Schneier, "Applied Cryptography", John Wiley & Sons (1994) ISBN 0-471-11709-9

[3]Xilinx, Inc : "XC6200 FPGA product description", 1997

[4] C. Adams, "Constructing Symmetric Ciphers Using the CAST Design Procedure", available on the Internet from http://www.entrust.com/

[5] B. Schneier, "Description of a New Variable-Length Key, 64-Bit Block Cipher (Blowfish)", Proc. of the Cambridge Security Workshop on Fast Software Encryption pp191-204, Springer-Verlag (1994)

[6] E. Biham, L. Knudsen, R. Anderson, "Serpent: A New Block Cipher Proposal", Proc. of the 5th International Workshop on Fast Software Encryption, Springer-Verlag (1998)

[7] L. Knudsen, "DEAL - A 128-bit Block Cipher", available on the Internet at http://www.ii.uib.no/~larsr/papers/deal2.ps.gz

[8] M. Kwan, "The Design of the ICE Encryption Algorithm", Proc. of the 4th International Workshop on Fast Software Encryption, Springer-Verlag (1997)

[9] D. Wheeler, R. Needham, "TEA, a Tiny Encryption Algorithm", available on the Internet at http://www.cl.cam.ac.uk/ftp/papers/djw-rmn/djw-rmn-tea.html (1994)

[10] R. Rivest, "The RC5 Encryption Algorithm", available on the Internet at http://theory.lcs.mit.edu/~rivest/rc5rev.ps (1997)

[11] M. Matsui, "New Block Encryption Algorithm MISTY", Proc. of the 4th International Workshop on Fast Software Encryption, Springer-Verlag (1997)

[12] R. Rivest, M. Robshaw, R. Sidney, Y. Yin, "The RC6 Block Cipher", available on the Internet at http://theory.lcs.mit.edu/~rivest/rc6.ps (1998)

[13] L. Brown, J. Pieprzyk, "Introducing the new LOKI97 Block Cipher", available on the Internet at http://www.adfa.oz.au/~lpb/research/loki97/loki97spec.ps (1998)

[14] B. Schneier, J. Kelsey, D. Whiting, D. Wagner, C. Hall, N. Ferguson, "Twofish: A 128-Bit Block Cipher", available on the Internet from http://www.counterpane.com/ (1998)

[15] J. Massey, "SAFER K-64: A Byte-Oriented Block-Ciphering Algorithm", Proc. of the Cambridge Security Workshop on Fast Software Encryption, Springer-Verlag (1994)

[16] B. Schneier, D. Whiting, "Fast Software Encryption: Designing Encryption Algorithms for Optimal Software Speed on the Intel Pentium Processor", Proc. of the 4th International Workshop on Fast Software Encryption, Springer-Verlag (1997)

[17] Xilinx, Inc. "A Fast Constant-Coefficient Multiplier for the XC6200", Xilinx Application Note (1997)

[18] A. Omondi, "Computer Arithmetic Systems", Prentice-Hall (1994) ISBN 0-13-334301-4

[19] R. Anderson, "A5 - The GSM Encryption Algorithm", available on the Internet at http://chem.leeds.ac.uk/ICAMS/people/jon/a5.html (1994)

[20] C. Ding, V. Niemi, A. Renvall, A. Salomaa, "TWOPRIME: A Fast Stream Ciphering Algorithm", Proc. of the 4th International Workshop on Fast Software Encryption, Springer-Verlag (1997)

[21] I. Goldberg, D. Wagner, "Architectural Considerations for Cryptanalytic Hardware", available on the Internet at http://www.cs.berkley.edu/~iang/isaac/hardware/ (1996)

An FPGA-Based Object Recognition Machine

Ali Zakerolhosseini, Peter Lee, Ed Horne

Electronics Engineering Laboratory,
University of Kent
Canterbury
Kent CT2 7NT, United Kingdom
az1@ukc.ac.uk

Abstract. The paper describes the architecture of a real-time invariant object recognition machine. The machine has been implemented on five XC4010 reconfigurable Xilinx Field Programmable Gate Array (FPGA) devices, operate with a PC host. The employment of FPGAs allowed compact implementation of a highly complex design with accelerated speed performance. Rotational invariance of the image is achieved by first performing projection process, and then a 32-point fast feature extractor, the Rapid Transform, is adopted. The machine can operate at up to 50 frames/sec using images received from a 128x128 camera.

1 Introduction

Object recognition systems usually require many computationally intensive operations to be performed on an image. For applications requiring real-time performance, the image need to be processed at video rates of at least 25 frames a second. Therefore, a fast realisation of such a computationally intensive operation is required.

Recent developments in Field Programmable Gate Array (FPGA) technology means that it is now possible to develop either a part or a complete object recognition system using these devices.

This paper presents the architecture of a real-time invariant object recognition system implemented using SRAM based FPGAs [1].

2 System Overview

The block diagram of the complete object recognition system developed is illustrated in Fig. 1. The image data is generated directly from a digital camera or from a Frame Grabber. At the preprocessing stage, the image is binarised and smoothed. The image is then passed to a projection stage where the normalisation for translation and positional movement is achieved. A fast feature extractor, the Rapid Transform (RT) is applied to the output of the projection. The features generated by the RT module become rotational and translation invariants. The classification is performed by a software based classifier.

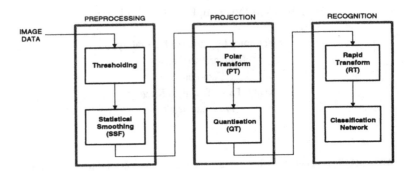

Fig. 1. Block diagram of the object recognition system

In section 2.1, the statistical smoothing filter algorithm is discussed. The implementation of this filter is described in section 3.1. A normalisation procedure, the projection algorithm is discussed in section 2.2 and its hardware implementation is described in section 3.2. The feature extraction algorithm and its hardware implementation are described in section 2.3 and 3.3 respectively.

2.1 Statistical Smoothing Algorithm

The Statistical Smoothing Filter (SSF) algorithm reduces the noise present in a binary image by *eliminating* small areas and *filling* small holes. This simple but efficient method uses a 3x3 operator or window, and is based on statistical decision criteria. The algorithm takes as an input a noisy binary image, $f(x, y)$, and produces as an output, a smoothed image $f'(x, y)$. It decides for each pixel in the image, if a level change is required or not, depending on the initial value of the pixel P_0 and those of its 8-nearest-neighborhood pixels as shown in Fig.2.

P_4	P_3	P_2
P_5		P_1
P_6	P_7	P_8

Fig. 2. 8-nearest-neighbourhood pixels configuration

The algorithm is defined by [2] as:

- If the centre point in the 3x3 window $f(x, y)$, $P_0 = 0$ then

$$P_0 = 0 \text{ in } f'(x,y), \text{ if } \sum_{n=1}^{8} P_n < 5 \text{ in } f(x,y) \text{ and}$$

$$P_0 = 1 \text{ in } f'(x,y), \text{ if otherwise}$$

- If the image pixel $P_0 = 1$ in $f(x,y)$, then

$$P = 1 \text{ in } f'(x,y), \text{ if } \sum_{n=1}^{8} P_n \geq 2 \text{ in } f(x,y) \text{ and}$$

$$P_0 = 0 \text{ in } f'(x,y), \text{ if otherwise}$$

where P_n, $n = 1, 2, ..., 8$ are the 8 pixels surrounding P_0.

Fig. 3(a) shows an original image and Fig. 3(b) is the corrupted image by 50 % of additive noise. Fig. 3(c) shows the smoothed image after applying SSF. The effectiveness of the SSF is demonstrated visually in these figures.

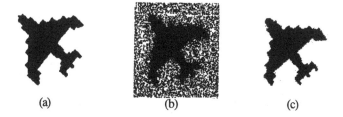

(a) (b) (c)

Fig. 3. (a) The original image (b) The corrupted image (c) The smoothed image

2.2 Projection Algorithm

The projection algorithm maps the input image plane into a projection plane such that the projection features become translation invariants [3]. The algorithm considered here consists of two stages, the Polar Transform (PT), and Quantisation Transform (QT).

Polar Transform (PT). The PT decomposes the rotational information of an image into the r and θ axes in the polar plane. Thus, any rotation of the object in the image plane becomes translation in the polar plane [4].

Let $f(x,y)$ be the function of a pixel (x,y) in the image. For any $f(x,y) > 0$, the amplitude r and the projection angle θ of the PT can be defined as:

$$r = \left[(x - \bar{x})^2 + (y - \bar{y})^2\right]^{1/2} \cdot f(x,y) \tag{1}$$

$$tan\,\theta = \left[(y - \bar{y})/(x - \bar{x}) \cdot f(x,y)\right] \tag{2}$$

where $(\bar{x}, \bar{y})$ is the centroid of the object.

Quantisation Transform (QT). In QT, the object area in the polar plane is divided into segments and the r's of the pixels in the object are partitioned into these segments. Let Q_i be the quantisation of the amplitudes r within segments where i indicates the segment number. The quantisation of the r values can be calculated as :

$$Q_i = \frac{1}{\eta_i} \sum_{\tan \Delta\theta_{i+1}}^{\tan \Delta\theta_i} r \cdot f(x,y) \quad , \quad (i = 0, 1, ..., R-1) \tag{3}$$

where $\Delta\theta = 2\pi / R$ is the segment's width, R is the number of segments and η_i is the number of r values included within a segment.

Implementation of equation (3), produces R 1-D projections surrounding the input plane as shown in Fig. 4. It can be observed from Fig. 4(b) that the QT has reduced the number of r's to 32 when $R = 32$. This *reduction of samples* makes the latter stages of the object recognition process, i.e. feature extraction and classification, less complex and computationally less expensive.

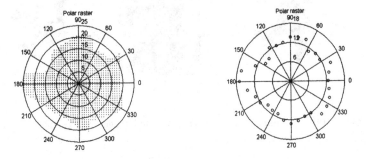

Fig. 4. (a) Polar plane for a 128x128 image. (b) Quantisation, $R = 32$

2.3 Rapid Transform

The Rapid Transform (RT) is a valuable tool for the purpose of feature extraction in pattern recognition systems [5] and [6]. The RT is invariant to cyclic shift, translation, and reflection of its input data sequence. The RT developed by Reithboeck and Brady [7], is based on the radix-2 butterfly. Fig. 5 shows a 4 point signal flow of the RT. It requires $N = 2^m$ real input variables, where m is a positive integer indicating the number of transformation steps required. The computation of the RT is also shown in Fig. 5 where N is the input sequence length, and X_i^m is the i-th component of the transformed data sequence. The number of points or input to the RT block effects the performance of the object recognition system. N is chosen to be 32 as the best compromise between performance and computational cost. The selection of this value was investigated using software and with $N = 32$, satisfactory results were obtained when applied to 1200 sample of images.

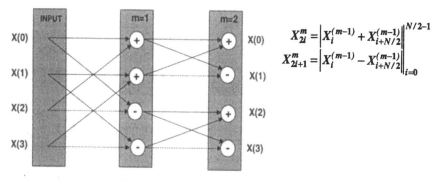

$$X_{2i}^{m} = \left| X_i^{(m-1)} + X_{i+N/2}^{(m-1)} \right|_{i=0}^{N/2-1}$$

$$X_{2i+1}^{m} = \left| X_i^{(m-1)} - X_{i+N/2}^{(m-1)} \right|_{i=0}^{N/2-1}$$

Fig. 5. RT signal flow for $N = 8$

3 FPGA Implementation of the System

The real-time object recognition system is implemented on 5 Xilinx XC4010 devices. The system is designed to operate with a PC host. The image input to the system has a resolution of 128x128, and generates 32 features.

3.1 SSF Implementation

The SSF has been designed with an existing digital camera and thresholding circuitry. The thresholding circuitry is a comparator which compares the grey scale values of pixels arriving from the digital camera with that of a pre-loaded threshold level.

Fig. 6 shows the 2D(3x3)SSF block diagram. The filter occupies just 89 CLBs when mapped into a single Xilinx XC4010 device.

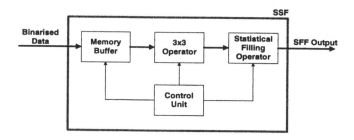

Fig. 6. The block diagram of 2D(3x3)SSF

The memory buffer shown in Fig. 7, consists of three 128x1 bits cascaded FIFOs, corresponding to 3 rows of a frame.

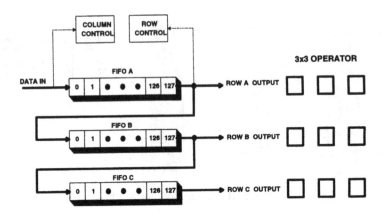

Fig. 7. The memory buffer block

A 3x3 window is created by shifting out the contents of the FIFOs 3 times. A shift at the output of the FIFOs causes the processing window to move one column to the right and every 128 shifts causes the content of a FIFO to move to the next FIFO in line. Hence the window is moved downward by one row. Using this technique the operator is applied to the entire frame.

The statistical filling operator of Fig. 6, consists of combinational logic which is the core of the SSF.

3.2 Projection Implementation

PT Architecture. The computation of equation (1) requires the calculation of both square and square root functions for each pixel. This is both complex and time consuming. However a simple and compact approximation [8] for equation (1) can be used without a significant reduction in overall system performance. This 'r' approximation is:

$$r = |AX| + 0.375|AY| \tag{4}$$

where AX is the larger magnitude of the pair and AY the smaller. The data format for 'r' approximation is a normalised 24 bit fixed point word with an 8 bit integer and 16 bit fractional part.

The implementation of equation (2) requires a divider. A 24-bit high precision signed serial/parallel divider was developed, based on the SRT algorithm [9]. The divider uses 111 CLBs and requires 24 clock cycles to produces a 24 bit result.

Fig. 8 below illustrates the block diagram for calculating the $tan\,\theta$ of an object area. The Y and X counters generate the pixel coordinates of the object area, and X_msb and Y_msb signals are the sign bits of the terms $(x - \bar{x})$ and $(y - \bar{y})$.

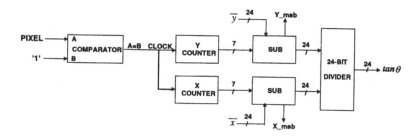

Fig. 8. Block diagram of $tan\,\theta$ operation

QT Architecture. The QT block diagram is shown in Fig. 9. From equation (3), the amplitudes (r) within a $tan\,\Delta6$ segment have to be quantised to new values of Q_i. The $tan\,6$ function is stored in a look-up table, LUT. The LUT holds 8 words of 24-bits wide corresponding to the maximum tangent values of 8 segments in a quadrant of a polar plane. Since $tan\,6$ values on all four quadrants are equal, values of only one quadrant need to be defined in the LUT. This resulted in reduction of LUT size by 75 %. The Y_msb and X_msb generated by the PT, are used as pointers to the appropriate quadrant.

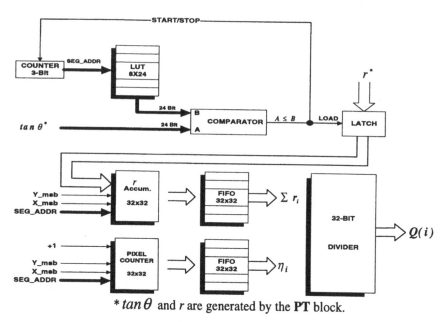

$*tan\,\theta$ and r are generated by the **PT** block.

Fig. 9. Quantisation, QT functional diagram

The 32 segments in the polar plane are searched and where $tan\,\theta$ value lies within a segment, the r value is accumulated and placed in a register RAM whose address is defined by the segment number and quadrant pointers. The accumulator has 32 words each 32 bits wide and includes a 32 bit parallel adder/subtractor and an accumulate register to store the progressive r sum. Implementing such an accumulator in a conventional form using flip-flops would require 512 CLBs. The RAM capability of the XC4010 series [1] is used to implement the registers required by the accumulator. This reduces the number of CLBs required to 32. Fig. 10 shows the block diagram of the accumulator employed in this design.

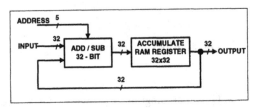

Fig. 10. Xilinx implementation of 32x32 accumulator

On each accumulation of r, a pixel counter is also incremented which has the same address input as the r accumulator. The output of the pixel counter η_i , reports the number of r values included within a segment. A divider at the output of the storage element (FIFO), generates the projection output Q_i which has a 32 bit fixed point format.

3.3 RT Implementation

The block diagram of a 32-point RT processor is shown in Fig. 11. The data format throughout the RT processor is a normalised 32 bit fixed point word with an 8 bit integer and 24 bit fractional part. The design is based on banks of 16x32 shift registers (PIPO) implemented using SRAM memory, and multiplexers. There are 4 PIPOs (PIPO1-4) of size 16 words of 32 bits each which are used for storing input sequence and intermediate results. The outputs of the RT processor are stored on a separate 32 deep by 32 wide FIFO in the same FPGA, so they can be read by the host processor or sent to another FPGA without disrupting the operation of the RT. Implementing the 16x32 PIPO or 32x32 FIFO utilised 52 and 66 CLBs respectively.

The 32 words of the input data sequence $X(i)$ are stored in PIPO1-2 with the least significant word in location zero of PIPO2. For the first iteration $m = 1$, the contents of PIPO1 and PPO2, i.e. X (31, 30, ..., 16) and X (15, 14, ..., 0) respectively, are added and subtracted from each other thereby completing the $N/2$ Radix-2 butterfly operations. The outputs of the first iteration are routed into PIPO3-4 with the least significant word in location zero of PIPO4. The roles of PIPO1-2 and PIPO3-4 are now interchanged. Data input to the ADD/SUB is form PIPO3-4 and the outputs are shifted into PIPO1-2. This process is repeated for $m = 5$ times and the final outputs are stored in an on-chip 32x32 FIFO.

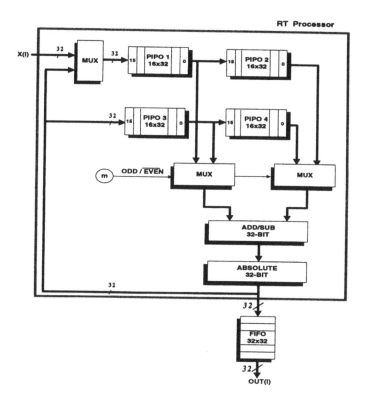

Fig. 11. Architecture of a 32-point RT processor

The 32 point RT processor implemented, requires 320 clock cycles in order to produce 32 features. With a system clock of 40 MHz, the RT is capable of processing a frame at a rate of 50 per second.

4 Results and Performance

The SSF implemented has a high sample rate. Real-time image processing requires filtering on the order of 50 frames/sec, and at this speed, the SSF could process an entire image in the required time scale. 29 clock cycles are required per pixel to perform all the processing steps necessary for the PT and QT circuits. This is largely due to the fact that, where possible, serial logic/arithmetic has been used. The integrated RT is a fast processor. The RT design has a parallel architecture and therefore the butterfly operation requires only 2 clock cycles. This results in an execution time of only 33 ns with a system clock of 66 MHz, compare to the FFT butterfly operation [10] of execution time of 320 ns. The overall system is capable of a throughput rate of 50 frames/second. Table 3, illustrates the CLB utilisation of major modules within the system.

Table 1. CLB Utilisation

Module	CLB
SSF	89
PT	384
QT	388
RT	390

5 Conclusion

An object recognition machine has been designed and normalised for position, translation, and rotation of its input image. The design highlights the potential for FPGAs to be used to perform computationally intensive operations needed for object recognition applications. To aim for real-time processing speed, pipeline structure has been created between the modules. This flexible architecture has been implemented on an FPGA array which enables the use of distributed memory and parallel processing to increase system throughput.

References

1. Xilinx, The Programmable Logic Data Book, 1996 Xilinx Inc.
2. Borghesi, P. "Digital Image Processing Techniques For Object Recognition and Experimental Results", *Proceedings of The Digital Signal Processing Conf. , Florance, Italy, September, 1984, pp. 764-768*
3. Ito, K., Hamamoto, M., Kamruzzaman, J., Kumaga, Y. "Invariant Object Recognition by Artificial Neural Network using Fahlman and Lebiere's Learning Algorithm", *IEICE T-Fundamentals, vol. E76-A, no. 7, pp. 1267-1272, July 1993*
4. Abu-Mostafa, Y., Psaltis, D. "Image Normalisation by Complex Moments", *IEEE T-PAMI, 1978, vol.7, No. 1, pp. 46-55*
5. Ma, J., Wu, C., Lu, X. "A Fast Shape Descriptor", *Computer vision, Graphics, and Image processing, 1986, vol. 34, pp. 282-291*
6. You, S., Ford, G. "Network Model for Invariant Object Recognition", *Pattern Recognition Letters, vol. 15, pp. 761-767, 1994*
7. Reithboech, H., Brody, T. P. "A Transformation with Invariance under Cyclic Permutation for Application in Pattern Recognition", *Information and Control 15, pp. 130-154, 1996*
8. Onoe, M. "Fast Approximation Yielding either Exact Mean or Minimum Deviation for Quadrature Pairs", *Proceedings IEEE, vol. 60, pp. 921-922, July 1972*
9. Robertson, J. E. "A New Class of Digital Division Methods", *IRE Trans. On Electronic Computers, 1958, pp. 88-92*
10. Mintzer, L. "Large FFTs in a Single FPGA", *Proc. Of ICSPAT,96*

PCI-SCI Protocol Translations: Applying Microprogramming Concepts to FPGAs

Georg Acher, Wolfgang Karl, and Markus Leberecht

Lehr- und Forschungseinheit Informatik X
Rechnertechnik und Rechnerorganisation /
Parallelrechnerarchitektur (LRR-TUM)
Institut für Informatik der Technischen Universität München
Arcisstr. 21, D-80290 München, Germany
{acher, karlw, leberech}@informatik.tu-muenchen.de

Abstract. The SMiLE project at LRR-TUM adopts and implements the Scalable Coherent Interface (SCI) interconnection technology to couple Pentium-II based PCs into a compute cluster with distributed shared memory. A custom PCI-SCI adapter has been developed for bridging the PC's PCI local bus with the SCI network. Such a PCI-SCI adapter intended for connecting PCI-based PCs via SCI involves complex protocol processing. In the paper we describe the rationale and implementation issues of our custom PCI-SCI adapter design. In particular, we demonstrate how traditional microprogramming techniques can be applied for a structured and simplified FPGA design.

1 Introduction

The Scalable Coherent Interface (SCI) is an interconnection technology for tightly and loosely coupled parallel systems. The SCI standard [6] specifies the hardware and protocols to connect up to 64 K nodes (multiprocessors, workstations or PCs, processors and caches, bridges or I/O adapters) into a high-speed and scalable network fabric. A 64 bit global address space across SCI nodes is defined as well as a set of related transactions for reading, writing, and locking shared regions, optionally supported by a directory-based cache-coherence protocol . In addition to communication via hardware-supported distributed shared memory (DSM), SCI facilitates fast message passing. Therefore, there is a wide range of SCI applications some of which are described in [7], [2], [8], and [3].

The SMiLE project[1] at LRR-TUM investigates high-performance cluster computing based on SCI interconnection technology [4]. Within the scope of this project, a SCI-based PC-cluster with DSM is being built. In order to be able to set up such a PC cluster we have developed our own custom PCI-SCI adapter for bridging the PC's PCI local bus with the SCI network. Pentium-II PCs equipped with these PCI-SCI adapters are connected to a cluster of computing nodes with NUMA characteristics (non-uniform memory access). Additionally,

---

[1] SMiLE: Shared Memory in a LAN-like Environment.

the PCI-SCI adapter allows the attachment of a hardware monitor, enabling research on data locality in NUMA systems. A detailed description of the PCI-SCI adapter implementation can be found in [1].

The PCI-SCI adapter has to translate PCI bus operations into SCI transactions, and vice versa. The interface to the PCI local bus is implemented by the PLX bus master chip PCI 9060 [9], the SCI side is handled by the LinkController LC-1 manufactured by Dolphin Interconnect Solutions. However, control and protocol processing between these two commercial chips have been implemented with two FPGAs.

The paper describes in detail the design and implementation of our custom PCI-SCI adapter targeted for clustering PCI-based PCs into a DSM system. In order to be able to manage the complex protocol processing, microprogramming concepts have been applied for a structured hardware design. Using the PCI-SCI protocol translations as an example, we show that these concepts simplify complex hardware designs for FPGAs in comparison with the use of state machines.

2 The PCI-SCI Adapter Architecture

As already mentioned, the Scalable Coherent Interface SCI has been chosen as the network fabric for the SMiLE PC cluster. Nodes within an SCI-based system are interconnected via point-to-point links in ring-like arrangements or are attached to switches. For the communication between SCI nodes, the logical layer of the SCI specification defines packet-switched protocols. An SCI split transaction requires a request packet to be sent from one SCI node to another node with a response packet in reply to it, thus overlapping several transactions and hiding remote access latencies.

For the SMiLE PC cluster, the PCI-SCI adapter serves as interface between the PCI local bus and the SCI network. As shown in Fig. 1, the PCI-SCI adapter is divided into three logical parts: the PCI unit, the Dual-Ported RAM (DPR), and the SCI unit.

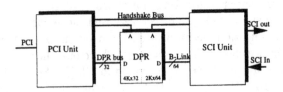

Fig. 1. PCI-SCI bridge architecture

The PCI unit (Fig. 2) interfaces to the PCI local bus. A 64 MByte address window on the PCI bus allows to intercept processor-memory transactions which are then translated into SCI transactions. For the interface to the PCI bus, the PCI9060 PCI bus master chip form PLX Technology is used. The main task of

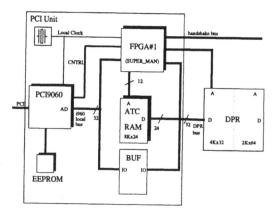

Fig. 2. Block diagram of the PCI unit

this chip is to transform PCI operations into bus operations following the Intel i960 bus protocol, and vice versa. Two independent bi-directional DMA channels are integrated, allowing direct memory transfers between PCI and SCI initiated by the PCI-SCI adapter.

The packets to be sent via SCI are buffered within the Dual-Ported RAM. It contains frames for outgoing packets allowing one outstanding read transaction, 16 outstanding write transactions, 16 outstanding messaging transactions using a special DMA engine for long data transfers between nodes, and one read-modify-write transaction which can be used for synchronization. Additionally, 64 incoming packets can be buffered.

The SCI unit interfaces to the SCI network and performs the SCI protocol processing for packets in both directions. This interface is implemented with the LinkController LC-1, which implements the physical layer and parts of the logical layer of the SCI specification.

Within both units, control and protocol processing is handled by an FPGA, respectively. The following section provides a detailed description of the design aspects for the FPGA which controls the PCI unit.

3 The SCI Upload/Packet Encoder Management FPGA (Super_MAN)

3.1 Choosing the right Technology

The previous description showed that despite the use of two specialized commercial ASICs, the main task of the PCI-SCI-bridge has to be done by custom hardware: The conversion from the bus oriented i960-protocol to a packet based B-Link protocol and vice versa. A quick approximation showed, that this task cannot be easily achieved with lower integrated CPLD techniques. The PCI unit has to handle reads and writes from the PCI side, as well as read and write requests from the SCI unit. Furthermore, the implementation of a semaphore/lock transaction and an efficient DMA block transfer would be very useful additions. In order to fully use the low SCI latency, none of these transactions (except the lock[2]) should need any additional software actions for packet encoding and decoding. Thus all encoding/decoding has to be implemented in hardware.

Eventually, the usage of SRAM based XC4000E-series FPGAs from Xilinx seemed to be the only way to implement the controlling parts of the PCI-SCI-bridge. Not only their relatively low cost and good performance, but also their reconfigurability in the environment of 'unknown' chips lead to this decision. Later on, this will also decrease the amount of work to implement new features. Synopsys VHDL was chosen for the design entry.

During the design phase, the RAM functionality of the XC4000E became very useful, because many details could be implemented very simply (namely the microsequencer described below).

3.2 Internal Structure of the FPGA

While evaluating the specifications for the controller, it became obvious that the somewhat complex dataflows and encoding/decoding actions in the PCI unit could be separated into five main parts (objects), communicating only with a few signals (commands).

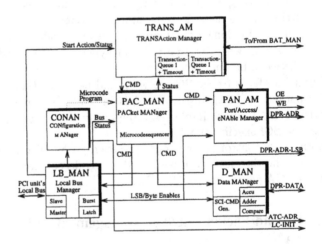

Fig. 3. Structure of SUPER_MAN

Referring to Fig. 3, these five main units are:

– **Local Bus Manager (LB_MAN)**: Controls the local bus, accepts accesses, generates a status, and starts accesses to the PCI9060 (started with a specific

---

[2] A SCI-lock transaction cannot be transparently handled through the PCI bus and the whole SCI network, therefore the packet **encoding** has to be done in software.

command). LB_MAN has no knowledge of the transferred data itself or any data flow concerning other busses than the i960 bus.

- **Data Manager (D_MAN):** This unit interfaces to the external DPR-bus. Depending on the command, it stores some fields of the read data or generates specific codes itself (e.g. the SCI-commands). It is also used as an ALU for the bounded add operation (needed for the lock transaction).

- **Port and Enable Manager (PAN_AM):** Although there seems to be a great number of possible dataflows between the i960 bus, the DPR, D_MAN, and the address translation RAM, complicated with different bit fields and offsets, they can be reduced to 15 simple flows. Depending on the command, PAN_AM sets the needed internal and external buffer enable and read/write signals, allowing adressing of some specific locations (bit fields, like the SCI command field) in a B-Link packet and combining with a source or sink.

- **Transaction Management (TRANS_AM):** The Transaction Management sets the DPR packet base address corresponding to the current LB_MAN-status (read/write from PCI) or to the next incoming packet. An arbiter selects between both possibilites. In some cases it is necessary to switch to another base (e.g. get read data from a read response), so there are specific 'override' commands.

As the SCI net supports split transactions[3] there are also two bookkeeping units for regular writes and DMA writes with 16 entries each.

The main task of TRANS_AM is the starting of the appropiate encoding/decoding action, the actions itself are controlled by the following unit:

- **Packet Manager (PAC_MAN):** In order to encode or decode a packet and to serve bus accesses this unit issues the right sequence of commands to the other four units. Depending on the needed action, this sequence can be linear, with waitstates or a few branches.

3.3 Implementation Issues

The separation of the five units with its distinct I/O signals allows the placement of 4 units with I/O (D_MAN, LB_MAN, PAN_AM and TRANS_AM) around the four edges of the die, surrounding the central PAC_MAN unit (see Fig. 4). Thus, the needed floorplanning was very simple and the external PCB-routing was also eased.

3.4 Structure of the Packet Manger as a Microcode Sequencer

As stated above, the various actions for packet encoding and decoding are controlled and coordinated in the Packet Management Unit. In general, its behavior can be described as a state machine consisting of about 60 states. Each state outputs the four 4bit commands to the other functional units. In total there are more than 80 state transitions, most of them unconditional. Yet, some transitions are more complicated e.g. waitstates or the initial dispatching of the 16 needed actions (e.g. generating single byte write requests).

---

[3] due to the PCI bus, this is only used for writes

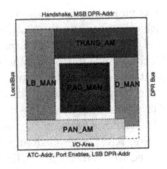

Fig. 4. Floorplanning of SUPER_MAN

The first approach in implementing this state machine was the conventional way, using the `case-when` construct in VHDL. After the first tests with only 30 states, it became evident, that this way is not feasible for an FPGA. The highly irregular structure of the state decoding and the relatively wide (16 bit) and dense packed command output were synthesized to a very large and slow logic (max. 14 MHz for an XC4013E-3). Because the target frequency 25 MHz was chosen, this result was considered inacceptable.

Although it would be possible to use a special tool for the FSM-synthesis[4] the simple command scheme of the other functional units and the RAM-capability of the FPGAs lead to another idea: The implementation of a small microcode programmable processor, helped by the circumstance that the program-like flow of the actions itself can very easily be translated into the microcode.

The usage of microcode for a program sequence is not very new, but mainly used in 'real' microprocessor applications. Older FPGAs without the RAM capability only had the possibility to implement microcode with external RAM (slow) or with lookup tables (ROM). For each change in the microcode, the design would have to be re-routed. Thus microcode in FPGAs is rare.

A detailed analysis showed that a very simple microcode sequencer could cover all needed state transitions and output signals, some of these without any need of explicit or very complex implementation (see Fig. 5):

- **Normal execution**: Comparable to some other microcode machines (e.g. the AM29xx series), the 'Next-PC' is encoded in the microinstruction word. Hence, there is no need for an adder and an additional branch logic. The necessary RAM for the 'Next-PC' is arranged as 64*6bit. The XC4000-series has 32*1bit RAM cells, accounting for 12 CLBs for the RAM itself and another 6 CLBs for the additional demultiplexers and flip flops for the clocked operation.
- **Command outputs**: Parallel to the PC RAM input, there are the four 64*4 bit RAMs for the command generation, their clocked output feeds the four other units. Each command RAM requires 12 CLBs.

---

[4] Under the tight time frame of this work, the usage of a totally unfamiliar tool also seemed not very useful.

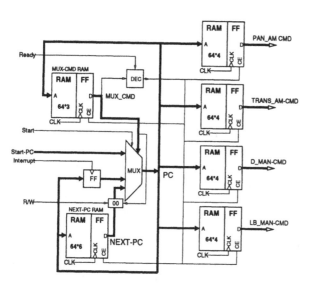

Fig. 5. Structure of the microcode sequencer

– **Starting a program**: For all encoding/decoding, TRANS_AM sets a 4 bit command, describing one of the 16 possible actions. In order to start, the microcode sequencer jumps at the first 16 locations in the control store, where each action has its entry point.
– **Changes in the program flow**
   • **Waitstates**: When a packet is encoded or decoded, the state machine has to wait until all data is accepted or delivered by the PCI-Interface or a response comes back from the SCI link.
   • **Interrupt and Return**: If a DMA write is aborted by the PCI9060, the unfinished packet must not be sent, until **all** 64 bytes are written into the packet. The next DMA-cycle has to return to that microcode position, where the aborted cycle left off (interrupt).
   • **Branch**: When directly accessing the DPR, the decision between read and write is made in the microcode, so a conditional branch is needed.
To accomplish the above tasks, there are another 3 bits in the microinstruction word (MUX_CMD), that control the feedback from the Next-PC output to the PC input, thus implementing the sequencer.
Because the XC4000-CLBs have clock enable (CE) inputs, the waitstate generation can easily be done by using the CE input in all RAM output flip flops. This avoids one logic level in the timing critical feedback.
The interrupt control consists of a register that latches the PC and outputs it to the sequencer multiplexer if a return is requested.
The 'branch' unit simply sets the least significant bits of the Next-PC to zero, if the condition is 'write', otherwise the execution continues. With the appropiate alignment this can be used as a conditional back jump.
– **Programming control**: There is an additional multiplexer input for the CLB-RAM address, allowing the simple reconfiguration of the microcode.

3.5 Microcode Examples

To show the ease of development for the chosen microcode architecture, the generation of a single byte read request (R_RQO) is shown[5]:

PC	Next-PC	PAN_AM	D_MAN	TRANS_AM	LB_MAN	MUX_CMD
2	19	TRANSADR_2_DPR	GEN_ADR_LSB	SEND_R_RQO	NONE	GO
19	20	TIDCMD_2_DPR	GEN_RRQ_CMD	NONE	NONE	GO
20	21	NONE	NONE	SET_RRSI	NONE	MUX_WAIT
21	63	DPR_2_DATAL	NONE	SET_RRSI	DATA_READY	GO
63	0	NONE	NONE	DONE	DONE	GO

The control flow is started with command '2', thus the sequencer begins at PC=2. In this step the translated address is written in the request packet, due to synchronisation stages the packet also can be 'sent' early, even when it is not completely assembled. In the second step the translated target ID (TID) and the read request command (RRQ) are written in the appropiate places. At PC=20 the execution waits until the response packet with the needed data arrives, then the packet address is set to the incoming packet (SET_RRSI) and the buffers are opened to the local bus. At this point, the waiting PCI9060-access can be finished (DATA_READY) and in the last step all actions are finished.

The most complex microprogram is the execution of a lock operation. It consists of 13 steps, implementing the read/modify/write cycle with sent arguments plus the additional response packet generation:

PC	Next-PC	PAN_AM	D_MAN	TRANS_AM	LB_MAN	MUX_CMD
/* Start the read cycle with a locked bus*/						
7	41	DPR_2_ADRGEN	NONE	NONE	NONE	GO
41	42	DPR_2_ADRGEN	LOAD_ADRLSB	NONE	NONE	GO
42	43	DPR_2_ADRGEN	NONE	SET_RSO	READ_LOCK	GO
/* Now wait for the data and write it in the response packet*/						
43	44	DATAL_2_DPR	NONE	SET_RSO	NONE	MUX_WAIT
/* Also load the data in the ALU*/						
44	45	NONE	LOAD_DATA	NONE	NONE	GO
/* Read upper bound */						
45	46	MAX_2_FPGA	NONE	NONE	NONE	GO
/* Read increment, latch upper bound */						
46	47	OP_2_FPGA	LOAD_COMP	NONE	NONE	GO
/*Latch increment and perform bounded add, start write back */						
47	48	DPR_2_ADRGEN	LOAD_ADD	NONE	WRITE	GO
/*Wait until data is accepted */						
48	29	FPGA_2_DATAL	STORE_DATA	SET_RSO	NONE	MUX_WAIT
/*Assemble response packet, swap source and target ID, early send */						
29	30	TIDCMD_2_DPR	GEN_R16_CMD	SEND_RSO	NONE	GO
30	31	SIDTRID_2_FPGA	NONE	SET_RSO	NONE	GO
31	32	FPGA_2_TIDTRID	LOAD_DATA	SET_RSO	NONE	GO
32	0	FPGA_2_TRID1	STORE_DATA	DONE_RSO	NONE	GO
/* Done... */						

This extract re-uses some parts of the response-outgoing (RSO) code part from the normal read action. Although the code has to deal with pipelining effects[6], the microcode approach shows its full elegance.

3.6 Results for the Microsequencer

While developing and testing the prototype, the reconfigurability of the microcode (without a new VHDL-synthesis) was heavily used for debugging. Nearly all unknown or uncertain behavior of the two ASICs could be analyzed. Even the real world robustness of the various data paths (setup/hold) could be tested with specific test (stress) patterns and sequences generated by the microcode.

---

[5] This textual description is processed by a simple parser, generating the binary patterns for programming.

[6] E.g. the Set-to-response-outgoing-packet (SET_RSO) has its effect in the next cycle, or a D_MAN load must occur one cycle after its corresponding PAN_AM read enable.

After getting the prototype to work, some (previously unplanned) features were implemented just by altering the microcode. In the same way, a few actions were tuned saving one or two clock cycles. Some other features presently not implemented such as support for remote enqueuing[7] and a touch-load[8]) should require only minimal changes in the hardware itself.

The total required logic resources for the microcode sequencer are about 80 CLBs from the 576 available CLBs of a XC4013, that is 14% usage. The VHDL description has only half the size of the incomplete first approach (with case-when). This results –with the highly regular structure– in a dramatically decreased synthesis and routing time. As a very pleasant side effect, the worst case frequency increased to more than 25 MHz.

Some care had to be taken for the routing: The PC bus has to be routed to about 50 CLBs. Due to the small bus width (6 bit) this seems not to be a resource problem at the first glance, but these nets are heavily loaded. Without manual intervention some nets had more than 25 ns delay time. This timing could be relaxed by using different nets to the 6 RAM blocks. Because the synthesis software tries to optimise this away, this could only be achieved with the manual instantiation of three-state buffers in the code. This reduced the net-load and the delay decreased to less than 15 ns. Due to some other critical nets and the future extensions, the final design uses now a XC4013E-2, making PAC_MAN performance even better. No further modifications were needed, keeping manual work very small.

Even without the manual tuning, the microcode sequencer design shows its superiority versus the conventional way of designing state machines, especially in this application with many linear, unconditional transitions, only a few input signals and wide output. Additionally, the possibility of reprogramming without a change in the synthesized hardware makes it very attractive for prototyping and debugging.

Unfortunately, the control store size (64 words) seems to be on the upper limit for the XC4013-FPGA, a a bigger size increases the needed nets drastically and would possibly result in a incomplete routing. Bigger CLB-RAMs or dedicated regular busses in the FPGA would solve this problem.

4 Some Preliminary Results

The logic of SUPER_MAN currently requires about 325CLBs (56% of the XC4013 CLB resources), thus leaving enough room for new features. The FPGA of the simple SCI-unit consist of a XC4005E-2 (about 53% CLB usage). Both units (and therefore the i960 bus and the B-Link) can run with 25 MHz[9].

The connection of two Pentium133-based machines via two PCI-SCI-bridges showed block transfer rates up to 40 MBytes/s and a bandwidth of 4 MB/s for

---

[7] The active messages layer [5] can be improved with the remote enqueue feature.

[8] Reducing the effective read latency.

[9] The SCI-link is clocked with 50 MHz, transmitting data on both edges.

normal (non-burst) shared memory writes over SCI. Moreover, the PCI-to-PCI-latency for these writes is (on a unloaded SCI-network) at about $2.7\mu s$, some orders below conventional networks (ethernet etc.).

5 Conclusion

In the paper, we described in detail the design aspects and implementation of the PCI-SCI adapter for the SMiLE PC cluster. Additionally, we demonstrated that with the application of traditional microprogramming concepts instead of complex state machines, the FPGA design can be simplified. New features can be integrated by adding the microcode with minimal hardware changes.

The PCI-SCI adapter allows the attachment of a hardware monitor which gathers detailed information about the run-time and communication behaviour of a program. The experience gained with the development of the PCI-SCI hardware will help us in designing and implementing the hardware monitor.

References

1. G. Acher. Entwicklung eines SCI Knotens zur Kopplung von PCI-basierten Arbeitsplatzrechnern mit Hilfe von VHDL. Diplomarbeit, Technische Universität München, Institut für Informatik (LRR-TUM), Oct. 1996. (in German).
2. CONVEX Computer Corporation, Richardson, TX. *Exemplar Architecture Manual*, 1993.
3. D. B. Gustavson and Q. Li. Local-Area MultiProcessor: the Scalable Coherent Interface. In *Proceedings The Second International Workshop on SCIbased High Performance LowCost Computing*, pages 131–166, Santa Clara University, Santa Clara, CA, Mar. 1995. SCIzzL, Association of Scalable Coherent Interface (SCI) Local Area MultiProcessor Users, Developers, and Manufacturers.
4. H. Hellwagner, W. Karl, and M. Leberecht. Enabling a PC Cluster for High-Performance Computing. *SPEEDUP Journal*, 11(1), June 1997.
5. H. Hellwagner, W. Karl, and M. Leberecht. Fast Communication Mechanisms–Coupling Hardware Distributed Shared Memory and User-Level Messaging. In *Proc International Conference on Parallel and Distributed Processing Techniques and Applications PDPTA*, Las Vegas, Nevada, June 30–July 3 1997.
6. IEEE Standard for the Scalable Coherent Interface (SCI). IEEE Std 1596-1992, 1993. IEEE 345 East 47th Street, New York, NY 10017-2394, USA.
7. T. D. Lovett, R. M. Clapp, and R. J. Safranek. NUMA-Q: An SCI based Enterprise Server. In *Proceedings The Sixth International Workshop on SCIbased HighPerformance LowCost Computing*, pages 25–30, Santa Clara, CA, Sept. 1996. SCIzzL.
8. H. Müller, A. Bogaerts, C. Fernandes, L. McCulloch, and P. Werner. A PCI-SCI bridge for high rate Data Aquisition Architectures at LHC. In *Proceedings of PCI5 Conference*, page 156 ff, Santa Clara, USA, 1995.
9. PLX Technology Inc., 625 Clyde Avenue, Mountain View, CA. *PCI 060 PCI Bus Master Interface Chip for Adapters and Embedded Systems*, Apr. 1995. Data Sheet.

Instruction-Level Parallelism for Reconfigurable Computing

Timothy J. Callahan and John Wawrzynek

University of California at Berkeley, Berkeley CA 94720, USA
http://www.cs.berkeley.edu/projects/brass/

Abstract. Reconfigurable coprocessors can exploit large degrees of instruction-level parallelism (ILP). In compiling sequential code for reconfigurable coprocessors, we have found it convenient to borrow techniques previously developed for exploiting ILP for very long instruction word (VLIW) processors. With some minor adaptations, these techniques are a natural match for automatic compilation to a reconfigurable coprocessor. This paper will review these techniques in their original context, describe how we have adapted them for reconfigurable computing, and present some preliminary results on compiling application programs written in the C programming language.

1 Introduction

In this work we consider compilation for a hybrid reconfigurable computing platform consisting of a microprocessor coupled with field-programmable gate array (FPGA) circuitry used as a reconfigurable accelerator. The FPGA is configured to provide a customized accelerator for compute-intensive tasks. This acceleration results in part from the parallel execution of operations, since the FPGA has no von Neumann instruction fetch bottleneck. The microprocessor is used for "random" control-intensive application code and for system management tasks. It also provides binary compatibility with existing executables, which eases the migration path to reconfigurable computing [4]. We assume support for rapid run-time reconfiguration to allow several different tasks in the same application to be accelerated [5].

For ease of programming these systems, it is best if a single, software-like language is used for describing the entire application, encompassing computation on both the microprocessor and the FPGA. But traditional imperative software languages are basically sequential in nature; starting from there, it is a challenging task to exploit the reconfigurable hardware's parallel nature. Previous efforts have corrected this mismatch by using languages with constructs to explicitly specify either data parallelism [8, 9] or more general parallelism [15, 2, 16]. However, the farther such a language's semantics deviate from those of sequential languages, the more difficult it is to train programmers to use it efficiently, and the more work is involved in porting "dusty deck" sequential code to it.

This work instead investigates automatic extraction and hardware compilation of code regions from dusty deck C code. While it is unlikely the resulting performance will be as good as if a human rewrote the code in a parallel style, this approach has its advantages: (i) it gives immediate performance benefit from reconfigurable hardware with just a recompilation, and (ii) it is useful in cases in which the execution time is spread across more kernels than are worth recoding by hand.

Automatic compilation of sequential code to hardware poses several challenges. In such code, basic blocks are typically small so that little instruction-level parallelism is found within each one. Also, operations difficult to implement directly in hardware, such as subroutine calls, are often sprinkled throughout the code. Finally, loops often contain conditionals with rarely executed branches that interfere with optimization.

These features of sequential code similarly caused problems for VLIW machines. A key technique used by VLIW compilers to overcome these obstacles was to optimize the common execution paths to the exclusion of all rarely executed paths. Applying these same techniques allows us to accelerate loops that could not otherwise be mapped to the coprocessor due to an operation that is infeasible to implement in hardware. Without the exclusion ability, an infeasible operation on even an uncommon path would prevent any of the loop from being accelerated. Furthermore, by excluding uncommon paths, the remaining paths typically execute more quickly, and in the case of reconfigurable computing, less reconfigurable hardware resources are required.

Our approach is greatly influenced by our target platform, the theoretical Garp chip [11]. The Garp chip tightly couples a MIPS microprocessor and a datapath-optimized reconfigurable coprocessor. The coprocessor is rapidly reconfigurable, making it possible to speed up dozens or hundreds of loops. If a desired configuration has been used recently it is likely still in the *configuration cache* and can be loaded in just a few cycles. The flipflops in each row of the Garp array are accessible as a single 32-bit coprocessor register; transfers between such a coprocessor register and a microprocessor register can be performed at a rate of one per clock cycle. The coprocessor can directly access the main memory system (including data cache) as quickly as can the microprocessor. Because of these features, the Garp coprocessor can accelerate many loops that would be impractical to implement with a more traditional FPGA coprocessor. It is also due to these features that we can easily off-load uncommon computations to the main processor, allowing the common cases to execute faster on the coprocessor.

2 VLIW Background

VLIW processors possess a number of functional units that can be utilized in parallel, connected to each other through a multiported register file. Builders of such machines long ago encountered difficulty extracting enough ILP from sequential programs to keep all of the functional units busy. Studies have shown that amount of ILP within a basic block is typically only 2–3.5 [7]. *Trace scheduling* [6] is a technique to enhance the amount of ILP by combining sequences of basic blocks along the most commonly executed linear path. This forms a larger unit for scheduling called a trace, within which more ILP is available. While this approach works well when there is a single dominant sequence, it is less successful when there are multiple paths that are executed with comparable frequency. The *hyperblock* [14] was developed to address this situation, and is the central structure we borrow from VLIW compilation.

A hyperblock is formed from a contiguous group of basic blocks, usually including basic blocks from different alternative control paths. For optimization purposes, a hyperblock will typically include only the common control paths and not rarely taken paths. By definition, a hyperblock has a single point of entry – typically the entry of an inner loop – but may have multiple exits. An exit may jump back to the beginning of the same hyperblock (forming a back edge of the loop); an exit may jump to an excluded path of the loop; or an exit may continue to other code, as in the case of a normal loop exit. Some basic blocks may need to be duplicated outside of the hyperblock in order for the single-entry constraint to be obeyed. Fig. 1 shows an example hyperblock.

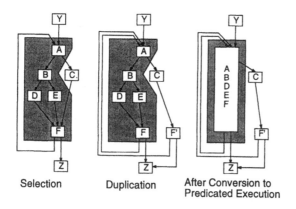

Selection   Duplication   After Conversion to
Predicated Execution

Fig. 1. Hyperblock formation for VLIW compilation.

The basic blocks selected to form a hyperblock are merged by converting any control flow between them to a form of *predicated execution*. We consider specifically *partially predicated execution* [13]. With partially predicated execution, the instructions along *all* of the included control paths are executed unconditionally (with the exception of memory stores), and *select* instructions are inserted at control flow merge points to select the correct results for use in subsequent computation (Fig. 2). If a select instruction's first operand (called a *predicate*) is true, the result is the value of the second operand, otherwise the result is the value of the third operand. The predicate is an expression of the boolean values that originally controlled conditional branches. The result is essentially speculative execution of all included paths; although this approach rapidly consumes resources, it also gives the best performance since it exposes the most ILP and reduces critical path lengths.

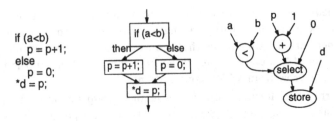

Fig. 2. C code, control flow graph, and partially predicated execution.

The challenge for the VLIW compiler is deciding which basic blocks should be included in each hyperblock. In general, rarely taken paths should be excluded. Excluding them allows the common cases to achieve higher performance, at the expense of causing the rare paths to execute more slowly due to the branch penalty of exiting a hyperblock. Factors considered when selecting the basic blocks to compose a hyperblock include relative execution frequencies, resource limitations, and the impact on the critical path.

3 Using the Hyperblock for Reconfigurable Computing

Our compiler uses the hyperblock structure for deciding which parts of a program are executed on the reconfigurable coprocessor as well as for converting the operations in the selected basic blocks to a parallel form suited to hardware. Being able to exclude certain paths from implementation on the reconfigurable coprocessor is very useful. Besides making the configuration smaller and often faster, it allows us to ignore certain operations that are impossible to implement using the coprocessor, e.g., subroutine calls, as long as they are on uncommon paths. If a loop body had to be implemented on the coprocessor as an all-or-nothing unit, the existence of a subroutine call even on an uncommon path would exclude the entire loop from consideration for acceleration using the coprocessor.

For each accelerated loop we form one hyperblock, which will be the portion of the loop body that is implemented on the reconfigurable coprocessor. Hyperblock exits are points where execution is transferred from the reconfigurable coprocessor back to the main processor. Each hyperblock eventually becomes one coprocessor configuration, and thus there is one configuration per accelerated loop. The partially predicated execution representation maps directly to hardware, with the select instructions implemented as multiplexors. The resulting dataflow graph is very similar to the "operator network" used in the PRISM-II compiler [1].

One adjustment in our use of the hyperblock is that a loop back edge from an exit directly back to the top of the hyperblock is considered to be *internal* to the hyperblock. This reflects the fact that normal loop iteration control is performed on the reconfigurable coprocessor with no intervention from the main processor. Thus such a back edge is not actually considered an exit. The remaining exits can be classified as either finished or exceptional. *Finished* exits are those that are taken because the loop has finished all its iterations (e.g., Exit 1 in Fig. 3). *Exceptional* exits are those that are taken because an excluded basic block must be executed (e.g., Exit 2 in Fig. 3). After an exceptional exit is taken, the hyperblock may be reentered at the beginning of the next iteration.

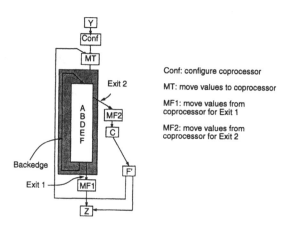

Conf: configure coprocessor

MT: move values to coprocessor

MF1: move values from coprocessor for Exit 1

MF2: move values from coprocessor for Exit 2

Fig. 3. Hyperblock formation for compilation to reconfigurable coprocessor. The hyperblock ABDEF is executed using the reconfigurable coprocessor, while all other basic blocks are executed on the microprocessor.

4   Execution Model

The unit of code that gets accelerated on the coprocessor is a loop[1]. General loop nesting is not currently supported. Thus accelerated loops cannot contain any inner loops on included paths. A loop that contains inner loops only on *excluded* paths can still be accelerated.

When an accelerated loop is reached in the program, the processor activates the correct configuration for the coprocessor, moves initial data into FPGA registers, and starts the coprocessor. The processor then suspends itself and does not wake up until the coprocessor is finished.

As the coprocessor executes, a simple sequencer keeps track of the current cycle in the iteration. The sequencer activates functional units that are scheduled for a specific cycle. In particular, a memory operation must execute during the correct cycle; during other cycles its address input may be invalid.

The sequencer is also used to determine when the end of the iteration has been reached. The number of cycles in the iteration is determined by the critical path through the hyperblock and is the same every iteration. At the end of an iteration, loop-carried values are latched for use in the next iteration.

---

[1] The execution model presented here is specific to our automatic compilation. It should not be inferred that this is the only model allowed by the Garp architecture.

Coprocessor execution will continue indefinitely until an exit is taken. An exit can occur at any cycle of an iteration, and a hyperblock may have several different exits. When any exit is activated, a builtin feature of the Garp reconfigurable array is used to halt the array instantaneously, freezing all values in registers. This action also awakens the processor.

Once the processor awakes, it must determine which exit was taken from the hyperblock. Once done, it moves any live values from the coprocessor back to the main registers. This transfer depends on which exit was taken, as there are likely different sets of live variables at different exits, and also different values for a given variable at different exits. If an exceptional exit was taken, the remainder of the iteration is completed on the processor, and at the start of the next iteration control is again transferred to the coprocessor.

5   Compiler Flow

Front End. We have used the SUIF compiler system [10] to implement our prototype C compiler targeting the Garp chip. SUIF's standard C parser and front end optimizations are utilized. A basic block representation of the code is then constructed using a control flow graph library [12]. This library includes natural loop analysis routines that allow us to recognize and process any kind of loop, even one formed by a backwards goto statement in the original source code.

Hyperblock Selection. At each loop an attempt is made to form a hyperblock. Initially all of the basic blocks in the loop are marked as included, and then blocks are systematically excluded. A basic block can be excluded from the hyperblock (i) because it contains an infeasible operation (floating-point, division, remainder, or subroutine call), (ii) because it is the entry of an inner loop (which will have its own hyperblock), (iii) because it needs to be excluded in order for the configuration to fit on the available resources, or (iv) simply to improve the performance of the remaining hyperblock. Currently (i) and (ii) are operational, and heuristics for (iii) and (iv) are under development.

The exclusion of one block often implies the exclusion of other blocks due to the *trimming* process. "Dead end" basic blocks – those blocks that ultimately lead only to excluded blocks – are trimmed. We also trim "unreachable" blocks – those that would only be reached by going through an excluded block. After this trimming we know that every remaining basic block is on a cycle contained completely in the hyperblock.

Hyperblock Duplication. We find it useful to duplicate all basic blocks selected for the hyperblock, retaining the complete original non-hyperblock version of the loop as well. This is in contrast to the VLIW approach, which only duplicates basic blocks as necessary to avoid re-entering the hyperblock. For our purposes, the non-hyperblock version is the "software" version of the loop, while the hyperblock copy is the "hardware" version. At an exceptional exit, control flows out of the hardware version and continues at the corresponding point in the software version.

The hardware version of the loop is a temporary construction; its presence aids in the construction of the interface instructions and the dataflow graph. Ultimately, however, the basic blocks in the hardware version will be deleted, since that computation will actually be performed in the FPGA.

Interface Synthesis. At the points where the hardware version of the loop interfaces with the rest of the program, interface code must be synthesized. This includes the instructions to load the correct configuration, to move values back and forth between the coprocessor and main processor registers, and to determine which exit was taken when the coprocessor finishes. When the data transfer code is synthesized, live variable analysis is used to avoid unnecessary transfers.

Dataflow Graph Formation. The computation in the basic blocks of the duplicated hyperblock is converted to partially predicated execution form as was shown in Fig. 2. This creates a dataflow graph where all of the control flow has been converted to explicit data transfer. This form maps very directly to the reconfigurable hardware. The "select" instructions are implemented in hardware as multiplexors and are analogous to the "merge-muxes" used in PRISM-II.

A number of optimizations are performed on the dataflow graph before it is written out for synthesis. The number of multiplexors can often be reduced at the expense of a small amount of extra boolean logic. Also, boolean signals (e.g., the results of comparisons) are identified and used to simplify multiplexors to gates, and to simplify comparisons to no-ops or inversions. We found that these cases arise frequently due to complex logical expressions typically found in C code.

The dataflow graph may contain multiple memory access operations. If it cannot be determined at compile time whether or not two memory operations access the same location, then they must be executed in the same order as they appear in the sequential program input, unless they are both loads. Such orderings are preserved using precedence edges in the dataflow graph; these edges indicate that the source node must execute before the destination node. Precedence edges are also needed between exits and memory writes to assure that writes don't occur when they shouldn't, or not occur when they should.

Synthesis. Each dataflow graph is written out and fed to the GAMA datapath synthesizer [3] to create the configuration for the coprocessor. GAMA looks for opportunities to merge neighboring operations (for example, an addition and an exclusive-or) to form a compound functional unit when this is smaller and/or faster than implementing each individually. GAMA also synthesizes a sequencer that counts the cycles in each iteration and activates modules appropriately.

Final Compilation and Linking. Assuming the synthesis is successful, the code is patched to direct control to the hardware version of the loop. The modified code is converted from SUIF back to C and cross-compiled with a modified version of **gcc** that understands Garp's extensions to the MIPS instruction set. The final executable links in the software object files along with the coprocessor configurations, which are in the form of integer array initialization data.

Execution. As the hardware is not currently available, the executable is run on the Garp simulator, which accurately models cache misses, configuration loading delays, and other important features to provide an accurate prediction of execution behavior.

6 Preliminary Results

The two primary benefits of the approach presented here are (i) increasing the performance of computation on the coprocessor, and (ii) increasing the fraction of a program that can be accelerated using the coprocessor. We will not be able to evaluate the magnitude of the first benefit until we complete development of heuristics for excluding basic blocks to get better performance. However, we have collected preliminary data regarding the second benefit – excluding parts of a loop that can't be implemented in hardware in order to allow the remainder of the loop to be accelerated.

The results are presented in Table 1. Execution cycles are classified into one of 5 categories, and the cumulative time in cycles in each category is reported for four application/dataset combinations. The categories are as follows:

- **Single Exit Loops** have a single exit and contain no infeasible operation.
- **Multi Exit Loops** have multiple exits and contain no infeasible operations.
- **Hyperblock Loops** have excluded blocks due to infeasible operations.
- **Unfruitful Loops** execute for too few cycles per exit to overcome overhead for using the coprocessor. We estimate a factor of two speedup using the coprocessor, and 25 cycles of overhead per exit. Thus loops that executed 50 cycles or fewer per exit on average would be slowed down using the coprocessor and fall into this category. This is admittedly a rough guess.
- **Other** Cycles not included above – straight-line code, code in library routines, and code in infeasible loops (loops that have an infeasible operation or inner loop on every path through their body).

With the **gzip** examples, we see that a large fraction of computation cycles are captured in the first two relatively simple classes of loops. This indicates that most loops in **gzip** don't contain infeasible operations. The hyperblock's ability to exclude some paths helps only a small degree.

With the **cpp** examples, however, the hyperblock approach allows a significant increase in the amount of computation that could be accelerated using the coprocessor. This is because many loops in **cpp** contain subroutine calls, e.g., to report errors. The three top time-consuming loops in **cpp** all contained infeasible operations, but in two of them, the infeasible operations were *never* executed, and in the third they were only rarely executed. This gives anecdotal support to the intuitive feeling that infeasible operations often occur on rarely executed paths.

256

Table 1. Execution time breakdown in cycles. Categories explained in text.

Test case	Single Exit Loops	Multi-exit Loops	Hyperblock Loops	Unfruitful Loops	Other	Total
gzip C source	530149 33.1%	586173 36.6%	143449 9.0%	134213 8.4%	209459 13.1%	1603443 100.0%
gzip English text	601187 28.6%	662164 31.5%	218534 10.4%	179781 8.6%	439624 20.9%	2101290 100.0%
cpp input 1	2949104 20.2%	2158983 14.8%	8423327 57.6%	213459 1.5%	878407 6.0%	14623280 100.0%
cpp input 2	1092072 18.5%	894918 15.2%	2179589 37.0%	265824 4.5%	1463763 24.8%	5896166 100.0%

7 Summary

We have adapted the hyperblock from VLIW compilation for our use in compiling to a reconfigurable coprocessor. Commonly-executed basic blocks are combined to form a large hyperblock, exposing instruction-level parallelism and allowing speculative execution to achieve high performance using the reconfigurable hardware. By excluding rarely-executed basic blocks, the compiler can produce configurations are smaller and faster, and can accelerate a greater number of loops than would be possible otherwise. Preliminary results show that in some cases our approach significantly increases the fraction of execution cycles that can be accelerated using the coprocessor when compiling dusty-deck C code.

8 Future Work

In future work we will develop hyperblock formation heuristics that integrate path profiling information and hardware estimation. We can then evaluate the performance benefit from intelligently excluding computation from the accelerated loop on the coprocessor.

9 Acknowledgements

This work benefited from discussions with others in the BRASS Research Group including John Hauser and André Dehon. We thank Randy Harr of Synopsys and the anonymous reviewers for their comments on earlier drafts of this paper.

This work is supported in part by DARPA grant DABT63-96-C-0048, DARPA/AFRL grant F33615-98-2-1317, Office of Naval Research grant N00014-92-J-1617, and National Science Foundation grant CDA 94-01156.

References

[1] L. Agarwal, M. Wazlowski, and S. Ghosh. An Asynchronous Approach to Efficient Execution of Programs on Adaptive Architectures Utilizing FPGAs. In *Proceed-*

ings IEEE Workshop on FPGAs for Custom Computing Machines, pages 101–10. IEEE Comput. Soc. Press, 1994. AN4754552.

[2] M. Aubury, I. Page, G. Randall, J. Saul, and R. Watts. Handel-C Language Reference Guide.

[3] T. J. Callahan, P. Chong, A. DeHon, and J. Wawrzynek. Rapid Module Mapping and Placement for FPGAs. In *Proc. ACM/SIGDA International Symposium on Field Programmable Gate Arrays*, pages 123–132, Monterey CA USA, 1998. ACM.

[4] A. DeHon. DPGA-Coupled Microprocessors: Commodity ICs for the Early 21st Century. In *Proceedings IEEE Workshop on FPGAs for Custom Computing Machines*, pages 31–9. IEEE Comput. Soc. Press, 1994.

[5] J. G. Eldredge and B. L. Hutchings. Density Enhancement of a Neural Network Using FPGAs and Run-Time Reconfiguration. In *Proceedings of IEEE Workshop on FPGAs for Custom Computing Machines*, pages 180–188, Napa, CA, Apr. 1994.

[6] J. R. Ellis. *Bulldog: A Compiler for VLIW Architectures*. MIT Press, Cambridge, MA, 1985.

[7] J. A. Fisher and B. R. Rau. Instruction-Level Parallel Processing. In H. C. Torng and S. Vassiliadis, editors, *Instruction-Level Parallel Processors*, pages 41–49. IEEE Computer Society Press, 1995.

[8] M. Gokhale and B. Schott. Data parallel C on a reconfigurable logic array. *Journal of Supercomputing*, pages 1–24, 1994.

[9] S. Guccione and M. Gonzalez. A Data-Parallel Programming Model for Reconfigurable Architectures. In *Proceedings IEEE Workshop on FPGAs for Custom Computing Machines*, pages 79–87. IEEE Comput. Soc. Press, 1993.

[10] M. W. Hall, J. M. Anderson, S. P. Amarasinghe, B. R. Murphy, S.-W. Liao, E. Bugnion, and M. S. Lam. Maximizing Multiprocessor Performance with the SUIF Compiler. *IEEE Computer*, Dec. 1996. See also http://suif.stanford.edu/.

[11] J. Hauser and J. Wawrzynek. Garp: A MIPS Processor with a Reconfigurable Coprocessor. In *Proceedings of IEEE Symposium on FPGAs for Custom Computing Machines*, Napa, CA, Apr. 1997.

[12] G. Holloway and C. Young. The Flow Analysis and Transformation Libraries of Machine SUIF. In *Proceedings of the Second SUIF Compiler Workshop*, Aug. 1997. Available from http://www-suif.stanford.edu/suifconf/suifconf2/.

[13] S. Mahlke, R. Hank, J. McCormick, D. August, and W. Hwu. A Comparison of Full and Partial Predicated Execution Support for ILP Processors. In *Proceedings 22nd Annual International Symposium on Computer Architecture*, pages 138–49, Santa Margherita Ligure, Italy, June 1995. ACM.

[14] S. Mahlke, D. Lin, W. Chen, R. Hank, and R. Bringmann. Effective Compiler Support for Predicated Execution Using the Hyperblock. In *Proceedings of the 25th International Symposium on Microarchitecture*, pages 45–54, Dec. 1992.

[15] I. Page and W. Luk. Compiling occam into FPGAs. In *FPGAs. International Workshop on Field Programmable Logic and Applications*, pages 271–283, Oxford, UK, Sept. 1991.

[16] N. Wirth. Hardware Compilation: Translating Programs into Circuits. *IEEE Computer*, 31(6):25–31, June 1998.

A Hardware/Software Co-design Environment for Reconfigurable Logic Systems

Gordon McGregor, David Robinson and Patrick Lysaght

Dept. of Electronic and Electrical Engineering,
University of Strathclyde,
204 George Street,
Glasgow, G1 1XW
United Kingdom

FAX: +44 (0)141 552 4968
email: g.mcgregor@eee.strath.ac.uk

Abstract. The design of reconfigurable systems is currently an area of intense interest within the programmable logic community. One of the main obstacles to the widespread adoption of this technology is the relative immaturity of the associated design methodologies and tools. This paper reports on a development environment and associated tools for the implementation and debugging of reconfigurable applications. These tools are part of a larger program of work to improve the construction of reconfigurable systems. The current environment is specific to a custom Xilinx XC6200 development board, but the principles are generic and portable to other reconfigurable systems and architectures.

1. Introduction

The development of reconfigurable applications typically proceeds in an ad-hoc manner, as there are very few CAD tools to accelerate or simplify the design process. If reconfigurable logic techniques are to be more widely accepted, application development procedures have to be better understood and become more structured. The current lack of CAD tools results in most examples being handcrafted [1], [2]. The consequent disadvantages are limited re-usability, restricted testability and the re-invention of design approaches. To address these issues new tools and methodologies are being researched to reduce the design effort involved in developing reconfigurable designs.

A design environment has been developed to compliment research into the simulation of reconfigurable systems. The Dynamic Circuit Switching (DCS) simulation tool [3] allows the simulation and specification of a reconfigurable design in its entirety. The interactions between reconfiguring and static circuits are modeled, along with normal circuit operation. With DCS, new designs can be investigated and solutions iterated upon much earlier in the design cycle than has been possible with other methods [4], [5], [6]. The amount of effort expended in evaluating candidate designs for implementation is thus greatly reduced. The original DCS tools are in the process of being enhanced and expanded to aid in several new areas of the design flow. Work has proceeded on methods to simplify and accelerate the co-design of software and hardware that interact with and control the reconfigurable application. The integration of these various tools provides a framework for the development of complete reconfigurable logic solutions from specification through to final implementation.

The paper is organised into five further sections. The next section presents an overview of the development environment and the design flow. The middle sections describe in more detail the component parts of our current system and the important features of the software API (Application Programming Interface). Section five presents an Interactive Design Tool (IDT) that builds upon the API to allow prototyping and debugging of the software and hardware routines. Conclusions and future work are discussed in the final section.

2. Overview of Development Environment

The underlying goal of the research was to provide a flexible and re-useable environment for the rapid investigation of dynamically reconfigurable applications. The development environment has been designed as a research tool, to allow the rapid investigation and production of proof-of-concept reconfigurable applications. The main objective was to raise the level of the development process above the level of the communication, configuration and management tasks that are inherent in reconfigurable systems. These goals have been achieved, allowing many more designs to be investigated more rapidly then was previously the case.

There are three main components to the development environment. These are the target reconfigurable architecture, a collection of software classes for programmatic control, and an interactive design tool. The target device is hosted on a custom PCI (Peripheral Component Interconnect) plug-in card, developed in the University of Strathclyde [8]. Software control of the card is encapsulated in C++ classes for ease of re-use and to allow abstraction from the implementation detail. The IDT provides the designer with access to the methods (C++ functions) of these classes, allowing the debugging of hardware operation and the development of reconfiguration algorithms.

3. Hardware Sub-system

The target system, shown in **Fig 1**, interfaces to the host via a Xilinx XC4013 FPGA, implementing a LogiCore PCI interface. A Xilinx XC6216 dynamically reconfigurable FPGA is the target device for reconfigurable applications. There is 1Mbyte of general purpose SRAM on the board, controlled via the XC6216 device. The card has two EEPROMs to allow serial configuration of either FPGA and the XC6216 can be (re)configured via the PCI bus, from configurations stored in the SRAM, or generated locally on either the XC6200 or XC4013 devices. The card is hosted in the Windows 95 operating system.

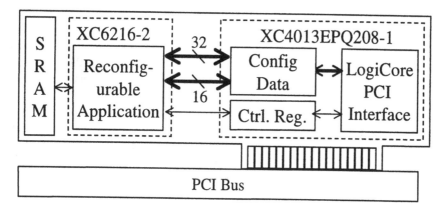

Fig 1 PCI plug-in card

The card communicates using PCI target mode for single data bursts between the card and host. Although initiator mode operation and interrupt services have been developed [7], they are not provided in the current revision of the system. Complete control of the XC6216 device operation is available via the XC4013 FPGA.

The design flow proceeds as follows.

- Designs are initially simulated using VHDL models that have been post-processed using the DCS simulation tools. VHDL simulation is then used to verify the operation of the reconfigurable design.

- When simulation is complete, each reconfigurable task is isolated from the design by hand. Methods to automatically extract reconfigurable tasks from the design files and then synthesise these tasks are being investigated, enhancing the DCS technique [7].

- The Velab VHDL elaborator tools are then used to convert the designs to EDIF netlists for placement and routing using the Xilinx XACT6000 design tools. The layout of reconfigurable tasks typically requires manual intervention, to ensure the consistent placement of logic across configurations. Current APR tools have no concept of layout across configurations so this task is the responsibility of the designer. Manual placement of logic blocks is specified using attributes.

Sections of the array can also be reserved, forcing logic to be routed around these areas. Logic may then be configured into these spaces at a later time. The non-reconfigurable portions of the design are automatically placed and routed as normal.

- The final stage of the design process is the generation of the bitstream files, using the Xilinx design tools.

For some designs, the bitstream generation tools produce very large, redundant configuration files and manual intervention is required to extract the relevant configuration information. The redundancy can be attributed to the APR tools being unaware of the reconfigurable nature of the design. Future tools will have to address these issues.

Improved estimates of removal and loading time [9] can be made from the configuration bitstream sizes and annotated into the DCS simulation. Work is currently ongoing to provide automated methods to generate accurate back-annotated timing simulation, through extensions to DCS.

4. Software API

An object-orientated API has been defined to simplify the control and management of reconfigurable applications. The interface encapsulates and hides the details of accessing the card, allowing work to proceed at a more abstract level when managing reconfigurable applications. The principal contribution of the API is support for event-driven reconfiguration of the target hardware.

The API is composed of three distinct layers. At the lowest level, a VxD (virtual device driver) controls access to the physical hardware, over the PCI bus. The next layer is the Hardware Abstraction Layer (HAL) that provides simple access functions. The Hardware Interaction Layer (HIL) layer builds upon the first two layers and provides more complex functionality. The designer uses a combination of these layers to interact with the underlying hardware. Applications typically interact directly with the HAL for data passing and use the HIL for configuration and reconfiguration management. An overview of the interaction between layers is shown in Fig 2. The IDT is also shown to indicate its relative location in the hierarchy.

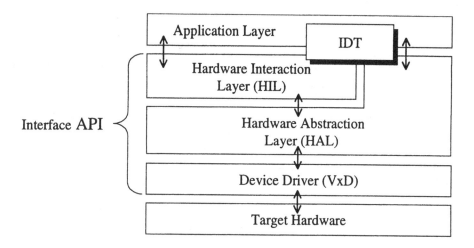

Fig 2 API Overview

The API has been designed to be easily re-targeted to other platforms. For example, support for other XC6200 prototyping boards would require changes to only the VxD layer. Targeting other FPGAs would require modification at the HAL layer but the methods in the HIL should remain substantially unaffected.

4.1. Device Driver / VxD

This layer of the API manages the initialisation and control of the hardware sub-system with the Windows 95 operating system. It obtains and stores configuration information, provided by the operating system, about the resources allocated to the hardware. The information is used by the VxD to mediate during data exchange. Application software cannot communicate directly with the underlying hardware. The VxD provides four hardware-specific methods to the HAL layer, to read and write an arbitrary location on the XC6216, and to read and write to the control register implemented in the XC4013. Although applications can communicate directly with the VxD, the access functions are greatly simplified in the HAL.

4.2. Hardware Abstraction Layer

The Hardware Abstraction Layer extends the basic functionality of the VxD layer. It provides more abstract access to the control register, implementing functions such as device reset, clock single stepping and data transfer. It reduces communications to the underlying hardware by maintaining copies of information on the current state of the device, e.g., map register contents or control register values. The HAL also performs address translation and validation.

Applications interact directly with this layer to pass single data words between an application and arbitrary locations on the target device. Address and data information are combined within a single object, simplifying the interfaces between methods. The address format is stored as either a numerical value or a symbolic name. The information in the symbol table produced by the XC6000 tools is used to locate named registers on the device. Registers are identified by the name used to instantiate them within the VHDL source code.

The ability to use symbolic register access greatly increases the readability and maintainability of source code. Relocation of interfaces in the hardware has no impact on the supporting application software. Removing the details of the hardware location from the application simplifies the interaction between the software and hardware portions of the design. The HAL maintains a database of the location of registers within the design, which is updated for each new configuration. Development time is also reduced, as the application software does not need to be recompiled as frequently to reflect hardware changes.

4.3. Hardware Interaction Layer

The Hardware Interaction Layer (HIL) extends the functionality of the previous two API layers, to provide configuration control and scheduling services. The main responsibilities of this layer include; configuration management, block data passing, advanced clock control, and reconfiguration control and scheduling.

Configuration management is encapsulated within three classes in the HIL. One of these classes encapsulates the format-dependent details for loading configuration files. Once loaded, the data is stored in an internal format that is used by the remainder of the API. A configuration can be pre-loaded for later use or immediately downloaded to the device. Using this feature, all configurations for an application can be pre-cached from disk to enhance performance. Methods also allow for downloaded configurations to be read-back and verified, taking into account device features such as wild-carding that allow multiple parts of the device to be configured with the same data, in a single access cycle.

Configuration objects are stored within managed list structures. Names are associated with each configuration to simplify retrieval. A configuration management class stores the list of configuration objects in the application and is used to reduce the amount of data transfer to the target device. If a request for a configuration that is currently active on the device is made, the management class suppresses the data transfer. If this feature is not suitable it can be disabled. Suppressing the configurations can only safely be done when it is known that configurations do not overlap, e.g., in applications where the entire device is being reconfigured on each configuration.

The HIL provides methods to enhance the transfer of blocks of data between software and hardware. Data objects are instantiated and associated with a location on the array. A data object can be either a disk file or a memory block. These are treated identically, exploiting the polymorphism of C++. Blocks of data can be passed between software and the reconfigurable hardware by calling methods in the data objects. The application software does not have to maintain the data structures or track the currently active location.

Support is provided within the HIL to setup and manage event-driven dynamic reconfiguration of the target reconfigurable subsystem. An event is defined by providing a location to inspect on the array and a trigger value. The event is triggered when the value on the array is equivalent to the assigned value. Each event has a vector table of configurations associated with it. When the event is triggered the first configuration in the list is downloaded to the array. The next time the event occurs, the next configuration in the table is used, and so on. The vector tables can be optionally set to loop back to their beginning when exhausted, or simply suspend when the end of the table is reached.

Managed lists of events are stored within the HIL. Event handling within the current system is non-optimal as the trigger values are polled from the array. A list is updated when called by the application software and all events within it are checked. Events are processed in the order in which they occur in the list, allowing priorities to be attached to reconfigurations on a first come, first served basis. More complex scheduling and prioritisation can be developed using multiple lists. The limitations introduced by polling do not represent a significant overhead in the interactive debugging tools, but an interrupt scheme is obviously more desirable for application development. Support for interrupt driven events would require explicit support in the reconfigurable hardware. The polled method places no onus on the designer to use special components, as the content of any arbitrary register is accessible by default.

The software API has been used in the development of several reconfigurable applications. Image processing and filtering applications have been produced, as well as examples of pattern matchers using data folding [10] principles. The experience of developing these applications prompted the creation of an interactive tool to accelerate the debugging and prototyping of applications.

5. Interactive Design Tool

An interactive design tool has been developed, building upon and extending the features of the software API. The tool's GUI provides the user with extensive control over all of the device functionality. The techniques used within this design tool are drawn from a combination of hardware emulation and software debugging methods. The user interface for the tool is shown in **Fig 3**.

To aid hardware debugging, the outputs of all cells in the array are observable. These values represent the combinatorial or sequential output, depending on the device configuration. Any arbitrary register can be set from software, with the proviso that the underlying logic has to be configured to accept data over the configuration bus. It is a feature of the XC6200 that any register can be configured to be accessible in this manner, without requiring routing to I/O pads.

Several flexible clocking methods are supported, allowing an arbitrary number of clock pulses to be sent to the array. Access to marked registers on the array can be configured to generate a notification pulse in the control logic, which can be routed into the application logic and used as a clock. This novel feature of XC6200 FPGAs is exploited to provide clock stepping during the transmission of data to the array. With slight modification, any synchronous design can be converted to allow single step control over the clock input.

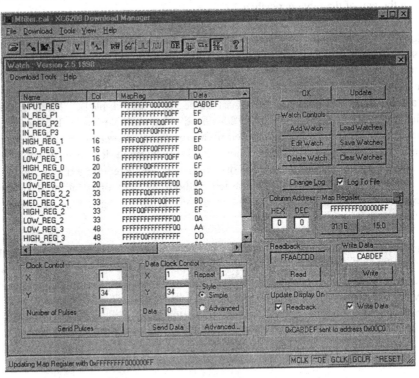

Fig 3. Debugging Interface

Inspection points or watches can be set on areas of the array. The values of these watches are updated on each clock transition. Breakpoint values can be associated with watches, which are analogous to the events described in the previous section. Using breakpoints, the system clock can be advanced until an event of interest occurs, then operation is suspended, allowing the designer to inspect the state of the target sub-system. At this point, new configurations can be loaded into the array, or logical values changed.

To aid in the prototyping of configuration algorithms, watches also support reconfiguration vectoring, as discussed previously. The order in which watches are entered in the debug tool affects the order in which they are updated, allowing the events to be prioritised. The interactive nature of the tool allows the rapid investigation of a variety of what-if scenarios for the control algorithms. When the algorithm is finalised, it can be quickly converted to a programmatic form, as the interface and methods are consistent between the API and the debugging tool. Application algorithms can also be prototyped in much the same manner, either by single stepping through the operation, or by transferring blocks of data until breakpoints are encountered. Full logging is provided of the selected watches, both at clock step points and during reconfiguration intervals.

6. Conclusions

The development environment has provided a flexible platform for research into reconfigurable systems. Many of the more novel features in this work are currently only supported by the XC6200 family of devices but it is anticipated that similar features will appear in next-generation FPGAs and that the techniques discussed can be migrated onto these devices.

The environment has proven a success for two main reasons. The more advanced features have allowed for rapid prototyping of complex systems. In particular, the integration of the application software with the underlying hardware has proven a simple task when using the API. The second main success has been the use of the IDT to simplify the introduction of relatively inexperienced users into the field of reconfigurable logic.

Closer integration of processor and FPGA would alleviate many of the speed penalties currently incurred by communicating over the relatively slow PCI bus [8]. The co-design environment has the potential to be of particular relevance for prototyping designs for some of the recently announced systems-level FPGA / microprocessor hybrid devices [6], [11]. As a result, complete software control and management of reconfiguration may prove a feasible solution for an increasing number of reconfigurable designs.

References

[1]   Hadley, J. D., & Hutchings, B. L.: Design Methodologies for Partially Reconfigured Systems, In Proceedings of IEEE Workshop on FPGA's for Custom Computing Machines, pp. 99-107, Apr 95

[2]   Eggers, H., Lysaght., P., Dick, H., McGregor, G.: Fast Reconfigurable Crossbar

Switching in FPGAs In R. W. Hartenstein, M. Glesner (Eds.) Field-Programmable Logic - Smart Applications, New Paradigms and Compilers, Springer-Verlag, Germany, 1996, pp. 297-306

[3]   Lysaght, P., Stockwood, J.: A Simulation Tool for Dynamically Reconfigurable Field Programmable Gate Arrays In IEEE Transactions on Very Large Scale Integration (VLSI) Systems, Vol. 4, No. 3, pp. 381-390, Sept. 96

[4]   MacKinlay, P.I., Cheung, P.Y.K., Luk, W., Sandiford, R.L.: Riley-2: A Flexible Platform For Co-design And Dynamic Reconfigurable Computing Research In Field Programmable Logic and Applications, Proceedings of FPL'97, pp. 91-100, W. Luk & P. Cheung Eds., Springer-Verlag, 1997

[5]   Kwiat, K., Debany, W.: Reconfigurable Logic Modelling, In Integrated System Design, December 1996 (www.isdmag.com)

[6]   Faura, J., Moreno, J. M., Madrenas, J., Insenser, J. M.: VHDL Modeling of Fast Dynamic Reconfiguration on Novel Multicontext RAM-based Field Programmable Devices In VHDL User's Forum in Europe 1997

[7]   Robinson, D., Lysaght, P., McGregor, G.: New CAD Tools and Framework for Detailed Timing Simulation of Dynamically Reconfigurable Logic, ibid.

[8]   Robinson, D., Lysaght, P., McGregor, G., Dick, H.: Performance Evaluation of a Full Speed PCI Initiator and Target Subsystem using FPGAs In Field Programmable Logic and Applications, Proceedings of FPL'97, pp. 41-50, W. Luk & P. Cheung Eds., Springer-Verlag, 1997

[9]   Lysaght, P.: Toward an Expert System for Apriori Estimation of Reconfiguration Latency in Dynamically Reconfigurable Logic In Field Programmable Logic and Applications, Proceedings of FPL'97, pp. 183-192, W. Luk & P. Cheung Eds., Springer-Verlag, 1997

[10]   Foulk, P. W.: Data Folding in SRAM Configurable FPGAs In IEEE Workshop on FPGAs for Custom Computing Machines, pp. 163-171, Napa, CA, Apr. 1993

[11]   Motorola: MPACF250 - MPA's CORE+ Reconfigurable System : Product Brief, Ref. MPACF250PB/D, Motorola, Inc., 1998

Mapping Loops onto Reconfigurable Architectures *

Kiran Bondalapati and Viktor K. Prasanna

Department of Electrical Engineering Systems, EEB-200C
University of Southern California
Los Angeles, CA 90089-2562, USA
{kiran, prasanna}@usc.edu
http://maarc.usc.edu

Abstract. Reconfigurable circuits and systems have evolved from application specific accelerators to a general purpose computing paradigm. But the algorithmic techniques and software tools are also heavily based on the hardware paradigm from which they have evolved. Loop statements in traditional programs consist of regular, repetitive computations which are the most likely candidates for performance enhancement using configurable hardware. This paper develops a formal methodology for mapping loops onto reconfigurable architectures. We develop a parameterized abstract model of reconfigurable architectures which is general enough to capture a wide range of configurable systems. Our abstract model is used to define and solve the problem of mapping loop statements onto reconfigurable architectures. We show a polynomial time algorithm to compute the optimal sequence of configurations for one important variant of the problem. We illustrate our approach by showing the mapping of an example loop statement.

1 Introduction

Configurable systems are evolving from systems designed to accelerate a specific application to systems which can achieve high performance for general purpose computing. Various reconfigurable architectures are being explored by several research groups to develop a general purpose configurable system. Reconfigurable architectures vary from systems which have FPGAs and glue logic attached to a host computer to systems which include configurable logic on the same die as a microprocessor.

Application development onto such configurable hardware still necessitates expertise in low level hardware details. The developer has to be aware of the intricacies of the specific reconfigurable architecture to achieve high performance. Automatic mapping tools have also evolved from high level synthesis tools. Most tools try to generate hardware configurations from user provided descriptions of circuits in various input formats such as VHDL, OCCAM, variants of C, among others.

---

* This work was supported by the DARPA Adaptive Computing Systems Program under contract DABT63-96-C-0049 monitored by Fort Hauchuca.

Automatic compilation of applications involves not only configuration generation, but also configuration management. CoDe-X [8] is one environment which aims to provide an end-to-end operating system for applications using the Xputer paradigm. General techniques are being developed to exploit the characteristics of devices such as partial and dynamic reconfiguration by using the concepts of Dynamic Circuit Switching [11], Virtual Pipelines [10] etc. But there is no framework which abstracts all the characteristics of configurable hardware and there is no unified methodology for mapping applications to configurable hardware.

In this paper we address some of the issues in the development of techniques for automatic compilation of applications. We develop algorithmic techniques for mapping applications in a platform independent fashion. First, we develop an abstract model of reconfigurable architectures. This parameterized abstract model is general enough to capture a wide range of configurable systems. These include board level systems which have FPGAs as configurable computing logic to systems on a chip which have configurable logic arrays on the same die as the microprocessor.

Configurable logic is very effective in speeding up regular, repetitive computations. Loop constructs in general purpose programs are one such class of computations. We address the problem of mapping a loop construct onto configurable architectures. We define problems based on the model which address the issue of minimizing reconfiguration overheads by scheduling the configurations. A polynomial time solution for generating the optimal configuration sequence for one important variant of the mapping problem is presented.

Our mapping techniques can be utilized to analyze application tasks and develop the choice of configurations and the schedule of reconfigurations. Given the parameters of an architecture and the applications tasks the techniques can be used statically at compile time to determine the optimal mapping. The techniques can also be utilized for runtime mapping by making static compile time analysis. This analysis can be used at runtime to make a decision based on the parameters which are only known at runtime.

Section 2 describes our Hybrid System Architecture Model(HySAM) in detail. Several loop mapping problems are defined and the optimal solution for one important variant is presented in Section 3. We show an example mapping in Section 4 and discuss future work and conclusions in Section 5.

1.1 Related Work

The question of mapping structured computation onto reconfigurable architectures has been addressed by several researchers. We very briefly describe some related work and how our research is different from their work. The previous work which addresses the related issues is Pipeline Generation for Loops [17], CoDe-X Framework [8], Dynamic Circuit Simulation [11], Virtual Pipelines [10], TMFPGA [14]. Though most of the projects address similar issues, the framework of developing an abstract model for solving general mapping problems is not fully addressed by any specific work.

2 Model

We present a parameterized model of a configurable computing system, which consists of configurable logic attached to a traditional microprocessor. This model can be utilized for analyzing application tasks, as regards to their suitability for execution on configurable logic and also for developing the actual mapping and scheduling of these tasks onto the configurable system.

We first describe our model of configurable architectures and then discuss the components of the model and how they abstract the actual features of configurable architectures.

2.1 Hybrid System Architecture Model(HySAM)

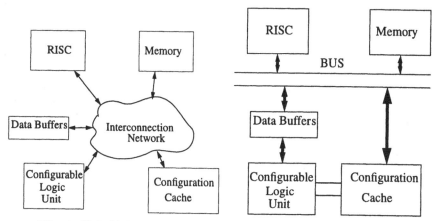

Fig. 1. Hybrid System Architecture and an example architecture

The *Hybrid System Architecture* is a general architecture consisting of a traditional RISC microprocessor with additional Configurable Logic Unit(CLU). Figure 1 shows the architecture of the HySAM model and an example of an actual architecture. The architecture consists of a traditional RISC microprocessor, standard memory, configurable logic, configuration memory and data buffers communicating through an interconnection network.

We outline the parameters of the Hybrid System Architecture Model(HySAM) below.

F : Set of functions $F_1 \ldots F_n$ which can be performed on configurable logic.
C : Set of possible configurations $C_1 \ldots C_m$ of the Configurable Logic Unit.
t_{ij} : Execution time of function F_i in configuration C_j.
R_{ij} : Reconfiguration cost in changing configuration from C_i to C_j.
N_c : The number of configuration contexts which can be stored in the configuration cache.
k, K : The reconfiguration time spent in configuring from the cache and external memory respectively.

W, D : The Width and Depth of the configurable logic which describe the amount of configurable logic available.

w : The granularity of the configurable logic which is the width of an individual functional unit.

S : The schedule of configurations which execute the input tasks.

E : Execution time of a sequence of tasks, which is the sum of execution time of tasks in the various configurations and the reconfiguration time.

The parameterized HySAM which is outlined above can model a wide range of systems from board level architectures to systems on a chip. Such systems include SPLASH [3], DEC PeRLE [16], Oxford HARP [9], Berkeley Garp [7], NSC NAPA1000 [15] among others. The values for each of the parameters establish the architecture and also dictate the class of applications which can be effectively mapped onto the architecture. For example, a system on a chip would have smaller size configurable logic(lower W and D) than an board level architecture but would have potentially faster reconfiguration times(lower k and K).

The model does not encompass the memory access component of the computation in terms of the memory access delays and communication bandwidth supported. Currently, it is only assumed that the interconnection network has enough bandwidth to support all the required data and configuration access. For a detailed description of the model and its parameters see [2].

3 Loop Synthesis

It is a well known rule of thumb that 90% of the execution time of a program is spent in 10% of the code. This code usually consists of repeated executions of the same set of instructions. The typical constructs used for specifying iterative computations in various programming languages are DO, FOR and WHILE, among others. These are generally classified as LOOP constructs.

Computations which operate on a large set of data using the same set of operations are most likely to benefit from configurable computing. Hence, loop structures will be the most likely candidates for performance improvement using configurable logic. Configurations which execute each task can be generated for the operations in a loop. Since each operation is executed on a dedicated hardware configuration, the execution time for the task is expected to lower than that in software. Each of the operations in the loop statement might be a simple operation such as an addition of two integers or can be a more complex operation such as a square root of a floating point number. The problems and solutions that we present are independent of the complexity of the operation.

3.1 Linear Loop Synthesis

The problem of mapping operations(tasks) of a loop to a configurable system involves not only generating the configurations for each of the operations, but also reducing the overheads incurred. The sequence of tasks to be executed have to be mapped onto a sequence of configurations that are used to execute these tasks. The objective is to reduce the total execution time.

Scheduling a general sequence of tasks with a set of dependencies to minimize the total execution time is known to be an NP-complete problem. We consider the problem of generating this sequence of configurations for loop constructs which have a sequence of statements to be executed in linear order. There is a linear data or control dependency between the tasks. Most loop constructs, including those which are mapped onto high performance pipelined configurations, fall into such a class.

The total execution time includes the time taken to execute the tasks in the chosen configurations and the time spent in reconfiguring the logic between successive configurations. We have to not only choose configurations which execute the given tasks fast, but also have to reduce the reconfiguration time. It is possible to choose one of many possible configurations for each task execution. Also, the reconfiguration time depends on the choice of configurations that we make. Since reconfiguration times are significant compared to the task execution times, our goal is to minimize this overhead.

Problem : Given a sequence of tasks of a loop, T_1 through T_p to be executed in linear order($T_1\ T_2\ \ldots\ T_p$), where $T_i \in F$, for N number of iterations, find an optimal sequence of configurations S ($=C_1\ C_2\ \ldots\ C_q$), where $S_i \in C$ ($=\{C_1,C_2,\ldots,C_m\}$) which minimizes the execution time cost E. E is defined as

$$E = \sum_{i=1}^{q}(t_{S_i} + \Delta_{ii+1})$$

where t_{S_i} is execution time in configuration S_i and Δ_{ii+1} is the reconfiguration cost which is given by R_{ii+1}.

3.2 Optimal Solution for Loop Synthesis

The input consists of a sequence of statements $T_1 \ldots T_p$, where each $T_i \in F$ and the number of iterations N. We can compute the execution times t_{ij} for executing each of the tasks T_i in configuration C_j. The reconfiguration costs R_{ij} can be pre-computed since the configurations are known beforehand. In addition there is a loop setup cost which is the cost for loading the initial configuration, memory access costs for accessing the required data and the costs for the system to initiate computation by the Configurable Logic Unit. Though, the memory access costs are not modeled in this work, it is possible to statically determine the loop setup cost.

A simple greedy approach of choosing the best configuration for each task will not work since the reconfiguration costs for later tasks are affected by the choice of configuration for the current task. We have to search the whole solution space by considering all possible configurations in which each task can be executed. Once an optimal solution for executing up to task T_i is computed the cost for executing up to task T_{i+1} can be incrementally computed.

Lemma 1. *Given a sequence of tasks $T_1'T_2'\ldots T_r'$, an optimal sequence of configurations for executing these tasks once can be computed in $O(rm^2)$ time.*

Proof: Using the execution cost definition we define the optimal cost of executing up to task T_i' ending in a configuration C_j as E_{ij}. We initialize the E values as $E_{0j} = 0$, $\forall j : 1 \le j \le m$.

Now for each of the possible configurations in which we can execute T_{i+1}' we have to compute an optimal sequence of configurations ending in that configuration. We compute this by the recursive equation:

$$E_{i+1j} = t_{i+1j} + min_k(E_{ik} + R_{kj}) \quad \forall j : 1 \le j \le m$$

We have examined all possible ways to execute the task T_{i+1}' once we have finished executing T_i'. If each of the values E_{ik} is optimal then the value E_{i+1j} is optimal. Hence we can compute an optimal sequence of configurations by computing the E_{ij} values. The minimum cost for the complete task sequence $(T_1'T_2'\ldots T_r')$ is given by $min_j[E_{rj}]$. The corresponding optimal configuration sequence can be computed by using the E matrix.

We can use dynamic programming to compute the E_{ij} values. Computation of each value takes $O(m)$ time as there are m configurations. Since there are $O(rm)$ values to be computed, the total time complexity is $O(rm^2)$. ⊙

Lemma 1 provides a solution for an optimal sequence of configurations to compute one iteration of the loop statement. But repeating this sequence of configurations is not guaranteed to give an optimal execution for N iterations. Figure 2 shows the configuration space for two tasks T_1 and T_2 and four possible configurations C_1, C_2, C_3, C_4. T_1 can be executed in C_1 or C_3 and task T_2 can be executed in C_2 or C_4. The edges are labeled with the reconfiguration costs and cost for the edges and configurations not shown is very high. We can see that an optimal sequence of execution for more than two iterations will be the sequence $C_1\ C_4\ C_3\ C_2$ repeated $N/2$ times. The repeated sequence of $C_1\ C_4$ which is an optimal solution for one iteration does not give an optimal solution for N iterations.

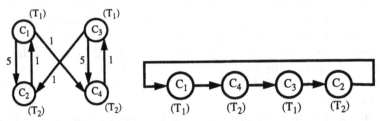

Fig. 2. Example reconfiguration cost graph and optimal configuration sequence

One simple solution is to fully unroll the loop and compute an optimal sequence of configurations for all the tasks. But the complexity of algorithm will be $O(Npm^2)$, where N is the number of iterations. Typically the value of N would be very high(which is desirable since higher value of N gives higher speedup compared to software execution). We assume $N \gg m$ and $N \gg p$. We show that an optimal configuration sequence can be computed in $O(pm^3)$ time.

Lemma 2. *An optimal configuration sequence can be computed by unrolling the loop only m times.*

Proof: Let us denote the optimal sequence of configurations for the fully unrolled loop by $C_1 C_2 \ldots C_x$. Since there are p tasks and N iterations $x = N * p$. Configuration C_1 executes T_1, C_2 executes T_2 and so on. Now after one iteration execution, configuration C_{p+1} executes task T_1 again. Therefore, task T_1 is executed in each of configurations C_1, C_{p+1}, C_{2*p+1}, ..., C_{x-p+1}. Since there are at most m configurations for each task, if the number of configurations in C_1, C_{p+1}, C_{2*p+1}, ..., C_{x-p+1} is more than m then some configuration will repeat. Therefore, $\exists y$ s.t. $C_{y*p+1} = C_1$.

Let the next occurrence of configuration C_1 for task T_1 after C_{y*p+1} be C_{z*p+1}. The subsequence C_1 C_2 $C_3 \ldots C_{y*p+1}$ should be identical to C_{y*p+1} $C_{y*p+2} \ldots C_{z*p+1}$. Otherwise, we can replace the subsequence with higher per iteration cost by the subsequence with lower per iteration cost yielding a better solution. But this contradicts our initial assumption that the configuration sequence is optimal. Hence the two subsequences should be identical. This does not violate the correctness of execution since both subsequences are executing a fixed number of iterations of the same sequence of input tasks. Applying the same argument to the complete sequence $C_1 C_2 \ldots C_x$, it can be proved that all subsequences should be identical.

The longest possible length of such a subsequence is $m * p$ (p possible tasks each with m possible configurations). This subsequence of $m * p$ configurations is repeated to give the optimal configuration sequence for $N * p$ tasks. Hence, we need to unroll the loop only m times. ⊙

Theorem 3. *The optimal sequence of configurations for N iterations of a loop statement with p tasks, when each task can be executed in one of m possible configurations, can be computed in $O(pm^3)$ time.*

Proof: From Lemma 2 we know that we need to unroll the loop only m times to compute the required sequence of configurations. The solution for the unrolled sequence of $m * p$ tasks can be computed in $O(pm^3)$ by using Lemma 1. This sequence can then be repeated to give the required sequence of configurations for all the iterations. Hence, the total complexity is $O(pm^3)$. ⊙

The complexity of the algorithm is $O(pm^3)$ which is better than fully unrolling ($O(Npm^2)$) by a factor of $O(N/m)$. This solution can also be used when the number of iterations N is not known at compile time and is determined at runtime. The decision to use this sequence of configurations to execute the loop can be taken at runtime from the statically known loop setup and single iteration execution costs and the runtime determined N.

4 Illustrative Example

The techniques that we have developed in this paper can be evaluated by using our model. The evaluation would take as input the model parameter values and the applications tasks and can solve the mapping problem and output the sequence of configurations. We are currently building such a tool and show results obtained by manual evaluation in this section.

The Discrete Fourier Transform(DFT) is a very important component of many signal processing systems. Typical implementations use the Fast Fourier Transform(FFT) to compute the DFT in $O(N \log N)$ time. The basic computation unit is the butterfly unit which has 2 inputs and 2 outputs. It involves one complex multiplication, one complex addition and one complex subtraction.

There have been several implementations of FFT in FPGAs [12, 13]. The computation can be optimized in various ways to suit the technology and achieve high performance. We describe here an analysis of the implementation to highlight the key features of our mapping technique and model. The aim is to highlight the technique of mapping a sequence of operations onto a sequence of configurations. This technique can be utilized to map onto any configurable architecture. We use the timing and area information from Garp [7] architecture as representative values.

For the given architecture we first determine the model parameters. We calculated the model parameters from published values and have tabulated them in Table 1 below. The set of functions(F) and the configurations(C) are outlined in Table 1 below. The values of n and m are 4 and 5 respectively. The Configuration Time column gives the reconfiguration values R. We assume the reconfiguration values are same for same target configuration irrespective of the initial configuration. The Execution Time column gives the t_{ij} values for our model.

Function	Operation	Configuration	Configuration Time	Execution Time
F_1	Multiplication(Fast)	C_1	14.4 μs	37.5 ns
	Multiplication(Slow)	C_2	6.4 μs	52.5 ns
F_2	Addition	C_3	1.6 μs	7.5 ns
F_3	Subtraction	C_4	1.6 μs	7.5 ns
F_4	Shift	C_5	3.2 μs	7.5 ns

Table 1. Representative Model Parameters for Garp Reconfigurable Architecture

The input sequence of tasks to be executed is is the FFT butterfly operation. The butterfly operation consists of one complex multiply, one complex addition and one complex subtraction. First, the loop statements were decomposed into functions which can be executed on the CLU, given the list of functions in Table 1. One complex multiplication consists of four multiplications, one addition and one subtraction. Each complex addition and subtraction consist of two additions and subtractions respectively. The statements in the loop were mapped to multiplications, additions and subtractions which resulted in the task sequence T_m, T_m, T_m, T_m, T_a, T_s, T_a, T_a, T_s, T_s. Here, T_m is the multiplication task mapped to function F_1, T_a is the addition task mapped to function F_2 and T_s is the subtraction task mapped to function F_3.

The optimal sequence of configurations for this task sequence, using our algorithm, was C_1, C_3, C_4, C_3, C_4 repeated for all the iterations. The most important aspect of the solution is that the multiplier configuration in the solution is actually the slower configuration. The reconfiguration overhead is lower for C_2 and hence the higher execution cost is amortized over all the iterations of the loop. The total execution time is given by $N * 13.055$ μs where N is the number of iterations.

5 Conclusions

Mapping of applications in an architecture independent fashion can provide a framework for automatic compilation of applications. Loop structures with regular repetitive computations can be speeded-up by using configurable hardware. In this paper, we have developed techniques to map loops from application programs onto configurable hardware. We have developed a general Hybrid System Architecture Model(HySAM). HySAM is a parameterized abstract model which captures a wide range of configurable systems. The model also facilitates the formulation of mapping problems and we defined some important problems in mapping of traditional loop structures onto configurable hardware. We demonstrated a polynomial time solution for one important variant of the problem. We also showed an example mapping of the FFT loop using our techniques. The model can be extended to solve other general mapping problems. The application development phase itself can be enhanced by using the model to develop solutions using algorithm synthesis rather than logic synthesis.

The work reported here is part of the USC MAARC project. This project is developing algorithmic techniques for realizing scalable and portable applications using configurable computing devices and architectures. We are developing computational models and algorithmic techniques based on these models to exploit dynamic reconfiguration. In addition, partitioning and mapping issues in compiling onto reconfigurable hardware are also addressed. Some related results can be found in [1], [4], [5], [6].

References

1. K. Bondalapati and V.K. Prasanna. Reconfigurable Meshes: Theory and Practice. In *Reconfigurable Architectures Workshop, RAW'97*, Apr 1997.
2. Kiran Bondalapati and Viktor K. Prasanna. The Hybrid System Architecture Model (HySAM) of Reconfigurable Architectures. Technical report, Department of Electrical Engineering-Systems, University of Southern California, 1998.

3. D. A. Buell, J. M. Arnold, and W. J. Kleinfelder. *Splash 2: FPGAs in a Custom Computing Machine*. IEEE Computer Society Press, 1996.

4. S. Choi and V.K. Prasanna. Configurable Hardware for Symbolic Search Operations. In *International Conference on Parallel and Distributed Systems*, Dec 1997.

5. Y. Chung and V.K. Prasanna. Parallel Object Recognition on an FPGA-based Configurable Computing Platform. In *International Workshop on Computer Architectures for Machine Perception*, Oct 1997.

6. A. Dandalis and V.K. Prasanna. Fast Parallel Implementation of DFT using Configurable Devices. In *7th International Workshop on Field-Programmable Logic and Applications*, Sept 1997.

7. J. Hauser and J. Wawrzynek. Garp: A MIPS Processor with a Reconfigurable Coprocessor. In *IEEE Symposium on FPGAs for Custom Computing Machines*, pages 12–21, April 1997.

8. R. Kress, R.W. Hartenstein, and U. Nageldinger. An Operating System for Custom Computing Machines based on the Xputer Paradigm. In *7th International Workshop on Field-Programmable Logic and Applications*, pages 304–313, Sept 1997.

9. A. Lawrence, A. Kay, W. Luk, T. Nomura, and I. Page. Using reconfigurable hardware to speed up product development and performance. In *5th International Workshop on Field-Programmable Logic and Applications*, 1995.

10. W. Luk, N. Shirazi, S.R. Guo, and P.Y.K. Cheung. Pipeline Morphing and Virtual Pipelines. In *7th International Workshop on Field-Programmable Logic and Applications*, Sept 1997.

11. P. Lysaght and J. Stockwood. A Simulation Tool for Dynamically Reconfigurable FPGAs. *IEEE Transactions on VLSI Systems*, Sept 1996.

12. Xilinx DSP Application Notes. The Fastest FFT in the West, http://www.xilinx.com/apps/displt.htm.

13. R.J. Petersen and B. Hutchings. An Assessment of the Suitability of FPGA-Based Systems for use in Digital Signal Processing. In *5th International Workshop on Field-Programmable Logic and Applications*, 1995.

14. S. Trimberger, D. Carberry, A. Johnson, and J. Wong. A Time-Multiplexed FPGA. In *IEEE Symposium on FPGAs for Custom Computing Machines*, pages 22–28, April 1997.

15. NSC NAPA 1000 URL. http://www.national.com/appinfo/milaero/napa1000/.

16. J. Vuillemin, P. Bertin, D. Roncin, M. Shand, H. Touati, and P. Boucard. Programmable Active Memories: Reconfigurable Systems Come of Age. *IEEE Transactions on VLSI Systems*, 4(1):56–69, March 1996.

17. M. Weinhardt. Compilation and Pipeline Synthesis for Reconfigurable Architectures. In *Reconfigurable Architectures Workshop RAW'97*. ITpress Verlag, Apr 1997.

Speed Optimization of the ALR Circuit Using an FPGA with Embedded RAM: A Design Experience

Sameh Asaad and Kevin Warren

IBM T. J. Watson Research Center
Yorktown Heights, NY 10598, USA
{asaad, kwwarren}@us.ibm.com

Abstract. The Active Line Repair (ALR) circuit is a specialized circuit to overcome some of the manufacturing imperfections in high resolution flat panel displays. In this paper, the design of the ALR circuit is presented. Speed bottlenecks for an FPGA-based implementation are identified and optimization alternatives are discussed. Results stress the importance of data representation and the match to the underlying hardware resources such as embedded RAM blocks. The optimized circuit runs at 63 MHz system clock, achieving a 40 % speedup over the original design.

1 Introduction

High resolution flat panel displays have recently surpassed the performance of CRT monitors in terms of pixel resolution. They are gradually displacing CRTs in the high-end desktop market because of the sharper image and the space and power savings they offer.

Although manufacturing yields of such displays have steadily improved over the past several years, higher resolution panels still suffer some manufacturing defects such as shorted lines and open lines, deeming the affected panels unusable [1]. The Active Line Repair (ALR) is a technique to overcome some of the panel imperfections using a hybrid of laser bonding on the panel and an electronic redriving circuitry.

The main focus of this paper is to report on the design experience gained while implementing and optimizing the speed of the ALR circuit using a Field Programmable Gate Array (FPGA).

2 The Active Line Repair Circuit

As shown in Fig. 1, high resolution flat panel displays are sometimes alternately driven from both ends, top and bottom (dual-bank drive). This is mainly due to fanout space limitation on the glass and driver clock frequency limitation. By driving the panel from top and bottom, two datapaths are formed, each driving half of the number of column lines thus halving the required bus frequency. Gate lines are each driven from both sides (double-sided drive) to reduce the voltage gradient on the line. A noteworthy side-effect of this double-sided drive is the inherent repair capability for open gate lines.

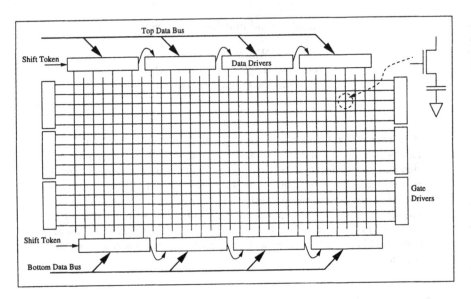

Fig. 1. Arrangement of a dual-bank, double-sided driven flat panel array

The panel is refreshed at video rates in scan line order from left to right and from top to bottom. Due to manufacturing defects, some of the array lines can be shorted together or can have discontinuities. According to [1], shorted lines can in general be repaired using laser cutting on the glass. While open gate lines don't pose a major problem since they are double-driven from both sides, open column lines cause all the pixels in the broken segment of the affected column to float. This problem can be minimized by redriving the broken segment from the opposite side of the panel with the same data. One way for achieving this is by rerouting the same driver output through extra wiring to the other side and patching the segment. This approach proved to be impractical [1] due to loading effects on the data driver and difficulty in data path routing. A better approach is to bond the floating segment to an unused driver output on the opposite side and to regenerate the same data stream on that particular driver output as illustrated in Fig. 2. This approach requires the insertion of a specialized circuit in the datapath before the panel to buffer and redistribute the required data to the opposite side of the panel, hence the ALR circuit.

The requirements for the ALR circuit can be summarized as follows: Data inputs to the circuit are the top and bottom pixel data busses. Each bus is 24 bits wide composed of 8 bits for each of the red, green and blue color components or subpixels. Data is latched at the rising edge of the pixel clock and is assumed to

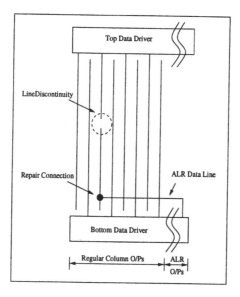

Fig. 2. The concept of the Active Line Repair Circuit

be valid only when the blank signal is not active. The circuit outputs the same data as the input after inserting a number of ALR pixels in the data stream at the end of each driver pair's[1] worth of data. The blank signal is shifted and stretched in time to match the output data stream. To make the behavior of the circuit transparent to the rest of the data pipeline, HSYNC and VSYNC signals are fed to the circuit and delayed by a proper number of clocks before output.

The circuit should include a programming port through which the ALR repair sites can be configured. Information pertinent to a specific panel layout such as the number of driver pairs, number of clock cycles (or shifts) per driver and the number of ALR shifts after each driver are also configurable through the programming port. The ALR repair sites tell the ALR circuit which subpixels to store and when to output them in the data stream after the current driver on the opposite bus. The circuit should run at a pixel clock of 55MHz or higher.

The next section will describe the design and implementation of the ALR circuit, showing where speed bottlenecks were encountered and the approaches taken to solve them.

3 Design and Implementation Issues

In general, a digital circuit can be divided into two parts: A datapath that implements the data flow in the circuit and a control circuit that acts on the datapath to control the flow of data. In case of the ALR circuit, this is no exception as illustrated in Fig. 3.

---

[1] A driver pair consists of a top data driver and a bottom data driver that are vertically aligned.

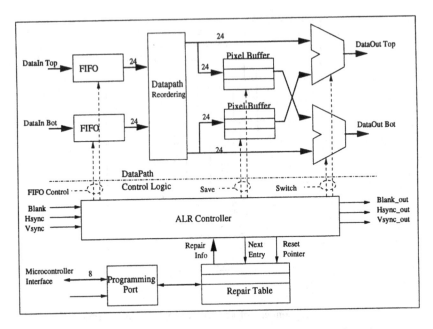

Fig. 3. ALR circuit design showing datapath and control sections

3.1 Datapath Design

Data enters the ALR circuit as two separate pixel streams, each 24 bits wide as shown in Fig. 3. FIFOs are required to buffer the data to maintain a constant data rate at the input while the ALR inserts the extra repair data after each data driver pair. Thus the minimum FIFO depth is equal to the number of extra ALR clocks for a complete horizontal line. Datapath reordering "reshuffles" the data for top and bottom to match the panel layout and therefore is panel-specific. During regular data time, the data comes out of this reordering step and feeds through the output multiplexers to the ALR outputs. At the same time, the controller captures the data intended to be redriven at the ALR time and saves them in the Pixel Buffers. At the end of each data driver time, the output multiplexers switch to the pixel buffers and output a predetermined number of ALR pixels. The crossing of the ALR data path before the output multiplexers is vital to the operation of the circuit since the repair data has to be redriven from the opposite side relative to the original data.

3.2 Control Logic Design

The ALR controller manages the FIFO read port, the operation of the Pixel Buffer, the output multiplexers and the reading from the Repair Table. The sequence of operation is repeated every horizontal line in the display and there is no knowledge of vertical sync except for delaying the VSYNC signal to match the pipeline delay of the circuit. The falling edge of the BLANK signal controls the writing of the FIFOs and signals the beginning of a new line to the controller. The controller issues a reset to the Repair Table pointer which holds the repair information originally organized as shown in Fig. 4. This is followed by reading the first repair site to determine the location of the first repair pixel in the incoming data stream. Now that the controller is ready with the first repair information, it starts the data flow by reading the pixels from the FIFOs. For every pixel clock it decrements the delta field of the current repair site until delta equals zero. This causes the controller to issue a hit signal qualified by which subpixel to save, which buffer (top or bottom) to use and the position of the saved subpixel in the ALR data time. Multiple subpixels can be saved and reordered during the same clock tick. The controller then loads the next repair site from the repair table which primes the delta counter with a new value for delta that corresponds to the number of remaining clock cycles until the next hit. This operation is repeated for the remaining repair sites. In parallel, the ALR controller sequences the operation of the output multiplexers by selecting the direct data paths for a number of clocks equivalent to the data driver width and then switching to the pixel buffer outputs for the ALR time. This process repeats for all data driver pairs, after which the end of line is reached.

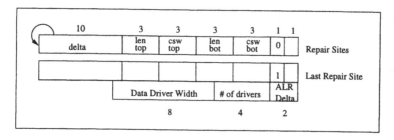

Fig. 4. Original data representation in the Repair Table

3.3 Implementation

The Altera Flex 10K [2] family of programmable logic devices was chosen to implement the ALR circuit mainly because of its embedded RAM blocks that were very suitable to hold the Repair Table information. Other deciding factors supporting this choice include its predictable timing, the availability of the design tools and our familiarity with its architecture. The circuit was designed in VHDL and synthesized using FPGA-Express logic synthesis tool from Synopsys [3]. The output from FPGA-Express was fed to Altera's MaxPlus II [4] design tools for place and route. Post layout information was then extracted and inspected for circuit speed, longest path delays, size and FPGA utilization. Several iterations were needed to optimize these parameters, most importantly the circuit speed which was required to run at 55 MHz.

After a number of initial runs experimenting with different synthesis settings, the timing reports showed a maximum speed of about 45 MHz. The remaining 10 MHz needed extra optimization effort and ultimately led us to redesign portions of the control logic as described in section 3.5.

Examining the longest paths in the synthesized circuit revealed that the problem resided in the control section and not the datapath design. In particular, the dependency between loading and decoding a new repair site from the Repair Table and the timing of the pixel flow limited the maximum allowable speed of the pixel clock. The worst case condition occurred when two or more adjacent lines needed repair. This translated to one or more consecutive repair sites with their delta field set to zero. In this case, the controller had to be able to detect the expiration of the current delta counter and also look ahead at the value of the next delta field from the Repair Table to see if it was also zero. For a 10-bit wide delta field as shown in Fig. 4, this scenario involved a RAM-block read operation, two 10-bit compare circuits and logic to set or reset the hit signal all in a single pixel clock cycle. This was difficult to achieve with the current technology.

3.4 Speed Optimization Techniques

A digital circuit can in general be regarded as a mixture of combinational circuits and sequential circuits (flip flops). Feedback paths must include at least one sequential element to avoid race conditions. In simple synchronous designs, all sequential elements are clocked using the same clock signal. The maximum speed of this clock is determined by the propagation delay of the longest combinational path between any two flip flops.

Given the above view, the job of optimizing circuit speed reduces to minimizing the propagation delay of the longest path. This can be achieved in a number of ways, such as: 1) Combinational circuit minimization techniques which try to find a logic representation with a minimal number of stages while preserving functionality [5]. 2) Retiming the circuit by repositioning the registers to make the combinational paths delay distribution more even [5]. 3) Adding new registers to break a long combinational path into smaller, hence faster, sections. These alternatives are in increasing order of difficulty and designer involvement. While most of the current synthesis tools use the first method quite extensively, they tend to leave the registers untouched and therefore do not take advantage of the other alternatives. Clearly the last method changes the overall pipeline latency of the design and thus needs some form of designer insight and intervention.

The main approach taken to optimize the speed was by manually adding register banks to break down long paths and adjusting the rest of the data pipeline accordingly (method 3 above). This was feasible in this design, since the overall latency of pixel data was not a major concern. In addition, the following tricks and observations were noteworthy:

The use of Registered I/Os: To ensure a "clean" interface with the rest of the system, it was a good practice to latch the primary inputs as soon as they entered the FPGA by instructing the place and route tool to utilize the registers in the I/O blocks. Obviously, the input latches had to be incorporated in the VHDL design. The same technique applied to the primary outputs, effectively hiding the delays from the I/O block to the core of the design and providing almost a whole clock cycle of setup time for the next stage in the system.

Synchronous Embedded RAM: It was found that keeping the interface between the embedded RAM and the rest of the circuit a synchronous interface consistently resulted in faster designs. This was accomplished by latching the address bus as well as the data input and output busses at the boundary to the RAM array.

Device Utilization Factor: An interesting observation was the relationship between the utilization factor of the FPGA and the overall speed. A low utilization, i.e. an FPGA with most of its resources unused, resulted in a relatively lower speed. This seemed at first counterintuitive since one would think that the place & route tool should have many options for optimization. The current explanation for this behavior is by assuming that the timing is affected by long interconnects as illustrated in Fig. 5. For a low utilization, the inputs and/or outputs have to travel longer distances to reach the I/O blocks with no retiming registers in between. On the other extreme, a design that consumed near the full capacity of the target FPGA was likely to become less optimized because of place and route problems.

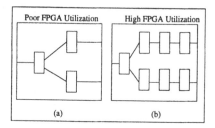

Fig. 5. Sparsely populated FPGAs (a) have longer interconnects between timing stages compared to highly populated FPGAs (b)

3.5   Redesign of Control Logic

To reach the target of 55 MHz a redesign of the control section was needed. The approach used was to "presynthesize" the control signals ahead of time using the repair site information. This can be done off-line either manually or by software. The result was a look-up table for the actions that needed to be performed by the controller on a cycle-by-cycle basis. So, in the new ALR design, the Repair Table of Fig. 4 is replaced by a new data representation as shown in Fig. 6. The control logic then became trivial: Every new line, the controller reset the LUT pointer and read in one entry every pixel clock. The contents of that entry were

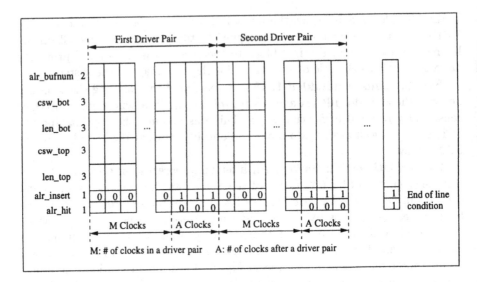

Fig. 6. New data representation in the Repair Table

simply the control signals that acted on the datapath such as the hit signal and the output multiplexer selector (alrinsert).

Although this approach seemed, at first, as a brute-force method, it achieved better results without loss of circuit generality. The number of data driver pairs and the number of ALR clocks after every driver pair were still programmable by means of adjusting the number of entries with alrinsert = 0 and the entries with alrinsert = 1, respectively. Consecutive repairs, that previously formed a bottleneck in the circuit, are now a regular case and easily expressed by consecutive entries with alrhit = 1. Due to the granularity of the Altera Flex 10K embedded RAM blocks, the penalty of having a relatively long LUT was not big. The original design used 24-bit wide repair sites and thus needed a minimum of three 8-bit wide RAM segments[2]. The modified design used 16-bit wide entries and could fit in four 8-bit wide RAM segments. A performance comparison between the original and the LUT-based designs is shown in Table 1.

4 Discussion

A number of lessons were learned from this design experience. These include:

H/W versus S/W tradeoff: Information that does not change during run-time, such as the configuration data of the display repairs, could be pre synthesized by software at compile time and fed to the H/W in a look-up table form. The extra software processing step is well offset by the simplification and hence the speedup of the resulting hardware circuit.

---

[2] The embedded array Blocks can be configured in one of the following sizes: 256x8, 512x4, 1024x2 or 2048x1

Table 1. Performance comparison between original and LUT-based ALR designs for a 208 pin Altera 10K20RC208-3 target device

	Max Clock Frequency (MHz)	FPGA Utilization (%)	
		Logic Cells	Memory Cells
Original Design	45	66	50
Modified Design	63	54	66

The Data representation problem: An important observation from this design experience is that the best way to represent the data set at hand depends on the optimization goal and the available resources. A compact representation will consume less memory to store and less bandwidth to transmit but will require more real-time processing power to extract and use the required information. On the other hand, a simpler data representation, like the "pre-synthesized" waveform LUT chosen in this implementation, takes up more storage space but needs very little processing circuitry. In our case, the latter approach proved to be more appropriate since it 1) matched the underlying hardware and 2) satisfied the speed goal.

Specialized cores versus uncommitted logic: In principle, most of the digital circuits can be realized using programmable logic devices. However, to achieve the desired efficiency, e.g. speed, area, power, a custom core is most likely an advantage. For FPGA device manufacturers, the tradeoff is between making a general purpose FPGA that will fit all purposes rather poorly versus making FPGAs with a mixture of special purpose cores and programmable logic that will fit a smaller number of applications (because of the specialized cores) but more efficiently. Among the challenges are what cores to embed, if any, and what is the right ratio between real estate spent on cores versus that for general purpose programmable logic. A current trend is to embed the most used functions in current state-of-the-art designs such as : Single and dual ported memory, bus interfaces such as PCI, microcontroller cores (e.g. 8051 family) and high speed off-chip communication cores (LVDS, GLM).

Synthesis tools: Synthesis tools impact the performance of the generated hardware in much the same way as code compilers do for the software. Therefore, in order for the hardware designer to use them efficiently, he should possess a thorough understanding of the inner workings of the synthesis tool and how to steer the synthesis process in order to achieve the desired results. Two issues stand out in particular: 1) How to write behavioral code in a hardware description language such as VHDL that translates to the desired netlist after synthesis (forward path) and, 2) given a synthesized netlist, how to relate a particular component or network to the source code construct responsible for generating it (backward path). The former issue requires understanding of how the tool infers library elements, such as registers and latches from the source code and the latter is a manifestation of the credit assignment problem that requires some analysis by the designer. The use of visualization tools that plot portions of the synthesized circuit annotated with identifiers from the source code can be of great help to the designer.

5 Conclusions

We believe that there are three major issues that the designer has to deal with when optimizing an FPGA-based synthesized design: *First*, a good understanding of the functional requirements of the circuit is needed along with a thorough analysis of how to best represent the data structures involved. *Second* , the underlying FPGA architecture has to be considered in order to be able to efficiently exploit its resources. This is because, unlike ASICs or custom circuits, the architecture of the FPGA is fixed a-priori and therefore the permitted programmability, connectivity, and routability is constrained by that architecture. *Last*, an intimate understanding of the synthesis tools is required. This is a byproduct of using a hardware description language to express the design rather than hand crafting the circuit by hand. A higher level of the design representation results in more portability across hardware platforms and reusability, but it becomes more insulated from the underlying hardware and harder to bridge that gap in order to optimize it. The current approach to resolve this issue is to incorporate architecture-specific optimizations in the synthesis tools thus keeping the source description at a high level while exploiting architecture-specific resources for a given target FPGA during synthesis. For more demanding applications, customizable FPGA cores may be the answer to this conflict. In this case, the whole design process is essentially raised one more level of abstraction with the basic building blocks shifted from gates and flip-flops to cores such as processor cores, bus interfaces and communication cores.

References

1. S.L.Wright et al.: Active Line Repair for Thin-Film-Transistor Liquid-Crystal Displays Research Report RC 20779, IBM Research Division, March 24, 1997.
2. Altera Corporation: 1997 Data Book Altera Corp. 101 Innovation Drive, San Jose, CA 95134
   http://www.altera.com/html/literature/literature.html
3. Synopsys Corporation: FPGA Express User's Guide v1.2 , September 1996 Synopsys, 700 East Middlefield Road, Mountain View, CA 94043
   http://www.synopsys.com
4. Altera Corporation: Max Plus II Development Software Users Manual v8.1, Altera Corp. 101 Innovation Drive, San Jose, CA 95134
   http://www.altera.com/html/literature/literature.html
5. Ellen M. Sentovich et al: SIS: A system for Sequential Circuit Synthesis Electronics Research Laboratory Memorandum No. UCB/ERL M92/41, University of California at Berkeley, CA 94720, May 1992
   ftp://ic.eecs.berkeley.edu/pub/Sis/SIS_paper.ps.Z

High-Level Synthesis for Dynamically Reconfigurable Hardware/Software Systems

Rainer Kress, Andreas Pyttel

Siemens AG, Corporate Technology, ZT ME 5
D-81730 Munich, Germany
{Rainer.Kress|Andreas.Pyttel}@mchp.siemens.de

Abstract. Dynamically reconfigurable hardware/software systems allow a flexible adaptation of their hardware part to the necessities of the application by reprogramming it at run-time. Traditional design methodologies do not support dynamic hardware structures efficiently. Thus the design space is not exploited thoroughly and the application might not be adequately implemented. In this paper we concentrate on the high-level synthesis of the hardware part including temporal partitioning to effectively use the dynamic nature of the target FPGA circuits.

1 Introduction

Dynamically reconfigurable FPGAs (DR-FPGAs) are mostly SRAM-based circuits, which can be reprogrammed during system operation. They may support partial reconfiguration or they can be reprogrammed in a full reconfiguration only. The partial reconfiguration can be *non-disruptive* or *disruptive*. According to Vasilko [7] non-disruptive means, that the portions of the system which are not being reconfigured, remain fully operational during the entire reconfiguration cycle. If the reconfiguration affects other portions of the system, it is called disruptive, e.g., there is a need for a clock hold.

The main reason to use DR-FPGAs is to save hardware resources by configuring only the part of hardware which is necessary at the actual time in an application or algorithm. This computation requires a *temporal partitioning* of the specification. This temporal partitioning divides the specification into a number of specification segments whose sequence of configuration and computation is controlled by a reconfiguration controller. The results of a specification segment, which have to be used in a future specification segment have to be saved in a memory. The reconfiguration time necessary to change from one specification segment to another reduces operation speed. By not interrupting the device during operation for loading a partially new configuration set, DR-FPGAs gain a potential speed advantage over traditional FPGAs.

Combining programmable hardware, such as field-programmable gate arrays (FPGAs) with microcontrollers or even digital signal processors (DSPs) results in an entirely adaptive system. However, a flexible, configurable hardware solution is also associated with costs in terms of area and timing performance when compared to pure ASIC designs. As a trade-off, hybrid embedded systems with partially fixed and partially adaptable hardware combined with a processor are employed.

Reconfiguration time and the time necessary to save and restore data is considered to be an overhead. To minimize this overhead scheduling techniques from the high-level synthesis scene can be used. Previous work in this area was done by Lysaght et. al., who reviewed a CAD tool for simulating reconfigurable systems in [4]. This tool may also be used for the synthesis of reconfiguration controllers. Vasilko et. al. [8] focus on the scheduling problem in architectural synthesis. They use a heuristic algorithm based on list scheduling. Kaul et. al. [2] use a 0-1 non-linear programming (NLP) formulation for the combined problem of temporal partitioning, scheduling, function unit allocation and function unit binding. The NLP formulation is linearized into a 0-1 linear programming (LP) model. Further, they select the best candidate variables upon which to branch-and-bound while solving the LP model. Their objective is to minimize the communication, that is, the total amount of data transferred among the partition segments, so that the reconfiguration costs are minimized.

Our approach differs in two main aspects: First, the target system is a hardware/software system comprising a Xilinx® XC6200 DR-FPGA [9] and a microprocessor, and second, we interleave the reconfiguration time and run-time in the programmable hardware part.

This paper is organized as follows: The next section gives a brief overview on our co-synthesis environment. Section 3 presents the high-level synthesis approach. The target architecture is shown in section 4. Our experiences are described in section 5.

2   Co-synthesis Environment

Our framework supports a software-oriented strategy for co-synthesis as we start from a Java specification and identify parts which are to be implemented in hardware (figure 1). Co-verification of the system prototype is integrated by co-emulation of the hardware/software architecture [1]. Verifying the correct interaction between software and hardware is a key problem in the design of a combined system. Thus, we use a design flow which includes a complete synthesis flow and accommodates fast prototyping. After identifying a suitable partitioning of the system, the appropriate hardware/software interface is generated by an interface generator. The software part is instrumented and bytecode is generated for execution on the Java virtual machine. The

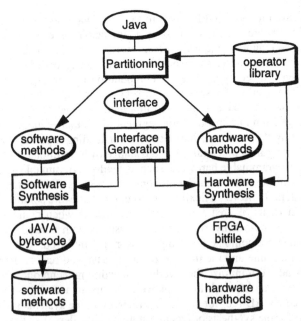

Fig. 1. Co-synthesis environment

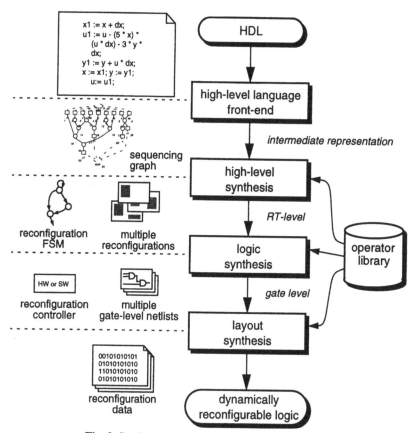

Fig. 2. Synthesis for dynamically reconfigurable systems

hardware part is synthesized and mapped to the reconfigurable FPGA target platform. The interface is partially realized in software and partially in hardware.

- *Hardware code generation*
  Code generation for the hardware part consists of three major steps: *High-level synthesis* (HLS) of the selected Java methods, which are to be implemented in hardware. *Register-transfer-level synthesis* of the VHDL description which has been generated by the HLS tool in the previous step, and logic optimization of the resulting netlist. *Layout synthesis* and generation of the configuration data for the target FPGA hardware platform. All steps are supported by an operator library containing the available operations.
- *Software code generation*
  Code generation for the software part is done using conventional compilation methods for JAVA source code.

In this paper, we focus on the high-level synthesis for the hardware part of the co-synthesis environment. Details on the hardware/software partitioning can be found in [1]. Designing dynamically configurable systems is different from conventional synthesis techniques. The higher flexibility complicates the overall synthesis process (figure 2). Like in traditional high-level synthesis (HLS), starting from a high-level description (a hardware description language or programming language) an intermediate representation is computed. This representation may be a control/dataflow graph (CDFG), or like in our case, a sequencing graph. Via high-level synthesis, the register transfer level (RTL) is reached. This step comprises the main difference to traditional HLS. Multiple configurations and a corresponding reconfiguration finite state machine (FSM) have to be generated instead of a single RTL description. Configuration overhead should be minimized while exploiting full and partial dynamic reconfiguration. We follow an approach from Vasilko [7], who tries to solve these problems following a strong library-based approach using a library of generic operators (figure 2). The operator library is also responsible for providing realistic estimates on technology dependent metrics like module area, latency, reconfiguration time, etc. at various stages during the synthesis process. Logic synthesis produces a gate level description of each configuration and the FSM. Finally, the layout synthesis generates the reconfiguration data.

3 High-Level Synthesis

High-level synthesis, also known as architectural synthesis, is the translation process from a behavioral description into a register-transfer level (RTL) structural description [3]. The core of this transformation comprises the following steps: *Scheduling* assigns operations of the behavioral description into control steps. *Allocation* chooses functional units and storage elements from a component or module library. There may be several alternatives available, regarding speed and area. *Binding* assigns operations to functional units, variables to storage elements, and data transfers to wires. These three tasks are usually closely interdependent.

Scheduling determines a precise start time of each operation. The start time must satisfy the dependencies between the operations which limit the amount of parallelization. Since scheduling determines the concurrency of the resulting implementation, it affects its performance.

Constraints can be classified into two major groups: *interface constraints* and *implementation constraints*. Interface constraints are additional specifications to ensure that the circuits can be embedded in a given environment. The following resources are constraint in the XC6200 FPGA architecture: the area and the interface for writing into the FPGA, as well as for reconfiguration.

- The area is limited. If more area is necessary, a part of a temporal segment has to be replaced by another temporal segment.
- The interface, in our case the processor interface, is constraint to a single operation at a time. Either a read or write operation can be performed or the interface can be used for reconfiguration.

```
do
    x1 := x + dx;
    u1 := u - (5 * x) * (u * dx) - 3 * y * dx;
    y1 := y + u * dx;
    x := x1; y := y1; u := u1;
while (x1 < a);
```

Fig. 3. Example

To determine a deadlock-free schedule and an optimized sequence of the temporal segments, the following strategy is used: First, an ASAP and an ALAP schedule is performed to compute the mobility. A list based resource constraint scheduling algorithm determines the time steps for the operations and the reconfiguration tasks. Then a reconfiguration controller is synthesized.

A sequencing graph $G_S(V, E)$ is a hierarchy of directed graphs, e.g. control/data-flow graphs. Usually, the control is modelled through the hierarchy and the data-flow is modelled by graphs. The graph has two major properties: first it is *acyclic*, and second it is *polar*. Acyclic dependencies suffice since iteration is modelled through the hierarchy. The graph is polar, i.e. there are vertices, called source and sink, that represent the first and the last task. Normally, they are modelled as no-operations (NOP), because there is no unique task to be executed first or last in the circuit specification.

In our case, the scheduling is restricted to basic blocks. So, no hierarchy of the sequencing graph has to be considered. Therefore, in the following, a non-hierarchical sequencing graph is considered. The vertex set $V = \{v_i; i = 0, 1, 2, ..., n\}$ of a sequencing graph $G_S(V, E)$ is in one-to-one correspondence to a set of operations, and the edge set $E = \{(v_i, v_j); i, j = 0, 1, 2, ..., n\}$ represents dependencies. The source vertex v_0 and the sink vertex v_n with $n = n_{ops} + 1$ are both no-operations. The set of execution delays is $D = \{d_i; i = 0, 1, 2, ..., n\}$ with $d_0 = d_n = 0$. It is assumed that the delays are data independent and known. Further it is assumed, that the delays are integers and multiples of the time step. With $T = \{t_i; i = 0, 1, 2, ..., n\}$, the start time of each operation is denoted. The vector notation $\mathbf{t}$ is used to represent all start times in a compact form. The *latency* λ of a schedule is the number of time steps required for the complete schedule, i.e. $\lambda = t_n - t_0$.

In the ASAP schedule, the starting time for each operation depends only on the dependencies between the operations. The vector $\mathbf{t}^S$ represents the starting times of operations. The latency bound $\overline{\lambda}$ is chosen to be the length of the schedule computed by the ASAP schedule, i.e. $\overline{\lambda} = t_n^S - t_0^S$. The ALAP scheduling provides the maximum values of the start times $\mathbf{t}^L$. The difference between the starting times computed by the ASAP and ALAP scheduling is called *mobility* $_i = t_i^L - t_i^S$; $i = 0, 1, ..., n$. Both schedules are outlined in figure 4 for the example in figure 3. For simplicity it is assumed that a multiplication of two variables consumes three time steps, the other operations a single time step.

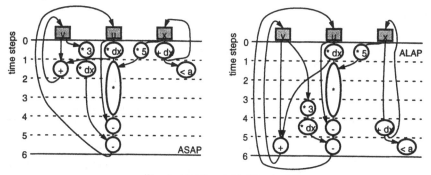

Fig. 4. ASAP and ALAP schedule

The mobility of the operations can be computed to (table 1):

operator	+	* 3	* dx	* dx	*	-	-	* 5	+ dx	< a
mobility	4	3	3	0	0	0	0	0	4	4

Table 1. Mobility of the individual operations

The list scheduling algorithm belongs to the heuristic methods. The minimum-latency resource-constraint scheduling can be solved by adjusting the priority function. A *priority function* or *priority list* is used to choose the operations to schedule in the current

```
LIST (GS(V, E), a) {
    l = 1;
    do {
        for (resource type k = 1; k <= nres; k++) {
            determine candidate operations Ul,k;
            determine unfinished operations Tl,k;
            select Sk ∈ Ul,k vertices, such that |Sk| + |Tl,k| <= ak;
            schedule the Sk operations at step l
                by setting ti = l ∀ i : vi ∈ Sk;
        }
        l = l +1;
    } while (vn is not scheduled);
    return (t);
}
```

Fig. 5. List scheduling algorithm for minimizing latency under resource constraints

time step from all candidate operations. In the following the list scheduling algorithm is sketched for the problem of minimizing latency under resource constraints.

The resource constraints are represented by the vector **a**, e.g. $a_1 = 2$ multipliers and $a_2 = 3$ ALUs. The operations whose predecessors have already been scheduled early enough, so that the corresponding operations are completed at time step l are called candidate operations $U_{l,k}$, with

$$U_{l,k} = \{v_i \in V : type(v_i) = k \text{ and } t_j + d_j <= l \; \forall \; j : (v_j, v_i) \in E\} \quad (1)$$

for any resource type $k = 1, 2, ..., n_{res}$. The unfinished operations $T_{l,k}$ are those operations of resource type k that start at an earlier cycle and whose execution is not finished up to time step l:

$$T_{l,k} = \{v_i \in V : type(v_i) = k \text{ and } t_i + d_i > l\} \quad (2)$$

Figure 5 shows the list scheduling algorithm. The operation S_k is the selected operation for the schedule in the current time step.

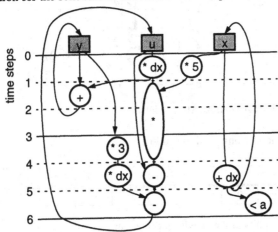

Fig. 6. Ressource constraint schedule

The selection of S_k is based on the priority list. In this case the operator is selected so that the resource constraints ($|S_k| + |T_{l,k}| <= a_k$) are satisfied. Other types of constraints can be achieved easily by changing the priority list. Having resource and relative timing constraints, the priority list reflects the proximity of an unscheduled operation to a deadline related to a maximum timing constraint. The algorithm satisfies the required constraint by construction, that means the list scheduling algorithm may not find an optimal solution. If the algorithm is applied to minimize resource usage under latency constraints, the mobility is used to rank the operations in the priority list. The resource constraint vector **a** has to be updated every time additional resources are required.

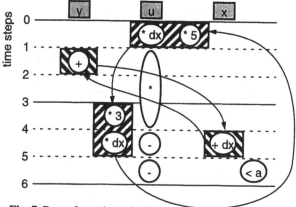

Fig. 7. Reconfiguration schedule

The result of the list schedule is given in figure 6. The used algorithm considers the resources: 1 multiplier, 1 subtractor, 2 constant multipliers, 1 adder, and 1 comparator. It is assumed that constant multipliers can be reconfigured to other constants during run-time. Time slots for reconfiguration are considered with second priority.

The selection of the temporal segments is library based. Due to the relative long reconfiguration times of today's FPGAs, the successing temporal partitions should not differ very much. If possible only routing switches should be changed. In our example the operator + is converted to $+dx$ and $*5$ to $*3$ (figure 7). The routing is updated accordingly. One time step is reserved for reconfiguration. The implementation of the individual temporal segments is done manually, since the place and route tools of the used FPGA require manual interaction. But these steps are done off-line during compile-time. The reconfiguration controller of our example is shown in figure 8.

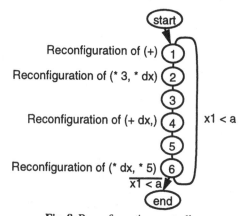

Fig. 8. Reconfiguration controller

4 Target Architecture

Our target platform is based on a board that is equipped with a Xilinx® XC6216 DR-FPGA and is called dynamically reconfigurable FPGA (DRF) board [6]. The microprocessor interface of the XC6216, which implements a 16 bit address bus, a 32 bit data bus, and control signals, is linked with a 96 pin connector. Through this connector the board can be coupled with a standard microprocessor system. Further components of the board are an 8 bit hex display, 6 LEDs and two 16-bit connectors that are linked with configurable IO pins. Besides the microprocessor interface the board has a serial interface that allows to configure the XC6216 by a serial PROM.

The DRF board is part of our HW/SW prototyping platform. Further components are the Weaver FPGA board, the memory board and the Weaver controller board. The Weaver FPGA board can be equipped with one to four statically reconfigurable Xilinx® XC4025(E) FPGAs or the pin compatible XC4028EX.

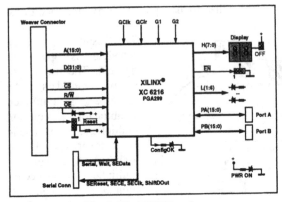

Fig. 9. The DRF Board

The Weaver memory board currently has 512 kByte SRAM and can be upgraded to 4 MByte. The Weaver controller serves as an interface between the Weaver boards and the host computer. Through the controller, configuration data can be sent to each FPGA on the connected boards. Besides the configuration of the FPGAs, the serial data interface can be used to send user data to the FPGAs or to receive them.

The DRF board requires a microprocessor interface to access the processor bus of the XC6216 FPGA. This interface is implemented by a processor design on the XC4025 FPGA of the Weaver board. This processor, which is called DRF processor establishes the data transfer between the host and the DRF board. Further it contains the reconfiguration controller. To accelerate the configuration of the XC6216 the

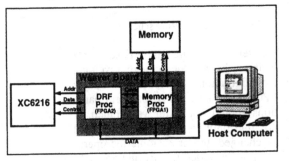

Fig. 10. DRF- and Memory Processor

configuration files are not directly loaded from the host to the XC6216, but stored on the memory board. The administration of these files on the memory is done by the memory processor, implemented on a second FPGA. Both processors interpret commands from the host and establish the communication between the host and the XC6216 FPGA.

5 Experiences

In the following, the investigation of different designs of operators for dynamic reconfiguration is described. We used the Xilinx® XC6216 DR-FPGA and the corresponding design software XACT6000™ (vers. 0.4.1b and 1.1b). Table 2 shows the number of functional units (FUs) as well as the number of addresses to be configured for 8 bit and 32 bit bus width of the processor interface (IF).

Design 1 is an 8 by 8 bit multiplier macro named *x8vscuc*, which is taken from the Viewlogic® library *x8vsuc*. It uses 256 FUs and requires 2215 (8 bit IF bus width) or 810 (32 bit) addresses to be written for the configuration. Assuming that one operand has a bit width of 4 bit only, 124 FUs are required, and 620 addresses (32 bit) have to be written (design 2).

If one operand is a constant, further FUs and write accesses for the configuration can be saved. Two different versions of constant multipliers are shown in table 2: one is array-based, the other adder-based. The array-based multiplier is derived from design 2. Instead of using a register for the 4 bit number, the constant is directly applied by setting the corresponding wire to logic zero or to logic one. The optimization is done by the XACT6000™ software. Unfortunately, the number of addresses necessary for the configuration does increase (design 3 and 4) and the number of FUs decreases only slightly. The constants in design 3 and design 4 are *13* or *3*, respectively.

Smaller designs can be achieved by using an adder-based multiplier which is already optimized during schematic entry. Design 5 to 7 show three constant multipliers requiring 73 FUs and 498 to 544 addresses to be written during configuration. They are smaller than the array-based multiplier. As a further comparison, an adder (design 8) and a combined adder/subtractor (design 9) are shown in table 2.

No. of design	design	# of FUs	bus width	
			8 bit	32 bit
1	Multiplier (8bit * 8bit)	256	2215	810
2	Multiplier (8bit * 4bit)	124	1508	620
3	Mult. array-based with Const. 13	120	1539	666
4	Mult. array-based with Const. 3	120	1500	637
5	Mult. adder-based with Const. 3	73	1305	505
6	Mult. adder-based with Const. 5	73	1305	498
7	Mult. adder-based with Const. 132	73	1374	544
8	Adder	52	1022	402
9	Adder / Subtractor	65	1274	517

Table 2. Number of necessary write accesses for configuration of the designs

For the dynamic reconfiguration of operators, the interesting data are the necessary write accesses to switch from one design to another. Table 3 shows six cases to reconfigure constant multipliers and the number of necessary configuration memory accesses. In the case of the adder-based multiplier, 37 or 44 addresses have to be changed for small constants. If the design switches from a small constant to a large one, 194 or 155 addresses have to be written. The array-based multiplier requires 147 or 176 addresses to be changed (32 bit bus width). If the multiplier of design 2 is used, only the register's content has to be reconfigured, which can be done within a single clock cycle. Compared to multipliers of two operands, constant multipliers save area, depending on the constant value and the implementation. The reconfiguration of the constant multiplier, however, requires more write accesses to the configuration memory.

switch from design ... to design ...	design	bus width	
		8 bit	32 bit
5 → 6	Mult. adder-based with Const.	65	44
6 → 5	Mult. adder-based with Const.	65	37
5 → 7	Mult. adder-based with Const.	326	194
7 → 5	Mult. adder-based with Const.	257	155
4 → 3	Mult. array-based with Const.	239	176
3 → 4	Mult. array-based with Const.	200	147

Table 3. Number of necessary write accesses to switch between different designs

In the Xilinx® application note XAPP 082 [10], a 8 by 8 bit multiplier is described which uses 68 FUs (including 8 bit input and 12 bit output registers). This multiplier is look-up table (LUT)-based and highly optimized by hand. Using such a multiplier, a constant can be reconfigured by 24 write accesses of 32 bit.

In our examples we do not use such hand-optimized designs. In industry, automatic tools are required in order to convince designers to use dynamically reconfigurable techniques. The work described in this paper was an attempt to save hardware area by reconfiguring operators during execution of the circuit. Hand-optimization of the design or extensive use of the XC6216 wildcard register in regular designs can improve the situation described above.

6 Conclusions

High-level synthesis for dynamically reconfigurable hardware/software systems is a powerful method to interleave run-time and configuration-time. But the DR-FPGAs are currently too small to be used efficiently. The run-time of the operators in one temporal segment must be at least in the same order as the reconfiguration-time in between. This can be achieved by

- larger DR-FPGAs,
- faster reconfiguration times,
- having only small changes in succeeding temporal segments, like
  - replacing a constant in a register, or
  - converting an adder to a subtractor using an adder/subtractor operator, or
  - pipeline morphing as done by W. Luk et. al. [5].

The presented high-level synthesis approach targets a hardware/software system. The realized prototype consists of two Xilinx® XC4025 which contain the processor and the interface to the memory and the host, and one XC6216 as DR-FPGA.

References

1. J. Fleischmann, K. Buchenrieder, R. Kress: A Hardware/Software Prototyping Environment for Dynamically Reconfigurable Embedded Systems; 6th International Workshop on Hardware/Software Codesign, CODES/CASHE'98, Seattle, March 1998
2. M. Kaul, R. Vemuri: Optimal Temporal Partitioning for Reconfigurable Architectures; Design Automation and Test Conference in Europe, DATE'98, Paris, Feb. 1998
3. Y.-L. Lin: Recent Developments in High-Level Synthesis; ACM Transactions on Design Automation of Electronic Systems, vol. 2, no. 1, Jan. 1997
4. P. Lysaght, G. McGregor, J. Stockwood: Configuration Controller Synthesis for Dynamically Reconfigurable Systems; IEE Colloquium on Hardware/Software Cosynthesis for Reconfigurable Systems, HP Labs., Bristol, UK, Feb. 1998
5. W. Luk, N. Shirazi, S. R. Guo, P. Y. K. Cheung: Pipeline Morphing and Virtual Pipelines; in W. Luk, P. Y. K. Cheung, M. Glesner (Eds.):Field-Programmable Logic and Applications, Lecture Notes in Computer Science 1304, Sept. 1997
6. A. Pyttel, A. Sedlmeier: HW/SW Systems Prototyping with Statically and Dynamically Reconfigurable FPGAs; Design Automation and Test Conference in Europe, DATE'98, Designer Track, Paris, Feb. 1998
7. M. Vasilko: Bournemouth University Page of Dynamically Reconfigurable Hardware; http://dec.bournemouth.ac.uk/dec_ind/decind6/drhw_page.html, Jan. 1997
8. M. Vasilko, D. Ait-Boudaoud: Architectural Synthesis Techniques for Dynamically Reconfigurable Logic; in Hartenstein, Glesner (Eds.): Field-Programmable Logic: Smart Applications, New Paradigms and Compilers, Lecture Notes in Computer Science 1142, Sept. 1996
9. N. N.: The Programmable Logic Data Book; Xilinx Inc., San José, CA, 1996
10. N. N.: A Fast Constant Coefficient Multiplier for the XC6200; Xilinx Application Note XAPP 082, Xilinx Inc., San José, CA, Aug. 1997

Dynamic Specialisation of XC6200 FPGAs by Partial Evaluation

Nicholas McKay[1] and Satnam Singh[2]

[1] Dept. Computing Science, The University of Glasgow, G12 8QQ, U.K.
nicholas@dcs.gla.ac.uk

[2] Xilinx Inc., San Jose, California 95124-3450, U.S.A.
Satnam.Singh@xilinx.com

Abstract. This paper describes preliminary results of dynamically specialising Xilinx XC6200 FPGA circuits using partial evaluation. This method provides a systematic way to manage the complexity of dynamic reconfiguration in the special case where a general circuit is specialised with respect to a slowly changing input. We describe how we address the verification and run-time support issues which are raised when one modifies a circuit at run-time.

1   Introduction

Imagine a decryption circuit with two inputs: the key and the data to be decrypted. The key (a few bytes) changes infrequently with respect to the data (megabytes). Imagine at run-time being able to specialise this circuit every time the key changes, *calculating* a circuit that decrypts only for the given key. This would incur a run-time cost i.e. the calculation needed to specialise the circuit description and then reconfigure the device. But in return it computes a circuit with a shorter critical path, allowing data to be decrypted faster. This paper describes a project which is developing technology to achieve exactly this kind of fine grain dynamic circuit specialisation.

Rather than solving the general problem of how to perform dynamic synthesis, we first select a special case of dynamic reconfiguration which is an easier problem to solve. In particular, we are researching how to specialise circuits systematically by taking a general circuit and some data known at run-time and then using this to *transform* the general circuit into a specialised circuit. By trying to solve this simpler problem which has useful structure and properties, we hope to get insight into how to solve more general problems in the area of dynamic reconfiguration.

Instead of devising a totally new methodology for dynamic circuit specialisation, we have borrowed from existing ideas in the areas of off-line constant propagation from HDL compiler technology and from partial evaluation techniques developed for the run-time specialisation of software.

We describe all the stages that make up our dynamic specialisation process, from high level language descriptions down to the level of programming data bits and multiplexor reconfigurations, allowing others to reproduce our experiments.

We also describe how we verify circuits that are modified at run-time, which is an issue that is often overlooked when one is typically struggling just to effect dynamic reconfiguration at all.

2   Dynamic Hardware Synthesis

FPGAs are currently used to rapidly prototype circuits and in niche markets where small production runs are expected. These applications configure the FPGA once on power-up, after which the circuit remains fixed. However, this does not fully exploit the reprogrammable nature of these new devices.

The XC6200 chips being used in our project can have their configuration state mapped onto the address space of the host system, so that reconfiguration under software control is as simple as assigning to variables in a program. This allows the dynamic reprogramming of subsections of the FPGA, even while the remainder of the chip is running. Circuits may be swapped into and out of the FPGA at will and at high speed. An analogy with virtual memory is appealing, and we call this technique *virtual hardware*.

However in addition to swapping in static, pre-compiled circuits, one could imagine synthesising circuits *dynamically*, on a need to use basis, before downloading them to the FPGA at run-time. For example, consider the example from the introduction of a device designed to decrypt a data stream with a given key. For each new session key, a specialised circuit can be dynamically synthesised which decrypts the associated stream with the relevant key. This circuit will be smaller and faster than a general circuit which stores the key in a register.

How we plan to exploit this novel idea is illustrated by the following example. Here is a simple 5 by 6 bit parallel multiplier circuit shown as a stylised XC6200 design:

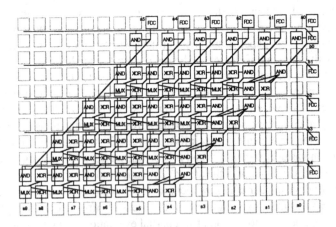

Figure 1 A stylised description of a shift-add multiplier

Assume we know at run-time that input b is going to be 6 for many subsequent iterations. It might therefore pay off to specialise this circuit at that time to:

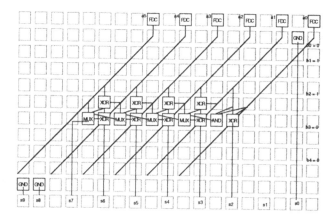

Figure 2 A shift-add multiplier specialised to multiply by 6

The circuit has been reduced to simply one addition operation and several long wires; the b register has disappeared. The critical path is now much shorter than the general parallel multiplier. No attempt has been made to compact cells; the specialised circuit still occupies the same area but it goes much faster.

In an experiment we used a partial evaluator proto-type developed at Glasgow University that can take a general shift-add 8-bit multiplier and specialise by performing run-time constant propagation. The general 8-bit multiplier has a critical path of 123ns. By propagating the constant 20 as the multiplicand through the general circuit and then modifying the programming information for the affected cells, yiels a design with a critical path of 53ns. The extreme case of propagating the multiplicand of 2 yields a circuit with a critical path of 11ns i.e. about ten times faster than the general circuit. It is exactly these kind of optimisations that we hope to achieve in an economical manner at run-time.

In this approach, the important question is when the cost of calculating new configurations are amortised over sufficient time to make the approach worthwhile. Consider a data stream consisting of a specialisation parameter followed by n data items:

In the encryption example mentioned above the specialisation parameter would be the key and the data items the message. Now suppose:

Ts   Time to synthesise hardware
Tp   FPGA programming time
Tc   Cycle time for specialised hardware

Tg   Cycle time of general purpose device
Tk   Time to load specialisation parameter

We are concerned with the ratio:

$$\frac{dynamic}{conventional} = \frac{(T_s + T_p) + nT_c}{T_k + nT_g}$$

One aim of this research will be to identify applications in which n is sufficiently large and Tc/Tg sufficiently small to make our approach worthwhile. For example, a circuit realising the DES ('Data Encryption Standard') [3] algorithm has the very useful property that under specialisation the combinatorial logic associated with the generation of the key schedule and transposition stages can be converted to a sequence of inverters, which them-selves can then be absorbed into a modified S-box. In this case 768 gates will have been replaced by wires and (in a design without pipelining) 16 gates delays removed from the critical path; Tc will be substantially smaller than Tg.

3   Verification

While dynamic synthesis seems appealing, it represents a major verification problem. How do we know if the dynamically generated circuit works as intended?

Even when current synthesis techniques are used, conventional verification relies on simulation—taking hours or days and often requiring human input and checking. Clearly such an approach is impossible in a system that will dynamically generate hardware and then use it for just a few milliseconds before discarding it.

An alternative is to use formal methods to verify the synthesised circuit. Here, again, user-guided methods are obviously inappropriate. Automatic techniques, for example those based on model checkers, can verify small to medium sized circuits; but even these still take far too long to execute for 'in the field' verification of synthesised circuits. In general, it is not feasible to perform a post-design verification of dynamically generated hardware, where 'post-design time' means a tiny gap between synthesis and downloading onto the FPGA.

We choose to verify the synthesis algorithm itself. The above decryption example provides an illustration of how we proceed. First, we use conventional techniques, complemented by formal methods, to convince ourselves that a general circuit which stores the key in a register works as intended. We then use formal techniques to prove that the specialised circuit synthesised from any given key is a legitimate replacement for the general circuit loaded with that key. This is a correctness property of the synthesis algorithm, which we need prove only once for all possible input keys.

Of course algorithm verification is in general very difficult. But we employ a very special kind of algorithm, analogous to the method of partial evaluation in functional programming [4], by which a general design can be specialised in the presence of partly known inputs. So far this has proved to be a relatively tractable formal verification task, although to date we have only considered circuits of modest complexity.

The formally-verified synthesis algorithm will, of course, be only one component in a complete applications system. We do not propose to use formal verification for the other components, but will rely on testing, simulation, and other conventional methods for these. That is, we will employ the *formal* effort only where it is the most appropriate choice for verification—namely, for addressing the correctness of the synthesised circuits, for which conventional simulation and testing is impossible.

In summary, the validation component of our research addresses the crucial issue of correctness with a novel combination of simulation and testing, established techniques in formal hardware specification and verification, and proof of algorithm correctness. In addition to being of intrinsic research interest, this work helps to establish dynamic synthesis as a trustworthy implementation method.

4 Low-Level Partial Evaluation

In the first stage of this project we have been implementing a very simple form of partial evaluation that corresponds to run-time constant propagation. By propagating known values at run-time, we can transform cells implementing logic functions like AND and OR into cells that just route wires, avoiding the delay incurred by going through the interior of the function block.

By turning cells into wires we get worthwhile time saving, but further savings are possible when we can spot that four cells in a 4x4 block are all converted into wires. This allows us to concatenate these 4 single cell wires into one length 4 flyover wire. This kind of optimisation brings the greatest time savings since a single length 4 wire has a very small delay.

5 A Simple Partial Evaluator

This section describes the implementation of a partial evaluator using the Xilinx XC6216 chip on the VCC Hotworks XC6200 board. This is a PCI board which contains an XC6200 FPGA and some static RAM. The RAM can be accessed over the bus or via the XC6216 chip.

Downloading the general design to the board is done via a CAL file. This file contains a series of address data pairs. The 16-bit address points to one of the XC6216 configuration registers. These registers control the function unit logic and the routing multiplexers on the chip.

In order to have access to the routing information we developed a program which partially evaluated the design at the CAL file level.

The C++ program sets up a structure which stores information on a net. This is a connection between two points in the circuit. The net information includes the x and y co-ordinates of the cell's source or destination and the number of inversions that the net is subject to. In the XC6200 architecture many of the routing multiplexors perform an inversion on their output signal. This is important when we come to perform the partial evaluation.

The Cell class is used to store information on the inputs and outputs of each cell on the FPGA together with the logic function that it implements.

Figure 3 shows a schematic of the cell structure. In the Cell class, variables x1, x2 and x3 hold the nets that are routed to the cell's X1, X2 and X3 inputs. Variables y2 and y3 hold information on the inversions applied to the inputs by the multiplexors on the left of the figure.

From knowledge of the x and y inputs the cell function can be deduced. This is also stored in the Cell class.

Lastly, an OutputList is generated for each cell. This is a linked list which contains information on all the locations that the output of the cell is routed to.

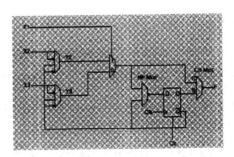

Figure 3 The architecture of an XC6200 FPGA cell

During the partial evaluation stage a list of the cells that have been changed is built up. To re-program the general circuit onto the chip the program also holds a copy of each cells non-partially evaluated function and inputs. When the general circuit is to be re-loaded the program looks through the list of changed cells and re-programs them according to the data held in these variables.

5.1 Class Initialisation

The partial evaluation program sets up a NxN array of Cell objects, where NxN is the number of cells on the chip. To obtain the data to write into the class members the program first connects to the VCC board and initializes the XC6216 chip. It then asks the user for a CAL file to download. The information in the Cell class is built up from the data that is sent to each of the configuration registers on the chip.

5.2 Constant Propagation

Once a picture of the general circuit has been constructed the program can use constant propagation to optimize the circuit.

Firstly, a net is labelled as being constant. The program then examines the data in all the Cell objects that the net is input to. For each net destination the program calls a function which performs the following steps:

- Finds out the value of the constant at the input to the cell. This depends on two things: The constant that the net was set to and the number of inversions that it goes through between it's source and destination.
- Retrieves the function of the cell from the Cell object.

The function then uses the above information to optimize the cell.

For example, if a cell performs an AND function on the inputs a and b and the constant input, a, is 0 then the cell is reconfigured to output a zero. If a is 1 then the cell is reprogrammed to be a buffer. The input to the buffer is provided by the other, non-constant input, b. The code shown below performs the optimisation. `value_a` is the constant input, while `fn` holds a local copy of the cell function variable. `cell[i][j]` is the cell object at co-ordinates (i,j).

```
if (fn == AND2) {
    if (value_a == ZERO) {
        cell[i][j].cell_function = ZERO;
        setFunction(i,j,ZERO, cell[i][j].input_a);
        return ZERO;
    }
    else if (value_a == ONE) {
        cell[i][j].cell_function = BUF;
        setFunction(i, j, BUF, cell[i][j].input_b);
        return BUF;
    }
}
```

The cell is reprogrammed by `setFunction`. This takes as its arguments the co-ordinates of the cell, the new function and, in the case of a buffer, the non-constant input `input_b`. The function reprograms the `x1`, `x2`, `x3`, `y2` and `y3` inputs to the cell's function unit, altering it's operation.

In the case of a buffer the `setFunction` function also tries to bypass the function unit completely. This is possible if the non-constant input arrives at the cell via one of the nearest neighbour routes. These routes (north, south, east and west) can be switched directly to the cell's output. This results in a bigger speed improvement.

If the result of the optimisation is a cell with a constant output the destinations of the cell are optimised. This process continues until no more reductions are possible.

5.3   Program Operation

The user can chose to partially evaluate on the output of a single cell or on the output of a column of cells. When a column of cells is selected the partial evaluation process is repeated for each cell in the column.

After all the constant inputs are partially evaluated the program looks for further optimisations. If, for example, a signal is propagated through four inverters or buffers it may be possible to replace them with a Length 4 line. The program checks through the circuit for such chains and, if the Length 4 line is available, reprograms the chip accordingly.

6   Case Studies

6.1   Parallel Multiplier

Figure 1 gave the layout of a simple parallel multiplier. The multiplier consists of a series of columns, each of which contains an n-bit adder and n AND gates. A N-bit by M-bit multiplier contains M columns each containing an N-bit adder. In the first column each bit of N is ANDed with the LSB of M and the result input into the adder. The other input of the adder is set to zero. The LSB of the adder output is routed to the LSB of the final output. In the next column each bit of N is ANDed with the next bit of M and input to the adder. The other input is given by bits 1 to N of the previous adders result and the final carry. This process is repeated M times.

If we partially evaluate on the M input then when a bit of M is zero the adder and the AND gates in the Mth column disappear. When M is equal to one then the AND gates are reduced to buffers.

A test circuit consisting of a multiplier fed from two input registers has been designed. The output from the multiplier is fed to an output register. All the registers are clocked by two pulses. The first pulse writes the input values to the registers, the second samples the multipliers output.

Table 1 gives the speed-up results for an 8-bit by 8-bit multiplier with the M input partially evaluated to a selection of constant values. The non-p.e. (non partially evaluated) row gives the maximum clock speed for the general multiplier circuit. The p.e. row gives the maximum clock speed after partial evaluation. Figure 4 displays the information in bar graph format.

Table 1. Multiplier Specialisation

	times 1	times 2	times 8	times 85
p.e.	23.5 MHz	23.5 MHz	23 MHz	16 MHz
non-p.e.	14 MHz	16.5 MHz	16 MHz	15 MHz
	times 126	times 128	times 170	times 255
p.e.	13.5 MHz	20 MHz	16 MHz	11 MHz
non-p.e.	11 MHz	14.5 MHz	13.5 MHz	11 MHz

6.2   Finite Impulse Response Filter

A systolic FIR filter is made up of a series of processing elements connected together via latches. Each stage consists of a multiplier and an adder. In this design we have used the parallel multiplier that was described in the previous section.

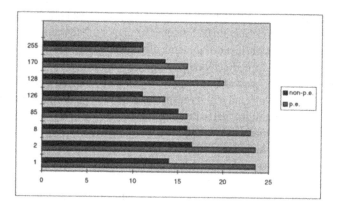

Figure 4 Data from Table 1 in bar graph form

The multiplier takes the input to the stage and multiplies it by a weight. The adder adds the output of the multiplier to the accumulated sum of the previous stages. The nth output of a N-tap filter is given below

$$y_n = w_0 \cdot x_n + w_1 x_{n-1} + w_2 x_{n-2} + \ldots\ldots\ldots + w_N x_{n-N}$$

Where x_n is the nth element of the input data stream and w_n is the nth weight. The systolic architecture has the advantage that the maximum delay path is limited to the delay through one of the processing elements.

A 12-tap 4-bit FIR filter was designed. The circuit takes its input from and writes its output to the on-board SRAM. The partial evaluator optimises each of the multipliers for a specific weight value.

In this case the partial evaluation produced no meaningful speed improvements. This is due to the fact that the slowest elements of the filter are the ripple carry adders that are used to sum the multiplier outputs. Partial evaluation does not have a significant effect on these as their inputs are not known.

7   Summary and Future Work

We have developed a proto-type partial evaluator which actually performs run-time constant propagation with the XC6200 devices. However, the first prototype takes too long to calculate circuit specialisations. Now that we have the technology to actually perform dynamic reconfiguration, we are investigating new algorithms and data structures which speed up partial evaluation.

So far we have achieved only modest speed improvements using localised partial evaluation and performing just one pass over the circuit. However, we are confident of achieving far better speed improvements by concatenating single wires into longer wires e.g. by using length 4 fly-overs. The implementation of a scheme for performing on-line partial evaluation is in itself a significant research result.

307

We are currently formalising and verifying the partial evaluation algorithm. Then we can use traditional verification techniques (formal or otherwise) on the general circuit and be reasonable confident of dynamically synthesising correct circuits.

Another barrier to immediately deploying this work in real systems is that we currently have no accurate way of knowing how fast a specialised circuit executes. To perform traditional timing analysis at run-time would take too long. We are investigating techniques for combining partial timing information quickly at run-time to get a safe estimate for the circuit delay. Once we have refined our run-time specialiser to operate quickly enough, we shall then concentrate further on the timing problem. Another alternative is to produce asynchronous circuits, perhaps realised on a special asynchronous FPGA.

All the circuits in this project have been described in the Lava language, which is a variant of the Ruby [6] algebraic hardware description language. This allows us to control circuit layout in a convenient manner [8]. In the future, we may consider porting our partial evaluation technology to VHDL descriptions.

This work is part of a project funded by EPSRC and the United Kingdom Ministry of Defence (MoD), managed by Satnam Singh (Xilinx Inc.), Tom Melham (University of Glasgow) and Derek McAuley (Microsoft Research Labs, Cambridge).

References

1. T. Kean, B. New, B. Slous. *A Multiplier for the XC6200*. Sixth International Workshop on Field Programmable Logic and Applications. Darmstadt, 1996.
2. H. T. Kung. *Why Systolic Architectures*. IEEE Computer. January 1982.
3. National Bureau of Standards. *Data Encryption Standard* (DES), Technical Report, National Bureau of Standards (USA), Federal Information Processing Standards, Publication 46, National Technical Information Services, Springfield, Virginia, April 1997.
4. N. D. Jones, C. K. Gomard, and P. Sestoft, *Partial Evaluation and Automatic Program Generation*, Prentice-Hall, 1993.
5. Jason Leonard and William H. Mangione-Smith. *A Case Study of Partially Evaluated Hardware Circuits: Key-Specific DES*. FPL'97. 1997.
6. M. Sheeran, G. Jones. *Circuit Design in Ruby*. Formal Methods for VLSI Design, J. Stanstrup, North Holland, 1992.
7. Satnam Singh and Pierre Bellec. *Virtual Hardware for Graphics Applications using FPGAs*. FCCM'94. IEEE Computer Society, 1994.
8. Satnam Singh. Architectural Descriptions for FPGA Circuits. FCCM'95. IEEE Computer Society. 1995.
9. Michael J. Wirthlin and Brad L. Hutchings. *Improving Functional Density Through Run-Time Constant Propagation*. FPGA'97. 1997.
10. Xilinx. *XC6200 FPGA Family Data Sheet*. Xilinx Inc. 1995.

WebScope: A Circuit Debug Tool

Steven A. Guccione

Xilinx Inc.
2100 Logic Drive
San Jose, CA 95124 (USA)
Steven.Guccione@xilinx.com

Abstract. *WebScope* is an interactive graphical tool used to probe and stimulate circuits in reconfigurable logic devices. *WebScope* is implemented using the *Java* programming language and features a graphical point and click user interface, remote access to hardware and a limited symbolic debug capability.

1   Introduction

Systems based on reconfigurable logic have been increasing in popularity. While various hardware platforms have been built [4] software support for these systems has lagged. In the area of software support, the emphasis has been almost exclusively on design tools. By contrast, little has been reported on debug environments for these systems.

Among the debug tools mentioned in the literature are the *systolic parallel C (spC)* debugger for the *Enable++* system [6], the *KRONO* and *ShowRB* debugger for the *PAM* system [2], the *T2* debugger for the *Splash 2* system [1], the *Hardware Promela Debugger (HPDB)* for the *PROMELA* system [7], the *DISC debugger (DDB)* for the *DISC* system [3] and the *CALLAS* debugger for *CHAMELON* [5].

While this is a substantial number of systems, none are discussed in detail, nor are supporting documents on such debug environments referenced.

WebScope attempts to fill this gap in the software development environment for reconfigurable logic based systems. *WebScope* provides a graphical, interactive interface to aid in the debugging of designs. While it is tempting to refer to *WebScope* as a debugger, it actually interfaces to the system at the hardware level and provides no direct support for software-style debugging.

In this respect *WebScope* more closely resembles *In-Circuit Emulators* (*ICEes*) popular in microprocessor development environments. While this system operates primarily at the hardware level, this permits *WebScope* to operate independently of other design tools or software packages. This also enhances the portability of the tool.

2   The System Architecture

WebScope is implemented in the *Java* programming language. Its implementation permits *WebScope* to run on a variety of hosts, from PCs to workstations, using the same small set of files. Additionally, *WebScope* may be run using local hardware, or remotely using hardware on another host. This is useful in situations where several users wish to share a board, or in cases where physical access to the hardware is not possible. To operate *WebScope* remotely, it is necessary to run a network server. This server negotiates network connections and provides the interface from the network to the physical hardware.

Finally, *WebScope* may be run as either a standalone application using a *Java* interpreter, or as an applet running from a Web browser such as *Netscape* or the *Microsoft Internet Explorer*.

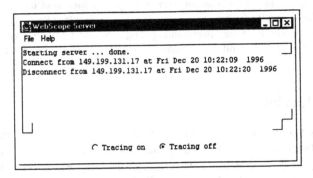

Fig. 1. The WebScope remote server.

The server supplied with *WebScope* is called *WsServer*. Like *WebScope* itself, this is a *Java* application. Figure 1 shows the server interface. All connections and disconnections to the hardware are logged, both to a window on the server and to a file. The *Tracing* option, when turned on, displays detailed information about the operations being performed remotely by *WebScope*.

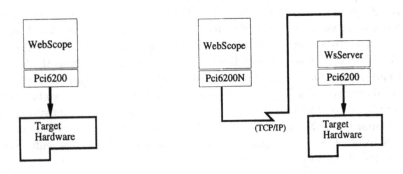

Fig. 2. Local and remote access to the target hardware.

Figure 2 shows the system architecture of *WebScope*. In this diagram, the local and remote access modes are illustrated. All access to the hardware occurs through a well defined interface. Currently, *WebScope* operates with the *XC6200DS* [9] hardware but is designed to port easily to other systems using the *XC6200* device [8]. The *Pci6200* interface is used in both modes to communicate directly with the hardware.

In the networked version of this interface, *Pci6200N* provides the message passing interface to *WsServer*, the remote server. Note that in turn, the server uses the same *Pci6200* class as the direct connection mode to communicate with the hardware.

3 The Command Panel

The primary control provided by *WebScope* is via the row of buttons across the top of the display. When *WebScope* is initialized, only the **Connect** button is enabled. Only after successfully connecting to the target hardware will the other command buttons become active.

The next button, **disconnect**, is used to terminate the connection with the target hardware. Once *WebScope* is disconnected from the hardware, all functions, except for the **connect** button, are disabled. Note that the state of the hardware remains unchanged even after **Disconnect**ing from the target. Reconnecting will resume the session where it was left off.

The **reset** button is used to reset the hardware to its default state. The **step** button is used to advance the state of the system. This stepping sends a single clock pulse to the hardware. In addition, symbol table information is accessed. This is discussed in more detail in the section on the symbol table below.

The **reload** button is used to re-read all of the data from the target and re-display the result. This is particularly useful when some external software has modified the state of the hardware.

The **display** button is used to toggle *WebScope*'s primary display. The software architecture for the *WebScope* displays is flexible and permits custom displays to be easily added. Currently, there are three displays. These are:

- **Graphical display**: The array of cells (default)
- **Symbolic display**: The symbol table
- **Waveform display**: Strip chart style traces of the symbol table variables

These displays are discussed in more detail in the sections below.

Finally, the **file** button is used to load files into the *WebScope*. When this button is clicked, a dialog box requesting a file name is popped up. The type of file to be downloaded is selected by the buttons in the display. Currently, *XC6200 CAL* design files and *SYM* symbol files can be downloaded.

4 The Cell Display

When *WebScope* is initialized, the default display is the graphical display. For the *XC6200*, this display consists of a grid of 64 x 64 squares, representing the

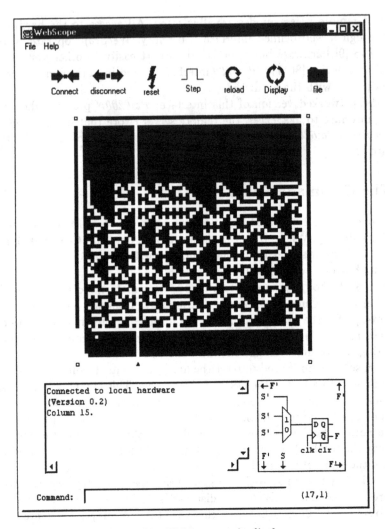

Fig. 3. The WebScope main display.

state of the logic cells in the *XC6200*. A green square represents a cell with a logic '1' output; a red square represents a logic '0'. The display in Figure 3 shows a linear cellular automata demonstration circuit. The unique "triangle" pattern produced by such automata is visible on the display.

The cell array is surrounded on its four sides by *bars*. The bar to the left of the cells represents the *Map register*. This register determines which cells in the *XC6200* are used during state accesses. Black cells indicate bits masked off by the Map Register, while white cells indicate enabled bits. Grey cells indicate bits that are enabled by the Map Register, but will not appear on the external bus, due to the current bus width setting. The bus width in Figure 3 is set to eight bits.

On the top of the cell array is the *Column Wildcard* register. This register determines which columns of the array are accessed during configuration. This permits multiple columns in the array to be written to simultaneously. Similarly, the *Row Wildcard* register is displayed as a bar on the right side of the array. Clicking on either wildcard register bar causes the value of the register to be printed in the *Status window* in the bottom portion of the display.

Below the cell array is a bar used to point to a given column in the array. Clicking on this bar highlights a column of cells in the array. Cells selected by the Map register are highlighted to help indicate their involvement in data accesses.

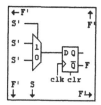

```
N: F'; S: F';
E: F'; W: F';
X1: S'; X2: S';
X3: S';
Y2: X2; Y3: X3;
RP: No protect;
CS: Q' M: X3'
(State: 0x0)
```

Fig. 4. The cell configuration status box.

Finally, clicking on cells in the array return their configuration value. This is displayed in the status panel at the lower right portion of the display. Note that this cell configuration panel has two modes. One displays textual information, the other displays a graphical representation of the circuit in the selected cell.

Clicking on the status panel toggles from one type of display to the other. Figure 4 shows the two modes for the cell configuration display. The graphical representation gives the four outputs of the cell (north, south, east and west), plus the extra "magic" output to the south. The three inputs to the primary cell multiplexer are also shown. In the textual display, the complete cell configuration is printed. This display is most useful to those intimately familiar with the *XC6200* cell.

5   The Symbolic Display

The second display in *WebScope* is the symbolic display. This display treats groups of cells in a column as a multi-bit variable and permits software-like symbolic access to the *XC6200* cells. Figure 5 shows the symbolic display used by the linear cellular automata demonstration circuit.

The variables are defined by the *name*, which is a symbolic name for the variable, a *column*, which indicates which column of cells in the *XC6200* is accessed, and a 64-bit bit pattern, specified by the *Map (high)* and *Map (low)* fields. These give the rows of the cells which combine to make the variable. Finally, the *Value* field displays the current value of the variable.

Name	Column	Map (high)	Map (low)	Value
clock	3	Oxffffffff	Oxffffff7f	0
clock	3	Oxffffffff	Oxffffff7f	1
random	5	Oxffffffff	Ox000000ff	0

Fig. 5. The symbolic display.

The symbol file format for *WebScope* is simply an ASCII text file containing the fields in the display, with an added field to indicate if the variable is a *read* or a *write* variable. *Read* variables are indicated by an "R", *write* variables by a "W". *Write* variables take a final parameter, the value to be written. This is only an initial value. It may be modified interactively from within *WebScope*. Figure 6 gives an example of a symbol file. Note that text following a hash character (#) are treated as comments and ignored.

```
#
#  Symbol file for WebScope
#  (for LCA demo)
#
# Name    Col     Map_high      Map_low     R/W     Value
#-----    ---     --------      --------     ---     -----
clock      3     Oxffffffff    Oxffffff7f     W        0
clock      3     Oxffffffff    Oxffffff7f     W        1
random     5     Oxffffffff    Ox000000ff     R
```

Fig. 6. The SYM file format.

On each **step** command, these variables are read or written in sequence, thus probing and stimulating the circuit. Note that in the example above, the same variable, *clock* is referenced twice, each time as a writable variable. This technique is used to produce a software-driven clock pulse on each **step**. Because the symbol table entries are read/written in the order in which they are listed, the cell at location (3,7) will be set to '0', then to '1'. This is used to clock the circuit in a software controlled manner.

6   The Waveform Display

The waveform display draws strip chart diagrams for the variables in the symbol table. This permits the history of the variable over time to be viewed. This is not only useful for spotting transient irregularities in data, but for Digital Signal Processing (DSP) applications as well. This display may also be favored by hardware engineers and others who are more comfortable with the digital waveform displays found in circuit simulators.

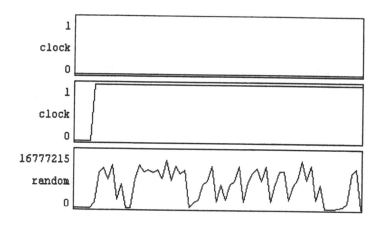

Fig. 7. The trace display.

As with the *Symbolic Display*, the *Waveform Display* is driven by the values in the symbol table. The example in Figure 7 shows the traces for the variables in symbol table in Figure 5. The value of the variable *random* contains bits in column 5, which is data produced by the circuit driving the linear cellular automata. These values are pseudorandom, as is indicated by the display.

7 The Command Line Interface

Finally, at the bottom of the screen is a command line interface. this interface permits complete access to the hardware. While not the preferred mode of operation, this interface is retained as legacy code from the original text-based interface to the *XC6200DS* hardware. This interface is still favored by some members of the design team.

On-line help is also available from the command line. This gives more detailed descriptions of the available commands and their syntax.

8 Conclusions

Perhaps just as significant was the tool itself is the process by which the software was developed. The original design contained a core functionality which simply displayed the state of cells in the *XC6200*. As the use of the tool increased, new features were requested and rapidly added. It is a testament to the power and flexibility of the *Java* programming language and support libraries that this tool was able to be developed in such a manner in less than 6 man months.

In addition, the number of bugs was surprisingly low. This is not so much attributed to the skill of the programmer as to the extensive compile and run-time checking in *Java*. Most programming errors were identified quickly and repaired. Finally, the object oriented nature of the language enabled new functionality to be smoothly integrated into the existing body of code. Seldom was it necessary to modify existing code objects to add new functionality.

WebScope represents a new level of support for circuit and system development using reconfigurable logic. A powerful interactive interface to reconfigurable logic designs has already proven to be helpful in finding design errors at all levels of the system. It has been used to alternatively debug user designs, the development tools, system level hardware and even the silicon itself.

References

1. Jeffrey M. Arnold. The splash 2 software environment. In Duncan A. Buell and Kenneth L. Pocek, editors, *IEEE Workshop on FPGAs for Custom Computing Machines*, pages 88–101, Los Alamitos, CA, April 1993. IEEE Computer Society Press.
2. Patrice Bertin and Hervé Toutai. PAM programming environments: Practice and experience. In Duncan A. Buell and Kenneth L. Pocek, editors, *IEEE Workshop on FPGAs for Custom Computing Machines*, pages 133–138, Los Alamitos, CA, April 1994. IEEE Computer Society Press.
3. David A. Clark and Brad L. Hutchings. Supporting FPGA microprocessors through retargetable software tools. In Kenneth L. Pocek and Jeffrey Arnold, editors, *IEEE Symposium on FPGAs for Custom Computing Machines*, pages 195–203, Los Alamitos, CA, April 1996. IEEE Computer Society Press.
4. Steven A. Guccione. List of FPGA-based computing machines. World Wide Web page http://www.io.com/~guccione/HW_list.html, 1997.
5. Beat Heeb and Cuno Pfister. Chamelon: A workstation of a different colour. In Herbert Grünbacher and Reiner W. Hartenstein, editors, *Field-Programmable Gate Arrays: Architectures and Tools for Rapid Prototyping*, pages 152–161, 1992. Proceedings of the 2nd International Workshop on Field-Programmable Logic and Applications, FPL 95. Lecture Notes in Computer Science 705.
6. H. Högl, A. Kugel, J. Ludvig, R. Manner, K. H. Noffz, and R. Zoz. Enable++: A second generation FPGA processor. In Peter Athanas and Kenneth L. Pocek, editors, *IEEE Symposium on FPGAs for Custom Computing Machines*, pages 45–53, Los Alamitos, CA, April 1995. IEEE Computer Society Press.
7. Alan Wenban and Geoffrey Brown. A software development system for FPGA-based data acquisition systems. In Kenneth L. Pocek and Jeffrey Arnold, editors, *IEEE Symposium on FPGAs for Custom Computing Machines*, pages 28–37, Los Alamitos, CA, April 1996. IEEE Computer Society Press.
8. Xilinx, Inc. *The Programmable Logic Data Book*, 1996.
9. Xilinx, Inc. *XC6200 Development System*, 1997.

Computing Goldbach Partitions Using Pseudo-Random Bit Generator Operators on an FPGA Systolic Array

Dominique LAVENIER[1], Yannick SAOUTER[2]

[1] IRISA, Campus de Beaulieu, 35042 Rennes, France
lavenier@irisa.fr
[2] IRIT, 118 route de Narbonne, 31062 Toulouse, France
saouter@irit.fr

Abstract. Calculating the binary Goldbach partitions for the first 128×10^6 numbers represents weeks of computation with the fastest microprocessors. This paper describes an FPGA systolic implementation for reducing the execution time. High clock frequency is achieved using operators based on pseudo-random bit generator. Experiments carried both on the R10000 processor and on the FPGA PeRLe-1 board are reported.

1 Introduction

In 1742 Goldbach claimed the following conjecture: "Every even integer greater than 3 is the sum of two prime numbers". This conjecture is known as the *binary Goldbach conjecture.* Today, it has been verified till the bound 4×10^{14} and partially near various powers of ten up to 10^{300} [3]. But the *exact number* of binary partitions has only been investigated up to 350 000 [1], because of high computation cost.

Such computations are useful for estimating the reliability of probabilistic models and testing their theoretical background. Historically, three models for the number of partitions have been proposed by Hardy and Littlewood, Brun, and Selmer. These three models are compared in [5] together with the values obtained from our FPGA implementation.

The solution we propose for speeding up the computation combines two technics: parallelization and customization.

- the **parallelization** allows to compute simultaneously N consecutive binary Goldbach partitions. It is implemented on a linear systolic array. Such regular arrays map well onto FPGAs: they are both made of locally interconnected regular elements. Furthermore, synchronous designs can reach very high computation speed.
- the **customization** maps into hardware a function which requires the use of several instructions on a sequential machine. Particularities of the function can be extracted to make the best use of hardware resources. In our case, a fast implementation has been achieved with arithmetic operators built with pseudo-random number bit generators and integer modular representation.

The next section introduces the binary Goldbach partition enumeration problem and section 3 shows the parallelization on a linear systolic array. Section 4 details the FPGA implementation and focuses on the pseudo-random bit generator operators. Section 5 compares the experimentations we have done with the R10000 processor and the PeRLe-1 board. Section 6 concludes with some perspectives.

2   Computing binary Goldbach partitions

Computing **one** binary Goldbach partition consists of counting, for an even number K ($K \geq 4$), all the possible ordered pairs such that $K = p_1 + p_2$ where p_1 and p_2 are two prime numbers. For instance, the binary Goldbach partition of 22 (denoted by $G_2(22)$) is 5 since there are five possibilities of getting 22 by summing two prime numbers (3+19, 5+17, 11+11, 17+5, 19+3).

Computing the binary Goldbach partitions of an even number K may be expressed by the following C function:

Algorithm 1:

```
int Goldbach_1(K) int K; {
    int G=0; int i=1;
    while (i<K) {
        if (prime(i) && prime(K-i)) G=G+1;
        i=i+2;
    }
    return(G);
}
```

The function `Goldbach_1(K)` returns $G_2(K)$. `prime(x)` is a function which returns true if x is a prime number and false otherwise. The complexity of this algorithm is equal to the numbers of times the loop is executed, that is: $K/2$ One may note the symmetry of the calculation for $i < K/2$ and $i > K/2$, leading to an optimized function:

Algorithm 2:

```
int Goldbach_2(K) int K; {
    int G=0; int i=K;
    while (i<K/2) {
        if (prime(i) && prime(K-i)) G=G+1;
        i=i+2;
    }
    G=G*2;
    if (prime(K/2)) G=G+1;
    return (G);
}
```

Since the case i=K/2 is not considered when executing `Goldbach_1(K/2)`, it is added to the body of the `Goldbach_2` function. The complexity is then lowered to $K/4$.

Now, the problem of computing N consecutive binary partitions can be stated as the calculation of N partitions in the interval [P .. P+2N-2]. The following C function stores the N results in the array G such as G[n]=$G_2(P + 2n)$.

Algorithm 3:

```
Goldbach_3(P,N,G) int P, N, *G; {
    int K,n;
    n=0;
    for (K=P; K<P+2*N; K=K+2) {
        G[n]=GoldBach_2(K);
        n=n+1;
    }
}
```

For P≫N (the general case) the complexity of algorithm 3, denoted by $G_{seq}(P, N)$ is equal to $N \times P/4$.

3 Parallelization

The computation of N consecutive binary Goldbach partitions can be parallelized on a linear systolic array of N processors as depicted by the figure 1. Each cell is responsible for the calculation of one binary Goldbach partition: The leftmost cell computes $G_2(P + 2N - 2)$ and the rightmost cell $G_2(P)$.

The array is supplied with two boolean vectors: V1 and V2. The vector V2 crosses the array at twice the speed of V1. The boolean vectors are formed as follows:

```
V1[i] = prime(2i-1)              0   <= i <  (P+2N-2)/2
V2[i] = prime (P+2N-2i-3)    (P+2N-2)/2  <= i <  (P+2N-2)/2 + N-1
```

A cell computing $G_2(k)$ receives two boolean values: prime(x1) and prime(x2) such that $k = x_1 + x_2$. When prime(x1) and prime(x2) are both true, a counter (G) is incremented by 1. At the end of the computation each counter holds the value of one binary Goldbach partition.

Performing the calculation of N consecutive binary partitions over the interval [P,P+2N-2] requires, for $P \gg N$, approximatively $P/2$ systolic steps (denoted by $G_{sys}(P,N)$). The speed-up compared with the sequential implementation, is thus given by:

$$S = \frac{G_{seq}(P, N)}{G_{sys}(P, N)} \times \frac{\delta_{seq}}{\delta_{sys}} = \frac{N}{2} \times \frac{\delta_{seq}}{\delta_{sys}} \tag{1}$$

δ_{seq} is the time for executing one iteration of the loop of algorithm 1. δ_{sys} is the time of one systolic cycle. From the above equation it can easily be seen that an efficient systolic implementation will aim to both increase N and to reduce δ_{seq}. These are the two sources of increased performance.

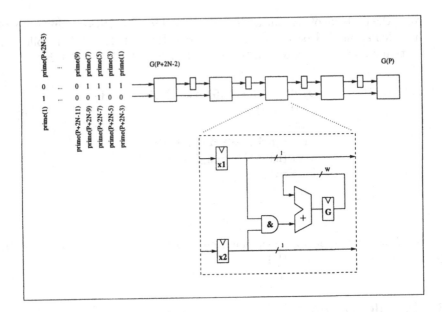

Fig. 1. Linear systolic array for computing N consecutive binary Goldbach partitions. It is composed of N cells, each cell computing one Goldbach partition. The array is supplied with two boolean vectors. The calculation perform by a cell consists simply in incrementing a counter if both inputs of the cell are true.

4 FPGA implementation

This section explains how the architecture of the systolic array has been tailored for the FPGA XC3000 Xilinx family. The three next sub-sections describe respectively the time optimization (how to get a high clock frequency), the space optimization (how to map a cell in a minimum of hardware), and the unloading of the results.

4.1 Time optimization

The clock frequency of a cell – and hence, the clock frequency of the array – is mainly determined by the speed of the counter. This depends of the number K for which $G_2(K)$ is computed. For example, finding the partition for numbers around 10^8 requires a 27-bit counter. Here, a ripple carry adder is too slow for achieving good speed performance, while a more sophisticated architecture, such as a carry save adder, requires too much space to reach a reasonable size array.

Instead of implementing a conventional counter, we use a mechanism which uses two main techniques: Pseudo-random bit generators and modular representation. The advantage is that no carry propagation occurs, allowing high frequency clock. On the other hand, the numbers are not in their natural representation and need to be post-processed before interpretation.

We use pseudo-random bit generator based on the following algorithm [2]:

```
Algorithm 4:    counter = 0;
                while (true) {
                  x = MSB(counter);              /* MSB */
                  counter = counter << 1;        /* shift left */
                  if (x==0) counter = counter ^ key;
                }
```

With a suitable *key* value, the successive values of the data can have a period long enough to be used as a counter. But interpreting the value of a W-bit counter based on this technique is not obvious: A lookup table of 2^W entries is required, which is unreasonable for the values of W we are considering ($W \geq 25$). On the other hand, retrieving natural representation by post-processing (in software) soft is too slow.

The difficulty can be surmounted by using two counters and using modular representation of integers: let p and q two numbers relatively prime to each other such that $M < p.q$. Then any number k in the interval $[1..M]$ is uniquely represented by the pair $(k \bmod p, k \bmod q)$.

The conversion from the pair representation to the plain integer representation is based on the following theorem:

Theorem 1:

Let p and q two integers relatively prime to each other. Let u and v be such that $u.p - v.q = 1$. A solution to the set of equation:

$$\begin{cases} k = n_1 \bmod(p) \\ k = n_2 \bmod(q) \end{cases}$$

is given by:

$$k = n_1 + (n_2 - n_1).u \bmod(p.q)$$

In other words, given the pair (n_1, n_2), the post-processing task for computing k consists simply of a modular multiplication which actually represents a small part of the overall computation. More details can be found in [5].

As an example, the hardware implementation of a 9-bit counter based on two pseudo-random bit generators and modular integer representation is shown on the figure 2. It is composed of two separate counters: A 4-bit counter and a 5 bit counter. According to Algorithm 4, the F_i functions implement the pseudo-random bit generator as follows:

$$F_i = inc.(\overline{x}.(k_i \oplus c_{i-1}) + x.c_{i-1}) + \overline{inc}.c_i \tag{2}$$

inc is true if the two inputs of the cell are true. x is the most significant bit of the counter. c_i and c_{i-1} are the current state of respectively the ith and the i-1th bits of the counter. $+, .$ and $\oplus$ stand respectively for logic OR, logic AND and logic exclusive OR boolean functions.

In such a counter, there is no carry propagation. The clock frequency is dictated by the computation time of one elementary 5-input F_i function.

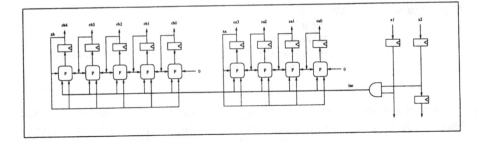

Fig. 2. Systolic cell: two pseudo-random bit generators of respectively 5 and 4 bit wide are used to form a 9-bit counter. The two generators are concurrently activated when input x1 and x2 are both true.

4.2   Space optimization

The goal is to fit a maximum of cells in a FPGA XC3000 Xilinx family component. Such components contain a matrix of CLBs, each CLB containing two 1-bit registers and either two 4-input boolean functions or one and 5-input boolean function.

If W is the width of the counter, a direct implementation of a cell requires W × 5-input functions (counter), one 2-input function (AND gate) and 3 × 1-bit registers, that is (W+2) CLBs (the 3 registers and the AND function fit into 2 CLBs). Note that this is an optimistic estimation since it does not consider the hardware for reading back the results.

One may notice that the counter contains two keys which remain stable during the whole computation. It is then possible to encode these keys and provide simpler F_i functions depending of the bit state k_i.

From equation 2, if k_i is equal to zero then:

$$F0_i = inc.c_{i-1} + \overline{inc}.c_i$$

On the same way, if k_i is equal to one, F_i becomes:

$$F1_i = inc.(\overline{x}.\overline{c_{i-1}} + x.c_{i-1}) + \overline{inc}.c_i$$

In this scheme, a counter is composed of two types of elementary functions: $F0_i$ or $F1_i$, according to the key. From a practical point of view, one CLB can now contain two $F0_i$ or $F1_i$ functions (which are respectively 3-input and 4 input functions), lowering a cell to (W/2 + 2) CLBs.

4.3   Unloading the results

The mechanism implemented for collecting the results (the values held by the counter) exploits the shift capability of the counter. Each $F0_i$ and $F1_i$ function is extended with a *read-back* input which acts as a switch:

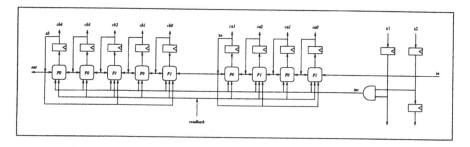

Fig. 3. Read-back mechanism: the shift capability of the counter is used to form a long shift register for outputing data serially.

$$F0_i = readback.c_{i-1} + \overline{readback}.(inc.c_{i-1} + \overline{inc}.c_i)$$

$$F1_i = readback.c_{i-1} + \overline{readback}.(inc.(\overline{x}.\overline{c_{i-1}} + x.c_{i-1}) + \overline{inc}.c_i)$$

Thus, reading back the results consists of connecting all the counters in a long shift register and outputing data serially. This is achieved simply as shown by the figure 3. This mechanism has the main advantage of requiring a very little extra hardware without affecting the clock frequency.

Note that the $F1_0$ function must be different: In the normal mode the shift register input is *zero*, and in the read-back mode its input is the most significant bit of the previous counter. Then the $F1_0$ function is:

$$F1_0 = readback.in + \overline{readback}.(inc.\overline{x} + \overline{inc}.c_i)$$

The $F0_i$ function is now a 4-input function, while the $F1_i$ function is a 5-input function. Consequently, the number of CLBs to fit a complete cell depends on the key since a CLB cannot simultaneously house two 5-input functions. Fortunately, the keys contain a small number of "1's", allowing hardware resources to be greatly minimized.

5 Experiments

A 256 cell linear systolic array has been successfully implemented on the PeRLe-1 board [4]. This board houses a 4×4 matrix of Xilinx XC3090 and is connected through a Turbo Channel interface to a 5000/240 Dec Station.

The counter, which is the critical point in terms of hardware resources, is 27-bit wide. It is split into two counters of 13-bit and 14-bit wide which require respectively a key set to 9 and 7. This configuration allows us to map 16 cells into a single Xilinx XC3090 component. The entire systolic array is then composed of 256 cells running at 30 MHz.

In addition to the systolic array, an interface composed of a small automaton, coupled with a serializer/deserializer mechanism has been implemented for managing the I/O connection with the Dec station. The host alternatively sends two sub-vectors of 16 boolean values corresponding to the two data inputs of the array. This compression mechanism avoids exceeding the Turbo Channel bandwidth.

The computation of the binary Goldbach partitions up to 128×10^6 was performed in 220 hours (9.2 days). The 64 first million binary Goldbach partitions are now available for comparing the three basic probabilistic methods. This mathematical study is beyond the scope of this paper and is not addressed here. Readers Interested by the estimation done on the reliability of the three probabilistic models mentioned in the introduction (Hardy and Littlewood, Brun, and Selmer) can refer to [5].

In order to evaluate the speed-up of the hardware approach, two programmable versions have been tested on a R10000 processor. We used one node of the *Power Challenge Array* of the Charles Hermite Center, Nancy, France. This supercomputer is composed of 40 R10000 processors scheduled at 195 MHz and sharing a common memory of 1.5 Gbytes. Experiments were performed for low values and extrapolated to 128×10^6 with respect to the complexity of the algorithms.

The first algorithm implemented is the naive one, that is, the algorithm presented in section 2 (complexity: $O(N^2)$, where N is the upper value for which the Goldbach partitions are computed). The second one has a lower complexity: For any pair of prime numbers below N, it computes the sum and adds one in the corresponding entry of an array containing the $N/2$ partitions. The prime number theorem states that the number of prime numbers below N is approximatively equal to $N/log(N)$. Consequently the complexity of the second algorithm is raised to $O((N/log(N))^2)$. Note that this algorithm requires an integer table of $N/2$ entries. The following table summarizes the execution time for the naive algorithm, the optimal algorithm and the systolic algorithm.

N	naive algorithm R10000	optimal algorithm R10000	systolic algorithm PeRLe-1
10^6	1:58:59	11:25	2:00
2×10^6	7:50:47	1:11:26	5:30
3×10^6		2:53:01	10:35
4×10^6		4:37:22	17:10
5×10^6		5:42:05	25:30
128×10^6	32500 hours (*3.7 years*)	2928 hours (*4 months*)	220 hours (*9.2 days*)

The last row – for the naive and optimal algorithms only – is an estimation of the execution time calculated as follows:

naive algorithm: $t_{naive} = 7.2 \times 10^{-9} \times N^2$

optimal algorithm: $t_{optimal} = 2.3 \times 10^{-7} \times (N/log(N))^2$

The two constants have been determined from the first measures. The systolic column reports the exact time.

One may have noticed that the comparison between the hardware and software doesn't rely on equivalent technology. The PeRLe-1 board is far from using up-to-date FPGA components compared with the R10000 microprocessor. The PeRLe-1 matrix (16 x XC3090 chips made of 16x20 CLB matrix) contains 10240 4-input boolean functions. This is approximatively the capacity of a single Xilinx XC40125XV component (10982 4-input look-up table)[6]. In other words, an up-to-date board will be able to house a much larger systolic array (4096 cells) which will certainly be clocked with a higher frequency. In that case, the execution time would be reduced to a few hours.

6 Conclusion and Perspectives

As in many other specific applications, the FPGA based co-processor approach has demonstrated its efficiency for enumerating the binary Goldbach partitions. In the present case, the execution time has been reduced from months to days.

Of course, such computation could have been performed on a parallel machine, or on a network of workstations. This is technically feasible. The drawback is just to find such computing resources, i.e. a parallel machine available for several tens of days, exclusively for that specific computation. Designing an ASIC is another solution which is no longer valid: once results have been obtained, the chip become useless. The FPGA technology appears as the right alternative for a domain of research which requires both intensive computation and one-time-use architecture.

Other than the architecture we proposed for enumerating Goldbach partitions, the systolic scheme can be applied to many other similar problems such as, for example, the test of the reliability of Schinzel's conjecture about pairs of prime numbers, or to verify the Hooley's conjecture on the sums of exact powers. Any of these applications would lead to very similar architectures, but operating on different bit-streams. Similarly, the specialization of operators based on pseudo-random bit generators can address other areas for optimizing the clock frequency and reducing the cost of certain circuits such as the Brent's polynomial greatest divider, the Huffman's systolic encoder, etc.

Short term perspectives of this work are concerned with automatic tools for implementing regular arrays onto FPGA. A a matter of fact, many time-consuming applications can be parallelized on a regular array. Generally, the critical section of code is a nested loop from which a parallel hardware co-processor can be synthesized. Being able to map onto a FPGA board an HDL description of a regular architecture, together with the host/co-processor communication interface will constitute a real gain of time and effort. We are currently developing such tools.

References

1. C.E. Bohman, J. Froberg. Numerical results on the Goldbach conjecture. BIT **15** (1975)
2. D. Knuth. The Art of Computer Programming: semi-numerical algorithms, Addison-Wesley (1969).
3. J-M. Deshouillers, Y. Saouter, H.J.J. te Riele. New experimental results concerning the Goldbach conjecture. Proc. of the Annual Number Theory Symposium, Portland, Oregon, USA, 1998.
4. J. Vuillemin, P. Bertin, D. Roncin, M. Shand, H. Touati, P. Boucard. Programmable Active Memories: Reconfigurable Systems Come of Age, IEEE Transactions on VLSI Systems, Vol. 4 No. 1 (1996) 56-69
5. D. Lavenier, Y. Saouter. A Systolic Array for Computing Binary Goldbach Partitions. IRISA report 1174 (1998)
6. Xilinx Products, XC4000XV family.
   http//www.xilinx.com/products/xc4000xv.htm

Solving Boolean Satisfiability with Dynamic Hardware Configurations

Peixin Zhong, Margaret Martonosi, Pranav Ashar, and Sharad Malik

Dept. of Electrical Engineering
Princeton University

NEC CCRL, Princeton NJ USA

Abstract. Boolean satisfiability (SAT) is a core computer science problem with many important commercial applications. An NP-complete problem, many different approaches for accelerating SAT either in hardware or software have been proposed. In particular, our prior work studied mechanisms for accelerating SAT using configurable hardware to implement formula-specific solver circuits. In spite of this progress, SAT solver runtimes still show room for further improvement.

In this paper, we discuss further improvements to configurable-hardware-based SAT solvers. We discuss how dynamic techniques can be used to add the new solver circuitry to the hardware during run-time. By examining the basic solver structure, we explore how it can be best designed to support such dynamic reconfiguration techniques. These approaches lead to several hundred times speedups for many problems. Overall, this work offers a concrete example of how aggressively employing on-the-fly reconfigurability can enable runtime learning processes in hardware. As such, this work opens new opportunities for high performance computing using dynamically reconfigurable hardware.

1 Introduction

Boolean satisfiability (SAT) is a core computer science problem with important applications in CAD, AI and other fields. Because it is an NP-complete problem, it can be very time-consuming to solve. The problem's importance and computational difficulty have attracted considerable research attention, and this prior research has included several recent attempts using configurable hardware to accelerate SAT solvers [9, 1, 10, 11].

In earlier work, we presented a novel approach to solving the SAT problem in which formula-specific hardware was compiled specially for each problem to be solved [11]. Implications are computed via Boolean logic customized to the formula at hand. Each variable in the formula was given a small state machine that dictated when new values should be tried for this variable. Control passed back and forth between different variables in this distributed, linearly-connected, set of state machines.

The advantages of our formula-specific approach are that the interconnect between clauses and variables are tightly specialized to the problem at hand. This leads to very low I/O and memory requirements. It also allows implication processing to be much faster compared to some previous approaches. As a result, we achieved order-of-magnitude speedups on many large SAT problems.

Our formula-specific approach, however, has two main disadvantages. First, the FPGA compile-time is on the critical path of the problem solution. This means that only long-running problems can garner speedups once compile-time is taken into account. A second problem is that the global interconnect and long compile-times make it inefficient to insert any on-the-fly changes to the SAT-solver circuit.

The second problem is particularly vexing because it precludes a key strategy employed by current software SAT solvers such as GRASP [7]: dynamic clause addition. In software solvers, as the problem is worked on, additional information about the formula is distilled into extra Boolean clauses which are added into the Boolean formula that defines the problem. These additional clauses allow one to more efficiently prune the search space, and they led to sizable performance improvements in the GRASP software SAT solver.

The work we describe here evaluates new designs for solving SAT in configurable hardware that use novel architectures and dynamic reconfiguration to allow us to circumvent the problems raised by our previous design. First, instead of an irregular global interconnect, a *regular* ring-based interconnect is used. This avoids the compile-time limitations of our prior approach. Second, by including generalized "spare" clause hardware in the design, we can add extra clauses as the solution progresses, which gives our approach the same advantages as GRASP's added clauses technique.

The remainder of this paper is structured as follows. In Section 2, we describe the SAT problem in more detail. Section 3 discusses design alternatives for solving it in configurable hardware, and then Section 4 proposes a particular hardware mapping that we evaluate further. Section 5 gives an overview of related work and Section 6 offers our conclusions.

2   The SAT Algorithm

The Boolean satisfiability (SAT) problem is a well-known constraint satisfaction problem with many practical applications. Given a Boolean formula, the goal is either to find an assignment of 0-1 values to the variables so that the formula evaluates to 1, or to establish that no such assignment exists.

The Boolean formula is typically expressed in conjunctive normal form (CNF), also called product-of-sums form. Each sum term (clause) in the CNF is a sum of single literals, where a literal is a variable or its negation. In order for the entire formula to evaluate to 1, each clause must be satisfied, *i.e.*, at least one of its literals should be 1.

An assignment of 0-1 values to a subset of variables (called a partial assignment) might satisfy some clauses and leave the others undetermined. If an undetermined clause has only one unassigned literal in it, that literal must evaluate to 1 in order to satisfy the clause. In such a case, the corresponding variable is said to be *implied* to that value. A variable is considered free if neither assigned nor implied. A conflict arises if the same variable is implied to be different values. This means that the corresponding partial assignment cannot be a part of any valid solution.

Most current SAT solvers are based on the Davis-Putnam algorithm [3]. This is a backtrack search algorithm. The basic algorithm begins from an empty assignment. It proceeds by assigning a 0 or 1 value to one free variable at a time. After each assignment, the algorithm determines the direct and transitive implications of that assignment on other variables. If no conflict is detected after the implication procedure, the algorithm picks the next free variable, and repeats the procedure (forward search). Otherwise, the algorithm attempts a new partial assignment by complementing the most-recently assigned variable (backtrack). If this also leads to conflict, this variable is reset to the free value and the next most-recently assigned variable is complemented. The algorithm terminates when: (i) no free variables are available and no conflicts have been encountered (a solution has been found), or (ii) it wants to backtrack beyond the first variable, which means all possible assignments have been exhausted and there is no solution to the problem.

Determining implications is crucial to pruning the search space since it allows the algorithm to skip regions of the search space corresponding to invalid partial assignments.

Recent software implementations of the SAT algorithm have enhanced it in several ways while maintaining the same basic flow [6, 2, 8, 7]. The contribution of the GRASP work [7] is notable since it applies non-chronological backtracking and dynamic clause addition to prune the search space further. Significant improvements in run time are reported.

2.1 Conflict Analysis

Much of the performance improvement reported by GRASP comes from their implementation of conflict analysis. When the basic Davis-Putnam algorithm observes a conflict, it backtracks to change the partial assignment. It does not, however, analyze which variable is the true reason for the observed conflict. The backtrack process may complement variables irrelevant to the conflict and repeatedly explore related dead ends. More sophisticated conflict analysis works to identify the variable assignments that lead to the conflict. Acting as a reverse implication procedure, conflict analysis identifies the transitive predecessors of the implied literals leading to the conflict.

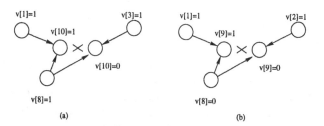

Fig. 1. Example of implication graphs. (a) Conflict after assignment v[8]=1. (b) Conflict after altered assignment v[8]=0.

Consider, for example, the partial formula $(\bar{v}_1 + v_8 + v_9)(\bar{v}_2 + v_8 + \bar{v}_9)(\bar{v}_1 + \bar{v}_8 + v_{10})(\bar{v}_3 + \bar{v}_8 + \bar{v}_{10})$. If v_1, v_2 ... and v_7 are previously assigned to 1 and then

v_8 is assigned 1, the resulting implication graph is shown in Fig. 1(a). A conflict is raised on v_{10}. The predecessors for the conflict are v_1, v_3 and v_8. Similarly, when v_8 is changed to 0 (Fig. 1b), it generates a conflict in v_9. The causes are v_1, v_2 and $\bar{v}_8$. At this point, we know either value of v_8 will lead to a conflict. The basic algorithm would change the value of v_7 to 0 and try again. It is, however, v_1, v_2 and v_3 that are actually responsible. Therefore, we can directly backtrack to the most recently assigned variable causing the dual conflict, i.e. v_3.

2.2 Dynamic Clause Addition

In the previous example, we showed how conflict analysis can deduce after the fact that if v_1, v_2 and v_3 are all 1, the formula can not be satisfied. This piece of information is not obvious, however, when these variables are assigned. To add such learned information into the solver's knowledge base, we can add a new clause $(\bar{v}_1 + \bar{v}_2 + \bar{v}_3)$ to the Boolean formula being solved. Adding this clause to the formula allows the solver to detect this conflict earlier and avoid exploring the same space in the future.

Conflict analysis and clause addition are relative easy to implement in software. When a new value is implied, it is added to a data structure summarizing the implication graph. When a conflict occurs, traversing the graph backwards identifies predecessors of the conflict. In the next section, we will show this can also be implemented in configurable hardware.

3 Design Alternatives

In designing configurable hardware to solve SAT, a number of design issues arise. Overall, the key is determining what functions are implemented on hardware and how they are implemented. Design decisions should be made on these questions:

- How do we choose which variable to assign next?
- How are logical implications computed?
- How are new implications sent to other units?
- How do we detect conflicts and backtrack?
- What further mechanisms do we harness for pruning the search space?

Our previous design compiles the problem formula and the solver into one custom circuit [11]. Covering the above design decisions, we note that this approach uses a statically-determined variable ordering based on how frequently each variable appears in the formula. The clauses are translated into logic gates to generate implications. All clauses are evaluated in parallel. Implications are communicated using hardwired connections. There is no analysis when a conflict is raised, and backtracking simply reverses the order of variable assignment.

Because so much of the formula is hardwired into the design, its run-time flexibility is limited. Here we discuss different alternatives for making dynamic modifications in SAT solver circuits. We identify the ability to dynamically add new clauses as the major objective in our new design. We have evaluated the following alternatives.

3.1 Supporting Dynamic Changes through Configuration Overlays

One way to achieve dynamic hardware modification is by implementing multiple configurations of each FPGA as overlays. An initial circuit is generated according to some static strategy. As this solver runs, new information is obtained and a better circuit can be designed and compiled. When the new circuit is available, the problem is then switched to run using it. This approach is very general for applications involving run-time hardware learning, and can clearly be applied to SAT clause addition. By adding conflict analysis to the hardware, it can direct new clauses to be added, and initiate new compiles of the improved designs. These compiles occur in parallel with further solutions using the current design.

This approach is particularly attractive with a system with multiple configuration capabilities and the ability to switch quickly between them. Extra memory can be used as configuration cache. While the solver is running, the cache is updated with a new design, and then we can quickly switch to the updated configurations. There are several drawbacks however. First, few commercial products currently support multiple configuration contexts, and those that do will inevitably pay a price in decreased logic density. This approach also requires very fast FPGA compilation; if the compilation is too slow, the newer circuit may be of little value by the time it is actually compiled.

3.2 Supporting Dynamic Changes through Partial Reconfiguration

Because of the difficulties inherent in approaches relying on configuration overlays, we chose to explore alternative techniques in which we redesign our base circuit to make it more amenable to partial configuration. In essence, we want to be able to modify only a small portion of the circuit and achieve the same performance goal as with full overlays.

Focusing on dynamic clause addition, we note that it would be natural to design each clause as a module. In this way, when a new clause is generated, a new module is simply added to the circuit. In our current design, this is difficult because we have implemented a variable-oriented, rather than clause-oriented, design. Section 4 discusses a mechanism for using partial reconfiguration by leaving "spare" clause templates in the solver and then customizing them into a specific added clause during runtime. A key aspect of using partial reconfiguration is implementing communication using a *regular* communication network; this ensures that no random global routing will be needed when a new clause is added.

4 Configurable Hardware Mapping

This section describes a hardware organization based on the partial reconfiguration approach from the previous section and evaluates a SAT solver algorithm based on it. We envision this hardware being implemented on an array of FPGA chips, because one FPGA does not provide the capacity necessary for interesting (i.e., large) SAT problems.

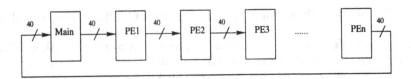

Fig. 2. Global topology of the SAT solver circuit

4.1 Hardware Organization

Global topology: The circuit topology is based on a regular ring structure as shown in Fig. 2. The ring is a pipelined communication network and the processing elements (PEs) are distributed along the ring. Each PE contains multiple modules with each module representing a clause. This regular, modular design allows for the easy addition of clauses during runtime. There is also a main control unit to maintain multiple control functions.

The communication network is used to send the updated variables to other units. Previously, we used direct wire connection between different variables. This direct approach has better performance for implication passing, but lacks the modularity needed to allow dynamic circuit changes.

The bus is 40 bits wide, so the FPGA chip will use 40 I/O pins for the incoming ring signals and another 40 pins for the output to the next FPGA. The bus consists of 32 data wires and 8 control bits. Signals are pipelined through a series of D-flipflops. All the variable data bits pass through the bus in a fixed order, with a synchronizing signal at the beginning.

In our design, the variable values are all rotating on the bus. Since each variable requires two bits ('00' denotes unassigned, '10' denotes a 1, and '01' denotes a zero) each stage can contain 16 variables.

Main control: The main control maintains the global state and monitors the ring for value changes and conflicts. When a variable changes from unassigned to either 1 or 0, the ordering of such changes must be recorded so that we know in what order to backtrack. These orderings are encoded in memory at the main control module. The main control also checks for conflicts by simply monitoring the ring for the '11' variable value that indicates a contradiction.

Implication Processing: Fig. 3 shown the connection between the bus and functional modules. Between each pipeline flipflop, there are only two levels of logic gates; this allows us to achieve a high clock rate.

Processing implications is generally compute-intensive, but as with our previous approach we employ large amounts of fine-grained parallelism. For each clause in the formula, we implement a module called a *clause cell*. The clause cell has a local counter to track which variables are currently on the bus. Each clause cell monitors the values of variables relevant to it, and uses them to determine when implications are needed. For an n-literal clause, if n-1 literals are set to 0, the other literal should be implied to be true, and this implied value is then propagated around the ring.

Conflict analysis: Since conflict analysis is the inverse of implication, it is natural to merge this function into each clause cell. When a new clause is generated, the cell stores its implication. In conflict analysis mode (initiated by

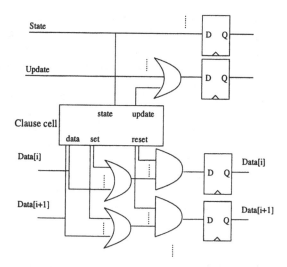

Fig. 3. One stage of the processing element

the main control), when the implied literal appears on the bus, it resets this variable and puts the predecessors on the bus.

4.2 Hardware SAT Algorithm

This hardware implements a SAT algorithm similar to software approaches. The major difference is that it tries to execute operations in parallel whenever possible. Since each clause is implemented as a separate cell in hardware, many clauses can be evaluated in parallel.

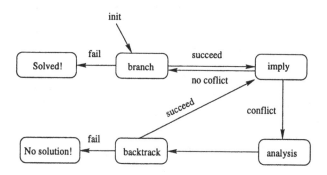

Fig. 4. Basic state diagram of the SAT solver

The basic flow diagram of the SAT solver is shown in Fig. 4. It includes four major states: Branch, Imply, Analysis and Backtrack.

Branch: After initialization (and whenever a partial assignment has successfully avoided a conflict), the circuit is in the branch state. The decision of which variable to assign (i.e., branch on) next, is determined by the main control. In the simple approach we simulate here, the variable ordering is statically determined, but more elaborate dynamic techniques are the subject of future research. It then proceeds to the Imply state. If no more free variables exist, a solution has been found.

Imply: This state is used to compute the logical implications of the assignment. The clause cells check the values and generate implications when necessary. The main control monitors the value changes. When implications have settled, it will proceed to branch on a new variable. It also monitors conflicts in variables, and initiates conflict analysis when needed.

Analysis: To indicate conflict analysis mode, both bits of the conflicted variable are set to 1, and all other data bits are set to 0. When the clause cells detect this mode, they generate predecessors for variables with an implied value. When this process settles, only the assigned variables responsible for the conflict will have a value on the bus. This list may be used by the main control to determine when to generate a new conflict clause cell. In our work, a new clause is generated only when both assignments for a variable end with a conflict. The backtrack destination is chosen to be the most recently-assigned variable of the ones responsible for the conflict. If there is no variable to backtrack to, there is no solution to the formula because the observed conflict cannot be resolved.

Backtrack: After conflict analysis, during backtrack, the bus is reset back to the variable values to allow further implication. Variables assigned before the backtrack point take on those values. Variables after the backtrack point are reset to free. When this is done, implications are tried again.

4.3   Performance Results

Problem name	FCCM98 design	New Design: No added clauses	New Design: Added clauses
aim-50-1_6-no-1	37806	93396	1552
aim-50-2_0-no-1	2418518	9763745	19749
aim-50-2_0-no-4	204314	294182	3643
aim-100-1_6-yes1-1	3069595	2985176	14100
aim-100-3_4-yes1-4	108914	775641	205845
hole6	32419	129804	129804
jnh16	84909	778697	513495
par8-1-c	176	700	700
ssa0432-003	194344	5955665	1905633

Table 1. Configurable SAT solver run-time in cycles

In order to evaluate the performance of this design, we built a C++ simulator and used DIMACS SAT problems as input [4]. Table 1 shows the number of hardware cycles needed to solve the problems. The first column of data shows the cycle counts for the FCCM98 formula-specific approach. The next column shows performance data for the newer design discussed here. This column includes conflict analysis and non-chronological backtracking, but does not include dynamic clause addition. The following column of data is the new design with the dynamic clause addition.

Although the run-time is expressed in number of cycles in each case, the actual cycle time is very different between the FCCM98 design and the current one. In the old design, long wires between implication units made routing difficult, and typical user clock rates were several hundred KHz to 2 MHz. In the newer design, the communication is pipelined and the routing is shorter and more regular. Initial estimates are that the clock rate should be at least 20 MHz. Therefore, speedups occur whenever the new design requires 10X or fewer cycles compared to the old design.

From the results, we can see the new design without clause addition has a speedup of about 1x to 10x. Speedups occur in this case due to (1) the improved clock rate and (2) the improved conflict analysis which leads to more direct backtracking.

Implementing dynamic clause addition offers benefits that vary with the characteristics of the problems. For some problems, there is marginal or no benefit. For the aim problems, the speed-up ration ranges from less than 4 times to about 500 times. The performance gain is especially significant in the unsatisfiable problems. In these cases, the dynamically-added clauses significantly prune the search space allowing the circuit to rule the problem unsatisfiable much earlier.

5 Related Work

Prior work includes several proposals for solving SAT using reconfigurable hardware [9, 1]. Suyama et al. [9] have proposed their own SAT algorithm distinct from the Davis-Putnam approach. Their algorithm is characterized by the fact that at any point, a full (not partial) variable assignment is evaluated. While the authors propose heuristics to prune the search space, they admit that the number of states visited in their approach can be 8x larger than the basic Davis-Putnam approach.

The work by Abramovici and Saab also proposed a configurable hardware SAT solver [1]. Their approach basically amounts to an implementation of a PODEM-based [5] algorithm in reconfigurable hardware. PODEM is typically used to solve test generation problems. Unlike PODEM, which relies on controlling and observing primary inputs and outputs, Davis-Putnam's efficient data structures also capture relationships between *internal* variables in a circuit; this reduces the state space visited and the run time significantly [6, 2, 7].

In prior work, we designed a SAT solver based on the basic Davis-Putnam algorithm, and implemented it on an IKOS Virtualogic Emulator This work was the first to publish results based on an actual implementation in programmable logic. We also designed an improved algorithm that uses a modified version of non-chronological backtracking to prune the search space [10]. This method indirectly identifies predecessors for a conflict, but is not as efficient as the direct conflict analysis we evaluate here. Finally, none of the prior configurable SAT solvers have employed dynamic clause addition.

Most importantly, all the prior projects involve generating formula-specific solver circuits. In these approaches, the compilation overhead can not be amortized among many runs. While they may have benefits on some long-running problems, the approach we describe here is much amenable to direct module generation and avoids much of the compiler overhead of prior work. We hope the work on fast module generation and the modular design methodology may lead to wider application of these input-specific hardware approaches.

6 Conclusions

This paper has described a new approach that takes advantage of dynamic reconfiguration for accelerating Boolean satisfiability solvers in configurable hardware. The design we evaluate is highly modular and very amenable to direct module generation. One of the key improvements of this design is its ability to dynamically add clauses. Overall, the approach has potential speedups up to 500X versus our previous configurable approach without dynamic reconfiguration. More broadly, this hardware design demonstrates the application of machine learning techniques using dynamically reconfigurable hardware.

References

1. M. Abramovici and D. Saab. Satisfiability on Reconfigurable Hardware. In *Seventh International Workshop on Field Programmable Logic and Applications*, Sept. 1997.
2. S. Chakradhar, V. Agrawal, and S. Rothweiler. A transitive closure algorithm for test generation. *IEEE Transactions on Computer-Aided Design of Integrated Circuits and Systems*, 12(7):1015–1028, July 1993.
3. M. Davis and H. Putnam. A Computing Procedure for Quantification Theory. *Journal of the ACM*, 7:201–215, 1960.
4. DIMACS. Dimacs challenge benchmarks and ucsc benchmarks. Available at ftp://Dimacs.Rut-gers.EDU/pub/challenge/sat/benchmarks/cnf.
5. P. Goel. An Implicit Enumeration Algorithm to Generate Tests for Combinational Logic Circuits. *IEEE Transactions on Computers*, C30(3):215–222, March 1981.
6. T. Larrabee. Test Pattern Generation Using Boolean Satisfiability. In *IEEE Transactions on Computer-Aided Design*, volume 11, pages 4–15, January 1992.
7. J. Silva and K. Sakallah. GRASP-A New Search Algorithm for Satisfiability. In *IEEE ACM International Conference on CAD-96*, pages 220–227, Nov. 1996.
8. P. Stephan, R. Brayton, and A. Sangiovanni-Vincentelli. *Combinational Test Generation Using Satisfiability*. Department of Electrical Engineering and Computer Sciences, University of California at Berkeley, 1992. UCB/ERL Memo M92/112.
9. T. Suyama, M. Yokoo, and H. Sawada. Solving Satisfiability Problems on FPGAs. In *6th Int'l Workshop on Field-Programmable Logic and Applications*, Sept. 1996.
10. P. Zhong, P. Ashar, S. Malik, and M. Martonosi. Using reconfigurable computing techniques to accelerate problems in the cad domain: A case study with boolean satisfiability. In *35th Design Automation Conference*, 1998.
11. P. Zhong, M. Martonosi, P. Ashar, and S. Malik. Accelerating boolean satisfiability with configurable hardware. In *FCCM'98*, 1998.

Modular Exponent Realization on FPGAs

Jüri Põldre | Kalle Tammemäe | Marek Mandre

Tallinn Technical University
Computer Engineering Department
jp@pld.ttu.ee

Abstract. The article describes modular exponent calculations used widely in cryptographic key exchange protocols. The measures for hardware consumption and execution speed based on argument bit width and algorithm rank are created. The partitioning of calculations is analyzed with respect to interconnect signal numbers and added delay. The partitioned blocks are used for implementation approximations of two different multiplier architectures. Examples are provided for 3 families of FPGAs: XC4000, XC6200 and FLEX10k

1 Introduction

Modular exponent calculations are widely used in Secure Electronic Trading (SET) protocols for purchasing goods over Internet. One transaction in SET protocol requires the calculation of six full-length exponents. Because of advances in factoring and ever-increasing computing power the exponent size has to be at least 1024 bits now and predicted 2048 in 2005 to guarantee the security [1].

The calculations with very large integers are managed in software by breaking them down to the host processor word size. The exponent is usually calculated by progressive squaring method and takes $2 \times N$ modular multiplications to complete. One modular multiply takes at least $(A / W) \times (N \times N)$ instructions to complete, where N is argument bit length, W is host processor word size and $A>1$ is a constant depending on the algorithm used. As exponent calculation demands N multiplications that leaves us with N^3 complexity.

As of now the need for SET transactions is about one per second. It is estimated to reach over 200 per second in servers after 18 months. Today the common PC Pentium 200 MHz processors can calculate one exponent in 60 msec. Taking 6 exponents per SET transaction we have 100% load in 2¾ SET transactions per second.

As the calculations are very specific it is not likely that they will become a part of general-purpose processors, although internal study by Intel Corporation has been carried out to find possible instruction set expansion for cryptographic applications in 1997. Sadly only abstract of that is available for public review. A separate unit in system for cryptographic calculations also increases security by creating "secure area" for sensitive information.

Recently many companies have come up with the product to solve this problem. Usually these consist of RISC processor core, flash ROM, RAM and exponent accelerator unit. Several products on the market are ranging from Rainbow CryptoSwift with 54 msec to Ncipher Nfast 3 msec per exponent. They also have different physical interfaces – Cryptoswift uses PCI bus and Ncipher is a SCSI device. Cryptoswift uses ARM RISC processors and Ncipher ASICs. Several other designs have been created including authors IDEA/RSA processor [7]. Prices for these products range from $1600 – $3000 per device.

Standards are being developed and new algorithms proposed, so the design lifespan of these accelerators is quite low. A solution here is to use a cryptography system library with certain functions being accelerated in reconfigurable hardware – FPGA.

FPGA based accelerator board supplied with PCI-interface is universal device, which can be plugged into any contemporary PC for accelerating RSA-key encoding-decoding task. Considering the fact, that Sun has already included PCI-interface into Ultrasparc workstation configuration, the board suits there as well, reducing computation load of main processor(s).

In the course of this work we will look into accelerating exponent calculations using two different methods. Both of them use progressive squaring, Montgomery reduction, and redundantly represented partial product accumulation. The difference is in the architecture of modular multiplier unit.

In following pages we:

- Select the appropriate exponentiation (multiplication) algorithm.
- Define the hardware building blocks for the algorithm.
- Analyze two different architectural approaches using the blocks from previous stage.

In every step the alternative approaches and reasoning behind selection are presented.

2 Modular exponentiation

will be handled by right-left binary method. It gives the possibility to run two multiplications per iteration in parallel and thus half the execution time if sufficient hardware resources are available. It can also be utilized easily for interleaved calculations as two arguments (N, P) are same for both multiplications

To find $C := M^e \bmod N$ proceed as follows:

Input:	base M; exponent e; moduli N;
Output:	$C := M^e \bmod N$
Temporary variable:	P
Exponent size:	h
Ith bit of e:	e_i

Algorithm:

1. $C := 1; P := M$
2. **for** $i = 0$ **to** $h - 2$
2a. **if** $e_i = 1$ **then** $C := C \times P \pmod{N}$
2b. $P := P \times P \pmod{N}$
3. **if** $e_{h-1} = 1$ **then** $C := C \times P \pmod{N}$
4. **return** C

Further possibilities for reducing number of multiplications are not considered in this work. These methods involve precalculated tables and short exponents [6]. The support for precalculated tables can be added at higher level of hierarchy using host processor. For the course of the article let the time for exponentiation be equal to number of bits in the exponent:

$$T_{exp} = h \times T_{mult} \tag{1}$$

h: number of bits in exponent,
T_{exp}: time for exponent calculation,
T_{mult}: time for multiplication.

3 Modular multiplication

is the only operation in exponentiation loop. The modular multiplication is multiplication followed by dividing the result by moduli and returning quotient:

$$C = A \times B \bmod N \tag{2}$$

$T = A \times B$
$Q = T / N$
$C = T - Q \times N$

We can calculate the multiplication and then divide by moduli, but these operations can also be interleaved. This reduces the length of operands and thus hardware consumption. The algorithms rank k is the amount of bits handled at one step.

The main updating line in interleaved k-ary modular multiply algorithm is:

$$S_{i+1} = S_i << k + A \times B_i - Q_i \times N \tag{3}$$

Not going any further into details [2] let us point out that most time-consuming operation is to find Q_i, what is S_{i-1} / N. Several approaches have been proposed. All of them use approximation to find Q_i. Some of them involve multiplication, others table lookup. All of them consume silicon resources, but mainly they increase cycle time significantly.

In 1985 Montgomery [3] proposed new method for solving the problem of quotient digit calculation. After some preprocessing it is possible to calculate the loop updating line as:

$$S_{i+1} = S_i >> k + \tilde{A} \times B_i + Q_I \times \tilde{N} \qquad (4)$$

Q_i is equal to k least significant bits of partial sum S_i. This comes at a price of transforming the initial arguments and moduli to Montgomery residue system and the result back. The transformations can be carried out using the same Montgomery modular multiplication operation (arguments conversion constant $2^{(2 \times h)}$ mod N is needed, but it can easily be calculated in software). Another restriction is that 2^k and N should be relatively prime. As application area is cryptography even N will never occur and thus this condition is satisfied.

The exponentiation process now takes two more multiplications to complete for transforming arguments. Because argument length h is usually large (more than 1024 bits) it is *ca* two tenths of percent. This introduced delay is negligible taken into account the cycle speedup and hardware savings.

4 Hardware blocks

To describe hardware architectures the main building blocks for them are needed. Montgomery multiplication (4) needs multiplication, summation and shift operators. Because the argument sizes are large and result is not needed in normal form before the end of the exponentiation it is reasonable to use redundant representation of arguments - 2 digits to represent one. The exact value of the digit is the sum of these two components.

Double amount of hardware is needed for handling redundant numbers, but it postpones carry ripple time until the result is needed in normal form. Even if we would construct a fast adder (CLA) it spends more than twice hardware and definitely has larger power consumption.

Shifting these digits is straightforward and involves shifting both numbers.

For addition normal full-adder cells can be used. Two such cells forms an adder for redundant numbers what is called 4-2 adder (Add4-2):

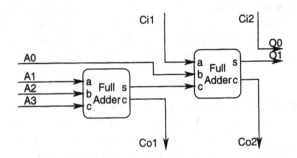

Fig. 1. 4-2 adder from two full adders

Connecting carries $ci \rightarrow co$ of h such blocks generates h-bit redundant adder. As it can be seen from the figure the maximal delay for such addition does not depend on argument length and equals to two full-adder cell delays.

Before making multiplier we will look at multiplicand recording. If both positive and negative numbers are allowed in multiplication partial product accumulation, then the number of terms can be halved. This process is called Booth encoding. Following table should illustrate the idea:

Table 1. Booth recording of 3-bit multiplicand

B	Term1	Term2
0	0	4×0
1	1	4×0
2	2	4×0
3	-1	4×1
4	0	4×1
5	1	4×1
6	2	4×1
7	-1	4×2

Calculating multiple of $A \times B$ in usual way requires 3 terms: A, $A \ll 1$, $A \ll 2$. By recording B differently we can do away with only two. The multiplication constants for terms are 0,1,2 and -1. Multiplications by $2,4,2^k$ can be handled with shift. Negation uses complementary code: $-A = ($not $A) + 1$. Carry inputs to partial sum accumulation tree structure are utilized for supplying additional carries.

One term of partial sum is thrown away by adding 4-input multiplexers (Mux4). The same method can be used to make $5 \rightarrow 3$, $7 \rightarrow 4$, ... etc. encodings. Generally we will have:

$$(N\text{-}1) \rightarrow N/2 \qquad\qquad (5)$$

Booth recorder is required for generating multiplexer control information from multiplier bits. As this circuit is small and only one is needed for multiplier we will not look into that more deeply.

The multiplier consists of Booth encoder, shifter and redundant adder tree. It has redundantly represented base N, Booth recorded multiplicand B and redundant result O. The terms from Booth encoders will be accumulated using tree of 4-2 adders. Carry inputs and outputs are for expansion purposes and for negation control at LSB end of digit.

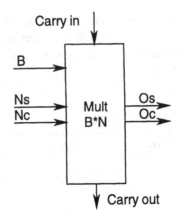

Fig. 2. $B \times N$ multiplier

The total component delay of this circuit is the sum of multiplexer delay and delay introduced by 4-2 adder tree. This delay is proportional to tree depth or log2 of size of B in digits. We can write delay as following:

$$T_{mult} = T_{mux4} + \log_2(\text{size}(B)) \times T_{add4\text{-}2} \tag{6}$$

T_{mult}	Time for multiplication.
T_{mux4}	Mux4 cell delay.
$T_{add4\text{-}2}$	Add4-2 cell delay.
Size(B)	size of Booth recorded number in digits.

The number of elements required for building such block is:

$$Count_{Mux4} = N \times 2 \times \text{size}(B) \tag{7}$$

$$Count_{Add4\text{-}2} = N \times 2 \times (\log_2(\text{size}(B)) - 1) + 1 \tag{8}$$

Here is an example to clarify the formulas:

Device is 4 booth digits × 8 bits or 7 × 8 bit multiplier. The result is calculated in $T_{mux4} + 2 \times T_{add4\text{-}2}$ time units. The number of 4 - input multiplexers is $8 \times 2 \times 4$ and the count of 4 - 2 adders is 16 + 1. The multiplier structure for one output bit is described in figure below.

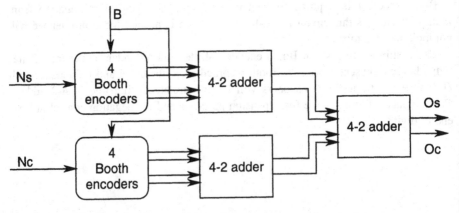

Fig. 3. 7×8 multiplier structure

Each 4-2 adder generates two carries. Booth encoder needs higher bits of previous operand to generate terms, adding two times the size of B carries for both input operands. The total is thus $3 \times 2 + 4 \times 2 + 2 = 16$ carries in and 16 carries out. The formula for counting carry signal numbers is:

$$(\log_2(size(b)) + size(b) + 1) \times 2 \qquad (9)$$

5 FPGA resources

For FPGA realizations the resource allocation formulas for these operators are needed. We will consider 3 series: Xilinx 4000, Xilinx 6200 and Altera FLEX10K. As all previously described blocks contain simple routing what is connected only to closest neighbors we will ignore the routing expenses in calculations and concentrate in CLB count.

The above described two operators demand the following hardware resources:

- MUX4 (may be built from two 2MUX cells).
- ADD4-2 (consists of two full-adder cells).

The following table will sum the resources needed to build these blocks in each of mentioned families:

Table 2. Cell hardware requirements

Cell name	XC4000	XC6200	FLEX10K
MUX4	1	2	2
ADD4-2	1*	6	2

* Actually it is 2 ADD4-2 cells per 2 blocks, because one block implements 2-bit full adder.

6 Architectural solutions

Having the blocks let us now consider different architectures for implementation.

6.1 Traditional k-ary algorithm

Calculates the Montgomery multiplication by directly implementing the loop updating statement:

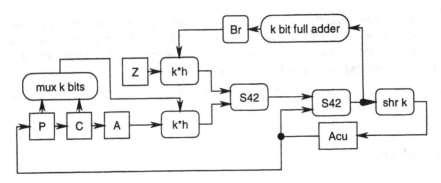

Fig. 4. Traditional architecture for calculating Montgomery multiplication

Z, A, ACU are h bit registers. $k \times h$ multiplier forming $B_I \times A$ is the multiplier cell described above. $Q_i \times Z$ is the same cell with only half of hardware, because Z is in normal (non-redundant) representation. Two 4-2 adders (S42) accumulate the results. By adding registers in accumulator structure it is possible to interleave two multiplications as described earlier. Control unit must multiplex B_i each clock tick from P or C. At the end of calculations C and P are updated. The updating of P is done conditionally depending on value of e_i, the ith bit of exponent.

6.2 K-ary systolic architecture

This approach uses array of identical blocks. Each block calculates digit(s) of result. By connecting these blocks it is possible to generate a hardware structure of arbitrary bitlength. Remarkable features of this approach are expandability and relative ease of construction. Once you have mastered the primitive block it is easy to place them on CLB array or silicon. The structure of systolic array multiplier consisting of $h / (2 \times k)$ cells implementing (4) is:

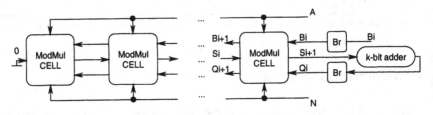

Fig. 5. Systolic multiplier structure

In each cell two terms of partial sum are calculated and summed [5]. Sum term is represented redundantly, but k-bit full adder converts it back to normal form. Therefore cell contains four $k \times k$ non-redundant input multipliers and accumulator tree of 4-2 adders (Fig 6). B, Q and S are k bit registers. Cell also contains carry memory what adds twice the number of S42 block count registers to cell memory requirements.

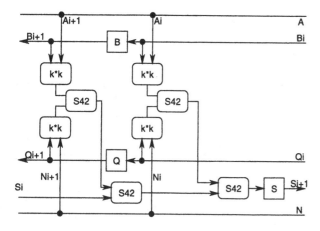

Fig. 6.. One systolic array cell

7 Analysis of implementations

Both the systolic and classical solution calculate the statement (2) with the same delay. As systolic solution is accumulating 2 terms it ads one S42 delay. Thus the formulas for calculating cycle length are (calculated in 4-2 adder delays):

$$T_{classic} = \log_2(k/2) + 1 \tag{10}$$

$$T_{systol} = \log_2(k/2) + 2 \tag{11}$$

We can further decrease time by adding registers at S42 outputs and using quotient pipeline [4]. This reduces cycle delay to one S42 cell delay. It can be reduced further, but registers in ASIC are expensive. This is not the case with FPGAs because the ratio of register/logic is high and flip-flops are already there.

Systolic array is made of $h / (2 \times k)$ cells and each cell consists of four $k \times k$ multipliers. Comparing that to standard approach with $1\frac{1}{2} k \times h$ multipliers:

$$4 \times (k \times k \times \frac{1}{2}) \times H/ (k \times 2) = 2 \times \frac{1}{2} \times k \times h = k \times h \tag{12}$$

In systolic array we have the result of multiplication in normal format, therefore we need 1/3 less hardware. The following table sums the hardware consumption for both architectures for 3 different algorithm ranks (k)

Table. 3. Hardware (CLB count) requirements for exponent calculator

bits	k	XC4000 systol	XC4000 classic	XC6200 systol	XC6200 classic	FLEX10K systol	FLEX10K classic	cycles systol	cycles classic
512	2	4096	6144	16384	24576	8192	12288	256	128
512	4	7168	10752	26624	39936	14336	21504	128	64
512	8	12288	18432	40960	61440	24576	36864	64	32
1024	2	8192	12288	32768	49152	16384	24576	512	256
1024	4	14336	21504	53248	79872	28672	43008	256	128
1024	8	24576	36864	81920	122880	49152	73728	128	64

The systolic structure calculates result in $2 \times N / k$ steps. For exponent calculations it is possible to either use twice the hardware or run two multiplications sequentially. In the table above hardware consumption for single multiplication is provided.

Cycle speed is increased by having to partition the design on several FPGAs, for large exponents do not fit into single FPGA. This additional delay consists of CLB→IOB→PCB→IOB→CLB path. Each component adds it's own delay. We will use the 20 ns safe figure here for this entire path. Thus the cycle times for chosen families are:

$$T_{4000} = 20 + (1 + \log_2(k)) \times 5 \qquad (13)$$

$$T_{6200} = 20 + (2 + 3 \times \log_2(k)) \times 4$$

$$T_{FLEX10K} = 20 + (2 + 2 \times \log_2(k)) \times 5$$

First term is communication delay, then 4mux delay for Booth encoder and finally logarithmic component for accumulator. The numbers behind parenthesis is CLB delay added to closest neighbor routing of fastest member in the family. These are optimistic values, but as structure is regular and routing is between the closest neighbors the expected results should not differ from calculated more than 10%. The values in the following table are exponent calculation times in msec.

Table 4. Exponent calculation timing

bits	k	XC4000 systol	XC4000 classic	XC6200 systol	XC6200 classic	FLEX10K systol	FLEX10K classic	cycles systol	cycles classic
512	2	3,9	2,0	5,2	2,6	5,2	2,6	256	128
512	4	2,3	1,1	3,4	1,7	3,3	1,6	128	64
512	8	1,3	0,7	2,1	1,0	2,0	1,0	64	32
1024	2	15,7	7,9	21,0	10,5	21,0	10,5	512	256
1024	4	9,2	4,6	13,6	6,8	13,1	6,6	256	128
1024	8	5,2	2,6	8,4	4,2	7,9	3,9	128	64

For partitioning the largest circuits from each family were used. These are at the current moment:

- XC6264 (16384 CLBs).
- XC4025 (1024 CLBs).
- EPF10K100 (4992 CLBs).

Utilizing them the following number of chips is needed for implementation (table 5). To compare the speed-up of calculations the data from RSA Inc. Bsafe cryptographic library is in table 6.

Table 5. Number of ICs for implementation

bits	k	XC4000 systol	XC4000 classic	XC6200 systol	XC6200 classic	FLEX10K systol	FLEX10K classic
512	2	4,0	6,0	1,0	1,5	1,6	2,5
512	4	7,0	10,5	1,6	2,4	2,9	4,3
512	8	12,0	18,0	2,5	3,8	4,9	7,4
1024	2	8,0	12,0	2,0	3,0	3,3	4,9
1024	4	14,0	21,0	3,3	4,9	5,7	8,6
1024	8	24,0	36,0	5,0	7,5	9,8	14,8

Table 6. Bsafe cryptolibrary execution benchmarks in seconds

Operand length in bits	Intel Pentium 90 MHz	Power Macintosh 80 MHz	Sun SparcStation 4 110 MHz	Digital AlphaStation 255 MHz
768	0.066	.220	.212	0.024
1024	.140	.534	.461	0.043

8 Conclusions

In this paper we have analyzed the implementation of modular exponent calculator on FPGAs. The appropriate algorithm for exponentiation and multiplication has been selected. Realizations on three families of FPGAs were considered.

While two XC6216 circuits would nicely fit onto PCI board and give over 10 times acceleration of calculations we must bear in mind that these circuits are quite expensive.

Maybe simpler approach would help? If we use 1-bit-at-a-time algorithm we can fit 1024 bit calculator into one package. $k = 1$ classic structure demands two 4-2 adders per bit and requires H steps to complete. 1024 bit exponent is calculated with $1024 \times 1024 \times 2$ cycles. As the structure is simpler the cycle delay can be decreased on condition that we stay in limits of one package. That leaves us with 512 bit for XC4K, 1024 bit for XC6264 and 2500 for FLEX10K. The clock frequency can now be lifted up to one CLB delay plus routing between closest neighbors. This can be as high 100 MHz calculating one exponent in 20 msec. This is comparable with Digital 255 MHz processor. This is approximately 50 Kgates of accelerator hardware running at twice slower speed.

As to now programmable hardware is still too expensive to be included on motherboards but these figure shows a clear tendency that the devices together with hardware-software co-development system and downloadable modules will become a part of functioning computer system in nearest future.

References

[1] *Schneier, Bruce. "Applied Cryptography Second Edition: protocols, algorithms and source code in C", 1996, John Wiley and Sons, Inc.*

[2] *Ç. K. Koç, "RSA Hardware implementation", RSA laboratories, 1995.*

[3] *Peter L. Montgomery. "Modular multiplication without trial division", Mathematics of Computation, 44(170):519-521. April 1985.*

[4] *Holger Orup. "Simplifying Quotient Determination in High-Radix Modular Multiplication", Aarhus University, Denmark. 1995.*

[5] *Colin D. Walter. "Systolic Modular Multiplication" IEEE transactions on Computers, C-42(3)376-378, March 1993.*

[6] *B.J.Phillips, N.Burgess. "Algorithms of Exponentiation of Long Integers – A survey of Published Algorithms", The University of Adelaide, May 1996.*

[7] *Jüri Põldre, Ahto Buldas: "A VLSI implementation of RSA and IDEA encryption engine", Proceedings of NORCHIP'97 conference. November 1997.*

Cost Effective 2x2 Inner Product Processors

Béla Fehér, Gábor Szedő

Department of Measurement and Information Systems
Technical University of Budapest
H-1521Budapest, Müegyetem rkp. 9.
feher@mit.bme.hu, szedo@mit.bme.hu

Abstract. Direct hardware realizations of digital filters on FPGA devices require efficient implementation of the multiplier modules. The distributed arithmetic form of the inner product processor array offers the possibility of merging the individual partial products, which leads to reduced logic complexity. Although this possibility can be exploited mainly in case of fixed coefficient multiplication and larger data set, for non-fixed, small sized, 2x2 arrays the integrated functional unit also results in significant achievements in area savings, especially in case of complex multiplication or Givens rotations in orthogonal filter structures. The proposed inner product processor uses the Canonical Signed Digit code for the representation of the multiplier operands.

Introduction

Hardware realization of digital filters allows application of special arithmetic units and number representation. In the past decade, many methods have been proposed to reduce the hardware complexity of the digital filter implementations. The FPGA technology widened these possibilities and opened the way for new methods, as the exceptional flexibility and user programmability of these devices made easier to synthesize any kind of coefficient dependent arithmetic circuitry.

FPGA implementations of fixed coefficient multiplication can benefit from the simplification of the general array multipliers based on different methods. For single operand hardwired operations the most obvious algorithms use the Canonical Signed Digit (CSD) code representation [1] of the fixed coefficient. The CSD code belongs to the family of Signed Binary Number Representation (SBNR), in which the coefficient value is given as a sum of signed power-of-two terms. (Without loss of generality, in the following, coefficient values are assumed to be integer. Fractional or mixed coefficient values can be made integer by multiplying it by an appropriate constant value.)

$$x = \sum_{r=0}^{B-1} s(r)2^r \qquad s(r) = -1, 0, 1 \qquad (1)$$

Generally, the SBNR is a redundant number representation, which means, that more than one possible digit series can represent the same numerical value. The CSD code on the other hand, is unique, and has the special feature, that it contains the minimal number of nonzero digits, such a way, that the product of two consecutive digits are zero. The average numbers of the non-zero digits are B/3.

For multiple operand, inner product (IP) type operation the different versions of the Distributed Arithmetic (DA) arrangement offers significant savings of logic resources. The well-known memory Look-Up Table (LUT) based algorithm of DA [2] uses pre-computed partial product sums to evaluate the result. This memory-based DA solution can be used in non-fixed coefficient applications also, only the appropriate LUT content should be generated and loaded to the RAM based memory. The number of the input data components determines the necessary size of the LUT memory, but the trade off of arithmetic and memory resources allows dramatic reduction of the memory size. Most of the current digital filter implementations are based on this method and its different variant. The typical basic IP module size is selected to 4 or 5 inputs, and the partial results are summarized by post adder stages.

Another DA architecture was introduced in [3], especially for FPGA implementations. That method is based on the CSD representation of the individual coefficients, and the whole IP architecture built up from only arithmetic components. The algorithm exploits the available digit pattern coincidences between the CSD codes of the coefficients. Using this algorithm the arithmetic complexity was transformed to the routing complexity. In case of FPGAs, where the available logic and routing resources are pre-determined by the internal architecture, this proved to be a useful transformation. Bit serial implementation of the CSD based IP functional units needs some pre-processing, for the calculation of the optimal order of the partial products.

Advantages of CSD representation can be retained for smaller, 2x2 size IP calculations, with variable operand type multiplications also. In CSD codes, the maximum number of nonzero digits are B/2, so on every second digit position the numerical value of the digits are zero. If one pair of the operands in a 2x2 IP is re-coded to CSD, it is possible to combine the two operations into one IP processors array. In this array the complexity of the basic multiplier cells are a little more complicated than in the traditional array multiplier, because the selection of the actual operand is necessary to generate the active partial product terms. If this overhead can be tolerated in the FPGA logic cell architecture (i.e. not requires more cells, than the original multipliers), than CSD based 2x2 IP processors are cost effective.

Many digital signal processing algorithm is based on calculations with complex numbers. Multiplication of complex numbers needs 4 real multiplications and two real additions/subtractions, according to the following expression (2).

$$(P + jQ) = (X + jY)(x + jy)$$
$$P = Xx - Yy$$
$$Q = Xy + Yx \qquad (2)$$

This complex multiplication is the kernel of the FFT butterfly operation and it can be observed in the signal flow graph of the orthogonal digital filters like the lattice filters [4] or resonator based filters [5]. In digital filtering the normalized complex multiplication is frequently called as Givens rotation. The computational flow graph of a normalized lattice filter stage from [4] is shown on Fig. 1.

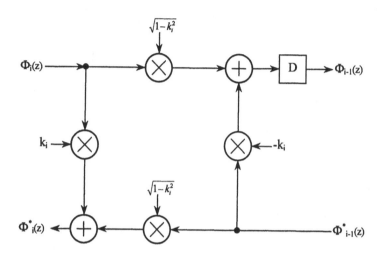

Fig. 1. The computation kernel of the normalized lattice filter

For the execution of one iteration, two 2x2 IP operation is necessary, of which the multiplier coefficients are the same, only the two multiplicand should be exchanged by each other.

2. The 2x2 size inner product multiplier array

2.1. The general structure

The 2x2 inner product array is based on the CSD code of the multiplier operands. As was mentioned in the earlier section, in the CSD code the numerical values are represented as signed power-of-two terms. The number of non-zero digits is upper bounded by B/2, and there are no two consecutive non-zero digits. The 2x2 size IP multiplier array exploits this feature and merges two independent CSD codes based multiplier. The general block diagram of the array is shown on Fig.2. The unit consists of two main blocks, the multiplier array and the CSD decoding circuitry. The function of the unit is given by (3).

$$P = Xx + Yy + C \qquad (3)$$

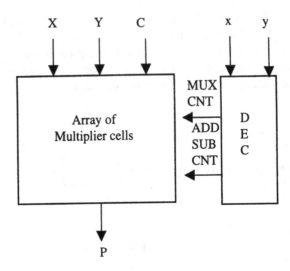

Fig. 2. The general block diagram of the 2x2 IP module

The array of multiplier cells directly calculates the sum of the two products. From the point of view of the operation, there is a slight difference on the internal rules of the ordering of the partial products from the Xx and Yy multiplications. The x multiplier operand is the master and it has priority over the y multiplier in the process of allocation of the partial product terms in the summation tree. The algorithm is the following: both multipliers are converted to CSD code. Two bit pairs $\{x_{Di}, x_{Si}\}$ and $\{y_{Di}, y_{Si}\}$ in every digit position represent the signed power-of-two terms of the internal CSD code words. One bit, x_{Di} and y_{Di}, stands for the non-zero digit, the other, x_{Si} and y_{Si}, designates the sign of them, respectively. These bit-pairs will determine the functionality of the array of the multiplier cells. Four different operation mode has been defined.

If there is no active digits in either of the two multipliers in a given binary weight, then there is now new partial product to summarize, so the array of multiplier cells will just pass the earlier partial products sums with the appropriate scaling.

If the x multiplier has no active digit at a given binary weight ($x_{Di}=0$), but the y multiplier has ($y_{Di}\neq0$), then that row of the array of multiplier cells is available for the Yy partial product summation.

If the x multiplier has an active digit at a given binary weight ($x_{Di}\neq0$), then that row of the array of multiplier cells will accumulate the partial product of the Xx operation, independently of the state of y_{Di}.

If in the last case the y_{Di} digit is also non-zero, then the execution of this Yy partial product calculation is postponed or shifted to the next available row of cells. The next row of the array multiplier cells will be always available, because of the properties of the CSD code.

This merged 2x2 IP module is also capable to add a C input constant value to the calculated product sum.

2.2. The multiplier cells

The basic cell of the multiplier array is similar to other binary multipliers. At each row in the array, one partial product of two input operands is generated and summed with the sum of the earlier partial products. Because of the signed properties of the CSD code digits, parallel adders/subtracters should be used in this array module. The parallel adders/subtracters can be realized by special arithmetic configuration modes of the FPGA logic cells, which results in efficient and high-speed operation. The configuration of the basic cell is shown on Fig. 3.

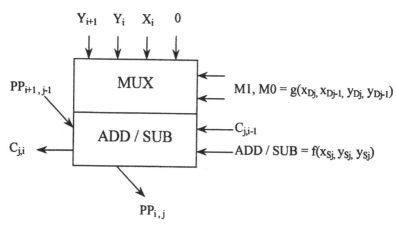

Fig. 3. The operation of the multiplier array cell

The modified multiplier cell consists of a 4:1 multiplexer and a controllable adder/subtracter. Inputs of the cell in the ith column and j^{th} row of the array are the X_i, Y_i, Y_{i+1} multiplicand bits and 0. The configuration of the multiplier cell is controlled by the logic functions of the CSD digits of the x and y multiplier operands, denoted by the f and g Boolean functions. These functions are illustrated on Fig. 4. and Fig. 5., respectively.

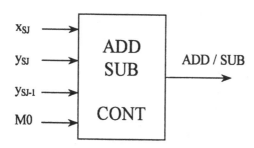

Fig. 4. The ADD/SUB control function of the multiplier cell

The ADD/SUB function output is simply the x_{sj} bit, if the multiplexer selects the X_i input (M0=0), in the other case the OR function of the two consecutive y_{sj} and y_{sj} sign bit. For positive or zero digits, the sign bits are zero, and for negative digits, the sign bits are one. Because these are neighboring digits of the CSD digits of y, only one could be active, so the OR function will properly determine the necessary operation in the cell.

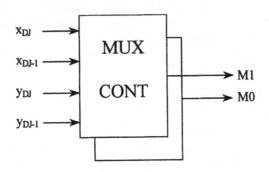

Fig. 5. The multiplexer control function of the basic cell

The MUX function is given in Table 1.

Table 1. The multiplexer control function

x_{Dj}	x_{Dj-1}	y_{Dj}	y_{Dj-1}	M1	M0	Selected
0	0	0	x	0	0	0
0	1	0	0	0	0	0
0	x	1	0	0	1	Y_i
0	1	0	1	1	1	Y_{i+1}
1	x	X	x	1	0	X_i

The table lists the possible combinations of the digit patterns in the jth and $(j-1)^{th}$ binary weights. The first two rows shows the situations, when there is no necessary operation on the given cells, except the scale down of the earlier partial product sum.

As mentioned earlier, an active x_{Dj} overrides any other operation digit codes, and forces the selection of the X operand for the partial product calculation. This is shown in the last row of the table. The third row indicates the other situation, when x_{Dj} inactive and y_{Dj} active. The input of the ADD/SUB unit is the Y operand, independently from lower weight x_{Dj-1} digit.

The most complicated input selection is shown in the fourth row. In this case there was a conflict at the $(j-1)^{th}$ weight, what should be resolved in this level. The input operand in this case will be the downscaled Y operand, because actually it is summed at a higher weight, than the original y_{Dj-1} multplier digit determines it. The calculated and summed partial product is $(Y/2)(2\ y_{Dj-1})$. To preserve the accuracy at the least significant bit position of the Y multiplicand, the array of the multiplier cells are extended by one extra column to accommodate the right shifted operand.

2.3. The CSD decoding module

There are different possibilities to convert the binary representation of the x and y multipliers to CSD code. In the 2x2 IP processor a parallel version of the converter has been developed. The input multiplier operands are represented in two's complement data format. In this data format, every bit represents positive values of the binary power-of-two weights, except the most significant bit, which carries negative sense. Equation (4) shows this representation, for simplicity only for the x multiplier operand. (The y operand has the same converter module also.)

$$x = -b(B-1)2^{B-1} + \sum_{r=0}^{B-2} b(r)2^r \qquad b(r) = 0,1; \qquad (4)$$

The definition of the binary-CSD conversion algorithm is given in [1], from which the appropriate logic circuits of the converter can be derived. The block diagram of the converter is shown in Fig. 6. Two bits, the x_{Dj} and x_{Sj} digit and sign bits represent the signed binary digits.

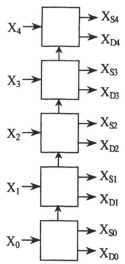

Fig. 6. The CSD converter module of the x multiplier operand

The output of the parallel converter will determine the partial product summation in the array of the multiplier cells. The complexity of the converter logic is comparable to any other arithmetic type circuits. It can be realized with a three input, two output block, with the appropriate cascading connection between the successive stages of the circuit.

Conclusion

The proposed CSD multiplier directly calculates xX+yY or xX-yY as necessary. The CSD code of the x and y multipliers can be calculated on the fly using parallel converter modules. In case of multiplication of complex numbers or Givens rotation, two 2x2 IP calculation is necessary. Simple exchange at the X and Y multiplicand inputs ensures the availability of the second product sum also.

It should be noted, that in case of adaptive applications, where the multiplier parameters are determined externally, the CSD conversion can be executed off-line, and directly loaded by the main computer into the multiplier array configuration control register of the reconfigurable co-processor board. This allows the elimination of the CSD decoder circuits.

The CSD type multiplier module can be used with fixed coefficient multiplication also. In this later case the maximal reduction of the logic complexity will available. This hardwired multipliers will need only some of the ADD/SUB units. The CSD code converters, the associated control logic and the input multiplexers of the multiplier cells can be cancelled. As a consequence, the proposed CSD IP module provides a cost effective alternative in realization of arithmetic functions in DSP, neural network or other highly computation intensive applications.

References

1. Reitwiesner, G. W.: Binary Arithmetic. Advances in Computers, vol.1.pp.232-308. Academic Press 1960.
2. White, S.A.: Applications of Distributed Arithmetic to Digital Signal Processing: A Tutorial Review. IEEE ASSP Magazine, July 1989. pp. 4-19.
3. Feher, B.: Efficient Synthesis of Distributed Vector Multipliers. 19th EUROMICRO Conference, September 6-9, 1993 Barcelona. Microprocessors and Microprogramming J., Vol. 38. No. 1-5. pp. 345-350.
4. Chung, J-G., Parhi, K. K.: Pipelined Lattice and Wave Digital Recursive Filters, Kluwer Academic Press 1996.
5. Péceli, G.:Resonator Based Filters, IEEE Trans. on Circuits Syst., vol. CAS-36, no. 1. Pp.156-159. Jan. 1989.

A Field-Programmable Gate-Array System for Evolutionary Computation

Tsutomu Maruyama, Terunobu Funatsu and Tsutomu Hoshino

Institute of Engineering Mechanics, University of Tsukuba
1-1-1 Ten-ou-dai Tsukuba Ibaraki 305 JAPAN
maruyama@darwin.esys.tsukuba.ac.jp

Abstract. In evolutionary computation, evolutionary operations are applied to a large number of individuals (genes) repeatedly. The computation can be pipelined (evolutionary operators) and parallelized (a large number of individuals) by dedicated hardwares, and high performance are expected. However, details of the operators depend on given problems and vary considerably. Systems with field programmable gate arrays can be reconfigured and realize the most suitable circuits for given problems. In this paper, we show that a hardware system with two FPGAs and SRAMs can achieve 50~130 times of speedup compared with a workstation (200MHz) in some evolutionary computation problems. With a larger system, we believe that we can realize more than 10 thousands of speedup.

1 Introduction

Evolutionary computation is based on ideas from genetic and evolutionary theory. In the computation, evolutionary operators (crossover, mutation, selection etc) are repeatedly applied to a large number of individuals (genes) in order to produce better individuals. One cycle of applying the operators is called a generation and more than several hundreds of generations are necessary.

The computation can be pipelined (evolutionary operators) and parallelized (a large number of individuals) by dedicated hardwares, and we can expect high performance gain. However, the details of the operators depend on given problems and vary considerably.

Field-Programmable Gate Array (FPGA) can reorganize its configuration and realize the most suitable circuits for given problems. The speed and size of FPGAs are drastically improved recently. Therefore a system with FPGAs is expected to achieve high performance for many problems of evolutionary computation. The size of FPGAs is especially important for evolutionary computation, because at least several dozens of individuals are necessary to form a small colony, and if we can not implement evolutionary operators that have interaction among the individuals in one chip, additional and fixed wirings on the printing board become necessary and this spoils the performance and flexibility of the system.

We are now developing a large system for evolutionary computation. To date, we evaluated the speedup by a system with two FPGAs and SRAMs using two problems of simple genetic algorithms and one problem of complex adaptive system. The speedup is 50~130 times compared with a workstation (SUN Ultra-Sparc 200MHz).

2 FPGA System

Figure 1 shows a block diagram of the FPGA system. In figure 1, FPGA-A executes evolutionary operators (crossover, mutation, selection), while FPGA-B executes evaluation of individuals. In the system, individuals stored in Memory-A (or B) are first read out, processed by FPGA-A/B and then stored back to Memory-B (or A). Scores of the individuals computed by FPGA-B are directly forwarded to FPGA-A. Memory-W is used as a work area by FPGA-B. Memory-C is used as a buffer in an island model of genetic algorithms (in section 3.3). All memories are SRAMs.

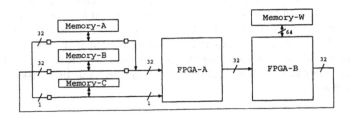

Fig. 1. The Block Diagram of the System

We are now designing the system using two FPGA boards (Power Medusa by Mitsubishi Microcomputer Software Inc.) with ALTERA EPF10K100. The board is square in shape and other FPGA boards and universal-boards can be connected to its four edges. All circuits described below work more than 33MHz. The critical path of the system is the speed of memory access.

3 Genetic Algorithms on the FPGA System

In this section, we show the results of two genetic algorithms. Many researches on genetic algorithms to date show that by combining with heuristic algorithms, genetic algorithms find good solutions in a limited amount of computation time. Simple genetic algorithms without any heuristic algorithms shown below require a lot of computation time (a large number of individuals and many generations), and are expected to converge to better solutions slowly.

3.1 Previous Works

Genetic algorithms have been implemented on FPGA systems in [1] and [2]. In [1], results of function optimization problems[3] were reported, and in [2], a travelling salesman problem was evaluated on Splash 2 [4]. The speedup by these researches was 3~5 times because of direct translation from software algorithms to hardware, and use of small size FPGAs.

3.2 Pipeline Processing of Genetic Algorithms

Figure 2 shows a pipeline for genetic algorithms. In figure 2, 32 individuals are processed in parallel bit by bit. Each individual is a bit string and the initial value of each bit is decided at random.

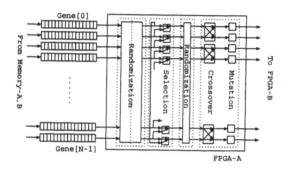

Fig. 2. Pipeline Stages for Genetic Algorithms

At the selection stage, tournament selection method[5] is used because of its simplicity. In tournament selection, first, two individuals are picked up at random from all individuals, and then better one is selected with a probability P. This method selects the best individual twice in average when P is 1.0, and has almost same features with rank selection [5]. In figure 2, individuals are shuffled at random in the randomization stage in stead of picking up individuals at random. This stage is implemented using a multi-stage network with some extra stages. Scores of two individuals are compared bit by bit at the selection stage, and one of them is selected. The scores are discarded at this stage, and the data of individuals are forwarded to next stages. After the selection, a randomization stage is used again in order to prevent same individuals from being sent to a same unit of the crossover stage. This stage can be much simpler than the first randomization stage.

The crossover stage exchanges a part of data between two individuals (for example, data from bit i to j are exchanged between two individuals). This stage can be implemented with counters, switches and pseudo random number generators. Each counter is set to a random number in a given range, and when the counter becomes 0, the switch is flipped. At the mutation stage, the value of each bit of individuals is changed at random with a probability Pm (for example, if the value of bit i is 0, it becomes 1). This stage can be implemented with pseudo random number generators and comparators.

3.3 Island Model

By using an island model[6], we can process more than 32 individuals on the system. In island models, individuals are divided into N groups of size M. Genetic algorithms are applied to each group, and some individuals are exchanged between the groups (for example one individual in every two generations). This model shows almost same or better results compared with a genetic algorithm applied to a group of size $M * N$. On the system, N groups are stored in Memory-A/B from different base addresses, and processed from group 0 to $N - 1$ sequentially. When storing individuals in each group into Memory-A/B, one individual is also stored into Memory-C in every other generations. In the next generation, when individuals in group K are read out from memory-A/B, an individual of group $(K + 1)\%M$ in memory-C is read out and used instead of an individual read out from memory-A/B.

3.4 Knapsack Problem

The goal of knapsack problem is to find the maximum value of objects in a knapsack, when N objects (each object has its own weight and value) are given and the weight of objects in the knapsack must be lower than threshold W.

Many sophisticated encoding methods have been proposed to date, but we choose the simplest one. The length of individuals is equal to N, and the i-th bit of each individual is 1 if object Ni is selected. In this encoding method, when the total amount of weight exceeds the threshold W, some penalty is added to the sum of values (if the penalty is too low, the search may converges to local optimum beyond the threshold, and too heavy penalty creates a steep cliff in the search space and make it difficult to find good solution for genetic algorithms).

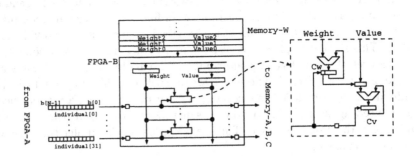

Fig. 3. The Evaluation Stage of Knapsack Problem

In the evaluation stage (figure 3), 64 adders (32 for value and 32 for weight) have to be implemented in FPGA-B (ALTERA 10K100). The width of the adders is 16-bit and they occupy about 21% of logic elements. The weight and value of each object are read out from Memory-W (suppose that they are stored in advance), and delivered to the adders. The value is added to registers Cv, and

Table 1. Performance: Knapsack Problem (32 individuals)

			time (sec)	speed up
Computation time in total	Workstation (Ultra-Sparc 200MHz)	lrand48()	16.6	0.0778
		random()	3.83	0.337
		mixed congruential method	1.29	1.00
	FPGA system (33MHz)	M-sequence	0.00956	135
Evaluation Stage	Workstation (200MHz) -		0.036	1.00
	FPGA system (33MHz) -		0.00865	41.6

the weight is subtracted from registers Cw (initialized to W in each evaluation) if the i-th bit of each individual is 1. When Cw becomes minus, the value begins to be subtracted from Cv. The penalty can be changed by shifting the value n-bit when the value is subtracted from Cv.

The maximum frequency of 16-bit adder of ALTERA EPF10K series is faster than 33 MHz, but we divided each adder into two adders. The upper half calculates the sum with one cycle delay. This makes the layout (especially the delivery delay of the weight and value) very easy. The speed down by this extra cycle is negligible when the problems size (the length of the individuals) is large enough (256 in the experiment below).

Table 1 shows the computation time for 1024 generations with 256 objects. In table 1, lrand48() and random() are functions in C standard libraries. In the mixed congruential method, all coefficients are chosen so that no multiply/divide operations are executed. In the FPGA system, M-sequence is used for pseudo random number generation. As shown in table 1, performance of workstation (SUN Ultra-Sparc 200MHz) depends on the methods for pseudo random number generation. We compared the performance of the FPGA system with the performance of the workstation with the mixed congruential method, because very high quality of pseudo random number sequence is not required in evolutionary computation. The speedup is 135 times in total computation time, and and 42 times in evaluation stage only (1.3 times per individual). This result shows that the pipelined and parallel processing works very well. With a larger number of individuals, we can expect to find better solutions. In this case, we can achieve more speedup by using a number of the systems and an island model that exchanges individuals between the systems.

3.5 Graph Partitioning Problem

The graph partitioning problem is to decompose a graph into two subgraphs so that the size of each subgraph is bounded and the cut size (the number of nets that connect to cells in both subgraphs) is minimized. Graph partitioning is an important process in many areas of computer science (e.g. design of circuits, mapping).

Suppose that cells are already divided into two groups (0 and 1). Then the cut size can benn counted as follows.

1. Prepare a table (Tn) that has net numbers connected to each cell.
2. Prepare a table T of size $NNets$ (the total number of nets). Each entry is 2-bit width and initialized to 0.
3. Reset counters CS and $G0$. CS counts the number of nets which connect two groups, and $G0$ counts the number of cells in group 0.
4. Apply the following procedures to all cells.
   (a) Increment $G0$ by 1, if cell Ci belongs to group 0.
   (b) Read out net numbers connected to cell Ci from the table Tn.
   (c) For all the net numbers, read out net status (Sk) from Table T and update Sk as follows.

Sk	New Sk	
	$Ci{=}{=}0$	$Ci{=}{=}1$
$00 \rightarrow$	01 ,	10
$01 \rightarrow$	01 ,	11
$10 \rightarrow$	11 ,	10
$11 \rightarrow$	11 ,	11

   New $Sk \leftarrow Sk \mid (1 << Ci)$

   (d) Increment CS by 1 when Sk becomes to 11 from 01 or 10, because this means that cells connected to net Nk belong to both groups.
   (e) Store Sk into Table T.
5. Calculate scores of all individuals. The score is given by the following in order to balance the number of cells in two groups.

   $$Si = CS/(G0*(\ Total\ Number\ of\ Cells\ -G0))$$

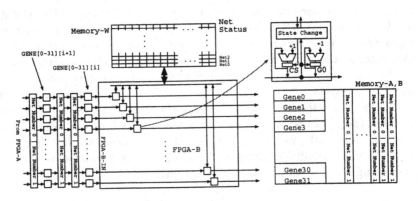

Fig. 4. The Evaluation Stage of the Graph Partitioning Problem

Figure 4 shows the evaluation stage of the graph partitioning problem. Memory-A and B store the table (Tn) (in figure 4, two net numbers are packed into one word). The contents of this table are read out by FPGA-A, and forwarded to FPGA-B. Memory-W stores the table T. The status of nets for 32 individuals are packed in one word of the table T. Table 2 shows the timing of the processing. In table 2,

Table 2. Timing of Evaluation of Graph Partitioning by FPGA-B

	FPGA-B-In	Memory-W	Status Update	
$t0$	$Na*$ & $Nb'*$			Na, Nb, Nc, Nd: net numbers
$t1$	Ci			Ci, Cj, Ck: cell numbers
$t2$		Read Sa		Sa, Sb, Sc, Sd: net status
$t3$		Read Sb	Update Sa	
$t4$	$Nc'*$ & $Nd*$	Write Sa	Update Sb	
$t5$	Cj	Write Sb		
$t6$	Ck	Read Sc		
$t7$		Read Sd	Update Sc	
$t8$	Na & Nc'	Write Sc	Update Sd	
$t9$		Write Sd		
$t10$		Read Sa		
$t11$		Read Sc	Update Sa	

Table 3. Performance: Graph Partitioning (32 individuals)

		time (sec)	speed up
Computation time	Workstation (Ultra-Sparc 200MHz)	2.13	1.00
in total	FPGA system (33MHz)	0.0261	81.6
Evaluation Stage	Workstation (Ultra-Sparc 200MHz)	1.24	1.00
	FPGA system (33MHz)	0.0261	47.5

1. Net numbers with $'$ (Nb' and Nc') are the last ones of the nets that are connected to Ci, Cj and Ck. FPGA-A begins to read net numbers for the next cell from Tn when these net numbers are read in.

2. * on net numbers means that the net is first accessed in the evaluation. By this bit, initialization of table T can be omitted.

As shown in table 2, one net can be processed in two clock cycles, because at least two cycles are necessary in order to read and store the status of each net, although update of net status and counters requires only one cycle.

Table 3 shows the computation time for 64 generations. The graph (2048 cells and 3096 nets) was generated using pseudo random numbers. Multiply and divide operation are necessary for calculating scores of the individuals. The operations are executed sequentially by repeating addition and subtraction using the counters (CS and $G0$).

The speedup of the evaluation stage is 48 times (1.5 times per individual), which is a bit higher than knapsack problem. The speedup of total computation is however a bit worse because the evaluation stage in FPGA-B requires more than one cycle for each bit of individuals, and during that, FPGA-A is idle.

4 Complex Adaptive Systems on the FPGA System

4.1 Iterated Prisoner's Dilemma Game

The Prisoner's Dilemma is a two-person nonzero-sum game where two prisoners (players) have to choose one of two moves: Cooperate (C) and Defect (D), where the payoff matrix is given in table 4. In the Iterated Prisoner's Dilemma Games (IPD), the choice is repeated. If the game is played once, or a fixed number of times, a rational player defects.

4.2 Evolution of IPD Agents

In the evolutionary computation of a group, suppose that all individuals play with all other individuals following the IPD game's rule, and their scores are given by the total point of the games. If all members of the group always cooperate, the group's score becomes the maximum (3 point in average). When an individual that always defects (called *all D*) comes into the group, the individual gets higher point than other individuals (5 points in average), and the number of *all D* continues to increase. However, as *all Ds* increase, *all Ds* have to play with other *all Ds* (1 point) and their scores begin to decrease. This gives a chance to increase to individuals with other choice strategies.

IPD model is used in many areas of complex adaptive systems, because it shows a very complex behavior like above in spite of its simplicity.

4.3 A Model for IPD with Noise

We implemented Lindgren's IPD model [7]. The model is easy to implement on hardware, though it shows very complex behaviors. Lindgren's model has the following features.

1. Each player has a history of moves of both players (5 bit at maximum, initially 1-bit(opponent's move)) and a table (32 bit at maximum, initially 2-bit). The player's next move is decided by the value of the table accessed by the history.
2. The history length is incremented or decremented with a probability Pl, and the table size is doubled (the content is copied) or shortened to half (the first half or last half is selected at random).
3. The value of the table is changed with a probability Pm.

Table 4. Payoff Matrix

	player-2 C	D
player-1 C	3/3	0/5
D	5/0	1/1

4. Communication channels between two players have noise. A player's move is transferred to another player by mistake with probability *Pt*. Therefore histories of two player are different.

5. All individuals play with all other individuals, and the total points of the games becomes their scores.

4.4 The Implementation of the Evaluation Stage

In figure 5, we show a pipeline for this problem. This pipeline works as follows.

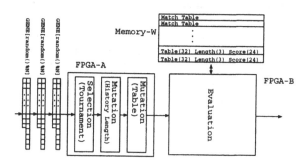

Fig. 5. Pipeline for IPD

1. The length of individuals is 59-bit (32-bit table, 3-bit history length and 24-bit score), and each individual is stored into two words of Memory-A (or B). FPGA-A selects a individual at random in every two clock cycles, and read out the individual.

2. The scores of two continuous individuals are compared in FPGA-A, and the better one is selected. The score is discarded at this stage.

3. There are two mutation stages. In the first stage, the size of history and table are changed, and in the second stage, the value of the table is changed.

4. All individuals are stored in Memory-W by FPGA-B.

5. Then FPGA-B reads out 32 individuals from Memory-W in fixed order (the order is stored in Memory-W in advance), and executes IPD games between the individuals. In each game, 2048 moves are repeated. FPGA-B repeats this cycle until all individuals play with all other individuals.

6. FPGA-B stores the individuals and their scores to Memory-A (or B), when all games finished.

7. Repeat the cycle above.

FPGA-B (ALTERA EPF10K100) can process 16 games (32 individuals) at once using internal RAMs and registers. Table 5 shows the computation time of 16 games. In this problem, the order of the evaluation is $N * N$, while the order of other stages is order N. Therefore, the performance of the evaluation decides the total performance. As shown in table 5, we can achieve 50 times speedup.

Table 5. Performance: IPD Evaluation Stage

	time(msec)	speedup
Work Station (Ultra-Sparc 200MHz)	7.23	1.00
FPGA system (33MHz)	0.135	53.6

The speedup for one game is about 3.3 times, which is larger than previous problems because two players are processed at the same time in FPGA-B. In the pipeline shown in figure 5, FPGA-A is idle when FPGA-B executes games between individuals. If FPGAs with very fast self-triggered reconfiguration are available, the speedup can be almost doubled by executing the games by FPGA-A and FPGA-B.

As shown in the evaluation of genetic algorithms, pseudo random number generation requires a lot of computation time on workstations. In the model that the communication channels have no noise, the speedup of one game decrease to 1.3 from 3.3. In this case, however, the history of two players are equal and we can use same internal memory for two players. Thus, we can process 32 games (64 individuals) at the same time and the performance gain becomes 42 times.

5 Conclusion

We are now developing a large system for evolutionary computation. To date, we evaluated the performance of a FPGA system consisting of two FPGAs and SRAMs using two problems of simple genetic algorithms and one problem of complex adaptive system. The speedup by the system is 50~130 times of a workstation (SUN Ultra-Sparc 200MHz). With a larger system, we believe that we can realize more than 10 thousands of speedup.

References

1. S. D. Scott, A. Samal and S Seth, "HGA: A Hardware-Based Genetic Algorithm", Int. Symposium on Field-Programmable Gate Array, 1995, pp.53-59.
2. P. Graham and B. Nelson, "Genetic Algorithm In Software and In Hardware - A Performance Analysis of Workstation and Custom Computing Machine Implementations", FPGAs for Custom Computing Machines, 1996 pp.216-225.
3. D.E. Goldberg, "Genetic Algorithms in Search, Optimization and Machine Learning", Addison-Wesley, 1989.
4. D. A. Buell, J.M. Arnold and W.J. Klenfelder, "Splash2: FPGAs in a Custom Computing Machine", IEEE Computer Society Press, 1996.
5. D.E. Goldberg, and K. Deb, "A Comparative Analysis of Selection Schemes Used in Genetic Algorithms" 1991, pp.69-93
6. V.S. Gordon and D. Whitley, "Serial and Parallel Genetic Algorithms as Function Optimizer", Fifth International Conference on Genetic Algorithms 1993 pp177-190.
7. K. Lindgren, "Evolutionary Phenomena in Simple Dynamics", Artificial Life II, pp.295-312, 1991.

A Transmutable Telecom System

Toshiaki Miyazaki, Kazuhiro Shirakawa, Masaru Katayama,
Takahiro Murooka, Atsushi Takahara

NTT Optical Network Systems Laboratories
Y-807C, 1-1 Hikarinooka, Yokosuka, 239-0847 JAPAN
e-mail: miyazaki@exa.onlab.ntt.co.jp

Abstract

We have developed a novel transmutable system for telecommunications, which features both reconfigurability and high performance. There are two key innovations. One is a board-level modularity concept that allows different functions to be implemented on different boards individually. The other is a high-speed serial link mechanism that provides excellent inter-board communications without sacrificing performance. Our system is distinguished from conventional ASIC emulators by its ability to provide a real-world execution environment, which enables us to connect the system to other telecommunications systems directly.

1 Introduction

Today, telecommunications systems require continuous enhancement to support various kinds of new multi-media services, and effecting enhancements in a timely manner is the key to surviving the time-to-market race. However, telecommunications systems are often constructed by dedicated hardware. This is because data transmission requires high data throughput and various bit-level manipulations, which micro-processors (MPUs) or digital signal processors (DSPs) cannot handle well. Hence the implementation of telecommunications systems is far from rich in terms of flexibility, and system enhancement takes a big effort.

To overcome these problems, we developed a telecom-FPGA (Field Programmable Gate Array) called *PROTEUS*[1] and several reconfigurable telecommunications systems utilizing it [2][3]. This approach succeeded in terms of providing some flexiblilty in the telecommunications area. Unfortunately, we have to implement all functions in the systems as FPGAs even though some parts of the functions, e.g. the SONET/SDH and ATM layer processing [4], can be replaced with commercially-available dedicated LSIs today.

To help remedy this situation, we developed an enhanced reconfigurable system called ATTRACTOR (A Transmutable Telecom system Realizing Actual Communications in a Timely manner with Other systems in the Real world). ATTRACTOR adopts a board-level modularity concept where each board is constructed as a function module, which enables free board combination using high-performance inter-board connections. Thus, we can add new functions in ATTRACTOR using suitable state-of-the-art LSIs as well as FPGAs.

1.1 Related Works

FPGA-based emulators [5][6] give us some hints on how to improve flexibility. They are widely used today when custom LSIs or ASICs (Application Specific ICs) are designed. Although their speed is around 1 MHz, which is much faster than software simulators, they cannot be applied to real-time telecommunication data processing, which often requires at least 20 MHz.

Recently, some emulators utilizing custom emulation chips have been also presented [7][8]. They mainly aim at accelerating the cycle-based simulation. The setup time of custom-chip emulators is improved compared with that of the FPGA-based emulators. This contributes to efficient debugging of target circuits. However, they are still developed for ASIC designs. Thus, they often require additional boards for, for instance, an I/O interface, when applied to system-level emulation. Unfortunately, the added boards degrade performance.

On the other hand, many reconfigurable custom computing machines utilizing FPGAs have been reported [9], and they are good at fine-grain parallel processing, such as number crunching and digital signal processing. For instance, "Splash-2" exhibits exceptional performance: it is more than 10,000 times faster than a conventional workstation, in searching a genetic database [10].

However, there are few systems tuned to telecom applications, especially to digital signal transport functions, such as IP (Internet Protocol) routing. For example, "DVC" (Distributed Virtual Computer) is an S-BUS card which has some FPGAs and high-speed communication links based on the Fibre Channel specifications [11]. The user can easily construct a distributed computing environment by installing "DVC" cards into several workstations and connecting them using coax cables. However, the "DVC" itself is a network interface card, not a heavy-job processing element. Another example is an FPGA-based protocol booster "P4" [12]. Although "P4" performs well as protocol booster, it does not have the flexibility to support other telecommunication functions such as network routing.

Our goal is to construct telecommunications equipment that is both flexible and fast, and is applicable to many aspects of a telecommunications network. ATTRACTOR respects our first attempt at realizing our idea. It can be transmuted into a *real* network node as well as a *real* end-level user terminal by changing the system configuration.

The rest of this paper is organized as follows: Section 2 overviews ATTRACTOR. Then, details of the hardware and the software in the ATTRACTOR are explained in Secs. 3 and 4. Finally, we conclude this paper with future works in Sec. 5.

2 ATTRACTOR

2.1 System Concept

For expandability and high-performance, ATTRACTOR adopts the board-level modularity concept. Figure 1 illustrates this concept. Any two boards have two kinds of common I/O interface connecting them, even if the functions of the boards are different among them. One is a direct link that connects two boards directly. The other is a system bus. The system bus is mainly used to broadcast signals from a board, and to communicate with the main control board, which totally manages this system. In other words, each heterogeneous function can be encapsulated by the common I/O interface, and we can access the function in the same way without worrying about the difference between the boards.

Furthermore, each board has an on-board controller to perform complicated signal handling and to manage the board.

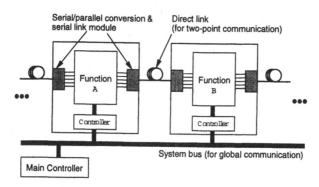

Fig. 1. The board-level modularity concept.

2.2 Implementation

An overview of ATTRACTOR is shown in Fig. 2. The system consists of heterogeneous boards for I/O, ATM (Asynchronous Transfer Mode) cell switching, common purpose look-up tables, data buffering, common purpose reconfigurable logic, and MPU. They are referred to as I/O, ATM-SW, LUT, BUFFER, FPGA, and MPU boards, respectively. Each board, except the "MPU", has a RISC-type MPU card (RISC card) as the on-board controller, and each card can be booted individually. All logic circuits in each board, except the functions realized by dedicated parts, are implemented as FPGAs. This results in board-level as well as system-level flexibility. The main MPU board contains the user interface and controls the whole system. There are five different ways to interchange information among boards, i.e., the CompactPCI bus [13], a local bus, direct back-board connections, the Ethernet, and 1-Gbps high-speed serial connections. Main data streams move between any two boards using the high-speed serial links. This simplifies the back-board wiring, since the actual wiring for the 1-Gbps serial links is in the form of coax cables connecting the front panel of each board. In addition, this is significantly advantageous for realizing a high-performance system compared with making inter-board connections utilizing flexible back-boards as in ASIC emulators. In flexible back-board implementation, wiring is certainly flexible, but many programmable-interconnect switches are often needed for full-mesh connection among boards with the limited number of assigned pins in each board connector, and the delay of the switches degrades system performance. The local bus corresponds to the system bus in Fig. 1, and is mainly used for interaction between the main MPU and other boards. Other connections are optional, and open to the user.

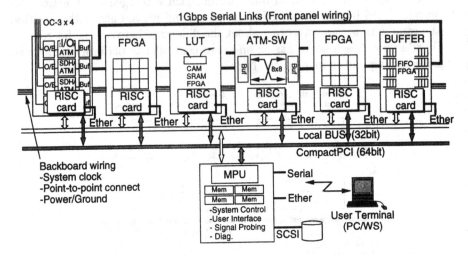

Fig. 2. An overview of ATTRACTOR.

We cannot install more than eight boards in a system. This limitation comes from the CompactPCI specification [13]. However, we can overcome this physical limitation by connecting more than two ATTRACTORs using the serial links. In this case, we cannot use any bus connections, but can use the Ethernet for communication among systems. In addition, each reconfigurable board has an external port for a synchronous clock from the outside, and there are equal-length wires for clock distribution on the back board. Thus, we can deliver a system clock from one system to another beyond the boundary of each ATTRACTOR system.

3 Hardware

Currently, we have five kinds of reconfigurable boards and a main MPU board. The specifications of the boards are summarized in Table 1. It also includes the specifications of the RISC card and the serial-link module, which are commonly used in each reconfigurable board. In each reconfigurable board, all logic circuits, except the functions realized by fixed parts such as ASICs and FIFOs, are implemented as FPGAs. Thus, there is board-level flexibility, which is why we call them *reconfigurable* boards. Furthermore, several of the same function units or channels corresponding to the number of serial-link I/O ports are realized on each reconfigurable board. This need mainly arises from implementation issues, but it enables us to make a large circuit using neighboring units on the same board. For example, the FPGAs on the FPGA board are basically divided into three groups corresponding to three serial links. However, if necessary, all FPGAs on the board can be used to construct a huge circuit without worrying about the boundary of each group.

We can select any seven boards maximumly, and set them into the system. (Actually, the system rack has eight slots, but one slot is dedicated to the main MPU board.) The connections among the boards are 1-Gbps serial links. Of course, new function boards can be added if necessary.

Table 1. Specifications of the reconfigurable boards

Board	Main parts	Functions	#S-L I/O
FPGA	12 FPGAs, 14 I-Cube PSIDs, 32 FIFOs (32Kx9b)	User defined logic, Signal probing	3
LUT	3 CAMs (256Kb), 21 SRAMs (128Kx32b), 21 FPGAs, 3 SARAMs (8Kx16b), 6 FIFOs (32Kx9b)	Network address resolution, Table look-up	3
BUFFER	12 FPGAs, 48 FIFOs (32Kx9b), 3 CAMs (256Kb)	Data reordering, Traffic shaping	3
I/O	4 OC-3 modules, 4 SONET/SDH chips, 4 ATM chips	OC-3 interface, SONET/SDH and ATM layer terminations	4
ATM-SW	155Mbps SW fabric, 16 FIFOs (32Kx9b)	ATM-cell self routing	8
MPU	R4000-compatible (66MHz, 64b bus), SDRAM (256MB), 100Base-T, RS-232C,	System control, User interface	1
RISC card	R3000-compatible (33MHz, 32b bus), DRAM (16MB), SRAM (1MB), Flash mem. (2MB), 100Base-T, RS232C	Controlling the mother board mounting this on	0
Serial-link module	HP S/P chip set, 2 FIFOs (4Kx18b), 2 SMB coax connectors	1/8 or 1/32 serial/parallel conversion, 1-Gbps signal sending/receiving	(1)

(Note) "#S-L I/O" means the number of the serial-link I/O ports. One serial-link I/O module has one pair of an input and an output port.

Figure 3 is a photograph of the buffer board. We adopt a 9U VME-style board whose size is 400mm(w) x 366.7mm(h). Parts constructing the main function are directly attached to the mother board, and a RISC card and several serial-link modules are mounted on the board as "daughter" cards. In the pictured buffer board, 48 FIFOs, 12 FPGAs, and MUX/DEMUX chips are directly attached on the surface on both side of the mother board, and a RISC card and three serial-link module cards are mounted on the mother board.

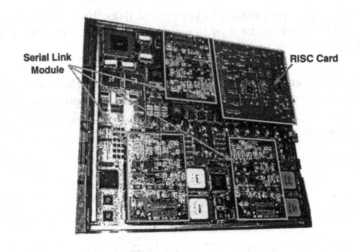

Fig. 3. A photograph of the buffer board.

3.1 FPGA Board

This is a general purpose board for realizing digital circuits, and it consists of arrayed FPGAs. Besides realizing user-defined circuits, this FPGA board has a pre-fixed function to probe signals moving through the board. The FPGA board has 14 field-programmable interconnect chips (I-Cube's PSIDs, programmable switch and interconnect devices) [16], and we can collect the signals moving between the FPGAs by reconfiguring the PSIDs. The collected signals are temporarily stored in the FIFOs on the FPGA board and transfered to the main MPU board via the CompactPCI bus. Thus, we can monitor the signals in AT-TRACTOR on a terminal screen. This board can easily be inserted between any two boards by changing the serial-link wiring.

3.2 LUT Board

The Look-Up Table or LUT board consists of high-speed SRAMs, Content-Addressable Memories (CAMs), and FPGAs. Data translations, according to input data, are often needed in telecommunications equipment. Looking up the routing-table in the IP (Internet Protocol) routers and the VPI/VCI (Virtual Path Identifier/Virtual Cannel Identifier) translation in the ATM (Asynchronous Transfer Mode) switches are typical examples. They require huge complicated look-up table functions, especially in equipment applied in a large network. Thus, an MPU and memories are often used to realize such functions, but the performance is not so good.

Our LUT board is designed to realize flexible and complicated table look-up functions without sacrificing their performance. Figure 4 shows a block diagram of the LUT board. The tightly-coupled FPGAs with CAMs and SRAMs provide a high-performance table look-up engine by installing a table look-up circuit in them.

In addition, Sequential Access/Random Access Memory (SARAM) [14] is prepared for each channel. Data sequentially written from the FPGA6 can be accessed randomly from the RISC card. This is often useful for getting some information from the main data stream, such as OAM (Operation, Administration, and Maintenance) cells in ATM applications.

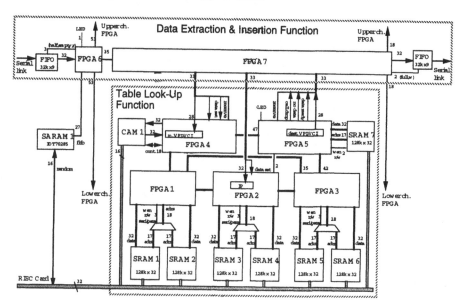

Fig. 4. A block diagram of the LUT board. This is for one channel. A LUT board contains three channels.

3.3 Buffer Board

The buffer board mainly comprises discrete FIFO chips and FPGAs. An outline of the buffer board organization is shown in Fig. 5(A). There are 16 FIFOs for each channel, and they construct four FIFO banks, "BANK0" to "BANK3". Each FIFO bank has a multiplexer and a demultiplexer (MUX/DEMUX) connected to four FIFOs as shown in Fig. 5(A). Thus, we can realize a variety of FIFO formations with different widths and lengths by changing the configuration of the FPGAs, and controlling the MUX/DEMUX appropriately. Figures 5(B) and (C) are two examples.

This board is useful in constructing a data reordering buffer as well as a simple FIFO. Data reordering is very important, and is often required in telecommunications. We can easily realize this function by controlling the MUXs/DEMUXs dynamically with the connected FPGAs.

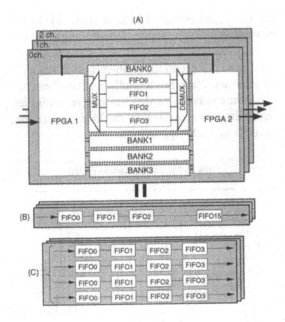

Fig. 5. An overview of the buffer board. (A) A block diagram for one channel. (B) A logical function (fully serial connection). (C) Another organization (four parallel FIFOs).

4 Software

Each reconfigurable board has a RISC card in which a commercial real-time OS (VxWorks [15]) is installed, and each card can be booted individually. All application software controlling ATTRACTOR is realized on VxWorks. The local bus and message queues are used for communication between the main MPU board and each reconfigurable board.

4.1 RISC Card for the Reconfigurable Board

Each reconfigurable board is managed by a RISC card mounted on it. The Vx-Works installed in the RISC card takes care of basic operations, such as handling interruptions and task scheduling. All tasks related to board reconfigurability are realized as application programs on the real-time OS. Of course, the tasks depend on the type of the reconfigurable boards. However, several functions are commonly included in every RISC card.

Command Interpretation is for reading data from the dual-port memory for the inter-board communication, and interpreting it as a command, and then, invoking the appropriate routine. This function is initiated whenever an interrupt signal is received.

Configuration allows a board to set itself up. This includes down-loading the configuration data into FPGAs, and writing initial data into SRAMs and CAMs mounted on the board. This function is called whenever ATTRAC-TOR is reset or booted up. Of course, the user can call this function explicitly if needed.

Status Report gives the current status of the board, i.e., the values of some status registers are sent to the main MPU board.

Diagnosis is for checking the board. The testing method depends on the reconfigurable board. For example, we apply a boundary-scan method, i.e, JTAG [17], to the FPGA board, and some add-hoc methods to the ATM-SW and buffer boards.

The kernel of the VxWorks is stored in a flash memory on the RISC card. Then, the RISC card is automatically booted up when the power is supplied. After the RISC card is booted up, a board initialization task is invoked, which includes the above configuration process. Large data, which cannot be stored in the on-board flash memory, such as the configuration data for FPGAs, are stored in a SCSI disk attached to the main MPU board. Each RISC card can access directly the SCSI disk as an NFS-mounted remote disk.

4.2 User Interface

We adopt the HTML in all user interfaces. An HTTP server runs on the main MPU board, and provides all user interface menus. Thus, the user can access ATTRACTOR using an HTML or WWW browser on a PC or workstation. In other words, any kind of user terminal can be used.

5 Conclusion

We have introduced a transmutable system targeting telecommunications applications. To provide both *flexibility* and *high performance*, different functions are packed on individual boards, and a high-speed serial link mechanism is adopted to connect them. Thus, the system can be completely reconstructed by using different board arrangements, depending on the applications.

One future task is to construct a system-level hardware/software codesign environment for the transmutable system. This is because the system utilizes multi-MPUs as well as FPGAs, making the system configuration complicated to handle manually.

Acknowledgment

The authors wish to thank Kazuyoshi Matsuhiro and all members of the High-Speed Protocol Processing Research Group for their helpful suggestions.

References

1. A. Tsutsui, T. Miyazaki, K. Yamada, and N. Ohta, " Special Purpose FPGA for High-speed Digital Telecommunication Systems," Proc. ICCD'95, pp. 486-491, October 1995.
2. K. Hayashi, T. Miyazaki, K. Shirakawa, K. Yamada, and N. Ohta, "Reconfigurable Real-Time Signal Transport System using Custom FPGAs," Proc. FCCM'95, pp. 68-75, April 1995.
3. K. Yamada, K. Hayashi and T. Fujii, "Achieving ATM Shaping Function using Programmable Adapter", Proc. GLOBECOM'96, pp. 67-71, 1996.
4. R. O. Onvural, "Asynchronous Transfer Mode Networks: Performance Issues — 2Rev. ed.," Readings, Artech House, Inc., 1995.
5. Aptix Corp., "Aptix System Explorer," Brochure, (http://www.aptix.com).
6. Quickturn Design Systems, Inc., "System Realizer M3000/M250", Brochure, (http://www.qcktrn.com).
7. Zycad Corp., "Paradigm XP," Data sheet, (http://www.zycan.com).
8. Quickturn Design Systems, Inc., "CoBALT Emulation System," Brochure, (http://www.qcktrn.com).
9. S. A. Guccione, "List of FPGA-based Computing Machines," (http:/www.io.com/~guccione/HW_list.html).
10. D. A. Buell, J. M. Arnold, and W. J. Kleinfelder, "Splash 2: FPGAs in a Custom Computing Machine," Readings, IEEE Computer Society Press, 1996.
11. Virtual Computer Corp., "Distributed Virtual Computer," Brochure, (http://www.vcc.com/products/dvc.html).
12. I. Hadžić and J. M. Smith, "P4: A Platform for FPGA Implementation of Protocol Boosters," Proc. FPL'97 (Springer LNCS 1304), pp.438-447, September 1997.
13. —, "CompactPCI Specification Short Form: PICMG 2.0 R2.0," PCI Industrial Computers Manufacturers Group, February 1997. (http://www.picmg.com)
14. Integrated Deveice Technology, Inc., "High Speed 128K (8k x 16 bit) Sequential Access Random Access Memory (SARAM)," IDT70825S/L Data sheet, December 1995. (http://www.idt/com)
15. Wind River Systems, Inc., "VxWorks Programmer's Guide 5.2," Manual, March 1995.
16. I-Cube, Inc., "IQ Family Data Sheet," December 1995.
17. —, "IEEE Standard Test Access Port and Boundary-Scan Achitecture," IEEE Std 1149.1, IEEE Computer Society, 1993.

A Survey of Reconfigurable Computing Architectures

B. Radunović, V. Milutinović

Department of Computer Engineering, School of Electrical Engineering, POB 35-54
11120 Belgrade, Yugoslavia
{vm,bokir}@galeb.etf.bg.ac.yu

Abstract. In this paper, a survey of reconfigurable computing is presented. There have been other surveys in this field, but none as exhaustive as this one tries to be. The main goal of this paper is to consider a large variety of different approaches to the field of reconfigurable computing, and to make a thorough classification. This classification is aimed at helping the understanding of the current systems, as well as the development of new systems. We first define the classification criteria and the classification itself. Each class is described briefly. Next, we classify the existing systems, based on their dominating characteristic, and finally we list each surveyed system under one of the classification classes. Each presented example is described using the same template (authors, essence of the approach, details of interest, advantages, drawbacks).

1 Introduction

Contemporary computer systems are based on simple instruction set microprocessors. Instructions have been chosen and optimized according to their frequency of occurrence in programs. For a vast majority of tasks, this approach fulfills the requirements. However, additional improvement can be obtained for some special-purpose, high-intensity computations, such as DSP, image manipulations, searching, etc. A solution for these applications is the usage of special-purpose architectures.

The FPGA technology leads to the new solution. The idea itself was proposed back in early 1960, by Gerald Estrin at UCLA, when he suggested a connection between a fixed and a variable structure computer [1]. Due to technological constraints, this idea could not be realized until recently. The biggest breakthrough in this field was brought by FPGAs with a static RAM programming technology. These FPGAs are reconfigured by changing the memory contents; namely, each programmable connection is controlled with a SRAM cell. In the classic FPGA approach, a configuration is loaded on startup. Furthermore, it can be loaded at runtime thus performing different operations during the execution of a single program.

Although FPGA is still the most common technology for implementing reconfigurable architectures, it is not the only one. In general, architecture of a reconfigurable unit can be described as a reconfigurable network of basic logic cells.

There are several benefits of using reconfigurable systems. Reconfigurable architectures present an inherently good solution for applications consisting of a large number of small processing units. Another advantage of reconfigurability is the reusability of resources. Furthermore, it brings fault-tolerance. Reconfigurability also makes developing and testing hardware systems cheaper and faster.

In the next section the classification criteria are given. Afterwards, each surveyed system is presented, classified according to the same criteria, and explained in details. However, some of the categories do not have an appropriate representative. That is mainly due to the following two reasons: a) Since this is a young and emerging technology, there are still some technology and economic obstacles, such as price, to overcome; in addition, b) All the systems are classified according to their dominating characteristics, though some of them express more than one observed characteristic.

2 Criteria

2.1 The aim of reconfiguration

First criterion represented here is the aim of reconfiguration. Some of the systems primarily focus on performance gain, while others focus on fault-tolerance. Therefore, one can observe the following two categories: *reconfigurable architectures for improving the runtime/execution performances (or speed improvement)* and *reconfigurable architectures for improving the manufacturing/exploitation performances (or fault tolerance)*.

2.2 Granularity

This criterion reflects the size and complexity of the smallest block of a reconfigurable device.

- *Fine grained* reconfigurable systems consist of small and simple basic logic block. Operations that are more complex can be constructed by reconfiguring this network, though not as efficient as in other approaches.
- *Medium grained* reconfigurable systems speed up the applications with intensive calculations of the same type. For that purpose, they have relatively complex basic cell able to do a significant part of calculations. The other types of calculations are implemented trough reconfiguration of the interconnection network. This approach is again complex and inefficient. Another drawback is that medium grained reconfigurable architectures are still new, not widespread on the market, thus more expensive than the fine grained ones.
- *Coarse grained* systems explore a different level of parallelism. Rather then executing bit or byte-level operations in parallel, they focus on cooperation of sophisticated execution units, each having its own instruction set, and executing its own program sequence. Although these systems resemble on multiprocessor architectures, their basic logic blocks are simpler than an ordinary microprocessor and are tightly integrate, thus achieving high communication speed.

2.3 Integration

Reconfigurable systems can also be classified by the way they are coupled with the host system.

- *Dynamic* systems are the ones that are not controlled by any external device [2]. They are bio-inspired, evolvable systems, and a list of possible configurations does not exist.

- *Static, Closely coupled* systems have reconfigurable units as execution units on a processor's datapath. It is also possible to use a standard system architecture (threads, context switches, multiple users) to support this approach. Nevertheless, this tight integration brings some limits in the sense of complexity of the units.
- *Static, Loosely coupled* systems have reconfigurable units attached to the host as a coprocessor, usually on a separate board. While this approach is highly efficient when processing a huge amount of data in the same way, it is inconvenient for program speedup in general.

2.4 Reconfigurability of the external interconnection network

One can also classify reconfigurable architectures after the way in which a larger number of reconfigurable units are connected.

- *Architecture with a reconfigurable external network* extends the concept of reconfiguration over several configurable circuits. However, going off-chip brings high performance penalty.
- *Architectures with a fixed external network[1]* are cheaper but less flexible way of building a large configurable system of several configurable integrated circuits.

Some of the systems presented in this survey have not been implemented in a technology suggested in a related paper. Often, cheaper test systems have been used instead. Having this in mind, presented systems are classified after the basic idea rather then the actual implementation. In addition, systems are classified according to their dominating characteristic, though some of them express properties of more than one category of a certain criterion.

3 The Olymp Classification

The previously explained classification is presented in the following paragraph. Furthermore, each category is named after an ancient Greek's god, according to its character. Example systems are listed next to each class name.

- Fault-tolerance (**ATHENA**)
  She is the most tolerant of all the Greek gods, and the one most likely to forgive.
- Speed
  - Coarse grained
    - Reconfigurable network (**DYONISIUS**)
      Zeus son, born out of wedlock, had a tough childhood. He constantly had to run away from Zeus wife Hera's revenge.
    - Fixed network (**PAN**) [3]
      He is the coarsest of all the goods and the only one who has died.
  - Medium grained
    - Fixed network
      - Dynamic (**HADES**)
        Brother of Poseidon. Independent. Lives secluded in his underground world and rarely utters his voice.

---

[1] Note that reconfigurable units always have a reconfigurable on-chip interconnection network

- Static
    - Closely coupled (EOS) [4, 5, 6, 7]
        The Dawn. She is not as refined as the 12 Olympic gods; is closely coupled to her brother, Helius. She waits for him devotedly.
    - Loosely coupled (HERA)
        Although one of the most powerful goddesses, she often uses cheap tricks. Though she loves him, jealously, she is rarely with her husband, Zeus, who fools around with other women.
- Reconfigurable network
    - Dynamic (POSEIDON)
        Brother of Hades. He lives in a world of his own and always clashes with the other gods.
    - Static
        - Closely coupled (HELIUS)
            The Sun. Brother of Eos. Like his sister, he is not too refined, and is closely bonded to her. While she awaits him, he strolls around the world.
        - Loosely coupled (ZEUS)
            As the most powerful god, he often plays tricks that are inadequate for his position and status.
- Fine grained
    - Fixed network
        - Dynamic (ARTEMIS) [9]
            Sister of Apollo. She pledged to eternal virginity. Upright but ruthless.
        - Static
            - Closely coupled (DEMETER) [15, 16, 17]
                Mother of Persephone. Closely coupled to her daughter, she once made the earth barren when Hades abducted Persephone.
            - Loosely coupled (HEPHESTUS) [11, 13, 14]
                Husband of Aphrodite. He is lame, and his wife unfaithful.
    - Reconfigurable network
        - Dynamic (APOLLO)
            Brother of Artemis. Musician and the handsomest of all gods. Independent and women-loving.
        - Static
            - Closely coupled (PERSEFONA)
                Daughter of Demetra. Closely related to her mother. She spends three quarters of the year with her while in winter she is with her husband.
            - Loosely coupled (APHRODITE) [18, 19]
                Wife of Hefest. She is the most beautiful goddess and she toys with her husband all the time.

4 The Papers (Listed by Groups):

Several papers are presented in the following paragraph, and are classified according to the criteria. Each one of them tends to show a different aspect of the belonging category.

4.1 Fault-tolerant

A field of fault-tolerance reconfiguration is one of the oldest and the most widely developed, and it goes beyond the scope of this paper. Therefore, we will not discuss it more detailed.

4.2 Speed, Coarse grained, Fixed external interconnection network

Different approach to the coarse grained, reconfigurable computing comes with the RAW project [3]. The Raw project is based on a processing unit consisted of simple, highly interconnected, replicated tiles. Each tile has instruction and data memory, and a pipelined data path with floating point and reconfigurable units (i.e., R2000 processor with additional logic). Each tile also has associated a switch with its own memory, controlling reconfiguration of the interconnection network. A speedup up to three orders of magnitude has been achieved. The Raw system has numerous advantages. By simplifying control logic and reducing hardware support for specific operations, the Raw system leaves more space for execution units, thus achieving higher level of parallelism, and it speeds up the clock. It also simplifies a verification process. Furthermore, a presence of a fine grained reconfigurable logic allows the evaluation of both bit and byte grained operations in each tile. Still, this system suffers from inefficiency in case of highly dynamic computations, where routing and data-dependencies can't be solved during the compile time. Authors have developed different methods for solving these problems but they haven't clearly showed the efficiency of the approach. However, this approach has opened promising new directions in development of reconfigurable architectures.

4.3 Speed, Medium grained, Fixed external interconnection network, Static, Loosely coupled

The MATRIX [4] is composed of an array of 8-bit units, connected with a reconfigurable interconnection network. Apart from being connected to the datapaths, network ports are connected to the control logic of the unit, and data from network port can control the functionality of the unit. Hence, most of conventional approaches can be used, such as systolic arrays, microcoding or custom VLIW. One of the major benefits of this system is better usage of available resources. Resources can be adjusted according to needs of a certain application, while in a case of classic architecture, an amount of a die used for memory, executional units and control logic has to be allocated during production time. Another advantage derived from the fact that one unit can directly control other is an increased speed of reconfigurability, as a unit is reconfigured in several cycles, depending of the type of network connection. However, a general drawback for this category remains. It is unsuitable for fine grained bit operations.

The MoM-3 system [5], as a representative of XPuter paradigm, is an array of reconfigurable ALUs in a mesh-type interconnection network with a specially designed address generator module [6]. An algorithm is mapped on this structure as a datapath. This system is adapted for medium granular computations. It is shown in [7] that an advantage of this system over a fine grained one is a lower space and time overhead on an interconnection network, due to a lower dependence on a generally imperfect placement and routing algorithms. Another advantage of this system is that it is ALU independent. Different types of operations can be implemented in a basic unit of the ALU array, depending on application requirements, while the rest of the system needs to be only insignificantly changed. However, the system is optimized for intensive computations while it doesn't offer a significant performance improvement for the general-purpose applications.

4.4 Speed, Medium grained, Fixed external interconnection network, Static, Closely coupled

The RaPiD [8] is a representative of a medium-grained, closely coupled architecture. It consists of an array of cells, placed on the datapath. Each cell has several different elements: ALUs, registers, multipliers, memory. All the elements are connected to the datapath bus. In future, the system should be integrated with a RISC microprocessor, so control signals will be generated by a RISC core. The RaPiD system is more efficient in the complex arithmetic operations than an FPGA-based circuit. Furthermore, due to its position on the CPU's datapath, the system can achieve parallelism on a finer-grained level. System is less effective in a bit-level parallelism then FPGA circuits. Another drawback is absence of the appropriate compiler, so users have to do mapping and routing manually.

4.5 Speed, Fine grained, Fixed external interconnection network, Dynamic

The Firefly [9] is an evolvable system based on cellular automata model that tends to produce uniform oscillations. The principles of evolution have already been used as an approach for software design. However, this is one of the first works in implementing these principles in hardware. The major advantages of an evolving system like this are massive parallelism, locality of cellular interactions, and simplicity of cells. These properties make it ideal for an FPGA implementation. A speedup of up to three orders of magnitude has been achieved, comparing to some software implementations. Still, this system is not open-ended, i.e. it has a predefined goal and no outside event can influence its behaviour. It also needs to prove itself on a larger variety of problems.

Another work in the field of evolvable hardware (or evolware) has come from Adrian Thompson [10]. He has used a FPGA circuit from Xilinx 6200 family to make it evolve to discriminate between 1kHz and 10kHz frequencies without any help from clock or any off-chip component. This work points out to the numerous advantages of evolvable hardware. When human designs a circuit, he has to follow different constraints, such as clock synchronization, modular design and handshaking between modules, in order that he could conceive it. On the other hand, evolvable hardware is free of all these constrains and therefore is likely to achieve a more optimal solution. Another interesting advantage is that evolvable hardware shows more fault tolerance than a conventional one, since it is less dependent of the underlying architecture. Still, evolvable systems are facing a problem of not-enough flexible hardware. Thus, they have to follow constraints of the current state-of-art reconfigurable technology, such as FPGA. Furthermore, different parameters of a system, such as fitness evaluation function and probability of genetic operators, vary from one application to another, and an evolving process for a sophisticated applications can consume more time than a conventional one. Nevertheless, this is one of the promising directions of development of the contemporary reconfigurable architecture.

4.6 Speed, Fine grained, Fixed external interconnection network, Static, Loosely coupled

As one of the first configurable systems, the SPLASH system [11] is a linear array of 32 Xilinx 3090 FPGAs, each coupled with 128kB RAM. Adjacent stages are interconnected with 68-bit data-paths. The first and the last stage are connected to the host computer through FIFO arrays. The SPLASH suffers from several drawbacks. For sake of simplicity, it has been implemented as a linear array. Software tools are rudimentary and requires knowledge of FPGA architecture and organization. Although more advanced and sophisticated researches in this field have been conducted afterward, the major importance of the SPLASH system is its breakthrough in the field of reconfigurable computing. It is simple and, most important, it shows significant advantage over existing conventional architectures.

Another pioneer among reconfigurable systems is the DECPeRLe-1 [12]. The DECPeRLe-1 board comprises 16 X3090 FPGA circuits forming a square grid. Each row and column of the grid is interconnected with a 16-bit bus, and are also connected to the host. Acting as an active memory, the DECPeRLe enables user to use the traditional memory architecture approach in order to exploit the advantages of reconfigurability. This idea is even more remarkable considering the fact that this is one of the first systems of its kind. Nevertheless, circuit design still requires user interaction; lack of an appropriate compiler represents the major stepping stone for shifting to the reconfigurable paradigm. Furthermore, the system consists of FPGA circuit, and consequently inherits the drawbacks of the FPGA circuits, mainly low efficiency of placement and routing.

A base of the PRISM-I [13] is a board consisted primarily by four Xilinx 3090 FPGAs, controlled by a processor board with a Motorola 68010 processor. User's code is transformed into dataflow graph and mapped onto FPGAs. Despite of the slow and inefficient architecture, this system has achieved a significant speedup, up to a factor of 50 for certain applications. Nevertheless, it has left a huge space for future improvements. Since the underlying hardware platform has small overall scale of integration, much improvement could be obtained by closely integrating a processor and reconfigurable areas. Yet another directions of improvement are compiler tools; an automatic algorithm mapping on hardware could lead to better performance with less human interaction. In addition, by improving the scale of integration and the reconfiguration speed of FPGAs themselves, different configurations could be used more frequently without getting a significant overhead. However, the major importance of this paper is a justification of the idea of reconfiguration.

One of the latest achievements in this category, RENCO [14] is a reconfigurable FPGA based architecture, completely programmable controllable trough the network. Rather then introducing new techniques, this board presents a platform for experimenting with various techniques for programming reconfigurable systems. Four present FPGAs gives more then half a million logic gates at one's disposal for implementing different algorithms. The number of gates is sufficient even for applications with high requirements, such as neural networks. On the other hand, this approach inherits the major drawback of its category, that is an inefficiency of implementing specialized computation, such as numerical calculation. This approach also hasn't addressed a problem of ease of programming. It requires hardware configuration to be supplied together with a program, in a classic way. While writing Java code, programmer still have to think about underlying hardware. However, the architecture itself leaves open possibilities for a solution of this problem.

4.7 Speed, Fine grained, Fixed external interconnection network, Static, Closely coupled

The Spyder processor [15] is a VLIW processor with a reconfigurable execution unit implemented on FPGA circuits. The biggest advantages of this approach is the idea of integrating reconfigurable units onto data-path of a von Neumann processor. This combines advantages of von Neumann processor in general-purpose applications and high efficiency of reconfigurable architectures in special purpose applications. However, major problem of this approach is an absence of a tool being able to hide all the hardware details form a user. This way, complex and error-prone software development keeps this approach from broader popularity.

An idea of a processor with a dynamic instruction set has been proposed trough the DISC project [16]. Each instruction is user-defined and loaded by a program during runtime. The main idea of this approach is partial reconfiguration. This platform is currently implemented in a medium-scale-integration technology; thus, it cannot demonstrate its full strength. It also suffers from a large number of memory accesses, since the absence of integrated, general-purpose registers. As many other reconfigurable systems, it lacks a unified software tool for both software and hardware code generation. Nevertheless, the concept has showed a significant speed improvement in certain applications and the idea presented in this approach opens wide directions for future research.

The GARP [17] is a processor based on MIPS-II instruction set with integrated on-chip reconfigurable logic. Following the idea of closely coupling reconfigurable units with a processor, the GARP project has managed to put a whole microprocessor together with a reconfigurable unit, on a same die. It has offered a possible solution for the present problem of efficient usage of an ever-growing number of transistors available in a modern microprocessor design. However, it still hasn't offered a cost-effective solution for programming these devices.

4.8 Speed, Fine grained, Reconfigurable external interconnection network, Static, Loosely coupled

The Splash2 [18] is based on 17 Xilinx XC4010 FPGAs and connected in a linear array, as well as to a crossbar switch that introduces larger flexibility than in the case of a simple linear array. Each one coupled is with 512kB of memory. The Splash 2 system has been developed to improve certain aspects of the SPLASH system: scalability, I/O bandwidth, and programmability. The whole system is controlled on a higher level, trough a language with a user-defined data types, strong type-checking, operator-overloading, functions, procedures and packages. One of the major drawback is that programming in VHDL requires a knowledge of the hardware and is complicated and error-prone, thus still far from being widely accepted by software industry. Although certain advantage has been made by introducing dbC, there is still al lot of space for future advance in a field of programming languages.

The SOP system [19] consists of multiple SOP boards. Each board consists of logic and memory elements, and switches. Memory element has been optimized for high-speed access and offers both associative and sorting operation ability. One of the major advantages of this system is its combining approach to medium and fine grained architecture. It also uses data-flow graph approach more efficiently than earlier works in that field, since it implements a hard-wired data-flow graph instead of simulating it. However, this paper doesn't propose the efficient solution to all the data dependency problems, thus it doesn't bring a significant improvement for general-purpose applications. Another drawback of this system is its high price.

Due to space limitations, a number of interesting approaches could not be mentioned in this survey. However, the full version of the survey can be found at http://galeb.etf.bg.ac.yu/~vm.

5 Conclusion

Reconfigurable approach still has numerous problems to solve. One of the bottlenecks is the speed of reconfiguration, as a capacity of devices limits the number of functions on chip at a time, and a reconfiguration is implemented through relatively slow serial paths. An interesting solution to this problem is the idea to keep more configurations for the single logic block on the chip. Another problem is making a compromise between bit and byte level operations. As shown in several papers, each approach has its own advantages, and they have to be combined in order to improve efficiency in general.

Software development for reconfigurable platforms is still another question of interest. Contemporary configware is missing of software tools that would cover both software and hardware aspect of programming these systems, through a single, high-level language. A presence of a tool like that would make reconfigurable architectures more popular among the huge population of software developers. On the other hand, hardware designers also have to change the point of view on designing systems. While in ASIC approach they tend to make a solution as flexible as possible, in reconfigurable systems, design should be highly optimized for a certain application. Several aspects of this problem are discussed in [20].

An intensive development of reconfigurable architectures has brought a large number of different approaches. Advantages of these systems have been clearly shown. Flexibility, speed, and economy of resources are some of them. Some of the systems have brought significant improvements in the application domain. Speedups of several orders of magnitude have been achieved for certain algorithms, still using a general-purpose hardware. Therefore, we hope that the systems, and their advantages and drawbacks we have pointed out in this paper, will help researches in this promising field of computer architecture; and that the idea of reconfigurability might be one of the directions in future development of the overall computer architecture.

Acknowledgements: Authors would like to thank to Abu Elhouni and Pedja Knežević for helpful remarks. We would also like to thank to Ksenija Simić for help in struggle with Greek gods. Special thanks to people from Logic System Laboratory, EPFL, Laussane, and proffesor Eduardo Sanchez for careful reading of the manuscript and his valuable comments, especially in the field of dynamic systems.

References

[1] G. Estrin, et al., "Parallel Processing in a Restructurable Computer System," *IEEE Trans. Electronic Computers*, December 1963, pp. 747-755.
[2] E. Sanchez, et al., "Static and Dynamic Configurable Systems," Submitted to *IEEE Transactions on Computers*, 1998.
[3] E. Waingold, et al., "Baring it all to Software: Raw Machines," *IEEE Computer*, September 1997, pp. 86-93.

[4] E. Mirsky, A. DeHon, "MATRIX: A Reconfigurable Computing Architecture with Configurable Instruction Distribution and Deployable Resources," *Proceedings of the IEEE Symposium on FPGAs for Custom Computing Machines*, April 1996, pp. 157 - 166.

[5] R.W. Hartenstein, et al, "A Reconfigurable Data-Driven ALU for Xputers," *IEEE Workshop on FPGAs for Custom Computing Machines*, FCCM'94, Napa, CA., April 1994.

[6] R. W. Hartenstein, et al., "A Novel Sequencer Hardware for Application Specific Computing," *ASAP'97*, Zurich, Switzerland, July 1997

[7] R. W. Hartenstein, "The Microprocessor is no more General Purpose: why Future Reconfigurable Platform will win," *Proceedings of the International Conference on Innovative Systems in Silicon*, October 1997.

[8] C. Ebeling, et al, "RaPiD – Reconfigurable Pipelined Datapath," Proceedings of the 6th International Workshop on Field-Programmable Logic and Applications, FPL '96, Darmstadt, Germany, September 1996.

[9] Moshe Sipper, et al., "The Firefly Machine: Online Evolware," *Proceedings, ICEC'97*, April 97, pp. 181-186.

[10] A. Thompson, "An evolved circuit, intrinsic in silicon, entwined with physics," Proc. 1st Int. Conf. Evolvable Systems: From Biology to Hardware (ICES96) (Lecture Notes in Computer Science). Heidelberg: Springer-Verlag, 1997.

[11] M. Gokhale, et al., "Building and Using a Highly Parallel Programmable Logic Array," *Computer*, January 1991, pp. 81-89.

[12] J.Vuillemin, et al., "Programmable Active Memories: Reconfigurable systems Come of Age," *IEEE Transactions on VLSI*, Vol 4, No. 1, March 1996.

[13] P. M. Athanas, H. F. Silverman, "Processor Reconfiguration Through Instruction-Set Metamorphosis," *IEEE Computer*, March 1993, pp. 11-18.

[14] J.-O. Haenni, et al., "RENCO: A Reconfigurable Network Computer," submitted to: *6th IEEE Symposium on FPGAs for Custom Computing Machines*

[15] C. Iseli, E. Sanchez, "Spyder: A SURE (SUperscalar and REconfigurable) Processor, "*The Journal of Supercomputing*, Vol 9. 1995, pp. 231-252.

[16] M.J. Wirthlin, B. L. Hutchings, "A Dynamic Instruction Set Computer," *Proceedings of the IEEE Workshop on FPGAs for Custom Computing Machines*, April 1995, pp. 99-107.

[17] J. R. Hauzer, J. Wawrzynek, "GARP: A MIPS Processor with a Reconfigurable Coprocessor," *Proceedings of the IEEE Symposium on FPGAs for Custom Computing Machines*, April 1997. pp. 12-21.

[18] D. A. Buell, J.M. Arnold, W.J. Kleinfelder, *Splash 2: FPGAs in Custom Computing Machine*, IEEE Computer Society Press, Los Alamitos, California, 1996.

[19] T. Yamauchi, et al., "SOP: A Reconfigurable Massively Parallel System and Its Control-Data-Flow based Compiling Metod," *Proceedings of the IEEE Symposium on FPGAs for Custom Computing Machines*, April 1996, pp. 148-156.

[20] A. DeHon, "Specialization versus Configuration," MIT Transit Note #113

A Novel Field Programmable Gate Array Architecture for High Speed Arithmetic Processing

N L Miller and SF Quigley

Digital Systems & Vision Processing Group,
University of Birmingham, School of Electrical & Electronic Engineering,
Edgbaston, Birmingham, UK B15 2TT.

Abstract. In this paper a novel Reconfigurable Arithmetic FPGA (RA-FPGA) architecture is presented. The FPGA employs novel logic cell structures (called Configurable Arithmetic Units CAUs) and an interconnection framework appropriate for high performance computer arithmetic. The FPGA architecture is both flexible, reconfigurable and is optimised for bit parallel processing of wide data. The proposed architecture is also scaleable supporting data of varying word length. Performance characteristics based on a 0.7μm CMOS process is presented.

1.0 Introduction.

The FPGA market has been a rapidly growing segment of the semiconductor component industry. Due to their low cost, flexibility and general purpose architecture FPGAs have found their way onto many digital applications [1]. Early devices offered very little in support for the implementation of arithmetic structures and were better suited for state machine and *'glue-logic'* implementations. FPGAs have developed considerably this decade such that they now include on-chip support for arithmetic processing. Digital signal processing in particular is one application area now targeted by leading FPGA manufactures [2,3]. Although FPGAs offer some support for computationally intensive applications they still have a general purpose architecture. The implementation of parallel arithmetic structures such as wide operand multipliers, dividers and adders or array structures can present difficulties. In many cases, bit-serial processing is employed due to limitations on routing resources [4-6]. In this paper a novel Reconfigurable Arithmetic FPGA (RA-FPGA) architecture optimised for bit-parallel computations is described.

2.0 Reconfigurable Arithmetic FPGA (RA-FPGA).

The proposed RA-FPGA architecture is partitioned into three configurable regions R_{Add}, $R_{Convert}$ and R_{Array} to implement high speed 2's complement addition, sign and magnitude to, 2's complement (vice versa) conversion, multiplication and division respectively. Three regions are proposed because it was found that a single common FPGA cell would lead to a complex and high granularity structure. By partitioning the FPGA in this way the physical chip area can be better utilised. The RA-FPGA is designed to implement arithmetic circuits for fixed point, sign and magnitude and two's complement operands. Additional resources are included within the R_{Array} region to support the implementation of general purpose logic. The proposed arithmetic FPGA architecture is scaleable and therefore can support applications with data of varying word lengths. For example, 8-bit for image processing and 16 or 32-bit for digital signal processing.

2.1 $R_{CONVERT}$, R_{ADD}, and R_{ARRAY} Regions.

The RA-FPGA assumes unsigned or sign-and-magnitude operands for multiplication and division. Two's complement operands, however, may be used provided they are converted prior to and after the data has been processed. This calls for a fast, parallel and scaleable converter. As a result a parallel operand conversion architecture based on the 2's complement algorithm is presented. A block conversion scheme is proposed in which wide operands are partitioned into nibbles. The conversion process is controlled by a complement signal, C_i, described by the following expression :

$$C_i = X_n \cdot H_1 \cdot {}^1X_{(i-1)} \tag{1}$$

The *hot 1* (H_1) input initiates the conversion process along with the sign bit (X_n) and ^1X the 1's complement representation of operand X. Fig. 1.A illustrates the block conversion process using an Operand Conversion (O_C) cell.

The purpose of the R_{ADD} region is to implement high speed adders for wide operands. The carry select method is preferred since other techniques have undesirable features of irregular structures and large granularity which will affect FPGA performance [7]. The carry select method generates two sets of results, the first is on the basis of an input carry equal to 1 and the second on the basis of an input carry equal to 0. This is implemented using the CAU illustrated in Fig. 1.B.

The R_{ARRAY} region is multi-functional in the sense that it can implement arithmetic and logic functions. This region employs the Arithmetic Logic (A_L) cell illustrated in Fig. 1.C. The A_L cell can be configured to enable the implementation of adders, multipliers and dividers. Outputs from the cell may be combinational and registered to support pipelined architectures.

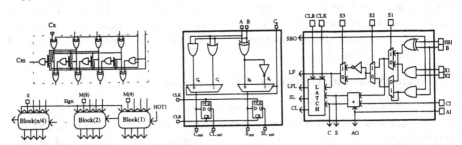

Fig.1.A (left), 1.B (middle), 1.C (right) n-bit block conversion using the O_C cell. The C_S Cell and the A_L Cell

The R_{Array} region implements multiplication using traditional carry save addition. Division is implemented using a similar array structure however, ripple carry techniques are employed. Fig. 2.A and 2.B illustrate how a divider and multiplier would be configured using the proposed CAUs. In both cases 2's complement operands are used and therefore are converted prior to and after (not shown) all computations. This post and pre-processing requires the used of both the logic operations and conversion circuits. In division the magnitude of the quotient must be packed with most significant zeros prior to converting back into a two's complement representation. The RA-FPGA architecture will support the implementation of a variation of narrow and wide operand multipliers and dividers. An *n-bit* architecture contains a minimum array of *n by n* A_L cells and at least of $2n$ C_S and O_C cells. These resources will permit the implementing of arithmetic building-blocks for digital systems such as FIR filters, DCTs and similar computationally intensive structures.

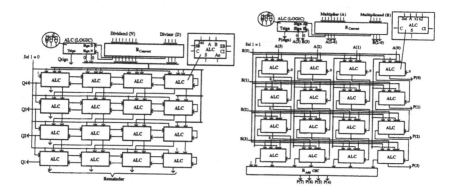

Fig 2.A (left) and 2.B (right). Implementation an array divider and multiplier

3.0 CAU Interconnection and Performance.

The routing architecture of an FPGA has been defined as : the manner in which the programmable switches and wiring segments are positioned to allow the programmable interconnection of the logic blocks [8]. A typical FPGA will employ a switch box or connection block within its routing architecture to permit the interconnection of individual logic cells. A similar approach is adopted for the RA-FPGA. The routing framework for the three regions contains predefined segmented wires in the vertical and horizontal directions. Interconnections between CAUs are made through small switching circuits controlled by a simple memory element (see Fig 3). In each region the only routing resources required is that to enable of the implementation of wide operand structures.

The RA-FPGA defines two types of switch boxes (SB_1 and SB_2) and a Transmission Gate Network (T_{GN}) also illustrated in Fig. 3. The first switch box SB_1 is essentially a 2:1 multiplexer which will selects one of two possible routing options via a programmable input. The second switch box SB_2 is a 3:1 multiplexer employing a combination of multiplexing and pass transistor techniques to selects one of three possible routing options via two programmable inputs. The T_{GN} offers a faster routing option and provides an interconnection between two points. The T_{GN} can vary in size depending on the arithmetic circuit being implemented, typically this will be four transmission gates wide. The $R_{CONVERT}$ region employs SB_1 within its local routing architecture to interconnect the Sign, HOT1 and C_m signals. The R_{Add} region employs SB_1 and a T_{GN} to interconnect C_s, C_{out}, CLR and CLK signals. The R_{Array} region employs all of the interconnect resources to implement arithmetic and general logic functions (including the interconnections shown in Fig 2).

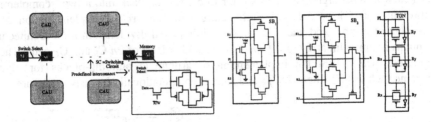

Fig. 3. CAU interconnection and Switching Circuits.

Interconnections between each of the three regions are made through the global routing framework. The global framework for a 32-bit architecture provides 64 wires for each of the three regions. Interconnections between the add, convert and array regions are made using CMOS switches. An overview of the global interconnecting framework is illustrated in Fig. 4.

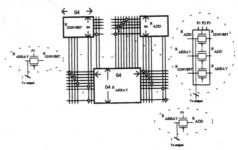

Fig. 4. Global Interconnect.

3.1 RA-FPGA Performance.

The proposed RA-FPGA cells have been implemented using a full-custom VLSI design and layout tool in order to extract physical characteristics. The propagation delay $\delta(t)$ for each CAU and switching circuits was measured using SPICE transient analysis. $\delta(t)$ is defined as the time difference between the 50% input transition and 50% of the output level. The transient analysis was run over a varied range of rise and fall times (0.5 to 4 ns) using slow, fast and typical SPICE models. These results are used to determine the speed of arithmetic circuits implemented using the proposed FPGA cells and interconnect. The performance of the RA-FPGA is summarised and contrasted with average performance characteristics stated by leading FPGA manufacturers in Table 1. Figures are also quoted for the RA-FPGA for various degrees of pipelining. The Table shows comparable results for combinational implementations of multiplier and adder circuits. It should be noted that it is difficult to make a like with like comparison. The commercial devices are, in general, implemented on a superior process technology to the proposed RA-FPGA. Also, there are significant architectural differences, which affect the number of logic blocks required implement an arithmetic function, especially where wide operands are involved. The RA-FPGA has been designed so as to efficiently handle bit parallel processing of wide operand data.

Table 1. Summary of the potential performance offered by the RA-FPGA. Key [a]Combinatorial, [b]Pipelined. RA-FPGA figures are based on 0.7μm CMOS process from ES2

δ_{ADD}(MHz)	RA-FPGA	XC3100	XC4000	XC4000E	Flex 10K	AT6000
16-bit Adder	74 (a) 417 (b)	36	49	70	79	28
32-bit Adder	36 (a) 417 (b)	-	-	-	-	11
4-Bit Multiplier	60 (a) 235 (b)	29	20	-	73	-
8-Bit Multiplier	33 (a) 147 (b)	-	-	43(a)	23	-
4-bit Divider	92 (b)	-	-	-	-	-
8-bit Divider	45 (b)	-	-	-	-	-

SUMMARY.

In this paper, the design a novel reconfigurable arithmetic field programmable gate array has been described. The overall architecture is partitioned into three regions, for operand conversion, high speed addition for wide operands, multiplication and division. Initial results obtained from circuit simulations show comparable results for combinational implementations of multipliers and adders. To maintain the flexibility the proposed architecture contains the features to support general purpose logic implementations.

References.

1. Frenzel.: "FPGA Applications." Tutorial Book of IEEE Symposium on Circuits and Systems. Chp. 1. pp. 1-10. Jun 95.
2. The Fifth Annual Advanced PLD and FPGA Conference Proceedings. May 95.
3. The Sixth Annual Advanced PLD and FPGA Conference Proceedings, May 96.
4. L Ferguson and J Rosenberg.: "Implementing DSP functions in FPGAs," IEEE Proceedings of WESCOM 95, pp. 250-255, Nov. 95.
5. Y.C Lim, J.B Evans and B Liu.: " An Efficient Bit Serial FIR Filter Architecture, Circuits Systems Signal Processing, Vol. 14, No. 5 pp. 639-651, 1995.
6. L Mintzer.: "FIR Filters with FPGAs." Journal Of VLSI Signal Processing, Vol. 6, No. 2, pp. 129-137, 1993.
7. Rose, A. El-Gammal, and A. Sangiovanni-Vincentelli.: "Architecture of FPGAs." Proceedings of the IEEE, Vol. 81, No. 7, pp. 1013-1027, Jul. 93.

Accelerating DTP with Reconfigurable Computing Engines

Donald MacVicar[1] and Satnam Singh[2]

[1] Dept. Computing Science, The University of Glasgow, G12 8QQ, U.K.
donald@dcs.gla.ac.uk
[2] Xilinx Inc., San Jose, California 95124-3450, U.S.A.
Satnam.Singh@xilinx.com

Abstract. This paper describes how a reconfigurable computing engine can be used to accelerate DTP functions. We show how PostScript rendering can be accelerated using a commercially available FPGA co-processor card. Our method relies on dynamically swapping in pre-computed circuits to accelerate the compute intensive portions of PostScript rendering .

1   Introduction

Imagine the office of a typical desk top publishing house: it will comprise of mid to high end PCs or Macintosh computers with large displays connected to a series of printers that can generate publication quality colour output at thousands of dots per inch (dpi). Rasterisation is the process of converting the high level page descriptions in PostScript into bitmaps that specify where to apply ink on the paper. This is a very compute intensive operation and is often performed by a separate computer or *Raster Image Processor* (RIP) system. The applications that graphic designers run include image processing packages like Adobe Photoshop that perform compute intensive operations such as convolution (e.g. Gaussian blur) over huge true-colour images. Image processing and printing are often very slow.

Imagine taking an off-the-shelf FPGA PCI card and slotting it into these machines to accelerate typical desk top publishing functions. That vision is exactly what we are striving for in our projects at the University of Glasgow in conjunction with Xilinx Inc. This paper concentrates on how we are working to accelerate PostScript rendering with reconfigurable technology. Other projects have shown that it is possible to extend and accelerate the filtering operations of Adobe Photoshop using exactly the same hardware.

This paper introduces the desk top publishing market and describes the PostScript rendering technology that we are currently developing. This includes an example of one of the circuits we have developed to accelerate the rendering process. The circuits are dynamically swapped onto the FPGA as and when required. It also includes a software architecture that manages the FPGA. Rather than providing a stand alone rasterisation application, we show how this system can be used with the Windows operating system to systematically provide seamless support for hardware based PostScript rendering.

2   Desk Top Publishing

Desk Top Publishing (DTP) is a rapidly growing area of the computer applications market. The increased use of high quality colour graphics has put an even bigger demand on the software and hardware used for DTP. The manipulation of a colour image to prepare it for printing using Postscript requires a significant amount of compute power to perform the operation in a reasonable amount of time.

Adobe Systems Inc. have recently introduced two solutions for PostScript printing. Adobe PrintGear [2] is a custom processor designed specifically for executing the commands in the PostScript language and is aimed towards desktop printers. The second solution is called PostScript Extreme [1], which is a parallel PostScript RIP system. It consists of upto ten RIP engines each of which processes one page before sending the rasterised page to the print engine. The first version of this system was built together with the IBM and costs arround $810,000 for printer and RIP system. This can produce 464 impressions per minute, on a RIP while printing basis, at 600dpi.

3   FPGA Technology

In the case of the FPGA PostScript project the Xilinx XC6200 FPGA is used to accelerate the compute intensive areas of the PostScript rendering process. The FPGA is only utilised when there will be a clear advantage over using software. It is not practical or possible to implement the entire PostScript rendering process on an FPGA therefore only the areas that can benefit from acceleration are concentrated on.

Since space is limited on the FPGA, we use the discipline of *virtual hardware* [4] to dynamically swap in circuits as they are required. Whenever possible, it helps to order rendering operations to avoid swapping, otherwise we might experience thrashing.

A brief overview of the rasteriser is given here a more complete description can be found in [8]. The system takes a PostScript print job as input and converts this into a PDF document which is then parsed to obtain the list of objects on each page. The bitmap for each page is then created using a combination of hardware and software. The final result is compressed before sending to the printer. Hardware is used to accelerate the following functions: matrix multiplication, rasterisation of lines, curves, circles and fonts, anti-ailasing, colour correction and compression. PDF is used as it provides a static page independant description of each page in a document unlike PostScript which allows variables to be dependant on later pages in a document.

4   A Case Study: Rendering Bézier Curves

Bezier curves are a parametric cubic curve and are used in both PostScript and PDF cf. $Q(t) = \left[x(t)y(t)\right]$, $y(t) = a_y t^3 + b_y t^2 + c_y t + d_y$, $x(t) = a_x t^3 + b_x t^2 + c_x t + d_x$, $(0 \le t \le 1)$ Curves are then defined in terms of control points which are substituted for a,b,c,d in the above equations.

The general technique for rasteristing curves is to approximate the curve with a number of straight line segments. After investigation it was decided that the best method to use was a recursive subdivision technique. Rather than performing complex straightness checks we use a fixed depth recursion. The distance between P1, P2, P3, P4 is used as a pessimistic estimate of the length of the curve. The distance P1, L4, P4 in Fig. 1 is used as an optimistic estimate of the length of the curve. The logarithm of each of the above lengths is found. The depth of recursion is then set to the average of the two logarithm values.

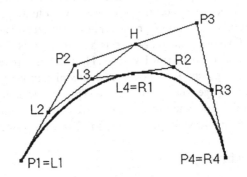

L2=(P1+P2)/2, H=(P2+P3)/2, L3=(L2+H)/2,
R3=(P3+P4)/2, R2=(H+R3)/2, L4=R1=(L3+R2)/2

Fig. 1 Splitting a Bézier Curve.

Fig. 1 shows how a curve (P_1, P_2, P_3, P_4) can be split into two curves (L_1, L_2, L_3, L_4) and (R_1, R_2, R_3, R_4) which represent the left and right halves of the curve respectively.

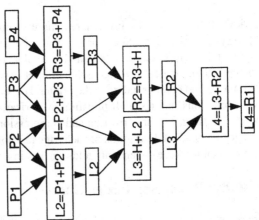

Fig. 2 Block Diagram of Bézier Dividing Circuit.

A circuit for dividing Bézier curves has been designed and built using only integer arithmetic but could be improved by using fixed point arithmetic. To perform the division of a curve two identical circuits are used one for the x components and one for the y components. The block diagram for one of the components is shown in Fig. 2.

All the circuits were implemented in an hardware description language called *Lava*, which is a variant of the relational algebraic hardware description language Ruby [3][5]. A key feature of this language is that it provides circuits combinators that encode circuit behaviour and layout. This allows us to specify circuit topology without explicitly calculating the co-ordinate of each cell. This in turn allows us to generate circuits which are far more likely to route in a reasonable amount of time.

5   Platform

Our target system is the VCC HotWorks board which contains a Xilinx XC6216 FPGA with 2MB of SRAM and a PCI interface. This card plugs into a Windows NT host. The driver model in Windows NT is a multi-level one with different levels having different operating environments. An FPGA accelerated system could be implemented at utilised in different levels of the print driver. The optimum level for implementing the FPGA-PostScript is at the print spooler level. The print spooler simply takes the data from the application level sending it down too the device level driver using a buffer to handle multiple print jobs.

Many printers can interpret the PostScript internally but this can be a very slow process. The FPGA system performs as much of the processing as possible and sends a bitmap to the printer which requires no further processing.

6   Performance

Using a test document which contains 15,768 lines totalling 92,262 pixels at a resolution of 72dpi the speed of the FPGA line drawing circuit was analysed. Using a simple implementation of Bresenham's line scan algorithm in C++ which simply renders the lines into a bitmap in memory it was measured to take approximately 1.73seconds to render the 15,768 lines at 72dpi. Assuming that the same image is to be rendered using the FPGA at a resolution of 1000dpi resulting in approximately 1,295,305 pixels must be rendered. The circuit can render at 5,000,000 pixels per second (using 16-bit arithmetic) thus takes 0.26s to render. The transfer of the data for each line will also affect the total rendering time. We shall use the measured data transfer rate of 0.7Mb/s for writing to registers on the XC6200. This results in a further 0.25s for data transfers giving a total time of 0.51s which is significantly faster than the software only version.

One of the severest limitations of our system is the very low performance of the PCI interface. Using one of the earlier VCC Hotworks boards, we have measured a transfer rate of just 0.7Mb/s, but the theoretical limit for PCI is 132Mb/s.

7   Accelerating Image Processing

PostScript rendering is just one of many desk top publishing functions that are suitable for hardware based acceleration. We have also developed plug-ins for Adobe Photoshop which use the same VCC Hotworks board to accelerate image processing operations like colour space conversion and image convolution. Some of these filters operate at around 20 million pixels per second on the board, but due to the PCI interface give a poorer performance to the user. However, all the hardware filters that we developed still ran several times faster than their software only versions.

8　Summary

In summary, we report that we are getting closer to our vision of a desk top publishing studio exploiting dynamically reconfigurable technology for commercial advantage. We have designed and implemented some of the most important circuits required for PostScript rendering. We have developed the methodology of virtual hardware allowing us to swap in circuits as required into the FPGA. We are developing a run-time system to manage the FPGA board resources and to present a high level interface to the application layer. And finally, we have investigated where in the Windows 95 and NT architecture would be the best place to install the rendering system.

The main barriers at the moment include the unsuitability of the VCC Hotworks board for our applications. In the next stage of the project, we will investigate using a board with a superior PCI interface, or one that has an alternative channel for communicating the image (e.g. AGP or FireWire). We also need far more image memory on the card, which might require us to move to DRAM instead of continuing with SRAM based cards. The TSI-TelSys cards are a likely system for us to investigate. They would allow us to cache enough circuits on the board to accelerate swapping virtual circuits. We are also re-implementing our circuits on the new Virtex FPGA from Xilinx. These devices have on-chip SRAM which helps to accelerate many operations that require multiple accesses to the same memory location e.g. Gaussian blur.

The authors acknowledge the assistance of Dr. John Patterson with Bézier curve rendering. This work is supported by a grant from the UK's EPSRC.

References

1. Adobe Systems. *Adobe PostScript Extreme White Paper.* Adobe 1997
2. Adobe Systems. *Adobe PrintGear Technology Backgrounder.* Adobe 1997
3. M. Sheeran, G. Jones. *Circuit Design in Ruby.* Formal Methods for VLSI Design, J. Stanstrup, North Holland, 1992.
4. Satnam Singh and Pierre Bellec. *Virtual Hardware for Graphics Applications using FPGAs.* FCCM'94. IEEE Computer Society, 1994.
5. Satnam Singh. Architectural Descriptions for FPGA Circuits. FCCM'95. IEEE Computer Society. 1995.
6. J.D. Foley, A. Van Dam. *Computer Graphics: Principles and Practice.* Addison Wesley. 1997.
7. Xilinx. *XC6200 FPGA Family Data Sheet.* Xilinx Inc. 1995.
8. S Singh, J. Patterson, J. Burns, M Dales. *PostScript rendering using virtual hardware.* FPL'97. Springer, 1997

Hardware Mapping of a Parallel Algorithm for Matrix-Vector Multiplication Overlapping Communications and Computations

C.N. Ojeda-Guerra[1], R. Esper-Chaín[2], M. Estupiñán,
E. Macías[1], and A. Suárez[1]

[1] Dpto. de Ingeniería Telemática U.L.P.G.C.
[2] Dpto. de Ingeniería Electrónica y Automática U.L.P.G.C.
e-mail: {cnieves}@cic.teleco.ulpgc.es

Abstract. The parallelization of numerical algorithms is very important in scientific applications, but many points of this parallelization remain open today. Specifically, the overhead introduced by loading and unloading the data degrades the efficiency, and in a realistic approach should be taking into account for performance estimation. The authors of this paper present a way of overcoming the bottleneck of loading and unloading the data by overlapping computations and communications in a specific algorithm such as matrix-vector multiplication. Also, a way of mapping this algorithm in hardware is presented in order to demonstrate the parallelization methodology.

1 Introduction

In parallel computing, one of the main bottlenecks is the input/output of data. In the I/O, massive storage devices are involved, which have lower data rate than the capability of computation and communication between processors. The value of the I/O time affects in the efficiency of the parallel algorithms because, even though the computation time can be decreased, this I/O time can reduce dramatically the gain of using parallel computation. So, in order to keep the advantages of parallel computation, not only the computation time must be diminished, but also the overlapping of computations and communications at the I/O should be studied [1].

In this paper a new methodology for mapping systolizable problems into hardware is presented. Our methodology [7] uses a mapping technique that can not be formalized by a linear mapping [5]. This methodology, which consists of four steps, has been used for programming multicomputer [7], [6] and our goal is to verify that it is efficient to map parallel algorithms into FPGA's. Once, the parallel algorithm and its implementation in a multicomputer are analysed, a specific data-flow controlled processor is developed to perform the same algorithm. This processor will overlap the computation and communication between processors and the I/O. For this implementation, a FPGA has been chosen, due to its high flexibility that allows medium complexity designs with reduced developing time, low cost and high avalaibility. In the next section, the software implementation of the algorithm of matrix-vector multiplication following the cited methodology is presented. In section 3, the hardware implementation is shown. Finally, in section 4, the results of this work are discussed.

2 Software Implementation

Let a matrix $A = (A_{i,j})$ of dimension $n \times n$ and a vector $b = (b_j)$ of dimension n ($n > 1$), its multiplication is obtained by $c_i = \sum_{j=0}^{n-1} A_{i,j} \times b_j$ ($\forall\ i = 0..n-1$) [4], where $c = (c_i)$ is the result vector of n elements.

2.1 Generation of Communication and Computation Graph

The first step in the methodology is the generation of communication and computation graph of the sequential algorithm (graph G). On any iteration of this algorithm, the processes to be executed and the data required for those processes are analysed. With this information the graph G is generated, where each node represents a point in the iteration space of the algorithm (processes executed in that iteration) and each arc represents the relationship between them (data needed). In figure 1(a), the communication and computation graph for a specific example of the matrix-vector multiplication is shown. The arcs in direction j represent the required element of the vector c between iterations of the main algorithm (flow dependencies) [2].

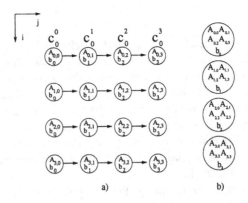

a)   b)

Fig. 1. a) Graph G ($n = 4$). b) Initial data distribution ($n = 4$)

2.2 Embedding and Data Distribution

The chosen architecture to perform the final parallel algorithm can be represented by another graph, where each node (processor+memory) is physically linked to one or more neighbour nodes by arcs (links or connections). In this step of the methodology, the embedding of the previous graph G in the graph of the architecture (graph H) is carried out. Based on the dependencies, the data are mapped on the line of processes $(i = j)$ of the graph G, which allows us to overlap communications and computations and avoid the repetition of b elements (fig. 1(b)). Supposing that the line $(i = j)$ is the graph H, the embedding has been made on a ring of processors.

2.3 Computation Distribution and Parallel Algorithm

The computation distribution is made depending on the data distribution and can be deduced from the sequential algorithm. For instance, from fig. 1(b) can be deduced that processor 0 performs the computation of $c_0 = A_{0,0} \times b_0 + c_0$, for $l = 0$. For $l = 1$, b_1 is needed and it is in the memory of the neighbour processor 1 (processor 0 and 1 should be connected), and $A_{0,1}$ is in the local memory of processor 0 and so on. Taking into account this study, the algorithm for a generic processor is:

```
do l=0,NP-2
    par
        send(b^l,↑); receive(b^{l+1},↓); computation c^l=c^l+A^l×b^l
    computation c^(NP-1)=c^(NP-1)+A^(NP-1)×b^(NP-1)
```

3 Hardware Mapping

The system architecture is defined by the parallel algorithm for matrix-vector multiplication. It has four PEs which performs the same computations in a syncronized way. This system is not limited to a fixed dimensions of the incoming matrix and vector. It computes the result vector in x steps, where x is the number of submatrices in which the original matrix is splited. In this particular implementation, the matrix is divided in blocks of 16×16 elements, and the vector in subvectors of 16 elements (16 must be multiple of n, adding zero rows if required). Because the system is composed by four PEs, a new division by rows of the matrix $A_{16 \times 16}$, so each processor will hold four rows of the submatrix and of the subvector, is needed.

While the computation is performed, the next block to be processed is incoming, matching the bandwidth of both operations, and keeping all the PEs always processing. The I/O data buses of the system are 16 bits wide, and internally the arithmetic operations are performed over 16 and 32 bits. The data of the matrix and vectors are represented in fixed point and 2-complement. For the off-chip communication through 40 pines are required, containing the incoming data bus, outgoing data bus, control bus and the system clock. In fig. 2(a) an overview of the implemented system is shown, where the four PEs are observed. They operate in parallel supervised by the control unit. Each PE is basically a multiplier and an adder plus their holding registers and the memories for storing the data. Although in the physical implementation, each set of memories belongs to one PE, the memory holding b can be accessed by all the processors to perform the data flow of b elements represented by solid lines in fig. 2(a) (the dashed lines represent the input/output data flow). The whole system is a data-flow controlled processor.

The multipliers/adders perform scalar operations of addition and substration of 16 and 32 bit wide, and shift operations [3]. The memory capability of each PE is 144 words, organized in five memories. These memories are two RAMs of 64×16 -block A-, two of 4×16 -block b- and a memory of 4×32 - block c-, in which the elements of the blocks submatrix-subvector, and the results are stored. The control unit is composed by a state machine, which hold the state of the system ($RESET\_S,\ PROCESS\_S,\ EXTRACTION\_S$ in fig. 2(b)), and three counters, which address the memories of the PEs, and generate control signals and operation commands. The final system has been designed to be included in a Xilinx's FPGA [1] [8] which have, among others, the advantage of carry small SRAMs, which will be used by the PEs to store the data in use.

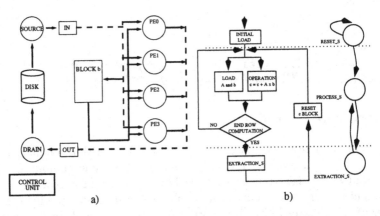

Fig. 2. a) Overview of the architecture of the system. b) Control unit state machine

4 Conclusions

This paper shows a way of optimizing the parallel algorithm of the matrix-vector multiplication by overlapping computations and comunications. Then, its mapping in hardware is studied, keeping the parallel nature of this algorithm. Our goal is to demonstrate that the regular parallel algorithms can be hardware implemented with slight difficulties due to the methodology used to parallel these algorithms. This can be of great interest for building specific processors. Should be notice that the parallel algorithm is directly mapped in hardware, making it suitable to be developed by a specific tool of automatic synthesis such as many of

---

[1] The authors wish to thanks the Centre for Applied Microelectronics for their support

those available today. The efficiency of the system is increased at the same time as the size of the matrices. However, due to the fact that when the size of the matrices is not a multiple of 16, it is completed with zeros in order to make then multiple of 16, the efficiency of the system is degraded when this case occurs, specially with small n, where the relative size of the extra zeros added are not neglictible compared with the total size of the matrix. Taking as unity time the time spent in one multiplication and addition (36 clock cycles), the efficiency η can be calculated as: $\frac{GainFactor}{TheoreticalGain} = \frac{9 \times n^2}{9 \times n'^2 + 16 \times n'}$, where $n \times n$ is the dimension of the matrix, and $n' = ((n-1) \ mod \ 16 \ + 1) \times 16$. As is shown in fig. 3, the efficiency of the system for small values of n has a sawtooth pattern, with relative maximums for n multiple of 16, and relative minimums for n multiple of 16 plus one.

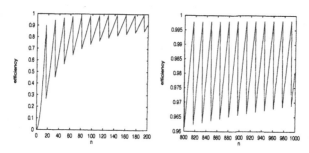

Fig. 3. Efficiency depending on n

References

1. Quinn M.J.: Parallel Computing. Theory and Practice. McGraw-Hill International Editions. (1994)
2. Banerjee U.: Dependence Analysis for Supercomputing. Kluwer Academic Publishers. (1988)
3. Booth A.D.: A Signed Binary Multiplication Technique. Quart. Journ. Mech. and Appl. Math vol. 4 part 2. (1951) 236–240
4. Golub G.H., Van Loan C.F.: Matrix Computations. Second edition. The Johns Hopkins University Press. (1989)
5. Moldovan D.I., Fortes J.A.B.: Partitioning and mapping algorithms into fixed systolic arrays. IEEE transactions on computers vol. C-35 no. 1. (1986)
6. Ojeda-Guerra C.N., Suárez A.: Solving Linear Systems of Equations Overlapping Computations and Communications in Torus Networks. Fifth Euromicro Workshop on Parallel and Distributed Processing. (1997) 453–460
7. Suárez A., Ojeda-Guerra C.N.: Overlapping Computations and Communications on Torus Networks. Fourth Euromicro Workshop on Parallel and Distributed Processing. (1996) 162–169
8. Trimberger S.N.: Field Programmable Gate Array Technology. Kluwer Academic Publishers. (1994)

An Interactive Datasheet for the Xilinx XC6200

Gordon Brebner

Department of Computer Science
University of Edinburgh
Mayfield Road
Edinburgh EH9 3JZ
Scotland

Abstract. In 1997, Lechner and Guccione introduced JERC: the Java Environment for Reconfigurable Computing. This consisted of a library of functions that permit logic and routing to be specified and configured in a reconfigurable logic device, making it possible for all design data to reside in a single Java source file. The first version of JERC involved some abstraction and simplification of the XC6200 architecture, which meant that many hardware resources of the XC6200 could not be harnessed. This paper reports on work that makes good the deficiencies, by integrating JERC with the author's SPODE environment. The resulting enriched environment is used to support a demonstration application. This is a useful tool that can described as an 'interactive datasheet'. This allows users to navigate technical information about the XC6200, and also to perform small experiments with a real XC6200 device, via a graphical user interface.

1 Introduction

In [4], Lechner and Guccione introduced JERC: the Java Environment for Reconfigurable Computing. This represented an interesting approach to hardware/software co-design for coprocessors based on reconfigurable logic. Specifically, the JERC environment consists of a library of functions that permit logic and routing to be specified and configured in a reconfigurable logic device. By making calls on these functions, circuits may be configured and reconfigured; additionally, programs can be written that interact with the reconfigurable hardware. Thus, it is possible for all design data to reside in a single Java source file. The platform for JERC is the XC6200DS development system, a PCI bus board containing a Xilinx XC6200 FPGA.

The first version of JERC had some drawbacks. These included the fact that abstraction and simplification meant that many hardware resources of the XC6200 could not be harnessed. Also, the question of adding some kind of graphical front-end was left as possible future work. This paper reports on work that has addressed both of these issues.

The solution to the problem of making the full hardware resource set of the XC6200 available was to make use of the author's own SPODE (Software

Person Oriented Design Environment) tool [3] to underpin JERC. SPODE is targeted at the XC6200, and is the descendant of an earlier, similar, programming environment (outlined in [1]) produced by the author for the Algotronix CAL technology. It is akin to JERC, in that it consists of a set of C functions that allow circuitry to be specified by calling the functions. The original version of SPODE, as reported in [3], caused configuration data for the XC6200 to be output to a file. A separate C library was then provided to allow the data to be loaded from the file, and the circuitry to be exercised under program control. In short, the overall effect was thus not unlike that of JERC, although lacking in the modernity of being Java-based.

In [4], it was suggested that JERC should be investigated as the basis for a traditional graphical CAD tool. There is no doubt that it is suitable as a fairly direct back-end for supporting a graphical tool for design at a low level, where the user specifies cell configurations and interconnectivity directly. Such a tool would have benefits not only for design, but also as a debugging aid for completed circuits. However, such a graphical design style is really only suitable for very small-scale designs, perhaps for educational purposes. The low-level specification method is most defensible when used in program mode, where programs can use function calls to specify and configure large, but regular, circuitry very efficiently. Indeed, the author has successfully designed non-trivial circuitry for both the Algotronix CAL and Xilinx XC6200 architectures using such methods (e.g., [1,2]).

As an extension to the idea of just having a useable (if somewhat low-level) design tool, the work described here has resulted in a novel tool that can be described as an 'interactive datasheet'. This tool allows a user to navigate information about the XC6200 part, and also perform simple experiments with the real part to check that they have correctly understood the supplied information. This represents a significant advance on having to fight with the terse and non-interactive descriptions contained in conventional hardcopy datasheets.

2 JERC plus SPODE

A new combined system has been produced, in which SPODE is used to underpin JERC, and the abstractions of JERC have been amended and extended to allow full use of the XC6200 hardware resources. Referring to [4], the original JERC system was organised as a two-level system. Level 0 consisted of abstractions corresponding to the bit-level reconfigurability of the XC6200. Level 1 consisted of abstractions corresponding to logic gates, registers and clock routing; it was implemented in terms of the Level 0 facilities. In the combined system, SPODE replaces JERC Level 0 as a 'Level 0.8' (approximately) facility. That is, it allows full access to the XC6200 resources, but is pitched at a level of abstraction not far below that of JERC Level 1. In particular, SPODE works at a configurable logic gate level, rather than a XC6200-specific configurable multiplexor level.

The major changes to SPODE and JERC to create a combined system capable of fully using the XC6200 were as follows:

- SPODE was enhanced so that it could write configuration data directly to a XC6200 chip, rather than just to an output file (this was very straightforward, given that appropriate code already existed);
- Java wrappers for SPODE's C functions were developed, so that the revised JERC could call them (this required a little specialist knowledge);
- JERC Level 1 was modified, so that it called appropriate SPODE functions, rather than directly accessing configurations (this was fairly intricate, to ensure a complete conversion — particular problems were that JERC stored configuration data for cells individually, and that JERC assumed certain default configuration settings);
- JERC Level 1's set of abstractions were extended in a manner consistent with existing abstractions, so that they addressed all of the XC6200's facilities (this required significant design work, motivated by the existing abstractions used by SPODE).

Unfortunately, space restrictions do not allow a full description of the final extended JERC facilities here, but documentation is available.

The result of the exercise is a substantially enhanced version of JERC (with working name of 'JERCng' — JERC next generation — pending further acronym development). This is suitable as a solid basis for higher-level design tools. Meanwhile, given the regrettable decision by Xilinx not to continue development of the XC6200 family, within Xilinx JERC has acquired the new, and more tasteful, name of 'JavaBits' and evolved into an environment targeted at the XC4000 and Virtex architectures instead.

3 Interactive Data Sheet

To demonstrate the new facilities of JERCng, a novel tool has been created. This can be used for graphical low-level design, but its main use is envisaged as an 'interactive datasheet'. In fact, the tool could have equally well been implemented directly over SPODE, omitting JERC, but this approach allowed the tool to be written in Java, based on an all-Java environment: JERC to access the XC6200 part, and the full range of Java APIs.

Any reader of FPGA datasheets will know how hard it is to describe the features of today's elaborate chips in print — the XC6200 datasheet is no exception in this respect. The idea behind the interactive datasheet is that, given a computer is equipped with the FPGA chip in question (here, the XC6200), a user can experiment with the information about the FPGA's properties by carrying out configuration activities and getting immediate feedback on their effects via a screen display. The author envisages that such a facility might become a standard part of the documentation distributed with FPGA chips. Such a facility is made particularly practical when FPGA technologies allow partial configuration, as does the XC6200. Without this, it is necessary to write full chip configurations, with only extremely small changes between writes.

The idea behind the interactive datasheet tool is that the user is presented with a cellular array, which can be viewed at several levels of detail:

- individual cell;
- 4 × 4-cell block;
- 16 × 16-cell block;
- whole array.

This choice was made to reflect the routing hierarchy of the XC6200. As well as allowing the exposition of length-4, length-16 and chip-length routing wires, it also allows a user to investigation interactions between neighbouring cells and neighbouring blocks. The whole-array level allows an exposition of input/output blocks.

For the individual cell level, the function is viewed at the logic-gate level of abstraction, rather than the lowest configuration level where interconnected multiplexors implement logic functions. This is consistent with the way the FPGA is presented in the XC6200 datasheet, for example. Experimental circuit configuration by the user is done by clicking on the displayed array, with menus indicating the allowable possibilities in each case. Basically, these menus are the interactive equivalent of the configuration options listed in the hardcopy datasheet. Additional textual information about any menu item is also available to the user, corresponding to the detailed descriptions of the options in the hardcopy datasheet. As a further bonus, the user may exercise the circuitry being constructed, to check that her/his interpretation of the datasheet is, in fact, correct. That is, particular inputs can be supplied by the user and the resulting outputs observed.

The individual-cell level will serve as a concrete example of the types of function presented to a user. In any cell, there are the following configurable components:

- the boolean or multiplexor function performed;
- the source of the inputs to the function unit;
- whether the D-type flip-flop is unused, read-only or read-write;
- the sources of the north, south, east and west outputs of the cell;
- the sources of the 'magic' output of the cell.

When the user chooses configrations for any these, the choice is superimposed on the generic cell diagram on screen. In the case of the function choice and flip-flop choice, this is a symbolic annotation. In the case of the various signal sources, this is shown as an explicit wire with the appropriate orientation in the cell.

For cells located on the boundaries of 4 × 4 and 16 × 16 blocks, there are extra choices for the north, south, east and west outputs. A cell with this more specialised nature can be selected for individual study by clicking on the appropriate cell at the 4 × 4-cell or 16 × 16-cell block levels. The 4 × 4-cell block level also allows a full presentation of the effect of the 'magic' wires, since these are not uniform at the individual cell level.

4 Conclusion

Both JERC and SPODE originated from similar viewpoints on how reconfigurable circuit design might best be carried out. These move beyond traditional hardware design-style tools, targeted at fixed architectures, and explore the ways in which software programs might intimately interact with soft circuitry. The combination of JERC and SPODE has led to a Java-based environment for the XC6200 that allows its complete functionality to be exercised. Hopefully, this will tempt more users from software backgrounds into attempting the design of reconfigurable circuitry.

The electronic datasheet concept seems a great advance in providing information about FPGA technologies to a user, not only aiding navigation of the information, but also allowing safe interaction with the real part to check understanding. Early experiments, using students unfamiliar with the XC6200, have shown that the new tool is of immense benefit in clearing up misconceptions. Tools like this should be a further way of tempting those from software backgrounds into a world that appears alien at first sight.

Acknowledgement

The author thanks Xilinx Inc., in particular Steve Guccione, for providing him with the source code and documentation for JERC, together with encouragement to develop it further. Thanks also to Richard Morrell for his efforts in helping to bridge the divide between the Java and C languages.

References

1. Brebner, "Configurable Array Logic Circuits for Computing Network Error Detection Codes", Journal of VLSI Signal Processing, **6**, 1993, pp.101–117.
2. Brebner and Gray: "Use of reconfigurability in variable-length code detection at video rates," Proc. 5th International Workshop on Field Programmable Logic and Applications, Springer LNCS 975, 1995, pp.429–438.
3. Brebner, "CHASTE: a Hardware-Software Co-design Testbed for the Xilinx XC6200", Proc. 4th Reconfigurable Architecture Workshop, ITpress Verlag, 1997, pp.16–23.
4. Lechner and Guccione, "The Java Environment for Reconfigurable Computing", Proc. 7th International Workshop on Field-Programmable Logic and Applications, Springer LNCS 1304, 1997, pp.284–293.

Fast Adaptive Image Processing in FPGAs Using Stack Filters

Neil Woolfries, Patrick Lysaght, Stephen Marshall, Gordon Mcgregor and
David Robinson

Dept. of Electronic and Electrical Engineering,
University of Strathclyde,
204 George Street,
Glasgow, G1 1XW
United Kingdom

Fax: +44 (0)141 552 4968
e-mail: n.woolfries@eee.strath.ac.uk

Abstract. Stack filters are a class of non-linear, digital filters whose behaviour is defined by Positive Boolean Functions rather than the multiply-accumulate, arithmetic operators that are widely used in conventional digital filters. The implementation of stack filters that can be adapted in real-time is feasible using dynamically reconfigurable FPGAs. This paper reports on efforts to map adaptive stack filter architectures for image processing onto current FPGAs and to assess the potential for more efficient filter synthesis with newer device architectures.

1. Introduction

Stack filters are non-linear, digital filters [1]. They function by decomposing their input data into streams of digital bits. A stack filter translates an input data sample, of value k, that is encoded as an n-bit, binary word, into a vector of 2^n-1 bits. The lower k bits of the vector are set to one while the remaining $(2^n$-$1)$-k bits are set to zero. The point at which the elements of a vector change from one to zero is defined as the vector threshold. The redundant re-coding of the input data is the key to the operation of the stack filter. Rather than processing streams of data words, the stack filter processes streams of consecutive data bits. Obviously, the stack filter must process more data windows due to the redundant coding, but the operation of processing bit streams is dramatically simpler than processing data words. These bit streams are processed using a subset of Boolean logic functions called Positive Boolean Functions (PBFs). A PBF is simply a Boolean function that can be expressed as a sum of products or a product of sums with no complemented terms. Crucially, individual data streams may be processed in parallel and their outputs combined so long as their relative order is preserved. This is the *stacking* property of stack filters.

The parallel, bit-level properties of stack filter algorithms appear to lend themselves to efficient implementation on FPGA architectures. The need for adaptive, real-time filters suggests that dynamically reconfigurable FPGAs could be exploited to fulfil this requirement in a novel way. This paper investigates the synthesis of adaptive stack filter architectures for image processing in current FPGAs. The next section introduces a stack filter architecture called the binary refinement architecture, which maps well to FPGAs. It presents the opportunities for fast filter implementation by extensive use of pipelined design techniques. Section three considers the use of FPGAs for adaptive image processing applications. The following section discusses the implications of dynamically changing the PBFs used by the filter to adapt its behaviour in real-time, based on studies using the Xilinx XC6216 FPGA. Section five concludes the paper.

2. Binary Refinement Architecture

Three main architectures have been proposed for stack filtering: threshold decomposition, input range compression and binary refinement. These architectures have been evaluated, and as shown in Table 1, the binary refinement has been demonstrated to be very efficient for hardware implementation [2]. Its main contribution is to reduce the requirement for PBFs, from the theoretical maximum of 2^n-1, to n PBFs.

Table 1. Architectural comparison: XC6216 FPGA erosion filter with a 3x3 window, processing 8 bit data

Architecture	Area Usage	Maximum Throughput
Threshold Decomposition	$\approx 80\%$	$\approx$ 15M Samples / Second
Range Compression	$> 100\%$	< 8M Samples / Second
Binary Refinement	< 20%	> 20M Samples / Second

The binary refinement architecture uses a binary search algorithm to find the required output vector threshold. The process successively halves the search space until only the result remains. This allows the architecture to filter n-bit data in n stages. These stages are identical and can be pipelined effectively.

The binary refinement architecture, as shown in Fig. 1, uses n PBFs to perform the filtering operation. The filter has the added advantages of being linearly scalable in both window size and number of bits. The critical path of the architecture consists of the delay through the PBF and the additional overhead of the inter-stage, inhibit signals. These signals mark values that have been evaluated as being outwith the search space.

The highly structured layout of the binary refinement architecture suggests a new form of adaptation. The number of sample bits (resolution), and the size and shape of the input window can be altered in real time in a predictable manner through dynamic reconfiguration. This presents a whole new area of novel applications.

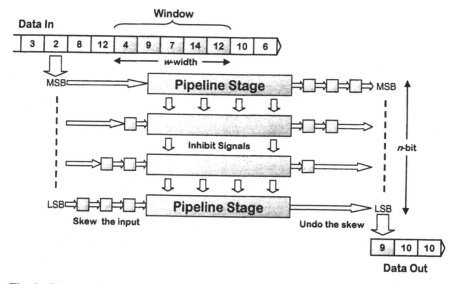

Fig. 1. Binary refinement architecture performing a median operation on 4-bit data, with window width of 5 samples

As the filter is required to hold a window of past input samples, for a window of width w, the filter will require a minimum of $w . n$ registers. If the filter is to be pipelined, this increases to $3 . w . n$ registers. Depending on the filtering function being performed by the stack filter, a range of different PBFs will be employed. The simplest of these can be used to implement the *erode* or *dilate* image processing operators while one of the more complex corresponds to the median operation [3]. For the pipelined architecture of Fig.1, the ratio of registers to two-input, combinatorial logic gates for the erode and dilate operations is close to unity. This suggests that fine-grained, register-rich FPGA architectures, such as the XC6216, are well suited to stack filter implementation.

3. Adaptive Image Processing

Many sophisticated image processing systems combine pure image processing operators with complex model matching algorithms. These systems have traditionally been implemented on specialised microprocessors. Present FPGA technologies certainly could not fulfil these roles, but future devices, comprising

FPGAs with tightly coupled microprocessors on a single chip will provide more suitable platforms for these systems.

Examples of such systems include automatic target recognition and feature recognition. Currently used throughout medical imaging, astronomy and radar systems, the number of applications of this type of system will escalate with the increasing availability of low-cost, digital video and home multimedia technologies.

One typical image processing operation is the use of adaptive filtering for noise reduction. This is achieved by periodically adapting the filter with reference to a known training set. For a digital video application, this may be achieved by sending video frames interspersed with known frames, which are not displayed but are used to optimise the filter for the transmission characteristics.

As the filter has two mutually exclusive modes of operation, the FPGA can be configured with slightly differing hardware for filtering and training. Training algorithms are often arithmetically complex, and would be better split between the FPGA and a microprocessor. The FPGA can be used to build up an array of statistics, which is then used by the processor to determine the optimal parameters and the appropriate PBF. The processor can then reconfigure the FPGA using this information.

4. Dynamic Adaptation of the PBF

The fine grained architecture of current dynamically reconfigurable devices results in a situation where the area and delay of the PBFs are highly dependent on the complexity of the particular function being implemented. An example of two representative PBFs is shown in Fig. 2.

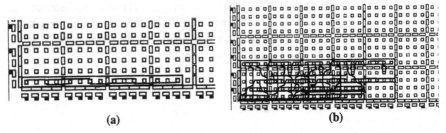

(a)   (b)

Fig. 2. Floorplans for (a) Erosion filter and (b) Median filter of window width 9 on the XC6216 FPGA

For most applications this is unlikely to be a problem, but for adaptive image processing, it is a major complication. Although dynamic reconfiguration can be used to adapt the PBF, and hence the behaviour of the filter, it is difficult to predict how much area must be reserved on the device for adaptation. Changing the operation of a filter can completely change the size and aspect ratio of the filter floorplan. This effect can be so severe that it negates any advantage gained in using dynamic reconfiguration.

As the PBF is simply a logic function with a known number of inputs, and one output, it could be implemented in a Look Up Table (LUT). Therefore, a dynamically reconfigurable FPGA that combines large numbers of registers and wide LUTs would provide a better solution. The adaptation of the PBFs could be realised with much less distortion of the floorplan of the filter. At present, there is no commercially-available, coarse-grained FPGA that is register rich and also dynamically reconfigurable.

5. Conclusions

Stack filters may be implemented efficiently on FPGAs because they rely on PBFs rather than arithmetic functions such as multiply-accumulate operations. The use of the binary refinement algorithm is significant because it reduces the number of PBFs required to the number of bits in the binary encoded input data.

The use of dynamically reconfigurable FPGAs allows considerable scope for the implementation of real-time, adaptive stack filter algorithms. To minimise floorplanning difficulties, operator adaptation would be best implemented with wide LUTs. This requires a class of dynamically reconfigurable coarse-grained FPGAs that is not available today. Opportunities exist for new devices combining microprocessors and FPGAs where the complementary processing power of the two processor types can be applied to different phases of the image processing algorithms.

6. References

1. Wendt P. D., Coyle E. J., Gallagher N. C., Jr.: Stack Filters, IEEE Trans. Acoustics, Speech, and Signal Processing, Vol. ASSP-34, no. 6, (1996) 898-911
2. Woolfries N., Lysaght P., Marshall S., McGregor G., Robinson D.:Non Linear Image Processing on Field Programmable Gate Arrays, NOBLESSE Workshop on Non-linear Model Based Image Analysis, Glasgow, Proc. NMBIA'98 (1998) 301-307
3. Dougherty E. R., Astola J.: An Introduction to Nonlinear Image Processing, Vol. TT 16, SPIE Optical Engineering Press, Washington, USA (1993)

Increasing Microprocessor Performance with Tightly-Coupled Reconfigurable Logic Arrays

Sergej Sawitzki, Achim Gratz, and Rainer G. Spallek

Institute of Computer Engineering
Faculty of Computer Science
Dresden University of Technology
D-01062 Dresden, Germany,
Phone: +49 351 463-8243, Fax: +49 351 463-8324
{sawitzki,gratz,rgs}@ite.inf.tu-dresden.de
WWW home page: http://www.inf.tu-dresden.de/TU/Informatik/TeI/english/

Abstract. Conventional approaches to increase the performance of microprocessors often do not provide the performance boost one has hoped for due to diminishing returns. We propose the extension of a conventional hardwired microprocessor with a reconfigurable logic array, integrating both conventional and reconfigurable logic on the same die. Simulations have shown that even a comparatively simple and compact extension allows performance gains of 2–4 times over conventional RISC processors of comparable complexity, making this approach especially interesting for embedded microprocessors.

1 Background and Motivation

The integration scale in the semiconductor industry is incessantly increasing. This trend allowed the implementation of increasingly complex systems on a single die. Dynamic instruction tracing and cache hit rate measurements show that the effectiveness of increased cache size and higher superscalarity is leveling off beyond a certain threshold. For instance, doubling the cache size from 64 to 128 KByte has been shown to increase the hit rate by only 0.4% [1] under certain loads. Average CPI values of commercial superscalar processors remain poor. A CPI of 1.2–3.0 was reported for quad-issue Alpha 21164 at 300MHz [2], a quad-issue HaL SPARC at 118MHz achieves 0.83 CPI under standard load [3]. These numbers can at least partly be attributed to bottlenecks in the memory sub-system, however the question arises whether the cost of larger caches and additional superscalar function units can be justified by these rather lackluster performance improvements.

Consequently, alternative approaches have been investigated, of which only a few can be mentioned here. Since memory is a major factor of system performance and the processor-memory gap is widening, integration of memory or additional special-purpose logic on the same die with a microprocessor core looks attractive. Projects like IRAM [2] and PPRAM [4] have shown promising results from this venue. Other researchers are abandoning the conventional computing paradigm in favor of a data-driven model. Xputer [5] and functional memories [6] may serve as well-known examples of these efforts.

Other bottlenecks in a microprocessor are created by the rigidity of the hardware structure itself and the resulting compromises. This situation could be remedied if parts of the processor were reconfigurable. Academic and industrial research picked up on this idea when it became technically and economically viable in the late 1980's with the availability of FPGA, producing a flurry of special purpose processors. Lately more conventional microprocessor cores with tightly-coupled programmable logic started to appear [7–9]. In this paper we propose a Common Minimal Processor Architecture with Reconfigurable Extension (CoMPARE), a simple and scalable microprocessor architecture.

2 Architectural Principles

CoMPARE is a RISC-like architecture with a reconfigurable extension that maintains close compatibility with the usual programming model. To simplify the design neither caches nor FPU and only 16 instructions and 16 registers on 8 bit wide, three-stage-pipelined data-paths were implemented. The reconfigurable extension is LUT based. These constraints are mostly determined by targeting an FPGA as a prototype, more complex implementations including cache and superscalar functional units are certainly possible.

CoMPARE uses a reconfigurable processing unit (RPU), which is a conventional ALU augmented by an LUT-based configurable array unit (CAU) used to implement additional, customized instructions. An LUT array that consumes the equivalent transistor count of a 2 KByte SRAM (100.000 transistors [10], smaller than many caches) provides a performance gain of a factor of 2–4 on average for the tested application kernels. Other FPGA technologies use different means for reconfiguration, but the overall complexity is comparable. The resulting architecture differs from the conventional RISC processor structure only in the use of a reconfigurable processing unit (RPU) in the place of the standard ALU. The hardwired instructions in the ALU are always available, but it only needs to provide the most basic instructions. Additional operations useful to accelerate different applications are provided by the CAU, whose structure is shown in the Fig. 1. In addition to the usual three-operand format the RPU can process at most four input operands and produce two results in one instruction. To avoid clutter in the instruction set, these operands are placed into adjacent registers.

The configuration context for an 8-bit CoMPARE uses 1984 Bytes. Up to 8 complete configurations can be stored in memory and loaded word-for-word into the CAU via the LCW (load configuration word) instruction. Therefore it takes 1984 clock cycles to configure the CAU before the application can use the extended instructions. It is possible to use partial configurations or to change only the differing bytes on a configuration context switch, thereby reducing this penalty. Several partial configurations can be merged within a single 2 KByte context, providing efficient reconfiguration.

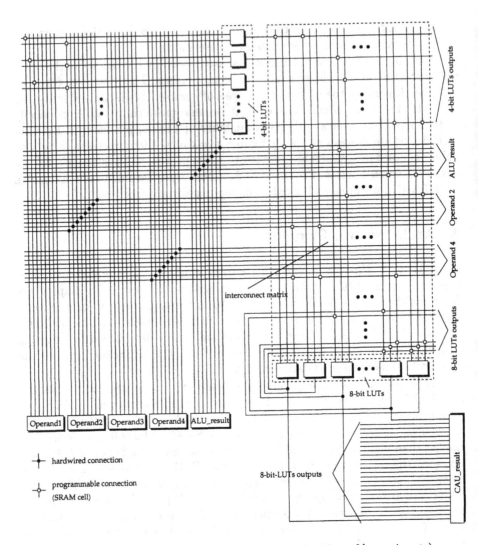

Fig. 1. CAU structure (x-bit-LUT $\equiv$ boolean function of $\log_2 x$ inputs)

3 Application Domain

The applications for CoMPARE-like architectures is widespread, but the comparatively high effectiveness and scalability suggests cost-driven designs especially in the embedded control market. We have used a VHDL model to simulate the inner loops of DSP, image processing, data compression and neural nets algorithms. The implementation of simple multimedia instructions known from instruction set extensions like MMX (Intel), MAX (HP), VIS (Sun), AltiVec (Motorola) or MDMX (MIPS) in reconfigurable logic seems to be an interesting application for CoMPARE. It has been shown that some multimedia instructions from PA-RISC MAX-1 [11] can be implemented straightforwardly within

Table 1. Cell complexity of CoMPARE prototype

Design unit	Cell count
FDU	185
Register file	1999
LSU	152
ALU	761
CAU	1118
DCU	230
Sum	4594

the CAU. Achievable speed-ups at the application level are estimated to fall into the range of 2–4 for a wide spectrum of applications, with much larger speedups possible in some cases. The algorithms consisting of one (or several nested) loop(s) with a small amount of basic operations including multiplications (or bit-shifting) and additions/subtractions which could be executed in parallel are best-suited for acceleration with CoMPARE.

4 FPGA Prototype

The actual performance of CoMPARE can be better evaluated with a prototype. We have chosen the Xilinx XC6200 family for prototype implementation. The Trianus/Hades CAD System developed at the Institute for Computer Systems (ETH Zürich, Switzerland) serves as design environment [12], the RTL and gate level description of the design were developed in Lola-HDL. We described and synthesized every design unit of CoMPARE separately to ascertain the complexity in terms of XC6200 cells. Table 1 summarizes the results of the synthesis process. A complete CoMPARE prototype will fit in at most 2 XC6216 FPGAs (4096 cells each). The better solution however would be to implement the design within a XC6264 circuit, which provides 16384 cells, so the CAU could be easily scaled. The simulation of the critical signal path within CoMPARE indicates that the 8-bit prototype can be clocked at about 11 MHz. Currently we are looking for a suitable FPGA board to start with real-world tests. Other FPGA architectures besides the Xilinx 6200 are also under consideration.

5 Conclusions and Further Work

We have shown that a very simple processor architecture extended with reconfigurable resources can provide a performance comparable to commercial RISC processors of similar complexity. A CAU capacity of a few KByte of configuration memory (SRAM-based LUTs) suffices to achieve the performance index of the factor of 2–4 compared to MIPS R2000 at the same clock frequency. Especially for embedded applications the inclusion of the CAU may prove more cost-effective than a cache of similar size. The integration of reconfigurable resources at the instruction level allows simple handling and maintains the common programming model for general purpose microprocessors. We hope to be able to evaluate the concept on a FPGA board and provide a suitable software environment soon.

The project has indicated several directions for further research. The LUTs contained in the CAU serve only as function generators. It may be advantageous to augment the LUTs by sequential logic, to implement automata. This approach however requires modifications to the data path structure of CAU. Furthermore other levels of parallelism should be supported. We intend to examine how CAU-like extensions to hardwired functional units can improve the performance of multithreaded and multiscalar architectures.

Acknowledgment. All product names etc. mentioned in this paper are registered trademarks of their respective owners.

References

1. Hennessy, J.L., Patterson, D.A.: Computer Architecture — A Quantitative Approach. Second Edition. Morgan Kaufmann Publishers, Inc. (1996)
2. Patterson, D.A. Anderson, T. et.al.: A Case for Intelligent RAM. IEEE Micro, 17(2):34–44 (March/April 1997)
3. Essen, A., Goldstein, S.: Performance Evaluation of the Superscalar Speculative Execution HaL SPARC64 Processor, in Proceedings of Hot Chips VII, p.3.1 (August 1995)
4. Miyajima, H., Inoue, K. et.al.: On-Chip Memorypath Architectures for Parallel Processing RAM (PPRAM). Technical Report PPRAM-TR-17, Department of Computer Science and Communication Engineering, Kyushu University (May 1997)
5. Ast, A., Hartenstein, R. et.al.: Novel High Performance Machine Paradigms and Fast Turnaround ASIC Design Methods: A Consequence of and a Challenge to Field-Programmable Logic, in Field Programmable Gate Arrays: Architectures and Tools for Rapid Prototyping, Vol. 705 of Lecture Notes in Computer Science, pp. 210–217, Springer-Verlag (1993)
6. Halverson Jr., R., Lew, A.: An FPGA-Based Minimal Instruction Set Computer. Technical Report ICS-TR-94-28, Information and Computer Sciences Department, University of Hawaii at Manoa (January 1995)
7. Wittig, R., Chow, P.: OneChip: An FPGA Processor With Reconfigurable Logic, in Proceedings of FCCM'96, pp. 126–135 (April 1996)
8. Hauser, J.R., Wawrzynek, J..: Garp: A MIPS Processor with a Reconfigurable Coprocessor, in Proceedings of FCCM'97, pp. 24–33 (April 1997)
9. National Semiconductor Corporation: NAPA 1000 Adaptive Processor. http://www.national.com/appinfo/milaero/napa1000/index.html
10. Razdan, R.: PRISC: Programmable Reduced Instruction Set Computers. PhD thesis, Harvard University, Cambridge, Massachusetts (1994)
11. Lee, R.B.: Accelerating Multimedia with Enhanced Microprocessors. IEEE Micro, 15(2):22–32 (April 1995)
12. Gehring, S.W., Ludwig, S.: The Trianus System and its Application to Custom Computing, in Proceedings of FPL'96 (September 1996)

A High-Performance Computing Module for a Low Earth Orbit Satellite using Reconfigurable Logic

Neil W. Bergmann and Peter R. Sutton

Cooperative Research Centre for Satellite Systems,
Queensland University of Technology,
GPO Box 2434, Brisbane 4001, Australia
n.bergmann@qut.edu.au, p.sutton@qut.edu.au

Abstract. A hierarchy of FPGAs, DSPs, and a multiprocessing microprocessor provide a layered high performance computing module which will be used to enhance the performance of a low-earth orbit satellite, FedSat-1, which will be operational in 2001. The high performance computer will provide additional hardware redundancy, on-board data processing, data filtering and data compression for science data, as well as allowing experiments in dynamic reconfigurability of satellite computing hardware in space.

1 Introduction

The Co-operative Research Centre for Satellite Systems (CRCSS) is a new research venture distributed over several universities, research labs and industrial partners across Australia, which commenced operations in January 1998 [1]. The mission of the CRCSS is to deliver a new, sustainable advantage for Australian industries and government agencies involved in services based on the applications of future generations of small satellites. Under the Centre's strategy, by focusing on affordable space missions which can be achieved in a relatively short time, Australia will regain experience in designing and operating space assets required for future commercial and public benefit applications. The budget for the Centre totals $A56 million over seven years, including contributions from government, research and industry participants.

The first major space project for the Centre will be a small, experimental scientific satellite, FedSat-1, to be operating in time to celebrate the Centenary of Federation of the Commonwealth of Australia (2001). The principal missions of FedSat-1 are currently as shown below.

- *Communications:* Ka-band satellite communications; experiments in multi-media data transmission, paging, remote area messaging and location service; relay of scientific data and control, innovative earth station design.
- *Space Science:* NEWMAG experiment in solar-terrestrial physics, to measure electrical currents and perturbations in the Earth's magnetic field.
- *Remote Sensing:* GPS occultation experiment for atmospheric sounding.

- *Engineering Research:* test of solar panel efficiency, new on-board processors, space qualification of GPS receiver.
- *Education and Training:* Researchers, students and engineers will gain experience in space technology and science, will design and test payloads and participate in experiments and research based upon the operation of those payloads.

This paper particularly addresses the design of a new high-performance computing module which incorporates reconfigurable logic.

2 Characteristics of Space Electronics

There are certain obvious characteristics of electronics systems for a typical small, low earth orbit satellite which greatly affect system design choices.
- The satellite operating environment is significantly different from that encountered in terrestrial systems. The near-vacuum conditions reduce convective cooling capability making temperature management more complex. Circuitry and packaging materials must be free from out-gassing (evaporation of volatile materials in vacuum).
- The lack of atmospheric protection increases the incident radiation which can produce soft and hard circuit faults.
- The circuitry undergoes extreme acoustic and mechanical vibration during launch.
- Hardware faults cannot be repaired, requiring high-reliability manufacture, assembly and operating techniques. Backup systems are needed for mission-critical sub-systems.
- Faults are difficult to diagnose due to limited observability of system components.
- For a small satellite reliant on photovoltaic power generation, total power is very limited. For our 0.125m³ satellite, only a 0.25m² surface area is presented to the sun. Overall, this provides only about a 10W average available power for all satellite services, payloads and communications.
- Our satellite has a total mass budget of 50 kg, of which only about 1/3 is available for payloads. Hence light, compact circuitry is preferred.
- Low earth orbit satellites might typically only be visible from a given Tracking, Telemetry and Control ground station for four to six passes of 10 minutes each per day. The availability of bandwidth for downloading telemetry data and uploading control information is limited.

Because of the unusual operating conditions, and the need for reliability, satellite electronics have typically used a very conservative design approach [2]. Specialised packaging and assembly techniques are used. Often, individual components for critical sub-systems must be specially space-qualified. Every subsystem of a planned satellite is typically tested in an environmental chamber to confirm its space-readiness. This conservative design approach is naturally in opposition to conventional computer design, which has very short product lifetimes and rapid adoption of the latest components.

3 Aims of the High Performance Computing Program

In order to further the mission of the CRC for Satellite Systems, the following aims have been developed for a High Performance Computing research project:

- To evaluate improvements in satellite performance enabled by the use of high performance computing technologies in space and on the ground.
- To develop computer architectures and algorithms for use in satellite systems which take advantage of reconf gurable computing technologies.

Our approach for achieving these aims is to develop a HPC architecture suitable for satellite use, evaluate performance gains through ground-based experiments across a range of satellite scenarios, and gain experience and mission-specific results through flying a HPC module onboard FedSat-1. We have therefore identified the following objectives for a FedSat-1 payload:

- To provide high performance processing onboard FedSat-1 - utilizing a combination of processors and reconfigurable logic - capable of implementing data compression, data filtering, communications baseband processing, message storage, and inter-experiment data computation.
- To conduct experiments on the practicalities associated with reconfiguration (including partial or dynamic reconfiguration) of hardware in space and to evaluate improvements in satellite performance offered by this approach.

The remainder of this paper investigates some details of how these aims might be achieved.

4 A Conventional On-Board Computer for a Small Satellite

Typically, on-board computers for satellites have been very conservatively designed [3]. Even recent small satellites might contain only an Intel 186 processor with 1 MByte memory. However, there has recently been a trend to incorporate extra intelligence in satellites, to perform mission activities more independently of ground control.

A typical, modern, small satellite would contain a modular data processing system which can be customised for a particular mission with selections from a range of individual cards or modules. Such a system might consist of the following modules:

- *Central Processing Unit,* which coordinates all the activities of the satellite, and deals with commands for core satellite activities such as attitude control, power management and health monitoring.
- *Redundant Processing Unit,* which is a backup processor for the CPU to increase system reliability. It might be an identical CPU module, or it may be a smaller, less powerful module which can still maintain a minimum of computing services.
- *Data Acquisition Unit,* which interfaces with the data streams to and from the payloads. Data from analog or digital interfaces is converted into data packets for transmission to the ground-station. Control packets are converted into appropriate

analog or digital control signals. Multiple modules may be needed to cope with a large number of different interfaces.

- *Mass Memory Unit*, which contains high-density solid-state mass memory for storage of remote sensing data awaiting transmission to ground.
- *Data Packet Handler*, which deals with the transmission of data packets to and from the controlling ground-station via the communications sub-system and routes these packets to the DAU or CPU as required.

For a small satellite, the on-board computer is typically in the range of 2-5kg in mass and 5 W power dissipation. This represents a substantial proportion of the total system mass and power budgets.

5   Design of a New High Performance Computing Module

In order to meet the aims of our research program, we are currently designing a new High Performance Computing card which would fit into the modular computing framework of our satellite, and service the high performance computing needs of the satellite payloads. The system design constraints of limited mass, volume and power, need for reliability and redundancy, and short design time have led to the following preliminary design decisions.

Firstly, a central processor running a multiprocessing operating system will provide access to other computing modules such as Data Acquisition or Mass Memory units via the system backplane. To increase overall system reliability, this processor will have the capability to take over control from the CPU in the event of failure of the main processor card. Otherwise, this processor will be available to provide enhanced system computing capability.

Secondly, a DSP chip will be used to provide dedicated real-time data processing for payloads, such as data processing, data filtering, or data compression. A key selection criterion here will be power consumption per MIP.

Thirdly, dynamically reconfigurable FPGAs will be used to provide a flexible data interface to payloads. High speed data streams will be able to be handled in real-time, with preliminary data processing and formatting implemented in hardware.

Software applications for the DSP subsystem, and programmable hardware configurations for the FPGA subsystem will be able to be uploaded to the satellite during the lifetime of the mission, to allow additional system flexibility.

At this stage, the tentative list of experiments which might use the High Performance Computing module includes the following:

- Digital filtering and modulation/demodulation of communications waveforms.
- Communications system error detection, correction and monitoring.
- Adaptive high-speed communications protocols.
- Data encryption and decryption.
- Data compression for remote sensing data.
- Position estimation for the satellite.
- Position estimation for mobile terrestrial transmitters.
- Emergency replacement of main platform computer, or other system components.

* Store and forward packet switching functions for low bandwidth remote-area communications.
* In-flight system reconfiguration via uplink communications channel.

6 Conclusions

The expected outcomes of the High Performance Computing project are improved satellite system performance across many different metrics:

* *Reliability:* Increased system flexibility to cope with individual component failures.
* *Flexibility:* Ability to deal with many different payload interfaces, increased flexibility for post-launch system upgrades, ability to reconfigure hardware support during different mission phases.
* *On-board Data Processing:* Ability to deal with real-time high speed data streams in a power efficient manner.
* *Received Data Throughput:* Increased amount of useful payload data transmitted to earth through data filtering (data analysed to send most useful samples), data compression, and adaptive communications channel coding (to make best use of available downlink bandwidth).
* *Design Time:* Reprogrammable logic allows late system changes to overcome problems encountered during system integration and test.
* *Power Optimisation:* Computations can be assigned to reprogrammable hardware or DSP software to optimise power consumption.
* *Mission Lifetime:* Flexible hardware configurations and interconnections can be used to make best use of available satellite resources throughout mission lifetime.

Acknowledgments: The support of the Australian government through the Cooperative Research Centres Program funding for the CRC for Satellite Systems is gratefully acknowledged.

References

1. Kingwell, J., Embleton, B.: Cooperative Research Centre for Satellite Systems, World Wide Web page at http://www.crcss.csiro.au/, (1998)
2. Jilla, C. D., Miller, D. W.: Satellite Design: Past, Present and Future, International Journal of Small Satellite Engineering, Vol. 1, No. 1, (1995) World Wide Web page at http://www.ee.surrey.ac.uk/EE/CSER/UOSAT/IJSSE/issue1/cjilla/cjilla.html
3. Wagner, D.J.: Spaceborne Processors: Past, Present and Future Satellite Onboard Computers, Proceedings of 49th International Astronautical Federation Congress, Melbourne (1998)

Maestro-Link: A High Performance Interconnect for PC Cluster

Shinichi Yamagiwa, Masaaki Ono, Takeshi Yamazaki, Pusit Kulkasem,
Masayuki Hirota, and Koichi Wada

Institute of Information Sciences and Electronics
University of Tsukuba
Tsukuba, Ibaraki 305
JAPAN
yama@wadalab.is.tsukuba.ac.jp

Abstract. Maestro is a distributed shared memory system currently being developed. In this paper, an architecture of the high performance network interface of Maestro is presented. Maestro consists of multiple PC(Personal Computer)s and dedicated network hardware for high performance message passing and maintaining cache coherency. IEEE1394, a high performance serial link, is used in the physical layer of Maestro network. The network interface is developed using FPGA(Field Programmable Gate Array)s. A network latency and a bandwidth between the network interface and PC are measured and discussed.

1 Introduction

A shared memory model is known as a powerful parallel programming model that provides a programmer a simple abstraction for information exchange among parallel tasks. A distributed system that has a capability to access globally shared data objects is called a DSM (Distributed Shared Memory) system [1][2][3][4]. A DSM system has an advantage in scalability as well as the easiness in parallel programming.

In realizing a shared memory on a distributed environment, access latency to the data that is owned by the other node is a critical issue. Generally, to reduce such access latency, the remote data are copied to the local cache or memory. This results in an another problem called coherency problem. Coherency should be maintained by exchanging messages to notify the action (e.g. writing to a local copy) that may violate the coherency. The communication protocol for maintaining coherency is called a cache coherency protocol. The performance of network strongly affects the time required for maintaining coherency, and hence, the access latency to the shared data.

Maestro is a distributed shared memory system that has a capability of high-performance message passing and coherency management. In this paper, a network architecture of Maestro is presented.

2 Design and Organization of Maestro System

The Maestro system has been designed to have following architecture.

- PC (Personal Computer) cluster
- IEEE1394 serial bus[5]
- Network Interface via PCI (Peripheral Component Interconnect) bus
- Dedicated hardware for DSM and fast messaging

One of the aims in the Maestro project is to develop a high performance parallel computer system based on the standardized technologies. PCs are used as high cost/performance node processors of Maestro. The IEEE1394 is gaining popularity as a next generation serial link. The bandwidth of the IEEE1394 is 200Mbps as yet, it is planned to be improved to more than 800Mbps.

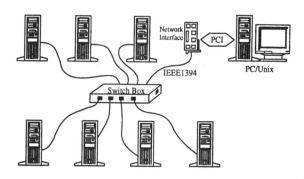

Fig. 1. Maestro Organization

The system organization of the Maestro is shown in Fig.1. The system is composed of PCs and a SB(Switch Box). The NI (Network Interface) is connected to the PC via PCI bus, and the NI is connected to the SB through IEEE1394. The NI has a dedicated hardware that performs a cache coherency protocol. The SB is in charge of switching messages issued from NIs.

3 Network Interface

The NI takes charge of: 1) communicating with the host PC through the PCI bus, 2) maintaining coherency for shared memory, and 3) receiving and sending messages through IEEE1394. The block diagram of NI is shown in Fig.2. The NI consists of PCI interface, NIC(Network Interface Controller), MCU(Memory Control Unit), DRAM, packet buffer, MLU(Maestro Link Unit), and IEEE1394 physical layer unit. The PCI9060[7], which is a commercial PCI Interface chip, are used to interface between PC and NI. NIC is an embedded microprocessor that performs a procedure for coherency protocol. MCU allows NIC to access

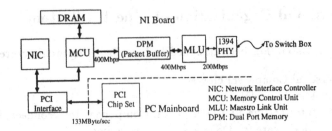

Fig. 2. Block diagram of NI

DRAM and the packet buffer. DRAM is used for storing a program of NIC and directory information of cached copies.

The board frequency is 25MHz, while the 1394PHY chip operates at 50MHz. The bandwidth between 1394PHY and MLU is 200Mbps. MCU and MLU are implemented using FPGAs. MLU is in charge of management of the packet buffer and provides support for a special protocol of Maestro link.

A block diagram of MLU is shown in Fig.3. The MLU is mainly composed of 1394PHY interface, link layer protocol controller, and packet buffer manager. We developed a special link layer protocol, called a piggybacked ack protocol, which improves the fairness to be a sender for both ends of the 1394 serial bus.

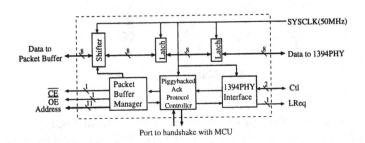

Fig. 3. Block diagram of MLU

4   Switch Box

The Switch Box(SB) is a multi-functional router that has a capability of high-performance message switching and directory management for distributed shared memory. The SB is designed using Altera's Flex10K devices[6].

The block diagram of SB is shown in Fig.4. Hardware modules for message analysis and switching are pipelined to realize fast switching operation. The modules depicted by shaded boxes are implemented by FPGAs. The SB consists of the following modules: CONE (Coupled Node Element), SBM (Switch Box Manager), and SWC (SWitch Controller). Each CONE manages two ports. MA

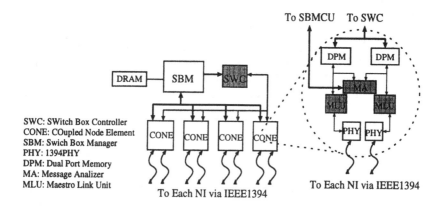

Fig. 4. Organization of Switch Box

(Message Analyzer) module extracts a message header from a message, then passes to SBM module. MA also analyzes a packet header to know whether the message is organized from a single packet or multiple packets. SWC establishes a direct connection between a source DPM and destination DPMs according to the commands from SBM.

5 Performance

To measure the throughput between PC and NI, 32Mbytes of data placed in the DRAM of NI are transferred to PC's main memory by DMA (Direct Memory Access). The obtained throughput was 63MBytes/sec. The throughput is determined mainly by the bandwidth of DRAM.

To evaluate the performance in communication, latency to transfer a packet from a sender's buffer to a receiver's buffer has been measured. The latency was approximately 1.1usec. The detailed timing in transferring a packet is shown in Fig.5. In the figure, CS indicates a check sum. Followings are the breakdown of the timing:

- 60nsec for bus acquisition
- 80nsec for setup
- 700nsec for sending Ack, packet, and check-sum
- 240nsec for transmission delay

6 Conclusion

In this paper, an architecture of the high performance network of Maestro, which is a distributed shared memory system currently being developed, is presented. Maestro consists of multiple PCs and a dedicated network hardware for maintaining cache coherency. IEEE1394, a high performance serial link, is used in

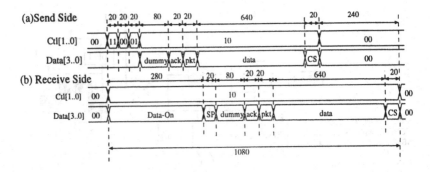

Fig. 5. Timing chart for packet transfer

the physical layer of Maestro network. The network interface is developed using FPGAs. One FPGA is in charge of memory control. The other FPGA operates functions on interfacing between IEEE1394 and the packet buffer.

The bandwidth between the network interface and PC, and the network latency are measured and discussed. It has been confirmed that the bandwidth for PC was 63MByte/sec and the latency of end-to-end packet transfer was 1.1usec.

Through the development of Maestro prototype, we confirmed that FPGA is usable device for high performance network interface. Moreover, Maestro network interface has many functions for supporting distributed shared memory. Flexibility of FPGA would be valuable when some modifications are required in those functions for optimizing system performance.

Future work is to develop a library for parallel programming that supports both massage passing and shared memory.

References

[1] K. Li, IVY: A Shared Virtual Memory System for Parallel Computing, Proc. of the 1988 Int'l Conf. on Parallel Processing (ICPP'88), Vol. II,pp. 94-101, Aug 1988.

[2] J. Kuskin etal, The Stanford FLASH Multiprocessor, Proc. of the 21th Annual Int'l Symp. on Computer Architecture (ISCA'94), pp. 302-313,Apr 1994.

[3] C. Amza and A. L. Cox and S. Dwarkadas and P. Keleher and H. Lu and R. Rajamony and W. Yu and W. Zwaenepoel, TreadMarks: Shared Memory Computing on Networks of Workstations, IEEE Computer, Vol. 29, Number 2, pp. 18-28, Feb 1996.

[4] J. P. Singh and T. Joe and A. Gupta and J. L. Hennessy, An Empirical Comparison of the Kendall Square Research KSR-1 and Stanford DASH Multiprocessors, Proc. of Supercomputing'93, pp. 214-225,Nov 1994.

[5] IEEE Standard Department, IEEE Standard for a High Performance Serial Bus Draft7.1v1, August 5, 1994.

[6] Altera Corporation, 1996 Data Book, 1996

[7] PLX Technology, PCI9060 Data Sheet VERSION1.2, December 1995.

A Hardware Implementation of Constraint Satisfaction Problem Based on New Reconfigurable LSI Architecture

Tsunemichi SHIOZAWA, Kiyoshi OGURI, Kouichi NAGAMI, Hideyuki ITO, Ryusuke KONISHI, and Norbert Imlig

NTT Optical Network Systems Laboratories
1-1 Hikari-no-oka, Yokosuka-shi, Kanagawa 239-0847 Japan
shiozawa@exa.onlab.ntt.co.jp

Abstract. The significant features of *Plastic Cell Architecture* (PCA) are autonomous reconfigurability and adaptable to the granularity of the application. By using these characters, it is possible to build the computing mechanism, which suits the granularity of the problem and the structure of it. We apply PCA to solve the Constraint Satisfaction Problem (CSP) that is typical combinatorial optimization problem, such as scheduling problem or image recognition.

1. Introduction

In general, when a given problem is solved with a conventional parallel computer, the divide-and-conquer method in which the final solution is obtained by solving smaller element problems is adopted. In this method, how efficiently this division and integration is done becomes the important point of the problem solving by parallel processing. Because the grain size of a element processor which executed processing in parallel was fixed in a general-purpose parallel computer, it was necessary to match the size of process executed on each processor to the granularity of it.

In this paper, we propose the method of solving Constraint Satisfaction Problems (CSP) which belongs to the combinatorial optimization problem. It is shown that the character of the reconfigurable and adaptable to the granularity of the given problem works effectively.

2. Plastic Cell Architecture

The Plastic Cell Architecture[1-3] (called PCA) is composed of the homogeneous cell connected mutually, and each cell consists of the built-in part and the plastic part. One or more plastic parts are configured and assembled to generate object that achieves functions of application on PCA. And the built-in part is a unit including static defined functions for message passing and reconfiguration. The built-in part and plastic parts of each cell are also connected via the connection path.

Differing from a popular programmable logic device such as FPGAs, PCA is in the point that the plastic part is reconfigured autonomous and in parallel by objects in PCA. Because the circuit generated in PCA reconfigures the circuit in autonomy using the built-in parts, it is possible only in PCA to achieve programmability corresponding to that by using software. The point of this that not only merit on the performance that the overhead for reconfiguration is reduced but also reconfiguration can be achieved in a distributed parallel manner. The unit of the function composed on PCA is called an object, and one or more object is utilized for the application.

3. Applied to CSP

3.1 Definition of CSP

Many artificial intelligence problems and scheduling problems can be formulated as constraint satisfaction problems that are NP-complete. Formally constraint satisfaction problem (CSP) is defined [4-6] as follows: Given a set of n *variables* $x_1, x_2, ..., x_n$ each with an associated *domain* $D_1, D_2, ..., D_n$ and a set of constraining relations $t_k = (x_i, ..., x_j)$ (1• i• • • n) each involving a subset of the variables, and all permitted or legal values for each t_k are given by $R_k = \{(u, ..., v)$• $D_i \times ... \times D_j$• $(u, ..., v)\}$, find one or all n-tuple $(d_1, d_2, ..., d_n)$ that is $\{(d_1$• d_2• ...• $d_n)$• $D_1 \times D_2 \times ... \times D_n$• • d_i• ..., d_j• • $R_k\}$ for all R_k(1• k• m). We consider only those CSPs in which the domains are discrete and finite. The pair (t_k, R_k) is simply called *constraint-pair*. The example of CSP and all the solutions are shown below.

[Example of CSP]

Variables• x_1, x_2, x_3, x_4, x_5
Domains• $D_1 = D_2 = D_3 = D_4 = D_5 = \{a, b, c, d, e\}$
Constraints• $t_1 = (x_1, x_2)$, $t_2 = (x_2, x_4)$, $t_3 = (x_1, x_3, x_4)$, $t4 = (x_2, x_5)$.
    $R_1 = \{(a, b), (b, a), (b, e)\}$, $R_2 = \{(a, d), (a, e), (e, a), (e, c)\}$,
    $R_3 = \{(b, b, e), (c, b, e), (b, c, a)\}$, $R_4 = \{(e, d), (a, d), (d, a)\}$.
Solutions• (b, a, b, e, d) and (b, e, c, a, d).

Many algorithms on the one or more processors, such as depth-first search [6] or breadth-first search by merging operation of constraints, have been used in *CSP solver* that solves the given CSP. Though improving the performance of *CSP solver* to use special hardware is proposed [5], these are only to eliminate the element of R_k by checking consistency between all *constraint-pair* which have common variables in t_k.

3.2 CSP solver on PCA

(1) Basic structure

CSP solver consists of one *root object* and the *constraint objects* which are generated corresponding to each *constraint-pair* $(t_1, R_1), ..., (t_k, R_k), ..., (t_m, R_m)$.

Constraint object **Restrict$_k$** corresponding to (t_k, R_k) receives the message $(d_1 \bullet d_2 \bullet \ldots \bullet d_n)$ in which all enable values of the variables are consistent to constraint-pair $(t_1, R_1), \ldots, (t_{k-1}, R_{k-1})$ from object **Restrict$_{k-1}$**. Where d_i is value of variable v_i. However, the message $(d_1 \bullet d_2 \bullet \ldots \bullet d_n)$ includes the disable value 'u' which indicates that corresponding variable is not assigned an enable value in the previous *constraint objects*.

Constraint object **Restrict$_k$** assigns the value to the variables, which have disable value and checks so as not to contradict *constraint-pair* (t_k, R_k). If consistent assignment is exist, the new assignment $(d_1', d_2', \ldots, d_n')$ is transfer to *Constraint object* **Restrict$_{k+1}$** as message. If two or more assignments exist, **Restrict$_k$** sends those assignments one by one. On the other hand, if consistent assignment is not exist, **Restrict$_k$** discards the message $(d_1 \bullet d_2 \bullet \ldots \bullet d_n)$.

Root object sends message $(d_1 \bullet d_2 \bullet \ldots \bullet d_n)$ in which all value d_i is disable to *Constraint object* **Restrict$_1$**, and then sends "End message" to **Restrict$_1$**. The last *Constraint object* **Restrict$_m$** sends consistent assignment $(d_1', d_2', \ldots, d_n')$ to *root object* if consistent assignment is exist. Moreover, the object, which receives the "End message", forwards it to the following object.

In the case of requiring single solution, when *root object* receives the assignment, *root object* deletes all *Constraint objects*. In the case of requiring all solutions, when *root object* receives the "End message", *root object* deletes others. In both cases, when *root object* receives only "End message", there is no solution for the given CSP.

(2) The use of dynamic reconfiguration
It is possible to think the above method to be a pipeline in which each stage is defined by *constraint-pair* and it composes the solution that satisfies *constraint-pair* in parallel. Each stage in the pipeline is operable in parallel and generally has the following characters.

a) It is in the tendency that the assigned results to the variable increases in a *constraint object* near the *root object*. (*growing stage*)

b) In *constraint object*, which locates near to the last *constraint object*, almost all assignments that are transmitted from the previous *constraint object* are discard. (*shrinking stage*)

Whether each *constraint object* is *growing stage* or it is *shrinking stage* changes dynamically in the influence of *constraint object* ordering in the pipeline, size of R_k and the number of variables that are newly assigned value in that *constraint object*. When the assignment to the value is generated a lot in the *growing stage*, pipeline hazard occurs because the processing time in the following stages grows. In order to execute all *constraint objects* efficiently, the copy of the object, which causes the pipeline hazard, is generated dynamically in PCA.

Figure 1 shows the example of describing the *Constraint object* corresponding to *constraint-pair* (t_k, R_k) of CSP, however k<m, by the enhanced HDL description which is based on SFL used in PARTHENON [7,8]. The description shown in Figure 1 is explained in detail. Line 1~4 are definitions of this object. In line 5, the following *Constraint object* is generated. The *par* statement of the line 6 is a very special feature of SFL which shows that the operations described in { } are executable in parallel. The user-defined function *empty* in line 7 is a function, which returns the truth-value

when the resource, such as input/output or register, specified by the argument is an empty state. The function *send* transmits the data stored in *out_buff* to the object specified by the first parameter as a message. Line 7~13 is interface of the object by which message is transmitted and received between other objects. The line 14~26 is done when the assignment of the value to the variable, which is consistent with *constraint-pair* (t_i, R_i) for all i<k, is received as a message. Line 15 shows that the line 16~19 is

```
1:class Restrict_k {
2:    input in;
3:    output out;
4:    object* dest = NULL; subset = NULL;
5:    if (dest == NULL) dest := new Restrict_{k+1};
6:    par {
7:        if (empty(out)) out := send(dest, out_buff);
8:        if (empty(in_buff)) {
9:            if (subset != NULL) forward(subset, in);
10:           in_buff := in;
11:       }/*if*/
12:       if (in_buff == "End message")
13:           if (empty(out_buff)) out_buff := in_buff;
14:       else {
15:           for ( λ∈R_k ) par {
16:               if ( consistent( in_buff, λ ) ) {
17:                   wait(empty(out_buff));
18:                   out_buff := merge( in_buff, λ );
19:               }/*if*/
20:           }/*for*/
21:           clear(in_buff);
22:           if ('empty(in_buff) && empty(out_buff)) {
23:               subset := new Restrict_k(lower(R_k));
24:               R_k := R_k - lower(R_k);
25:           }/*if*/
26:       }/*else*/
27:   }/*par*/
28:}
```

Fig. 1. HDL description of constraint object with dynamic load balancing

executed for all local assignments λ which satisfy the *constraint-pair* (t_k, R_k). User-defined function *consistent*, which is implemented by using comparator, is a function that returns true value when value of the variable included in the t_k does not contradict the value in *in_buff*. Function *wait* is a function which suspends processing until the parameter value becomes true, and this function behaves as an arbiter to whom only the demand of one suspending operation is resumed in the same clock period in order to resume the suspended operation, which waits for same resource, without contradiction. The *merge(in_buff, λ)* is a function which sets the value assigned in λ for variable that is assigned disable value in *in_buff* and returns the result of new assigned values.• This function is composed of the circuit, which merges bit strings.

In figure 1, when the next message has been received from previous object and a buffer which transmit a message to the following object is empty at the end of for-loop, *Constraint object* is

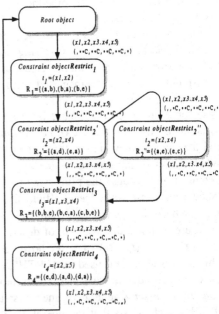

Fig. 2. Dynamic configuration of object

generated dynamically in line 23. *lower* is a function which gives partial sets of *constraint-pair* (t_k, R_k), and the original object and newly generated object process each *constraint-pair* which is divided disjunctively in the line 23~24.

Figure 2 shows this example. *constraint-pair* (t_2, R_2) is divided into *constraint-pair* (t_2, R_2') and *constraint-pair* (t_2, R_2'').

The method described in section 3.2 (1) corresponds to the conventional method by which merge operation is repeated on single or multiprocessor. But it is known that the size of R_k obtained from a result of merge operation in parallel processing is often larger than the case processed in serial order with a single processor. In the merge operation of *constraint-pair* on PCA, an increase in the number of the inconsistent assignment of variables is restrained since the assignment, which is consistent with constraint in previous pipeline stages, is propagated to the next *constraint-pair*. This example shows a typical problem that the sub-problem, which consists of some small problems, is assigned to the calculation mechanism that the grain size of a function is as large as that of the processor and it is processed. The method of section 3.2 (2) makes processing by more fine grain size than that of section 3.2 (1).

4. Conclusion

In this paper, we proposed the method of solving the constraint satisfaction problems in parallel by using the fine grain hardware logic on Plastic Cell Architecture. By using the Plastic Cell Architecture, it is possible to solve the imbalance of the load according to usable resource.

The examination of first PCA implementation is getting on. In addition, the design environment (high-level hardware description language, simulator, and logical synthesis tools, etc.) for the plastic cell architecture are being developed.

References

[1] K. Nagami, K. Oguri, T. Shiozawa, H. Ito and R. Konishi, "Plastic Cell Architecture: Towards Reconfigurable Computing for General-Purpose," Proc. of FCCM, 1998.

[2] H. Ito, K. Oguri, K. Nagami, R. Konishi, and T. Shiozawa, "The Plastic Cell Architecture for Dynamic Reconfigurable Computing," Proc. of RSP, pp39-44, 1998.

[3] N.Imlig, K. Oguri, H. Ito, K. Nagami, R. Konishi, and T. Shiozawa, "General Purpose Computer Architecture Based on Fully Programmable Logic," ICES,, 1998.

[4] A. K. Mackworth, "The logic of constraint satisfaction," Artificial Intelligence, no. 58, pp3-20, 1992.

[5] P. R. Cooper, "Arc consistency: parallelism and domain dependence," Artificial Intelligence, no. 58, pp207-235, 1992.

[6] R. M. Haralick and G. L. Elliott, "Increasing Tree Search Efficiency for Constraint Satisfaction Problems," Artificial Intelligence, no. 14, pp263-313, 1980.

[7] Y. Nakamura, K. Oguri and A. Nagoya, "Synthesis From Pure Behavioral Descriptions," High-Level VLSI Synthesis, Edited by R. Camposano and W. Wolf, Kluwer Academic Publishers, pp.205-229, 1991/06.

[8] "PARTHENON Home Page," http://www.kecl.ntt.co.jp/car/prthe/

A Hardware Operating System for Dynamic Reconfiguration of FPGAs*

Pedro Merino[1], Juan Carlos López[1] and Margarida Jacome[2]

[1] Departamento de Ingeniería Electrónica
Universidad Politécnica de Madrid, Madrid, Spain.
{merino|lopez}@die.upm.es
[2] Department of Electrical and Computer Engineering
University of Texas at Austin, Austin TX 78712
jacome@ece.utexas.edu

Abstract. This paper proposes a hardware operating system which provides a number of basic resource management services aimed at facilitating the use of dynamically reconfigurable devices in the design and implementation of effective reconfigurable systems. In particular, a number of tedious and error prone low level resource management tasks are automatically supported by the proposed operating system, thus becoming transparent to the designer of the reconfigurable system. The several components of the operating system, as well as their implementation in a hardware *reconfiguration controller*, are described in some detail.

1 Introduction

Dynamically reconfigurable FPGAs allow for a selective updating of the device's programmable logic and routing resources while the remaining resources continue to function [1]. Since FPGA reconfiguration delays are typically non-negligible, the ability of overlapping execution and reconfiguration opens new possibilities in terms of achievable raw performance.

In general, dynamic reconfiguration has been considered in the design of some experimental systems. In [2], a neural network is implemented using dynamic reconfiguration for the training phase. A microprocessor with a mutable instruction set is implemented in [3]. The design of a microprocessor with three reconfigurable processing units is presented in [4].

On the other hand, the development of new dynamically reconfigurable FPGAs, such as the Xilinx XC6200 family, the Atmel AT6000 and the FIPSOC FPGA (currently under development) [5], opens new possibilities in the design of reconfigurable systems.

New approaches based on the XC6200 family are currently appearing. In [6], a pipelined architecture is modified in run-time. A software operating system that assists in dynamic reconfiguration of functional units is proposed in [7].

* This work is partially sponsored by NATO (Grant No. CRG 950809) and by the European Commission (project HCM CHRX-CT94-0459).

The goal of the Hardware Objects Technology (HOT) [8] is to be able to *call* hardware routines from a C program.

The system that is presented in this paper is intended to simplify the design of dynamically reconfigurable systems by means of an operating system which will be dedicated to offer services to the user (application) tasks. Our proposal, however, is significantly different from those in [7] and [8]. For efficiency reasons, the operating system (also denoted *reconfiguration controller*) is fully implemented in hardware. This idea borrows some basic concepts that have been used by *traditional* Operating Systems (OS) for years, and has been properly adapted to the specifics of our technology of interest, i.e., dynamically reconfigurable systems.

In the remainder of this paper, the problem that has been addressed in this work and some basic issues related with design of such reconfigurable systems are introduced. Then, the basic functionality of our hardware operating system is described. Finally, some conclusions are drawn.

2 Problem Formulation

A dynamically reconfigurable system includes at least one reconfigurable area where blocks of logic can be loaded in run-time. The design of a system that takes advantage of this possibility poses a number of problems:

- The partitioning of a high-level system description into blocks that can be swapped into/out of the reconfigurable area.
- The search for an optimal reconfiguration schedule for those blocks.
- The determination of a set of services that helps to properly execute the required functionality.

We may refer to the mentioned blocks as *tasks* as they implement a small piece of functionality inside a more complex algorithm. This concept was previously used by Lysaght and Stockwood [9] to develop a simulation technique called *Dynamic Circuit Switching* (DCS). In our work, we will use these tasks as key elements to develop a specific methodology for the design of dynamically reconfigurable systems.

The critical issue in this approach is the implementation of a controller able to handle the reconfiguration of all these tasks. This controller should offer (OS-like) services such as tasks loading/removing, tasks scheduling, etc.

For the sake of completeness, in the remainder of this section we will briefly discuss some basic concepts that are essential to understand the whole methodology in which the design of a hardware OS makes sense. More information related with these issues can be found in [10, 11].

2.1 Task Based Partitioning

As a result of a previous research [10], it has been observed that the partitioning of a system into tasks causes a very important increment in the number of ports

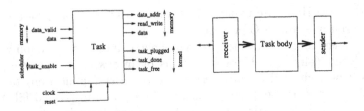

Fig. 1. The Task Template

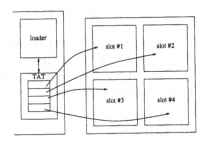

Fig. 2. System layout with the reconfigurable slots

and registers (then resources) that have to be implemented. The obtained figures drove us to look for a different way for task implementation.

The definition of a *task template* arises as a possible solution to the communications problem [11]. A task template is a standardized implementation scheme for all the tasks. Specifically, each task is implemented using three processes, two of which (input and output) are standard, that is, they are directly used by all the tasks. The third process is thus the only one the designer needs to take care of. In other words, its functionality has to be explicitly specified (see Figure 1).

2.2 System Floorplan

In order to allow the reubicability of the modules [3], we divide the dynamically reconfigurable FPGA into several areas, called *reconfigurable slots*, where the tasks can be loaded. These areas have the same size and their ports[1] are placed in the same relative position. Thus, the tasks will fit exactly inside them, since the use of the task template concept *standardizes* the user tasks' I/O ports.

Figure 2 illustrates the system floorplan. A *Task Allocation Table (TAT)* has been considered to keep track of which task is currently loaded in every slot.

3 A Hardware Operating System

As it has been discussed above, the aim of our work is to develop a *Hardware Operating System (HOS)* to give run-time support to dynamic reconfiguration.

---

[1] A port is the contact point between the routing channels and the reconfigurable slot.

The enormous complexity of reconfigurable systems and the design methodology proposed in [11] have motivated the realization of such a system. Using the services that the HOS offers, the designer can take advantage of using reconfiguration, at the same time that gets rid of facing all the cumbersome related details.

This HOS, called *FOCA (FPGA Operating system for Circuit Autoconfiguration)*, has been specified as a set of VHDL processes that implements specific services that helps designers in the realization of reconfigurable systems. The result, conversely, for instance, to the system described in [7], that needs a CPU, is an external dedicated hardware controller, resident in a static FPGA.

In the remainder of this section, some HOS basic functions will be described, in terms of the specific hardware (VHDL processes) that implements them.

3.1 FPGA Configuration

The dynamically reconfigurable FPGA initial configuration may be performed during the system startup. In order to generalize the concept of the HOS and provide a complete emulation of a software OS, we have designed a process called init that takes charge of the FPGA initialization by creating routing channels and the reconfigurable slots.

The main functionality implemented by the module loader is to read tasks and to configure them into the FPGA at run-time. In order to do this, loader has to look for the task data in an external memory, find out an empty slot by addressing the TAT, and store the task data into the FPGA.

The access to the configuration pins is controlled by a process called muxing.

3.2 Data Storage

The data storage is managed by a couple of processes. The first one, store, emulates a register file, while the second one, mutex, will guarantee *mutual exclusion* in the access to store by the different tasks (reconfigurable slots). This is accomplished by means of a priority-based access mechanism.

3.3 The Control of a FOCA–based System

The run-time control of the whole reconfigurable system is done by the processes kernel and scheduler. kernel's main functionality consists in providing services to the user's tasks. To properly perform its job, it is essential that kernel keeps track of which tasks are working in every slot. This is done by means of the TAT.

kernel is also in charge of loading new tasks whenever it is needed. To do that, a command to loader is then issued. Finally, kernel offers a *message passing* mechanism between tasks, as well as a way to introduce data from outside.

The process scheduler will enable tasks whenever they are needed. It passes a message to kernel and, if the task is not present in any of the slots, kernel will issue a command to load it.

4 Conclusions

Taking advantage of dynamic reconfiguration of FPGAs is one of the most important topics in the FPGA research area. Many examples are being designed, but not many of those are really suitable to this kind of implementation, due, mainly, to the long reconfiguration time.

This fact highlights the importance of defining a good strategy for the partitioning and scheduling of these systems. Otherwise, inefficient implementations will be obtained. But this strategy, and the use of the subsequently defined methodology, forces the designer to deal with new problems that may make the realization of a reconfigurable design quite difficult.

In this paper, a Hardware Operating System has been presented as a natural way of dealing with the resource management issues that result of applying the mentioned methodology. A number of services to handle tasks reconfiguration has been specified and the corresponding hardware has been designed.

References

[1] Patrick Lysaght and John Dunlop, "Dynamic Reconfiguration of FPGAs", in *More FPGAs*. Abingdon EE&CS Books. pp. 82–94. 1993.

[2] J. D. Hadley and Brad L. Hutchings. "Designing a Partially Reconfigured System". *FPGAs for Fast Board Development and Reconfigurable Computing. Proc. SPIE 2607*. pp. 210–220. 1995.

[3] Michael J. Wirthlin and Brad L. Hutchings. "DISC: The dynamic instruction set computer". *FPGAs for Fast Board Development and Reconfigurable Computing. Proc. SPIE 2607*. pp. 92–103. 1995.

[4] Christian Iseli. "Spyder: A Reconfigurable Processor Development System". *PhD Thesis No. 1476*. Polytechnic Federal School. Lausanne. 1996.

[5] Julio Faura, et al. "Multicontext Dynamic Reconfiguration and Real Time Probing on a Novel Mixed Signal Device with On-chip Microprocessor". *7th International Workshop on Field Programmable Logic and Applications*. 1997.

[6] W. Luk, et al. "Pipeline Morphing and Virtual Pipelines". *7th International Workshop on Field Programmable Logic and Applications*. pp 111–120. 1997.

[7] Gordon Brebner. "A Virtual Hardware Operating System for the XC6200".*6th International Workshop on Field Programmable Logic and Applications*. pp 327–336. 1996.

[8] Steve Casselman, et al. "Hardware Object Programming on a Reconfigurable Computer". Virtual Computer Corporation 1996.

[9] Patrick Lysaght and Jon Stockwood, "A Simulation Tool for Dynamically Reconfigurable Field Programmable Gate Arrays", in *IEEE Trans. on VLSI Systems*, Vol. 4, No. 3, September 1996.

[10] Pedro Merino, Juan Carlos López and Margarida Jacome, "Task Partitioning for Reconfigurable Systems". *Sixth BELSIGN Workshop. Behavioural Design Methodologies for Digital Systems*. Aveiro (Portugal). pp 127–130. October 1997.

[11] Pedro Merino, Margarida Jacome and Juan Carlos López, "A Methodology for Task Based Partitioning and Scheduling of Dynamically Reconfigurable Systems". *IEEE Symposium on FPGAs for Custom Computing Machines*. April 1998.

High Speed Low Level Image Processing on FPGAs Using Distributed Arithmetic

Elena Cerro-Prada[1] and Philip B. James-Roxby[2]

[1,2] Digital Systems and Vision Processing Group
School of Electronic and Electrical Engineering
The University of Birmingham, Birmingham B15 2TT, United Kingdom
[1] cerroe@ee-wp.bham.ac.uk   [2] P.B.James-Roxby@bham.ac.uk

Abstract. A method of calculating the 3x3 mask convolution required for many low level image processing algorithms is presented, which is well suited for implementing on reconfigurable FPGAs. The approach is based on distributed arithmetic, and uses the symmetry of weights present in many filter masks to save on circuit space, at the expense of requiring custom circuitry for each set of coefficients. A four product example system has been implemented on a Xilinx XC6216 device to demonstrate the suitability of this reconfigurable architecture for image processing systems.

1   Introduction

The spatial convolution process uses a weighted average of an input pixel and its immediate neighbours to calculate an output pixel value. For a 512x512 image, the number of multiply-accumulate operations needed to perform a 3x3 mask convolution is around 2.4 million. At a frame rate of 25 frames/sec, real-time processing requires 59 million operations per second. Normally, to meet this computational requirement, fast dedicated parallel multipliers and accumulators are needed.

We consider the use of current FPGAs for performing these multiply accumulate operations; in particular, we examine the capabilities of the Xilinx XC6200 series devices. It is clear that fast parallel multipliers are not suitable due to their large size. Instead, we consider the use of distributed arithmetic, and investigate current methods of implementing distributed arithmetic elements on the 6200 series devices.

2   Distributed Arithmetic for FPGA Based Filters

Multiply accumulate (MAC) structures can be implemented on devices with limited space by using Distributed Arithmetic (DA) techniques [1,2], Partial products are stored in look-up tables (LUTs) which are accessed sequentially, and summed by a single accumulator.

In implementing masks where several weights are the same, it is possible to exploit symmetry to reduce the size of the partial product LUTs. This can be performed by accumulating the inputs prior to accessing the look-up table using a serial adder [3]. At the expense of slightly larger LUTs, it is also possible to use full width addition resulting in faster circuits, which is the approach used here. Also since all weighted results are produced at the same time, this unifies the control process for filters containing different symmetries. An example block structure for a 3x3 mask convolution process is shown below in figure 1.

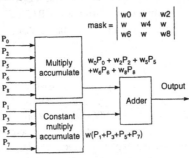

Fig. 1. Block structure for a 3x3 mask convolution

3   Design Implementation

A four product example system using distributed arithmetic has been produced to illustrate the method of implementing LUT-based circuits on the XC6200. The design can be used to calculate the inner products of a mask for four common coefficients, and is shown in figure 1 as the constant multiply accumulate block.

The XC6200 series devices offer a fine-grained sea of gates, with dynamic partial reconfiguration and a dedicated microprocessor interface [4]. The cells can implement any 2 input function with a register if required. Unlike other RAM based Xilinx devices, no demonstration of the use of RAM embedded on the device by other parts of the device has yet been shown. Thus, to implement storage on the XC6200 series devices, it is necessary to explicitly design circuits capable of being addressed and producing the appropriate data word. This is of great significance when implementing LUTs on the XC6200.

In implementing the constant multiply accumulate block, the most important aspect is the implementation of the look-up table. The other components are quite simple to design. Briefly, the adder prior to the look up table provides the sum of 4 input bits, and occupies 9 cells. For a system using 8 bit pixel values, and 4 bit weights, the DA accumulator occupies a bounding box of size 5 x 12, though the routing within the box is fairly sparse.

A number of methods are suitable for implementing look-up tables on the XC6200, depending on whether the contents of the look-up tables are known at synthesis time. If the contents are to be changed to any arbitrary value at run time without any software support for pre-computing values, then a series of loadable registers and multiplexors must be used. This will clearly use a lot of the FPGA real estate; for example, a 256 entry look up table storing 8 bit values would consume all the area of a 6216 device.

If the contents of the LUT are known at synthesis time, it is possible to get smaller implementations. In [5,6], a technique of embedding the bits of the look-up table in the logic gate available in the 6200 series cell is presented. We have used this technique to implement LUTs by constructing a generator which accepts the required stored values as input and produces a LOLA description [7] of the required circuit complete with placement information. This can subsequently be processed by the Lola Development System tools to produce configuration data as shown in figure 2. LOLA is in effect used by the generator as an intermediate language, which can then be further processed by device specific tools, in a similar manner to the bytecode used by Java interpreters.

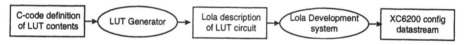

Fig. 2. Design flow for LUTs

To clarify the flow used in [5,6], an example will be discussed. Consider a LUT required to store the 4 unsigned values <13,9,2,4>. Clearly the address of the LUT will be 2 bits (a_1a_0), and four bits will correctly represent the output $(d_3d_2d_1d_0)$. Firstly, a table is constructed showing the binary pattern required for each of the output bits. The required logic function to implement each output bit given the two input bits is identified by reading down the column for each bit as shown in table 1.

Table 1. Example of LUT construction

a_1a_0	d_3	d_2	d_1	d_0
00	1	1	0	1
01	1	0	0	1
10	0	0	1	0
11	0	1	0	0
Function	$\sim a_1$	$\sim(a_1 \cdot a_0)$	$a_1 * \sim a_0$	$\sim a_1$

Since the logic of a 6200 cell can implement any 2 input function, LUTs containing any bit pattern can be constructed this way. Implementing LUTs requiring more bits per entry is simply a matter of duplicating the process for as many additional bits as are required. Implementing LUTs with more than 4 entries requires multiplexors on the outputs of multiple LUTs using the additional address bits as selectors, as discussed in [5].

The LUTs produced by the generator match the sizes reported in [5]. For example, a 64x4 bit LUT requires 124 cells. In general for a LUT of size 2^k x 4m, the cell usage is given by $m(2^k+4(2^{k-2}-1))$.

In the case of a 5xM LUT, as is required in the example system, a second LUT containing the value when a_2 is set could be used together with the multiplexor. Since the value is independent of a_0 and a_1, this LUT would simply contain hardwired 1's and 0's. It is possible to use constant propagation to reduce the storage requirements by merging these hardwired units with the logic of the multiplexors. Since each of the required functions for multiplexing in a 0 or 1 can be implemented using a single cell, this saves a third of the required area. For instance, a 5x8 bit LUT can be implemented in 8 cells.

To evaluate the performance of the four product example system, an XC6200 FPGA card was used, which allows data to be written and read over a system PCI bus. The pixel data was transferred to and from internal registers using the FastMap interface of the 6216 present on the board. Though it is possible for user logic to determine that a register has been accessed using the FastMap interface, and hence start working [8], a separate software controlled clock was used. Using 8 bit pixels, two write accesses were required (1 for pixel data, 1 for the clock) before the result could be read back.

Using the functions supplied in the boards API for transferring data to and from columns on the XC6216 device, the performance was limited to 60,000 results per second on a 100 MHz Pentium machine. By pre-computing target memory addresses and re-writing the assembly code using the API as a base, 700,000 results per second could be calculated. As noted in [8], this could be further improved by using the SRAM on the board. However, extra circuitry would be required to control the transfers to and from the SRAM.

This result is an order of magnitude short of the real time processing requirements of the 6.5 million pixel results per second required to process 25 512x512 frames every second. The problem is now I/O bound by the performance of the PCI interface. However, due to the small size of the system, it is possible to process a number of pixels simultaneously, and since the mask slides over the target image, this will actually reduce the amount of I/O required, and hence speed up the overall execution.

4 Changing Weights : Exploitation of Reconfigurability

Changing the weights can be performed in two ways, which on the XC6200 series are actually rather similar. Considering first the address bus format for the XC6216 device, described in [4], if mode(1:0) is set to 00, this allows access to the cell configuration and the state of the cell register.

If a register and multiplexor method is used to implement the look-up tables, the new weights are loaded into the registers by writing into the region of device's memory map which maintains the state of the cell register. This is performed by setting the column offset to 11 and writing to the appropriate columns.

If the bits of the look-up tables are embedded within logic functions, as described in section 4, new weights are loaded by writing pre-computed configuration data into internal cell routing registers for each cell. This is performed by setting the column offset to 01 or 10, and writing to the appropriate row and columns. The configuration data must be pre-computed using the generator described in section 4, to give the correct logic functions.

For image processing systems requiring adaptive changes to weights, pre-computing configuration data is impractical. In addition, the configuration overhead is significant. For image processing systems requiring a small number of changes to the weights, the pre-computing of configuration data is not such a problem. Also techniques are available for compressing the configuration bitstream to minimize the reconfiguration overhead [9].

As well as the changing of individual weights within a mask, it is important to consider changing the symmetry of the mask. In the worst case, each mask value is different, requiring a single large LUT to hold the partial products. Currently, we are investigating techniques for minimizing the reconfiguration overhead between different mask symmetries, and hope to have results shortly.

5 Conclusions and Future Work

Distributed arithmetic techniques can successfully be implemented on devices without explicit support for embedded storage. By using techniques to save on LUT entries, it is possible to reduce the space required for the LUTs, without affecting the performance of the system. It is possible to exploit partial reconfiguration to change weight values, and in the future, we wish to quantify the effects of changing the symmetry of masks in terms of the reconfiguration overhead.

6 References

1. Jaggernauth, J., Loui, A.C.P., Venetsanopoulos, A.N.: "Real-Time Image Processing by Distributed Arithmetic Implementation of Two-Dimensional Digital Filters", IEEE Trans. ASSP, Vol. ASSP - 33, No. 6, pp. 1546-155, Dec. 1985
2. Goslin, G.R.: "Using Xilinx FPGAs to design custom digital signal processing devices", available at http://www.xilinx.com/appnotes/dspx5dev.htm
3. Mintzer, L.:"FIR Filters with Field-Programmable Gate Arrays", Journal of VLSI Signal Processing, Vol. 6, pp.119-127, 1993
4. Xilinx Inc., "XC6200 field programmable gate arrays", available at http://www.xilinx.com/partinfo/6200.pdf
5. Xilinx Inc., "A fast constant coefficient multiplier for the XC6200", available at http://www.xilinx.com/xapp/xapp082.pdf
6. Duncan, A., Kean, T : "DES keybreaking, encryption and decryption on the XC6216", Proc. 6th Annual IEEE Symposium on Custom Computing Machines, 1998
7. Wirth, N. : "Digital circuit design", Springer-Verlag Berlin Heidelberg, 1995
8. Singh, S, Slous, R. : "Accelerating Adobe Photoshop with reconfigurable logic" Proc. 6th Annual IEEE Symposium on Custom Computing Machines, 1998
9. Hauck, S, Z. Li, Schwabe, E. : "Configuration compression for the Xilinx XC6200 FPGA" Proc. 6th Annual IEEE Symposium on Custom Computing Machines, 1998

A Flexible Implementation of High-Performance FIR Filters on Xilinx FPGAs

Tien-Toan Do, Holger Kropp, Carsten Reuter, Peter Pirsch

Laboratorium für Informationstechnologie,
University of Hannover,
Schneiderberg 32, 30167 Hannover, Germany

{toan, kropp, reuter}@mst.uni-hannover.de
http://www.mst.uni-hannover.de/

Abstract. Finite impulse-response filters (FIR filters) are very commonly used in digital signal processing applications and traditionally implemented using ASICs or DSP-processors. For FPGA implementation, due to the high throughput rate and large computational power required under real-time constraints, they are a challenging subject. Indeed, the limitation of resources on an FPGA, i. e. , logic blocks and flip flops, and furthermore, the high routing delays, require compact implementations of the circuits. Hence, in lookup table-based FPGAs, e. g. Xilinx FPGAs, FIR-filters were implemented usually using distributed arithmetic. However, such filters can only be used where the filter coefficients are constant. In this paper, we present approaches for a more flexible FPGA implementation of FIR filters. Using pipelined multipliers which are carefully adapted to the underlying FPGA structure, our FIR filters do not require a predefinition of the filter coefficients. Combining pipelined multipliers and parallely distributed arithmetic results in different trade-offs between hardware cost and flexibility of the filters. We show that clock frequencies of up to 50 MHz are achievable using Xilinx $XC40xx - 5$ FPGAs.

1 Introduction

Belonging to the so called low-level DSP-algorithms, finite impulse-response filtering represents a substantial part of digital signal processing. Low-level DSP-algorithms are characterized by their high regularity. Nevertheless, on the other hand, they require a high computational performance. Yet, if the processing has to be performed under real-time conditions, those algorithms have to deal with high throughput rates.

An N tap FIR filtering algorithm can be expressed, like many other DSP-algorithms, by an arithmetic sum of products:

$$y(i) = \sum_{k=0}^{N-1} h(k) \cdot x(i - k) \tag{1}$$

where $y(i)$ and $x(i)$ are the response and the input at time i, respectively; and $h(k)$, for $k = 0, 1, ..., N - 1$ are the filter coefficients.

Hence, the implementation of an N tap FIR filter expressed mathematically in equation (1) requires the implementation of N multiplications, which are very costly regarding hardware and computational time. However, in many cases of digital signal processing where symmetric FIR filters are required, the number of multiplications can be reduced. For the coefficients of such filters, the following relations are valid [1]:

$$h(k) = h(N - k - 1), \quad \text{for} \quad k = 0, 1, 2, ..., N - 1 \qquad (2)$$

Utilizing relation (2) can almost halve the number of required multiplications. Thus, only symmetric FIR-filters are considered here.

Further, filters whose coefficients are constant can be implemented at a low hardware cost using bit-plane-structures, distributed arithmetic (DA) [2] or lookup-table multipliers (LUTMULT) instead of conventional hardware multipliers. Especially, for FPGAs where lookup tables (LUTs) are the underlying logic blocks, e. g., Xilinx FPGAs [3], DA techniques [4] and LUTMULT can be invoked as a convenient way for low-cost realization of FIR-filters with constant coefficients. Nevertheless, such filters would be not used, if the filter coefficients should be frequently varied. This is the case when, e. g., emulating algorithms, where influences of such variations of the algorithm parameters on the quality of the processed signals must be investigated.

Hence, in this paper, we present approaches leading to an efficient, flexible and modular realization of symmetric FIR-filters on Xilinx $XC40xx$ FPGAs. FPGA-implementations of pipelined filters using parallely distributed arithmetic and implementation results will be discussed in sections 2. In section 3, the alternative approach for an implementation using conventional hardware multipliers which are carefully adapted to the underlying FPGA structure is considered. In Section 4 concluding remarks will be provided.

2 Distributed-Arithmetic FIR Filters

In essence, distributed arithmetic (DA) is a computation technique that perform multiplication using lookup table-based schemes [5]. DA-techniques permit computations in form of sum of products as expressed in equation (1) to be decomposed into repetitive lookup table procedures, the results from which are then accumulated to produce the final result.

Since Xilinx $XC4000$ FPGAs are based on lookup tables, distributed arithmetic is a convenient way to implement the multiply-intensive algorithms like FIR filters, provided that one of the multiplication operands is constant. The bits of the other operand are then used as address lines for looking up a table which is, in fact, a storage, e. g. ROM, RAM, where the potential products from the multiplication of the first operand by the potential values of the second operand are stored (Fig. 1). FPGA-implementation of FIR filters using serial distributed arithmetic has been proposed in [4] and [6], where implementation results are also described.

We realize fully parallel DA FIR filters on Xilinx $XC4000$ as depicted in figure 1 where an 8 tap 8 bit symmetric filter is sketched. To assure a compact realisation of the circuit, the LUT sizes are tailored to the required precision for the output data. So, for a given precision, the LUT sizes are not uniform [6], but depend on the positions of the individual bits, i. e. LUTs for the less significant bits are smaller. Furthermore, in order to obtain high performance, the filters are pipelined after every 4 bit adder whose timing amounts about 18 ns to 20 ns on a $XC4000 - 5$. The number of required CLBs for the 8 tap 8 bit symmetric FIR filter depicted in figuge 1, which can run at frequencies up to 50 MHz on a $XC4000 - 5$, is 140. The latency of the above filter is 14 clock cycles

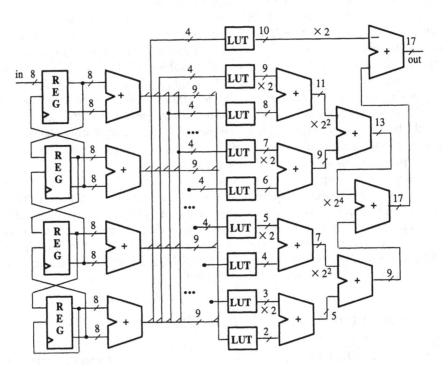

Fig. 1. Distributed-Arithmetic FIR Filter on Xilinx $XC4000$

While the fully precise filtering requires data stored in every LUT to be 10 bit-wide and outputs 19 bit data, the maximal absolute error ($= 1024$) caused by our 8 bit 8 tap FIR filter depicted in fig. 1 is quite the same as it caused by the coressponding Xilinx DA filter ($= 1022$), where the LUTs are uniformly wide and require 36 CLBs. The number of CLBs for all the LUTs in our design is 27.

Hence, high-performance digital filters can be implemented at a low hardware cost on LUT-based FPGAs using DA technique. The main drawback of this approach is that DA technique requires the predefinition of the filter coefficients. In many application FPGAs for DSP, e. g. hardware emulation of DSP algorithms, filters are needed which allow a frequent and flexible modification of the filter coefficients.

3   FIR Filters with Conventional Hardware Multipliers

Though multipliers are costly, involving them is inevitable for filters whose coefficients should be frequently varied. Hence, we have investigated an efficient FPGA-implementation of FIR-filters using pipelined array multipliers.

For the processing at a sample rate comparable to that of the above DA filter, the $8 - by - 9$ multipliers of the filter are two-rows pipelined [7] as illustrated in figure 2, and their structure is adapted and carefully mapped onto the target architecture, i.e. Xilinx FPGA. Further, for the same precision as for the above DA filter, the eight right most product bits from the multiplication (max. absolut error $= 1023$) are cut off. The filter has a latency of 13 clock cycles and requires 390 CLBs. The achievable frequency for this filter on a $XC4000 - 5$ is about 45 MHz - 50 MHz. In comparison with a parallely distributed arithmetic FIR-

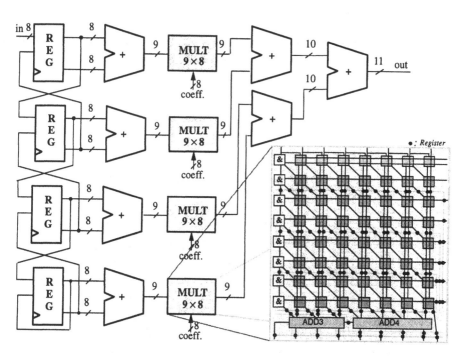

Fig. 2. FIR Filter with conventional multipliers on Xilinx $XC4000$

filter (Fig. 1), the hardware cost for the FIR filter with conventional hardware multipliers (Fig. 2) is increased, while the performance is quite the same.

Because the achievable frequencies for the above DA filters and filters with conventional hardware multipliers are about the same, they can be combined in a "hybrid" approach leading to different trade-offs between hardware cost and flexibility.

4 Conclusions

Using Xilinx XC40xx-5 FPGAs, clock frequencies up to about 45MHz - 50MHz for FIR filters are achievable. While the DA technique approach leads to low-cost implementations of FIR filters on lookup table-based FPGAs, FIR filters with conventional hardware multipliers are more flexible. In spite of the high cost, such filters are desirable in many cases where the filter coefficients should be frequently varied. An example for that is hardware emulation of algorithms where influences of variations of the algorithm parameters, e.g., filter coefficients, on the processing have to be investigated. Combining the above approaches will lead to different trade-offs regarding hardware costs and flexibility.

Acknowledgment

One of the authors, T.-T. Do, receives a scholarship from the German Academic Exchange Service (Deutscher Akademischer Austauschdienst - DAAD). He is grateful to this organization for supporting his research.

References

1. A. V. Openheim, R. W. Schafer: *Digital Signal Processing*, Prentice Hall (1975)
2. P. Pirsch: *Architectures for Digital Signal Processing*, John Wiley & Sons (1997)
3. Xilinx Inc.: *The Programmable Logic Data Book*, (1996)
4. L. Mintzer: *FIR Filters with Field-Programmable Gate Arrays*, IEEE Journal of VLSI Signal Processing (August 1993) 119–128
5. C. S. Burrus: *Digital Filters Structures described by Distributed Arithmetic*, IEEE Trans. on Circuits and Systems (1977), 674–680
6. Xilinx Inc.: *Core Solutions*, (May 1997)
7. T.-T. Do, H. Kropp, M. Schwiegershausen, P. Pirsch: *Implementation of Pipelined Multipliers on Xilinx FPGAs - A Case Study*, 7th International Workshop on Field-Programmable Logic and Applications, Proceedings (1997)

Implementing Processor Arrays on FPGAs

István Vassányi

Department of Information Systems, University of Veszprém, Hungary
vassanyi@madmax.terra.vein.hu

Abstract. Fine grain FPGAs offer a suitable medium for the implementation of bit level processor arrays. This paper describes a layout method, and a parametrized tool based on it, for designing two-dimensional array structures on FPGAs. The use of the tool is demonstrated by an example application in morphological image processing. The tool observes high-level array structure, and thus it can find better layouts for arrays on the XC6216 FPGA, than the tool of the FPGA vendor (XACT 6000). Additionally, non-rectangular (distorted) layouts were found to perform better than rectangular ones.

1 Introduction

FPGAs naturally fit the array structure of two-dimensional (2-D) cellular arrays, built up from identical Processing Elements (PEs). There are several case studies in the field of signal and image processing that prove the applicability of FPGAs for fine grain, regular processor arrays [1], [2], [3], [4], etc. These studies present manually designed processor arrays on FPGAs. However, they do not give a general framework and methodology for the theoretical (geometrical) and practical (layout-related) problems of FPGA-based processor array design.

The most important new contributions presented in this paper are the application of planar tiling theory for finding the possible types of FPGA-based processor arrays, and the adaption of existing FPGA CAD methods to support the design of 2-D array layouts.

2 Geometrical Properties of FPGA Tilings

A 2-D processor array implemented on a CLB-matrix can be modelled by a tessellation with copies of a tile (so-called *prototile*) over a discrete plane. We require that the tiles cover the plane without gaps and overlaps. Furthermore, to ensure proper operation of the processor array, a PE-tile must have an input port where, and only where, the adjacent PE-tile has an output port. Then, each tile must have either 4 or 6 symmetrically positioned neighbours, and the neighbourhood pattern must be the same for all tiles. Further, the tiling must be *periodic* (i.e. it must have two nonparallel translations that copy the tiling onto itself), and the minimal period parallelograms must have the same area as the PE-tile used in the tiling. These properties follow simply from established results of planar tiling theory [5].

In the practice of signal/image processing array algorithms, the required processor array is normally rectangular, e.g. $N/2 \times N$ processors, where N is the problem size. In order to implement such an array or a part of it, on a square matrix of CLBs, we need a layout that is contained by a rectangle parallel to the CLB grid. Otherwise, large sections of the chip area are lost.

Theorem 1. *There are two grid types which have a container rectangle that is parallel to the CLB grid:*

- *rectangular grid: both coordinate axes of the PE grid are parallel to the CLB grid.*
- *hexagonal grid: only one of the PE grid axes is parallel to the CLB grid. The period of the tiling in this direction must be an even number (measured in CLBs).*

In both grids, the area, or CLB-count, of the prototile can be expressed as the product of two natural numbers (the horizontal and vertical periods, P_v and P_h).

The proof of this theorem is omitted for brevity. The four possible combinations of neighbour numbers and grid types are shown in Fig. 1.

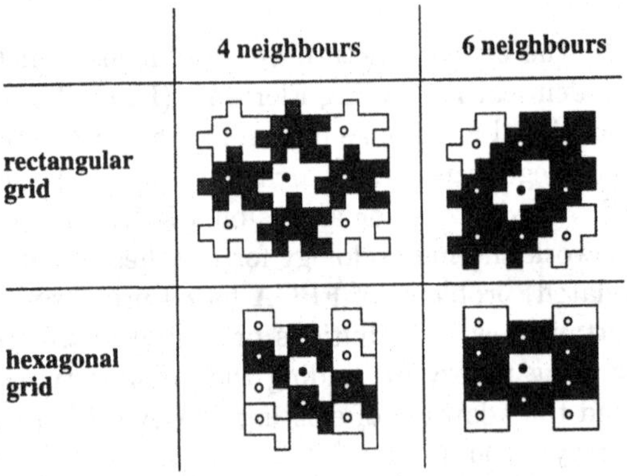

Fig. 1. The four possible neighbourhood/grid type combinations of FPGA-based tilings. The neighbours of the central PE are shaded

When designing an optimized layout for a PE, all delays, whether they arise inside a PE or on a link connecting two PEs, must be considered. This would require the analysis of an area much larger than the PE, although all PEs are laid out the same way. The proposed solution to this problem is the use of a *wrapped-around plane*. It is easy to see that a tiling can be reproduced by cutting and multiplying any rectangle of height P_v and width P_h of the tiling, no matter how eroded or elongated the shape of the prototile is. This is illustrated in Fig. 2 for a 6-neighbour rectangular grid. For hexagonal grids, the same concept can be used except that the connections of abutting border CLBs are shifted with half-period in the direction of the PE grid axis that is not parallel to the CLB grid.

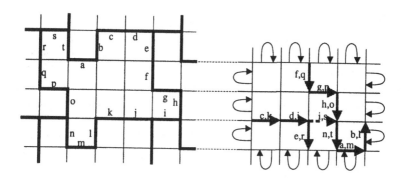

Fig. 2. Tile boundaries on a wrapped-around plane. Bent arrows show the connections of abutting border CLBs. The original tile (left) and its representation (right). Letters a,b, etc. represent edge correspondances

On the period rectangle (right in Fig. 2), we mark the borderlines of the tiles that the rectangle intersects and we assume that the rectangle wraps around like a torus (this is shown by bent arrows). Then, the usual placement methods can be used with the following simple rule: when we cross the borderlines, we enter one of the neighbour tiles. For six neighbours, we have three types of directed borderlines, shown by gray, black, and dashed black arrows in the figure.

On the torus surface, the inter-PE links to far PEs can be defined by paths that cross a number of borderlines of prescribed types a prescribed number of times. The order of border crossings is irrelevant.

3 An Algorithm and a Tool for Regular Array Layout

There is relatively little support in today's FPGA CAD systems for the extra layout requirements of 2-D array structures. A notable exception is the XACT step 6000 system, which preserves the hieracrhical structure of the design throughout the layout process. The PE can be placed and routed, then multiple copies of this layout can be instantiated. However, inter-PE links must be routed at the top level, one-by-one. Thus, inter-PE nets, which in most cases form a part of the post-layout critical delay path of the circuit, cannot be taken into account when designing the internal layout of the basic PE tile.

The proposed algorithm uses the wraparound plane concept shown in Fig. 2, so it can choose a layout that optimizes the post-layout critical path of the whole array while designing a single PE.

The input of the algorithm is made up by the partitioned netlist of the PE, the specification of inter-PE links, grid type and geometrical parameters and constraints (e.g. required periods). Then, the CLBs of the PE are placed in an initial, minimally distorted tile using the mincut algorithm. After this, random distorsion steps are performed to improve the estimated critical path of the array. Each such step makes an overlap between abutting PEs. At the end of this step, the shape of the tile is fixed. The last step in the placement is a standard simulated annealing procedure. Finally, the PE is routed using a maze routing algorithm and the post-layout critical path is measured.

This algorithm has been implemented in a tool called Array Mapper (ARM). The tool uses a parametrized, fine grain CLB model that uses only local routing resources. Regional and global routing can be used to propagate global control signals to PEs, without interfering with local routing. Also, the use of regional routing would make position-independent layout design impossible. However, a fine grain, bit-level PE is expected to occupy only a small area, for which regional routing resources are not very important.

4 Experimental Results

The ARM tool was run on a PE array for binary morphology from [6]. This array represents a fine grain benchmark with a tile geometry of $P_v = P_h = 3$. The operation of this array is similar to [1], see also [7]. Figure 3 shows a layout

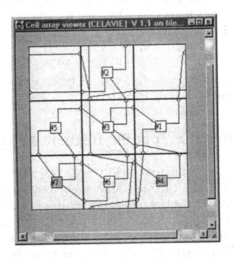

Fig. 3. The layout of the morphological PE, shown in the Celavie viewer. This array has a 4-neighbour rectangular grid. PEs in the array are connected to the four nearest neighbours via bidirectional links. The PE shown has 7 functional CLBs, numbered #1..7. Note that nets exiting at the border of the PE enter at a symmetrical position in the abutting PE

for the morphological array in the Cell Array Viewer (Celavie) that belongs to the ARM tool. A 3 × 3 sub-array of PEs with this layout was transported in the XACT 6000 system, which measured a critical path delay of 17.67 ns in the layout (clock to setup). We note that when only the placement of CLBs was specified, the XACT router was unable to route the array with only local connections, although such a routing exists (see te figure). When the use of regional and long nets was allowed, the XACT software could route the array of 3 × 3 PEs. The resulting clock-to-setup critical path was 22.34 ns. However, inter-PE links took long detours *outside* the PE array, using an irregular combination of lenght 4 and global nets. Such an arrangement would be impossible for larger arrays of PEs, let alone a PE array that fills the entire CLB matrix. The increase in the CP was also caused by an internal net that was forced to detour outside the array.

In other experiments the tile shapes were limited to rectangles to check the effect of tile distorsions. For small benchmarks, such as the morphological PE, there was no change in the critical path, and the routability degraded. However, for larger (6 × 6) PEs there was a statistically significant increase in the critical path of 7.6%, compared to the distorted tile shapes. This shows that although non-rectangular shapes are harder to route, they can be more favourable than rectangles, if the overlaps between abutting PE tiles are not too deep.

5 Conclusions and Future Work

The paper presented a method and a tool for layout design of fine grain array structures. The core of the method is the uniform treatment of inter- and intra-PE nets. Exploiting the extra information that comes from array structure, the tool can find better layouts than a general-purpose CAD tool.

Further work on the ARM tool includes a better interface to the XACT 6000 system, and an improved routing algorithm.

References

1. Chaudhuri, A.S., Cheung, P.Y.K., Luk, W.: A Reconfigurable Data-Localised Array for Morphological Algorithms. In: Proc. 7th Int. Workshop on Field-Programmable Logic and Applications. Springer-Verlag, (1997) 344–353
2. Marnane, W.P., O'Reilly, F.J., Murphy, P.J.: Compiling Regular Arrays onto FPGAs. In: Proc. 5th Int. Workshop on Field-Programmable Logic and Applications. Springer-Verlag, (1995) 178–187
3. Jebelean, T.: Implementing GCD Systolic Arrays on FPGA. In: Proc. 4th Int. Workshop on Field-Programmable Logic and Applications. Springer-Verlag, (1994) 132–137
4. Vassányi, I.: FPGAs and array algorithms: Two implementation examples. J. Systems Architecture **43** (1997) 23–26
5. Grünbaum, B., Shepard, G.: Tilings and patterns. W.H. Freeman & Co., New York (1987)
6. Vassányi, I.: An FPGA-based Cellular Array for Binary Morphological Operations. In: Proc. 2nd Workshop on Computational Modelling in Biosciences. Kecskemét, Hungary, (1995) I.17–25
7. Erényi, I., Fazekas, Z.: Image Processing Applications and their Parallel Aspects. Computing and Control Eng. J. of the IEE (1994) **5** 71–74

Reconfigurable Hardware – A Study in Codesign

Samuel Holmström and Kaisa Sere

Turku Centre for Computer Science, Åbo Akademi University,
Department of Computer Science, FIN-20520 Turku, Finland
{Samuel.Holmstrom,Kaisa.Sere}@abo.fi

Abstract. The role of software methods, especially programming, is achieving a more and more important role in system design. This paper demonstrates how an algorithm can be implemented partly in hardware and partly in software on a special FPGA-based reconfigurable computing system platform. We start with an abstract formal specification of the algorithm. Thereafter we show, without being very formal, how the specification is mapped into an implementation. Moreover, the specification helps us in identifying the different software and hardware partitions.

1 Introduction

Reconfigurable computing systems can be defined as systems consisting of a combination of SRAM-based FPGAs, memory and CPUs [3]. Used together with a CPU, the FPGA can be seen as a fast and flexible coprocessor that can be used in order to speed up the execution of time-critical portions of algorithms.

A hardware description language, e.g. VHDL or Verilog, can be used as a starting point for codesign [10]. In our work we start from an abstract high-level specification of the algorithm. Guided by this we create the hardware and software partitions. Even though we are not entirely formal in our reasoning in this paper, we use the formal specification to transform it into an implementation.

2 A Reconfigurable Computing System

In this study we used the HARP-2 which was developed by the Oxford Hardware Compilation Group at the University of Oxford. The HARP-2 consists of a 32-bit RISC-style microprocessor (a T425 transputer) and a Xilinx XC3195A FPGA. 4 MB of DRAM and 128 kB of SRAM is also available. Several HARP boards can be connected together via contacts and transputer links [9].

The transputer executes an occam program which is stored in DRAM. The program takes care of downloading suitable configurations to the FPGA as well as establishing proper clock speed by programming the frequency generator. Handel-C, defined as a codesign tool or a CASE-tool [1, 4], can be used in order to model an implementation on the HARP-2. After simulating the model, it probably needs to be partitioned. A separate Handel-C program must be written (pasted) for each hardware partition. These programs will result in downloadable configurations. Software partitions are rewritten in occam. The original Handel-C model is used for verification purposes.

Input:	$P_L, P_R \in \{0, 1, \ldots, 2^{32} - 1\}$
	$K_0, K_1, \ldots, K_{15} \in \{0, 1, \ldots, 2^{16} - 1\}$

Output:	$C_L, C_R \in \{0, 1, \ldots, 2^{32} - 1\}$

Variables:	$L, R \in \{0, 1, \ldots, 2^{32} - 1\}$
	$r_0, r_1, r_2, r_3, k_0, k_1, f_0, f_1, f_2, f_3 \in \{0, 1, \ldots, 2^8 - 1\}$
	$j \in \{0, 1, \ldots, 7\}$

Operations:

$$L = P_L \oplus (K_8, K_9) \tag{1}$$
$$R = P_R \oplus (K_{10}, K_{11})$$

$$j = 0 \tag{2}$$
while $(j \le 7)$:
$\quad (r_0, r_1, r_2, r_3) = R$
$\quad (k_0, k_1) = K_j$
$\quad f_2 = r_2 \oplus r_3 \oplus k_1$
$\quad f_1 = ((r_0 \oplus r_1 \oplus k_0) + f_2 + 1) \bmod 256$
$\quad f_2 = (f_2 + \mathrm{Rot2}(f_1)) \bmod 256$
$\quad f_0 = (r_0 + \mathrm{Rot2}(f_1)) \bmod 256$
$\quad f_3 = (r_3 + \mathrm{Rot2}(f_2) + 1) \bmod 256$
$\quad R = L \oplus (\mathrm{Rot2}(f_0), \mathrm{Rot2}(f_1), \mathrm{Rot2}(f_2), \mathrm{Rot2}(f_3))$
$\quad L = (r_0, r_1, r_2, r_3)$
$\quad j = j + 1$
end while

$$L = R \oplus L \tag{3}$$
$$C_L = R \oplus (K_{12}, K_{13})$$
$$C_R = L \oplus (K_{14}, K_{15})$$

Fig. 1. Specification for the FEAL-8 algorithm

3 Specification of the FEAL-8 Algorithm

In this section, the FEAL-8 algorithm is described as a set of *inputs, outputs, operations,* and internal *variables*. In the implementation stage, the operations will be implemented in the same order as they are specified. The specification method used here is based on a hardware specification method that can be found elsewhere [5]. In here, an expression $(A, B, \ldots)$ means concatenation of bit-vectors A and B etc., where the the leftmost vector contains the MSB.

The FEAL-8 algorithm (specified in Fig. 1) takes binary encoded plaintext and keys as input. The plaintext is divided into a left half (P_L) and a right half (P_R). The text is enciphered by using rotations and 16-bit keys. In the specification, Rot2 represents rotations of two bits to the right for 8-bit vectors. The creation of extended keys is not described here. The enciphered text comes out from the FEAL-8 algorithm as two 32-bit vectors C_L and C_R.

4 HARP-2 Implementation of FEAL-8

Because the FEAL-8 algorithm could not be implemented as one single hardware partition for the Xilinx XC3195A FPGA, it had to be divided into several partitions. Our goal was to implement as much as possible of the algorithm in hardware by using as few configurations as possible. In this case study, three different configurations[1] are used. These configurations follow naturally from the formal specification in Fig. 1. The first configuration does some initial encipherment for the binary encoded plaintext P_L and P_R. The second configuration continues the job of the first configuration by implementing the loop (2) specified in the FEAL-8 algorithm. The third configuration fine-tunes the encipherment and stores the final results C_L and C_R.

The binary encoded plaintext is divided into blocks and the FEAL-8 algorithm is used for each of these. The extended keys $K_0, \ldots, K_{15}$ are stored in SRAM, memory locations 0 to 15, while the binary encoded textblocks are stored in memory locations 17 to 2046. The left part of block $n \geq 0$ is stored in location $2n+17$ whereas the right part is stored in location $2n+18$. The number of blocks are limited to a maximum of 1015. The expression $\text{Rot2}(x)$ in the specification is mapped into the expression $(x<-6)@(x\backslash\backslash 6)$ in Handel-C. The variables of the formal specification are mapped onto variables in the Handel-C program via the abstraction relation $\mathbf{R}$ [7]:

$$\mathbf{R} \cong \mathbf{R_K} \wedge \mathbf{R_P} \wedge \mathbf{R_C} \wedge \mathbf{R_r}$$

where the predicates $\mathbf{R_K}, \mathbf{R_P}, \mathbf{R_r}, \mathbf{R_C}$ are defined below.

$$\mathbf{R_K} \cong K_0 = sram[0] \wedge \ldots \wedge K_{N+8} = sram[15]$$
$$\mathbf{R_P} \cong P_L = (sram[17] \wedge sram[19] \wedge \ldots \wedge sram[2045])$$
$$\wedge \; P_R = (sram[18] \wedge sram[20] \wedge \ldots \wedge sram[2046])$$
$$\mathbf{R_r} \cong r_0 = R.(24..31) \wedge r_1 = R.(16..23) \wedge r_2 = R.(8..15) \wedge r_3 = R.(0..7)$$
$$\mathbf{R_C} \cong C_L = (sram[17] \wedge sram[19] \wedge \ldots \wedge sram[2045])$$
$$\wedge \; C_R = (sram[18] \wedge sram[20] \wedge \ldots \wedge sram[2046])$$

When the Handel-C code below is completed together with appropriate declarations and placed inside the void main function, compilation of the code would result in a model that can be simulated. Communication channels between the Handel-C program and the outside world are declared as parameters to the void main function. The target technology for the program/circuit is also declared as a parameter to void main. When split up in three partitions, each partition is placed in a separate file in its own void main. Each of these provides the same interface and uses the same target technology, however.

---

[1] Actually, two more configurations are needed — one to store data in SRAM and another to bring the results back from SRAM — but, because they are rather trivial, we do not describe them here.

```
/* Partition 1 */
i = N+9;
STDIN ? max;   /* Wait for signal from transputer */
  while (i != max) {
    L        = sram[i];
    R        = sram[i+1];
    tmp16    = sram[N].(0..15);
    L        = L ^ (tmp16 @ sram[N+1].(0..15));
    tmp16    = sram[N+2].(0..15);
    R        = (R ^ (tmp16 @ sram[N+3].(0..15))) ^ L;
    sram[i]  = L;
    sram[i+1] = R;
    i        = i + 2;  }
  STDOUT ! any;  /* Notify transputer */     }

/* Partition 2 */
STDIN ? max;
i = N+10;
while (i != max) {
  R, j = sram[i], 0;
  while (j.MSB != 1) {
    f2        = R.(8..15)^sram[0@j].(0..7)^R.(0..7);
    f1        = (R.(16..23) ^ sram[0@j].(8..15) ^
                R.(24..31)) + f2 + 1;
    f2        = f2 + ((f1<-6)@(f1\\6));
    f0, f3    = R.(24..31)+((f1<-6)@(f1\\6)),
                R.(0..7)+((f2<-6)@(f2\\6))+1;
    R         = sram[i-1] ^ (f0<-6) @ (f0\\6) @ (f1<-6) @ (f1\\6) @
                (f2<-6) @ (f2\\6) @ (f3 <- 6) @ (f3 \\ 6);
    L, j      = sram[i], j+1;
    sram[i-1] = L;
    sram[i]   = R;  }
  i = i + 2; }
STDOUT ! any;

/* Partition 3 */
i = N+9;
STDIN ? max;
while (i != max) {
  L         = sram[i];
  R         = sram[i+1];
  L, tmp16  = R ^ L,  sram[N+4].(0..15);
  R         = R ^ (tmp16 @ sram[N+5].(0..15));
  tmp16     = sram[N+6].(0..15);
  L         = L ^ (tmp16 @ sram[N+7].(0..15));
  sram[i]   = R;
  sram[i+1] = L;
  i         = i + 2; }
STDOUT ! any;
```

As mentioned before, an occam program downloads configurations etc. By using the code below, the program downloads the third configuration and communicates with the FPGA. More details are given in our technical report [8].

```
SEQ
  configure.fast(config.calc,length,clk.off,good)
  data.to.fpga ! max        -- send index for last block
  data.from.fpga ? any      -- receive notification
  data.to.fpga ! 0
  more.to.send.2 ! FALSE     -- terminate sending
  more.to.receive ! FALSE    -- terminate receiving
  data.from.fpga ? any
```

5 Conclusions

In this case study we used a formal specification to guide us in the selection of the hardware partitions and also plan for reconfiguration for a reconfigurable target system. The latter is visible from the way we mapped the variables of the formal specification into the SRAM of the HARP-2 system in order to reuse data between configurations. This paper is our first step in our goal to use formal techniques in developing correct FPGA-based systems. We have been partly influenced here by the work done in the ProCoS-group [6] as well as in our own group on using the *Refinement Calculus* [2].

Acknowledgement The work reported here was supported by the Academy of Finland via the Cocos-project.

References

1. M. Aubury, I. Page, G. Randall, J. Saul, R. Watts: Handel-C Language Reference Guide. Oxford University Computing Laboratory, August 28, 1996.
2. R.J.R. Back, K. Sere: From Action Systems to Modular Systems. Software-Concepts and Tools (1996) 26-39. Springer-Verlag.
3. D. van den Bout, et al.: Anyboard — An FPGA-Based Reconfigurable System. IEEE Design & Test of Computers, Vol. 9, No. 3, 21-30.
4. Embedded Solutions. Handel-C Preliminary Product Information Sheet. http://www.embedded-solutions.ltd.uk/ProdApp/handelc.htm, (ref. 15.8.97)
5. M. D. Ercegovac, T. Lang & J. H. Moreno: Introduction to Digital Systems. Academic Publishing Service, 1996 (draft 6/96)
6. C.A.R. Hoare, I. Page: Hardware and Software — The Closing Gap. Proceedings of the 5th Nordic Workshop on Program Correctness (1994) 1-23
7. C.A.R.Hoare: Proof of Correctness of Data Representations. Acta Informatica (1972) 1:271-281
8. S. Holmström, K. Sere: Reconfigurable Hardware — A Case Study in Codesign. Turku Centre for Computer Science. TUCS Technical Report No. 175, 1998.
9. A. E. Lawrence: HARP (TRAMple) Manual Volume 1, User Manual for HARP1 and HARP2. Version 0.1 (draft). Oxford University, 18.12.1996.
10. M. B. Srivastava & R. W. Brodersen. Using VHDL for High-Level, Mixed-Mode System Simulation. IEEE Design & Test of Computers, Vol. 9, No. 3, 31-40.

Statechart-Based HW/SW-Codesign of a Multi-FPGA-Board and a Microprocessor

Claude Ackad

TU Braunschweig, Department of Integrated Circuit Design (E.I.S.),
Gaußstraße 11, D-38106 Braunschweig, Germany,
ackad@eis.cs.tu-bs.de,
WWW home page: http://www.cs.tu-bs.de/eis/ackad/welcome.html

Abstract. The codesign of hardware and software is an up-to-date issue. For increasing network data rates high performance communication subsystems are needed. This paper discusses an approach of a semi-automated HW/SW-implementation using a microprocessor and an FPGA-based flexible hardware platform. Moreover, an increasing productivity in implementing such systems efficiently and correctly is needed. Therefore, the semi-automated approach is applied to an implementation of a modern communication protocol on the flexible platform.

1 Introduction

For increasing network data rates high performance communication subsystems are needed. Many applications have been developed that require high performance, e. g. multimedia applications. In order to properly serve these applications, suitable communication subsystems are required including network and transport layer protocols. Various implementation techniques have been developed over the years [1].

Considering the increased gap between the growth of physical network bandwidth and the growth in processing power available for protocol processing, multiprocessor platforms including dedicated hardware are attractive. Especially, a design incorporating standard processors as well as specific hardware (FPGAs) can lead to an efficient and flexible implementation platform.

The approach presented in this paper is based on a protocol engine that can be used to implement dedicated functions in programmable hardware. Functions that are not performance critical are implemented in software. Within the project, an FPGA-based flexible engine is designed and implemented. This platform will be used for various experiments, e.g. in the area of semi-automated HW/SW-protocol implementations.

Semi-automated designs of HW/SW-protocol implementation could lead to a higher productivity in the implementation and evaluation of communication subsystems.

2 Semi-automated HW/SW-implementation of communication protocols

In order to increase the correctness and productivity of protocol implementations, automated implementations from high-level specifications have been addressed in various research projects. Some projects focus on efficient SW implementations using SDL [2]. [3] synthesizes a HW/SW-implementation of a communication system starting with an SDL description. Fine-grain parallelism cannot be specified because each process is sequential by nature as opposed to statecharts [4]. Statecharts employ parallel hierarchical finite state machines (FSMs) to describe a system.

[5] describes a HW/SW-implementation architecture for statechart models. A model is implemented by a HW part (FPGA) with an associated SW part (standard microprocessor).

2.1 Using Statecharts to model protocols

Statecharts allow the modeling of complex, reactive systems using parallel, hierarchical FSMs, which synchronously execute transitions and communicate using global variables and abstract events.

Because of the decomposition of parallel protocols into communicating FSMs, statecharts seem to be well suited as a modeling language.

2.2 Semi-automated implementation

The communication system is viewed as a set of modules providing individual services that are composed to become the complete communication service. These modules may be complete protocols or single protocol functions. Performance intensive modules are downloaded to a flexible hardware platform.

The main objective of our design flow is to stay as long as possible with a relatively abstract statechart model which allows fast changes to be applied, and is well suited for simulation and debugging. From this model, code without manual interventions is generated. Changes of the protocol behavior occur only at the statechart level, followed by a code generation step.

First, the protocol specification is modeled using statecharts. Statemate [7] is used to develop the statechart model. It is in wide-spread use in industry. After the model is developed, it can be simulated and animated in a step-by-step simulator. The dynamic test tool DTT checks the absence of deadlocks and races. Code generators transform the debugged model into software C and to some extent into hardware VHDL code.

After debugging the model, protocol parameters are estimated. The protocol contains some protocol parameters, which are not determined by the protocol specification but must be estimated through simulations. For example, the error correction of the protocol is based on the selective reject mechanism. A small number of outstanding unacknowledged packets leads to poor performance. The maximum number corresponds to the length of a list which consumes resources of the implementation.

Then, the model is partitioned into SW, HW and some additional glue behavior. The time-critical parts of the statechart model are part of the HW partition while the remaining behavior is part of the SW partition. The granularity of the partitioning is relatively coarse, in that not single transitions but FSMs as a whole are moved to the selected partition. The decision is based on analysis of the message flow and simulation profile data. Statecharts which maximally contribute to the overall delay for transmitting data packets will be contained in the HW partition.

Because of the abstract nature of the statechart descriptions, comprehensible models for complex protocols can be developed leading to inefficient circuit implementations without manual refinement. For example, large lists can be modeled with statechart arrays, which do not fit on a single FPGA. Therefore, they are swapped to an external RAM component.

Unfortunately, the HW code generation possibilities of Statemate are very limited. On refining the statechart model we redesigned it using a very similar tool, Speedchart [Spee96] which includes a more matured code generator. This generator translates the statechart model into VHDL code which is synthesized by the Synopsys Design Analyzer to a netlist, placed and routed using the Xilinx XACT toolkit and downloaded to the FPGAs.

The SW portion is translated into C code and compiled using a C code cross compiler (gcc) for the target microprocessor.

3 Implementation example

To demonstrate the practicability of our design flow, we implemented the parallel transport subsystem Patroclos [6] on a HW/SW-platform consisting of FPGAs, a microprocessor and standard components, e. g. an ATM interface card.

3.1 Patroclos

The parallel transport subsystem Patroclos was developed for high performance communication systems. The left side of figure 1 shows the coarse structure of Patroclos. The application sends transport service data units via the transport interface. Protocol data units are sent/received by the send control and receive control protocol function, respectively.

To improve the achievable performance, Patroclos is not a layered protocol but composed of communicating FSMs; each FSM defines one protocol function. In this way, individual protocols can be composed by selecting respective FSMs. Patroclos provides for acknowledged or unacknowledged connection establishment, optional flow control, selective retransmission (window or rate based), segmentation, reassemblation, and virtual connections.

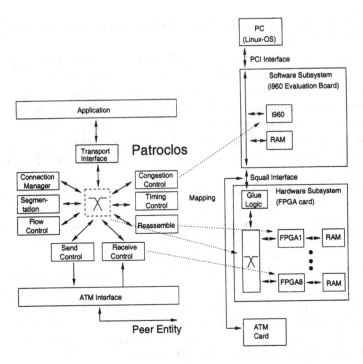

Fig. 1. Structure of Patroclos and implementation environment

3.2 Implementation environment

The implementation environment consists of two connected hosts exchanging video data at a high data rate. Each host consists of a PC with Linux-OS, a software and hardware subsystem (figure 1, right side). The software subsystem is connected to the PC via the PCI interface. The i960 evaluation board consists of an i960 standard processor as well as dynamic RAM. The hardware subsystem is connected via the Squall interface of the evaluation board. The FPGA card consists of eight XC4020 FPGAs with a local dual-ported, synchronous RAM memory each. The FPGAs communicate with each other and with the software part through the connection component as well as some glue logic.

3.3 Partitioning the statechart model

There are many objectives possible for the acceleration of protocol process- ing, e. g. small connection establishment delay. We focus on small average data transmission delay. Therefore we only accelerate protocol functions which are frequently used for the transmission of data, e. g. segmentation as opposed to connection management protocol functions.

We analyzed the model and selected all FSMs which are involved in data packet processing.

In figure 1, one possible mapping of the FSMs of the statechart model on the SW and HW subsystem is illustrated.

3.4 Refining the HW partition

Each FSM in the HW partition must be implemented by one FPGA and its associated RAM which holds incoming messages as well as protocol data.

In the statechart model, communication between FSMs is synchronous: the sender waits until the receiver accepts the message. This can degrade the performance when the receiver is often busy. To speed up the communication in the HW partition it was refined to an asynchronous one. When two FSMs communicate, the receiver puts the message in a FIFO for later processing.

The FSMs must keep large amounts of protocol data for each connection, e. g. sequence counters. These data are modeled using arrays. Because of the limited FPGA resources, these protocol data are mapped to the dual-port RAM in figure 1. The statechart model is refined, so that the read/write accesses reference the external RAM rather than the on-chip variables.

4 Conclusions and future work

In the paper an approach towards semi-automated HW/SW-implementation of high-performance protocols has been presented. The prototype platform consists of several FPGAs for the HW part and an i960 processor for the SW part.

Future project problems with the proposed design flow have to be considered and possible improvements should be searched for. Furthermore, the performance bottleneck of the implementation must be identified together with possible extensions to our approach.

References

1. Abbott, M., Peterson, L.: Increasing Network Throughput by Integrated Protocol Layers. IEEE/ACM Transactions on networking, Vol. 1, No. 5 (1993)
2. Henke, R., König, H., Mitschele-Thiel, A.: Derivation of Efficient Implementations from SDL Specifications Employing Data Referencing. Integrated Packet Framing and Activity Threads. Eighth SDL Forum, North-Holland (1997)
3. Carle, G., Schiller, J.: High-Performance Implementation of Protocols using Cell-Based Error Control Mechanisms for ATM Networks (in German). GI Fachtagung Kommunikation in verteilten Systemen (KiVS), Braunschweig, Germany (1997)
4. Harel, D.: Statecharts: a Visual Formalism for Complex Systems. Science of Computer Programming, Vol. 8, August 1987
5. Buchenrieder, K., Pyttel, A., Veith, C.: Mapping Statechart Models onto an FPGA-Based ASIP Architecture. Euro-DAC96, Geneva, Switzerland (1996)
6. Braun, T.: A parallel Transport Subsystem for cell-based high-speed Networks (in German). Dissertation, University of Karlsruhe (1993)
7. Statemate Magnum Reference Manual. i-Logix Inc., Andover, USA (1997)
8. Speedchart Reference Manual. Speed Electronic Inc., Switzerland (1996)

Simulation of ATM Switches
Using Dynamically Reconfigurable FPGA's

A.Touhafi, W. F. Brissinck, E.F. Dirkx

Atouhafi@info.vub.ac.be, wfbrissi@info.vub.ac.be, efdirkx@info.vub.ac.be
Vrije Universiteit Brussel,TW-INFO,Pleinlaan 2,1050 Brussels ,Belgium

Abstract. In this article we will discuss a new approach for efficient simulation of queuing systems by using the configurable computing paradigm. One of the classical approaches to optimize the simulation of queuing systems is by implementing co-processors for the hard parts of the simulation algorithm using Asics or FPGA's. The approach that we are proposing is different from the previous one in the sense that we are not using FPGA's to optimize the simulation algorithm but we implement an equivalent system of the one that has to be simulated in the FPGA. As a case study we have made a simulator for ATM switching fabrics. Our research shows that dynamically reconfigurable FPGA's like the 6200 RPU of XILINX can be efficiently used for the simulation of queuing systems.

1 Introduction

Discrete Event simulation is a widespread simulation technique used in a broad range of applications. All systems of which the state changes only at discrete time stamps can be simulated by this technique.A type of systems, simulated this way, are queuing-systems. An example of a queuing system is a car-wash where cars enter and wait in a queue until the car-wash is available. This car-wash can be modeled using a few basic building elements which are: a queue in which car's can wait until they arrive at the point where they will be surved, a source that simulates the arrival of a car and a service point in which a car enters and leaves after it has been served (washed). One of the observations immediately made is the fact that this system contains some natural parallelism. Many simulation algorithms try to exploit this natural parallelism found in the system. This led to some sophisticated simulation tools [1] that are ran on a parallel computer which is built up with a set of interconnected workstations. Such a parallel simulation system is very efficient for models or systems, which have an enormous lookahead. For systems with a small lookahead which are very communication intensive it is known that the communication bottleneck lowers the efficiency of the simulation. In this paper we are focussing on these systems that suffer from a small lookahead and will certainly not perform well on a coarse granular parallel computing system.The approach that we are proposing to simulate queuing systems with a small lookahead is based on the mapping of the model of a physical system onto a reconfigurable computing system. In this article we will first explain how this mapping is done in general and more specific how it is done for some ATM switch fabrics. By the end we will present some performance results and give our experiences with using this methodology.

2 From queuing model to a hardware equivalent system

A queuing model is built using six basic blocks. The challenge is to find a correct minimal hardware equivalent of these blocks such that a new physical system can be built up from the hardware equivalents. If this equivalence is satisfied than the queuing model theory guarantees that this new physical system and the real system of which the model has been extracted will show the same statistical behavior.For this basic components the behavior is briefly discussed and a hardware equivalent will be extracted:

The Source: Different types of sources exist, the design parameters here are the distribution and the load of events generated by the source. This means that sources are random generators with a certain behavior. We have implemented some very large Psuedorandom M-sequence generators [2] with a varying load and uniform distribution.

The Sink: This component is used to test if no events disappeared in the simulator. The sum of all events swallowed by the sinks must be equal to the sum of all events generated by the sources. Basically this component is a counter that counts all incoming events.

The Queue: A queue has one input and one output port where events can respectively enter or leave the queue. The parameters of a queue is its queue length (Qmax), if more events are entering the queue than can be handled by the queue an overflow occur and events get lost.

The Server: The parameter of a server is the service time: this is the time needed by the server to handle one packet. During the time a packet is being served, no other packets are accepted.

The Multiplexer: The parameter here is the number of input channels. Important here is the timing behavior of the multiplexer. The internals of the multiplexer scan the input channels and put an event at the output if an event appears at any input channel. This means that the scanning speed of the multiplexer depends on the number of input channels and the time between two waves of events presented to the input of the multiplexer. For a multiplexer with n inputs and an occurrence time of events Dt the scanning frequency is n x (1/Dt). This makes that very large multiplexers will slowdown the overall simulation-speed. We have implemented some 4-channel multiplexers that have a scanning speed of 64 MHz. This means that the overall simulation speed of the system can be maximally 16 MHz. Our experience taught us that real systems mostly need only very small multiplexers.

The Demultiplexer: This component is almost the opposite of the multiplexer. This component has a single input and multiple output channels. It is mainly used for routing packets to a certain destination. Packets entering the demultiplexer are put at a certain output channel depending on the routing address.

3 From Model to Simulator

ATM switching fabrics based on Multistage Interconnection Networks: Multistage ATM switches [3] are conceptually based on multistage interconnection networks (MIN). The switch architecture is built by using small shared memory switches as switching elements (SE) which are arranged in a MIN. Multistage Interconnection Networks can be classified into two categories: The internal blocking and the internal non-blocking switches. Internally non-blocking switches contain enough internally routing paths to ensure that two or more cells at different input ports can reach the desired output port as long as the output ports are distinct. This is not the case in an internally blocking switch, internal contention of cells can occur which means that there is need for buffering packets. In this article we will concentrate on an internally blocking switch architecture of which the used MIN is classified as a Banyan network.

An ATM switch simulator:

As a case study we have made some library's for the simulation of ATM switches based on a Banyan network. This library's are available in LOLA [5] and as schematics for the Xilinx XACT step tools [6].

The experiments done by now are based on the VCC HOTWORKS [6] configurable computer. This configurable computer contains one XC6216 Reconfigurable Processing Unit (RPU) [7] and one Megabyte of RAM. A few experimental simulations have been executed of which the most important remarks and performance results are given.

Simulation one: Simulator for a 64x64 ATM switch with Central queuing SE's.
One switching element needs only 48 cells of the XC6216 RPU. The SE contains a multiplexer, demultiplexer, a central queue and some logic to generate random routing addresses for the ATM cells. The implementation of the 64x64 ATM simulator on one XC6216 RPU. contained the sources, the three stages and some logic to measure the cell loss.

A first important remark is that all blocks have been preplaced, this was necessary because none of the available tools was able to find a placement and routing solution without placement hints. This makes LOLA very useful since the placement hints are calculated by the model itself, which relieves the user of the library from unnecessary intervention in the design of the basic queuing elements.

Secondly we have to remark that a simulation is only useful if the simulator generates statistics. Due to limited space on the XC6216 RPU only a few statistics are generated during a simulation run. This means that different netlists must be generated and separately run on the configurable computer to obtain all necessary simulation results.

Performance issues for experiment 1

The scanning speed of the multiplexers used in the SE's is 64Mhz. Since every SE has four inputs the occurrence frequency of cells at the input can be max. 16 MHz. This means that every 63 ns a new input stream of ATM packets is sent to the inputs of the ATM switch fabric. Remark that these 63 ns form a virtual timeslot for one ATM packet.

In steady state almost all the SE's will be active, which means that every 63 ns about (16 x 4 x 3) events are handled. This results in a simulation speed of three events per ns. Due to the limited space on the used RPU nine simulation runs must be performed to collect all the necessary simulation results. On a parallel computing system that is based on 8 Pentium II PC's interconnected by a Fast Ethernet switch, simulation speeds of one event per 5 Microseconds can be obtained. This means that the configurable computing system simulates about 1100 times faster compared to the coarse granular parallel computer.

Simulation 2: Simulator for a 16x16 ATM switch with output queued SE's.
The output queued SE's needs 148 cells of the XC6216 RPU. Since the RPU architecture provides an array of 64x64 cells it is impossible to implement a 64x64 ATM switch based on the output queued SE's. A 16x16 ATM switch could be implemented using less than 50 % of the available RPU resources; the other resources are used to implement counters to measure the packet loss of the switch.
Performance issues for experiment 2: In this simulation experiment the occurrence frequency of incoming packets is also 16 MHz. The maximal obtainable simulation speed for this model is 2ns per event, which is less than in experiment one. This lower performance is a result of the fact that the 16x16 ATM switch contains less parallelism compared to the 64x64 switch. On the other hand only one simulation run was needed to collect all the needed simulation statistics which leads to almost the same net speedup.

Simulation 3: Simulator for a 64x64 ATM switch with output queued SE's.
In the previous experiment we remarked that the used RPU is to small to simulate a 64x64 ATM switch with output queued SE's. This problem can be solved using the dynamically reconfigurable properties of the XC6216 RPU.
Since the ATM switching fabric has a regular pipelined architecture it becomes possible to perform a simulation by implementing only one stage in the RPU. Therefor the used SE's must be modified in such a way that it becomes possible to change the initial value of the queues and the outputs of the stage must be stored in an output register. Also the sources must be modified such that they can be given fixed values.

Performance issues for experiment 3: In this experiment one iteration took about 4 microseconds. This gives a simulation performance of 48 events per microsecond, which is still more than a factor 200 faster compared to the results obtained by a coarse grain parallel computing system. The performance loss we see has two reasons: The fact that less parallelism can be exploited during one simulation cycle and the fact that the reconfiguration time is long compared to an execution period.

4. Conclusion

In this paper a new approach for the simulation of queuing systems has been presented. As a case study a simulation platform is built for ATM switching fabrics. Simulations can be done by making a hardware equivalent of the model that has to be simulated. This can be done by some libraries that have been implemented. We have investigated how the partial reconfigurability of the used RPU can be exploited as a mean to simulate models that do not fit on one RPU. By the end we have given some results about the simulation performance that can be obtained. Here we can conclude that the performance depends on the number of cells needed to calculate one event. The more area per event is needed (which implies that less parallelism can be exploited) the less the performance. An important performance loss is seen ones the hardware equivalent of the model does not fit on one RPU. But still important speedup (more than a factor 200) is achieved compared to a coarse granular parallel computing system.

References

[1] W.Brissinck & all. A hierarchical Approach to distributed Discrete Event Simulation., Proceedings IASTED conference on modeling and simulation,Signapore1997.
[2]V.N. Yarmolik, S.N. Demidenko, Generation and Application of Pseudorandom Sequences for Random Testing. ISBN 0-471-9199-3
[3]Martin De Prycker, Asynchronous Transfer Mode,
Solution for Broad Band ISDN, ISBN 0-13-342171-6
[4]A. Touhafi & all. The Implementation of a Field Programmable Logic Based Co-Processor for the acceleration of discrete event simulators. LNCS Proceedings FPL '96 Darmstadt Germany 1996
[5]Stefan Hans, Melchior Ludwig, Hades: Fast Hardware Synthesis tools and a Reconfigurable Co-processor , Doctoral Thesis1997.
[6] http:\\www.vcc.com
[7]Xilinx, The programmable Logic Databook, version 1996

Fast Prototyping Using System Emulators

Tero Rissa[1], Tommi Mäkeläinen[2], Jarkko Niittylahti[1], and Jouni Siirtola[2]

[1] Tampere University of Technology, Signal Processing Laboratory, P.O. Box 553,
FIN-33101 Tampere, Finland
{tero.rissa, jarkko.niittylahti}@cs.tut.fi
[2] Nokia Research Center, Electronics Laboratory, P.O. Box 100.
FIN-33721 Tampere, Finland
{tommi.makelainen, jouni.siirtola}@research.nokia.com

Abstract. A novel concept for fast prototyping of embedded systems is presented. This concept combines utilization of dedicated configurable hardware blocks, a programmable processor core, and a general purpose Field Programmable Circuit Board as an implementation platform. The use of programmable and reconfigurable components enables flexible partitioning and development of the system functions as well as realistic testing of the system prototype. In this paper, we introduce one possible solution how to combine a rack of several DSP boards with FPGAs including I/O FPGAs for protocol handling and Field Programmable Interconnection Circuits for handling the routing between other components.

1. Introduction

Typical embedded systems like the ones designed for wireless telecommunication products, are getting more and more complicated. The amount of end-user services to be implemented into new products is drastically increasing. Due to the large variety of cellular standards, there exists a need to provide products capable of supporting multiple physical level communication methods. The radio frequency allocations are different for different standards, requiring that the products must be capable of multi-band operation.

Due to this great versatility the forth-coming products must support, it is getting increasingly important to have a flexible way to test new concepts. The design cycle must be flexible, so that the iteration from the algorithm design to the emulation and prototyping is fast, thus allowing easy testing of new ideas on a realistic environment in the early stage of development.

Traditionally, a common concept for testing and verifying the new products has been to build several custom prototypes. However, this method is time-consuming and the iteration cycle from design board to the test platform is long. Another well-known solution, the workstation-based software simulation, is still far too slow for large full speed digital system simulations.

Recently, the use of configurable prototyping platforms has been increasing [1]. A configurable platform can be either a processor based software accelerator, a VHDL hardware accelerator, or a FPGA-based prototyping environment. In addition, combinations of these solutions have been introduced, of which most notable ones containing processor(s) and FPGA(s). In this paper, we describe a fully configurable prototyping platform architecture with parallel communication links between the hardware and software parts.

2. A flexible platform for system prototyping

A block diagram of our system architecture is shown in Fig. 1. The main parts are a rack for DSP boards and an APTIX prototyping board. A simple buffer card has been inserted between these two to prevent damages in case of malfunctions. The system is controlled from a UNIX-workstation. The FPGAs on the Aptix board can be programmed via a Xilinx Xchecker cable. A Host Interface Module (HIM) both programs FPICs in the board and controls the Logic Analyzer.

The configurable hardware in our solution is the following. There is an Aptix System Explorer MP3A FPCB [2] with FPICs and Xilinx 4020/4025 FPGAs in it. The software platform is a Pentek DSP board of four Texas Instrument TMS320C40s [3]. The system can be expanded to employ several DSP boards because the communication link protocol of C40 is not dependent on the DSP configuration.

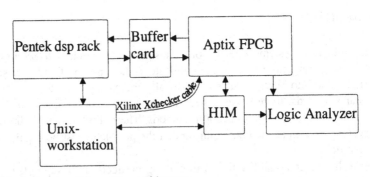

Fig. 1. A block diagram of the system architecture.

In our solution, we utilize the communication links of the DSPs to create a communication channel between hardware and software parts working in parallel. This also greatly improves the flexibility of the system. This is illustrated in Fig. 2.

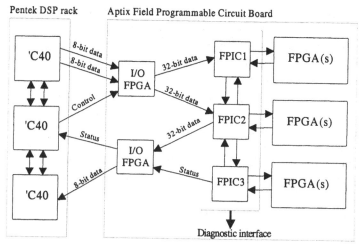

Fig. 2. The parallel communication arrangement of the system.

When designing this communication arrangement, our first task was to create a flexible way to handle the handshaking protocols between a DSP and a FPGA. In the DSP end of the link we use Texas Instruments (TI) C40, whose bi-directional communication links have total of 12 lines each: 8 for data, 2 for handshaking, and 2 for token exchange. In the FPGA side of this link, there is an Aptix FPCB, which has 142 hardwired I/O connections to its two I/O FPGAs. The I/O FPGAs handle the handshaking and demultiplex 8-bit data signals to 32-bit data signals. Furthermore, these I/O FPGAs are used to implement the necessary handshakes with other FPGA blocks on the board. Figure 3 illustrates the handshaking operations described above.

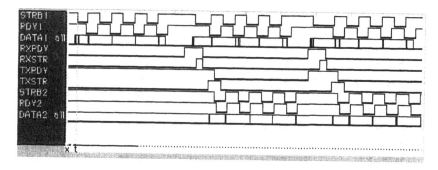

Fig. 3. Handshakes and data flow.

With this configuration, changes in quantity of other FPGAs in the board have a little of influence to the contents of I/O FPGA. Naturally, there is a limit how many data lines I/O FPGAs can handle due to its limited number of I/O pins. When using true bi-directional and/or asymmetric FPGA structure, we can use up to five 32-bit bi-directional data paths. In most cases, the disadvantages of bi-directional data paths are greater than the advantages in it. For example, if we use a configuration where three

DSPs are linked to several FPGAs, it is best to use six fixed data paths. In that case, each DSP has its own link through which to send and to receive.

A slight problem associated with bi-directional data paths is the default direction setting in DSP's links. If a DSP is resetted without a reset in FPGAs, the direction of data links may change without a token exchange. In the worst case, this means that both ends of the line are sending at the same time. This leads to serious problems or even destruction of equipment. For that reason, we used buffering equipment between the DSP and Aptix. In addition, we don't need token exchange lines in fixed directional data paths and this increases the routing capacity.

One typical problem in PCB prototypes is a poor visibility to the system. In this configuration, there is a possibility to monitor all data lines routed through FPIC devices. Moreover, it is possible to change the level of the desired signal. This function is most useful when testing and debugging the design.

3. Results

Theoretically, a single C40 link can send or receive 160-megabit per second [5]. When using configuration described above, we have easily achieved 32-megabit per second for one link. The maximum clock rate of an Aptix FPCB is 25MHz and this is the limiting factor of the transfer capacity. However, this speed is sufficient to satisfy the needs of many telecommunication applications. There are certain ways to increase the transfer capacity if necessary. For example, we have used synchronous data transmission even if a C40 link uses asynchronous one. If we made the handshaking asynchronous in both ends of the data path, we could increase transfer speed few megabits. Additionally, if there are more than one data source, the transmission speed is multiplied with the number of sources available. Of course, this must be within the routing capacity of Aptix as mentioned earlier. However, we have to keep in mind that this kind of prototyping environment is meant for the first prototype validation and system development phase for which purpose it is quite adequate.

When exploring different partition alternatives, a dedicated embedded DSP/ASIC board offers similar attributes as this system does. However, a standalone platform's verification cycle is remarkably slower and more expensive.

The presented concept was found excellent for our purposes. Once the interface problem between a DSP and an I/O FPGA was solved, there was little of trouble to modify the design. This is the key feature of our system providing the highest degree of flexibility. A small drawback of this concept is the uncertainty caused by the lack of experience with such new systems. The effects of the delay caused by FPIC devices and relatively long data paths are not identical to the ones in PCB prototypes. Furthermore, the young generation of software available in this field of research introduces some problems. However, the high flexibility and decreased verification time are such advantages that overrun these disadvantages.

After the code to the signal processors and the hardware description language to the FPGAs have been written and compiled, it takes only few hours to run the first tests. At this point, the real value of this environment is revealed. When testing different partitioning options, it is a simple process to modify the design. After the code and HDL have been rewritten to match the new partition, they must be compiled. The code for a signal processor usually does not require major changes, because function calls can be initially made to use communication links. The HDL of I/O FPGAs remains basically the same, but other FPGA blocks must naturally be completely redesigned with the exception of handshaking signals. In this kind of environment, there is no need to allocate I/O pins on FPGA blocks, because of the configuration capability of a FPCB. This gives a FPGA designer a higher degree of freedom to iterate the design block by block. In some cases, this improves speed and functionality. The Aptix's software creates routing information from netlists created by a compilation tool. The only task left to the user is to create a file describing where the blocks are located in the board. These are the only steps required for one iteration cycle, and an engineer is able to run the new prototype immediately after design is completed without waiting for a PCB to be manufactured.

The presented design flow is slightly more complicated than the one of an embedded DSP/ASIC PCB prototype environment. On the other hand, it provides comfort and speed which attempts to explore the different system component allocation and partitioning possibilities.

4. Conclusions

In this paper, we have described a novel concept for fast system prototyping. It is a platform based on highly configurable components providing large flexibility. It is easy to expand the platform with additional DSPs or FPGAs with no major modifications required to the software and hardware descriptions of the actual system that is to be prototyped. The presented solution is most suitable for fast exploration of system design issues by hardware emulation thus providing an alternative for slow software simulations. A system similar to the one presented here has been constructed and tested with several design cases and found to be a valuable tool for embedded system design.

References

1. H. L Owen, U. R. Kahn, and J.L. A. Hughes, "FPGA- based Emulator Architectures", In W. Moore and W. Luk, editors, *More FPGA*, Abingdon EE&CS Books, UK, 1994.
2. R. First, Aptix; Reconfigurable System Prototyping, MP3 System Explorer User's Manual. Relase 3.6a November 1997
3. PENTEK operating manual, Model 4284, TMS320C40 Digital Signal Processor MIX Baseboard for VMEbus Systems, Pentek Inc., Sep 1996.
4. H. Hakkarainen, Prototyping of Asic Based Systems, Master's Thesis, 106 pages, Tampere University of Technology, Finland Jun 1996
5. Texas Instruments Inc., TMS320C4x, *User's Guide*, 1994

Space-efficient Mapping of 2D-DCT onto Dynamically Configurable Coarse-Grained Architectures *

Andreas Dandalis and Viktor K. Prasanna

Department of Electrical Engineering-Systems
University of Southern California
Los Angeles, CA 90089-2562, USA
Tel: +1-213-740-4483, Fax: +1-213-740-4418
{dandalis, prasanna}@usc.edu
http://maarc.usc.edu/

Abstract. This paper shows an efficient design for 2D-DCT on dynamically configurable coarse-grained architectures. Such coarse-grained architectures can provide improved performance for computationally demanding applications as compared to fine-grained $FPGAs$. We have developed a novel technique for deriving computation structures for *two dimensional* homogeneous computations. In this technique, the speed of the data channels is dynamically controlled to perform the desired computation as the data flows along the array. This results in a space efficient design for 2D-DCT that fully utilizes the available computational resources. Compared with the state-of-the-art designs, the amount of local memory required is reduced by 33% while achieving the same high throughput.

1 The Problem

Coarse-grained configurable architectures consist of a small number of powerful configurable units. These units form datapath-oriented structures and can perform critical word-based operations (e.g. multiplication) with high performance. This can result in greater efficiency and high throughput for coarse-grained computing tasks.

The *2D-DCT* of a $N \times N$ image U is defined as [8]:

$$v(k,l) = \sum_{m,n=0}^{2N-1} \sum_{m,n=0}^{2N-1} u(m,n) c_{k,l}(m,n)$$

where $C = c_{k,l}(m,n)$ is the $N \times N$ cosine transform matrix and $0 \leq k,l < N$.

* This research was performed as part of the MAARC project (Models, Algorithms and Architectures for Reconfigurable Computing, http://maarc.usc.edu). This work is supported by the DARPA Adaptive Computing Systems program under contract no. DABT63-96-C-00049 monitored by Fort Hauchuca.

The 8×8 $2D\text{-}DCT$ is a fundamental computation kernel of still-picture and video compression standards. Efficient solutions (mapping schemes) must achieve high computational rates. In addition, since in coarse-grained configurable architectures, the functional units are word-based, the amount of chip area available for local storage is limited. Hence, the designs should be space-efficient as well.

In this work we derive computation structures for 8×8 $2D\text{-}DCT$. These structures match the datapath-oriented nature of the target architectures and lead to efficient mapping. The characteristics of the derived structures are:

- Scalability with the size of $2D\text{-}DCT$,
- Partitionability with the image size $N \times N$,
- Maximum utilization of computational resources, and
- Space efficiency.

2 Our Approach

The design methodology is based on a model of a configurable linear array. The array consists of identical powerful PEs, connected in a pipeline fashion with word parallel links between adjacent PEs. The data/control channels can be configured to communicate with each other at different speeds. The PEs can also be configured to have various internal organization (*functionality*). The parameters of the model include p, the number of PEs, m the amount of total memory in each PE and w the data width. An external controller/memory system is assumed to provide the required data/control signals and can store results computed by the array. I/O operations can only be performed at the left and right boundary of the array. Several research groups are currently building such configurable coarse-grained architectures [2, 6, 7, 9].

The key idea of our approach is dynamic interaction between data streams. The dataflow is determined by the speed and the connectivity of the datapaths. The configuration of the data paths schedules the computations to be performed onto a data stream along the array. Furthermore, the functionality of the PEs can be changed by reconfiguring the connectivity among their functional units, local memories and data channels.

The parameters of the target architecture p, m, and w are given as input and are assumed to be independent of the problem size. The three major steps of the approach are:

Step 1 (Algorithm selection): Selection of an appropriate algorithm for the considered task.

Step 2 (Primitive structure): Derivation of a "primitive" computation structure which is independent of the parameters p and m. The derived multirate linear array determines:

- Internal structure of the PE,
- Control/communication scheme,
- Schedule of Data/Control streams, and
- Speed of Data/Control channels.

Step 3 (Partitioning): "Fitting" the solution obtained in *Step 2* into the target architecture. Partitioned schemes are derived by efficient utilization of the local memory in the *PEs*. The new solution depends on the parameters p and m.

3   2D-DCT on Coarse-Grained Architectures

Given a $N \times N$ image U, we partition it into 8×8 submatrices ($U_{8\times8}$) and then compute the *2D-DCT* of each of them as $V_{8\times8} = CU_{8\times8}C^T = [C(CU_{8\times8})^T]^T$ [8]. C is the 8×8 cosine transform matrix. This approach reduces the complexity of the problem from $O(N^4)$ to $O(N^3)$ [8]. It also leads to decomposition of the *2D-DCT* into two *1D-DCT* blocks. Each block performs the *1D-DCT* transform and transposes the computed matrix as well.

Correspondingly, the *2D-DCT* array (Fig. 1a) consists of two identical computational blocks of 8 *PEs* each. Each block computes and transposes the result of a 8×8 matrix multiplication (Fig. 1a). Data and control travel through the *PEs* via differential speed channels (*fast/slow* channels). The regular nature of the computation makes the control of the array uniform and simple.

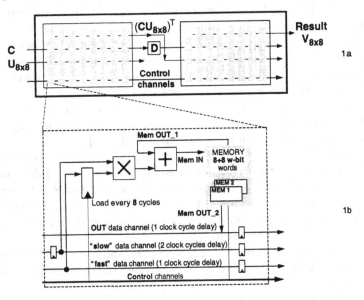

Fig. 1. The 2D-DCT array (1a) and the PE organization (1b).

Figure 1b shows the *PE* structure. In each *PE*, one column of the input submatrix commutes with all the 8 rows of the cosine transform matrix C. Thus, 8 results are computed per *PE*. Two 8-word banks of local memory are used per *PE* for storing the intermediate results. The contents of each memory bank are updated for 64 cycles alternatively. The memory contents are read in order 8 times during this time period via *Mem OUT_1*. The values read by *Mem OUT_1* get updated by the incoming data values and are stored back via

Mem IN. The memory bank that is not updated, uploads in order its contents on *OUT* via *Mem OUT_2*. Each memory bank is *flushed* every 128 cycles for 8 consecutive cycles. The memory contents are uploaded in a repetitive manner along the array, starting from the leftmost to the rightmost *PE*.

The cosine transform matrix *C* is fed into the slow data channel (Fig. 1a) in column-major order. The submatrix $U_{8\times 8}$ is fed into the fast data channel in row-major order. Figure 1a shows the way in which the data and control streams are transferred between the two computational blocks. The matrices *C* and $(CU_{8\times 8})^T$ are fed to the second block via the *slow* and *fast* data channels respectively. In addition, a delay (D) of 56 clock cycles is added to the datastream of matrix *C*. By inserting this delay, the datastreams of the two matrices are synchronized at the input of the second block. This synchronization can also be performed by using a new data channel. This new channel *transports* matrix *C* from the leftmost *PE* of the array to the second block. The delay is now distributed among the first 8 *PEs* (9 clock cycles per *PE*). Similar delays are inserted in the control channels as well.

The order in which the results are computed in each block, assures that the output matrix is the desirable one. No additional block for transposing the result of matrix multiplication is needed. Moreover, the uploading mechanism leads to full utilization of the computational resources of the array. *I/O* operations are performed only at the right/left boundary of the array. Thus, the required *I/O* bandwidth is constant.

The latency of the resulting array is 144 clock cycles while its throughput is same as the clock rate of the array. The multiply-add-update operation inside the *PEs* (Fig. 1b), is the most time consuming part of the computation and determines the clock rate of the array. By pipelining the datapath of this operation, the clock rate can be increased up to the computational rate of the slowest functional unit (multiplier, adder, memory). By replacing matrix *C* with its transpose C^T, the same structure can compute the inverse *2D-DCT* transform without any additional changes. On the average, the array requires 3 external memory accesses and 18 local memory accesses per clock cycle (i.e. 1.13 local accesses in each *PE* on the average).

For the sake of illustration, we compare our solution with that proposed for RaPiD (a coarse-grained configurable architecture) [6]. Both solutions are based on the row/column decomposition of *2D-DCT* to two *1D-DCTs*. The time performance is asymptotically the same. The key difference is the amount of local memory required and the number of local memory references.

In [6], matrix *C* is stored locally among the *PEs* and additional memory is needed for matrix-transpose operations. A total of 384 words of memory is used (i.e. $m = 24$ per *PE*). On the average, 20 local memory accesses/cycle are required. Our solution uses 256 words of local memory for storing intermediate results. On the average, it requires 18 local memory accesses/cycle. However, it also requires 3 (compared with 2 in [6]) external memory accesses/cycle. This is not a limiting factor since RaPiD can support at most two reads and one write to the external memory per cycle [6].

4 Conclusion

Coarse-grained configurable architectures offer the potential for high computational efficiency and throughput for coarse-grained computing tasks. In this paper, a *2D-DCT* structure for such architectures was derived, using our dynamic data path interaction technique. Space efficiency, high throughput and constant I/O requirements, are the main advantages of the derived array.

Our technique is based on dynamic interaction of data streams via differential speed data channels. It also leads to scalable and partitioned mapping schemes for similar matrix-oriented computations (e.g. matrix-multiplication [4]). These schemes achieve high computational rates while the required I/O bandwidth is constant (independent of the size of the array). Moreover, their space efficiency makes them an attractive solution for coarse-grained configurable architectures.

The work reported here is part of the USC MAARC project. This project is developing algorithmic techniques for realising scalable and portable applications using configurable computing devices and architectures. Computational models and algorithmic techniques based on these models are being developed to exploit dynamic reconfiguration. In addition, partitioning and mapping issues in compiling onto reconfigurable hardware are also addressed [1, 3, 4, 5].

References

1. K. Bondalapati and V. K. Prasanna, "Mapping Loops onto Reconfigurable Architectures", *Int. Workshop on Field Programmable Logic and Applications*, Sep. 1998.
2. D. C. Chen and J. M. Rabaey, "A Reconfigurable Multiprocessor IC for Rapid Prototyping of Algorithmic-Specific High-Speed DSP Paths", *IEEE Journal of Solid-State Circuits*, 27(12):1985-1904, Dec. 1992.
3. Y. Chung, S. Choi and V. K. Prasanna, "Parallel Object Recognition on an FPGA-based Configurable Computing Platform", *Int. Workshop on Computer Architectures for Machine Perception*, Oct. 1997.
4. A. Dandalis and V. K. Prasanna, "Mapping Homogeneous Computations onto Dynamically Configurable Coarse-Grained Architectures", *IEEE Symposium on Field-Programmable Custom Computing Machines*, Apr. 1998.
5. A. Dandalis and V. K. Prasanna, "Fast Parallel Implementation of DFT using Configurable Devices", *Int. Workshop on Field Programmable Logic and Applications*, Sep. 1997.
6. C. Ebeling, D. C. Cronquist, P. Franklin and C. Fisher, "RaPiD - A configurable computing architecture for compute-intensive applications", *Technical Report UW-CSE-96-11-03*, Nov. 1996.
7. R. W. Hartenstein, R. Kress, H. Reinig, "A Scalable, Parallel, and Reconfigurable Datapath Architecture", *6th Int. Symposium on IC Technology, Systems & Applications*, Sept. 1995.
8. A. K. Jain, "Fundamentals of Digital Image processing", Prentice-Hall Inc., Englewood Cliffs, NJ, 1989.
9. A. Agarwal et al., "Baring it all to Software: The Raw Machine", *MIT/LCS Technical Report TR-709*, March 1997.

XILINX4000 Architecture - Driven Synthesis for Speed

I.Lemberski, M.Ratniece

Riga Aviation University ,1,Lomonosova iela, Riga LV-1019, LATVIA
lembersk@vlsi.rau.lv

Abstract. Architecture-driven (instead of LUT-driven) method of boolean functions logic synthesis for speed is proposed. It takes XILINX4000 architectural features (heterogeneous LUTs of 3 and 4 inputs) into account and includes two step decomposition. In the first step, two-level logic representation is transformed into a graph of at most 4 fanin nodes (after this step, each node can be mapped onto 4 input LUT). In the second step, selected 4 fanin nodes within a critical path are re-decomposed into 3 fanin nodes to ensure mapping onto 3 input LUTs. Re-decomposition task is formulated as substituting node two fanins for exactly one fanin. Either existing node or one especially created, is considered as a fanin to be substituted for. The extended PLA format describing a multi-level boolean network, is proposed. Based on this description, substituting is formulated in terms of a covering task.

1 Introduction

LUT FPGA-based logic synthesis methods developed don't consider architectural features of LUT FPGAs[1] (as exception, the paper [2] can be mentioned where decomposition methodology is oriented on XILINX3000 and 4000 structure). Instead of it, two-level logic is transformed into the set of sub-functions, where each one depends on the restricted number of inputs. Usually, this number doesn't exceed the number of LUT inputs. Therefore, each sub-function can be implemented onto one LUT. For optimization , methods to minimize the number of sub-functions are considered (LUT-driven synthesis).

However, such approach may be not optimal for FPGAs having several heterogeneous LUTs with specific connections between them.

In this paper, architecture - driven (instead of LUT-driven) approach to logic synthesis for speed targeting XILINX4000 structure is offered. It takes heterogeneous LUT architecture (two type LUTs of 3 and 4 inputs) into account and includes two step decomposition to ensure minimization of the number of logic blocks (rather than the number of LUTs) within the critical path.

2 XILINX4000 Architecture and Mapping

XILINX4000 logic structure bases on cooperating Configurable Logic Blocks (CLBs) (fig. 1) (minimum 64 CLBs per module). A CLB consists of 3 look-up-tables (LUTs) (function generators), namely, LUT of type F, G and H (further, F-LUT, G-LUT, H-LUT).

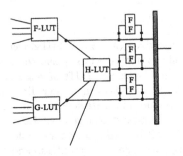

Fig.1. Configurable logic block structure

F-LUT and G-LUT can implement any function of up to 4 variables . H-LUT implements up to 3 input function, where two inputs are F-LUT and G-LUT outputs (internal inputs), but the third input is external. CLB has two external outputs . Any two of three LUT outputs can be connected to CLB outputs either directly or through flip-flops (FF).

Let decomposed logic functions PO=f(PI) be represented by a directed acyclic graph D: D=(PI, PO, G), where PI, PO - set of primary input and output nodes, G - set of nodes obtained as a result of decomposition. We call the node $g_{i-1} \in RI \cup G$ as a fanin of the node $g_i \in G \cup PO$, if there is an arc from g_{i-1} to g_i (fig.2). Let sup (g_i), $g_i \in G \cup PO$, be the set of g_i fanins. Suppose, that $|sup(g_i)| \leq 4$ for each $g_i \in G \cup PO$. Therefore, each node can be mapped onto F- or G- LUT (fig.1). We call such mapping as trivial. Let τ be CLB propagation delay. Then, the critical path propagation delay d :d=n×τ, where n - number of nodes within the critical path. To increase performance, H-LUTs should be used for mapping. Suppose: $|sup(g_i)| \leq 3$ (fig.2) and g_{i-1}, g_i are in the critical path. The nodes g_{i-1} and g_i can be mapped onto the same CLB (F- or G- LUT and H-LUT respectively). As the CLB delay remains the same, the propagation delay within the critical path is reduced : d= (n-1)*τ.

Therefore, our goal is to develop decomposition technique, to map as many as possible nodes within the critical path onto H-LUTs. The approach may include generating a graph where each node has at most 3 fanins. However, in this case, logic capacities of 4-input (F-,G-) LUTs will be not used in the best way. As a result, the total number of nodes may be increased.

To ensure optimal implementation we propose two step decomposition. In the first step, a graph D: $|sup(g_i)| \leq 4$, $g_i \in G \cup PO$ is obtained and optimized for area and speed using SIS tool [4]. In the second step, selected 4 fanin nodes are re-decomposed into 3 fanin nodes to map them onto H-LUTs.

3 Re-decomposition via Substituting

Given a 4 fanin node g_i (fig2). To transform it into a 3 fanin one, we substitute its 2 fanins (say, g_{i-3}, g_{i-4}) for an exactly one fanin g_j while preserving functionality and acycle.

While substituting, two type of nodes may be considered: substituting for an existing node g_j, $g_j \in G$ and a new node : $g_j \notin G$ especially created and introduced into the graph: $G=G\cup\{ g_j \}$. Clear, that for a new node: $|\sup(g_j)| \leq 4$. However, in the last case, an additional node is introduced and the total number of nodes is increased. Therefore, we give preference to substituting for an existing node. If such a node can't be find, substituting for a new node is considered.

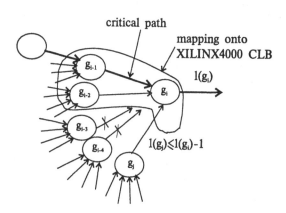

Fig.2. Substituting for a node

4 Substituting as a Covering Task

Usually, two- level logic is represented by the PLA table (fig.3a) of dimension p*(n+m), where n= | PI |- number of primary inputs, m=| PO | - number of functions, p- number of input vectors for which functions are described (for simplification, two-valued vectors are considered).

The main advantage of the PLA format is joined description of all the functions. It ensures compactness, clearness, convenience for analysis.

After decomposition by SIS, the set G of node sub-functions is generated (fig.3b). Each sub-function is described separately, by ON-set vectors (complement vectors belong to OFF-set) together with the list of input and output names (keyword .names). Taking the advantage of the PLA format into account, it is expediently to describe sub - functions by the extended PLA table using as a starting point, a table of two-level representation.

We represent the decomposed logic by the extended PLA table of dimension $p*(n+|G|+m)$, where $|G|$ - number of additional columns describing sub-functions from the set G .The procedure of the PLA table extension is as follows. In each step, a sub-function g_i is described in the PLA table, $g_i \in G/G_i$, $sup(g_i) \subset (PI \cup G_i)$, G_i - set of sub-functions already described in the PLA table during the previous steps. To describe g_i , for each PLA table row, an embedded vector of $sup(g_i)$ variables is checked if it is covered by a vector from the sub-function g_i ON-set . If yes, the value 1 is put on the crosspoint of this row and the column g_i. Otherwise, the value 0 is put. For example (fig.3), to describe g_1 ,we check PLA table embedded vectors of $sup(g_1) = \{x1,x3\}$ variables and put value 1 in the 2-nd (embedded vector 01 is covered by ON - set vector -1) and in the 4 - 8- th rows (fig.3c).

Let $l (g_i)$ be a node g_i level (maximal number of nodes between PI and g_i). In case of substituting for an existing node (fig.2) , we search for a node to be substituted for, among the set $S_i= PI \cup G/g_i$. In addition, this node has to satisfy the conditions as follows: after substituting, the graph remains acyclic and node level doesn't exceed $l(g_i)-1$.

Let $S'_i \subset S_i$ be the set of fanins satisfying above conditions. The selection matrix is arranged where columns are associated with the sub-function g_i all possible (ON-, OFF-) seed dichotomies [5] ,but rows - with the variables from the set S'_i. To substitute, we try to cover columns uncovered by g_{i-1}, g_{i-2} , using exactly one variable from the set S'_i / g_{i-3} , g_{i-4}. To substitute for a new node, (ON-, OFF-) seed dichotomies not covered by g_{i-1} , g_{i-2} are merged to one dichotomy describing the sub-function g_i .Let $S'_i , S'_i \subset S_i$, be the set of fanins that can be potentially assigned to the node g_j (after assigning , the node g_j satisfies above conditions) . To compute $sup(g_i) \subset S'_i$, the covering procedure [5] is applied and solution is accepted , if $|sup(g_i)| \leq 4$.

X_1	X_2	X_3	F_1
0	0	0	1
0	0	1	0
0	1	0	1
0	1	1	0
1	0	0	1
1	0	1	0
1	1	0	0
1	1	1	1

a)

. names X_1 X_3 g_1

1	-	1
-	1	1

. names X_2 X_3 g_2

1	1	1

. names g_1 g_2 F_1

0	0	1
1	1	1

b)

X_1	X_2	X_3	g_1	g_2	F_3
0	0	0	0	0	1
0	0	1	1	0	0
0	1	0	0	0	1
1	1	1	1	1	1
1	0	0	1	0	0
1	0	1	1	0	0
1	1	0	1	0	0
1	1	1	1	1	1

c)

Fig.3. PLA table (a), nodes description (b), extended PLA table (c)

5 Experimental Results

XILINX4000 architecture driven re-decomposition procedure for speed is implemented and tested on some FSM examples (fig.4).

For state encoding, the procedure [5] is used. In the fig.4 , one can see that the re-decomposition for speed reduces significantly the CLB number within the critical path (c.p.).

| Example | XILINX4000 | | | |
| | Re-decompo-sition | | Trivial | |
	#CLB c.p.	#CLB total	#CLB c.p.	#CLB total
ex2	2	10	4	12
ex3	2	5	4	5
ex4	2	13	3	14
ex5	2	4	3	5
ex6	3	26	5	32
ex7	2	4	3	4
beecount	2	7	4	8
dk14	2	15	4	17
coprodes	2	8	3	10
Total:	23	128	43	146
Percentage:	53,5%	87,7%	100%	100%

Fig.4. Experimental results

References

1. Cong, J,Ding ,Y. :Combinational Logic Synthesis for LUT Based Field Programmable Gate arrays . ACM Trans. on Design Automation of Electronic Systems, Vol.1, No. 2, April (1996) 145-204
2. Abouzeid, P., Babba, B., Crastes de Paulet, M., Saucier, G.:Input-Driven Partitioning Methods and Application to Synthesis on Table-Look-up-Based FPGA's. IEEE Trans. CAD, Vol. 12, No. 7, July (1993) 913-925
3. Murgai, R., Brayton, R., Sangiovanni-Vincentelli, A. :Logic Synthesis for Field-Programmable Gate Arrays. Kluwer Academic Publishers (1995)
4. Sentovich, E..et al: SIS: a System for Sequential Circuit Synthesis. Electronic Research Laboratory Memorandum No. UCB/ERL M92/41(1992)
5. Grass, W., Lemberski,I.: Support-Based State Encoding targeting FSM Optimal LUT FPGA Implementation.- Int.Workshop on Logic and Architecture Synthesis, Grenoble, France (1997)97-104

The PLD-Implementation of Boolean Function Characterized by Minimum Delay

Valeri Tomachev

Institute of Engineering Cybernetics, Logical Design Laboratory,
220012 Minsk, Belarus
Toma@Newman.Basnet.Minsk.by

Abstract. Let a Boolean function be represented by the SOP (sum-of-products) which involves q products. Let there be only p, there $p<q$, product terms per combinatorial macrocell of given PLDs. It is shown how to implement that SOP as a one-level logic circuit characterized by minimum delay. The main idea is to use the dynamic output enable control tools for switching the combinatorial macrocells of PLDs. The output enable product terms are chosen so that only one of them is true at every instant. To find these product terms the SOP of Boolean function is converted by factorization into the next form $SOP=k_1(SOP_1)\vee...\vee k_r(SOP_r)$. Every SOP_i, is chosen so that it can be implemented by single combinatorial macrocell. The factor-products $k_1,...,k_r$ are ortho to each other, and $k_1\vee...\vee k_r\equiv 1$. The factor-product k_i is used for output enable/disable control of the macrocell where SOP_i is implemented.

1 Introduction

The PLDs and some modern CPLDs have a rather limited number of product terms per combinatorial macrocell. This involves some difficulties if Boolean function to be implemented depends on the great number of products. To overcome these difficulties we are obliged to built multilevel circuit, which is distinguished from one-level one by more significant delay.

Let a Boolean function $f(x_1,...,x_n)$ be presented by the Sum of Products SOP_f involving q products. Suppose n is not greater than a number of inputs of PLD under consideration.

The question is how to implement such Boolean function on combinatorial macrocells of PLDs if there are only p product terms per output in each combinatorial macrocell and $p<q$, where q is the number of products in the SOP_f.

2 Two-Level Implementation

The ordinary way to implement such Boolean function using PLDs is to divide the set of products formed the SOP_f into $]q/p[$ subsets so that each of them consists of p products (may be with the exception of the last subset).

The products belonging to the distinct subsets are placed into the separate combinatorial macrocells. An additional macrocell is used to combine the outputs of $]q/p[$ macrocells mentioned above. There is precisely an element which forms the second level of the circuit. Note that at minor $]q/p[$ a single PLD will be sufficient to implement f with the help of internal feedback tools. As a matter of fact, such implementation should be considered as a two-level circuit too. The output of the additional macrocell represents a value of the Boolean function f.

In general, the two-level implementation of Boolean function is characterized by the double delay in relation to one-level case.

3 New Approach

At first site, if $q>p$, only two-level implementation of the SOP_f exists and there is no way to decrease the delay which is caused by the presence of tow-levels in the circuit. However, an unexpected solution of this problem is suggested here to increase the delay of the PLD-implementation of the SOP_f on condition $q>p$.

The PLDs such as PAL-type devices[1] and similar ones have an output enable tools which allow to place some output in the high-impedance state (three-state). In other words, it is way to disable the corresponding output buffer. The output enable/disable signal may be generated by special product term of the combinatorial macrocell of PLD . The output buffer is disable if the special product term is FALSE (has the logical LOW state).

The disable/enable control tools are common to increase a number of inputs by transformation some outputs into inputs. For this purpose the corresponding control product term remains to be equal to zero. Hence the output will be disable constantly. By contrast, to enable an output constantly, the corresponding control product term should be equal to 1 (TRUE) identically.

The dynamic disable/enable control (when the state of the output essentially depends on input's variable values) is less common.

It is suggested that these tools should be used for the implementation of Boolean function, whose SOP depends on great number of the products, in one-level logic characterized by minimum delay.

The main idea[2] is to apply the dynamic output enable control tools for switching the combinatorial macrocells of the PLDs. The output enable product terms are chosen so that only one of them is true at every instant. To find the product terms for output buffer control it is necessary to convert by factorization the SOP_f of Boolean function f into the next form:

$$SOP_f = k_l(SOP_l) \vee ... \vee k_r(SOP_r). \qquad (1)$$

Every SOP_i is chosen so that it can be implemented by single combinatorial macrocell. In other words, each SOP_i involves no more than p products. The factor-products $k_l,...,k_r$ are ortho to each other, and $k_l \vee ... \vee k_r \equiv 1$. Every factor-product k_i is used for enable/disable control of the output buffer of the corresponding to SOP_i macrocell.

After implementation of all SOP_i on the separate macrocells its output pins are combined like «hook-up OR». But the «hook-up OR» contact does not take place in fact since one, and only one, product amongst k_i is equal to 1 (is TRUE) at every instant.

4 About Algorithm

In order to implement Boolean function using PLDs as a one level circuit we need to transform the SOP_f into the form (1), where the factor-products $k_l,...,k_r$ are ortho to each other, and $k_l \vee ... \vee k_r \equiv 1$. Such transformation can be named by «a partially orthogonalization of a SOP».It is obvious that this problem has a lot of solutions similar to other combinatorial problems.

A simple heuristic algorithm is discussed here. It is proposed to complete a factoring of the initial SOP_f step-by-step recursively until each SOP_i will be involved not greater then p products.

The recursive step which deals with some current SOP consists in choosing some variable x for the next factorization act. As a result the current SOP is represented in the form (2).

$$SOP = x(SOP_x) \vee \bar{x}(SOP_{\bar{x}}). \qquad (2)$$

The problem is that to choose a variable for factorization more correctly. Let us point a few rules which are worth to take as a guide in choosing a variable for factorization.

- It is desirable to choose such variable x which is present as x or $\bar{x}$ into the greatest number of products of the current SOP. If some product t does not involve x or $\bar{x}$ it should be represented by the sum $t = xt \vee \bar{x}\,t$. This transformation increases the overall number of products and as a result an additional macrocell would be expected to be demanded.
- It is not desirable to choose variable x if we have an empty (or near-empty) sets of products involving x or $\bar{x}$ as well. Otherwise the corresponding macrocell will be empty (or near-empty) too what is inefficient.

5 Example

As an example consider the transformation of the Boolean function $f(x_1,...,x_5)$ represented by the SOP (3)

$$f(x_1,...,x_5) = x_1 \ \overline{x_2}x_5 \vee x_3 x_4 \ \overline{x_5} \vee \overline{x_1}x_2x_4x_5 \vee \overline{x_2}x_3 \ \overline{x_4}x_5 \tag{3}$$

to the form (1) assuming that $p=2$.

Consider also it's implementation for hypothetical PLD, which combinatorial macrocell contains only two product terms and an additional one for enable/disable control of the output buffer status.

Let us choose x_2 as a variable for factorization at the first step. Since variable x_2 is not involved in the product $x_3 x_4 \ \overline{x_5}$ it is need to represent it as the sum of two products involving x_2 in an explicit form.

$$x_3 x_4 \ \overline{x_5} = x_2 x_3 x_4 \ \overline{x_5} \vee \overline{x_2}x_3 x_4 \ \overline{x_5}. \tag{4}$$

After factorization the expression (3) by x_2 the representation (5) is obtained.

$$f(x_1,...,x_5) = \overline{x_2}(x_1 x_5 \vee x_3 x_4 \ \overline{x_5} \vee x_3 \ \overline{x_4}x_5) \vee x_2(\ \overline{x_1}x_4x_5 \vee x_3 x_4 \ \overline{x_5}). \tag{5}$$

There is no need for a further factorization of the SOP on x_2 because this SOP can already be implemented by our hypothetical combinatorial macrocell. On the other hand the SOP on $\overline{x_2}$ is needed for the further factorization. As a result of the simple transformation the expression (6) is obtained.

$$f(x_1,...,x_5) = \overline{x_2} \ x_5(x_1 \vee x_3 \ \overline{x_4}) \vee \overline{x_2} \ \overline{x_5}(x_3 x_4) \vee x_2(\ \overline{x_1}x_4x_5 \vee x_3 x_4 \ \overline{x_5}). \tag{6}$$

Here each SOP into parentheses consists of no greater than two products. Hence it can be implemented by the separate combinatorial macrocell. The products preceding the SOPs closed into parentheses are due to be implemented by the control product terms of the corresponding macrocells.

References

1. PAL® Device Data Book and Design Guide. Advanced Micro Devices (1995)
2. Tomachev, V.F.: The Minimization of the Delay in the PAL-Implementation of Boolean Function. In: Zakrevskij, A.D. (ed.): Logical Design, Vol.2. Institute of Engineering Cybernetics of NAS of Belarus, Minsk (1997) 52-58 (in Russian)

Reconfigurable PCI-BUS Interface (RPCI)

A. Abo Shosha, P. Reinhart, F. Rongen

Central Laboratory for Electronics (ZEL), Research Centre Juelich (FZJ),

D-52425, Germany

http://www.kfa-juelich.de/zel

Abstract. In this paper the Peripheral Component Interface PCI is presented as a target/master reconfigurable interface, based on Programmable Logic Devices PLDs (the Field Programmable Gate Arrays FPGAs and the Complex Programmable Logic Devices CPLDs are collectively referred to herein as PLDs). The core of the PCI interface design is implemented on the 1428 PCI-Interface board Rev. 3.00 using XC4028EX device, package 208 with speed grade 3C. The main transaction of the PCI compliant interface and the principle characteristics of the PLDs based interface are introduced. The analysis of the software driver algorithm is explained. Also, the main technical notes of the PCI interface design implementation and its corresponding diagnosis software tools are discussed.

1 Introduction

During the recent years PLDs have received much attention in the research communities, practical applications and the media. Elegant have been accomplished powerful solutions to problems in the field of Digital Signal Processing [1], through PLDs which, exhibit a surprising number of advantages and characteristics. The main characteristic is the ability for reconfiguration. The application areas are; reconfigurable logic microprocessors [2], configurable memory architectures [3], and flexible bus Interfaces [4]. The incorporation of the PLDs into the system interface domain may yield great benefits in terms of interface flexibility and reliability for digital signal manipulation and processing. Almost all PLDs vendors realised the PCI interface using their own products, and all of them ensure that these products are 100% compatible to the PCI timing compliant, such as Actel FPGAs based PCI-Compliant Family [5], Altera CPLDs based PCI-BUS application [6], Lucent FPGAs based PCI-Application [7], Xilinx FPGAs based PCI Core Solutions [8], ...etc. The implementation of the PCI-BUS interface using PLDs products proves the powerful capabilities of these products in accessing and manipulating high speed digital signals. The main characteristics of the PCI-BUS interface are; 1) *Automatic configuration,* 2) *Low power consumption,* 3) *High performance data transfer.* the PCI offers high performance (132 Mbyte/sec.) 32/64 bit multiplexed mode (address/data) that reduces the number of pins, also the PCI supports processor independent data transfer and an optional burst mode that provides accelerated throughput of data across the bus. Devices connected to the PCI interface achieve performance comparable to that of devices directly connected to the processor local bus [9]. In section II, the PCI interface design criteria will be presented. Section III, will explain the design implementation strategy. Section IV will present the basic algorithm of the software driver (PCI-BUS Charger). Finally section V, shows the project notes, and discussion of the PLDs based PCI interface implementation.

2 PCI interface design criteria

The PCI interface requires a minimum of 47 pins for target-only devices and 49 pins for a master to handle data and addressing, interface control, arbitration, and system functions. The data communication on the PCI-BUS is accessed in three logic spaces, the first is the configuration space that is intended to define the PCI communication protocol and carries the PCI interface characteristics. The others two spaces are I/O space and memory spaces that deal with the Add-on user application interface. The configuration space must be accessible at all times in contrary to Add-on user application interface space that can be controlled to handle data or not. The Add-on user application interface is handled through I/O space and memory space. The base addresses of these spaces are defined in the configuration space header. The data Transfer can be accessed directly through the I/O or memory space but the memory space must be predefined (mapped) to enable the system to handle it. In general the PCI transaction is multiplexed (address/data), (**Fig. 1.** Shows the main PCI-Bus transaction for burst transfer mode multiple data cycles/single transaction).

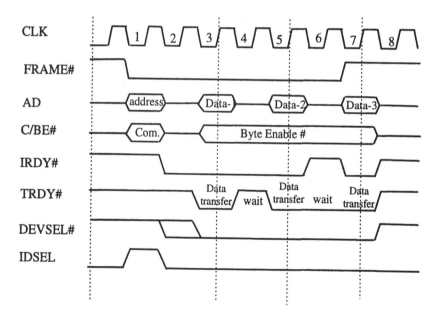

Fig1. PCI-BUS transaction

The first cycle of the transaction is the address phase and the other cycle(s) is data phase (according to the data transfer mode, single or burst data transfer modes). The transaction starts with the address phase which occurs when FRAME# is asserted

(# active low) for the first time. During the address phase, AD-bus contains a valid address and (C/BE#)-bus contains a valid bus command. For the configuration cycles an extra signal IDSEL is asserted (active high) during the address phase. After the address phase, the initiator (the master) asserts IRDY# that means the initiator is ready to receive data (read transaction) or AD-bus contains valid data (write transaction). The target replies by asserting the TRDY# signal and DEVSEL# that means the AD-bus contains a valid data (read transaction) or the target is ready to receive data (write transaction). During the data phase the C/BE# bus contains the suitable Byte Enable BE# that is used to arrange the byte sequences of the data transfer. The DEVSEL# is asserted till the end of the transaction. The data transfer occurs only if the IRDY# and TRDY# are asserted, wait cycles may be inserted in the data phase by either the master or the target when IRDY# or TRDY# is deasserted (cycles 4,6 figure 3). The latest cycle occurs when both IRDY# and TRDY# are asserted and FRAME# is deasserted (cycle 7). The PCI device can access the transaction according to its operation mode. If the PCI device is target, it will receive FRAME#, IDSEL, address on AD, C/BE# and IRDY# signals. The target sends TRDY#, and DEVSEL#. If the PCI device is master, the device must request the mastership (Only one Master may control the PCI bus at a given time [10]) from the PCI-BUS agent (by asserting REQ# signal) and wait till the PCI-BUS agent grants the mastership of the device (the agent asserts GNT# signal). After that the device accesses the transaction as a master. The master sends the FRAME#, IRDY#, C/BE#, address on the AD signals, and receives TRDY#, DEVSEL# signals. The data transfer take place from target to master at read and from master to target at write.

3 Implementation of the PCI transaction using PLDs

Because each PCI design is unique, PLDs provide an ideal solution for PCI designs. The 1428 PCI-Interface board **Fig. 2** is based on the XC4028EX device package 208 with speed grade 3C, this device is interfaced with Am29F010 128 K Byte, speed grade 120 flash memory (as a permanent design storage). On this card the device can be configured using two modes of configurations (down loading the design to the XC4028EX device). The first is the slave serial mode, and the second is the master parallel mode. The slave serial mode is used for design prototypes and testing only whereas, the master parallel mode is used for down loading the design from the permanent design storage. The output of design routing format that is supported by this design is (Intel MCS-86 Hexadecimal object file format code 88) that can be down loaded by the software driver to the flash memory. The time synchronization of the overall design is the most demanding factor of the PCI interface design. As the XC4028EX is 100% compatible to the PCI timing specifications the basic interface does not need too much timing control. With the large scale designs, the need of controlling the internal time constraints is essential. Almost all PLDs vendors support a User Time Constraints (UTC) that describes the timing behavior of the internal components such as, time delay, buses, timing groups, I/O speed rates, ...etc. So, the designers need a high experience to handle these constraints specially with highly sensitive interfaces like the PCI. The XC4028EX supports adequate resources for the primary PCI-BUS Interface. Due to logic complexity or the design extension , the designer can depend on an other device that has more resources or multiple device architecture designs [2].

Fig. 3 1428 PCI-Bus Interface board

4 Software driver of the PCI interface

The software programming of this PCI interface includes two drivers. The first is the PCI interface driver that mainly is used to define the board in the Windows environment and deals with the interface utilities like PCI-BIOS ROM routines, configuring the device, ...etc. The second is the application driver that deals with the application itself and controls the measurements and data acquisition that is carried out by the application core. The PCI interface driver at first defines the basic information of the board and the basic PCI interface. The PCI interface driver (PCI-BUS Charger) depends on Labview as a graphical programming tool. The powerful hardware diagnosis tools of the C++ can support the access of the PCI-BIOS routines. The integration between Labview and the C++ Dynamic Link Libraries (DLLs) leads to compact PCI software diagnosis. The PCI-BUS driver allows full automation of the board reconfiguration without causing any conflict with the operating system. Due to on line reconfiguration, Some designers use a second device on the board because not all operating systems (Win 95, NT, ...ect.) take kindly to a device being taken off line [8].

5 Discussion and comment

Through the PCI implementation steps, some important notes must be recognised. At first, timing synchronisation of design blocks, is a first priority because the timing factor plays the vital rule in PCI multiplexed transactions accesses. The second note, is the simplicity of the PCI interface, because in a real world we do not need to implement all PCI compliant functions. The third note, is the flexibility of the PLDs to reconfigure the PCI interface board (On or Off line reconfiguration) in not more 20 sec. On the other side, the PLDs are less dense than the custom logic. In general the simplicity of reconfiguration and development indicates the powerful facilities of PLDs based DSP systems. From the previous discussion, we can conclude that the PLDs based digital system will play an important role especially for the flexible powerful interface designs.

References

1. Goslin, G. R. „Using Xilinx FPGAs to Design Custom Digital Signal Processing Devices", Proceedings of the DSP 1995 Technical Proceeding pp.595-604,12 Jan 1995.
2. R. D. Wittig," One Chip: An FPGA processor with reconfigurable logic", Dep. Of Electrical &Computer Engineering University of Toronto, Sep. 1995.
3. S.J.E. Wilton, J. Rose, Z.G. Vranesic ``Memory/Logic Interconnect Flexibility in FPGAs with Large Embedded Memory Arrays," IEEE Custom Integrated Circuits Conference , May 1996.
4. H. Saleh, P. Reinhart, R. Engles, R. Reinartz, „A Flexible fully compatible PCI Interface for Nuclear Experiments", Nuclear Science Symposium and Medical Imaging Conference, Albuquerque, New Mexico, USA., 9-15 Nov. 1997.
5. Actel FPGA Application Briefs „ACT 3 PCI Compliant Family,, 22 Dec. 1997. http://www.actel.com/
6. Altera Applications, „(PCI Compliance of Altera Devices), ver. 2,, May 1995. http://www.altera.com/
7. Lucent Technologies „ ORCA Series FPGAs in PCI BUS Master (with Target) Applications," http://www.lucent.com/micro/fpga/
8. Xilinix Logic Core, „PCI master & Slave Interfaces Version 2.0", Oct. 1997. http://www.xilinx.com/
9. PCI Special Interest Group, „PCI Local Bus Specifications Revision 2.1", 1 June 1995.
10. AMCC „PCI Controller Data Book", SPRING, 1996.

Programmable Prototyping System for Image Processing

Andrej Trost, Andrej Žemva, Baldomir Zajc

University of Ljubljana, Faculty of Electrical Engineering, Tržaška 25, 1000 Ljubljana, Slovenia

Abstract. In this paper, we present a programmable prototyping system for hardware implementation of image processing algorithms. The system is composed of a PC, reconfigurable prototyping card with 2 FPGA circuits, microcontroller and memory circuit board. Programmable devices are used for implementing the designed algorithm and the interface circuit for communication between the implemented design and the PC. The software for an automatic interface circuit synthesis allows users to design and implement digital circuits without specific knowledge of the structural details of the system. The implementation of the image processing chain is described to demonstrate the operation of the programmable system.

1 Introduction

For the real time image processing, high speed processors and ASIC circuits are often required for an efficient implementation [1]. However, ASIC circuits require extensive designing and manufacturing efforts resulting in the increasing production time and financial risk incurred in the development of a new product. An alternative solution to the time-to-market and risk problems are FPGA integrated circuits since they, due to the recent progress in microelectronics technology, provide instant manufacturing and low-cost prototypes [2]. The reprogrammability of FPGAs is particularly explored in programmable systems, an environment for a fast prototyping implementation of complete circuit designs in a real time [3]. Designs implemented on the programmable system are flexible for any changes just by recompiling hardware devices with software programs [4].

In this paper, we present a programmable reconfigurable system for prototyping hardware realizations of different image processing algorithms. The proposed system provides a thorough hardware verification of the implemented design before it is embedded into the real time image processing system. An user friendly software supports the design and implementation of digital circuits without a specific knowledge of the structural details of the programmable system.

The paper is organized as follows. First, the architecture and the functionality of the system is presented. A typical design flowchart and hardware verification procedures are described next. In the second part, the implementation of the image processing chain is described as a case study for the operation of the presented system. The paper concludes with the final remarks and guidelines for the future work.

2 Hardware Prototyping Environment

The hardware components of the programmable prototyping system are presented in Figure 1. The system is based on a reconfigurable prototyping card with 2 FPGA circuits (LCA1 and LCA2) used for implementation of the prototyping design and interfaces. We used Xilinx XC4010 FPGA devices with the capacity of up to 10.000 equivalent logic gates. The reconfigurable card is inserted in a PC ISA bus and externally connected to the microcontroller and memory board.

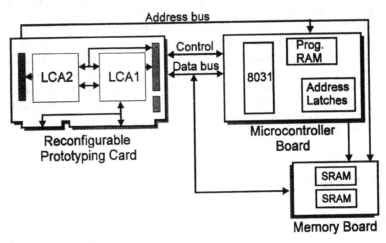

Fig. 1. Prototyping hardware components.

The PC is used for sending test vectors and reading design responses through the 16 bit ISA bus and the interface circuit inside FPGAs. The FPGA circuits are not suitable for emulation of larger memory blocks which are extensively used in the image processing designs. External memory modules have to be used, with the size and configuration of the memory depending on the particular design. We used the microcontroller and memory board with additional interface circuits for emulation of any memory configuration required for a specific image processing algorithm. The total size of emulated memory modules is limited to 512×8 bits of memory on the external board, which can be easily expanded.

The required interface circuits for each prototyping design are automatically synthesized and implemented in the FPGA devices together with the designed circuit. The software for interface circuit synthesis extends the approach introduced for the prototyping system based on XC3000 devices [5].

Figure 2 illustrates a typical design flowchart on the reconfigurable system. The design process starts with a study of the selected image processing algorithm. We use Matlab for the study, simulation and evaluation of the image processing algorithm on sample images. After evaluating the performance of a specific algorithm, the hardware architecture is derived. We explore the possibility of pipelined or other parallel implementations by considering timing and architectural constraints. An architecture dependent simulation using the same software environment is performed next.

The next step is the design of the processing elements with a schematic entry or VHDL design tools. Functionality of the designed processing elements is verified using the simulation software on the PC. Rather than performing a timing simulation as a software program on the PC, we speed up this step by performing a hardware verification, denoted as hardware verification I in Figure 2. For this purpose, the interface circuit netlist is automatically synthesized and merged with the design netlist. The single netlist is then partitioned and technology mapped using XACT tools resulting in a configuration file for both FPGA devices. Delays and device utilization are known in this step. The user friendly software support allows the designer to interactively set test vectors, execute hardware verification, and observe and compare results with the simulation results. Designer can take digital image file as an input and observe the result as an image.

Once all processing elements are designed and verified, the complete circuit architecture is implemented by connecting processing elements and additional memory control logic. The hardware verification, denoted as hardware verification II in Figure 2, is performed in a similar manner after interface synthesis and technology mapping.

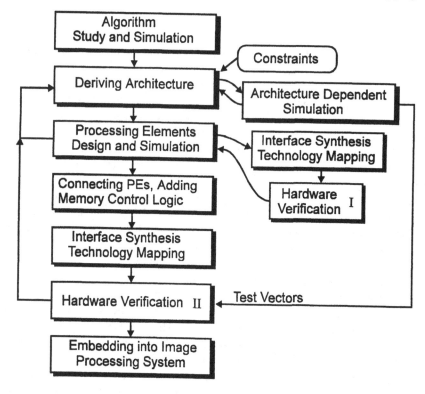

Fig. 2. Design flowchart.

It is important to note that the test vectors used for the architecture dependent simulation are also used for comparing the simulation and hardware verification results. In case of any violation of the design specifications, the design cycle is repeated, otherwise the designed circuit can be embedded into the image processing system.

3 Applications of the Reconfigurable System

In this section, we demonstrate the application of the proposed programmable system by designing a circuit performing an edge-based image segmentation. We designed, implemented and tested several image processing operators on the reconfigurable board. The pipeline architecture was used in the operators, which can be then cascaded to form an image segmentation chain, as presented in Figure 3.

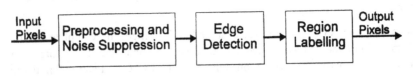

Fig. 3. Image processing chain.

The first stage includes preprocessing and noise suppression operators to remove any noise captured in the image. A nonlinear pseudomedian operator was used for noise suppression, since it is better in preserving the real edges than a low-pass filter [6].

The basic idea for edge-detection techniques is the computation of the local derivative operator. We used Sobel operator with 3x3 convolution matrices for obtaining horizontal and vertical gradients. The final gradient value is then calculated by the infinite norm. The threshold filter produces at last a binary image with edge and background pixels. The pipeline implementation of the Sobel operator requires two line FIFO memories.

Once the edges between the regions are found, the regions grouping the pixels with the same characteristics should be identified and labeled. The regions are identified in two passes. In the first pass, background pixels are labeled by choosing either a new label or a label of a neighboring pixel. The labeling algorithm is based on a set of cases depending on the current values of the input pixel and the two neighboring pixels. A FIFO memory is used for producing the value of already labeled upper neighbor of the current input pixel. Equivalences between the already labeled pixels are written into the equivalence memory. Pixels are delayed by another FIFO memory before entering the resolving architecture in the second pass. The final labels are obtained by the two consecutive indirect addressing operations on the equivalence memory bank. Two equivalence memory banks are required for the real time implementation. One equivalence memory bank is used in the first pass for the current image frame while the other one is used in the second pass for the previous frame. The banks are switched at the beginning of each new image frame.

Technology mapping results of the designed circuits are shown in Table 1. For each operator, we report the number of CLBs utilized for the hardware implementation, number of CLBs required for the interface circuit and in the last column, the worst case delay as reported by XACT.

Algorithm	Device Utilization (CLBs)		Timing (ns)
	Operator	Interface	
Pseudomedian Filter (3x3)	98	31	210
Sobel Edge Detection	199	48	280
Region Labelling	132	34	150

Table 1. Device utilization of image processing circuits.

4 Conclusions

The presented programmable system can be efficiently used for prototyping the hardware implementation and verification of different image processing algorithms. The same computer can be used for simulating the image processing algorithm as well as for providing an environment for the hardware verification of the algorithm implemented as a digital circuit. An automatic synthesis of the interface circuit simplifies the design flow and enables the designer to focus onto the real design issues. Based on our current experiences, our efforts are oriented towards a larger prototyping environment consisting of multi-FPGA programmable boards. The new environment will retain all the features of the presented system while providing additional flexibility to implement image processing circuits of various complexities.

References

[1] E. R. Davies: Machine Vision: Theory, Algorithms, Practicalities. Academic Press, London, 1990

[2] S. D. Brown, R. J. Francis and J. Rose: Field-Programmable Gate Arrays. Kluwer Academic Publishers, Boston, 1992

[3] M. Wendling and W. Rosenstiel: A Hardware Environment for Prototyping and Partitioning Based on Multiple FPGAs. European Design Automation Conference '94, 77-82, September 1994

[4] L. E. Turner and P. J. W. Grauman: Rapid Hardware Prototyping of Digital Image Processing Circuits. 5th International Workshop on Field Programmable Logic and Applications, 68-77, 1995

[5] A. Trost, R. Kužnar, A. Žemva and B. Zajc: An Experimental Programmable Environment for Prototyping Digital Circuits. 6th International Workshop on Field Programmable Logic and Applications, 337-345, 1996

[6] H. E. Burdick: Digital Imaging. McGraw Hill, USA, 1997

A Co-simulation Concept for an Efficient Analysis of Complex Logic Designs

J. Fischer[1], C. Müller[2], H. Kurz[2]

[1] Institute of Semiconductor Electronics II, Technical University of Aachen,
Sommerfeldstr. 24, D-52056 Aachen/Germany
jfischer@iht-ii.rwth-aachen.de
[2] AMO GmbH, Huyskensweg 25, D-52074 Aachen/Germany
{mueller, kurz}@amica.rwth-aachen.de

Abstract. The focus of this paper is the presentation of our work on developing a novel co-simulation concept for synchronous logic designs. The growing complexity of programmable devices (FPGAs and CPLDs) requires complex test environments to find design and implementation errors as early in the design process as possible. In most cases it is the system environment that determines the performance requirements of the design and its behavior under dynamic workloads. Our approach takes advantage of the fact that the circuit design and simulation can be implemented with standard hardware description languages (HDLs). To model and simulate the system environment, however, we have used a state-of-the-art simulation language. Both simulations are tied together through a simple communication structure. The simulators constantly exchange state information, which provides dynamic feedback to simulate realistic workloads. As an application example we will describe how this concept was applied during the development of the controller logic for an optical high-speed network adapter.

Introduction

System designers applying programmable logic have a set of tools at their disposal, which let them implement their designs with relative ease and limited risk when compared to the complexity of developing an ASIC. In order to take advantage of the flexible implementation process, it is mandatory that the design can also be rapidly validated, both in terms of correctness, i.e. that the hardware behaves according to the specifications, and in terms of performance. Otherwise the validation phase will become the bottleneck in the development cycle. Many complex logic designs have a common structure in that they are synchronous implementations of a state machine. The dynamic behavior of the hardware is described by the assumed states and their transitions, as well as through its input and output streams. State transitions occur at fixed intervals in reference to a clock signal. The system environment in which the hardware operates can likewise be model as a synchronous design. The logic itself is mostly designed by means of software tools. Rather then conducting in-circuit tests on a hardware prototype, it is far superior to validate a design through a additional simulation step when changes in the design carry little delay. Validating the design means to exercise the hardware by providing a stimulus at the inputs and to verify that it produces the expected outputs. In the simplest form, these stimuli are static test vectors. A static test vector, however, does not allow to capture the dynamics of a system's environment. To test the design under realistic conditions, which allows to reveal design flaws much more reliably, requires to model the dynamics of the environment. The tools available with the design front ends of programmable logic mostly focus on the behavior of the hardware itself. To create a realistic model of the hardware environment can turn out to be a task even more complex than creating the system design itself. Moreover, if the same hardware development tools are used, the designer of the test tool needs at least as much experience in hardware design as the system designer. Thus the required process is either very complex or the required add-on components are extremely expensive.

Our approach therefore has been to model and implement the system's environment with a state-of-the-art simulation language. The design of our hardware is captured and simulated in VHDL [2] while the system environment is modeled and implemented in MODSIM III [1], a high level object oriented simulation language. The communication between both tools is based on the exchange of symbols from a predefined set using a simple file stream model. Within the VHDL simulator, an integrated interpreter translates the symbolic information into the corresponding device signals. Within the MODSIM simulator, independent state machines are used to provide the required stimulus for the programmable logic implementation. This architecture also allowed us to generate additional trace information, which we used to locate error conditions in the complex waveform representation of the underlying digital design.

Co-simulation Analyzer

The co-simulation analyzer concept (CoSimA) was developed to validate the implementation of an adapter board's controller logic (GigaNet) implemented with two high capacity FPGAs. The GigaNet board effectively is a bus bridge between a PCI bus and an SCI interconnect. PCI (Peripheral Component Interconnect) [4] buses are found in most modern PC and workstations. SCI (Scalable Coherent Interface) [3] is an IEEE standard that was specified to provide bus-like services to support distributed shared memory environments. In addition to the standard documents, the SCI standard uses C code to unambiguously specify SCI functionality.

The CoSimA concept itself can be applied to any synchronous logic design. CoSimA was designed with the following objectives in mind:

- to validate the hardware's correct implementation of the bus specifications
- to evaluate the performance (latency) of the hardware
- to take advantage of the SCI standard's simulation model (C source code)

- to provide an easy-to-implement and reusable communication structure
- to allow a distributed simulation approach
- to make the validation tool's implementation independent from the VHDL design

As such there were a number of design choices. Primarily the question of how to implement the simulation environment was of interest. We have chosen to implement CoSimA in MODSIM III, an object oriented simulation language, which is commercially available. Other simulation languages can certainly be used (for more information, see e.g. [6]). The advantage of MODSIM III is that existing C and C++ libraries can easily be incorporated, because the MODSIM III compiler generates C++ code that is compiled in a second step. This allowed to tie in the relevant parts of the SCI C code very easily. CoSimA could have been implement using a general purpose language, alas with more effort. There are libraries available that provide additional functionality for simulation purposes [5] that are not provided in the standard libraries of a language.

Another question is how to communicate time information. Both simulators work with an internal clock. System state changes occur in reference to these clocks. The two co-simulators must make the other system aware of any state changes. To avoid causality errors and to evaluate the performance of the hardware, there needs to be a way to relate the state change information to elapsed simulation time. One possible way to solve this problem is to exchange messages that are sent whenever a system advances time. Since both simulators work synchronously, however, we have combined the exchange of state change information with the time advance indications. In order to do that the simulators exchange a defined set of symbols. In our case these symbols are ASCII character strings. The symbols themselves carry the state information while the mere exchange of these symbols synchronizes the two simulators and therefore serves as a time advance indication. In the case of SCI, this has been rather straightforward. Information sent around an SCI interconnect is contained in packets that consist of 16 bit symbols. An additional flag bit is transmitted which serves as a packet delimiter. Represented as an ASCII string, this yields something like "0xFFEF 1", where "0xFFEF" is the 16 bit symbol (in C notation) and "1" represents the flag value.

In the case of PCI the mapping is not quite that obvious. PCI is a backplane bus that uses signal lines to handle the handshaking during the exchange of information. Thus we had to define a mapping between the signal lines of the PCI bus that would be equivalent to the information exchanged on the SCI side. By mapping the state of the relevant signal lines at every rinsing edge of the PCI bus clock to a set of symbols, we are able to provide that mapping. The allowed sequence of symbols can then be capture by an extended state machine. In addition to its states, an extended state machine uses internal variables to capture state information, which reduces the number of required states. The second piece of information in the ASCII strings is the data that is exchanged during a PCI bus cycle. A third symbol represents the request/grant lines of the PCI bus, because CoSimA also acts as the PCI bus arbiter. Figure 1 illustrates the mapping of the PCI signal lines to symbols for a PCI read cycle, whereas table 1 shows the corresponding symbol stream that will be exchange for both the PCI master and the PCI target.

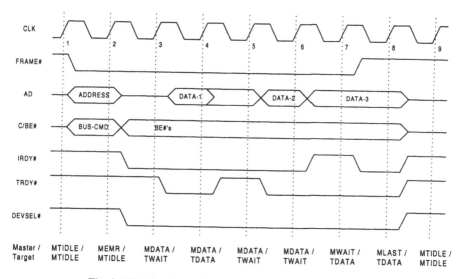

Fig. 1. PCI Read Cycle (Source: [4]) with Symbol Mapping

Master Output Symbols			Target Output Symbols		
MTIDLE	0x00000000	GNT0	MTIDLE	0x00000000	REQ0
MMEMR	0x1C000064	GNT0	MTIDLE	0x00000000	REQ0
MDATA	0x00000000	GNT0	TWAIT	0x00000000	REQ0
MDATA	0x00000000	GNT0	TDATA	0x11111111	REQ0
MDATA	0x00000000	GNT0	TWAIT	0x00000000	REQ0
MWAIT	0x00000000	GNT0	TDATA	0x22222222	REQ0
MLAST	0x00000000	GNT0	TDATA	0x33333333	REQ0
MTIDLE	0x00000000	GNT0	MTIDLE	0x00000000	REQ0

Table 1. PCI Symbol Stream

The simplest way to exchange the symbols is to use a file stream model. Files can be shared across networks which supports a distributed simulation environment. Moreover most simulation environments including VHDL tools allow file-based I/O independent from the operating system on which they run. The ASCII strings are written to a file by one simulation program and read by the co-simulator. To avoid file access conflicts, each file is read-only for one simulator and write-only for the other. To support bi-directional information exchange, two data files (inputs and outputs) are needed per bus interface. Access to the files is blocking, which ensures proper synchronization between the simulators. File synchronization has been implemented through two additional control files per data file. The control files are also used to exchange ASCII strings, implementing a two state handshake protocol. The handshake protocol disable/enables access to the data files, while an aging protocol ensure that the data is current. In order to avoid deadlock, care must be taken as to the sequence in which the data files are access. The simplest way to avoid deadlock is to first read all inputs into the simulation and then to provide all outputs for every bus cycle.

Summary and Future Work

Validating complex synchronous designs can efficiently be handled through co-simulation. Timing and state information is exchanged between the co-simulators via synchronized files. File-based I/O is supported by most development tools. State information needs to be mapped to appropriate symbols. The mapping of signal lines for the PCI bus was demonstrated as an example. The co-simulation has several advantage over in-circuit testing or the implementation of a test bench with hardware development tools:

1. the test environment uses a completely independent code base; thus design flaws will not propagate into the test bench.
2. interpretation errors are easily uncovered, because the independent design of the system and its environment will otherwise cause interoperability problems.
3. the system environment can be modeled to any level of detail/abstraction as require
4. statistically distributed stimulus can be generated and outputs can be analyzed
5. the observable window of information is larger than with hardware analyzer tools
6. the hardware's performance can be analyzed to evaluate design alternatives

We have applied the concept successfully during the development of the GigaNet board. The concept is valid, however, for any complex synchronous logic design.

Our simulation environment solely runs on Windows NT. We therefore plan to encapsulate the communication functionality in some form of reusable module, e.g. a dynamically linked library (DLL). Moreover, we want to evaluate different communication mechanism alternatives. The communication mechanism should yield as little performance overhead as possible and must not buffer the data, so that the data in the shared medium is available to the other simulator as soon as it is written.

And lastly, the performance data recorded for the hardware can also be used for system level simulations to evaluate throughputs and latencies of the entire interconnect of multiple nodes.

References

[1]MODSIM III Reference Manual, CACI Product Company, La Jolla, CA 92037, USA, 1996
[2]IEEE "IEEE Standard VHDL, Language Reference Manual", 1993, Standard 1076-1993
[3]IEEE "IEEE Standard Scalable Coherent Interface (SCI)", 1992, Standard 1596-1992
[4]PCI Special Interest Group, "PCI Local Bus Specification", Revision 2.1, 1995
[5]Aachen University of Technology, Aachen/Germany, Dept. of Electrical. Engineering, Communication Networks, "Communication Networks Class Library - CNCL", http://www.comnets.rwth-aachen.de/doc/cncl.html
[6]USENET comp.simulation archive: http://tebbit.eng.umd.edu/simulation/gen_archive.html

Programming and Implementation of Reconfigurable Routers[1]

Andreas C. Döring, Wolfgang Obelöer, Gunther Lustig

Medical University of Lübeck, Institute of Computer Engineering
Ratzeburger Allee 160, D-23538 Lübeck, Germany
E-Mail: doering/obeloeer/lustig@iti.mu-luebeck.de

Abstract. Clusters made from standard PCs or workstations interconnected by a high-speed network form a high-performance parallel computer. High-speed networks consist of routers switching the data via several wire segments. In order to allow flexible use of the network the routers have to be reconfigurable. Such a router is described as an application of reconfiguration techniques and standard devices like FPGAs. The presented approach is based on the use of sets of rules to describe the router's behavior in a flexible manner. The rule set is translated to generate configuration data for the hardware.

1 Introduction

Many problems in industry, research, medicine etc. can only be solved by using parallel computer systems. They consist of a high number of computation nodes interconnected by a fast network. Due to a good price/performance ratio PC or workstation clusters become more and more important in this area. For the nodes of a cluster, off-the-shelf PCs or workstations are used. The nodes are connected to the network via a network adapter (typically placed in a standard bus like the PCI bus). For high performance computing the network has to provide both low latency (sub microsecond range) and high throughput (Gbps). Using ready-made solutions for such a network is not always possible. To avoid the bottleneck of bus-like networks (e.g. Ethernet) no single medium is applied. The network contains routers (or synonymously switches) interconnected among each other and to the network adapters by wire segments called links. Data, injected into the network by an adapter, is guided by the routers across several links to the destination node (adapter). Hence, the properties of the links, the adapters, and especially the behavior of the routers have a strong impact on the network performance. Since the whole system can be constructed in a compact way (all components located in one room), error rate and wire delay are quite low. Therefore the use of protocol stacks as in LANs can be

---

[1] This work was sponsored by the German Research Council DFG (MA 1412/3) in cooperation with SFB 376 "Massive Parallelität" at the University of Paderborn, Germany.

avoided. Mostly performance issues and not protocols determine the design of the routers.

Looking at the speed demands it is obvious that no software solution is possible for network router controlling. Hence, most existing routers are dedicated hardware implementations which are only able to perform relatively simple or specialized methods for message guiding (routing algorithm). By using these fixed routers it is very difficult or even impossible to adapt the behavior of the network to the requirements of the used hardware or software. Solutions for these problems are described in terms of sophisticated routing algorithms, e.g. [1], considering different topologies [4], adaptivity information, real-time capabilities, fault-tolerance etc. But because of their complexity they are not applicable in current high-speed networks with methods used so far. The description of these aspects of routing is complex [2], therefore a method for a clear description is presented next. It is shown how a routing algorithm given this way can be executed in hardware. Some aspects of a router architecture are discussed. Furthermore some notes on the implementations under work are given.

2 Rule-Based Routing

In this context the aim of RBR (Rule Based Routing) is to provide an approach which makes it possible to:
- describe complex routing algorithms (and therewith the behavior of the routers) on a high abstraction level
- enable fast hardware execution of the high-level description
- reconfigure the behavior of a router in a wide range

As the common basis for the whole project a rule-based description method developed at our institute is used to describe the routing algorithms. Here IF-THEN-Rules are applied to specify the router behavior.

```
IF a = d THEN use_link <- computation_node;
IF abs(a-d)< n div 2 AND a>d THEN use_link<-ring_left;
IF abs(a-d)< n div 2 AND a<d THEN use_link<-ring_right;
IF abs(a-d)>=n div 2 AND a>d THEN use_link<-ring_right;
IF abs(a-d)>=n div 2 AND a<d THEN use_link<-ring_left;
```

This very simple rule base defines the path of a message within a two-way ring topology with n nodes, increasingly numbered from left to right. At the beginning of a message there are some bits containing information about the message. In this so called message header the position of the destination d is located. In the rule base there are two comparisons of d to two constants depending on the actual position a and the ring length n. The results lead to one of three outputs (left, right and attached computation node). Note that the absolute value computation can be eliminated in the translation process without introducing additional comparisons.

This approach makes it relatively easy to implement a new routing algorithm and in addition the rule-based description method has a well-defined semantic which allows automatic processing including mapping for fast execution on hardware. The rule base is used to describe everything which is necessary to make good direction decisions including estimating load distribution in the network and propagating fault states. The data transport inside the router works in a similar way for all routing algorithms and thus is outside the rule based description. This allows an independent optimization of the router's data path.

3 Router Structure

The connection of a flexible control part and the data transport is shown in Fig. 1. For brevity assume that steering the data transport is done by control registers. Vice versa the rule interpreters have access to status registers that contain information about the data path and the present messages. Typically, a routing algorithm is described by several sets of rules which are processed independently and exchange information via variables. In order to address this, there are several rule interpreters to allow node internal parallelism. For storing the variables, registers are provided.

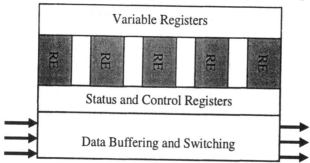

Fig. 1. Router structure (RE = Rule Evaluator)

Network latency demands inhibit a sequential processing of the rules, hence their interpretation consists of only three steps. At the first one all logic terms in the premises of the rules are evaluated in parallel. In the above example these are only two comparisons between d and node-dependent constants with three possible outcomes for each. For typical routing algorithms one rule base contains about 5-10 of such basic logic expressions. The results are encoded in bit vectors that are combined so as to give a key (or index) to the required rule. In this case equality of only one comparison matters, which allows compacting the other two results. The encoding can be done by concatenating, by linear combination or similar methods. The conclusions of the rules are stored in a table. The key is used as an index into this table giving the encoded conclusion, which is executed in the third step. In total the time for a rule evaluation is dominated by the table access and the premise operations and takes some tens of nanoseconds (50 ns in an ALTERA EPF10K50-3).

Altogether for a fast and flexible rule evaluator the following components have to be configurable:

i. Choice of input values to use: the individual routing algorithms use different sets of parameters for their routing decision, e.g. header fields of messages, queue usage or links state.
ii. Evaluation of arithmetic or similar functions found in the premise: Beside of common functions like addition or comparison some more uncommon functions, e.g. maximum in a finite order or selection of a minimal element in rated sets have to be provided.
iii. Rule evaluation: the commands from the conclusions are some kind of micro-instructions that initiate writing to registers, further executions of rules or routing-related actions like switch setting. Similar to i) there is a huge set of possible actions that has to be encoded in an efficient way for a given routing algorithm.
iv. Register structure: The rule base contains the declaration and access to variables, which may have the structure of arrays. They are concurrently accessed by several rule interpreters.

Though all four topics are complex and worth a treatment on its own, only the first and the last point are covered in the following paragraphs.

The first component is spread among several units of the router. For example, every router contains memory in order to be able to store data arriving at one of its input links while all output links are in use. The information how much data this memory contains is valuable for the routing algorithm because it is an evidence for the network load. To avoid expensive multi-port memories, this buffer is normally structured into several small buffers, whose individual usage provides further insight. It is clearly advantageous to transport only those buffer usage values to the rule evaluator that are actually needed for the current rule base. Because it is impossible to do this for all values at the same time, the rule evaluators contain registers which are associated with the appropriate parameters. Most of these parameters change slowly compared to the router operation. Only some of them are time critical, e.g. the message header. The sources of these parameters, e.g. the buffer managers are connected to the rule interpreters by a set of busses. The structure of this interconnection system allows optimizing the router design with respect to hardware cost and execution speed. The values used by the routing algorithms are stored at the parameter sources. They are automatically transmitted when they have changed and the associated bus gets free. Note that this configurable interconnection problem differs from standard programmable logic devices since there is a fixed set of sources and a fixed set of destinations (the rule interpreters). Furthermore the knowledge of the urgency of the individual values allows saving much hardware cost compared to direct wires.

One challenging problem is the use of registers. Routing algorithms often need some variables to hold a state. This way previous decisions can be considered and balancing of network resources is eased. These registers are written by instructions in the rule conclusions and read when they are part of rule premises. To guarantee determinism the use of the variables has to be synchronized in some way. One option is the association of registers with semaphores. This is a typical problem for many designs where the sequence of operations can not be precomputed

For the realization two target technologies are considered. An early implementation is a prototype based on FPGAs. It is possible with our structured approach to implement a complete router for complex routing algorithms in one FPGA (e.g. with limited functionality and small buffers: XILINX XC4085; later XC40125). Compared to the Telegraphos project [3], where a switch was built also using XILINX-devices (15), the advances in technology allow this. For FPGA-based hardware the rule-based description of a routing algorithm is translated into structural VHDL. The generation of the configuration data still needs the manufacturers' back-end tools incorporating hand-optimized macros for the performance-critical data path. This way the configuration capability of RAM-based FPGAs are exploited. Therefore additional flexibility (by higher number of rule evaluators) requires only a small amount of additional hardware. The limiting factor is the integration of buffer memory. Hence, programmable logic devices with a heterogeneous structure (fine-grained cells, PAL structures and flexible RAM) would suit to the router's demands very well. As second option we developed an architecture for a fast rule evaluator with a standard cell ASIC in mind. Thereby the number of ports is limited by packaging. The die area is determined by the pad-spacing too. The advantage of this technology is the more efficient implementation of regular structures like buffer RAM. In a typical router this consumes most of the hardware effort.

4 Conclusion

The area of high-speed communication networks requires reconfigurable elements, namely routers. They can be built by standard FPGAs but the dedicated demands suggest the design of an ASIC with reconfigurable structures for control and fixed and highly optimized modules for data transport and buffering. In both cases the generation of the configuration data from sophisticated routing algorithms is a challenging task which can be mastered by the application of the presented rule-based approach.

References

[1] C.M. Cunningham, D. Avresky: Fault-Tolerant Adaptive Routing for Two-Dimensional Meshes. Proc. First Int. Symposium on High Performance Computing Architecture, 122-131, IEEE Computer Society Press 1995

[2] A.C. Döring, G. Lustig, W. Obelöer, E. Maehle: A Flexible Approach for a Fault-Tolerant Router. Proc. Workshop on Fault-Tolerant Parallel and Distributed Systems FTPDS 98, Lecture Notes on Computer Science 1388, 693-713, Springer Berlin, 1998

[3] E.P. Markatos, M.G.H. Katevenis: Telegraphos: High-Performance Networking for Parallel Processing on Workstation Clusters. Proc. Symposium on High-Performance Computer Architectures, 1996

[4] S. Rosner, S. Danz, M. Scholles: Minimal Routing in Reconfigurable Communication Networks. Proc. Int. Conference on Massively Parallel Computing Systems, IEEE Computer Society Press 1996

Virtual Instruments Based on Reconfigurable Logic

María José Moure[1], María Dolores Valdés[2], Enrique Mandado[2]

[1] Departamento de Tecnología Electrónica, Universidad de Vigo, Apartado de Correos
Oficial Universidad, 36.200, Vigo, Spain
mjmoure@uvigo.es
http://www.dte.uvigo.es
[2] Instituto de Electrónica Aplicada "Pedro Barrié de la Maza", Universidad de Vigo,
Apartado de Correos Oficial Universidad, 36.200, Vigo, Spain
{mvaldés, emandado}@uvigo.es

Abstract. A virtual instrument results from the combination of a general
purpose computer with a generic data acquisition system in order to emulate a
traditional measurement instrument. The data acquisition hardware of the
virtual instruments provides computers with input/output capability and is
usually based on the integration of standard circuits with fixed architecture.
Meanwhile the software defines the analysis and processing of the acquired
data that is the function of the generated virtual instrument. As a consequence,
the virtual instruments are characterized by their versatility and low cost but
they lack of performance of the application oriented hardware architectures. In
this paper, we present a virtual instrument system based on reconfigurable
hardware that improves the features of virtual instruments preserving their
versatility and low cost.

1   Introduction

The traditional instruments are application specific systems based on fixed hardware
and software resources so their function and applications are defined by the
manufacturer. These instruments are complex systems and therefore they become
expensive and difficult to manage.
The widespread usage of personal computers in many scientific and technological
fields make them an ideal hardware and software platform for the implementation of
measurement instruments. By adding a simple data acquisition system, a personal
computer can emulate any instrument. The instruments generated in this way are
called virtual instruments because they do not have exclusive access to hardware and
software resources. Different instruments can be implemented over the same
hardware by only reprogramming the software. The virtual instruments offer plenty of
advantages the most important of which is the low cost due to the reusability of
hardware and software resources [1]. The above characteristics and the continuous
evolution and cheapening of the personal computers make the virtual instruments a
valuable alternative to traditional ones.

Nevertheless, there are two main factors which limits the application of virtual instruments. By one hand, the data capture is reduce to slow rates because of the more common operating systems of the general purpose computers are not oriented to real-time applications. By other hand, the data acquisition system is not an application oriented system but a generic one. Therefore, our proposal is focused on the enhancement of virtual instruments by the replacement of the generic hardware with a reconfigurable data acquisition system, as it is shown in Figure 1. By this way, some data process can be implemented by hardware reducing the data flow to/from the computer and rising the maximum sample rate.

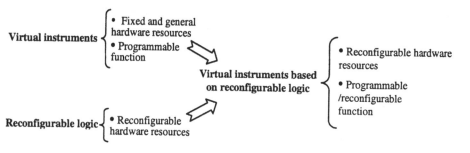

Fig. 1. Virtual Instruments based on reconfigurable logic.

The benefits of virtual instruments based on reconfigurable logic are the following:
- The bandwidth of the instruments can be increased implementing the more time critical algorithms by hardware.
- The input/output capacity can be reconfigured according to the application. In special, FPGAs devices are characterized by a great number of input/output pins providing virtual instrument with the capacity to observe and control a wide number of signals.
- The computer interface can be reconfigured according to the available resources (Plug&Play peripherals).
- Different instruments can share software and hardware design modules increasing their reusability.

2 Reconfigurable data acquisitions systems

We propose the implementation of a reconfigurable data acquisition system using FPGAs. This system operates like a reconfigurable coprocessor oriented to the capture, generation and analysis of digital signals. The combination of this hardware with a general purpose computer results in a reconfigurable virtual instrumentation system where the end user determines the software and hardware resources required for each particular application.

2.1   General description

The more essential blocks of a data acquisition system are represented in Figure 2. As an application oriented system, most of these modules must be scalable (increasing or decreasing the number of input/output pins) according to different applications. For example, the capacity of the acquisition memory varies with the requirements of the instrument.

At the same time, if the device provides with enough resources, several instruments can be active simultaneously. In this case, some blocks of the structure shown in Figure 2 must be multiplied accordingly while others can be shared among instruments. For example, an unique computer interface block multiplexed in time is generally more efficient because less input/output pins are dedicated to the communication tasks.

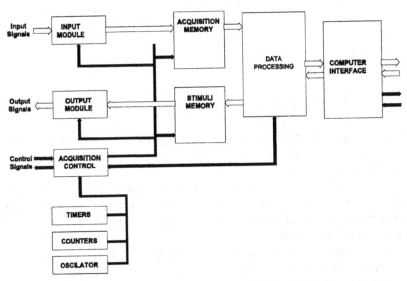

Fig. 2. Block diagram of a generic data acquisition-generation system.

In the computer side, the software is dedicated to the storage and visualization of data, and also to the configuration and control of the hardware. The first tasks are implemented at application level and take advantage of multitask operating systems and their advanced graphic interfaces. The second tasks are mainly implemented as extensions of the operative systems and in this way they are closely linked to the hardware.

The blocks represented in Figure 2 are briefly described in the next sections. Also, the characteristics of the configurable devices (SRAM FPGAs) required for the implementation of these blocks are indicated.

2.2   Input/Output modules

The input/outputs modules conform the interface with the real world. The input/output blocks of the reconfigurable device must be bidirectional, with tri-state capability and internal registers for faster capture rates [3].

2.3   Acquisition control block

The data capture is usually synchronized with some external or internal events and this task is developed by the acquisition control module. As a consequence, the routing of this control signals to the input/output blocks and to the internal logic becomes very important. An architecture with several low skew and great fan-out distribution networks is mandatory for this purposes [4].
At the same time, several inputs and outputs usually share common control signal so a device with a peripheral bus carrying control signals is suitable for this application [5].

2.4   Timing blocks

The timing blocks (oscilator, timers and counters) provides internal control signals to the data acquisition system. Special attention was dedicated to the design of counters in order to reach maximum operating frequencies.

2.5   Memory blocks

The memory blocks operate as a temporary storage of the acquired/generated data. This memory blocks isolate the data acquisition process from the transference through the computer interface. Therefore these storage devices are implemented as dual-port FIFOs with different clocks for push/pop operations.
The memory blocks can be implemented like internal or external units to the FPGA. The first case is more desirable because the design offers best performance, consumes less power and is less error prone. Therefore, the FPGAs with embedded dual port memory blocks are more suitable for these purposes[5].

2.6   Data processing Unit

The data processing unit performs a real-time pre-processing of the acquired data. This unit implements the more critical algorithms that determine the data throughput while the others can relay over software control (in the computer side).
An exhaustive analysis of which algorithms must be implemented in hardware and which must be implemented in software was made for each different instrument. For example in a logic analyzer, the detection logic of the trigger patterns must be

implemented in hardware for better performance meanwhile the data conversion formats of data (assembling, disassembling) can be done in the computer.

2.7 Computer Interface

There are two different options for the interconnection of the reconfigurable data acquisition board with the computer, one using of a direct expansion/local bus connection and the other using of a serial/parallel communications interface. In the first case, instruments with a great data throughput can be obtained but this kind of interface consumes many resources of the FPGA (logic and input/output pins) and limits the physical distance between the interconnected systems. On the opposite side, serial/parallel communications interfaces limit the binary rate of the transference but consume less logical and input/output resources and permit the physical isolation between devices. This last characteristic is important for the implementation of portable instrumentation and also isolate the acquisition hardware from the noisy environment of general purpose computers. By this reason, the developed system actually implements the standard IEEE-488 (ECP mode) as the communication interface with the computer.

3. Conclusions

Several prototype boards using Xilinx (XC400E) and Altera (FLEX10K) were developed for the implementation of a virtual logic (state and timing) analyzer. A performance of more than five was obtained over virtual instruments implemented using a commercial data acquisition board.

References

1 Moure M.J., Rodriguez L., Valdés M.D., Mandado E.: An Interactive Environment for Digital Learning and Design. Educational Multimedia/Hypermedia and Telecommunications, AACE, 1997.
2 Valdés M.D., Moure M.J., Mandado E.:Using FPGAs for the Rapid Prototyping of Programmable Interfaces Oriented to Microcontroller Systems. Proceedings of the XII Design of Circuits and Integrated Systems Conference, Sevilla 1997.
3 XC4000 Series, Xilinx, September 1996.
4 Field Programmable Gate Arrays Data Book, Lucent Technologies, October 1996.
5 FLEX 10K Embedded Programmable Logic Family, Altera, June 1996

The >S<puter: Introducing a Novel Concept for Dispatching Instructions Using Reconfigurable Hardware

Christian Siemers[1] and Dietmar P.F. Möller[2]

[1]Fachhochschule Westküste, University of Applied Sciences, Rungholtstr. 9, D-25746
Heide, siemers@fh-westkueste.de
[2]Technical University Clausthal, Institut für Informatik, Julius-Albert-Str. 4, D-38678
Clausthal-Zellerfeld, moeller@informatik.tu-clausthal.de

Abstract. A novel model for executing programs inside microprocessors is introduced, based on the integration of programmable structures in the dispatch and execution unit. These structures enable the highest degree of instruction parallelism while maintaining the strong sequence of results. The new model is introduced but not limited to register-based processors, while the requested compiler technology proves to be the same as for superscalar processors.

1 Introduction

In the 1970s and 1980s, research and development on control-flow based processors has led from 'normal' kinds using several cycles per instruction to the RISC-architectures with 1 cycle per instruction. This rate resulted still in keeping both instruction and result sequence. The newest development in this sector – the superscalar processors – has now reached a performance of more than 1 instruction per cycle [1]. These speeds are no longer obtainable by sequential execution.

This paper introduces a new superscalar processor model using programmable structures. This model executes programs faster than a conventionally designed superscalar processor. This new processor model is called >S<puter, while the main part inside, the functional unit, is designed by the s-paradigm-model.

2 The Block Structure Level of the >S<puter

Figure 1 shows the block structure of the >S<puter. This model is not limited to integer processing, but for simplification the floating point part has been omitted. The memory interface connects the data cache for the data streams (on the right handside) as well as the predecode unit and the instruction buffer for the instruction flow (on the left handside) to the main memory. A first level instruction cache has been integrated

into the instruction buffer, where instructions are already in process. The predecode unit examines the first decodes on the instructions in preparation for the later stages.

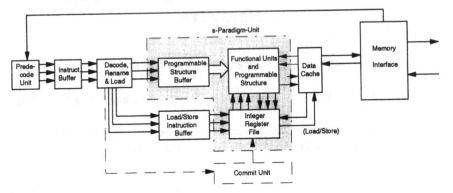

Fig. 1: Microarchitecture of the >S<puter

Inside the Decode, Rename and Load unit, the final translation is performed on all instructions. While all arithmetical and logical instructions and moves are processed inside this unit, conditional and unconditional branches are handled inside the Predecode Unit and the Instruction Buffer – these aspects are beyond the scope of this paper. Load and store instructions are routed to the corresponding instruction buffers and will control the data flow between the register file and the external memory.

The remaining part of the instruction stream, consisting of arithmetical/logical instructions and moves between registers, is stored in the Programmable Structure Buffer for further processing. Due to the internal structure of the >S<puter, the format of this class of instructions in the Programmable Structure Buffer is different from the common instruction format and will be explained in the next section.

3 The Register Transfer Level of the Functional Unit

The scope of this section will be focused on the s-Paradigm-Unit of the >S<puter shown in fig. 1 as the core part of the model. The first step will be to classify the typical instruction sets of nearly all microprocessors:

1. Data-flow instructions, such as arithmetical and logical instructions, for computing new values from register sources including moves between registers.
2. Load/store instructions for data transfer between registers and (external) memory.
3. Control-flow instructions like branch and jump instructions. This class also includes also other instructions like NOP, Wait, Stop etc.

The ability of executing several instructions (of type 1) in parallel corresponds to a basic block, which is defined as a block of consecutive instructions without any control flow operation such as branches. Later, this ability is extended to hyperblocks, which can be derived by code transforming from branches to predicated instructions [2]. The model's objective is now to establish a network inside the s-Paradigm-Unit to execute all instructions of this basic block simultaneously.

This network consists of the registers as the data sources and drains as well as a set of switching units. While the data transfer into the (drain) registers is synchronized, all links inside the network are coupled in an asynchronous way. The network matches the instructions of the basic block for the short period of executing the block and will conform to the next block after reload. Fig. 2 explains the functionalities inside the s-Unit, which are needed to establish the data flow network.

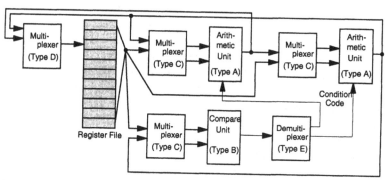

Fig. 2: Principal structure of one functional unit of the s-paradigm-model

The subunits inside the functional unit and the register file are connected by a great number of data connections and multiplexers. These connections consist of data busses with the system immanent width (e.g. 32 bit) with the exception of condition codes, which are implemented as bit lines (shown as thin lines in fig. 2). Five types of subunits exist inside the functional unit, while the network may be of complete or partial type:

- *Arithmetic Unit* (AU, type A): Differing from the Arithmetical-Logical-Unit (ALU), the AU includes just one or some (configurable) computations, for example, adding two integer values. The AU is characterized by two input busses, one output bus and, if necessary, by configuration and conditional bits.
- *Compare Unit* (CoU, type B): This subunit generates conditional bits inside the network used for the conditional execution of computations or moves. Characteristics for the CoU are two input busses, one conditional bit as an output and the possibility for configurable compares.
- *Multiplexer* (Mul_C, type C): Type C Multiplexer are used to route sources to the inputs of AUs and CoUs with two input busses (of full bus width).
- *Multiplexer* (Mul_D, type D): The routing of a number of possible sources to a certain register can be done by a multiplexer with only one output bus.
- *Demultiplexer* (Demul, type E): The results from the comparison units (CoUs) are routed to the corresponding AUs by these demultiplexers.

All arithmetical and logical instructions including moves are translated into a structure of hardware connections which relate closely to the programming sequence. The configuration bits represent the network structure; regardless of the location, where they are produced, these bits are stored in the instruction buffer and – directly before execution starts – in the structure buffer of the function unit.

4   Effects and Extensions of the >S<puter Architecture

Inside most superscalar architectures, the dispatcher unit is based on the data flow principle realized by reservation stations. One of the greatest advantages of the s-unit as the kernel part of the >S<puter is the fact that waiting time is omitted by the execution of a complete instruction block, which fits into the s-unit network. The s-unit uses data forwarding as a central feature of the network.

The second advantage is the use of arithmetic units of lower complexity. The same hardware resources as used for one complex ALU is expanded into several AUs and usable in parallel. The structure of multiple but small AUs increases the availability of hardware resources significantly resulting again in more performance.

The third advantage is also a result of the structured network: There is no need for a re-order unit, because results will be stored in the registers in the correct order and the functional unit processes the instruction block like one super-instruction.

For obtaining greater instruction blocks without branches, the method of code translation from branches to predicated instructions, also known as if-conversion [2] may be used. This is possible, if pxx-instructions like PEQ (predicate flag if equal) are added to the instruction set of the >S<puter and predicated instructions like

movp <Dest>, <Source>, <Dest. bit>

are available. This instruction for example will execute and copy the source register into the destination register, if the <Dest. bit> is true, otherwise it will act as a no operation instruction. The combination of pxx- and predicated instructions translates the control flow into data flow forming hyperblocks.

5   Results of Simulation of the >S<puter

A small implementation of an s-Unit inside the >S<puter containing 12 arithmetic units, 4 compare unit and 16 registers was simulated with typical code parts implementing conditional assignment and matrix operations [3]. The network – of complete connectivity – inside this s-Unit is configurable by 204 bits. All applications are written in C and translated in the following optimizing steps:

1. The C sourcecode is translated using a 'normal' optimizing compiler.
2. The blocksize is increased by the substitution of conditional branches by predicated instructions. This process forms hyperblocks [2].
3. Two loops are summarized to a greater loop (Loop Unrolling) with additional dependancy analysis resulting in a (compile time) register renaming.

The results in fig. 3 are valid under the assumption that – independent of the way – the network will need only one clock cycle for all data flows inside This is valid only for simple cases, and in practice a good solution for optimal number of cycles will be a runtime detection inside the network by special signals.

Application:	Level:	Superscalar CPU	>S<puter
Conditional assignment	First	6 cycles, 1.5 instruction/cycle	-
	Second	4 cycles, 2 instructions/cycle	3 cycles, 2.66 instructions/cycle
	Third	4 cycles, 3.75 instructions/cycle	3 cycles, 5 instructions/cycle
Matrix operation	First	5 cycles, 2 instruction/cycle	-
	Second	5 cycles, 2 instructions/cycle	3 cycles, 3.33 instructions/cycle
	Third	5 cycles, 3.2 instructions/cycle	3 cycles, 5.33 instructions/cycle

Fig. 3: Simulated results for superscalar CPU and >S<puter

6 Conclusion

The >S<puter and the s-Paradigm-Unit were introduced as an alternative micro-architecture for superscalar microprocessors. The focus of the >S<-puter-architecture is set to implement a processor capable of executing one instruction block at a time like one dynamically formed super-instruction. This architecture uses FPL-like structures and presents a possible performance win limited to roughly 2.

The compiler technology for superscalar microprocessors may be used for >S<puter implementations without nearly any modification. The only exception is the post assembler run to extract the structure information from the control flow.

On the other side, the >S<puter has some relations to the R&D scene in Hardware/Software Co-Design as well as ASIPs (Application Specific Instruction Set Processors) and CCMs (Customized Computing Machines) [4]. Compared with reconfigurable CCMs like the Xputer, the >S<puter fits its structures in a *program-dynamical* way and could be viewed as a dynamical reconfigurable ASIP.

References

[1] James E. Smith, Gurindar S. Sohi, "The Microarchitecture of Superscalar Processors", Invited Paper in *Proceedings of the IEEE, Special Issue on Microprocessors*, Vol. 83 (12), p. 1609 .. 1624, 1995.

[2] W. Hwu Wen-Mei et. al., "Compiler Technology for Future Microprocessor",. Invited Paper in *Proceedings of the IEEE, Special Issue on Microprocessors*, Vol. 83 (12), p. 1625 .. 1640, 1995.

[3] C. Siemers, D.P.F. Möller, "The >S<puter: A Novel Microarchitecturemodel for the Execution of Instructions inside Processors", in: Xu De, K.-E. Großpietsch, Ch. Steigner (Eds.): Proceedings of the Second Sino-German Workshop on Advanced Parallel Processing Technologies APPT '97, Koblenz, September 1997, p. 75 .. 82. Fölbach Verlag, Koblenz, 1997.

[4] R.W. Hartenstein, J. Becker, R. Kress, "Custom Computing Machines vs. Hardware/Software Co-Design: From a Globalized Point of View", *6th Int. Workshop on Field Programmable Logic and Appl., FPL'96*, Darmstadt, Sept. 1996, Lecture Notes in Computer Science 1142, Springer 1996.

A 6200 Model and Editor
Based on Object Technology

L.Lagadec, B.Pottier

Université de Bretagne Occidentale, 6 av. Le Gorgeu, Brest, France
{Loic.Lagadec, Bernard.Pottier}@univ-brest.fr

Abstract. This paper presents an open programmable editor for the XC6200 using object-oriented technology. A motivation for this work is to obtain full control on the path between configurable hardware and high-level programming. The paper also shortly discusses the direction followed for architecture synthesis.

Introduction

The design of an FPGA development system generally appears as a consequence of choices on circuit architecture: editor, place and route, support tools are built taking into account the description of chip features. This approach leads to important costs and delays for software availability because everything becomes specific and needs to be redesigned for a new hardware.

In opposition with this situation, object-oriented (OO) methodology recommands to make early decisions on reusable components, to design these components, then to specialize for the specific application. OO engineering is an incremental process where components remain available for further developments with an increased cost during the first designs.

We are investigating the opportunities provided by this approach with the case of the 6200 circuit as a test-bed. The first part of the paper explains the object support for the XC6200 editor and basic tools. the second part is a summary of the way used to synthesize modules from the Smalltalk-80 environment.

6200 architecture

The 6200 is a family of fine-grain, sea-of-gates FPGAs [4]. An XC6200 is composed of a large array of simple configurable cells. Each cell contains a logic unit (two or three inputs producing a single output) and a routing area for inter-cell communication.

The structure is simple, symmetrical, hierarchical and regular. At the lowest level of hierarchy lies an array of simple cells. Neighbor connected cells are grouped into blocks of 4 × 4 cells which themselves form a cellular array, communicating with neighbor 4 × 4 cells blocks.

The same hierarchical organization is replicated at levels 16, 64, ... Each level of the hierarchy has its own associated routing resources.

This architecture enables partial reconfiguration: sections of the device can be reconfigured with circuits running on other sections.

An obvious interest of the 6200 architecture is its public definition. The internal aspects of the components can be accessed directly (register contents, configuration ...).

At every level, higher level routing resources may be considered such as diffusion resources or pass-through resources. This brings flexibility but leads quickly to routing bottlenecks.

Modelization

The software architecture relies on separate sets of classes for:

- FPGA architecture description,
- circuit modules, routing channels ... conforming to the FPGA architecture
- control operations that can be applied to these components
- visual interface that allows to manipulate the controls

All these components are independent one to each other. Higher level functionalities are produced by encapsulation and message bindings to the components.

An FPGA architecture is described as a 2-d data structure embedding connectivities and basic logic functions.

Configuration description uses the same basic structure: a module, or a routing channel is a specialization of cells at different levels of the chip architecture, plus geometrical coordinates.

Algorithm design follows the abstract chip hierarchy. For efficiency, the rule is to take into account the whole set of features proposed at each level of the FPGA hierarchy.

The only interface constraints to the components is the understanding of some messages. The constraints have been chosen as weak as possible in order to strictly isolate the architecture description from activities such as routing, geometric operations, graphic representations, support for logic synthesis...

Editor structure

A graphical programmable editor has been realized which interacts with the hardware model through the control interface. The editor is object oriented and provides naming mechanisms on so-called "modules". Modules can be extracted from the design by copy/cut functions. They can be part of a high level object having a HLL specification. They can be manipulated by Smalltalk-80 programs to describe regular architectures.

Editor functionalities are:

- Copy/Cut/Paste on cells, object, cell assembly

- Module creation from external EDIF, a specific format, or interactive selection. Output to EDIF.
- Geometric operation on modules: flip, mirror, rotate...
- Point to point signal routing
- A generic place and route algorithm is under design

Most of these functions are built in the control interface so that they can be used independently of the editor, and could be used for similar FPGA architectures. Run-time circuit control is another potential application of the editor: any modification on the model, possibly coming from an application or system activity, generates the accurate modifications on the visual representation. In facts, the user interactions are executed by the control interface on the model, that feeds back modifications to the visual part.

All the operations of the control interface are programmable using standard Smalltalk-80.

```
|module|
module := (self blocks at: #adder) performRotateRight.
#(0 12 23) do:[:x| self putBlock: module at: x@50].
```

This code extracts a named module from a dictionary. It performs a replication of a rotated module at different positions enumerated using the **do:** iterator. The module description is written at the specified positions.

Datapaths can be manipulated in the same way to enable to build complex structures. Modules can either be pasted over the model or merged to this model.

Extensibility

Further interactions with the model can be described as follow:

- place and route
  Intent: Allocating resources in order to convert a logical description into a physical one
  Primal Forces: Management of functionality, of change, of performances
  Solution: Definition of support for logic description, of a conversion mechanism. The model enumerates accessible points from a given source.
  Benefits: It allows to keep a link between the high-level behavioral description and the final circuit.
- support for debug/runtime
  Intent: Enabling the upper layers or the user to simulate/ interact with the reality
  Primal Forces: Management of functionality
  Solution: Gateway between the hardware and the model
- system aspects
  Intent: Producing a support for resources system management
  Primal Forces: Management of functionality and change

Solution: Definition of swap operation; management of several configurations

All the tools (control, router, ...) relying on the model have been designed in such a way that they are decoupled from the model itself. In the opposite, any underlying model reusing these tools must conform to a defined interface. This architecture allows to reuse tools for a given hardware architecture as well as to prospect hardware requirements using tools as quality estimators.

FPGA module synthesis

The development of a model and low level tools for a public FPGA architecture is part of a larger project on OO architecture integration. One objective is to build a complete OO development system from high level behavioral descriptions to physical circuit and execution control within the object world.

An important difference with conventional CAD tools is the absence of internal layers represented by file formats. The environment allows a high level process to carry its circuit description, physical state or specification.

On top of the model described in this paper, the generic place and route is expected to use every available resource in a particular architecture, provided that the elementary circuit pattern has a restricted complexity.

The place and route will fill the gap between logic synthesis and FPGA architecture. it can be commanded to build particular module geometries for operators or regular designs.

Logic synthesis

Imperative language support is not the main focus of the project. OO languages are able to describe execution concurrency in a better way than languages reflecting the sequential execution model.

The first choice of the project has been to find a general way to generate circuit elements. The main requirement was a 100% control on hardware description from the high level environment. A benefit is portability over practical architectures since there is no dependency on operator libraries.

Smalltalk-80 is used for the developments and also for behavioral description. This choice is motivated by the level of abstraction and the absence of types that can be provided lately to allow a context specific recompilation of a model. The logic synthesis grain is a Smalltalk *block*, that will be represented by a circuit component, combinational or sequential, with a good efficiency at a grain in the order of 10 inputs 10 outputs.

There is no other restriction in the nature of the code appearing in the blocks. Blocks can call complex software tools such as lexical analyzers, pattern matching engines, external C code etc..., bringing hardware supports for these functions. After place and route they become circuits modules.

Synthesis process

Logic synthesis uses the Sis package of UC. Berkeley[2] and is descibed in [3]. In the case of combinational circuits, there are 4 stages:

1. **Production of a lookup-table**
   Each entry in the block definition set is computed and produces a resulting object. This table could be used as a high level replacement for the block.
2. **Translation into a PLA**
   Each entry into the table is transformed using the appropriate binary encoders. The output is produced as a file format suitable for the logic minimization package.
3. **Logic minimization and technology mapping**
   Depending on the target technology, the logic network is reduced and split according to LUT or gate library for the technology.

In the case of sequential circuits, 2 additional steps are required. We consider the block as a finite state automaton whose states are recorded into the remote variables. The first preliminary step is to sweep exhaustively the state space starting with the remote variable initial values. Then, the lookup table is built by adding the state transitions in the input and in the output of the block. The synthesis result is a circuit element suitable to build operators and regular arrays. After place and route, this block becomes a model for the editor tools.

Such circuit elements can appear as leaves in iterative or recursive algorithms. They are hardware primitives for a compiler that handles the data set streaming over the element network.

Conclusion

Our concern is to establish an analysis of FPGA development with the idea to fix knowledge and designs in flexible, reusable, component descriptions or tools. For this reason it is important to investigate seriously the whole translation from behavioral specification to working circuits. The opportunity of the public 6200 architecture has been taken to achieve these investigations. A partial result is a set of tools usable as a standard graphic editor or as a basis for further research on FPGA architecture and control [1].

References

1. Loïc Lagadec. http://ubolib.univ-brest.fr/llagadec/poster.html. (Snapshot of the editor view).
2. Sentovich Ellen M. and al. Sis: A system for sequential circuit synthesis. Technical Report Memorandum No. UCB/ERL M92/41, Electronics Research Laboratory, UC Berkeley , CA 94720.
3. Pottier and Llopis . Revisiting smalltalk-80 blocks, a logic generator for fpgas. In IEEE, editor, *FCCM'96*, April 1996.
4. Xilinx. *XC6200 Data Sheet*, January 1997.

Interfacing Hardware and Software

M. Eisenring, J. Teich

Computer Engineering and Communication Networks Lab (TIK)
Swiss Federal Institute of Technology (ETH)
Gloriastrasse 35, CH-8092 Zurich, Switzerland
email: {eisenring, teich}@tik.ee.ethz.ch

Abstract. The paper treats the problem of automatic generation of communication interfaces between hardware devices such as FPGAs and ASICs and software (programmable) devices such as microprocessors. In [2], we introduced an object-oriented approach to interface generation starting from a coarse-grain process graph specification level to the final device-dependent implementation. Here, we present generic templates of how to implement hardware/software interfaces, in particular in the scope of rapid prototyping environments that use reconfigurable hardware devices such as FPGAs. The major concerns here are 1) efficiency of communication protocols (speed), 2) low implementation complexity (area), 3) synthesizability, and 4) low power dissipation.
Keywords: automatic interface synthesis, low power design, hardware/software codesign, rapid prototyping

1 Introduction

Embedded systems impose strong constraints on design criteria such as area, speed and power dissipation. These often force a mixed implementation consisting of microcontrollers and microprocessors for implementing software functionality, and ASICs and FPGAs for hardware processes.

In order to find an appropriate solution which best fits the specification, design space exploration is neccessary. With the advent of configurable computing paradigms and the availability of powerful compiler and synthesis tools, the exploration of different design alternatives in the design space (rapid prototyping) has become a reachable goal. However, automatic interface synthesis, which generates a link between the communicating processes, becomes of increasing interest and importance and hence a key factor for rapid prototyping.

In [2], we introduced an object-oriented approach to automatic interface generation: Starting with a graphical specification in the form of a data flow graph (i.e. SDF graph [5]), and given a partition of tasks (nodes) onto hardware and software modules, we explained how the required communication channels as implied by the arcs in the graph may be refined such that the required interfaces in hardware and software (drivers) could be automatically synthesized. Due to the restricted communication semantics of the underlying data flow graph model (uni-source, uni-sink FIFO-buffered channels with blocking read, non-blocking write semantics), the refinement could be done in a completely automated manner.

Here, we want to focus on implementation aspects of hardware/software interfaces of a particular class of target architectures that use reconfigurable hardware devices such as FPGAs. In this area, the generated interface must satisfy the following requirements:

- *efficiency* of communication protocols (speed),
- *low implementation complexity* (area),
- *synthesizability*, and
- *low power dissipation*.

First, the communication should not slow down severely the application. Second, the interface should occupy the least amount of chip area possible. Also, the generated interface code should be synthesizable using existing compiler and hardware synthesis tools. Finally, there are sometimes power constraints that dictate a certain implementation. With these concerns in mind, we introduce 1) an efficient interface protocol, 2) an interface template for communication on and with reconfigurable hardware devices. 3) A gated-clock implementation is proposed for minimizing the power dissipation of the functionality that is implemented in hardware.

In the following, we present an efficient protocol for synchronizing two communicating partners in hardware (Section 2), a generic hardware template for interfacing a reconfigurable hardware device with a microprocessor, and an efficient and power saving implementation of hardware using a gated-clock technology (Section 3). Finally, we describe how these interface techniques are embedded into our object-oriented interface generation tool HASIS [2].

2 Templates for hardware/software communication

In [3], we described different interface models for communication between processors and hardware components. Here, we propose a special efficient interface protocol for two communication partners being mapped onto hardware devices being clocked with the same clock and a generic hardware/software interface template.

2.1 An efficient synchronization protocol

Between independent subsystems we use a handshake protocol as described in [7] for synchronisation. In the context of this paper, we assume that subsystems use the same clock and that the exchange of data is synchronized to this clock. Each subsystem has a request line for each channel to request a transmission and an acknowledge line to get the request of the communication partner. The events on that lines are described as follows:

req+ : ready to transmit data at the next active clock edge

req- : no further data to transmit

The communication takes place at the next active clock edge if both communication partners have released an event req+. The protocol has the following properties: 1) symmetric, 2) communication within one clock cycle possible, 3) request remains valid until it is acknowledged, 4) easy to implement.

Example 1. Figure 1 presents the synchronisation between two synchronous subsystems A and B of unknown computation time. Each node signals a request for communication by emitting req+, e.g. reqA+. The communication takes place at the next rising clock edge where both events reqA+ and reqB+ have been emitted (see in Fig. 1 times X, Y and Z).

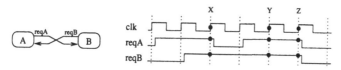

Fig. 1. Synchronisation between two synchronous subsystems

2.2 Generic hardware/software interface template

Similar to [6], we use a configurable interface template between hardware nodes and programmable software devices, e.g. microprocessors. It consists of three concurrent parts (see Fig. 2a) which allows to switch off power of unused circuit parts and is generated by HASIS [2] for various processors.

1. The *address decoder* decodes the addresses and enables parts of the controller logic if an appropriate address has been used by the microcontroller. This block contains combinational logic and an optional address register in case of a shared bus for address/data.
2. The *controller logic* contains state machines to implement a specific microcontroller bus protocol and the state machines for the request lines (see Section 2.1) of the connected hardware nodes.
3. The *data I/O* part is a (de)multiplexer for the access to the shared resource microcontroller data bus. There exist three different unidirectional transfer elements (see Fig. 2b) which may be instantiated as input or output. They are activated by the enable signal *e* through the controller logic. The *TRI-STATE switch* realizes a direct link between the data bus and an internal channel. With the *asynchronous register*, data may be stored at any time. The *synchronous register* allows to save a data value at the next active clock edge.

3 Reduction of power consumption of hardware nodes

Power dissipation of sequential circuits is proportional to the used clock frequency and is a design constraint for embedded systems. Numerous approaches like [4] and [1] present solutions to reduce power. Here, we propose a *gated-clock* [1] (see Fig. 3a) which allows to switch off parts of a sequential circuit that are actually not in use.

Our implementation makes use of the handshake protocol between synchronous subsystems as proposed in Section 2.1. The idea is to stop the clock of a hardware node if there is no further computation to do. Therefore, a node has two different modes.

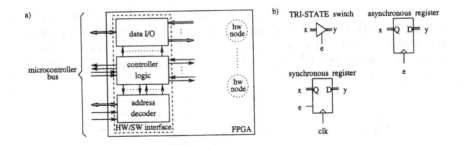

Fig. 2. a) HW/SW interface template, b) data I/O components

- *node enabled*: The node is running by executing its task.
- *node disabled*: The node is waiting for data transmission on all of its channels and therefore the clock is disabled. The clock is reenabled if at least one request for data transmission is acknowledged.

An implementation of a *gated-clock* power saving scheme may be described as follows. To each subsystem, a clock circuit is added which observes the node

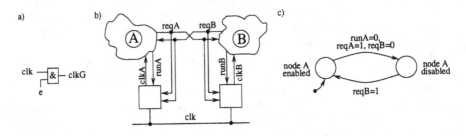

Fig. 3. a) Gated-clock, b) circuit structure, c) modes of node A

state and the request lines of all channels of the node, e.g. Fig. 3b).

Example 2. Figure 3b) presents two nodes A and B connected via one channel (only request lines shown). Each node has an additional clock circuit and an output signal (e.g. *runA*) which shows the node activity (i.e. *runA*=1: node A runs, *runA*=0: no further computation for node A). The clock circuit disables the node clock (e.g. *clkB*) if there is no computation to do.

Example 3. Figure 3c) presents the two node states of node *A* in Fig. 3b). The node remains disabled as long as its request isn't acknowledged. For simplicity, only conditions which force a state transition are shown.

Example 4. Figure 4a) shows a possible circuit implementation. If the system is implemented on an FPGA, e.g. the XILINX XC4062XL, each gated-clock circuit requires only one CLB (configurable logic block). If the node clock (e.g. *clkA*) is enabled, it has one gate delay compared to *clk*. Figure 4b) shows parts of the timing diagram for the gated-clock circuits in Fig. 4a). At time **X** node A releases *reqA+* which is not acknowledged at the next clock edge. Therefore *clkA* has been disabled (see **Y**). It is reenabled if node B releases its *reqB+* (see **Z**).

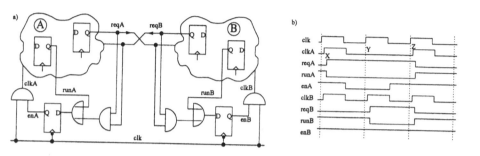

Fig. 4. a) Circuit for gated-clocks, b) timing diagramm for gated-clock

To satisfy the setup/hold conditions between a hardware/software interface and a hardware node, the *req+* event of the interface is delayed for a half clock period.

4   HASIS, a hardware/software interface generator

An object-oriented approach is taken for the generation of interfaces [3]. The major advantage of the object-oriented approach was to define classes for abstract communication interfaces such as via I/O ports, shared-memory communication, using DMA or interrupt facilities, etc., which are supported by almost any kind of microprocessor family on the market. In order to allow code generation for a new microprocessor, only few device-specific parts of the code generation classes have to be reconfigured or rewritten because of class inheritance, see [2],[3].

References

1. L. Benini and G. De Micheli. Transformation and synthesis of FSMs for low-power gated-clock implementation. *Int. Symp. on Low Power Design*, pages 21–26, 1995.
2. M. Eisenring and J. Teich. Domain-specific interface generation from dataflow specifications. In *Proceedings of Sixth International Workshop on Hardware/Software Codesign, CODES 98*, pages 43–47, Seattle, Washington, March 15-18 1998.
3. M. Eisenring, J. Teich, and L. Thiele. Rapid prototyping of dataflow programs on hardware/software architectures. In *Proc. of HICSS-31, Proc. of the Hawai'i Int. Conf. on Syst. Sci.*, volume VII, pages 187–196, Kona, Hawaii, January 1998.
4. Shyh-Jye Jou and I-Yao Chuang. Low-power globally asynchronous local synchronous design using self-timed circuit technology. In *International Symposium on Circuits and Systems*, volume 3, pages 1808–1811, June 1997.
5. E.A. Lee and D.G. Messerschmitt. Synchronous dataflow. *Proceedings of the IEEE*, 75(9):1235–1245, 1987.
6. B. Lin, S. Vercauteren, and Hugo De Man. Constructing application-specific heterogeneous embedded architectures for custom HW/SW applications. In *ACM/IEEE Design Automation Conference*, June 1996.
7. Ad M.G. Peeters. *Single-Rail Handshake Circuits*. PhD Thesis, Eindhoven University of Technology, 1996.

Generating Layouts for Self-Implementing Modules

James Hwang, Cameron Patterson, S. Mohan,
Eric Dellinger, Sujoy Mitra, and Ralph Wittig

Xilinx, San Jose, CA 95124 USA

Abstract. Recent advances in FPGA density allow system-level implementations in programmable logic. However, traditional FPGA design tools do not scale well to large complex designs containing substantial datapaths, control logic, and memories, in part because they mostly ignore hierarchy and treat complex circuits as flat netlists. Many FPGA designers have adopted synthesis-based approaches to deal with design complexity, but unfortunately, synthesis technology is not sufficiently advanced to make best use of the target FPGA. As a result, libraries of modules with optimized implementations are essential for high-performance system-level FPGA design [1], [2], [3]. In this paper we describe an object-oriented framework for module generation, focusing on a novel approach to specifying and computing layouts for parametric modules.

1 Background

Creating high-performance parametric modules requires a high level of expertise in FPGA design, especially when the modules must target multiple FPGA architectures. To create, maintain, and extend libraries of such modules requires a flexible framework as well as data representation. Recent work has begun to address module generation based on object-oriented design. Generators described in [3] emphasize high-performance circuits. Another system described in [4] focuses on flexibility and simulation capabilities rather than performance of the generated modules. We have independently developed an object-oriented framework and library of module generators that is extremely flexible, treating modules as interacting objects, but making no sacrifices of circuit performance for flexibility.

2 Self-Implementing Modules

Self-implementing modules (SIMs) are parametric module generators that compute their logical and physical structure at instantiation time to optimize circuit performance in global context. As an example, an "FIR" SIM might generate an FIR filter using either serial- or parallel-distributed arithmetic depending on parameters that specify timing and area constraints. SIMs generate simulation models and technology mapped netlists containing detailed placement information. Whereas existing modules have parameters that are essentially variables (*e.g.* a filter coefficient), a SIM parameter is an arbitrary symbolic expression. A SIM can defer evaluation of the symbolic expression until the time of instantiation, using dynamic scoping to compute the expression's value.

SIMs are inherently hierarchical, and exploit object-oriented language features to express dynamic configuration. They compute their physical layout using the well-established Strategy design pattern[5]; a SIM designer can assign distinct strategies to any SIMs in the logical hierarchy. A strategy can be as simple as "apply one of a set of precomputed fixed footprints", as malleable as "place this SIM's children in a horizontal linear order with abutment," or as general as "place children within a fixed device region using simulated annealing." SIMs address some of the problems arising from static module definition, and by use of hierarchy, help address problems of design complexity.

A SIM framework and library has been designed in Java, although SIMs can be implemented in any high-level programming language that supports object-oriented design. The library contains SIMs for complex functions such as filters and correlators, and is commercially available[6], so that FPGA designers can incorporate SIMs with existing design methodologies. In this paper we briefly describe Application Program Interfaces (APIs) that were used to create our SIM library. Once finalized, the APIs will be made public to facilitate user-constructed SIMs.

The *Logical API* provides full design capture functionality in Java, and supports dynamic structural modifications, such as adding or deleting child SIMs, ports, or nets depending on parameter values or context. The *Placement Directives API* provides layout patterns that are particularly well-suited to datapath and other structured logic. This API provides Java classes to represent structured layouts, coordinate-free relative placement directives, and common transformations on structures.

3   SIM Placement Directives

Layout directives are specified by creating *containers*, or aggregates of components, and assigning an *arrangement* to each container. Elements of a container can be any instantiated component, including other containers; hence, containers can be composed to define arbitrary floorplans. A container with an arrangement that defines an ordered linear structure is called a *VectorTemplate*. VectorTemplates support simple geometric "place A to the left of B to the left of C", as well as more complex positional relations. VectorTemplates have customizable attributes that direct the SIM back-end during coordinate computations, including *alignment*, row or column *orientation*, *stride*, which defines spacing between template elements, *direction*, which specifies the direction implied by the linear order, and *fold* attributes that specify in either device coordinates or vector indices the point at which a vector should be folded. In addition, transformations on a vector such as rotation and reflection can be specified.

Other template types include the *OverlapTemplate*, a container whose elements are overlaid without resource sharing or contention, the *InterleaveTemplate*, a VectorTemplate whose elements are shuffled according to a specified interleave pattern, and the *RemapTemplate*, whose combinational elements are combined through technology remapping and optimization. Relationally placed macros (RPMs), containers whose elements are each given specific relative locations in device coordinates, are also supported. Taken in combination, these containers provide a rich framework for specifying relative placements and facilitate reuse (via composition) of optimized modules.

Template containers specify relative placements in abstract coordinates (*i.e.* vector indices) rather than device coordinates. Consequently the shapes of the template elements need not be known until the overall floorplan is resolved into device coordinates. This allows SIMs to defer the evaluation of the precise physical footprint until more contextual information is available. It also means that a single floorplan specification can be valid for a range of module parameters, or indeed for implementations on distinct target architectures. In effect, the placement directives specify the structure in an abstract coordinate space; it is up to the SIM back-end to resolve these coordinates into device coordinates.

SIMs are written in Java, but many FPGA designers prefer to design circuits in an HDL. We support a VHDL-to-SIM flow by providing placement directives in VHDL-93 syntax and a compiler that translates a VHDL module into a Java SIM. Templates are specified as instantiated components having generics that define template attributes. Template entities are portless and have no effect on simulation, but unlike embedded comment syntax, will not be stripped away by any program that filters comments from source.

4 Examples

We present an example of a parametric SIM that implements a registered read-only memory (ROM). Although simple, it demonstrates how templates can simplify layout specification by replacing arithmetic expressions embedded in structural VHDL generics by simple template indices. It shows how optimized modules can be combined hierarchically to build other optimized modules.

The basic elements comprising the ROM are 4-input lookup tables (LUTs), each of which can implement a 16x1 ROM, and edge-triggered D-flip flops (DFFs), each of which can store one bit. We assume a target architecture having two LUTs (f and g), and two DFFs (ffx and ffy) per configurable logic block (CLB), as in the Xilinx 4000 family[7].

The module was originally written in VHDL, with placement information stored in component generics as x, y, and site locations. When the module is compiled into a netlist, these properties are interpreted to generate the proper device location for the component. The floorplan for the ROM is created by constructing an array of CLBs, inserting 16x1 ROMs in alternating f-LUT and g-LUT resources, and DFFs in alternating ffx and ffy sites. For odd N, the top CLB is treated as a special case.

```
architecture original of rom16xNreg is
  constant    size : integer := N/2 + N mod 2;
begin
clb_array: for i in 0 to N/2-1 generate
    rom_f : rom16x1 generic map(x=>x, y=>y+size-i-1, site=>f_lut);
    dff_x :     dff generic map(x=>x, y=>y+size-i-1, site=>ff_x);
    rom_g : rom16x1 generic map(x=>x, y=>y+size-i-1, site=>g_lut);
    dff_y :     dff generic map(x=>x, y=>y+size-i-1, site=>ff_y);
  end generate;
clb_odd: if (N mod 2 = 1) generate
    rom_f : rom16x1 generic map(x=>x, y=>y, site=>f_lut);
    dff_y : dff     generic map(x=>x, y=>y, site=>ffx);
  end generate;
end original;
```

The arithmetic expressions for the y-coordinates are relatively simple; however for more complex modules, such expressions can be more difficult to establish or comprehend.

The SIM version is hierarchical, with the top-level consisting of a register and combinational ROM SIM. All SIM ports and nets have parametric width. The addPort method creates a named port having a direction, a width, and a net to which the port is attached, and the ripNet method on the Net class returns the ith strand of a net. The VectorTemplate method addSim adds the argument SIM to the template in the next position of the linear order, and registers the SIM as a child of the constructed SIM.

The register's layout is defined as a column of DFFs by instantiating a VectorTemplate with column orientation.

```
public class Register extends Sim {
    public Register(int N, Net din, Net clk, Net q) {
        addPort("din", Port.IN,  N, din);
        addPort("clk", Port.IN,  1, clk);
        addPort("q",   Port.OUT, N, q);

        VectorTemplate column =
            new VectorTemplate(this, COLUMN);

        for (int i = 0; i < N; i++)
            column.addSim(new DFF(din.ripNet(i),
                          clk, q.ripNet(i)));
    }
}
```

The combinational ROM has similar structure, hence the code is omitted.

The top-level SIM consists of a register and ROM sub-SIM contained in an Overlap Template. The constructor creates ports, instantiates an OverlapTemplate, then allocates and adds the register and combinational ROM. The template method computeLayout evaluates the OverlapTemplate (and sub-arrangements) and generates locations for all elements comprising the module.

```
public class ROM16xNreg extends Sim {
    public ROM16xNreg(int N, Net addr, Net clk, Net out) {
        addPort("addr", Port.IN,  4, addr);
        addPort("clk",  Port.IN,  1, clk);
        addPort("out",  Port.OUT, N, out);

        // Create internal net between the ROM and register
        Net din = new Net("din", N);

        OverlapTemplate layout = new OverlapTemplate(this);
        layout.addSim(new Register(N, din, clk, out));
        layout.addSim(new ROM16xN(N, addr, din));
        layout.computeLayout();
    }
}
```

5 Discussion

SIMs provide a flexible framework for hierarchical library design. The template-based placement directives provide a powerful means of specifying and computing layouts for SIMs, and are equally applicable to other module generators. They enable floorplan specification in abstract coordinates that can be independent of the sizes of the circuit elements. Overlap and Remap templates enable reuse via composition of optimized modules into higher level optimized modules, providing flexible support for libraries of high performance parametric modules that target multiple FPGA architectures.

For lack of space, we did not address the dynamic aspects of SIM instantiation. However, we note that SIM constructors can incorporate run-time information, and there are SIM methods for modifying existing implementations based on context. SIMs are particularly well-suited for high-performance modules used in DSP applications, and have been successfully incorporated in a commercial product.

References

1. Steven Kelem and Jorge Seidel. Shortening the Design Cycle for Programmable Logic Devices. IEEE Design & Test of Computers, December 1992.
2. EDIF LPM Subcommittee. Library of Parameterized Modules (LPM), Version 2 0. Electronic Industries Association, EIA/IS-103, May 1993.
3. O. Mencer, M. Morf, and M. J. Flynn. PAM-Blox: High Performance FPGA Design for Adaptive Computing. FCCM 1998, Napa, CA.
4. M. Chu, K. Sulimman, N. Weaver, A. DeHon, and J. Wawrzynek. Object Oriented Circuit-Generators in Java. FCCM 1998, Napa, CA.
5. E. Gamma, R. Helm, R. Johnson, and John Vlissides. Design Patterns. Addison-Wesley, 1995.
6. S. Mohan, R. Wittig, S. Kelem, and S. Leavesley. The Core Generator Framework. FPD '98, Montreal, June 1998.
7. The Programmable Logic Data Book. Xilinx, Inc. 1998.

Author Index

Lecture Notes in Computer Science

For information about Vols. 1–1386

please contact your bookseller or Springer-Verlag

Vol. 1424: L. Polkowski, A. Skowron (Eds.), Rough Sets and Current Trends in Computing. Proceedings, 1998. XIII, 626 pages. 1998. (Subseries LNAI).

Vol. 1425: D. Hutchison, R. Schäfer (Eds.), Multimedia Applications, Services and Techniques – ECMAST'98. Proceedings, 1998. XVI, 532 pages. 1998.

Vol. 1427: A.J. Hu, M.Y. Vardi (Eds.), Computer Aided Verification. Proceedings, 1998. IX, 552 pages. 1998.

Vol. 1429: F. van der Linden (Ed.), Development and Evolution of Software Architectures for Product Families. Proceedings, 1998. IX, 258 pages. 1998.

Vol. 1430: S. Trigila, A. Mullery, M. Campolargo, H. Vanderstraeten, M. Mampaey (Eds.), Intelligence in Services and Networks: Technology for Ubiquitous Telecom Services. Proceedings, 1998. XII, 550 pages. 1998.

Vol. 1431: H. Imai, Y. Zheng (Eds.), Public Key Cryptography. Proceedings, 1998. XI, 263 pages. 1998.

Vol. 1432: S. Arnborg, L. Ivansson (Eds.), Algorithm Theory – SWAT '98. Proceedings, 1998. IX, 347 pages. 1998.

Vol. 1433: V. Honavar, G. Slutzki (Eds.), Grammatical Inference. Proceedings, 1998. X, 271 pages. 1998. (Subseries LNAI).

Vol. 1434: J.-C. Heudin (Ed.), Virtual Worlds. Proceedings, 1998. XII, 412 pages. 1998. (Subseries LNAI).

Vol. 1435: M. Klusch, G. Weiß (Eds.), Cooperative Information Agents II. Proceedings, 1998. IX, 307 pages. 1998. (Subseries LNAI).

Vol. 1436: D. Wood, S. Yu (Eds.), Automata Implementation. Proceedings, 1997. VIII, 253 pages. 1998.

Vol. 1437: S. Albayrak, F.J. Garijo (Eds.), Intelligent Agents for Telecommunication Applications. Proceedings, 1998. XII, 251 pages. 1998. (Subseries LNAI).

Vol. 1438: C. Boyd, E. Dawson (Eds.), Information Security and Privacy. Proceedings, 1998. XI, 423 pages. 1998.

Vol. 1439: B. Magnusson (Ed.), System Configuration Management. Proceedings, 1998. X, 207 pages. 1998.

Vol. 1441: W. Wobcke, M. Pagnucco, C. Zhang (Eds.), Agents and Multi-Agent Systems. Proceedings, 1997. XII, 241 pages. 1998. (Subseries LNAI).

Vol. 1442: A. Fiat. G.J. Woeginger (Eds.), Online Algorithms. XVIII, 436 pages. 1998.

Vol. 1443: K.G. Larsen, S. Skyum, G. Winskel (Eds.), Automata, Languages and Programming. Proceedings, 1998. XVI, 932 pages. 1998.

Vol. 1444: K. Jansen, J. Rolim (Eds.), Approximation Algorithms for Combinatorial Optimization. Proceedings, 1998. VIII, 201 pages. 1998.

Vol. 1445: E. Jul (Ed.), ECOOP'98 – Object-Oriented Programming. Proceedings, 1998. XII, 635 pages. 1998.

Vol. 1446: D. Page (Ed.), Inductive Logic Programming. Proceedings, 1998. VIII, 301 pages. 1998. (Subseries LNAI).

Vol. 1447: V.W. Porto, N. Saravanan, D. Waagen, A.E. Eiben (Eds.), Evolutionary Programming VII. Proceedings, 1998. XVI, 840 pages. 1998.

Vol. 1448: M. Farach-Colton (Ed.), Combinatorial Pattern Matching. Proceedings, 1998. VIII, 251 pages. 1998.

Vol. 1449: W.-L. Hsu, M.-Y. Kao (Eds.), Computing and Combinatorics. Proceedings, 1998. XII, 372 pages. 1998.

Vol. 1450: L. Brim, F. Gruska, J. Zlatuška (Eds.), Mathematical Foundations of Computer Science 1998. Proceedings, 1998. XVII, 846 pages. 1998.

Vol. 1451: A. Amin, D. Dori, P. Pudil, H. Freeman (Eds.), Advances in Pattern Recognition. Proceedings, 1998. XXI, 1048 pages. 1998.

Vol. 1452: B.P. Goettl, H.M. Halff, C.L. Redfield, V.J. Shute (Eds.), Intelligent Tutoring Systems. Proceedings, 1998. XIX, 629 pages. 1998.

Vol. 1453: M.-L. Mugnier, M. Chein (Eds.), Conceptual Structures: Theory, Tools and Applications. Proceedings, 1998. XIII, 439 pages. (Subseries LNAI).

Vol. 1454: I. Smith (Ed.), Artificial Intelligence in Structural Engineering. XI, 497 pages. 1998. (Subseries LNAI).

Vol. 1456: A. Drogoul, M. Tambe, T. Fukuda (Eds.), Collective Robotics. Proceedings, 1998. VII, 161 pages. 1998. (Subseries LNAI).

Vol. 1457: A. Ferreira, J. Rolim, H. Simon, S.-H. Teng (Eds.), Solving Irregularly Structured Problems in Prallel. Proceedings, 1998. X, 408 pages. 1998.

Vol. 1458: V.O. Mittal, H.A. Yanco, J. Aronis, R-. Simpson (Eds.), Assistive Technology in Artificial Intelligence. X, 273 pages. 1998. (Subseries LNAI).

Vol. 1459: D.G. Feitelson, L. Rudolph (Eds.), Job Scheduling Strategies for Parallel Processing. Proceedings, 1998. VII, 257 pages. 1998.

Vol. 1460: G. Quirchmayr, E. Schweighofer, T.J.M. Bench-Capon (Eds.), Database and Expert Systems Applications. Proceedings, 1998. XVI, 905 pages. 1998.

Vol. 1461: G. Bilardi, G.F. Italiano, A. Pietracaprina, G. Pucci (Eds.), Algorithms – ESA'98. Proceedings, 1998. XII, 516 pages. 1998.

Vol. 1462: H. Krawczyk (Ed.), Advances in Cryptology - CRYPTO '98. Proceedings, 1998. XII, 519 pages. 1998.

Vol. 1464: H.H.S. Ip, A.W.M. Smeulders (Eds.), Multimedia Information Analysis and Retrieval. Proceedings, 1998. VIII, 264 pages. 1998.

Vol. 1465: R. Hirschfeld (Ed.), Financial Cryptography. Proceedings, 1998. VIII, 311 pages. 1998.

Vol. 1466: D. Sangiorgi, R. de Simone (Eds.), CONCUR'98: Concurrency Theory. Proceedings, 1998. XI, 657 pages. 1998.

Vol. 1467: C. Clack, K. Hammond, T. Davie (Eds.), Implementation of Functional Languages. Proceedings, 1997. X, 375 pages. 1998.

Vol. 1469: R. Puigjaner, N.N. Savino, B. Serra (Eds.), Computer Performance Evaluation. Proceedings, 1998. XIII, 376 pages. 1998.

Vol. 1473: X. Leroy, A. Ohori (Eds.), Types in Compilation. Proceedings, 1998. VIII, 299 pages. 1998.

Vol. 1475: W. Litwin, T. Morzy, G. Vossen (Eds.), Advances in Databases and Information Systems. Proceedings, 1998. XIV, 369 pages. 1998.

Vol. 1482: R.W. Hartenstein, A. Keevallik (Eds.), Field-Programmable Logic and Applications. Proceedings, 1998. XI, 533 pages. 1998.